THE
RIDLEY SCOTT
ENCYCLOPEDIA

Laurence Raw

THE SCARECROW PRESS, INC.

Lanham • Toronto • Plymouth, UK

2009

Published by Scarecrow Press, Inc.
A wholly owned subsidiary of The Rowman & Littlefield Publishing Group, Inc.
4501 Forbes Boulevard, Suite 200, Lanham, Maryland 20706
http://www.scarecrowpress.com

Estover Road, Plymouth PL6 7PY, United Kingdom

British Library Cataloguing in Publication Information Available

Library of Congress Cataloging-in-Publication Data

Raw, Laurence.
  The Ridley Scott encyclopedia / Laurence Raw.
    p. cm.
  Includes bibliographical references and index.
    ISBN 978-0-8108-6951-6 (cloth : alk. paper) — ISBN 978-0-8108-6952-3 (ebook)
    1. Scott, Ridley—Encyclopedias. I. Title.   PN1998.3.S393R39 2009
  791.4302'33092—dc22   2009015582

Printed in the United States of America

CONTENTS

IT IS A PLEASURE to have been asked to write the foreword to this book. Quite simply, Ridley Scott is among the finest directors to have emerged from the long and fairly illustrious history of British cinema. His breadth of vision, as well as the sheer range and diversity of his work—from *Blade Runner* to *Thelma & Louise*, from *Body of Lies* to *Gladiator*, mark him out as an extraordinarily gifted man.

Ridley was one of a group of British directors, which included Alan Parker, Hugh Hudson, Adrian Lyne, and of course his brother Tony Scott, who emerged from the world of advertising during the 1970s. They all had a highly developed visual sense which represented something of a departure from the generation that had immediately preceded them. Their post-war outlook, forged in the sixties, encouraged them to interpret the world in a very different way from that of Karel Reisz, John Schlesinger, and Tony Richardson, some of the dominant names of British cinema just a few years earlier.

I began working with Ridley on the development of a couple of screenplays: *The Duellists*, and a pretty grim version of "The Gunpowder Plot" in 1975.

Alan Parker's *Bugsy Malone* was presented at the Cannes Film Festival the following year and received an ecstatic response; walking down the red carpet following that gala screening, David Picker (then president of Paramount Pictures) called over to me and said: "Boy, oh boy, that Parker's an extraordinary talent. Do you know anyone else like him?" And I shot back, "Yes, I'm working with a chap named Ridley Scott." To which he replied, "I'd really like to meet him."

I went straight from the cinema, phoned Ridley at home, and suggest that he jump on a plane first thing the next morning. Lunchtime the following day we were having lunch on the beach—not all that unusual in Cannes—making a deal. When we got to the crux of what film it would be (we had the two scripts) it became clear that one was likely to cost two million dollars, and the other we felt we could make for around $1.2 million. David Picker gave the matter about thirty seconds thought and said, "I'll take the cheaper one." We both nodded, and six months later were on the set of *The Duellists*.

I think those early films made by Ridley and his peers just looked more handsome, because they owed nothing to what at the time were the dominant television drama or documentary traditions.

Over the next three decades Ridley has proved to have the most extraordinary ability to recreate and reimagine the world.

Early on I remember someone criticizing his work, saying "the images are too perfect." For me that was a bit like suggesting that Vermeer or Rembrandt painted too well. In the end he has this quite extraordinary eye. What would you do, deny it? Pretend not to have it? I should be so lucky!

Amongst his work you will find at least half a dozen really great movies. Ridley has made a massive contribution to world cinema, and to the British film industry in particular. This encyclopedia, itself the result of meticulous and painstaking scholarship, is a fitting tribute to the breadth of Ridley's work and his extraordinary contribution to the history and improvement of the moving image.

ACKNOWLEDGMENTS

I WOULD LIKE to thank the staffs at the British Film Institute and the British Library, who dealt with my seemingly endless requests for material in a calm and professional manner. John Tibbetts of the University of Kansas gave me the chance to read out some parts of this work at the Literature/Film Association Conference in 2007; Rezzan Kocaöner Silkü provided a similar opportunity at the Studies in English (IDEA) conference in İzmir, Turkey, in 2008. To Stephen Ryan, my editor at Scarecrow Press, much thanks—not only for commissioning this work but for remaining patient while the manuscript was completed. Special thanks go to Lord Puttnam, Scott's first producer on *The Duellists*, who generously contributed a foreword to this book. My dear friend (and partner in many projects) Jim Welsh, Emeritus Professor of English at Salisbury University was provided a stimulus for discussion as well as unceasing encouragement. I'd also like thank other colleagues involved in adaptation studies who in their various ways have been equally encouraging—Richard J. Hand, Dennis Cutchins, Diane Lake, Iain Smith, Deborah Cartmell, and Imelda Whelehan. When I first undertook this project, I was at a loss as to how to shape the material; for his help in overcoming this difficulty I'd like to thank my friend and colleague Thomas Leitch of the University of Delaware. Lastly, I'd like to pay special thanks to my parents, John and Margery Raw, who not only listened to my endless discourses on Scott (running up huge telephone bills in the process), but provided hospitality and encouragement during my lengthy stay in London, while researching this project. This book is dedicated to them.

INTRODUCTION

RIDLEY SCOTT'S long career as a director has formed the subject of several surveys in the past, most notably by James Clarke, Richard Alan Schwarz, and Paul M. Sammon. We also know a considerable amount about his life—his origins in South Shields, his early years at London's Royal College of Art, and his television work with the BBC and Independent Television—from books such as Laurence F. Knapp's and Andrea F. Kulas's *Ridley Scott Interviews* (2005). What is perhaps less known, however, is the sheer range of activities in which Scott has been involved—as a director (of feature films, commercials, and television dramas), designer, producer, film mogul, and advertising executive. This *Ridley Scott Encyclopedia* is the first book focusing on all aspects of his work in a career lasting nearly fifty years.

The entries in the encyclopedia come from four basic categories. The first is Ridley Scott's work as a director, encompassing not only all his feature films but also some of his work in television and in commercials. Every major feature film produced for the cinema and television from *The Duellists* (1977) to *Body of Lies* (2008) is covered, as well as some unrealized projects ("The Hot Zone," "Tripoli," and "I Am Legend"). Some unrealized projects ("The A Team," "Diamond Dead," "Mary Queen of Scots," and "Stones") are omitted on the grounds of lack of information: many of them exist only as announcements in past issues of *Variety* or *The Hollywood Reporter*. With the help of IMDb.com, the Internet Movie Database, the encyclopedia also provides information on some of Scott's early television work as director and designer. Included is the first major analysis of "The League of Uncharitable Ladies," an episode in the spy series *Adam Adamant Lives!* (1966). All entries incorporate factual information about the genesis of each production, a selection of reviews (from newspapers and online), and a short critical analysis relating individual works to some of Scott's major thematic preoccupations.

The Ridley Scott Encyclopedia breaks new ground in analyzing Scott's work as a producer as well as a director. Through his various companies, such as Percy Main and Scott Free, he has been involved in several projects, all of which develop some of the themes covered in his work as a director. This is particularly true in recent years, where television series such as *Numb3rs* and films such as *Tristan + Isolde* focus on the political issues raised in *Kingdom of Heaven* and *Body of Lies*. As a producer, Scott has also been responsible for comedies such as *Monkey Trouble* and *Where the Money Is*, which tends to disprove the theory (raised by many critics at the time of *Matchstick Men*'s release) that he is only really at home with adventure films or epics. The encyclopedia also analyzes some of Scott's most famous television commercials. In a recent interview he claims to have directed over three thousand of them; this encyclopedia looks at only twenty-five (which are accessible either in libraries or online). Many of the themes raised in Scott's films are also evident in many commercials, which might dispel the notion once and for all that he is purely interested in visuals.

The second category in this encyclopedia encompasses the people who have been involved in Scott's projects. They include actors, directors, producers, designers, writers, and other creative personnel. Many of them have made perceptive comments about Scott as a director or producer in interviews; where appropriate, extracts are included in each entry. In the past, critics have often claimed that Scott is primarily concerned with visuals, taking little note of other aspects of the mise-en-scène (performances, music). The encyclopedia shows that this is certainly not the case. Several creative people—Russell Crowe, Hans Zimmer, Sigourney Weaver—have regularly worked for Scott in the belief that he can provide them with opportunities not found elsewhere. This encyclopedia shows why.

The third category focuses on general thematic issues raised in Scott's oeuvre. They encompass gender construction, political issues (which assume particular significance after 9/11), and geographical locations. Many of his films—with Scott as either producer or director—have used specific locations (Los Angeles, New York, Provence) to reinforce particular themes. This is not only characteristic of familiar works (*Blade Runner*) but also influences the ways in which episodes of *Numb3rs* are filmed.

Finally, the encyclopedia incorporates entries on films by other directors who have influenced Scott's approach to his work as a director or producer. This includes not only classic works such as *The Seventh Seal* or *The Third Man* but also more recent films such as *The Good Shepherd*. In the case of *1492: The Conquest of Paradise*, space has been allotted to the rival film *Christopher Columbus*, produced by the Salkind brothers, which was released at the same time as the Scott film (and flopped at the box office). Such entries demonstrate Scott's enduring respect for other directors, both past and present, who have contributed to the enrichment of cinema as an art form.

Each entry is followed by a bibliography of published sources, both in print form and online. Perhaps uniquely, Scott has understood the potential of the Internet to reach his audiences both for his film and television work. Many of the interviews he has given—particularly in recent years— have been published online and can be readily accessed. On the other hand, many of them tend to say much the same thing (especially when they are publicizing an individual film); with this in mind, I have included only a selection of them in this encyclopedia. Readers seeking further published interviews with Scott online are encouraged to search for themselves. Nonetheless, the bibliography included in this work remains the most comprehensive yet published on Scott's work both past and present.

Ridley Scott has always been an exceptionally busy person and remains so to this day. As I write this introduction (in March 2009), I discover from the *Internet Movie Database* that he is currently involved in nine projects, ranging from *Tell-Tale* (an adaptation of Edgar Allan Poe's "The Tell-Tale Heart") to *Into the Storm* (a sequel to *The Gathering Storm*) and *Welcome to the Rileys* (directed by Jake Scott), not to mention another series of *Numb3rs* (which is currently being broadcast on CBS). Perhaps future editions of *The Ridley Scott Encyclopedia* will incorporate entries on these works, as well as updating the bibliographies.

I must admit that writing this encyclopedia proved a most enjoyable task. Scott has always been reliable—someone who could be trusted to helm a big-budget project and turn in a profit. Hopefully this encyclopedia will show that he is also a great director/producer, whose oeuvre has a lot to say to today's audiences about living in the post-9/11 world.

ABOUTBUL, ALON (1965–)

Israeli actor whose films include *Munich* (2005), *Noodle* (2007), and *BODY OF LIES*. Cast as the extremist leader Al-Saleem, Aboutbul offers a penetrating study of an intelligent man who believes that his cause is worth fighting for. "Non-believers" such as Roger Ferris (LEONARDO DICAPRIO) must be executed for the wrongs they have committed against Muslims in the past. The best course of action for them is "to pray. The time has come. God is great." Al-Saleem's behavior proves the truth of W. H. Auden's lines (included as a preface to the film): "I and the public know/ What all schoolchildren learn/ Those to whom evil is done/ Do evil in return."

ADAM ADAMANT LIVES!

GB 1966 TV series, 29 × 50-min episodes, b/w. *Production Company*: British Broadcasting Corporation. *Producer*: Verity Lambert. *Directors*: Moira Armstrong (seven episodes), Philip Dudley (four episodes), Ridley Scott (three episodes), Paul Ciappessoni (three episodes), Henri Safran (three episodes), Roger Jenkins (two episodes), Leonard Lewis (two episodes), Laurence Bourne (two episodes). *Writers*: Dick Vosburgh (two episodes), Tony Williamson (nine episodes). *Production Designers*: Peter Kindred (five episodes), Michael Young (five episodes), Evan Hercules (four episodes). *Music*: David Lee. *Cast*: Gerald Harper (*Adam Adamant*), Juliet Harmer (*Georgina Jones*), Jack May (*William E. Simms*).

Adam Adamant Lives! was conceived as an escapist adventure series, the BBC's answer to the highly successful Independent Television (ITV) series *The Avengers*. The BBC's head of drama, Sydney Newman, had originally planned to adapt the stories of Sexton Blake, a comic-book hero created in 1893, which had already been successfully broadcast on radio. However, the rights could not be secured, so Newman created a series from scratch. The name Adam Adamant came from the mineral adamantine, which is "tougher than diamonds." The series was conceived as a prestige drama. Newman invited the British singer Kathy Kirby to record the theme tune in an orchestral arrangement strongly reminiscent of Shirley Bassey's "Goldfinger" (1962).

Adam Adamant (GERALD HARPER) was an Edwardian adventurer who had been frozen in a block of ice for sixty years. His attitudes and values were entirely different from those of the 1960s: one of the series' chief premises was to show how he was both entranced and appalled by the contemporary world. He was especially shocked by what he perceived as a lack of morality where women were concerned. He could not adjust to the fact that many of them felt quite capable of choosing their own destinies. He found it particularly difficult to understand the behavior of his sidekick, Georgina Jones (JULIET HARMER), a typically free-spirited 1960s woman who always wanted to be in the thick of the action.

As with *The Avengers*, the plots of *Adam Adamant Lives!* were generally far-fetched, with Adam rescuing the weak and oppressed from villains who sought to take over the world. The villains were often portrayed as slightly camp—in contrast to Adam's gentlemanly appearance. In several episodes there was also an evil female accomplice, someone who could twist Adam around their little fingers. In a 2006 documentary, the series producer VERITY LAMBERT stressed that such women epitomized the spirit of the 1960s, where people sought new forms of self-expression. Nonetheless Adam usually emerged victorious by outwitting these women, or—if that strategy failed—by striking them down (accompanied by an apology for doing so). He would subsequently save the world from certain doom by vanquishing the villains.

The series ran for two seasons, 1966–1967, when the BBC canceled it because it had not attracted sufficiently high ratings. It remained forgotten until the 2007 release of all the surviving episodes in the BBC archives—plus a documentary on the making of the series—in a five-DVD set. It provides a fascinating example of an era in British television history—the so-called "swinging sixties"—when it really did seem as if new possibilities were being created, especially for women. Ridley Scott directed one episode in series one: "THE LEAGUE OF UNCHARITABLE LADIES" (broadcast 22 September 1966) and two in series two—"Death Begins at Seventy" (broadcast 18 February 1967) and "The Resurrectionists" (broadcast

11 March 1967). Although primitively filmed (directors were given a maximum of two days' studio time to shoot each 50-minute episode), it provides a fascinating record of Ridley Scott's early attempts at directing.

Reference

Verity Lambert, interviewed in *This Man Is the One* (documentary celebrating the fortieth anniversary of *Adam Adamant Lives!* (London: BBC Worldwide, 2006).

AFFLECK, CASEY (1975–)

Casey Affleck made his debut in *To Die For* (1995) and teamed with BRAD PITT on all three *Oceans* films—*Ocean's Eleven* (2001), *Ocean's Twelve* (2004), and *Ocean's Thirteen* (2007).

Cast as Robert Ford in *THE ASSASSINATION OF JESSE JAMES BY THE COWARD ROBERT FORD*, Affleck plays a sniveling little crawler whose life revolves around following in Jesse James's (BRAD PITT's) footsteps. In director ANDREW DOMINIK's screenplay, Ford conceives himself as a nobody—someone paling into insignificance beside a man such as Jesse James. Once he has murdered James, however, his character changes completely; no longer the subordinate, he barnstorms across the Broadway stage, reenacting the crime for appreciative audiences. The screenplay describes the climax to his performance thus: "The house lights dim with darkness. Then rise on a stage which contains only Robert Ford. He slings his gun and proclaims with gravity: 'And that's how I killed Jesse James.'" Although the narrator (HUGH ROSS) tells that by the end of his life Ford "was ashamed of his persiflage, his boasting, his pretensions of courage and ruthlessness," this is clearly not the case; Ford revels in his celebrity status. Like James, he willingly courts death as he removes his cartridge belt, winds it around his gun and rests it against the cash register of the Omaha Club. This provides an open invitation for Edward Patrick O'Kelly (Michael Copeman) to assassinate him.

References

"About the Production," http://party931.com/common/movies/notes/54706-1-full.html (accessed 12 August 2008); Andrew Dominik, "The Assassination of Jesse James by the Coward Robert Ford," Final White Draft Screenplay dated 17 August 2005, www.simplyscripts.com/oscar80.html (accessed 5 February 2009); Damon Wise, "Casey Affleck Is the Coward Robert Ford," *Empire* 221 (November 2007): 146–47; Damon Wise, "Casey, the Brother," *The Times: The Knowledge*, 24 November 2007, 6–7.

ALIEN

GB 1979 r/t 124 min col. *Production Companies:* Brandywine Productions and Twentieth Century-Fox Productions. *Producers:* Gordon Carroll, David Giler, and Walter Hill. *Director:* Ridley Scott. *Writers:* Walter Hill and Dan O'Bannon.

Director of Photography: Derek Vanlint. *Music:* Jerry Goldsmith. *Production designer:* Michael Seymour. *Cast:* Tom Skerritt (*Dallas*), Sigourney Weaver (*Ripley*), Veronica Cartwright (*Lambert*), Harry Dean Stanton (*Brett*), John Hurt (*Kane*), Ian Holm (*Ash*), Yaphet Kotto (*Parker*).

The then-head of Twentieth Century-Fox, Sandy Lieberson, saw *THE DUELLISTS* and decided to look for a project Ridley Scott might find attractive. One such project was a script co-written by WALTER HILL and DAN O'BANNON, originally entitled *Star Beast*. After several rewrites and a name change to *Alien*, the screenplay was optioned by a Fox-related company Brandywine Productions, founded by Hill, DAVID GILER, and producer GORDON CARROLL. Giler and Hill rewrote O'Bannon's screenplay, preserving the original plot but altering the dialogue. They made several changes, including switching the gender of the central character from a man to a woman. It was this script that Scott eventually agreed to direct with Hill, Giler, and Carroll as producers. The budget was fixed at $8 million, a substantial increase on *The Duellists*, which cost $900,000.

The film itself has its roots in 1950s horror films such as *THE THING FROM ANOTHER WORLD* (1951) and *INVASION OF THE BODY SNATCHERS* (1956), as well as comic books. The cartoonist RON COBB, whose previous work included creating several creatures for George Lucas's *Star Wars* (1977), was hired to design *Alien*'s human spacecraft, the mechanisms within it, and everything else connected with the human world. The spacesuits were designed by the French artist Jean Giraud (aka Moebius); the alien itself was created by the Swiss painter and sculptor H. R. GIGER. The designs featured the creative use of bones in the architecture (the set constructors used real bones in making the interior of the alien ship). The design of the creature, with strong Freudian sexual overtones and multiple phallic symbols, provides a compelling androgynous image, conforming to images in horror films that often redraw gender lines.

JERRY GOLDSMITH was responsible for the score; but Scott remained unhappy with some of it. Some of the cues scored for *Alien* were replaced with ones Goldsmith composed years earlier for John Huston's *Freud* (1961). According to PAUL M. SAMMON, Scott substituted Goldsmith's end-credit music with an extract from Howard Hanson's Symphony No. 2 ("Romantic") in the belief that Hanson's "feminine" music ended the film on a hard-won but triumphant note.

The film caused a great stir on its American opening (despite Frank Rich's rather tepid review in *Time* which considered the piece "a cinematic bastard, and a pretty mean bastard at that. *Alien* contains a couple of genuine jolts, a barrage of convincing special effects and enough gore to gross out children of all ages. What is missing is wit, imagination and the vaguest hint of human feeling." The London *Daily Mirror* invited some of its readers to share a special preview experience of the film which "is breaking all box-office records in America"; one of them was quoted as saying that "It's [the film is] the most wonderful experience in the world. He [H. R. Giger] may paint strange pictures, but he's no madman." The reviews were equally enthusiastic: the *Sunday Express* critic felt that "the hairs pricked on the back of my neck . . . and I swear I heard them do so." Nigel Andrews felt that there had never been a movie "which looks as resplendent as this since [Kubrick's] *2001*." Philip French believed that while the film was "not a particularly elevating experience . . . it is a uniquely cinematic one, and as a piece of professional filmmaking it reflects credit on everyone concerned."

The film was a great financial success, and won the Academy Award in 1979 for Best Visual Effects, as well as receiving a nomination for Best Art Decoration—Set Decoration. The Academy of Science Fiction, Fantasy and Horror Films, USA, named it the Best Science Fiction film of the year and Ridley Scott Best Director, and it won the Hugo Award for Best Dramatic Presentation. In 2002 the United States National Film Registry incorporated it into its collection on the grounds that the film was "culturally, historically or aesthetically significant." In 2003 the film was rereleased as THE DIRECTOR'S CUT. The film continues to exert an influence today. The critic Andrew O'Hehir wrote in 2006 that "almost every horror film since *Alien* has ripped it off in some way, but most of the imitations have focused on details." In 2007 *Empire Magazine* named the "chestbuster" scene the greatest R-rated movie moment ever.

Alien represents a radical departure from Scott's previous work. He had never done a science fiction film, even though he had some experience of time-travel subjects while directing episodes of the BBC series *ADAM ADAMANT LIVES!* Nonetheless, *Alien* contains distinct echoes of *THE DUELLISTS*. The spaceship in the film is called *NOSTROMO*—a conscious borrowing from JOSEPH CONRAD's novel that reminds us of Scott's interest in his work. Although a matter of conjecture, it might be argued that *Alien* resembles *Nostromo* in its portrayal of characters that never change. Ian Watt argues that Conrad's purpose lies in demonstrating the importance of action, for it is only when people act that "they will find, or probably fail to find, the realization of their ideas and aims as individuals." The same applies to the characters in *Alien*, as Scott shows how authority and power are ceded to people irrespective of sex, solely in regard to their position and function. The film takes for granted Ripley's (SIGOURNEY WEAVER's) assumption of command, her right to order and boss the men around. Her most effective ally is Parker (YAPHET KOTTO), a black male worker committed to action, especially when it comes

to destroying the alien. Ripley herself spends the last seventeen minutes of the film making her own—successful—stand against it.

The Conradian echoes in *Alien* are also evident in its focus on duty and responsibility. In *The Duellists*, the two protagonists are obsessed with the idea of correct procedure to sustain their HONOR, even if that means sacrificing their humanity. In *Alien* Ripley displays similar traits, as she refuses to open the airlock through which the stricken Kane (JOHN HURT), Dallas (TOM SKERRITT), and Lambert (VERONICA CARTWRIGHT) might pass to safety. Her insistence on the rules leads her to sacrifice friends, colleagues, and (in Dallas's case) loved ones. Initially we are encouraged to sympathize with Ash (IAN HOLM), who takes a chance by opening the airlock, even if he incurs Ripley's wrath as she accuses him of neglecting his responsibilities as a science officer. Scott emphasizes Ash's apparent humanity as he shows the science officer wringing his hands in anxiety, on the verge of breaking into a cold sweat.

As the action unfolds, however, we gradually understand that Ripley's concern for the rules has been prompted by her suspicion about Ash's competence for the job. Compare this clear-headed attitude with Dallas's and Ash's emphasis on the protocols laid down by the Company. "The money's safe!" exclaims Dallas as he leaves the mother ship to explore the alien planet. For his part, Ash seems more preoccupied with conducting exhaustive tests on the alien than protecting human life. Scott observes in the DVD commentary to the film's 2003 release that Ash's preoccupation with the job reveals that "he has an agenda . . . no one knows what it is." Parker understands his shortcomings; at one point when Ripley assigns a duty to the two of them, Parker insists he will do it alone.

The sheer futility of adhering to Company rules is revealed when Parker and Ash discover that Ash is a robot, planted on the spaceship for the express purpose of controlling the crew. Those who blindly live by rules without exploring their implications will end up like Ash—automatons with no capacity for self-determination. In the Company's view, such people are expendable, so long as the alien can be brought back to earth without damage.

Alien also makes some telling points about the fragility of gender roles. If Ash has been implanted into the spaceship's womb, Kane, when the alien is in his stomach, is impregnated. The male has become feminized, quite literally devoured by it. Other male members of the crew suffer a similar fate: Brett (HARRY DEAN STANTON) and Dallas are covered in mucus, transformed into wombs to fertilize alien eggs. Lambert dies because she is traumatized by the alien's perceived "threat," being unfamiliar with its predatory MASCULINITY. The alien is also a good example of how CHILDHOOD can be corrupted if the "parents" (in this case, Kane and the alien) are corrupt. It is not just the protagonists who are victims of "gender trouble." "Mother," the spaceship's computer, not only symbolically gives birth to the crew, but has the power to dispense with them at the end of the film. By destroying the spaceship, Ripley curtails "Mother's" malevolent power; no longer a vehicle for producing and sustaining human life, it has been programmed simply to destroy human beings once they have outlived their usefulness. The same logic governs Ash's behavior; he is not a human being at all, but an android, an asexual being identified with "Mother." Having fulfilled his appointed task—to capture the alien and organize its safe passage to Earth—he has no other function in the film, and can thus be destroyed.

But perhaps the film's politics are not quite as radical as a first viewing might suggest. At one point Ash tries to kill Ripley by forcing a rolled-up pornographic magazine down her throat. Scott has described this sequence in the Director's Commentary as evidence of the robot's destructive sex-drive; he does not have a penis, so he has to find other means of asserting his MASCULINITY. More significantly, this scene shows how male violence has been equated with science and progress. The Darwinian concept of the survival of the fittest is clearly emphasized: as men are stronger, they believe they have the "natural" right to assert their authority. Stephen Mulhall sums up this view of life thus: "rapacious, inherently violent and violating." Significantly, the only way in which the alien can be destroyed is through "masculine" methods, as Ripley buries a harpoon in its heart and sends it spinning into outer space. She might emerge victorious by nullifying the alien's perceived "threat," but achieves it at the expense of her femininity. She herself becomes "rapacious, inherently violent and violating."

The final sequence can be interpreted optimistically, as Ripley returns to the womb of the module to look after the cat Jones, and hopefully to hibernate during the six weeks it will take to return to Earth. She recovers her maternal instincts as she cradles the cat in her arms, and thereby shows how life in the cosmos is not inimical to humanity. On the other hand, there are certain elements that seek to undermine the tranquility of this sequence. Ripley might have recovered her femininity, but it is significant that she enjoys a close relationship with an animal rather than a human being. Moreover, her isolation recalls the end of *The Duellists*, when D'Hubert (HARVEY KEITEL) looks out over the landscape like Napoleon, proud but inescapably alone. In the earlier film Scott used this image to show how the soldier's obsession costs him everything: friendship, career, and self-respect. In *Alien* Ripley is certainly characterized as a strong woman, but throughout the previous two hours the notion of strength has been associated with the alien—the penis-shaped organism emerging from Kane's stomach, the beast crushing Parker like a pygmy. Ripley might triumph in the end, but she has herself been transformed into an alien—someone committed to the Darwinian notion of the survival of the fittest.

Alien has been the subject of considerable critical comment since its release. Peter Lev (1998) believes that this film and Scott's subsequent work in *BLADE RUNNER* "project a future of oppressive institutions." Thomas B. Byers develops the point by identifying the Company as symptomatic of many modern capitalist organizations valuing commodities above human life. On this view, "human beings have become the true aliens." This picks up a point first made in 1980 by Jeff Gould, who identified the alien as resembling "nothing so much as that other superorganism, and victor in an evolutionary struggle: the multinational (soon to be interstellar) corporation. In the system of the narrative, the Alien is the double . . . of the Company."

Other critics have seen the film as a comment on late 1970s America. William Paul, among others, suggests that its social structure "is based on something corrupt because corruption actually exists at the top. After Watergate the loss of a head of state (with Nixon's resignation) and the greatly weakened presidency that followed it, provoked an anxiety about leadership that permeated the culture. American society had become a social body without a head."

James H. Kavanagh identifies *Alien* as a feminist parable, portraying Ripley as "a strong woman . . . a new type of humanist hero—this, after literally chewing up all other differences existing within the space of the human." In contrast, Judith Newton argues that the film's ending invests Ripley with "traditionally feminine qualities. . . . we see her stripped to her bikini underpants . . . exposing a long, and lovingly recorded, expanse of marvellous body . . . [She] is not only divested of coalition and reinvested with feminity [*sic*], she is also confirmed as a Company Woman." This essentially patriarchal strategy has also been developed by Barbara Creed, who identifies the alien as an example of the "monstrous-feminine"—a being which cannot be contained within Freudian, masculinist discourse: "the monstrous creature is constructed as the phallus of the negative mother . . . What is horrific is her desire to cling to her offspring in order to continue to 'have the phallus.' Her monstrous desire is concretized as the figure of the alien; the creature whose deadly mission is . . . to reincorporate and destroy all life." The sign of Ripley stripping at the end of the film represents the (male) director's belief that "the monstrousness of women" has been controlled "through the display of woman as reassuring and pleasurable sign . . . The final sequence works, not only to dispose of the alien, but also to repress the nightmare image of the monstrous-feminine within the text's patriarchal discourses." Catherine Constable develops Creed's thesis by arguing that "human reproduction [in the film] is represented as scientific or sterile, in clear contrast to the alien's physical materiality, thus setting up an opposition between the human and the monstrous." On this view, the monstrous-feminine alien is also the most fertile being on the ship, which would suggest that Scott's attempts to contain it at the end of the film are ultimately futile.

Nonetheless, the director appears to make strenuous efforts to contain his material within a patriarchal framework. Annette Kuhn suggests that the special effects sequences—for example, the alien emerging from Kane's stomach—"invite the [male] spectator's awed gaze . . . What sort of appeal to scopophilia is being made in such displays of cinema's codes of visibility?" Jenny Wolmark approaches the film from a POSTMODERN perspective, arguing that the combination of male and female traits in Ripley's character allows "for the development of an alternative framework for thinking about [sexual] difference, one that is not characterized by polarities and hierarchies, but which is contingent, on the edges of the possible."

Pamela Church Gibson argues that, while there has been a considerable amount of comment on the film itself, little has been published on the ways in which audiences react to it. She argues that "avowed fans . . . —unlike many academics—are invariably familiar with the work of the artist H. R. Giger . . . This might be because Giger's work is too unsettling, too transgressive, or too phallic . . . The disregard for Giger's work could also be the result of artistic snobbery—his work seen as second-rate, as not coming within any recognized canon. But really there seems to be a lack of knowledge, rather than a considered judgment, among film scholars."

Alien's narrative sources have been explored by Robbie Robertson. They include Joseph Conrad, H. P. Lovecraft, popular literature of the nineteenth century (*The War of the Worlds*, for example), American B pictures of the 1950s, and short stories such as A. E. Van Vogt's *The Voyage of the Space Beagle* (1950).

References

"Alien: Day One," *Daily Mirror*, June 11, 1979, 4; Nigel Andrews, "Alien Corn," *Financial Times,* 2 September 1979, 3; Richard Barkley, "When a Space Crew Answers a Strange Signal," *Sunday Express,* 4 September 1979, 30; Thomas B. Byers, "Commodity Futures" (1987), in *Alien Zone: Cultural Theory and Contemporary Science Fiction Cinema*, ed. Annette Kuhn (London: Verso, 1990), 40; Catherine Constable, "Becoming the Monster's Mother: Morphologies of Identity in the *Alien* Series," in *Alien Zone II: The Spaces of Science Fiction Cinema,* ed. Annette Kuhn (London: Verso, 1999), 173; Barbara Creed, "*Alien* and the Monstrous-Feminine," (1986), in Kuhn, *Alien Zone*, 139–40; Philip French, "Something Misty in Space," *The Observer,* 4 September 1979, 36; Pamela Church Gibson, "You've Been in My Life So Long I Can't Remem-

ber Anything Else: Into the Labyrinth with Ripley and the Alien," in *Keyframes: Popular Cinema and Cultural Studies,* ed. Matthew Tinkcom and Amy Villarejo (London and New York: Routledge, 2001), 43–45; Jeff Gould, "The Destruction of the Social by the Organic in *Alien,*" *Science Fiction Studies* 7, no.3 (1980): 283; James H. Kavanagh, "Feminism, Humanism and Science in *Alien*" (1980), in Kuhn, *Alien Zone*, 86; Annette Kuhn, "Introduction: Spectators," in Kuhn, *Alien Zone,* 148; Peter Lev, "Whose Future? *Star Wars, Alien* and *Blade Runner*," *Literature/Film Quarterly* 26, no.1 (1998): 34; Stephen Mulhall, *On Film* (London and New York: Routledge, 2002), 30; Judith Newton, "Feminism and Anxiety in *Alien*" (1981) in Kuhn, *Alien Zone,* 86; Andrew O'Hehir, "The Horror, The Horror," *Salon* 1 November 2003, http://dir.salon.com/story/ent/movies/review/2003/11/01/alien/index.html?CP=IMD&DN=110 (accessed 9 January 2008); William Paul, *Modern Hollywood Horror and Comedy* (New York: Columbia University Press, 1994), 395; Frank Rich, "Sell Job," *Time*, 4 June 1979, 15; Robbie Robertson, "Some Narrative Sources of Ridley Scott's *Alien*," in *Cinema and Fiction: New Modes of Adapting 1950–1990,* ed. John Orr and Colin Nicholson (Edinburgh: Edinburgh University Press, 1992), 171–80; Paul M. Sammon, "The Beast," in *Ridley Scott: Close Up* (New York: Thunders Mouth Press, 1999), 56; Ridley Scott, "Director's Commentary to *Alien*" in *Alien Quadrilogy* (Los Angeles: Twentieth Century-Fox Home Entertainment Inc., 2003); Ian Watt, *Joseph Conrad: Nostromo* (Cambridge: Cambridge University Press, 1988), 82; Jenny Wolmark, *Aliens and Others: Science Fiction, Feminism and Postmodernism* (Iowa City: University of Iowa Press, 1994), 53.

Bibliography

Anthony Ambroglio, "*Alien:* In Space, No One Can Hear Your Primal Scream," in *Eros in the Mind's Eye,* ed. Donald Palumbo (Westport, CT: Greenwood Press, 1986), 169–79; Robert Baird, "The Startle Effect: Implications for Spectator Cognition and Media Theory," *Film Quarterly* 53, no.3 (Spring 2000): 12–24; Michele Aina Barale, "When Lambs and Aliens Meet: Girl-Faggots and Boy-Dykes Go to the Movies," in *Cross-Purposes: Lesbians, Feminists and the Limits of Alliance,* ed. Diana Heller (Bloomington: Indiana University Press, 1997), 95–106; Rebecca Bell-Martereau, "Woman: The Other Alien in *Alien,*" in *Women Worldwalkers: New Dimensions of Science Fiction and Fantasy,* ed. Jane B. Weedman (Lubbock: Texas Tech Press, 1995), 9–24; Ellen Bishop, "Alien Subject/ Alien Thought: The Female Subject in the *Aliens* Films" in *Critical Studies on the Feminist Subject,* ed. Giovanna Covi (Trento: Dipartimento di Scienze Filologiche e Storiche, 1997), 127–63; Thomas B. Byers, "Kissing Becky: Masculine Fears and Misogynist Moments in Science Fiction Films," *Arizona Quarterly* 45, no.3 (1989): 77–95; Donald Carveth, Naomi Gold, "The Pre-Oedipalizing of Klein in (North) America: Ridley Scott's *Alien* Re-Analyzed," *PsyArt: An Online Journal for the Psychological Study of the Arts*. www.clas.ufl.edu/ipsa/journal/1999_carveth03.shtml (accessed 3 August 2008); Mark Clark, "Pets or Meat: *Alien, Aliens* and the Indifference of the Gods," in *Science Fiction America: Essays on SF Cinema,* ed.

David J. Hogan (Jefferson, NC and London: McFarland and Company Inc. [Publishers], 2005), 233–46; Patricia Clough, "The 'Final Girl' in the Fictions of Science and Culture," *Stanford Humanities Review* 2, nos. 2–3 (1992): 57–69; John L. Cobbs, "*Alien* as an Abortion Parable," *Literature/Film Quarterly* 18, no.3 (1990): 198–201; C. Carter Colwell, "Primitivism in the Movies of Ridley Scott: *Alien* and *Blade Runner*," in *Retrofitting Blade Runner: Issues in Ridley Scott's Blade Runner and Philip K. Dick's Do Androids Dream of Electric Sheep?* ed. Judith B. Kerman (Bowling Green: Bowling Green State University Popular Press, 1991), 124–31; Michael Davis, "What's the Story, Mother?" *Gothic Studies* 2, no.2 (August 2000): 245–57; James Delson, "*Alien* from the Inside Out: Part II," in *Ridley Scott Interviews*, ed. Laurence F. Knapp and Andrea F. Kulas (Jackson: University Press of Mississippi, 2005), 11–32; Thomas Doherty, "Genre, Gender and the *Aliens* Trilogy," in *The Dread of Difference: Gender and the Horror Film*, ed. Barry Keith Grant (Austin: University of Texas Press, 1996), 181–99; C. Ximena Gallardo and C. Jason Smith, *Alien Woman: The Making of Lt. Ellen Ripley* (New York: Continuum, 2004); Tabitha Goode, "Abstract Representational Space: Uncanny Aliens and Others (Pandora, or Prometheus' Return)," *Camera Obscura* nos. 40–41 (1997): 245–74; Michael Grant, "'Ultimate Formlessness: Cinema, Horror and the Limits of Meaning," in *Horror Film and Psychoanalysis: Freud's Worst Nightmare*, ed. Steven Jay Schneider (Cambridge: Cambridge University Press, 2004), 172–88; Harvey R. Greenberg, "Fembo: Aliens' Intentions," *Journal of Popular Film and Television* 15, no.4 (1988): 165–71; Harvey R. Greenberg, "Reimagining the Gargoyle: Psychoanalytic Notes on *Alien*," *Camera Obscura* 15 (Fall 1986): 86–109; Steffen Hantke, "In the Belly of the Mechanical Beast: Technological Environments in the *Alien* Films," *Journal of Popular Culture* 36, no.3 (2003): 518–46; Chad Hermann, "Some Horrible Dream About (S)mothering: Sexuality, Gender and Family in the *Alien* Trilogy," *PostScript* 16, no.3 (Summer 1997): 36–50; Kelly Hurley, "Reading Like an Alien: Posthuman Identity in Ridley Scott's *Alien* and David Cronenberg's *Rabid*," in *Posthuman Bodies*, ed. Judith Halberstam and Ira Livingston (Bloomington: Indiana University Press, 1995), 203–24; Ros Jennings, "Desire and Design: Ripley Undressed," in *Immortal, Invisible, Lesbians and the Moving Image*, ed. Tamsin Wilton (London and New York: Routledge, 1995), 193–206; T. J. Matheson, "Triumphant Technology and Minimal Man: The Technological Society, Science Fiction Films and Ridley Scott's *Alien*," *Extrapolation* 33, no.3 (Fall 1992): 215–29; Steve Nolan, "Worshipping (Wo)Men, Liturgical Representation and Feminist Film Theory: An *Alien/s* Identification," *Bulletin of the John Rylands Library of Manchester* 80, no.3 (Autumn 1998): 195–213; Mary Phar, "Synthetics, Humanity and the Life Force in the *Alien* Quartet," in *No Cure for the Future: Disease and Medicine in Science Fiction and Fantasy*, ed. Gary Westfield and George Slusser (Westport, CT: Greenwood Press, 2002), 145–62; Rolando J. Romero, "The Postmodern Hybrid: Do Aliens Dream of Alien Sheep?" *PostScript* 16, no.1 (1996): 41–52; Janice Hocker Rushing, "Evolution of the 'New Frontier' in *Alien* and *Aliens*: Patriarchal Co-optation of the Feminine Archetype," *Quarterly Journal of Speech* 75, no.1 (1989): 1–24; Amy Taubin, "The *Alien* Trilogy: From Feminism to AIDS," in *Women and Film: A Sight and Sound Reader*, ed. Pam Cook and Philip Dodd (London: British Film Institute, 1993), 93–100; Robert Torry, "Awakening to the Other: Feminism and the Ego-Ideal in *Alien*," *Women's Studies: An Interdisciplinary Journal* 23, no.4 (1994): 343–63; Colleen Tremonte, "Recasting the Western Hero: Ethos in High-Tech Science Fiction," *Journal of the American Studies Association of Texas* 20 (1989): 94–100; Jeffery A. Weinstock, "Freaks in Space: 'Extraterrestrialism' and 'Deep-Space Multiculturalism,'" in *Freakery: Cultural Spectacles of the Extraordinary Body*, ed. Rosemarie Garland Thompson (New York: New York University Press, 1996), 32–37.

ALIEN: THE DIRECTOR'S CUT

GB/US 2003 117 min col. Rerelease of the original film with several minor changes. They include a new scene where the crew hear an unearthly signal from the planet and look at each other as if uncertain as to its identity. Lambert (VERONICA CARTWRIGHT) calls it a planetoid, while Ash (IAN HOLM) thinks that people can walk on the planet.

The Director's Cut includes more panning shots of the alien's lair, and a closer shot of the membrane and skin. It also incorporates an extra sequence in which Parker (YAPHET KOTTO) asks how Kane (JOHN HURT) can breathe with the face-hugger on his features. Meanwhile Dallas (TOM SKERRITT) is angry at Ripley for refusing his order to let the infected Kane into the *NOSTROMO*, even though Dallas has disregarded Company policy by permitting it in the first place.

The Director's Cut has a new version of Brett's (HARRY DEAN STANTON's) death, as the creature's claws move slowly into frame, then lift him up and away. Parker and Ripley rush into the room, and look up to see the alien and the empty airlock. Drops of blood fall on to the camera lens. Scott cuts back to Parker and Ripley holding their hands out to catch the blood, and Parker dropping his weapon onto a bloodstained floor. The sequence ends with a close-up on Jones the cat as Parker screams "Brett!!"

Most significantly, the Director's Cut restores the sequence created by Scott in collaboration with special effects designer NICK ALLDER, in which Ripley discovers Dallas and Brett in an underground cavern being converted into alien spores. Originally cut from the 1979 version on the grounds that it impeded plot-development, this sequence provides an explanation as to why the alien poses such a threat to the crew's future.

Because of the shortening of certain sequences, the Director's Cut is actually forty-six seconds shorter than the original. The *Cinefantastique* reviewer described it as "a harrowing and truly unique piece of art rather than commerce."

Reference

Jeff Bond, "Interstellar Scenes," *Cinefantastique* 35, no.6 (December 2003): 14.

ALIEN QUADRILOGY

The *Alien Quadrilogy* is a four-movie, nine-DVD box set of *ALIEN, Aliens, Alien 3* and *Alien: Resurrection*. Released by Twentieth Century-Fox on December 2, 2003, following the rerelease of *Alien* in theaters on Halloween 2003. This nine-disc set replaced the five-disc set of the series, *The Alien Legacy*.

Created by DVD producer CHARLES DE LAUZIRIKA, the *Alien Quadrilogy* features each of the four movies with two discs; one contains the theatrical and director's cut/special edition of the movie, and the second includes bonus features such as "making of" documentaries. The ninth disc includes bonus features for the entire franchise, such as an edited version of "Alien Evolution," a documentary made by the UK's Channel 4. The *Alien Quadrilogy* was well received by DVD critics and went on to win several awards, including the DVD Exclusive Award for Best Classic Movie (including all extras) and Best Audio Commentary for *Alien*, as well as landing on several top ten DVD lists. In 2005, for the twenty-fifth anniversary, the *Alien Quadrilogy* was rereleased in Alien-head packaging, with the DVDs stored inside the head.

ALIEN (VIDEO GAME)

Alien is a game produced by Argonaut Software in 1984 and released by Argus Press—it is based on the film *ALIEN* directed by Ridley Scott. The game used very simple black and green graphics, with a little extra color for some text and for the location of the characters.

Alien was a slow-moving but suspense-heavy strategy game. An omniscient, menu-driven game, the player was put in charge of all of the crew members of the *NOSTROMO*. The game started with one of the crew members being killed by the alien, which mirrored the death of Kane (JOHN HURT) when he gave birth to the alien in the movie. The player moved the characters around on a map-grid representation of the ship as they searched for the alien. Littered around the map were various useful objects such as nets, incinerators, laser pistols, and oxygen tanks. The player could order one of the crew members to pick up such objects and use them when needed.

The game-play was challenging in that, based on the current situation, the emotional status of your crewmen could change. The emotional status could range from confident, stable, uneasy, shaken, hysterical, and broken. This meant that the crew members would not always obey the player's orders and could be frozen by fear or unwillingness to enter a hazardous situation. Ordering characters to pick up weapons could positively affect their emotional status and make them more likely to follow orders. Sending a character off alone could negatively affect emotional status, causing the character to perform poorly.

One of the crew members was secretly an android and he would turn on the other crew when the player least expected it. When the crew was reduced to three, there was the option of self-destructing the ship and escaping in the *Narcissus*.

ALIEN VS. PREDATOR

Two highly successful franchises brought together by Paul Thomas Anderson in 2004. Throughout the film there are references to *ALIEN*; for example, the altars in the Chamber of Sacrifices are arranged in the same fashion as the hibernation pods at the beginning of Scott's film.

The follow-up film *Aliens vs. Predator: Requiem* (2007) likewise contained references to Scott's film. DAN O'BANNON and RON SHUSETT took credit on both films for the original story.

ALIEN WAR

A "total reality" experience based on the *ALIEN* trilogy, which opened in London in 1993. Created by a pair of Glaswegians, Gary Gillies and John Gorman, this "living theatrical exhibition" recreates the experience of *Alien* employing costumes, props, and other memorabilia from SHEPPERTON STUDIOS. Twelve customers at a time were led through by Colonial Marines for a tour of the base owned by Weyland Yutani, the so-called company that owned the *NOSTROMO*. The attraction failed to find a large enough public and closed fairly soon afterwards.

References

"Aliens Ahoy!" *Empire*, November 1993, 12.

ALIENS NOVELS

The Aliens novels are an extension of the *ALIEN* franchise. Up until 1998, the novels were published by Bantam Books and were mostly adaptations of various comics previously published by Dark Horse Comics. The most recent run of novels, which began in 2005, consists of original stories being published by Dark Horse Comics under their DH Press imprint. They include *Earth Hive* (1993), *Nightmare Asylum* (1993), *The Female War* (1993), *Genocide* (1994), *Alien Harvest* (1995), *Labyrinth* (1996), *Rogue* (1995), *Berserker* (1998), *Original Sin* (2005), *DNA War* (2006), *Cauldron* (2007), *Steal Egg* (2007), *Criminal Enterprise* (2008), and *No Exit* (2008).

ALL THE INVISIBLE CHILDREN—"JONATHAN"

France, Italy 2005 17 min (total r/t 129 min) col. *Production Companies*: RAI, Adriana Chiesa Enterprises, and UNICEF.

Producers: Maria Grazia Cucinotta, Chiara Tilesi, and Stefano Veneruso. *Director:* Ridley Scott. *Writer:* Jordan Scott. *Director of Photography:* James Whitaker. *Production Designer:* Ben Scott. *Music:* Ramin Djawadi. *Cast:* David Thewlis, Kelly Macdonald, Jordan Clarke, Jack Thompson, Joshua Light.

One of an omnibus of seven short films on the subject of CHILDHOOD made by different directors (the other six were Mehdi Charef, Emir Kusturica, Spike Lee, Katia Lund, Stefano Veneruso, and JOHN WOO) as part of an initiative supported by the children's relief charity UNICEF. Scott's contribution—"Jonathan"—told of the eponymous hero, a photojournalist (DAVID THEWLIS) whose work has left him disillusioned and unhinged. Retreating from what he has experienced, he regressed back to when life was at its best, seeking renewal through a return to childhood. The children he meets on the way inspire him to embrace life again. The film deals once again with the theme of journeys and spiritual renewal, ideas which have been characteristic of Scott's work since *LEGEND*. The film was well received, particularly by filmgoers outside Italy; by 2006 it was the highest-grossing Italian film abroad.

All the Invisible Children has honorable intentions. But its unevenness means it feels more like several standalone films than an illuminating riff on one theme. Standouts are Spike Lee's incisive "Jesus Children of America," about an HIV-positive teen and "Joao and Bilu," Katia Lund's vibrant portrait of Sao Paolo's street kids. "Ciro," Stefano Veneruso's paean to Neapolitan street children, suffers an uncertain script although it boasts authentic non-professional performances. Less compelling are the plodding "Tanza" from Mehdi Charef; Jordan and Ridley Scott's unresolved war photographer episode "Jonathan"; and John Woo's over-schmaltzy "Song Song and the Little Cat." Portmanteaus can be hard to market. *All the Invisible Children* also lacks the edge that persuaded some audiences to try the likes of the similarly structured *11'09"01*.

Bibliography

"All the Invisible Children," *Cineforum* 449 (November 2005): 32–33; Roberto Chiesi, "All the Invisible Children," *Cineforum* 453 (April 2006): 44–45 (articles in Italian); Lee Marshall, "All the Invisible Children," *Screen International* 1541 (24–30 March 2006): 22.

ALLDER, NICK

Special effects supervisor for *ALIEN*. He was heavily involved in the making of a sequence cut from the original release but restored in THE DIRECTOR'S CUT (2003) in which Ripley (SIGOURNEY WEAVER) discovers Dallas (TOM SKERRITT) partially devoured yet still alive, glued to a niche in a wall with a sticky pitch-like substance. On the opposite wall, what remains of Brett (HARRY DEAN STAN-

TON) is being transformed into one of the alien spores. Shaking with fear, Ripley accedes to her captain's plea for an act of mercy and destroys the entire room with a flamethrower. Scott recalled in an interview with Don Shay that the sequence provided "a way of explaining what had happened on the derelict [spaceship] and what was now happening on the *NOSTROMO*. And I think it provided some explanation for the alien's killing spree . . . it has a very limited life span in which to reproduce itself. It also helped explain why it didn't attack Ripley in the *Narcissus*. Its days were over." Scott eventually decided that the sequence slowed up the film's plot-development, and ultimately removed it. Nick Allder also collaborated with ROB BOTTIN on the creation of the special effects for *LEGEND*.

References

Ridley Scott, quoted in Don Shay, "Creating an Alien Ambience," in Don Shay and Bill Norton, *Alien: The Special Effects* (London: Titan Books, 1997), 43.

ALLMAN, GREGG (1947–)

Rock and blues singer, best known as a founding member of The Allman Brothers Band. Allman provided the vocals for the title song in *BLACK RAIN*, a David Paich-produced "I'll Be Holding On," a power ballad so formulaic that his band Toto wouldn't have touched it, according to the *All-Music Guide Review*.

References

"Black Rain Soundtrack," *All-Music Guide Review*, www.artist direct.com/nad/store/artist/album/0,,53145,00.html (accessed 18 June 2008).

ALTMAN, BRUCE (1955–)

Born in the Bronx, New York, Altman's early screen career included roles in *Regarding Henry* (1991) and *Glengarry Glen Ross* (1993).

Cast as the therapist Dr. Klein in *MATCHSTICK MEN*, Altman offers a convincing portrait of a sympathetic person paid to listen to and advise Roy (NICOLAS CAGE). The only suggestion we might have that Klein might not be what he seems is that he smokes a pipe; as Scott and the co-writers NICK AND TED GRIFFIN suggest in the Director's Commentary to the DVD release of the film, anyone who smokes is not really trustworthy. In August 2008 Altman appeared as himself in an episode of AMC's *Cinemania* devoted to *Matchstick Men*. Hosted by comedian Regan Burns, this trivia competition—broadcast during the commercial breaks of the film—pitted two diehard fans against one another to see who knew the most about the actors, specific quotes and other details relating to *Matchstick Men*.

Reference

Ridley Scott, Nick and Ted Griffin, Director's Commentary to the 2004 DVD release of *Matchstick Men* (London: Warner Home Video UK, 2004).

AMERICAN FIGHTER PILOT

US 2002 TV series 7 × 60 min episodes (only two broadcast) col. *Production Companies*: Columbia Broadcasting System, Skip Film, Warfront Pictures, and Zeal Pictures. *Executive Producers*: Ridley Scott, Tony Scott, Jesse Negron. *Producers*: Maria Baltazzia, Jennifer Bresnan, Sean T. Coughlin, David Goffin, Erica Hanson, Geoff Mazer, Andy Meyer. *Writer/Director*: Jesse Negron. *Music*: Harry Gregson-Williams, Steve Jablonsky, John E. Nordstrom, and Andrew Rollins. *Cast*: Tod Giggy, Mike Love, Marcus Gregory, Robert Garland, Chris Penn (*narrator*), Regina Pope (*narrator*).

This reality series carries on from where *BLACK HAWK DOWN* left off, in its portrayal of the US Army. It followed three male US Air Force officers as they attended flight school at Tyndall Air Force Base in Panama City, Florida. If they passed the course, which lasts several months, they would become pilots of F-15 fighter jets. The series featured classroom training, practical exercises, and interviews with instructors. Viewers also saw how the officers' wives and families were affected by the high-stress environment. The series covered similar ground to that of British Second World War documentaries such as *FIGHTER PILOT*.

The series began life as a film but, once CBS expressed interest in broadcasting it, creator JESSE NEGRON decided to turn it into a reality show. Photography on the series was filmed in 2000, and during that time Negron was granted unprecedented access by air force and Navy alike. He followed his subjects into the classroom, aboard F-16s, inside diving tanks and everywhere else their training took them. He even managed to film the solo party, a ritual hitherto unseen by television viewers to celebrate the students' first solo flight in an F-15. According to US Air Force reports, the crew worked on the project for two years. To get the necessary aerial footage, crews filmed from the backseats of F-15s and affixed cameras to aircraft to capture training sessions. In addition to from-the-cockpit shots, camera crews followed these Top Guns-in-training from their homes to churches to local businesses in order to capture the culture and lifestyles of fighter pilots. The production was overseen by TONY SCOTT, who had been responsible for *TOP GUN* (1983), a fictionalized account of similar activities starring TOM CRUISE.

After filming was completed, the production was left on the shelf until CBS agreed to air the series in March 2002, as a way of fulfilling the White House's demand for "morale building" productions. In November 2001 Karl Rove, President George W. Bush's top White House adviser, was dispatched to Hollywood to discuss how its producers and celebrities could contribute to the war effort. Rove sought from Hollywood a commitment to patriotic material while the White House conducted its war on terrorism.

While *American Fighter Pilot* was filmed entirely before 9/11, the producers claim the event had little effect on the show. "Our project would have stayed the same," claimed director Negron in a prebroadcast interview: "What changed was people became much more interested in who our warriors were and who is defending our country." Nonetheless he did add some extra material, such as recalling the terrorist attacks in a title sequence at the beginning of each episode, plus post-9/11 interview footage of the pilots (some of whom apparently fought in the war in Afghanistan). The Pentagon was reportedly thrilled with the show: "It's important to them that the American public sees this with the black eyes in it—that this is the way our warriors are made," claimed Negron in an interview quoted in the *Michigan Daily*.

The publicity reinforced the jingoistic mood: "The show is a *Top Gun*-like reality series that follows three men from different walks of life as they train to become F-15 fighter pilots . . . As these heroes prepare to take control of some of the most complex and expensive planes in the world, they come face to face with the life-threatening reality of their chosen career." Sadly, the reviewers did not share this view: Caryn James in the *New York Times* described the series as "one long, unconvincing commercial for the Air Force . . . The series tries to make up for its lack of stirring characters with music-video editing and graphics, but the effect is haywire—not lively." Regional newspapers such as the *Michigan Daily* thought that the characters "offer little humor depth to the show, at least outside of . . . vomiting on one of the test flights." The *Pittsburgh Post-Gazette* went further by claiming that "editing chores on this choppy program were apparently farmed out to CBS's sister network MTV, which never met two seconds of film it couldn't slice into nanosecond clips." As a result, "the show's look, simply put, is repulsive." Viewers responded equally unenthusiastically to the series: only 4.8 million people watched the first show on 29 March 2002, and CBS canceled it after two episodes.

Nonetheless, the series reinforces thematic concerns characteristic of Ridley Scott's other work. MASCULINITY and male bonding are intrinsic to the *Fighter Pilot's* life. In the transcript of the two broadcast programs, one of the instructors says that he is looking for recruits "that have the hearts of a lion," who can "take this jet [the F-15] off and kick the crap out of any MIG-29 on the planet." Once they have learned to fly solo, they can be admitted "to the brotherhood." However, the recruits have to learn how to be strong; to put up with "the crap" thrown at them by the instructors: "Maybe an IP [Instructor Pilot] will refer to a student as a maggot because it's the lowest form of life that ever has the hope of flying." At the end of each week pilots gather to drink in the camp bar; this, they are told, is a means of learning more about flying "than you will on any flight." It also provides a means "for bonding and storytelling . . . This is a fraternity that you are attempting to enter, and as a student, you haven't entered it yet." At the beginning of the series, the three featured recruits—Mike Love, Marcus Gregory, and Todd Giggy—are even deprived of their male identities; in the self-enclosed world of the camp "they really don't have a tactical call sign [like the qualified pilots]. Somewhere over the course of that six-week [induction] period, they will do something that earns them a certain call sign. So in the meantime, we just name 'em [boners] . . . and just the boner with a number."

Anyone who deviates from these group norms is perceived as inadequate. Giggy turns up for training with bleached hair; the instructors claim—falsely—that he is "a complete wuss," as he has let his wife Lori change his hair color. One instructor claims that "if you want to highlight yourself in less than optimum or negative ways [by bleaching your hair], you're gonna incur some wrath, especially if you don't have any clout to stand on at all." As a devoted family man, Gregory finds it difficult to socialize with his fellow pilots, particularly when they bring women in for entertainment because "it lightens up the atmosphere, and . . . the guys like it after a long day." He has to learn the importance of "working together and trying to succeed together" in spite of his personal likes and dislikes.

Eventually the three recruits emerge triumphant by passing the grueling 112-day course. They acquire their particular identities (Marcus "Patch" Gregory, Mike "Getsno" Love, and Todd "Merkin" Giggy), while understanding at the same time the importance of remaining part of a group dedicated to protecting their families from enemies seeking to kill their wives and children. The experience of training teaches them "how to trust people and get to know them, [especially] the kind of guys to go to war with." In the final episode the entire group of pilots are shown coming together and chanting "We are warriors!" in an assertion of masculine strength and pride.

Although the three recruits remain devoted family men, they have a fixed concept of gender roles. While they consider it their duty to go out and fight for their country, their spouses are expected to stay at home and support them or look after their children. The concept of LOVE VS. DUTY, so important to many Scott films, is not an issue. Love describes his wife Mauri as "the most fantastic mother to my children that I could have ever found, and she does that while still being a great wife to me." Mauri herself finds her existence difficult, to say the least: "On the average I see

Michael for two hours, you know, an evening, if that, and mainly just for dinner. It's very hard to be alone and in a new place, and the only people that you have are your children . . . I really wanted a husband who worked a nine-to-five job." However, she devotes herself to Love: "Michael wanted it [to be a fighter pilot] so bad, and that, just, to me, that was the big thing that turned me around." Giggy admires his wife Lori who understood "from the get-go . . . what my schedule was like." Gregory's spouse Sunni is about to have a baby but is denied the experience of "the baby story" when "the husband goes to all their appointments and they have a lot of that fun bonding." Her husband tries to set aside some time "to talk and stuff" but he is usually so tired after a hard day that he has to rest, "to get enough sleep for the next day."

All three recruits are devotes to the ideals of AMERICANISM, most succinctly defined by their senior pilot instructor, Robert Garland: "Faith in God, your love of your family and then your country, an opportunity to defend your country, one nation under God, is the highest calling that a man can have." Gregory is seen worshiping in church and listening to the minister telling him that "when we disobey God, there are always consequences." Gregory responds: "Now there's hostility and there's disobedience in the world, and . . . [there's] the account of Cain killing Abel. Now there's hatred and murder springing up . . . Everyone seeks to find their purpose." His purpose, as he sees it, is to eliminate hostility and disobedience by removing those enemy forces that threaten the liberty of all Americans—including his family. Love insists that he always puts his family first. One of the instructors describes the entire series as a journey, "a challenging time in our life [and the recruits' lives] and our service to our country." Another recruit believes himself in a fortunate position to be able to respond to the events of 9/11: "This is what I am here for. This is why I serve. I'm an American fighter pilot. We're not gonna let that [disaster] happen again." At the beginning of the episode the narrator (Chris Penn) sums up the series thus: "In the end, war awaits, and a nation is calling for heroes. Tonight the [three recruits'] quest to be top gun continues."

American Fighter Pilot positions itself squarely as one of the FILMS AFTER 9/11. Each episode begins with an image of the disaster—for example, one of the hijacked planes hitting the Twin Towers, and a shot of the Stars and Stripes fluttering in the breeze. A montage follows, containing other images of the disaster and shots of Osama bin Laden. On the soundtrack the voice of President George W. Bush can be heard intoning the following speech: "We're the brightest nation for freedom and opportunity in the world. And no one will keep that light from shining. Our country is strong. A great people have been moved to defend a great nation." The implication is clear: when the recruits have finished their training, they will undertake the great task of defending their country. In the light of such noble intentions, it is sad that the series bombed.

The complete series of *American Fighter Pilot* was released on DVD in late 2005, including the two episodes already broadcast plus five hitherto unseen episodes. The three-disc set also includes a "Making of ..." documentary with Negron, Tony Scott, and co-executive producer Leon Melas. Sadly, the customer reviews were not much different from those of the newspapers three years earlier. One customer on the Amazon website described the series as containing "the worst editing I have seen. You will enjoy it if you suffer from schizophrenia or suffer from Attention Deficit Disorder, since no single video clip lasts for more than one second." Another, more sympathetic, reviewer believed that it was a "great documentary if you like fighter jets and what it takes to get there[; if you do,] then this series is well worth it." Unfortunately, the majority seemed to agree with the *Pittsburgh Post-Gazette* reviewer who summed up the series as "virtually unwatchable."

References

"*AFP—American Fighter Pilot: Publicity*," www.pazsaz.com/afp .html (accessed 7 August 2008); Caryn James, "Trying to Make Sense of Her Life before It Ends," *New York Times* 29 March 2002, http://query.nytimes.com/gst/fullpage.html?res=9E03E3D71E3BF9 3AA15750C0A9649C8B63&scp=1&sq=afp%20american%20fighte r%20pilot&st=cse (accessed 27 December 2008); *Amazon.com Customer Reviews: American Fighter Pilot* www.amazon.com/review/ product/B0007XG4D2/ref=cm_cr_dp_all_helpful?%5Fencoding =UTF8&coliid=&showViewpoints=1&colid=&sortBy=bySubmission DateDescending (accessed 29 December 2008); Rob Owen, "On the Tube: There's Nothing 'Neat' about CBS Reality Show *American Fighter Pilot*," *Pittsburgh Post-Gazette*, 29 March 2002, www.post-gazette.com/tv/20020329owen2.asp (accessed 27 December 2008); Jim Schiff, "*American Fighter Pilot*: Heavy Handed with Patriotism," *Michigan Daily*, 29 March 2002, www.michigandaily.com/ content/american-fighter-pilot-heavy-handed-patriotism (accessed 27 December 2008); Transcript of the dialogue in the first two episodes of *American Fighter Pilot*, http://worf.dyndns.org/AFP/ #The_Goods (accessed 27 December 2008).

AMERICAN GANGSTER

US 2007 r/t 156 min col. *Production Companies*: Universal Pictures, Imagine Entertainment, Relativity Media, and Scott Free. *Producers*: Brian Grazer and Ridley Scott. *Director*: Ridley Scott. *Writer*: Steven Zaillian, based on an article by Mark Jacobson. *Director of Photography*: Harris Savides. *Production Design*: Arthur Max. *Music*: Marc Streitenfeld. *Cast*: Denzel Washington (*Frank Lucas*), Russell Crowe (*Det. Richie Roberts*), Chiwetel Ejiofor (*Huey Lucas*), Josh Brolin (*Detective Trupo*), Armand Assante (*Dominic Cattano*), Ruby Dee (*Mama Lucas*), Cuba Gooding Jr. (*Nicky Barnes*).

The story was first inspired by an article in *New York* magazine written by MARK JACOBSON. He was introduced to the real Frank Lucas by author and filmmaker NICHOLAS PILEGGI, writer of the 1995 film *Casino*. Not long afterwards, Pileggi encouraged STEVEN ZAILLIAN to write an adaptation of Jacobson's article. While Zaillian was working on this, producer BRIAN GRAZER bought the rights to the project. Antoine Fuqua was originally set to direct the film in 2004 with DENZEL WASHINGTON and Benicio Del Toro starring, but production was halted one month prior to shooting after Universal Pictures canceled the film over budget concerns. A year later Terry George was brought in to rewrite Zaillian's script in the hope of reducing costs; George had planned on reuniting with his *Hotel Rwanda* lead DON CHEADLE to portray Lucas. However, the project foundered once again, so producer Grazer rehired Zaillian to redraft another screenplay, and pursued Ridley Scott as his director. According to an interview in the film's production information, Grazer "charged forward with all [his] energy and full commitment to get it made. I'd taken the script to Ridley Scott seven or eight times, but the timing was never right for him. This time—the ninth or tenth time, he said— 'Yes.'" Scott himself suggests in the commentary to the film's 2008 DVD release that he first became interested in the project while filming *KINGDOM OF HEAVEN*. While filming *A GOOD YEAR*, both he and RUSSELL CROWE discussed the project, which led to them signing on. Washington was reengaged to play Frank without taking a fee (having previously signed a contract for the aborted film which guaranteed him his twenty million-dollar salary whether it was made or not).

Filming took place in all five boroughs of New York City, primarily in practical locations. There were also a few days' filming in upstate NEW YORK and suburban Long Island. While there were inherent difficulties in re-creating the Harlem of the early 1970s, Scott knew New York City quite well, having worked there during the late 1960s. In the production information he was quoted as saying that he "knew what to do with Harlem ... finding little nooks and corners and crannies of what Harlem must have been." In collaboration with designer ARTHUR MAX he tried to recreate the world portrayed in classic 1970s GANGSTER FILMS such as *THE FRENCH CONNECTION* and *SERPICO*. The crew subsequently decamped to northern Thailand, where Scott re-created Lucas's visits to the drug barons in southeast Asia. The four-month shoot was described by Scott in the director's commentary as one of the most ambitious of his career, involving 360 scenes filmed in 180 different locations.

The film opened in late 2007 to largely enthusiastic reviews. Derek Malcolm, a longtime critic of Scott's previous films, observed that "the film-making is, on the whole, less determined to show its virtuosity ... No one could call him overtly flashy this time. He is aided not just by Washington and Crowe but by some outstanding character actors." Roger Ebert called it "an engrossing study, told smoothly and well, and Russell Crowe's contribution is enormous." J. Hoberman in the *Village Voice* believed that the film acknowledged "the key texts of the day: Scott . . . draws on the quintessential New York dope opera so closely that his movie might have been subtitled *The 'French Connection' Connection*. . . . The movie never spins out of control." Inevitably, the film had its detractors as well: for the *Sight and Sound* reviewer the seventies allusions demonstrated the film's conservatism, the work of "a director not renowned for experimentation." Anthony Quinn in the London *Independent* felt that the film was far inferior to seventies classics such as Coppola's *Godfather*. "It's a rags-to-riches story that almost tries to bypass the inconvenient fact that its hero was indirectly responsible for the deaths of thousands, probably tens of thousands . . . This repulsively stupid and self-important movie doesn't begin to understand the nature of its subject."

Few filmgoers took much notice of such comments: *American Gangster* was a considerable hit on both sides of the Atlantic. On its opening weekend in the United States, it recouped two-fifths of its budget of $100 million; to date it has taken $130 million in America and £10 million in Great Britain, with a total overseas gross of $136 million. The film also caused considerable controversy: the London *Times* reported in early 2008 that three retired Drug Enforcement Agency agents had filed a libel suit against Universal Pictures for $50 million, in the belief that they had been "besmirched" by the film's version of the raid on Frank Lucas's home on 28 January 1975. One of them, Gregory Korniloff, described it as "a total fabrication . . . [During the raid] I did not shoot his [Lucas's] dog, beat his wife or steal his money." Universal responded with a statement insisting that "*American Gangster* does not defame these, or any, federal agents." The suit was dismissed on 15 February 2008, even though the federal judge in charge of the case stated that the film got its facts wrong.

Screenwriter Zaillian originally wrote the film as two separate stories, one involving Frank Lucas, the other the detective Richie Roberts. Scott, in an interview for the film's production information, described wanting to use the GANGSTER FILM to "explore two universes—hopefully making them both fascinating and gradually bringing them together. They're carefully intercut, because every time you intercut between these two worlds, they're getting closer together." Richie Roberts's (Crowe's) world is one where police officers routinely take bribes and turn a blind eye to the drug dealing around them. Roberts's sidekick Javier Rivera (JOHN ORTIZ) observes in Zaillian's script that such policies are not wrong, but represent "part of the salary for getting shot at. For that, certain courtesies are shown. In

gratitude . . . A discount on a TV, a doughboy in the backyard, a new dress for your girlfriend." Detective Trupo (JOSH BROLIN) takes this to extremes, either demanding a share of every drug deal within his particular area of New York City, or payments from the dealers in exchange for his silence. Corruption is not only rife within the police; it dominates all of America's major law-enforcement institutions who "don't want this to stop. It [dope] employs too many people. Cops, lawyers, judges, probation officers, prison guards. The day dope stops coming into this country, a hundred thousand people lose their jobs." Anyone (like Richie) who does the right thing and turn in any money obtained from drug deals is routinely treated like a pariah. In one sequence he is shown lifting weights in a police gymnasium; some fellow officers enter, only to leave once again when they see him. Nor can he expect much support from his wife Laurie (Carla Gugino), who believes that Richie refused bribes only in order to "buy being dishonest about everything else. And that's worse than taking money nobody gives a shit about—drug money, gambling money nobody's gonna miss. I'd rather you took it and been honest with me. Or don't take it, I don't care. But don't then go cheat on me."

However, Richie resembles Clarice Starling in *HANNIBAL* in his dedication to his work. There is no conflict between LOVE VS. DUTY in his world; he spends all his time on the trail of errant-drug dealers. Scott shows this through frequent shots of him in his lonely converted church, staring at the photographs of would-be suspects on the board in the hope of finding inspiration. Home life for him is a lonely existence with sandwiches and beer interspersed with frequent one-night stands. He makes a half-hearted attempt to retain custody of his son Michael (Skyler Fortgang), but at length acknowledges that his job prevents him from fulfilling his parental responsibilities: "This is no place for him. Around me. The further away the better. For him."

By contrast, Frank Lucas's life seems orderly and legitimate, as he lives in a luxurious New Jersey mansion with his brothers, cousins, mother, and wife. This is well summed up through a shot of them all gathered together for Thanksgiving, with Frank carving a huge cooked turkey and putting it onto a plate that is subsequently passed from hand to hand. He goes to church every Sunday and sits in the same pew, accompanied by Mama Lucas (RUBY DEE). Frank likewise runs his business as a family concern, with himself as the "father"—following the example of his mentor Bumpy Johnson (Clarence Williams III) who "ran one of the biggest companies in New York City for almost fifty years." Frank himself spent "fifteen of them [those years] looking after him, taking care of things, protecting him, learning from him"; and expects the same kind of loyalty from his brothers. Anyone stepping out of line—such as his brother Huey

(CHIWETEL EJIOFOR)—is brutally dealt with. In one sequence Frank crushes Huey's head in a piano as a punishment for disrupting one of his parties. Frank's world resembles that of a Sicilian family.

When Frank defends his country and beliefs ("This is where my family is. My business. My mother. This is my place. This is *my* country. This is America"), he is speaking with just as much passion and fervor as the service personnel fighting for America's future in *BLACK HAWK DOWN* or *AMERICAN FIGHTER PILOT*. However, Scott and Zaillian expect us to appreciate the irony of the situation; in a sequence deleted from the theatrical release Frank's sidekick Charlie Williams (Joe Morton) criticizes the Special Investigations Unit (led by Richie) for its lack of ethics.

Frank's world possesses clearly defined notions of gender; to be a true representative of MASCULINITY one must dress fashionably but not ostentatiously to sustain the image of being a respectable businessperson. Those who dress flashily draw attention to themselves as potential criminals—which might thereby threaten the future of Frank's organization. He denounces his brother Huey for choosing to wear a parrot-green suit, gold chains, and a hat: "The guy making all the noise in the room [both visually and verbally] is the weak one . . . Like a girl." However, Frank fails to listen to his own advice and attends the Muhammad Ali/Joe Frazier fight at Madison Square Garden dressed in an expensive chinchilla overcoat. This unwise choice precipitates his own downfall; Richie immediately takes notice of him as an influential representative of the underworld.

From then on Frank's behavior becomes increasingly desperate as he tries to shore up the damage done to his families both at home and at work. He resolves to kill Detective Trupo, but by doing so angers his mother who reminds him that an honorable man does not shoot police officers. She chides him for his lack of responsibility towards his brothers who "all came here [to New Jersey] because of you. You called and they came running. They look up to you. They expect you to always know what's best . . . Do you really want to make things so bad for your family they'll leave you? Because they will." Although a frail person, Mama Lucas slaps him across the face—a fitting punishment for someone who has forgotten everything he has been taught about family loyalty.

Zaillian's script brings the two men together in a police cell. At first there seems to be little communication between them: at one point the script has Frank searching Richie's face for some clue as to what he is thinking about. Eventually the two of them understand that they have a shared antipathy towards corrupt police officers: Frank wants revenge against those millions of people who "put my money in their pockets," while Richie offers him the chance to name "every cop you ever paid off. Everyone who ever stole from you." In *AMERICAN GANGSTER: EXTENDED EDITION*, released on DVD in 2008, Scott includes a final scene in which the two meet again after Frank has been released from prison. The sequence incorporates distinct echoes of a BUDDY MOVIE, as they walk down the much-altered Harlem streets, with Richie promising Frank that he will not let him starve, even though he can barely take care of himself. In another interview with Wilson Morales, Scott emphasized that this scene was based on actual fact: "[W]hen Frank was released from prison, he did seventeen years, the first person to meet him coming out was Ritchie [*sic*] Roberts with a jacket and clothing . . . Because Frank Lucas had actually turned in the state's evidence and instead of giving him 135 years, where Ritchie could have brought in everything from statutory crime, first-degree murder, etc. they kept that out of it in exchange for information on the corrupt police department."

In an online review of the film the Australian critic Julie Rigg observed that "Ridley Scott has taken Steve Zaillian's screenplay about the rise and rise and ultimate fall of Frank Lucas—who rose in the seventies to become Harlem's heroin drug lord, beating the Italo-American mafia at their own game—and cast it as one great big metaphor for badass American capitalism." In many ways she is right: the film includes numerous references to how AMERICANISM and American values became corrupted in the drug culture of the early 1970s. At the beginning Bumpy Johnson criticizes the world of contemporary America, which he believes lacks "pride of ownership" and "personal service." Such sentiments might be justified, were it not for the fact that the "personal service" provided by Johnson's (later Frank's) organization creates ghettos like the Stephen Crane Projects—a debris-strewn place redolent of hopelessness. On another occasion Mafia boss Dominic Cattano (ARMAND ASSANTE), informs Frank that "monopolies are illegal in this country, Frank, because no one can compete with a monopoly . . . That's un-American." Wise sentiments indeed; but Cattano uses them simply as a way of forcing Frank into an unwanted alliance to guarantee "peace of mind"—in other words, sharing Frank's profits in return for his safety. On several occasions we see archive footage of the Vietnam War, including battle sequences, demonstrations, and comments made by Presidents Johnson and Nixon. Scott juxtaposes these images with short sequences showing (unnamed) American generals in Vietnam accepting bribes in return for permitting heroin to be smuggled into America in the coffins of dead soldiers. This emphasizes the hollowness of the attorney's (Roger Bart's) words as he criticizes Richie for trying to root out corruption in the US MILITARY by "desecrating the remains of young men who've given their lives in the defense of democracy." In the world of *American Gangster*, these young men died for nothing.

On the other hand, *American Gangster* portrays the early 1970s as a time when African Americans were at last finding a voice for themselves. Archive film of Muhammad Ali is juxtaposed with images of Frank's emergence as a force to be reckoned with—someone who defies the attorney's myopic assumption that "no nigger has accomplished what the American Mafia hasn't in a hundred years!" Many groups—the Mafia included—despise Frank not only because of his abilities as a businessperson, but for what he represents; the emergence of a new force in American social and political life. Richie confidently predicts that once Frank has been imprisoned, "things can return to normal," with the white Americans reassuming their position of power. The last three and a half decades of American history have proved him wrong.

Apart from reviews of the film, the only articles to deal with *American Gangster* is J. Madison Davis's "Living Black, Living White: Cultural Choices in Crime Films," which focuses on the issue of color and race relations in Zaillian's script. Nick James's "Dealing Dope and Death" argues that the film makes a direct connection between Richard Nixon's handling of the Vietnam War and George W. Bush's conduct in Iraq, "through the now hackneyed method of having every television seen show the news."

References

American Gangster: Production Information (Los Angeles: Universal Pictures, 2007), 6, 12; James Bone, "Movie Chefs Face $50m lawsuit as Police Claim, 'We've been Framed,'" *The Times*, 18 January 2008, 46; J. Madison Davis, "Living Black, Living White: Cultural Choices in Crime Films," *World Literature Today* 82, no.3 (May/June 2008): 9–13; Roger Ebert, "American Gangster," *Chicago Sun-Times*, 2 November 2007, http://rogerebert.suntimes.com/apps/pbcs.dll/article?AID=/20071101/REVIEWS/711010303/1023 (accessed 11 February 2009); Ryan Gilbey, "American Gangster," *Sight and Sound* 18, no.1 (January 2008): 56; J. Hoberman, "CEO of Smack," *Village Voice*, 23 October 2007, www.villagevoice.com/2007-10-23/film/ceo-of-smack/ (accessed 11 February 2009); Nick James, "Dealing Dope and Death," *Sight and Sound* 17, no.12 (December 2007): 38; Derek Malcolm, "A New King of New York," *Evening Standard*, 15 November 2007, 39; Wilson Morales, interview with Ridley Scott (6 November 2006), www.blackfilm.com/20061103/features/ridleyscott.shtml (accessed 8 August 2008); Anthony Quinn, "American Gangster," *The Independent Film*, 16 November 2007, 6–7; Julie Rigg, "*American Gangster*" (10 January 2007), www.abc.net.au/rn/movietime/stories/2008/2135587.htm (accessed 10 February 2009); Ridley Scott, "Director's Commentary" to *American Gangster 2-Disc Extended Collector's Edition* (Los Angeles: Universal Studios, 2008); Trivia for *American Gangster*, *The Internet Movie Database*, www.imdb.com/title/tt0765429/trivia (accessed 10 February 2009).

Bibliography

"American Gangster Aims to be a Big Shot," *Cinema Business* 36 (July 2007): 47; "*American Gangster*. Location—Brooklyn, New York," *Empire* 220 (October 2007): 88–89; Ian Freer, "*American Gangster*. Russell and Denzel Reteam. Well, It's Better Than Virtuosity," *Empire* 222 (December 2007): 54–56; Nick James, "Dealing Dope and Death," *Sight and Sound* 17, no. 12 (December 2007): 36–40; Will Lawrence, "My Scraps with Russell Crowe," *Daily Telegraph*, 2 November 2007, 32; Martyn Palmer, "Original Gangsters," *Empire* 221 (November 2007): 114–24; Steven Zaillian, "*American Gangster*. Final Shooting Script" (27 July 2006), www.roteirodecinema.com.br/scripts/files/american_gangster.htm (accessed 8 February 2009).

AMERICAN GANGSTER—EXTENDED EDITION

DVD version of the film, released in April 2008. It includes the theatrical release (running at 156) minutes and an extended edition of the film with an extra eighteen minutes of footage. This includes extra lines of dialogue from Bumpy Johnson (Clarence Williams III), and some more shots of Richie Roberts (RUSSELL CROWE) and his team doing surveillance. One new scene shows Richie being informed that as a result of his investigation he now has a price on his head, which helps to explain the character's changed attitude to paranoia and fatalism. The biggest difference is the ending, which extends the closing shot for several minutes and follows with an exchange between Richie and Frank Lucas (DENZEL WASHINGTON), during which Richie promises to take care of Frank, even though he can scarcely take care of himself. All of the extra material is incorporated in STEVEN ZAILLIAN's "Final Shooting Script" of July 27, 2006.

Bibliography

Steven Zaillian, "*American Gangster*. Final Shooting Script" (27 July 2006), www.roteirodecinema.com.br/scripts/files/american_gangster.htm (accessed 8 February 2009).

AMERICANISM

In films such as *ALIEN* and *BLADE RUNNER* Scott is sharply critical of certain American values such as capitalism (which he believes leads to the creation of dystopic cities such as the futuristic LOS ANGELES of *Blade Runner*). *MATCHSTICK MEN* focuses on similar issues by suggesting that Roy Waller's (NICOLAS CAGE's) success as a conman arises from the fact that most of his victims are rapacious, searching for something for nothing in a money-dominated world. Monica Cyrino argues that *GLADIATOR* is equally critical of American values such as the family as moral force, the multiple roles of women, televised sports (which are identified with the ancient games), and modern trends towards agrarianism and the apocalypse. She notes the way in which Commodus's (JOAQUIN PHOENIX's) behavior—particularly his emphasis on trying to be liked by the people, even if it means wasting money on endless spectacle—prefigures media images of George W. Bush. In the Ridley Scott-produced television film *THE LAST DEBATE*, director JOHN BADHAM returns to this theme by showing how the broadcast media reduce contemporary America into a DYSTOPIA, a dog-eat-dog world dedicated to surface images in which values such as HONOR and integrity no longer exist. The same also applies to *HANNIBAL*, where the "New World" of the United States is portrayed as lawless and corrupt; where drug-dealers such as Evelda Drumgo (Hazelle Goodman) are prepared to put their children at risk to avoid arrest by the police; and where the police themselves are impossibly corrupt, even though they try to project an image of efficiency and fair-mindedness on television. The same world forms a backdrop to the action of *AMERICAN GANGSTER*, where the NEW YORK police officers are even more corrupt than the drug dealers who regularly provide them with "gratuities," to avoid arrest. In *THE ANDROMEDA STRAIN* the American obsession with capitalism has put the planet in danger from a mysterious (and apparently incurable) virus. Scott even has a sly dig at the Americans in *A GOOD YEAR*, as an unnamed couple (Mitchell Mullen, Judy Dickerson) arrive in a French restaurant and try to order Salade Niçoise with Ranch dressing, topped off with bacon bits and croutons. Needless to say, Max Skinner (RUSSELL CROWE) refuses to serve them, offering the contemptuous retort in MARC KLEIN's script: "McDonald's is in Avignon. Cod and chips in Marseille."

America is also viewed somewhat cynically by the Somalis in *BLACK HAWK DOWN*. Atto (George Harris) likens the American raid on Mogadishu to "gunfight at the K. O. corral [*sic*]" in which they are trying to catch General Aidid by putting up wanted posters. In KEN NOLAN's script, Atto believes the Americans do not understand that the country's future lies with its people, and "without a lot of Arkansas white-boy's ideas in it." Firimbi, a Somalian fighter, offers the American soldier Durant (Ron Eldard) a cigarette; when Durant refuses, the Somalian observes cynically, "None of you Americans smoke anymore. You all live long, dull, uninteresting lives." Other non-American characters in Scott's work denounce the country for similar reasons: in *THE COMPANY*, the agent Lilli (Alexandra Maria Lara) criticizes the central character Jack McCauliffe (CHRIS O'DONNELL) for strutting about with "false confidence . . . as if you own the world." The Soviet spy Yevgeny (RORY COCHRANE) calls Americans "foolish and greedy, yes, but not insane. Americans are very good at self-preservation." Such comments might be true; but they might also be part

of an illusion created by American spies in order to outwit their Soviet rivals during the Cold War.

BODY OF LIES can be seen as an overt criticism of contemporary American policy in the Middle East. While Roger Ferris (LEONARDO DICAPRIO) tries his best to build diplomatic bridges between himself and Hani, the head of the Jordanian Secret Service (MARK STRONG), he finds himself hamstrung by Ed Hoffman, his boss at the CIA (Russell Crowe), who has no interest in anything except exterminating the enemy as soon as possible and by whatever means necessary. For him the "war on terror" can be seen in black-and-white: "These people [the terrorists] do not want to negotiate. Not at all . . . They want every infidel converted or dead."

In *BLACK RAIN*, however, Scott celebrates the basic American trait of individualism through the central character, Nick Conklin (MICHAEL DOUGLAS), who refuses to listen to orders given by the Japanese superintendent Ohashi (SHIGERU KOYAMA), preferring instead to trust in his "balls," as he puts it—in other words, follow his instincts. Sometimes this gets him into trouble: he is put on a plane and told to return to New York (an order he blissfully ignores). However, his persistence eventually pays off as he brings the *yakuza* leader Sato (YUSAKU MATSUDA) to justice and persuades his Japanese colleague Masahiro (KEN TAKAKURA) to join him. Both are rewarded for their efforts with a medal—even if they have broken the rules to achieve their goal. HANS ZIMMER's song "I'll Be Holding On" plus other songs on the soundtrack including UB40's "The Way You Do the Things You Do" vindicate Nick's course of action by celebrating those brave enough to live their lives according to their own system of values. Whether the film achieves its purpose or not is debatable: the *Empire* reviewer Andy Gill observed that this "subtext" failed to convince, rendering *Black Rain* "pretty dull fare indeed." *RKO 281* looks at the seamier side of individualism by showing how Orson Welles (LIEV SCHREIBER) and William Randolph Hearst (JAMES CROMWELL) are so wrapped up in themselves and their own self-images that they remain totally oblivious to people around them. The famous lines from *Citizen Kane*—which are quoted in *RKO 281*—apply to both of them: "You want love on your own terms, don't you, Charlie? Love according to your own rules. And if anything goes wrong and the game stops, then you've got to be soothed and nursed, no matter what else is happening, and no matter who else is hurt!" In *THE ASSASSINATION OF JESSE JAMES BY THE COWARD ROBERT FORD*, the eponymous central character (BRAD PITT) has become a celebrity—a living icon of bravery and individualism. However, his personal life is a mess; no one can get close to him, and he mistrusts everyone around him. Eventually he is driven to depression and welcomes death as a merciful release from a lonely existence. Like Welles, he can never enjoy his life.

THELMA & LOUISE adopts a more positive view of America by adapting the conventions associated with classic Hollywood ROAD MOVIES. Thelma (GEENA DAVIS), who has never gone away without her husband, says, "I always wanted to travel, I just never got the opportunity." When she escapes with Louise in the car, she fulfills her dream of freedom and individuality. The moment the two of them decide to hit the open road, they are no longer part of established society (and the conventions that restrict them). Not only do they become individuals; they develop a desire for one another which might be lesbian or heterosexual (the film allows for both interpretations). Whatever the nature of that desire, it is clear that they can't (or won't) go back to the patriarchal society that imprisoned them. The final sequence, showing them taking off from Grand Canyon in mid-air, symbolically shows them "leaving" that society for a new world in which anything might be possible. They have left their men and the world of men behind for a world in which friendship exists between women—a relationship customarily represented in Hollywood films as competitive or jealous. Leilani Nevarez Luce uses Jung to come to the same conclusion; the two women's decision to "continue their journey can be read, both symbolically and literally, as a squaring of the circle, as a union with the Chthonic Mother, the Grand Canyon." This is no ordinary Hollywood film; rather, it represents the triumph of two individuals in finding a lifestyle of their own.

According to *Black Hawk Down*, as well as the reality show *AMERICAN FIGHTER PILOT* (broadcast one year later in 2002), good Americans should remain loyal to their nation, recognize the presence of God in their lives, and fight to preserve freedom in the world. In the director's commentary to the 2004 DVD release of *Black Hawk Down*, Scott paid tribute to the Americans, who often had to "go it alone" in trying to bring peace to the world, without the help of other nations. Similar precepts are set forth in *KINGDOM OF HEAVEN*, even though it is set in the time of the Crusades. Godfrey of Ibelin (LIAM NEESON) sets forth the knightly code of belief thus: "Be brave and upright that God may love thee, speak the truth always, even if it leads to your death. Safeguard the helpless and do no wrong, that is your oath."

References

Monica S. Cyrino, "*Gladiator* and Contemporary American Society," in *Gladiator: Film and History*, ed. Martin M. Winkler (Malden, MA and Oxford: Blackwell Publishing Ltd., 2004), 136–48; Andy Gill, "Son of His Father," *Empire*, October 1991, 104; Marc Klein, "*A Good Year:* Screenplay" (Draft dated 5 September 2005), www.dailyscript.com/scripts/A-GOOD-YEAR-2.pdf (accessed 26 January 2009), 4; Leilani Nevarez Luce, ". . . We Don't Live in That Kind of World, Thelma," *Film and Philosophy* 3 (1996): 166; Herman Mankiewicz and Orson Welles, *Citizen Kane*, Original Script, www.godamongdirectors.com/scripts/citizenkane.shtml (accessed 23 November 2008); Ken Nolan, *Black Hawk Down: The Shooting Script* (New York: Newmarket Press, 2002), 6–7, 101; Ridley Scott, Director's Commentary to the 2-disc DVD release of *Black Hawk Down* (Los Angeles: Revolution Studios Distribution Company LLG & Jerry Bruckheimer, Inc., 2004).

Bibliography

Amelia Arenas, "Popcorn Circus: *Gladiator* and the Spectacle of Virtue," *Arion: A Journal of the Humanities and Classics* 9, no.1 (Spring/Summer 2001): 1–12; Glenn Man, "Gender, Genre and Myth in *Thelma and Louise*," *Film Criticism* 18, no.1 (Fall 1993): 36–53; Jeffrey T. Nealon, "Empire of the Intensities: A Random Walk Down Las Vegas Boulevard," *Parallax* 8, no.1 (Jan-Mar 2002): 78–91; Brian Opie, "Android Textuality, or Finding a Toad in the Desert of America," in *Remembering Representation*, ed. Howard McNaughton (Christchurch: University of Canterbury, Department of English, 1993), 76–89.

AMURRI, FRANCO (1958-)

The films of director Franco Amurri include the comedy *Il Ragazzo del Pony Express* (1986). Born in Rome, Amurri studied art and architecture before beginning his film career as one of Fellini's assistants for *City of Women* (1978). Amurri worked as an assistant director to Fellini for two years and then continued to work in that capacity for Paul Mazursky's *The Tempest* (1982) and for Dan Curtis's *The Winds of War* (1983). Amurri began writing for television and feature films in 1978.

MONKEY TROUBLE, which Amurri co-wrote with Stu Krieger, was originally slated to be produced by Warner Bros. However, they passed on the project, and Ridley Scott stepped in to produce the film.

Amurri directs the film at a fast pace, allowing for plenty of incident and car-chase sequences, but also allowing for a focus on the central character Eva (THORA BIRCH). Amurri's subsequent work includes *Amici Ahrarara* (2001). He has a daughter with the actress SUSAN SARANDON.

ANCIENT EPICS

Epics set in ancient times—whether in Greece, Rome, or biblical times—have always been a staple of Hollywood. From the days of silent film, they have been used to make statements not only about the past, but also about the present. For example, Hollywood epics of the Cold War period in the late 1940s and early 1950s—*Quo Vadis* (1951) or *The Robe* (1953)—frequently cast British theater actors as villainous Egyptian pharaohs or Roman patriarchs and American film stars as their virtuous Jewish or Christian opponents. For Maria Wyke, Hollywood's histories of Rome became a huge, many-faceted metaphor for Hollywood itself: "The reconstruction on screen and exhibition of ancient Rome came to stand for Hollywood's own fantastic excess—its technological and aesthetic innovations, its grandeur and glamour, its ostentation, and the lavishness of its expenditure and consumption. And spectators of Hollywood's widescreen epics were invited to position themselves not only as pure Christians but also as Romans luxuriating in a surrender to the splendors of film spectacle itself."

Ridley Scott is widely credited with reviving the genre with GLADIATOR, even if the plot is lifted almost wholesale from THE FALL OF THE ROMAN EMPIRE. The film's pressbook made much of the fact that "it has been four decades since chariots raced across movie screens in epic dramas of a time long past. Now, director Ridley Scott brings the glorious battles of the ancient Roman arena back to the big screen in a sweeping story of courage and revenge." Writer DAVID FRANZONI chose to compare his characters to recognizable Hollywood figures and said, "Promoter Proximo [OLIVER REED] is a sort of Mike Ovitz, and Commodus [JOAQUIN PHOENIX] is a sort of Ted Turner. And Maximus [RUSSELL CROWE] is the hero we all wish ourselves to be: the guy who can rise above the mess that is modern society." Martina Nagel criticizes Franzoni's script on the grounds that it made Maximus a superhero: "Allowing the characters of an epic to degenerate into fantasy superheroes immediately undermines the film's validity as an epic . . . The high price of Maximus's invulnerability is the viewer's emotional empathy . . . and with that, any real hope of suspense."

The film was a considerable financial success, as a result of its DVD sales coupled with the overseas box-office receipts. Martin Winkler observes that *Gladiator* inaugurated a veritable renaissance of classical antiquity on American and European cinema and television screens, including *KING ARTHUR* (2004) and the television miniseries *Rome* (2005). As with the Hollywood epics of the past, *Gladiator* tells us more about the spirit of contemporary America at the beginning of the third millennium AD than about the history of the Roman Empire.

References

David Franzoni, quoted in James Russell, *The Historical Epic and Contemporary Hollywood: From Dances with Wolves to Gladiator* (New York and London: The Continuum International Publishing Group Inc., 2007), 159, 172; Martina Nagel, "The Misuse of Cinematic Convention," *ScriptWriter* 4 (May 2002): 30; Martin M. Winkler, "Introduction," in *Troy: From Homer's Iliad to Hollywood Epic*, ed. Winkler (Malden, MA and Oxford: Blackwell Publishing Ltd., 2007): 3–4; Maria Wyke, *Projecting the Past: Ancient Rome, Cinema and History* (New York and London: Routledge, 1997), 22, 30–31.

Bibliography

Monica Silveira Cyrino, *Big-Screen Rome* (Malden, MA and Oxford: Blackwell Publishing, 2005).

ANDREI RUBLEV

USSR 1966 r/t 200 min b/w. *Production Company:* Mosfilm. *Director:* Andrei Tarkovsky. *Writers:* Andrei Tarkovsky and Andrei Mikhalkov-Konchalovsky. *Director of Photography:* Vadim Yusov. *Production Designer:* Evgeni Cherniaev. *Music:* Vyacheslav Ovchinnikov. *Cast:* Anatoli Solonitsyn (*Andrei Rublev*), Ivan Lapikov (*Kirill*), Nikolai Grinko (*Daniil the Black*), Nikolai Sergeyev (*Theophanes the Greek*), Irma Raush Tarkovskaya (*Deaf and Dumb Girl*), Nikolai Burlyaev (*Boriska*), Rolan Bykov (*Buffoon*).

Epic chronicle of the Russian hero (c.1370 – c.1430), who defended his country against repeated attacks from the Tartars while coping with warring factions within his own army. According to Philip Strick, Tarkovsky recreated the world of fifteenth-century Russia for 1960s audiences "to show, through the eyes of a poet, the wonderful and terrible age when the great Russian nation was taking form and shape."

Ridley Scott acknowledged the film as inspiration for *KINGDOM OF HEAVEN*, particularly in the battle sequences showing Balian's (ORLANDO BLOOM's) valiant defense of Jerusalem against Saladin's (GHASSAN MASSOUD's) army.

References

Andrei Tarkovsky, quoted in Philip Strick, "The Shaping of *Rublev*," in Andrei Tarkovsky, *Andrei Rublev*, trans. Kitty Hunter Blair (London: Faber and Faber, 1991), xiv.

THE ANDROMEDA STRAIN (1971)

US 1971 r/t 131 min col. *Production Company:* Universal Pictures. *Producer:* Robert Wise. *Director:* Robert Wise. *Writer:* Nelson Gidding, from the novel by Michael Crichton. *Director of Photography:* Richard H. Kline. *Production Design:* Boris Leven. *Music:* Gil Mellé. *Cast:* Arthur Hill (*Dr. Jeremy Stone*), David Wayne (*Dr. Charles Dutton*), James Olson (*Dr. Mark Hall*), Kate Reid (*Dr. Ruth Leavitt*).

Highly popular science-fiction thriller about a satellite crashing back to earth, carrying with it an unknown but deadly organism. All but two of the residents of the small town of Piedmont, New Mexico, have been killed by the organism. It is the responsibility of a team of scientists working in the Nevada desert laboratory known as Wildfire to study and eliminate it. The film exploited Cold War fears of an unknown invasion, much like Wise's earlier thriller *The Day the Earth Stood Still* (1951). The film was nominated for two Oscars in Best Art Direction and Best Film Editing. It was remade in 2008 (with the same title) with Ridley Scott as executive producer.

THE ANDROMEDA STRAIN (2008)

US 2008 TVM r/t 167 min col. *Production Companies*: A. S. Films, Scott Free, and Traveler's Rest Films. *Executive Producers*: David W. Zucker, Ridley Scott, Tony Scott, Mikael Salomon, and Tom Thayer. *Producers*: Clara George, Malcolm Reeve, and Ron Binkowski. *Director*: Mikael Salomon. *Writer*: Robert Schenkkan, from the novel by Michael Crichton. *Director of Photography*: Jon Joffin. *Production Designer*: Jerry Wanek. *Music*: Joel J. Richard. *Cast*: Benjamin Bratt (*Dr. Jeremy Stone*), Eric McCormack (*Jack Nash*), Christa Miller (*Dr. Angela Noyce*), Daniel Dae Kim (*Dr. Tsi Chou*), Viola Davis (*Dr. Charlene Barton*), Andre Braugher (*General George W. Mancheck*), Ricky Schroder (*Major Bill Keane MD*).

Producer Tom Thayer first had the idea of remaking *The Andromeda Strain* in the late 1990s and eventually he secured Scott's interest. At first they thought of making another film, but there was little interest from the major studios, so they planned a miniseries instead. Another series, *The Burning Zone* (UPN, 1996-97), had dealt with similar subject matter, but the network had canceled it after only nineteen episodes. John Kenneth Muir described the series as "an unceasing (but ill-advised) attempt to blend science and religion into a cohesive TV formula." Nonetheless other networks took a serious look at reviving *The Andromeda Strain*, including NBC and the Sci-Fi Channel. In 2004 the latter company announced that the series would be broadcast with the Scott brothers (Ridley and Tony) and Frank Darabont as co-executive producers. When that project fell through, the brothers teamed up once again with David W. Zucker and director MIKAEL SALOMON, who had all worked on *THE COMPANY*. Universal—which owned the rights to the book—signed a deal for distribution rights; the broadcasting rights were sold to the American cable company A&E. However, the production itself was financed largely by Zucker, Thayer and the Scott brothers, who used their own money for the production completion bond.

In an interview with Scott Eastman, Ridley Scott expressed interest in remaking *The Andromeda Strain* on account of its contemporary resonance: "It seems just as potent because there is a combination of things—what we have done to our planet and global warming. Under that massive heading there are questions about whether we have really done it or whether it is reversible or not. Then there is what have we done to ourselves politically, religiously, economically. We have really messed up in several measures, and fundamentally a lot of it is greed." He had previously worked with similar material in the aborted project to film Richard Preston's best-selling novel *THE HOT ZONE*, dealing with the efforts of USAMRID (US Army Medical Research Institute of Infectious Diseases) virologists to deal with an outbreak of Ebola; an incurable virus killing nine out of ten of those infected.

Mikael Salomon began filming *The Andromeda Strain* directly after finishing work on *The Company*. Two principal cast members—Barry Flatman and Ted Atherton—had also been involved in that production. Filming took place between June and September 2007, in and around Vancouver in British Columbia, Canada (considered the cheapest and most practical substitute for the Utah locations in Robert Schenkkan's script). The production team worked under tight budgetary constraints: much of the fifteen million-dollar cost had to be spent on special effects which were added in post-production at the UPP VFX and PostProduction House in Prague, Czech Republic. The nine hundred special shots included recreating the deadly Andromeda virus in the scientists' laboratory, the attack of the killer birds on some unfortunate members of the National Guard, a sequence where a snake attacks a rabbit, and most of the scenes involving aircraft. David Vána, UFP vfx supervisor, takes up the story: "There were no real F16s available for shooting. We had two possibilities: to use existing reference material from our databanks or to create our own F16 in 3D. We decided to go for our own model as this gave us much more flexibility to take in to account the various visual elements that Mikael [Salomon] was looking for. We are particularly happy with the scene where real footage of the pilot in the cockpit merged with our CG F16."

The Andromeda Strain premiered on A&E on 26 and 27 May 2008, to largely indifferent reviews from the major newspapers. The *New York Times* felt that the action "never grows quite suspenseful enough, and it rests on the rather un-sci-fi-ish idea that the future is a benign force, like a mentor uncle with something meaningful to teach us about our venality and callous disregard for the Earth." The *San Francisco Chronicle* particularly disliked the second installment, giving it "four thumbs down" on account of its predictability and "pointless, we're-on-cable swearing." The *Boston Globe* agreed, describing the remake as "a paint-by-numbers techno-thriller" with long passages of meaningless dialogue, transforming the action into "a long lesson in pseudoscience."

Reaction from the specialist websites was more enthusiastic: Sarah Stegall of *SF Scope* approached the adaptation on its own terms as "a re-visioning, a reassessment not just of what we know of the world but how we view it and our place in it." The *Film Critics United* reviewer found it "an entertaining, very well made and quick-moving bit of Sci-Fi escapist fare . . . not a bad way to spend a couple of evenings." Audiences appeared to like it, too: part one averaged 4.8 million viewers, making it the second most-watched A&E program ever broadcast, while part two averaged five million viewers. *The Andromeda Strain* was nominated for six Emmys including Outstanding Miniseries, Outstanding Cinematography, and Sound Editing, but failed to win any awards.

Although based on THE ANDROMEDA STRAIN (NOVEL), this version of Michael Crichton's book has strong visual echoes of ALIEN. A group of five scientists are buried deep below the ground in a laboratory codenamed Wildfire. Like the spaceship NOSTROMO in the earlier film, this is a claustrophobic space resembling a womb, with long, narrow, vaginal passages leading off from it. In the film's climactic moments Doctors Stone (BENJAMIN BRATT), Chou (DANIEL DAE KIM), and Keane (RICKY SCHRODER) climb up one of these passages in a desperate attempt to shut down the laboratory's computer system and hence prevent a nuclear explosion. This particular emergency has been precipitated by Dr. Charlene Barton (VIOLA DAVIS) opening the vial containing the alien virus (codenamed Andromeda), which subsequently eats its way through the laboratory, destroying everything—including human beings—in its wake. Dr. Stone finally destroys it by closing the computer system and thereby enabling the US military forces—led by General Mancheck (ANDRE BRAUGHER)—to neutralize its power with a bacterium found only on thermal vents. As in *Alien*, the film creates a nightmare scenario of the "monstrous-feminine," with the virus implanted in the womb (represented by the laboratory) and subsequently reincorporating and destroying all human life. The film suggests that it can only be neutralized by strong, virile men—like Mancheck's squadron of pilots—who spray the landscape with the bacterium using long, penis-shaped hoses.

As in many of Scott's earlier films—*Alien* included—*The Andromeda Strain* has some harsh things to say about AMERICANISM and contemporary America. Senior army officers embark on a campaign of disinformation about how the Andromeda Strain was picked up by a secret research mission to a secret wormhole that has since collapsed. Worse still, they are prepared to kill anyone who seeks to uncover the truth, such as the campaigning journalist Nash (ERIC McCORMACK). Although the army ultimately plays its part in neutralizing the virus, it is clear that its leaders do not take kindly to public humiliation. Both Mancheck and his sidekick Colonel Ferrus (Justin Louis) are murdered in cold blood by an unknown assailant—despite their efforts, they have been made scapegoats for what has happened.

Corruption in the highest levels of the army has a knock-out effect on the troops' ability to carry out their duties. The army makes valiant attempts to defend the country but remains powerless to resist the virus's malignant effect. Early on in the film a team sent to investigate a fallen satellite in the town of Piedmont, Utah, arrives to find everyone dead, save for one man—Kyle Tobler (Tom McBeath)—frantically yelling at them. They have no time to respond, because in seconds they are too are dead, the victims of the deadly virus. Salomon's film incorporates distinct visual echoes of BLACK HAWK DOWN, with soldiers climbing

into helicopters and mounting elaborate military operations in an attempt to counteract the virus. However, all their efforts are doomed to fail; they are either burned to death or are driven to such a state of distraction that they shoot one another. One sequence shows an unnamed lieutenant driving his vehicle through a military encampment and being shot at by his comrades as a potential terrorist. As an example of FILMS AFTER 9/11, *The Andromeda Strain* suggests that America is particularly vulnerable to a major attack, particularly when many of its armed forces have been deployed in other countries such as Iraq.

The film also criticizes the Homeland Security Act and the USA Patriot Act, both of which are invoked as ways of preventing Nash from finding out more about the army's conduct. In one scene Nash is shown defying the corrupt Colonel Ferrus, who threatens him with the kind of treatment from which the Fourth Amendment no longer protects the American people: incarceration without legal representation, revocation of *habeas corpus*, and a possible "disappearance" from society. Nash expresses the view of many liberals in an angry outburst: "Listen to me you little tin-pot fascist; I'm not some hapless Middle-Eastern exchange student with an out-of-date visa. I'm an American citizen with a very public profile."

It seems that no aspect of American society is immune from corruption. In a long expository scene we learn that the only way to eradicate the Andromeda Strain is to obtain the bacterium, which can be grown in the scientists' laboratory but can only be found in large quantities at the bottom of the Pacific Ocean. However, the future of that substance has been threatened by thermal vent-drilling, which, while providing capitalist organizations with a sizable income, nonetheless affects the earth's environmental balance. On at least two occasions we see demonstrations mounted against the American government by pressure groups determined to stop vent-mining. All these protests prove fruitless: at the end of the film President William Scott (Ted Whittall) reaffirms his commitment to mining, with scant regard for the future of the environment.

In this kind of society the president is nothing more than a figurehead—someone more concerned with reelection than governing the country. One sequence shows him giving a press conference in the White House about the potential consequences of Andromeda; director Salomon cuts to a shot of his advisers, led by Charles "Chuck" Beeter (Barry Flatman), who are desperately embarking on a campaign of damage limitation, designed to save the government's face while keeping as much of the truth about the virus from the public as possible. The sequence recalls political dramas such as THE LAST DEBATE, where image takes precedence over an ability to govern. The president's basic lack of knowledge is summed up in one exchange where he advises Beeter to pray to God in an attempt to restrain the apparently inexorable spread of the Andromeda Strain. William Paul's comment—referring to *Alien*—could equally well apply to Salomon's *Andromeda Strain*: "[It] is based on something corrupt because corruption actually exists at the top . . . [as a result of a] greatly weakened presidency . . . [the film] provoked an anxiety about leadership that permeated the culture. American society had become a social body without a head."

In this anarchic world, SMALL TOWNS like Piedmont, Utah (which embody certain virtues of American society such as family, community, and friendliness), have been destroyed. Our only salvation, Salomon suggests, is to rely on scientists such as Stone, Chou, and Keane. The film incorporates long sequences where the team discovers ways in which the Andromeda Strain can be counteracted. Many of their hypotheses prove wrong; and it seems that their task is futile in view of the fact that the samples of Andromeda in the laboratory seem to be communicating with one another to fight back against attempts to kill them. Eventually Chou comes up with the solution as he decodes a secret message encoded in the actual molecules of the substance. He finds out that Andromeda was sent through the wormhole in the universe from our own future, in an attempt either to wipe out all human beings or (in the best scenario) to warn everyone about what will happen unless greater care is taken to preserve the environment. The message also provides the scientists with the necessary clues to help them find the bacterium to neutralize the invading virus. While these sequences are fundamentally undramatic—provoking the *San Francisco Chronicle* reviewer to criticize the film's "ceaseless love of geek-speak"—they demonstrate the scientists' patient dedication to their work. Like James Angleton (MICHAEL KEATON) in *The Company*, they understand the virtues of patience in finding the exact solution rather than accepting the quick-fix requests demanded of them by the government.

While Salomon's film updates Michael Crichton's book to the contemporary era, it sustains the fundamental theme of his work: we must be very, very careful in finding solutions to our own problems, especially when we interfere with ecological systems.

To date there has been no published work on the remake of *The Andromeda Strain*. Paul Ramaeker's article "Notes on the Split-Field Diopter" looks at the cinematography of the original version. Dan Donlan's "Experiencing *The Andromeda Strain*" looks at how well the novel works in the high school classroom. Arthur B. Evans's and R. D. Mullen's "North American College Courses in Science Fiction" shows how both book and film are widely studied in North American educational institutions. John Woodcock asserts that both book and film are critical of the government, which has produced "a professional culture of ingenious people and marvelous machines, but in the process has generated side effects beyond the capabilities of those people and that machinery to control." Michael Crichton's 1999 article "Ritual Abuse, Hot Air, and Missed Opportunities" looks at how scientists are often adversely portrayed in films. Salomon's film tries to rectify such stereotypes. M. Z. Ribalow's response asserts that Wise's *Andromeda Strain* "makes thrilling a scientific search that lasts the length of the film." The same could also be said of Salomon's version.

References

Christopher Armstead, "The Andromeda Strain," *Film Critics United* (May 2008): http://filmcriticsunited.com/andromeda strain.html (accessed 13 February 2009); Gina Bellafante, "Earth's End Is Near Again: Crichton's Brain Squad Is Back," *New York Times*, 26 May 2008, www.nytimes.com/2008/05/26/arts/television/26andro.html?_r=1&scp=1&sq=andromeda%20strain&st=cse (accessed 13 February 2009); Michael Crichton, "Ritual Abuse, Hot Air and Missed Opportunities," *Science* n.s. 283, no. 5407 (5 March 1999): 1461–63; Dan Donlan, "Experiencing *The Andromeda Strain*," *The English Journal* 73, no.6 (1974): 72–73; Scott Eastman, "Interview: The Great Ridley Scott Speaks with Eclipse by Scott Eastman," *Eclipse Magazine*, 3 June 2008, http://eclipse magazine.com/hollywood-insider/interview-the-great-ridley-scott-speaks-with-eclipse-by-scott-essman/5812/ (accessed 12 August 2008); Arthur B. Evans and R. D. Mullen, "North American College Courses in Science Fiction, Utopian Literature, and Fantasy," *Science Fiction Studies* 23, no.3 (November 1996): 437–528; Tim Goodman, "TV Review: Andromeda Strains Its Credibility," *San Francisco Chronicle*, 26 May 2008, E1; John Kenneth Muir, *Terror Television: American Series 1970–1999* (Jefferson, NC and London: McFarland and Company Inc., Publishers, 2000), 458; William Paul, *Modern Hollywood Horror and Comedy* (New York: Columbia University Press, 1994), 395; Paul Ramaeker, "Notes on the Split-Field Diopter," *Film History: An International Journal* 19, no.2 (2007): 179–98; M. Z. Ribalow, "Swashbucklers and Brainy Babes?" *Science* n.s. 284, no.5423 (23 June 1999): 2089; Sarah Stegall, "Encoding Humanity," *SF Scope* (May 2008): http://sfscope.com/2008/05/encoding-humanitya-review-of-t.html (accessed 14 February 2009); David Vána and Tara Bennett, "*The Andromeda Strain*: The Virus Spreads in VFX," *VFX World*, 6 June 2008, www.vfxworld.com/?atype=articles&id=3661 (accessed 14 February 2009); Joanna Weiss, "Doomsday Plot of 'Andromeda' Stands the Test of Time," *Boston Globe*, 26 May 2008, www.boston.com/ae/tv/articles/2008/05/26/doomsday_plot_of_andromeda_stan (accessed 13 February 2009); John Woodcock, "Disaster Thrillers: A Literary Mode of Technology Assessment? *Science, Technology and Human Values* 4, no.26 (Winter 1979): 40.

Bibliography

"Terra Incognita: The Making of *The Andromeda Strain*," included on the 2-disc DVD release of *The Andromeda Strain* (Los Angeles: Universal Studios, 2008).

THE ANDROMEDA STRAIN (NOVEL)

First published in 1968 by Michael Crichton, who wrote it principally to comment on the state of scientific research in America at that time: "the events [in the book] were a compound of foresight and foolishness, innocence and ignorance . . . This country [America] supports the largest scientific establishment in the history of mankind. New discoveries are constantly being made, and many of these discoveries have important social or political overtones. In the near future, we can expect more crises on the pattern of Andromeda. Thus I believe it is useful for the public to be made aware of the way in which scientific crises arise, and are dealt with." In both film versions of the novel (1971 and 2008) directors have followed the author in reshaping the material to comment on contemporary events.

Reference

Michael Crichton, *The Andromeda Strain* (London: Jonathan Cape, 1968), 3.

APPLE COMPUTERS

US 1984 Commercial r/t 1.5 min col. *Production Company*: RSA Films for Chiat Day Inc. *Producers*: Chiat/Day. *Director*: Ridley Scott. *Writers*: Steve Hayden and Lee Clow. *Cast*: Anya Major (*The Heroine*), David Graham (*Big Brother*).

This commercial was made for $900,000 for Apple Computers. When it was first shown to the company directors, they hated it. Despite the board's dislike, Apple's Steve Jobs supported it, and it was finally shown just once on network television on the night of Super Bowl on 22 January 1984. It was designed not only to advertise the new Apple personal computer, but also to portray Apple as the representatives of freedom resisting the attempts by its rival IBM to monopolize the computer market. This strategy was deliberately planned by Apple's CEO Steve Jobs; in a speech introducing the commercial to his employees given in late 1983, he asked whether George Orwell was right about 1984, in view of the fact that "The Big Blue" (i.e., IBM) sought to take over the industry.

Filmed at SHEPPERTON STUDIOS, England, this commercial, inspired by SYD MEAD's designs for *BLADE RUNNER*, evokes the mood of George Orwell's novel. It begins with a shot of rows of people moving along a subway, looking straight ahead, while a voice-over (representing Big Brother) tells them, and us, that "today we celebrate the first glorious anniversary of the information purification collective." Scott cuts to a quick shot of a woman in a white tank top and red shorts, carrying a sledgehammer and pursued by legions of police officers. The people move towards a large movie theater and sit down, apparently transfixed by the sight of Big Brother speaking directly to them from the screen about their "all-powerful nation" comprised of "one people, one resolve,

one cause." The gray lighting and costumes emphasize the conformity of this state. Suddenly the scene is interrupted by the woman's unexpected entrance as she throws her sledgehammer at the screen with a grunt. The screen explodes, and the camera pulls back to show the aghast faces of the audience witnessing this unexpected sight. A voice informs us: "On January 24 [1984], Apple Computer will introduce Macintosh, and you'll see why 1984 won't be like *1984*."

In an interview recorded soon after the commercial's broadcast, Scott suggested that its design was also inspired by William Cameron Menzies's design for the 1936 version of H. G. Wells's *Things to Come*. Big Brother was initially conceived as resembling Karl Marx, but was changed once a suitable actor had been found. The gray, anonymous nature of the corridors (where the people move towards the auditorium) also recalls the *Nostromo* in *ALIEN*; this (according to Scott) was a deliberate decision to make the corridors look businesslike. As with many of Scott's films, the main concern was not only to tell a story, but to emphasize the commercial's look or design. The director of photography on this commercial was ADRIAN BIDDLE, who fulfilled a similar role on *THELMA & LOUISE* and *1492: CONQUEST OF PARADISE*. The commercial and its impact has been featured in the film *PIRATES OF SILICON VALLEY*, focusing on the relationship between Steve Jobs and Bill Gates.

References

Steve Jobs, speech to Apple employees, late 1983, www.youtube.com/watch?v=AD2Xs0Spj_8 (accessed 4 February 2008); Ridley Scott, interviewed in "The Making of the Apple Commercial, 1984," www.youtube.com/watch?v=AD2Xs0Spj_8 (accessed 4 February 2008).

Bibliography

Adelia Cellini, "The Story behind Apple's '1984' TV Commercial: Big Brother at 20," *MacWorld* 21, no.1 (January 2004): 18; Linda Scott, "'For the Rest of Us: A Reader-Oriented Interpretation of Apple's '1984' Commercial," *Journal of Popular Culture* 25, no.1 (Summer 1991): 67–81.

ARMSTRONG, SU (?–)

Producer of films such as *Mad Max Beyond Thunderdome* (1985) and *Good Will Hunting* (1997).

As producer of *RKO 271*, Armstrong was faced with the responsibility of keeping the budget within the $10 million specified by HBO (the original theatrical release envisaged by Scott was budgeted at three times that amount). Armstrong was enthusiastic about the project, not only for its potential interest to audiences, but because of the historical events it discussed. In an interview with the magazine *Televisual* she suggested that the film was "about the events behind it [*Citizen Kane*] and the personalities involved . . . It meshes history and mythology into a dramatic script, with parallels and circularities at every turn: the film within a film, the search for the motives and character of Welles, and the recurring theme of power and the media . . . [*Kane* is] the number one popular film at the American Film Institute, but when you actually talk to people, they've heard of it but there are many who've never seen it."

Armstrong planned a theatrical outing for the film, but only to limited outlets in Los Angeles and New York. The film was also released theatrically in Spain, Norway, Italy, Belgium, and the Netherlands.

Reference

Keely Winstone, "*RKO 281* Revisited," *Televisual*, September 1998, 24.

ARRIGHI, LUCIANA (1940–)

Began her career in Australian films such as *My Brilliant Career* (1979), and moved on to British films such as *Privates on Parade* (1982), *The Ploughman's Lunch* (1983), and *Madame Sousatzka* (1988). During the 1990s she worked on historical dramas from a variety of historical periods including *Surviving Picasso* (1996), *A Midsummer Night's Dream* (1999), and *Anna and the King* (1999).

As designer for the Ridley Scott-produced film *THE GATHERING STORM*, Arrighi was faced with the challenge of re-creating the House of Commons at SHEPPERTON STUDIOS. She described this experience in an interview with *Broadcast* magazine: "Recreating the 1930s Commons was quite a challenge . . . We had to go back to the original Pugin drawings with all their wonderful Victorian gothic detail and from that we modelled it in plaster. I'm very proud of it [the 1930s House of Commons set]."

Reference

Matthew Bell, "Location Story: A Lonely War Brings Churchill Back to Life," *Broadcast B+*, 7 December 2001, 3.

ASSANTE, ARMAND (1949–)

Born in New York. Made his name in *Private Benjamin* (1980) and *Belizaire the Cajun* (1986). Cast as Sánchez in *1492: CONQUEST OF PARADISE*, Assante plays a Spanish grandee obsessed with diplomacy who is willing to exploit everyone else for his own ends. When he extracts from Brother Buyl (John Heffernan) the confession that Columbus has been mistreating his crew and his fellow Spaniards, he smiles in triumph. Robert Thurston's novelization of the screenplay explains why: "His goal has been to start breaking her [Isabel's] confidence in Columbus . . . Sánchez waited with his usual patience. He was calm, even at the point of victory." Assante essays a creditable mid-Atlantic accent, and manages to remain expressionless throughout the film as befits someone concerned to maintain relations at court with Queen Isabel (SIGOURNEY WEAVER). He was quoted

in the pressbook as saying that Sánchez was "the guiding force of the reason of state in the film . . . He speaks the truth, but dreamers like Columbus don't want to hear the truth. Eventually, Sánchez comes to realize that dreamers do have a place within the state and must be nurtured." This was especially true in the final sequence, as Sánchez leaves the grand hall at the University of Salamanca, where the academics have just credited the discovery of America to Vespucci, not Columbus. Sánchez observes to one of his fellow courtiers that if ever he (Sánchez) will be remembered in the future, it would only be because of Columbus (GÉRARD DEPARDIEU). In an interview with the fanzine *Movieline*, Assante admitted that he liked men such as Columbus: those "not always understood in their own times, but eventually lauded for their vision."

Typifying the mafioso of the early 1970s, Armand Assante plays Dominic Cattano in *AMERICAN GANG-STER*, the powerful thorn in the side of Lucas who, like everyone else, is shocked that a black power player has usurped the structure and brought less expensive, purer heroin to the streets.

References

Martha Frankel, "Armand Assante Is Not Who You Think He Is," *Movieline* X, no.11 (August 1999): 66; *Pressbook: 1492: Conquest of Paradise* (Los Angeles: Paramount Pictures Corporation, 1992), 5; Robert Thurston, *1492: Conquest of Paradise Based on a Screenplay by Roselyne Bosch* (London: Penguin Books, 1992), 176.

THE ASSASSINATION OF JESSE JAMES BY THE COWARD ROBERT FORD

US 2007 r/t 160 min col. *Production Companies*: Warner Bros. Pictures, Jesse Films, Inc., Scott Free, Plan B Entertainment, Alberta Film Entertainment, and Virtual Studios. *Producers*: Jules Daly, Dede Gardner, Brad Pitt, David Valdes, and Ridley Scott. *Director*: Andrew Dominik. *Writer*: Andrew Dominik, from the novel by Ron Hansen. *Director of Photography*: Roger Deakins. *Production Designers*: Patricia Norris and Richard Hoover [uncredited]. *Music*: Nick Cave. *Cast*: Brad Pitt (*Jesse James*), Casey Affleck (*Robert Ford*), Sam Shepard (*Frank James*), Mary-Louise Parker (*Zeralda "Zee" James*), Sam Rockwell (*Charley Ford*), Hugh Ross (*Narrator*).

The film originated with writer/director ANDREW DOMINIK, who read Ron Hansen's book *THE ASSASSINATION OF JESSE JAMES* (NOVEL), and admitted that he was drawn to it "as a story of people and emotions that were vivid and realistic . . . Few people even know Robert Ford's real story. For him, it was about a young man's desperation to become everything he wasn't and everything he worshiped." Although based on comprehensive research, Dominik's screenplay deliberately speculated on the relationship between Jesse James and Robert Ford, in an attempt to stir the imagination rather than impose a point of view on the audience.

Funding for the film was difficult to find until BRAD PITT joined the project as leading actor and co-producer through his company Plan B Entertainment. Ridley Scott subsequently acted as co-producer through his company SCOTT FREE. He liked the film on account of its imaginative possibilities: "The universe of Robert Ford can only be imagined, as can Jesse James's dilemma towards the end of his life, his private thoughts and possible regrets. The film raises questions best answered by each individual in the audience. Andrew [Dominik] poses the possibilities." Dominik and Pitt collaborated to produce what Dominik himself described as an anti-Western that debunks some of the more cherished myths that have grown up around the supposed heroes of the American West. In this version Jesse James (played by Pitt himself) was portrayed as a media celebrity, whose image as a romantic OUTLAW—largely invented by a hack journalist called John Newman Edwards—concealed the fact that he was "a volatile killer who shot dead at least seventeen people during his twelve-year outlaw spree." James himself was not at all comfortable with this image: "You see him throughout the movie struggle with the idea of protecting himself . . . He seems really indecisive about whether he wants to live or die." Meanwhile Bob Ford (CASEY AFFLECK) spends his whole life seeking celebrity, eventually achieving it through killing James. However public opinion soon turns against him: "Bob was able to cash in for a brief period, until the legend [of Jesse James] rose up and swamped him." Co-producer Dede Gardner summed up the story thus: "It's about how someone's adoration for another has to be examined within the context of both their lives and individual needs. Hero worship cannot exist in purity. There are outside influences at work long before the two people in question even meet."

Filming took place in western Canada between August and December 2005. However, the film's release was delayed, allegedly because Pitt and Dominik could not agree about the fine details of the final cut. Pitt explained in an interview that "this [film] is a very complex, slow burn, seventies-style of storytelling and it deals with a lot of psychology, so it had to be just right . . . The first version was four and a half hours long and I thought it was fantastic." The style was very much reminiscent of TERRENCE MALICK's work in its emphasis on visuals.

The reviews—especially in the British press—were largely enthusiastic. The London *Daily Telegraph* described it as "an essay on fame" which must have proved extremely relevant to a superstar like Pitt. *Sight and Sound* called it "a finely honed character piece," while *Time Out* saw it as "an unorthodox psychodrama, almost a study in myopic dependency, pathological or otherwise." As a New Zealand-born Australian director, Dominik brought an outsider's perspective to the Western genre—especially in Jesse James's death scene, which according to the London *Guardian* had "a bizarre mysticism . . . like some parody-version of Thomas More or Thomas Becket." The London *Times* thought it almost inevitable that Pitt would receive an Oscar nomination for his performance: "Pitt's ability to look through characters like a pane of glass has taken years to perfect. Few actors in Hollywood have the charisma to bring him down. His screen paranoia chimes perfectly with the times. It must be miserable acting opposite the American actor in such an arrogant mood." The only sour note was expressed by Derek Malcolm in the *Evening Standard*, who warned readers not to be taken in by the film's "intended depth and psychological realism . . . there's a fake myth-making quality to it that, because of its inordinate length, could be mistaken for grandeur."

The thirty million-dollar film opened to enthusiastic reviews at the Toronto Film Festival but failed at the American box office. By January 2008, some four months after its opening, it had only taken just under $4 million. The British take was not much better; after three weeks in December 2007, its total receipts totaled just over £500,000. In box-office terms, the film suffered by being released almost at the same time as the Coen Brothers's Oscar-winning adaptation of CORMAC MCCARTHY's *NO COUNTRY FOR OLD MEN*.

The Assassination of Jesse James takes a long hard look at celebrity culture, pointing out its advantages and disadvantages. On the one hand, Dominik's screenplay transforms Jesse James into a figure of myth with "a face as smooth and innocent as a schoolgirl. His blue eyes, very clear and penetrating, are never at rest. His form is tall and graceful and capable of endurance and great effort." While Jesse himself dismisses such phrases as "all lies," he nonetheless glories in his celebrity status. At one point he takes off his hat and coat and sits down, and "no one talks as [he] . . . moves—it's as if his acts are miracles of invention wondrous to behold." On another occasion he appears as a Christlike figure in the doorway of Elias's grocery store, the afternoon sun blazing behind him like a halo. Jesse declares, "all America thinks highly of me"; however, being a celebrity can prove an extremely isolated life: at the end of one sequence he crosses his legs and puts his hands deep into his pockets, observing rather bitterly to Charley Ford (SAM ROCKWELL) that "you ought to pity me too." His behavior is routinely misrepresented by the narrator (HUGH ROSS), who seems more concerned with telling a good story than reporting events in a balanced manner: "He [Jesse] camouflaged his depressions and derangements with masquerades of extreme cordiality, courtesy and goodwill towards others." Thus it comes as no surprise to find Jesse feeling "cornered and just plain ornery," which persuades him to accept death rather than continue to live. Once he has passed away, however, his celebrity value increases: the narrator gleefully tells us how two-dollar photographs of his corpse provided "the models for the lithographed covers on a number of magazines," while another photograph of "the renowned American bandit nestled in a bed of ice . . . was most available in sundries stores and apothecaries, to be viewed in a stereoscope alongside the Sphinx, the Taj Mahal and the Catacombs of Rome." Note the narrator's choice of terms here: James has now become public property as "the renowned American bandit" and thereby deprived of his identity. No one really cares for James the man anymore, but appreciate what he *represents*.

Bob Ford spends his whole life modeling himself on Jesse James, to such an extent that he keeps a box under his bed stuffed with lurid nickel books about the James gang, Civil War photographs, yellowed newspaper articles, and other souvenirs. James asks him at the end of one sequence: "Do you want to be like me, or do you want to be me?" We know what the answer is, but Bob deflects the question: "I'm just making fun, that's all." However, Bob exploits his fame at the end of the film as Jesse James's killer; with his brother he recreates the death-scene on the Broadway stage, portraying himself as the good guy charged with the responsibility of bringing Jesse to justice. As a result he achieves a celebrity status of sorts, as he and his girlfriend Dorothy Evans (Zooey Deschanel) promenade down the snowy streets of the SMALL TOWN of Creede, dressed "like a dandy in his gentleman's clothes and cane. *Shopkeepers* and *citizens* greet him, defer to him. He is like a king in this town." As James's reputation increases following his death, so Bob fades into oblivion. The narrator's rhetoric reveals his obvious enjoyment in reporting Bob's decline: "No people would crowd the streets in the rain to see his funeral cortège; no biographies would be written about him, no children named after him, no one would ever pay twenty-five cents to stand in the rooms he grew up in." Unlike James, Bob will never become public property, which (in the narrator's opinion) deprives him of celebrity status.

Dominik suggests that to achieve celebrity, James has to assert his individuality, something which in many Scott films has been identified with AMERICANISM. His exploits have transformed him into an American hero (with the help of the pulp fiction writers), but they have taken their toll on him. Bob watches him taking a bath, and seems shocked by the fact that this thirty-four-year-old legend "seems old, prematurely decrepit, the scars on his body stand[ing] out as red as slaughter." James has no friends; in fact, he suspects that every member of the gang wants to bring him to justice. This explains why he murders Ed Miller (Garret Dillahunt), and will do the same to Dick Liddil (Paul Schneider) if he

gets the chance. Even his brother Frank (SAM SHEPARD) has deserted him to pursue the life of a respectable married man in Baltimore. True to form, the narrator reports this development in typically florid language: "He [Frank] had spurned his younger brother for being peculiar and temperamental, but once he perceived he would never see James again, Frank would be wrought up, perplexed, despondent." Everyone mistrusts Jesse; no one wants to make friends with him. As Bob observes, "friendship [with Jesse] could put you under the pansies." Dominik sums up James's existence in one sequence, where he looks out of a barred window at his daughter Mary's (Brooklynn Proulx's) shoe lying on the grass. The image suggests isolation—although a hero to millions of admirers and a devoted family man, he remains a prisoner of his own celebrity.

The Assassination of Jesse James has some cynical things to say about friendship—and by doing so exposes the shortcomings of the BUDDY MOVIE. At the beginning we learn that the much-heralded James Gang actually comprises "hooligans mainly, boys with vulgar features and sullen eyes . . . They are known collectively as *The Crackerjack Boys* and are just here to provide 'atmosphere' at the robbery and easy prey for the sheriff afterwards." In Frank's view they do not even deserve to be called "men": "Look at those fools. They're going to trip and shoot each other into females." The so-called "inner gang" of Wood Hite (JEREMY RENNER), Charley, Dick, and Ed are not much better—far from bonding together, they compete for Jesse's favor while plotting against him at the same time. Everyone is "suspicious and unnerved" while desperately trying and failing to preserve a façade of normality. Dominik includes at least three sequences in which members of the gang guffaw at James's jokes (even though they are not really funny) as proof of their loyalty to him. The last of these is particularly savage: Jesse shows his contempt and distrust for Bob by snapping his skull back and putting a knife to his throat. Then, his temper altering abruptly, he shoves Bob rudely forward and begins to laugh uproariously. Both Bob and Charley join in, even though they do not feel like doing so. The James Gang's lack of concern for one another is summed up in two sequences: in the first, the brothers throw Wood Hite's naked corpse into a snow-filled ravine like a rag-doll and kick clods of earth over it; in the second, James takes Ed Miller for a ride, lets him ride ahead and then shoots him through the chest.

In this dog-eat-dog world, there does not seem to be any real point in living—particularly when human affairs seem so insignificant in the overall scheme of things. Dominik and his director ROGER DEAKINS suggest this by means of repeated shots of the sky, with the clouds eddying by (denoting the passage of time), or through long shots depicting the characters as mere specks on the vast American (actually Canadian) prairie. In THELMA & LOUISE, the eponymous central characters' flight into the landscapes of Arizona and New Mexico is seen as a way of achieving freedom from social convention. By contrast, in *The Assassination of Jesse James* the landscape engulfs the characters; as seen in one sequence—comprised of a series of long takes—where James and Charley cross a frozen lake somewhere in Nebraska. We can scarcely identify them as they remain in the rear of the frame, concealed in the graying light of dusk. All we can do is to listen to them talking on the soundtrack as Charley talks airily about the James Gang's future plans—involving Bob, of course—while James comments in melancholy fashion on the futility of his existence: "You won't fight dying once you've peeked over to the other side; you'll no more want to go back to your body than you'd want to spoon up your own puke." Bearing this speech in mind, it is clear that James wants Bob to shoot him at the end of the film. He ostentatiously removes his holster, lays it on the bed "as if creating an exhibit," and turns his back on Bob to look at the picture of Skyrocket while observing in a matter-of-fact tone that it seems very dusty. Bob acts on cue by drawing his gun and killing him.

To date there has been scant critical comment on the film. Piers Handling contributed a penetrating summary to the Toronto Film Festival program (where the film received its premiere), suggesting that Dominik "distances us [the audience] from the tale through the use of an omnipresent narrator while also constructing the story through a series of tableaux, reminiscent of paintings or studies of the past." Michael Barson's nostalgic look back at the history of the Western (2008) refers to *The Assassination of Jesse James*, as well as other examples of JESSE JAMES ON SCREEN.

References
"About the Production," http://party931.com/common/movies/notes/54706-1-full.html (accessed 12 August 2008); "The Assassination of Jesse James by the Coward Robert Ford," *The Guardian Film and Music*, 30 November 2007, 7; Michael Barson, *True West: An Illustrated Guide to the Heyday of the Western* (Fort Worth: TCU Press, 2008); James Christopher, "Murder Behind the Myth," *The Times 2*, 29 November 2007, 14; Andrew Dominik, "The Assassination of Jesse James by the Coward Robert Ford," Final White Draft Screenplay dated 17 August 2005, www.simplyscripts.com/oscar80.html (accessed 5 February 2009); David Gritten, "The Assassination of Jesse James by the Coward Robert Ford," *Daily Telegraph*, 30 November 2007, 33; Wally Hammond, "The Assassination of Jesse James by the Coward Robert Ford," *Time Out*, 28 November 2007, 68; Piers Handling, "Film Description and Director Biography," *Toronto Film Festival Program* 2007, www.tiff07.ca/filmsandschedules/filmdetails.aspx?id=706291238481386 (accessed

5 February 2009); Derek Malcolm, "How Jesse Shot to Hero Status," *Evening Standard*, 29 November 2007, 43; "Brad Pitt Interview: *The Assassination of Jesse James*," www.indielondon.co.uk/Film-Review/the-assassination-of-jesse-james-by-the-coward-robert-ford-brad-pitt-interview (accessed 5 February 2009); Kate Stables, "The Assassination of Jesse James . . . ," *Sight and Sound* 18, no. 5 (May 2008): 93; Paul Whittington, "The Big Interview: Andrew Dominik, *The Assassination of Jesse James*," *Irish Independent*, 30 November 2007, www.independent.ie/entertainment/day-and-night/the-big-interview-andrew-dominik-the-assassination-of-jesse-james-1233098.html (accessed 6 February 2009).

Bibliography
Jim Kitses, "Twilight of the Idol," *Sight and Sound*, 17 no. 12 (December 2007): 16–20.

THE ASSASSINATION OF JESSE JAMES BY THE COWARD ROBERT FORD (NOVEL)
Ron Hansen's 1983 novel combines historical material and fiction to reconstruct the real West of Jesse James and his death at the hands of Robert Ford. The book was filmed twenty-four years later with Scott as producer and BRAD PITT in the leading role.

AVALON
GB 1982 Video r/t 4 mins 30 secs col. *Directors*: Ridley Scott and Howard Gard.

Avalon, released in June 1982, was BRYAN FERRY and Roxy Music's eighth studio album; it is generally regarded as the culmination of the smoother, more adult-oriented sound of the band's later work. It was a huge commercial success, hitting number one in the UK (for three weeks) and staying on the album charts for over a year. Although in the US it only climbed as high as number fifty-three, *Avalon* is notable as the band's only platinum record in America. It is also Scott's only rock video.

Continuing a Roxy Music tradition, Ferry's girlfriend Lucy Helmore appears in the video wearing a medieval helmet and carrying a hawk. The image evoked King Arthur's last journey to the mysterious land of Avalon. Ferry himself appears in the video with a red rose, signaling his affection for her. The lush arrangements and synthesizer-drenched sound of *Avalon* later found its way onto Bryan Ferry's solo follow-up album, *Boys and Girls* (1985).

The title track was released as the album's second single and also became a UK Top Twenty hit.

Reference
Roxy Music: Avalon (includes copy of the video), www.dailymotion.com/video/x21d94_roxy-music-avalon_music (accessed 26 February 2009).

BADHAM, JOHN (1939–)

British-born director of films such as *Saturday Night Fever* (1975), followed by *Whose Life Is it Anyway?* (1983). He also directed *Blue Thunder* (1983) and *War Games* (also 1983). In the 1990s his films included *Another Stakeout* (1993) and *Nick of Time* (1995). Badham's chief motivation as a director has been to focus on the film's visual aspects: "I use my knowledge of the history of art every single day in the movie business . . . All day long I'm using that knowledge in composition (of the camera angle), in painting and construction (of the sets and overall visual look of the film." This made him an ideal candidate to direct THE LAST DEBATE, produced by Scott, with its emphasis on interiors and painstaking reconstructions of television studios and presidential suites. Badham also appears in a small role as the news anchor Don Beard, whose contract with a leading network is abruptly terminated as executives decide to employ Joan Naylor—one of the four panelists involved in exposing Republican candidate Richard Meredith's (Stephen Young's) shady past—on account of her celebrity status. The fact that Badham, a director often overlooked by Hollywood as they search for more "hip" talent, chose to play this role says a lot about the ways in which experience counts for nothing in the contemporary media.

References

John Badham, quoted in the pressbook for *War Games* (Los Angeles: MGM/UA Entertainment, 1983), 3.

BALLARD, ALIMI (1977–)

Born in New York, Ballard's early credits include the television series *Sabrina the Teenage Witch* (1996) and *Dark Angel* (2000-2001). Cast as Agent David Sinclair in the television drama *NUMB3RS*, Ballard provides a safe, dependable presence as someone dedicated to his job and only occasionally swayed by sentiment: for example, in the episode "Checkmate" (Series 4, Episode 14), in which he allows his concern for a teenage boy's welfare to blind him to the fact that the boy is being used by a gangland leader to pass on secrets. Sometimes Sinclair has to put his personal feelings aside and

commit himself to his job—as in "Contenders" (Series 3, Episode 16), when he discovers that one of his childhood friends has been accused of murder.

BANA, ERIC (1969–)

Born Eric Banadinovich in Melbourne, Australia, Bana made his name as a stand-up comic before taking the central role in the film *Chopper* (2000). It was on the strength of this performance that JERRY BRUCKHEIMER and Scott cast him as Hoot in *BLACK HAWK DOWN*.

Bana's Hoot is the ideal soldier—one who never knows when to give up. When everyone else has collapsed, exhausted, after eighteen hours of nonstop fighting, Hoot resupplies himself and strides out once again into the fray, determined to find more wounded American soldiers. KEN NOLAN's script gives him the chance to express the soldier's creed: "When I go home . . . and people ask me, hey Hoot? Why do you do it, man? Why? You some kind of war junkie? I won't say a god damned word. Why? Because they won't understand . . . They won't understand, it's about the man next to you . . . and that's it . . . that's all it is." Bana himself remarked in an interview that Hoot is "pretty calculated, experienced, battle-hardened—and I wanted him to be jaded without being too negative. If I didn't feel that I got the levels within that absolutely perfect, I couldn't have lived with myself."

References

Ken Nolan, *Black Hawk Down: The Shooting Script* (New York: Newmarket Press, 2002), 126; Fred Schruers, "The Way We War," *Premiere* 15, no.6 (February 2002): 53.

Bibliography

Ben Marshall, "Anger Management," *The Guardian Guide*, 28 January 2006, 4–6.

BANCROFT, ANNE (1931–2005)

Born Anna Maria Louisa Italiano in the Bronx, New York, she made a name for herself on the New York stage before winning the Oscar for Best Actress in 1962 for her performance in *The Miracle Worker*. Other major roles for her were in *The Pumpkin Eater* (1964) and in *The Graduate* (1967), probably her best-known film, in which she played Mrs. Robinson opposite Dustin Hoffman.

By the mid-1990s, when she played Senator DeHaven in *G.I. JANE*, she had become an established and reliable star. Scott claimed that she was the first choice for the role, as he wanted someone "who's a representative of strength and intelligence and women's rights." He had originally modeled the character on Senator Ann Richards of Texas, who first came to national attention in 1988 when she delivered the keynote address at the Democratic National Convention. However, Bancroft was largely given free rein by Scott to create her own "*grande dame* character . . . she [Bancroft] might not like to hear that, but she really was great." Bancroft herself was quoted in the pressbook as saying that hitherto she had been "playing a lot of women who stay at home, a mother, a great aunt, a grandmother. Here was a glamorous woman with a great sense of herself who is out in the world. It was nice to pull that out of myself."

Bancroft has some notable moments, especially at the beginning when, while chairing a Senate hearing on women in the US armed forces, she takes great pleasure in tormenting Theodore Hayes (Daniel von Bargen), who is endeavoring to preserve the status quo: "Well, I'm just an old dame without much time left, so you'll pardon me if I jump right in here before they discontinue my blood-type. I am deeply concerned over the navy's seemingly incontrovertible attitude toward women in the military." A stage direction in DAVID TWOHY's script observes that "*she's roasting his* [Hayes's] *nuts over an open fire, and everyone knows it*." However, DeHaven recedes into the background once O'Neil (DEMI MOORE) comes on the scene. The final confrontation between the two is peremptorily curtailed, as O'Neil threatens to expose DeHaven's hypocrisy (the senator originally supported the idea of women in the armed forces, but now is prepared to endorse O'Neil's expulsion from military training) to the media. The script describes DeHaven's reaction once she hears O'Neil's threat: "The last image we have of DeHaven is her whirling back, startled." This does not seem consistent with the character as depicted earlier on the film: someone willingly prepared to defeat the military in pursuit of sexual equality.

References

"*G.I. Jane*: Production Notes" (Los Angeles: First Independent Distributors, 1997), 6; Ridley Scott, quoted in Paul M. Sammon, "Joining the Club: Ridley Scott on *G.I. Jane*," in *Ridley Scott Interviews*, ed. Laurence F. Knapp and Andrea F. Kulas (Jackson: University Press of Mississippi, 2005), 142, 159; David Twohy, "*G.I. Jane*: First Draft" (6 August 1995), http://sfy.ru/sfy.html?script=gi_jane (accessed 21 October 2008), 2, 90.

BARCLAYS BANK

GB Commercial r/t 1 min col. *Production Company*: RSA Films. *Director*: Ridley Scott.

One of a series of commercials advertising the British bank; this one begins with a young man climbing into a car in an underground car park and addressing the camera directly: "There's always someone at Barclays who can help." He picks up a red rose and looks at it while informing viewers that if they apply in-branch, they can have the money in as little as ten minutes. The action cuts to a tracking shot a of a blonde-haired woman; the young man reacts, gets out of the car and moves towards her, while informing viewers that they can also apply for loans via telephone and the Internet. Even if they can't meet the customer's requirements, "a member of the staff will be able to explain other ways they can help you." The young man smiles at the camera; in the background we see the young woman climbing into her car. We cut to a close-up of her opening a box with an engagement ring and the words "Marry Me?" on the inside. The commercial ends with intercut close-ups of the young woman and the man, who finishes by saying "Believe me, you'll be glad you did" as he embraces her.

BARCLAYS BANK—FLUENT IN FINANCE

GB 1998 Commercials 6 × 40 sec episodes col. *Production Company*: RSA for BBH. *Director*: Ridley Scott.

A series of commercials, premiering on 7 April 1998, all featuring actor Samuel L. Jackson and set in various locations such as an amphitheatre, baseball stadium, and golf course. They are designed to promote the bank's combined mortgage and current account Openplan, using the slogan "Fluent in Finance."

BARCLAYS BANK QUERY

GB Commercial r/t 1 min col. *Production Company*: RSA Films. *Director*: Ridley Scott.

This commercial creates a DYSTOPIA of the future, where a customer climbs out of his flying car and enters a bank to be screened by security staff. He runs down some stairs packed with vagrants and puts his hand on an identification screen, giving his number as he does so. The screen lights up with the words "Bank Entry." He then goes from screen to screen enquiring about a personal loan, but can never find the answer. He does not have any idea what kind of loan he wants, but simply wants to talk to someone. Eventually he enters an office and encounters what he thinks is a human being, who asks him, "What kind of business loan?" Increasingly frustrated, the protagonist replies, "I don't know. That's why I just want to talk to someone." The official checks the appointments book for the next month, turns around, and is revealed to be a REPLICANT-like figure with an electric cable coming out of the back of his head. The protagonist screams, pulls the cable out, and causes an explosion, screaming, "*I just want to talk to someone!!*" The action dissolves to a shot of an office, with a friendly official inviting the protagonist to sit down and discuss the loan. A voice-over (spoken by IAN HOLM) informs viewers that Barclays's Customer Service program will give expert advice and will visit customers personally if necessary.

The commercial incorporates distinct echoes of *BLADE RUNNER* in its portrayal of a mechanized world in which human beings have been reduced to robots.

BARKER, RONNIE (1929–2005)

British writer and comic actor, most famous for his appearances on television in shows such as *Porridge* (BBC 1974–1977), *The Two Ronnies* (BBC 1971–1986) and *Open All Hours* (BBC 1981–1985).

Unexpectedly lured from retirement to play Winston Churchill's (ALBERT FINNEY's) butler, Inches, in *THE GATHERING STORM*, produced by Scott, Barker gave a low-key performance as a servant devoted to his job yet painfully aware of his employer's foibles—his bad temper, his bouts of manic depression, his tendency to change his mind at the last moment. Barker's Inches is always there to smooth Churchill's feathers, even if he finds the job somewhat onerous. Barker liked working with Finney, someone who seemed to respect the comic actor as a performer: "It [filming] was easy and enjoyable and I acted with him and Celia Imrie, which was very good."

Reference

Bob McCabe, *Ronnie Barker: The Authorised Biography* (London: BBC Books, 2004), 230.

BARRY LYNDON

GB 1975 r/t 183 min (original theatrical release) col. *Production Company*: Peregrine/Hawk Films. *Producers*: Jan Harlan, Stanley Kubrick, and Bernard Williams. *Director*: Stanley Kubrick. *Writer*: Stanley Kubrick, from an original novel *The Memoirs of Barry Lyndon, Esq.* by William Makepeace Thackeray. *Director of Photography*: John Alcott. *Production Designer*: Ken Adam. *Cast*: Ryan O'Neal (*Barry Lyndon*), Marisa Berenson (*Lady Lyndon*), Patrick Magee (*The Chevalier*), Hardy Kruger (*Captain Potzdorf*), Steven Berkoff (*Lord Ludd*), Gay Hamilton (*Nora*), Michael Hordern (*Narrator*).

Stanley Kubrick's massive eleven-million-dollar epic, filmed in Ireland and England, provided much of the inspiration for *THE DUELLISTS*. This is evident both in terms of theme and technique; both films focus on the conflict of LOVE VS. DUTY, particularly concerning the central characters, while emphasizing the importance of the duel (and the code of HONOR attached to it) as a way of resolving disagreements between soldiers.

Stylistically, both films adopt a painterly approach to their material. Kubrick endeavors to recreate the atmosphere of Thomas Gainsborough in many of his landscape shots, while Scott models his film on early nineteenth-century French works such as Géricault's "Mounted Officer of the Imperial Guard" (1812). Both films employ long continuous shots which focus attention on the landscape, as well as tracking shots and slow zooms in and out which concentrate on the characters' relationship to that landscape. Both directors employ a voice-over narrator: Michael Hordern (*Barry Lyndon*) and STACY KEACH (*The Duellists*). This strategy draws attention to the "surface quality" of both films, in the sense that they quote directly from their original literary causes.

Barry Lyndon and *The Duellists* are remarkably similar in the way they photograph their respective duels. Kubrick has one taking place by a river at daybreak: the sunlight illuminates the landscape, while on the soundtrack we hear birds, the rustle of jackets being removed, and the ominous sound of a drum. Redmond/Barry Lyndon (Ryan O'Neal) and Quin (Leonard Rossiter) are shown in long shot facing one another and then firing one shot. Kubrick cuts to a close-up of Quin's petrified face just before he collapses to the ground, dead. In the second duel of *The Duellists*, Scott employs similar strategies—the landscape photographed at dawn, accompanied by a multilayered soundtrack of bird song, horses' hooves, and the seconds' idle chatter. The duel—this time with swords—is shot in close-ups and two-shots, with the soundtrack foregrounding the clash of steel. As in *Barry Lyndon*, this is a fight to the death (or near-death, as D'Hubert retires badly wounded).

Bibliography

Charles Shiro Tashiro, "The Bourgeois Gentleman and the Hussar," *The Spectator: University of Southern California Journal of Film and Television Criticism* 13, no.2 (Spring 1993): 37–38.

BARTY, BILLY (1924–2000)

Born William John Bertangetti in Millsboro, Pennsylvania, Billy Barty began performing at age three and making pictures in 1933. He had a small role in *Gold Diggers of 1933* (1933). He played Mickey Rooney's little brother in the "Mickey McGuire" comedy shorts series. Barty was equally adept at both comedy and drama; he was also a noted crusader for the greater public knowledge and social acceptance of dwarfs.

As Screwball in *LEGEND*, Barty has the chance to show off his talent as someone who does not know the meaning of limitation. He becomes the dominant fairy, not only marshaling Gump (DAVID BENNENT) and Brown Tom (CORK HUBBERT) but encouraging Jack (TOM CRUISE) to maintain his courage in the face of adversity. This role is typical for Barty, who spent years endeavoring to fight discrimination and attitudinal and social barriers in pursuit of his chosen career.

Bibliography
"Billy's," www.billybarty.com/billybio.html (accessed 13 May 2008).

THE BATTLE OVER CITIZEN KANE
US 1996 r/t 118 min b/w and col. *Production Companies*: Lennon Documentary Group, in association with WGBH Boston. *Producer*: Michael Epstein. *Director*: Thomas Lennon. *Writer*: Richard Ben Cramer. *Music*: Maurice Wright. *Director of Photography*: Michael Chin.

Award-winning compilation documentary that chronicles the dramatic events surrounding the production of Orson Welles's *Citizen Kane*, which was nearly destroyed before it could be released. Archival footage is intercut with interviews with some of the people involved, as well as Welles himself (in a 1982 recording). Among those interviewed include Douglas Fairbanks Jr., Peter Bogdanovich, Frank Mankiewicz, and Robert Wise. This film provided the inspiration for *RKO 281*, the Ridley Scott-produced drama recounting the same events, which was filmed by HBO and the BBC in 1999.

THE BEE GEES
The Bee Gees were a singing trio of brothers—Barry, Robin, and Maurice Gibb. They were born on the Isle of Man to English parents and lived in Chorlton-cum-Hardy, Manchester, England; during their childhood years they moved to Brisbane, Australia, where they began their musical careers. Their worldwide success came when they returned to the United Kingdom and signed with producer Robert Stigwood. During the late 1970s they contacted Scott about making a film—a medieval romp provisionally titled "Castle Accident." Scott himself recalled, "My contact in their management company told me, 'The boys are in disarray. We need to do a movie that will put everything back on track. You know, like [the Beatles film] *A Hard Day's Night* . . . I was very much enamored of medieval tales. . . . Then something happened financially and they decided not to do it. I was very disappointed."

Reference
"Scott Penned Medieval Musical for the Bee Gees," www.imdb.com/news/ni0578994/ (accessed 25 October 2008).

BEGHE, JASON (1960–)
Born in New York, Beghe played a small part of the State Trooper in *THELMA & LOUISE*; other early roles included Jeffrey Lindley in the television series *Melrose Place* (1994).

Cast as Jordan O'Neil's (DEMI MOORE's) boyfriend Royce in *G.I. JANE*, Beghe experiences a clear conflict of LOVE VS. DUTY as he discovers the conspiracy to ensure that she does not complete her military training. Although DAVID TWOHY's script has him showing concern for O'Neil (at one point he exclaims "I want to kill the guys who made you cry like this"), it is clear that her success represents a threat to his own position. This is revealed in a significant exchange earlier on. O'Neil observes, "Royce. We're the same age, we started the same time—and now you're sitting in the upperdecks while I'm still down in the bullpen . . . I'm topped out at Intel." Royce responds by insulting her ("so dump on me") and then calling her "a ball-breaker." He obviously cannot contemplate the prospect of a strong woman, and it is therefore unsurprising that their relationship should be heading for the rocks: "Thank you, Royce. It was shaping up like such a tough call—and then you go and make it so goddam easy. Really, thank you so much." For women, it is often those closest to them who prove the most reluctant to contemplate any changes in their roles—particularly in the military.

Reference
David Twohy, "*G.I. Jane*: First Draft" (6 August 1995), http://sfy.ru/sfy.html?script=gi_jane (accessed 21 October 2008), 11–12, 80.

LA BELLE ET LA BÊTE (BEAUTY AND THE BEAST)
France 1946 r/t 93 min (original US release); 94 min (European release) b/w. *Production Company*: DisCina. *Producer*: André Paulvé. *Writer/Director*: Jean Cocteau. *Director of Photography*: Henri Alekan. *Production Designers*: Christian Bérard and Lucien Carré. *Music*: Georges Auric. *Cast*: Jean Marais (*La Bête/The Prisce/Avenant*), Josette Day (*Belle*), Mila Parely (*Félide*), Nane Germon (*Adelaide*), Raoul Marco (*The Usurer*).

Cocteau's famous version of the fairy tale by Madame La Prisce de Beaumont asks its audience to accept its practical magic. Beauty is seen looking into a mirror and her face is replaced by that of the Beast—a fitting metaphor for the potential of any young woman to possess a dark side to her nature. Belle is also kept in a castle, pacing through the Beast's melancholy hallways while she awaits his nightly visit as a statue behind her. The film's effect is purely visual—completely different in atmosphere and style from anything previously released, especially in the commercial cinema.

The film has a dreamlike quality, achieved by slow, flowing continuous shots and the use of curtains fluttering in the wind. Cocteau also has a flair for photographing objects: the mirror into which Beauty stares, reflecting her narcissism; the marble statue separating Beauty from the Beast in one sequence. Above all, the Beast is portrayed as sympathetic;

even though he can never persuade her to marry him, he impresses himself so much on her mind that she eventually rejects her lover and returns to the place where he died. This shows her giving in to her animal nature, which in this film is equated with instinct rather than reason. Scott was inspired by *Beauty and the Beast* when he came to create *LEGEND*. There is not only a shared concern for visual impact, but the director also shows Lily (MIA SARA) being strangely attracted to the Beast-figure Darkness (TIM CURRY) even while she claims to be repelled by him. However, Darkness is completely unlike Cocteau's Beast: one remains a sympathetic character; the other casts a frightening aura over his lair.

Bibliography

Derek Malcolm, "Jean Cocteau: La Belle et la Bête," *The Guardian*, 1 July 1999, 37.

BENNENT, DAVID (1966–)

The son of actor Heinz Bennent and former dancer Diane Mansart. At age nineteen, Bennent starred as Honeymoon Gump in the film *LEGEND* with TOM CRUISE. His role is that of an imp who remains fundamentally self-willed, even if he strives to help Jack (Cruise) in his quest.

BERENGER, TOM (1949–)

Born Thomas Michael Moore in Chicago, Berenger made his debut in the daytime drama *One Life to Live* (1967). He acquired a reputation as a dependable supporting player in films such as *The Big Chill* (1983) and *Platoon* (1986), which encouraged Ridley Scott to cast him as the cop Mike Keegan in *SOMEONE TO WATCH OVER ME*.

Berenger gives a workmanlike performance in the film as a basically decent personality who, though married, falls in love with Claire Gregory (MIMI ROGERS). His range of facial expressions remains limited; even the pain of separation from his wife Ellie (LORRAINE BRACCO) barely shows in his face. Rather, he expresses his disquiet through intense activity—for example, going for a long nighttime run to overcome the fact that he can no longer see his son Tommy (Harley Cross) on a regular basis.

Mike remains a fundamentally optimistic person—one who believes that it is possible for him and Ellie to restart their relationship even after everything that has happened. Whether this will prove true is debatable: if Mike has fallen in love with another woman once, he might do so again, in spite of the fact that he and Ellie seek to escape from their Queens neighborhood and live somewhere else. The film's ending remains inconclusive. Mike believes his main role in life is to protect women from potential danger; ironically, Mike may need someone to watch over *him* to ensure his future as a married person.

BIDDLE, ADRIAN (1952–2005)

Began his career as director of photography on *Aliens* (1986), *The Princess Bride* (1987), and *The Tall Guy* (1989). Previously he had worked with Scott as a loader on *THE DUELLISTS* and as a focus puller on *ALIEN*, a role that required his constant presence at the camera and made him a silent witness to everything going on around him. Biddle first worked as Scott's director of photography on the famous commercial for APPLE COMPUTERS (1984) which recreated George Orwell's DYSTOPIAN world in the studio. Scott also introduced Biddle to James Cameron, the director of *Aliens*.

As Scott's director of photography on *THELMA & LOUISE*, Biddle was responsible for the film's distinctive look—a landscape of oil rigs, cheap motels next to the highway, and nondescript roadside coffee houses. The film's open horizons invest the story with an epic quality that heightens the story's significance. As the two women drive on the road, their progress is continually interrupted by signifiers of the road as male territory—a street-cleaner spraying with them with water, huge trucks blocking their path, a stop sign, a bulldozer, and a herd of cattle. At one point he shows a crop-duster plane flying over the two women's car in a shot strongly reminiscent of Hitchcock's *North by Northwest* (1959) and which here is used to suggest how men seek to "control" women, even when on the open road. The open landscape is not a site of freedom, but a series of obstacles designed to impede women's progress.

However, the film uses the landscape to show how Thelma and Louise ultimately transcend such barriers and achieve some form of liberation. The setting moves from the generic western landscape to shots of Canyonlands and subsequently the lower end of the Grand Canyon in Arizona. When Louise (SUSAN SARANDON) stops the car on the women's last night as fugitives and stands among the cliffs and rock formations, the camera shows how much she has been transformed; no longer a waitress confined to a monotonous job, this tanned, rugged woman now seems at one with the landscape. Scott commented in the pressbook that he and Biddle sought to "create a world which was a reflection of the characters, an environment that mirrored the drama, humor or pathos that they were experiencing at any given moment, around any given curve in the road."

Biddle's achievement was likewise recognized in the pressbook: "Set against the backdrop of the expansive yet vanishing landscapes of America's Southwest, T&L is a cinematic journey filled with friendship, character and truth. If there is one word that could be used to describe the film it would have to be 'moving.' As is the case with all of Ridley Scott's films, *Thelma & Louise* is without question visually moving. And as the story of two women whose innocent road trip becomes a passage into a world of new discoveries, greater freedom and deeper friendship, it is certainly emotionally moving."

Biddle also worked as Scott's director of photography on *1492: CONQUEST OF PARADISE*. They spent months scouting locations in Spain and Costa Rica before eventually choosing the latter country because it provided pristine beaches, islands, and jungle environments. As in *Thelma & Louise*, Scott generally shot with two cameras, focusing especially on aggressive movements to pump visual energy into the film. There were also many handheld shots on the ships: "Ridley wanted the audience to feel what it was like on those small ships bouncing around the ocean." Interior shots on the ships were generally photographed by candlelight, torches or the occasional fireplace, lending the film an intimate quality appropriate for such scenes, where Columbus (GERARD DEPARDIEU) tries to prevent a mutiny among his increasingly frustrated crew.

Both Scott and Biddle loved the outdoor locations: "There have been only two set-ups on the picture where we haven't put in some sort of atmosphere—mist or smoke, rain or fire—to enhance the general scene." To portray the Indians Columbus encountered in the New World, Scott and Biddle photographed 170 indigenous people of Costa Rica, comprising four tribes.

References

Adrian Biddle, interviewed in Bob Fisher, "*1492: Conquest of Paradise*: Epic Film Recounts Legendary Epoch," *American Cinematographer* 73, no. 10 (October 1992): 31; *Pressbook, 1492: Conquest of Paradise* (Los Angeles: Paramount Pictures Corporation, 1992), 8; Ridley Scott, interviewed in the pressbook for *Thelma & Louise* (London: United International Pictures [UK], 1991), 2–3, 6.

Bibliography

"Adrian Biddle," *Daily Telegraph*, 28 January 2006: 27; "Adrian Biddle," *The Times* (London), 17 December 2005: 65; Howard Guard, "Adrian Biddle: Cinematographer at the Cutting Edge of Hollywood Style," *The Guardian* (London), 19 January 2006, 34.

BIRCH, THORA (1982–)

Born in Los Angeles, Birch made her acting debut at the age of four, and subsequently moved into a television series *Day by Day*, followed by *Hocus Pocus*.

Birch made *MONKEY TROUBLE*, produced by Scott, when she was eleven years old. She admitted in an interview seven years later that the film was "a particular favorite . . . I was that way. I wasn't acting at all." In the pressbook, producer MIMI POLK described casting Birch as a stroke of good fortune: "Thora is able to act and react in a most natural way. We were also impressed with her ability to focus, which was crucial since she would spend most of the filming surrounded by four animal trainers in addition to the usual distractions of making a movie." Polk was excited about casting Birch because "she's a realistic nineties kid who can play vulnerable, but also has a nice edge to her when she needs it. What's also unique is that you don't often see a little girl at the heart of a film. We wanted to show that a little girl could be just as interesting, have just as much adventure, and get into just as much jeopardy as a little boy."

References

Thora Birch, interviewed by Neil Norman, "Fearless Thora," *Evening Standard*, 10 April 2001, 29; *Pressbook, Monkey Trouble* (London, Entertainment Film Distributors Ltd, 1994), 13.

BIRNBAUM, ROGER

Born in Teaneck, New Jersey, Birnbaum ran Caravan Pictures, an independent subsidiary of Disney from 1996 onwards. He was formerly vice president of A&M Records and Arista Records, president of the Guber/Peters Company, and executive vice president of Twentieth Century-Fox.

It was Birnbaum who green-lighted the project to film *G.I. JANE* by securing DEMI MOORE's services and engaging Scott to direct. Birnbaum was quite voluble about the project, pointing out in the pressbook that "in order for the movie to appear realistic, the actors in the film would actually have to go through some of the training exercises on film . . . They needed to be prepared for their roles both psychologically as well as physically." He was especially enthusiastic about Moore, who he believed had undertaken "one of the most challenging roles I think any actor—regardless of whether the actor is a man or a woman—has probably had to go through. But she is extraordinary. She put her whole heart and soul into this, and she was there every single moment for the film."

Reference

"*G.I. Jane*: Production Notes" (Los Angeles: First Independent Distributors, 1997), 7–8.

BISSELL, JIM (1952–)

Jim Bissell is a graduate of the University of North Carolina at Chapel Hill with a BFA in Theater. After working in New York and LA on commercials and low-budget features, he won an Emmy Award in 1980 for his work on *Palmerstown, USA* (1982), followed by a BAFTA nomination for production design on Steven Spielberg's *ET: the Extra-Terrestrial* (1982).

It was Bissell's designs that were chiefly responsible for creating the unique style in *SOMEONE TO WATCH OVER ME*—a style contrasting the lush interiors of Fifth Avenue with the grimy rain-washed pavements of Manhattan and the drab exteriors of downtown Queens. Richard Corliss of *Time* magazine described Bissell's designs and Scott's direction thus: "[they] know . . . how to mix sleaze and sleek . . .

set loose in New York City [they] create . . . a Deluxe color version of an Old Hollywood vision: Manhattan in the 1940s, with its twin thrills of grandeur and menace."

Reference

Richard Corliss, "High-Risk Love in an Alien World," *Time*, 12 October 1987, 27.

BLACK DOG

Production company formed by Scott for the creation of new talent in both the film and advertising industries. Its films include *Yoorinal: An Insider's Guide to the World of the Gent's Toilet* (2000). JOHN MATHIESON began his career working for the company.

Bibliography

Richard Natale, "Commercial Break" (1999), in *Ridley Scott Interviews*, ed. Laurence F. Knapp and Andrea F. Kulas (Jackson: University Press of Mississippi, 2005), 172–79.

BLACK HAWK DOWN

US/GB 2001 r/t 144 min col. *Production Companies*: Revolution Studios, Jerry Bruckheimer Films, and Scott Free. *Producers*: Jerry Bruckheimer and Ridley Scott. *Director*: Ridley Scott. *Writer*: Ken Nolan, from the book of the same name by Mark Bowden. *Music*: Hans Zimmer. *Director of Photography*: Slawomir Idziak. *Production Design*: Arthur Max. *Cast*: Josh Hartnett (*Eversmann*), Ewan McGregor (*Grimes*), Tom Sizemore (*McKnight*), Eric Bana (*Hoot*), William Fichter (*Sanderson*), Ewen Bremner (*Nelson*), Sam Shepard (*Garrison*).

Black Hawk Down was based on a 1999 book by MARK BOWDEN, which gave an account of a raid by US soldiers to capture Somali General Aidid and members of his Habr Gidr clan. Their target was the Olympic Hotel in downtown Mogadishu. The story of the abortive raid was well told in Bowden's book, but perhaps more significant—at least for the production of the film—was the media's reaction to it. Aidid celebrated his victory by dragging the naked body of a US ranger through the streets of Mogadishu: Ryan C. Hendrickson discusses how this image was broadcast across the United States and the rest of the world and sent shockwaves through the American body politic. "The people who are dragging American bodies don't look very hungry to the people of Texas," commented Republican senator Phil Gramm, reacting to thousands of telephone calls to Capitol Hill demanding the withdrawal of US forces. John McCain, then a member of the Armed Services Committee, exhorted, "Clinton's got to bring them [the troops] home." Not only did Congress put pressure on the president to consider a pullout from Somalia, the images had their own direct effect in the White House. National Security adviser Anthony Lake

commented, "The pictures made us recognize that the military situation in Mogadishu had deteriorated in a way that we had not frankly recognized." Eventually President Bill Clinton decided to withdraw: according to Thomas Rid, the media was not becoming just part of the battlefield; it had become a strategic factor in the political environment in Washington, a factor that could determine the progress of the war itself.

Bowden's book was bought by the producer JERRY BRUCKHEIMER, who asked him to write a screenplay. According to Bowden, one of Bruckheimer's lieutenants called him and admitted to being "pleasantly surprised [with Bowden's draft]. *We might even be able to use some of this.*" Eventually the script was turned over to young writer KEN NOLAN, who worked on the project for over a year. Other contributors to the finished script included STEVEN ZAILLIAN, Steven Gaghan, and SAM SHEPARD, who largely wrote his own lines. Bruckheimer showed the script to Scott (who had worked with him in the past on commercials). Scott well remembered the events of October 1993 as described in Bowden's book. He recalled to a *Premiere* interviewer that he "recall[ed] watching BBC News and seeing this tragic sight of what was clearly two bodies that were being seriously mauled . . . I knew that it would be a giant shock to the system, seeing that being pushed into the forefront of their [the viewers'] lives on the television sets at home." He agreed to do the film, with the proviso that he could create a story of combat that eliminated all information except what was occurring during the eighteen-hour battle. In the film's production notes he emphasized his intention to show "how these guys [the American army] function under that kind of fire . . . I think the military are a world apart. They police for us, look after our backs."

To prepare for their roles, the cast were sent to the actual military bases used by American service personnel: Fort Benning, Georgia, for the Rangers; Fort Bragg, North Carolina, for Special Forces including the Delta Force; and Fort Campbell, Kentucky. Bruckheimer commented in the production notes, "We wanted the actors to have respect for the military and understand the physical challenges they go through. If you talk to any soldier who has been through a battle, they'll tell you that the only thing that saved their lives was either the man next to them or their training."

As filming in Somalia proved impractical, both for travel and safety purposes, filming took place in two Moroccan cities—the capital Rabat and the ancient city of Sale, across the Bou Regreg River from Rabat, which bore remarkable architectural similarities to the Somalian capital Mogadishu. Several sets were specially constructed, while others were added on to existing buildings or basically used as found. Filming took ninety-two days, with the crew being assisted throughout by military advisers Harry Humphries (a former Navy SEAL) and Colonel Thomas Matthews, air commander of the mission that circled above the battle in the Command and Control Black Hawk. Matthews recalled in the production notes that he did not relish the prospect of returning to Somalia, but felt obliged to do so "for the memory of the soldiers who were killed in that combat operation and their families."

Other members of the military actually participated in the film. Major Brian Bean worked closely with Scott on the aerial sequences, "making sure we understood his vision and executed it to our standards and safety." He was pleased with the outcome: "We really enjoyed the professionalism of the production company, and they've showed us that they totally care about the memory of our men."

Prior to the film's US release in December 2001 (in time for the Academy Award nominations), Scott showed it to selected audiences in US military bases. According to the "Director's Commentary" to the film's DVD release, their largely enthusiastic reaction encouraged the director to believe that he had "got it right"—in other words, provided a balanced view of one of America's largest ground offensives in recent years. Reviews for the film focused principally on its visual style. The London *Times* described it as "100 Ridley minutes [actually 144] of juddering, blood-soaked panic," while the *Evening Standard* drew attention to Scott's ability to set up "an emotional response that no amount of rationalizing can temper while in its grip. War is hell but it's still goddamn exciting to watch." The London *Daily Telegraph*'s East Africa correspondent complained that, while the film was exciting, it still retold "bad history"; but this did not seem to affect Somalian audiences, who apparently cheered when they saw their victory over the Americans retold on film.

Other critics also took Scott to task for creating "bad history." Ann Talbot of the *World Socialist Review* condemned Scott for not showing how the US had helped to create the civil war in Somalia through its support of the deposed dictator Siad Barre. In Talbot's view the director was doing little more than "propagandizing for a particular political position . . . its spirit still reflects the increasingly reactionary outlook of a section of the American élite." Still other critics voiced their opinions more bluntly: the commander of Malaysian forces in Somalia at that time, retired Brigadier-General Abdul Latif Ahmad, was quoted by the AFP news agency saying that the record needs to be set straight, otherwise "Malaysian moviegoers will be under the wrong impression that the real battle was fought by the Americans alone, while we were mere bus drivers to ferry them out." Yusuf Hassan of the BBC's Somali service believed that the Somalis were not actually fighting the Americans but "were just people in the neighborhood who got caught up in this fire and were trying to defend their homes, as they thought they were under attack." Scott argued

in the "Director's Commentary" that he had "no problems" about intervention: despite the fact that the Somalian invasion brought no prestige to the Americans, its purpose (i.e., to remove the Fascist dictator Aidid and bring relief to a starving population) was justified.

Whatever the merits of the film's portrayal of historical events, it was nonetheless a considerable box office hit. The film was nominated for four Oscars and won two for Best Editing (PIETRO SCALIA) and Best Sound. It cost $90 million to make; by April 2002 it had recouped its costs on the US box office alone. Like many similar FILMS AFTER 9/11, audiences welcomed its positive images of American service personnel showing extraordinary courage in adverse situations. Deputy Secretary of Defense Paul Wolfowitz declared *Black Hawk Down* to be a "powerful film." The DVD version was released later that year, followed by the *BLACK HAWK DOWN—EXTENDED CUT* in 2006. The events of October 1993 were also the subject of a documentary *BLACK HAWK DOWN: THE TRUE STORY.*

In contrast to other Scott films such as *GLADIATOR*, *Black Hawk Down* associates MASCULINITY with the group ethic, rather than with individual acts of heroism. Soldiers can only function effectively in battle if they look out for one another. This aspect of their training is emphasized again and again in Ken Nolan's script. Eversmann tries to inspire his men with a stirring cry: "We're Rangers . . . We're elite. Let's act like it out there [in battle]." By contrast, Major Garrison wishes his troops good luck but tells them also to "be careful . . . no one gets left behind." The film contains several sequences in which Rangers and Delta forces observe this dictum, as they risk life and limb to rescue their colleagues—whether alive or dead—from the battlefield. Sometimes this group ethic is put under severe strain: in one sequence Thomas (Tac Fitzgerald) is ordered by his superior officer Struecker (Brian Van Holt) to go out and rejoin the fray. Petrified with fear, the younger man stammers "I can't go back out there," to which Struecker replies, "Thomas, everyone feels the same way you do, all right? It's what you do right now that makes a difference. It's your call." Despite his misgivings, Thomas overcomes his misgivings and follows his fellow soldiers into battle. Even when the odds are stacked against them, officers such as McKnight believe the group ethic gives the troops the strength to succeed: "We're going home. Let's go . . . We're gonna be home in a second, we're gonna be home in a second. Hang on! God dammit, you guys hang on!"

While individual acts of male heroism are condoned, they should always be carried out for the benefit of the group. Hoot, understanding this, returns from one maneuver, slaps in a magazine, grabs a bunch of night-vision goggles, and returns immediately to the battlefield. He does the same thing at the end of the film: Eversmann asks him in astonishment, "You're going back in?" Hoot replies, with disarming candor, that "there's still men out there" who have to be rescued: "[I]t's about the man next to you . . . and that's it . . . that's all it is." Eversmann makes a move to join him, but Hoot claims that he's better on his own, "just another soldier, one of the dogs of war." To emphasize their group loyalty, the soldiers employ the battle cry "Hooah" (similar to the phrase "strength and honor" used in *Gladiator*), whenever they have to undertake a particular maneuver. Eversmann tells his men, "We're gonna hold the perimeter. We're gonna hold the strongpoint," stares into their "wide, scared eyes" and shouts "Hooah!" All of them respond in unison. They are dedicated to their professional responsibilities as members of the US Army—even at the expense of their personal lives. As the Ranger creed puts it: "Readily will I display the intestinal fortitude required to fight on to the Ranger objective and complete the mission, though I be the lone survivor." The conflict of LOVE VS. DUTY that dominates so many Scott films simply does not exist in *Black Hawk Down*. The only time we get to hear about the soldiers' lives back in America is when they are about to die—as, for example, when Wex (Kim Coates) asks McKnight to "tell my girls they'll be okay," or Smith asks of Eversmann, "You tell my parents, that I fought well today."

At the same time, the film's construction of masculinity also permits a considerable degree of compassion. The timing of the raid on Mogadishu is thrown into chaos when Blackburn (ORLANDO BLOOM) falls forty feet to the ground from a helicopter. However, it is far more important for the US Army to look after one of their own: two men place Blackburn on a stretcher and place him in one of the military vehicles (known as Humvees). Hoot and his men assume the responsibility of ensuring his safe return to base ("I'll go! I'll take my team, make sure they [the wounded] get back okay"). Even in a hopeless situation—during Smith's (Charlie Hofheimer's) death sequence—the troops try their best to console him. Eversmann kneels next to him and murmurs: "You don't have anything to be sorry for . . . You did perfect . . . This is nothing.'" As he dies, Smith grips Eversmann's hand in a symbolic act of companionship.

Such acts of tenderness allow for a more compassionate view of masculinity, especially when compared with Scott's earlier films (*G.I. JANE*, for instance). By contrast, women are consigned to the margins; they are no longer necessary in a world where men combine both masculine and feminine qualities. In *Black Hawk Down* they are portrayed as passive—as when, for example, the sixteen-year-old Somali teacher cowers in the corner when Yurek (Thomas Guiry) bursts into her classroom and motions her to be quiet. She obliges meekly. Other women are rapidly exterminated on the grounds that they pose a threat to the troops' safety. In a sequence strongly reminiscent of *HAN-*

NIBAL, in which a drug-dealer carrying a baby fires on Clarice Starling (JULIANNE MOORE), one unnamed woman crosses the street and starts shooting at the troops. Kurth (Gabriel Cassens) kills her with a single bullet.

What sets *Black Hawk Down* apart from other war films is its documentary-style representation of the soldiers' experiences during the eighteen-hour period covered by the raid. Thomas Matthews suggests in the commentary to the 2006 DVD release that the troops would not have survived had it not been for their training and their group loyalty. Many of these themes were later explored in the Ridley Scott-produced television series *AMERICAN FIGHTER PILOT*. While the Somalian campaign contained many specific acts of bravery, no one tried to promote themselves at the expense of their fellow soldiers; they were simply carrying out their responsibilities. Although the film is not political per se, it nonetheless pays tribute to the professionalism of certain individuals—as suggested in the title cards at the end, which list the nineteen soldiers who perished in the conflict, and tell us that Delta sergeants Gary Gordon and Randy Shughart were the first soldiers to receive the medal of honor posthumously since the Vietnam War.

Despite Bowden's and Nolan's professed concern to maintain an even-handed point of view in their script, the film follows *BLACK RAIN* in depicting non-American peoples as deficient in both loyalty and compassion. While Nolan's script describes the Somalis as "little skinny bastards" and "mother fuckers," both Shughart and Gordon are likened to angels as they appear from nowhere and try to rescue Durant. Cribbs (Steven Ford) describes the Somali leader Atto (George Harris) as "urbane, sophisticated [and] cruel"; later on, Firimbi (Treva Etienne) reinforces the truth of this idea when he says, "There will always be killing . . . This is how things are in our world." This gives rise to the belief—held by several American troops—that "if one skinny kills another skinny, his clan owes the dead guy's clan a hundred camels" ("skinny" being the pejorative phrase used to describe the Somalis). Even those Somalis who help to further the American cause are regarded as second-class citizens: the taxi-driver who locates Aidid's house for the troops is not called by his given name but variously referred to as "Tie-Dye," "Abdu" and "Avi."

Several critics have charged the film with racism. Jonathan Markowitz believed that Scott portrayed the Somalis as "an absolutely undifferentiated and unthinkingly brutal threat. The Americans, forced to fight for their lives, are faced with never-ending hordes of Somalis intent on their deaths. . . . The dehumanization of Somalis is so complete as to be causal and automatic: It is even reflected in the language of the soldiers, who consistently refer to them as "skinnies.'" He concluded that "the Hollywood film that comes closest to *Black Hawk Down* in terms of its reliance on racist stereotypes of unthinking brutality is D. W. Griffith's *Birth of a Nation* (1915), and like *Black Hawk Down* plays off highly racialized fears in shaping and disseminating a new national mythology of victimization." Thomas Doherty likens the Somalis to "crocodile meat . . . [who] evoke nothing so much as the swarming aliens in the series originated by Ridley Scott and reinvented in sci-fi combat by James Cameron." Robin Andersen notes that the film offers new constructions of masculinity, but castigates Scott for promoting the idea "of ill-conceived military adventures and the deaths of US soldiers on ill-defined missions with little measurable success."

By contrast, Rebecca Bell-Metereau approaches *Black Hawk Down* as a commentary on new masculinities. The soldiers "express their love and tenderness, but only within the context of death. It is only when comrades fall and lie in each other's arms, ready to die or already dead, that the hero can express his love for his comrade." This, she believes, is characteristic of a war film which has "homoerotic appeal . . . Women are unnecessary . . . because all the real romance, intimacy, and physical thrills occur between men . . . The intimacy accomplished by a single silent gaze from one suffering man to another speaks much louder to many male audience members than the romantic prattle of a woman ever could."

David Machin and Theo van Leeuwen compare the film with the video game, released soon after the film's US release. They stress how both place in the foreground "the qualities of the elite forces: high combat skills, superior technology and team work, the absolute priority of looking after wounded members of the team, and a stress on the speed, the meticulous timing, of the operation and the quick and efficient 'insertion' and 'extraction' of the force. The enemy, meanwhile, is represented differently, as under the sway of a despotic warlord, tyrant or super-terrorist, and as ill-disciplined and ill-equipped by comparison to the US soldiers."

References

Robin Andersen, *A Century of Media, A Century of War* (New York: Peter Lang Publishing Inc., 2006), 226; Rebecca Bell-Metereau, "The How-To Manual, the Prequel and the Sequel in Post-9/11 Cinema," in *Film and Television after 9/11*, ed. Wheeler Winston Dixon (Carbondale: Southern Illinois University Press, 2004), 152–53; Mark Bowden, "Foreword" to Ken Nolan, *Black Hawk Down: The Shooting Script* (New York: Newmarket Press, 2002), ix; James Christopher, "Down and Rout in Africa," *The Times* Section 2, 17 January 2002, 12–13; Jonathan Clayton, "Young Somalis Cheer Their Film Victory over US," *The Times*, 24 January 2002, 16; Thomas Doherty, "The New War Movies as Moral Rearmament: *Black Hawk Down* and *We Were Soldiers*," in *The New War Film*, ed. Robert Eberwein (New Brunswick, NJ, and London: Rutgers University Press, 2005), 216; Jonathan Fryer, "Jingoism Jibe over *Black Hawk Down*," *BBC News*, 21 January 2002; Ryan C. Hendrickson, *The Clinton Wars: The Constitution, Congress and War Powers* (Nashville, TN: Vanderbilt University Press, 2002), 192; David Machin and Theo van Leeuwen, "Computer Games as Political Discourse: The Case of *Black Hawk Down*," in *The Soft Power of War*, ed. Lilie Chouliaraki (Amsterdam and Philadelphia: John Benjamins Publishing Company, 2007), 126; Jonathan Markowitz, "Reel Terror Post 9/11," in *Film and Television after 9/11*, 214–15, 219; Ken Nolan, *Black Hawk Down: The Shooting Script* (New York: Newmarket Press, 2002), 7, 17, 26, 34, 54, 62, 87–88, 102, 109–10, 116, 175; Neil Norman, "Dodging Bullets—and Politics," *Evening Standard*, 17 January 2002, 31; Scott Peterson, "Black Hawk Down—Good Box-Office but Bad History," *Daily Telegraph*, 21 January 2002, 18; "Production Notes: *Black Hawk Down*," repr. in Nolan, *The Shooting Script*, 157, 163, 171–74; Thomas Rid, *War and Media Operations: The US Military and the Press from Vietnam to Iraq* (London and New York: Routledge, 2007), 93; Ridley Scott, "Director's Commentary" to the 2-disc DVD release of *Black Hawk Down* (Los Angeles: Revolution Studios Distribution Company LLG & Jerry Bruckheimer, Inc., 2004); Ridley Scott, quoted in Fred Schruers, "The Way We War," *Premiere* 15, no.6 (February 2002), 85; Ann Talbot, "*Black Hawk Down*: Naked Propaganda Masquerading as Entertainment," *World Socialist Review*, 19 February 2002, www.wsws.org/articles/2002/feb2002/hawk-f19.shtml (accessed 31 December 2008).

Bibliography

Jean Baudrillard, "Pornography of War," *Cultural Politics* 1, no.1 (March 2005): 23–27; Tom Charity, "Do the Fight Thing," *Time Out*, 9–16 January 2002: 24–27; Michael Boughn, "Representations of Postmodern Spaces in *Black Hawk Down*," *West Coast Line* 39, no.1 (2005): 5–16; Tom [Thomas] Doherty, "The New War Movies as Moral Rearmament: *Black Hawk Down* and *We Were Soldiers*," *Cineaste* 27, no.3 (Summer 2002): 4–8; Giles Foden, "You Can't Diddle with the Truth," *The Guardian*, 11 January 2002, 8; Joe Fordham, "Under Fire," *Cinefex* 89 (April 2002): 43–60, 135–63; Philippa Gates, "Fighting the Good Fight: The Real and the Moral in the Contemporary Hollywood Film," *Quarterly Review of Film and Video* 22, no.4 (October 2005): 297–310; Harlan Jacobson, "Bad Day at Black Rock," *Film Comment* 38, no.1 (January–February 2002): 28–31; Charles Laurence, "When the Enemy Is Schmaltz," *Sunday Telegraph Review*, 23 December 2001, 9; "Leave No Man Behind: The Making of *Black Hawk Down*," in Nolan, *Shooting Script* (New York: Newmarket Press, 2002), 151–75; Peter Malone, "War Movies and Political and Social Agendas," *Cine and Media* no.1 (2002): 10–12; Trevor B. McCrisken and Andrew Pepper, *American History and Contemporary Hollywood Film* (Edinburgh: Edinburgh University Press, 2005), 187–211; Adam Smith, "Empire on Set: *Black Hawk Down*," *Empire*, January 2002, 30; Guy Westwell, "Lights, Camera, Military Action," *Vertigo* 2, no.5 (July 2003): 28–92; Yvonne Tasker, "Soldiers' Shoes: Women and Military Masculinities in *Courage under Fire*," *Quarterly Review of Film and Television* 19, no.3 (July 2002): 209–22.

BLACK HAWK DOWN—EXTENDED CUT

US 2006 r/t 151 min col. Rerelease of the original 2001 film, with about seven minutes of extra footage which had been already included in the "Deleted and Alternate Scenes" accompanying the 2004 DVD release. An early sequence shows the Rangers and Delta operators during the calm before battle: Hoot (ERIC BANA) talks shop with Sanderson (WILLIAM FICHTNER); Maddox (Michael Roof) behaves in a threatening way; and Kowalewski (Brendan Sexton II) gets called back to base. Another sequence shows Schmid (Kim Coates) examining Sizemore's (Matthew Marsden's) broken arm; this shows Sizemore's stoicism towards his injury in addition to preparing the audience for a later scene in which he threatens to cut off his cast so that he can join his comrades in battle.

Other restored material centers on the battle; the Task Force Rangers encounter some confusion as they move on the target building. The Delta operators raid the wrong structure, then the Rangers mistake their Delta comrades for enemies and open fire on them. In other sequences set at night, Eversmann (JOSH HARTNETT) kills time with his comrades in conversation before Hoot arrives to provide added security, while Steele (JASON ISAACS) vents his concerns about the progress of the conflict over the radio. Another sequence in the soccer stadium allows most of the surviving main characters some extra time, so as to help the audience understand who is still alive. The sequence also enhances Steele's reaction to the number of American casualties suffered.

Bibliography

"*Black Hawk Down*: The Extended Cut," www.dvdmg.com/blackhawkdownextended.shtml (accessed 31 December 2008).

BLACK HAWK DOWN: THE TRUE STORY

US 2002 TVM r/t 52 min col. *Production Companies*: Wild Eyes, 44 Blue Productions and Flashback Television. *Producer/Director*: David Keane.

Documentary on the failed raids of the American troops in Mogadishu to capture the warlord General Aidid, looking at the events and the consequences both on the ground and for future American foreign policy. The documentary focuses in particular on the idea of American exceptionalism and how the raid questions people's beliefs in it. Produced a year after *BLACK HAWK DOWN*, this documentary offers a factual interpretation of the events covered in Scott's film.

Bibliography

John Lewis, "Hawks and Doves," *Time Out*, 13 August 2003, 39; Trevor B. McCrisken, *American Exceptionalism and the Legacy of Vietnam: US Foreign Policy since 1974* (New York and Basingstoke: Palgrave, 2003), 153–54, 166–69.

BLACK RAIN

US 1989 r/t 120 min col. *Production Companies*: Paramount Pictures and Pegasus Film Partners. *Producers*: Sherry Lansing and Stanley R. Jaffe. *Director*: Ridley Scott. *Writers*: Craig Bolotin and Warren Lewis. *Director of Photography*: Jan de Bont. *Production Designer*: Norris Spencer. *Music*: Hans Zimmer. *Cast*: Michael Douglas (*Nick Conklin*), Andy Garcia (*Charlie Vincent*), Ken Takakura (*Masahiro*), Kate Capshaw (*Joyce*), Yusaku Matsuda (*Sato*), Shigera Koyama (*Ohashi*), John Spencer (*Oliver*), Yuya Uchida (*Nashida*), Tomisaburo Wakayama (*Sugai*).

Black Rain was offered to Scott by Paramount executives SHERRY LANSING and STANLEY R. JAFFE, who had to find another director for the project after their original choice Paul Verhoeven had turned it down. Scott told the *New York Times* that he wanted to use the film to explore whether "East [is], East; and West, West, or are we all part of the Family of Man?"

Filming began in Osaka, JAPAN, in October 1988, but Scott was forced to move his operation back to the United States in January 1989 owing to well-publicized production difficulties. The *New York Times* reported that many businesspeople objected to having their houses used as places frequented by the yakuza, or Japanese gangs, for fear it would "reflect badly on them." When the producers wanted to film nighttime scenes, they had to agree to do so over a number of days, in the quiet hours between 3:00 and 6:00 AM, instead of completing it all in one session. Associate producer Alan Poul did not have "a lot of kind things to say about the Japanese police, except they ultimately let us do it [film]." Producer Stanley R. Jaffe recalled in an interview for the film's DVD release that in the American crew's view, Japan was a very hostile place to make a film.

Although Scott suggested to the *New York Times* that working with the Japanese actors was "brilliant . . . I got very good, balanced, very contemporary, very real performances," he recalled in a 1999 interview with PAUL M. SAMMON that both he and the American crew found it difficult to work efficiently. They misunderstood "the Japanese order . . . The way they function and the way they work . . . I also think there was a misunderstanding of how costly it would be in Japan." Filming was eventually completed in Manhattan and New York's Silvercup Studios; areas around LOS ANGELES doubled up for the Japanese locations. The final chase sequence was shot near San Francisco, with an American vineyard converted into a sake firm. Principal photography wrapped in March 1989; the film was released in September of the same year.

Reviews for the film's original release were mixed. Roger Ebert of the *Chicago Sun-Times* believed that Scott must have been "bewitched by memories for the futuristic Los Angeles he created for *BLADE RUNNER* . . . The production design . . . is so overwhelming that the characters seem lost and upstaged." The *Washington Post* criticized the director for losing sight of the story "in this artistic barrage of blood and guts. It's [the film is] a gorgeous, erratic movie most definitely not for those with an aversion to cutlery." Vincent Canby of the *New York Times* criticized the script which "plays as if it has been written during the course of production. There appears to have been more desperation off the screen than ever gets into the movie." Even so, he complimented Scott on his ability to "capture the singular look of contemporary urban Japan." The film seemed unimportant, however, when compared with a Japanese film released in New York at the same time (also with the title *Black Rain*), exploring the legacy of the atomic bomb that exploded over Hiroshima in 1945. The critic of the Asian film magazine *Cinemaya* (published in India) complained that Scott was consciously orientalist in his portrayal of Japan: "Must the Oriental always serve as a foil to the Hollywood American character in terms of group loyalty versus independence, restrictions versus initiative, reserve versus the 'good ol' boy'?"

British reviewers' opinions ranged from enthusiastic appreciation of Douglas's performance (he was "not Mr. Nice Guy" anymore), to a grudging observation that the Japanese characters in the film were "portrayed as the ultimate Aliens." Derek Malcolm of *The Guardian* saw the film as "an art director's movie elaborated by a film maker who never achieves an unwatchable movie but seldom matches eye and brain."

In spite of its weaknesses, Scott's *Black Rain* found favor with American audiences. It grossed a respectable $45 million during its initial run, and was considered a decent hit. In common with several of his films, *Black Rain* was rereleased in a "Special Collector's Edition" in the United States in early 2007, including a variety of extras such as a documentary on the making of the film. Producer Lansing recalled that approximately thirty-five minutes of scenes were removed from the final print: the original cut of the film ran 160 minutes. Unfortunately, the DVD does not contain any evidence of the lost material.

Black Rain explores several themes characteristic of Scott's earlier work. Prominent among these is a concern for the importance of HONOR (which dictates the protagonists' behavior in *THE DUELLISTS*). Sugai (TOMISABURO WAKAYAMA) stresses the point to Nick Conklin (MICHAEL DOUGLAS): "Unlike our syndicates, your criminals don't understand the words 'honor' and 'duty' . . . We can't afford not to deal with them." The finished film develops this point by stressing that Nick has committed a "dishonorable" act by stealing counterfeit dollars from Sato's (YUSAKU MATSUDA's) house; when Nick later admits that he took a bribe from the mafia bosses in New York,

Masahiro (KEN TAKAKURA) calls him a disgrace. The Japanese police officer will never appreciate that New York is "just one big gray area"; in a world governed by traditions of honor, both social and personal, the notions of right and wrong are absolute.

Japanese codes of honor also force Sato to undergo the ritual of yubitsume, in which the joint of the little finger is sliced off to atone for a mistake. The original script places this scene at the end, when Sugai captures Sato and delivers him to Nick. By contrast, the final version uses the ritual to suggest that Sato has bowed to the older yakuza leader's authority. He places his finger on a table—a guard slices the top off, places it in a handkerchief and gives it to Sugai. Throughout the whole grisly sequence Sato's face remains impassive: the code of honor demands that he betray no emotion. However, Sato gets his revenge soon afterwards, as his followers overpower Sugai's men and take over the sake factory. Sammon comments that such sequences, performed "with a sardonic and gleeful intensity," render *Black Rain* one of Scott's most violent films. This might be true, but such rituals are commonplace in a culture dominated by traditions of honor.

Whether Scott approves of such traditions is another matter. Throughout the film he contrasts Japanese notions of group identity with American individualism, and it is clear where his sympathies lie. The original script has Kobo/Sato saying with some bitterness that for "a couple of thousand years they've [the Japanese] been bound by these little rules. Always afraid. Ugly little lives . . . Where you [Nick] come from a man can stand out. It's expected. Here a man is made to look a fool for standing out." The finished film has Masahiro being suspended from the police force for disobeying Superintendent Ohashi's (SHIGERU KOYAMA's) orders and observing cynically, "I belong to a group. They [the police] will not have me anymore." Once Sato has been arraigned and brought to Ohashi's office, the camera tracks along the endless rows of identical desks in a shot strongly reminiscent of Billy Wilder's *The Apartment* (1960). In this world individualism counts for nothing; people cannot be separated from their workstations. By contrast, the American way of life is celebrated in a newly created scene in a karaoke bar where Charlie (ANDY GARCIA) gets up and sings Ray Charles's classic 1959 hit "What I'd Say" while persuading Masahiro to join in the choruses. The song celebrates personal initiative—something Masahiro obviously admires, as he decides to flout convention and "go for it" by assisting Nick in his quest to arrest Sato. Such notions of individual self-determination are part of the film's celebration of AMERICANISM.

In the *New York Times* interview published immediately prior to the film's American release, Scott stated that the film's plot centered on "the conflict between police methods

. . . Conklin—is a New York homicide detective with a certain disgruntlement, a certain dissatisfaction with the system and a certain renegade quality . . . Ken [Masahiro], on the other hand, is a thorough, by-the-book, hardline bureaucrat who is part of what seems to be this wonderful machine in Japan." However, this contrast is not really evident in the finished film which, according to the *Entertainment Weekly* reviewer, "couldn't be more brainlessly racist unless he had called it *Black Lain . . . Black Rain* is designed to punch the xenophobe's buttons."

Black Rain also recalls earlier Scott films in its representation of the urban landscape. Like the futuristic Los Angeles in *Blade Runner*, Osaka (as photographed by JAN DE BONT) is a threatening place awash with neon lights, whose citizens wander aimlessly along the sidewalks. Cheap restaurants sell hot food to those who can afford it; overdecorated bars provide temporary solace for tired businesspeople. In one sequence Nick and Charlie are shown walking along a deserted street illuminated by flashing lights. Suddenly they are assailed by several black-clad bikers who drive up close to them uttering wolf-whistles as they do so. They are members of Sato's gang seeking, quite literally, to scare the police officers stiff. It is at moments like this that Charlie and Nick understand just how far from home they are.

As in *SOMEONE TO WATCH OVER ME*, the central character Nick Conklin is something of a maverick, devoted to his family but unable to sustain a happy MARRIAGE. Nick is proud of his MASCULINITY—a long sequence at the beginning of the finished film shows him racing with fellow bikers along the banks of the Hudson River. The fact that he emerges triumphant is significant in terms of the ensuing action: when he tries to catch Sato at the end, we instinctively feel he will succeed. On his arrival in Japan, Nick behaves boorishly, expecting everyone to follow his orders even though he is nothing more than a "*gaiijin*; an outside person; a foreigner; a barbarian." As he comes to understand Masahiro, Nick gradually becomes more acclimatized to Japanese culture; the original script has him learning to slurp while he eats his noodles with chopsticks, a sign of enjoyment according to local custom. The finished film replaces this with two sequences—in the first of these Nick finds it difficult to use chopsticks but graciously allows an (uncredited) Japanese woman to show him the way. In the second, taking place at the airport prior to Nick's departure, he manipulates his chopsticks like a native. He might be proud of his American identity, but like Deckard in *Blade Runner* he has learned to empathize with alternative cultural values.

Nonetheless, *Black Rain* remains resolutely unadventurous in its representation of gender. It follows the convention of the BUDDY MOVIE by endorsing male bonding: Nick and Charlie remain partners through thick and thin, and when Charlie meets a bloody end (in the finished version he is ritualistically beheaded by Sato in an underground car park), Nick vows revenge. Despite their cultural differences, Nick and Masahiro forge a new bond of friendship—as seen in the way the Japanese police officer casts aside his inhibitions and joins Nick in the hunt for Sato. This decision should inevitably bring retribution from Ohashi; but in a wish-fulfilling ending, Scott has the two police officers being decorated for their efforts with two golden suns presented by the superintendent. As in *Someone to Watch Over Me*, friendship among male police officer is something desirable that sustains individuals both personally and professionally. By contrast the female characters remain sketchily drawn: Joyce (KATE CAPSHAW), an American expatriate reluctant to leave Osaka, serves both as Nick's token love interest and a means to advance the plot (as she provides Nick with vital information as to Sugai's whereabouts). This is certainly surprising for a director who seems so preoccupied with FEMINISM and female roles in *ALIEN*, and who would subsequently release the female ROAD MOVIE *THELMA & LOUISE*.

Critical material on the film includes an essay by Gerald Fitzgerald drawing attention "to the range of 'cultural signifiers' deployed throughout the film"—for example, the "mingled dark . . . and glistening . . . tones [that] produce an atmosphere of ambiguities and complication, which are absolutely appropriate for its themes of 'cultural' dissolution and intersection." He highlights Scott's use of "'doublings' of episodes/scenes that correspond to or echo each other" designed to focus on the theme of cultural difference. Scott also focuses on "cultural appropriation, borrowing, [and] imitation, of which both Japan and America may be seen as zealous practitioners." Richard Schwartz prefers instead to focus on the characters; for him, Sato represents "a shadow figure for Nick . . . He represents what Nick could become if he succumbed fully to his dark side." However, just as Deckard in *Blade Runner* emerges as a better person for his confrontation with Batty, "Nick is redeemed and revitalized by his conflict with his shadow figure, Sato, and by his association with his better self, as embodied in the honorable and incorruptible Masahiro."

References

Craig Bolotin and Warren Lewis, "*Black Rain*: Draft Script" (November 1987), http://sky.ru/sfy.html?script=black_rain_ds (accessed 8 June 2008); Tim Appelo, "Black Rain," *Entertainment Weekly* (1990), www.ew.com/ew/article/0,,317146,00.html (accessed 12 June 2008); Vincent Canby, "Police Chase a Gangster in a Bright, Menacing Japan," *New York Times*, 22 September 1989, http://query.nytimes.com/gst/fullpage.html?res=950DE4DA103DF931A1575AC0A96F948260&scp=3&sq=black+rain+vincent+canby&st=nyt (accessed 11 June 2008); Donald Chase, "In Black Rain, East Meets West with a Bang! Bang!," *New York Times*, 17 September

1989, B7; Roger Ebert, "Black Rain," *Chicago Sun-Times*, 22 September 1989, http://rogerebert.suntimes.com/apps/pbcs.dll/article?AID=/19890922/REVIEWS/909220301/1023 (accessed 11 June 2008); Linda C. Ehrlich, "Black Rain," *Cinemaya* 6 (Winter 1989–90): 29–30; Gerald Fitzgerald, "Black Rain: Ridley Scott's 'New' Cinema," *Metro* 84 (Summer 1990–19): 14–15; Aljean Harmetz, "2 Movies called 'Black Rain,'" *New York Times*, 27 September 1989, http://query.nytimes.com/gst/fullpage.html?res=950DE0D9163EF934A1575AC0A96F948260&scp=4&sq=black+rain+vincent+canby&st=nyt (accessed 11 June 2008); Stanley R. Jaffe, interviewed in "*Black Rain*: The Making of the Film Part 1," Special Feature included in the Special Collector's Edition DVD release of *Black Rain* (d. Laurent Bouzereau) (Los Angeles: Paramount Pictures, 2006); Rita Kempley, "Black Rain," *Washington Post*, 22 September 1989, www.washingtonpost.com/wp-srv/style/longterm/movies/videos/blackrainrkempley_a09fde.htm (accessed 11 June 2008); Derek Malcolm, "Orient Expressed," *The Guardian*, 25 January 1990, 24; Pauline McLeod, "Douglas Not Mr. Nice Guy," *Daily Mirror*, 20 January 1990, 27; Suzanne Moore, "Black Rain," *New Statesman Society*, 2 February 1990, 44; Richard Alan Schwartz, *The Films of Ridley Scott* (New York: Praeger Publications, 2001), 78; Ridley Scott, quoted in Paul M. Sammon, *Ridley Scott Close-Up: The Making of His Movies* (New York: Thunder's Mouth Press, 1999), 92.

BLADE RUNNER

US, 1982 r/t 117 min col. *Production Companies*: Tandem Productions/ Norman Lear, The Ladd Company and The Shaw Brothers. *Producer*: Michael Deeley. *Director*: Ridley Scott. *Writers*: Hampton Fancher and David Peoples, from the original novel *Do Androids Dream of Electric Sheep?* by Philip K. Dick. *Director of Photography*: Jordan Cronenweth. *Production Designer*: Lawrence G. Paull. *Music*: Vangelis. *Cast*: Harrison Ford (*Rick Deckard*), Rutger Hauer (*Roy Batty*), Sean Young (*Rachael*), Edward James Olmos (*Gaff*), M. Emmet Walsh (*Bryant*), Daryl Hannah (*Pris*), William Sanderson (*J. F. Sebastian*), Brion James (*Leon Kowalski*), Joe Turkel (*Eldon Tyrell*), Joanna Cassidy (*Zhora*), James Hong (*Hannibal Chew*).

The origins and production history of *Blade Runner* have been outlined in detail by PAUL M. SAMMON.

Scott first heard about the project when producer MICHAEL DEELEY brought him the script of PHILIP K. DICK's *DO ANDROIDS DREAM OF ELECTRIC SHEEP?* (1968). At this point the screenplay had been written by HAMPTON FANCHER and Brian Kelly, who had asked Deeley to find a suitable director. According to Sammon, Scott liked the screenplay because it dealt with "the near future . . . there was a real character in there, rather than what is frequently a two-dimensional cardboard character." At first Scott declined the project as he was committed to other films, including an adaptation of Frank Herbert's

DUNE (which was eventually directed by David Lynch). But personal difficulties led Scott back to *Blade Runner*, a project he hoped to begin immediately in the wake of *ALIEN's* success, although it was fully one year before shooting began. *Blade Runner* was to be produced through a small outfit, Filmways Productions, on a limited budget of $13 million. But before photography could proceed, the script needed to be reworked. Another writer, DAVID PEOPLES, was hired to work on it: one of his principal contributions was to coin the term REPLICANT to describe the characters manufactured by the Tyrell Corporation. As the script was being finalized in December 1980, Filmways withdrew from the project; Deeley managed to arrange alternative financing from the Ladd Company (funding $7.5 million through Warner Brothers), Sir Run Run Shaw (who put up the same amount in exchange for foreign rights) and Tandem Productions, run by Norman Lear, Bud Yorkin and Jerry Perechino, which put up $7 million for the ancillary rights. Tandem served as bond guarantors with the right to take over if the budget went 10 percent over the projected amount.

Principal photography began on 9 March 1981 and was completed four months later. By all counts, it was a torturous shoot: Hollywood was unprepared for Scott's style of filmmaking, while Scott did not understand the way of life in unionized Hollywood. There were also personal difficulties: Scott did not see eye to eye with HARRISON FORD; SEAN YOUNG also clashed with the leading actor. Meanwhile, Tandem Productions became increasingly upset with Scott's approach to directing, which revealed itself through endless retakes. By the end of shooting, the film was $11 million over budget; according to the terms of the original agreement, Tandem took over the production. Both Scott and Deeley lost their authority and had to accept the company's wishes.

Disastrous previews were held in Denver in February and March 1982, with criticism centered in particular on the film's narrative confusion, slow pace and muddled editing. As a result Tandem insisted that explanatory narration should be introduced in the form of voiceovers delivered by Deckard (Ford). Tandem also recommended a happy ending in which Deckard and Rachael (Young) soared over verdant landscapes in a series of outtakes borrowed from Stanley Kubrick's *The Shining*.

Blade Runner opened in the United States on 25 June 1982 to mixed reviews. Pauline Kael of the *New Yorker* admitted that such a visionary film "that has its own look cannot be ignored," but added that "if anybody comes around with a test to detect humanoids, maybe Ridley Scott and his associates should hide." British reviewers such as Nigel Williams praised the film's "excellent atmospheric scenes," but at the same time criticized Scott's "Hovisitis" (a reference to his television commercial for HOVIS BREAD)—more precisely defined as the "desire to soft-focus at the merest hint of any emotion." Nigel Andrews of the *Financial Times* believed that "atmospherics are all" in the film, while Tom Hutchinson wrote more prophetically that its major strength was "its sense of dislocation . . . [it] may well be a glimpse of the way things are going. For, stepping out into a wino-littered Leicester Square heaped with unswept rubbish, I began to wonder if the things to come I had just seen were here already." *The Sunday Telegraph* thought that the film had "all the marks of a solid hit."

Such predictions failed to materialize: in the United States the film's opening weekend receipts totaled $6.15 million while its gross earnings on its initial theatrical run—in the United States and elsewhere—totaled only $14 million, or half its production budget. However, the film refused to go away: Warner Bros. pulled it from theatrical distribution and broadcast it on cable television as well as releasing it on video, where it became one of the most popular rented tapes. It appealed not only to science fiction buffs but to wider audiences as well. In 1982 *Cityspeak*, the first fanzine dedicated to the film, appeared; a year later, *Blade Runner* was voted the third favorite science fiction film of all time (following *Star Wars* and *2001: A Space Odysssey*) at the World Science Fiction Convention.

The story of how the film was rereleased ten years later as the *BLADE RUNNER*: THE DIRECTOR'S CUT and how that version differed from the other available versions has been told in detail by William M. Kolb. The Director's Cut opened in fifty-eight theaters in the United States, with the highest box office that weekend. After five weeks, the number of screens climbed to ninety-five and the film remained in the top fifty grossing pictures for ten weeks, earning $3.7 million during this period alone. The American release was followed by openings in Europe, Great Britain, and Japan. Critical response was again mixed, but Scott declared in an interview with *Starburst* that he was "glad that, at long last, it's [the film is] getting seen as I'd always wanted it to be seen. It's about time." But that was not the end of the story: By 2001 Scott and his DVD producer CHARLES DE LAUZIRIKA agreed to assemble a special edition, plus a newly edited version of the film for a limited theatrical run. The project was abandoned due to copyright issues; however, de Lauzirika kept the idea afloat, drawing up a list of all the visual and audio adjustments Scott might like to make for a new version. Scott added his own ideas, and the result was *BLADE RUNNER*: THE FINAL CUT, which was released first in theaters and subsequently in a five-disc DVD set (containing all the previous versions of the film plus many extras) in late 2007. Whereas in 1992 Scott had insisted that the Director's Cut was definitive, now he was not so sure. He told Geoffrey Macnab in October 2007 that the experience of working on the film again resembled "fin-ishing a painting—you never really do . . . You still walk into a room and look at it."

Blade Runner shares with *THE DUELLISTS* and *Alien* a concern for the notions of LOVE VS. DUTY. When Deckard comes to realize that his love for Rachael is more important than loyalty to his job, he is perceived as an extraordinary person in a degraded social sphere where it no longer seems possible to separate the real from the artificial. The city skyline is dominated by mass advertisements—Coca-Cola signs, an oriental face promoting drugs, and a host of other displays. A large floating screen invites the citizens of LOS ANGELES to "off-world colonies," with the chance to "begin again in a golden land of opportunity." The pertinence and uniqueness of time and space, of illusion and reality, no longer exist; in their place a new POSTMODERNISM reigns, dictated by the logic of pastiche, which allows and promotes quotations of a synchronic and diachronic order. Giuliana Bruno observes that the film's "recollections and quotations from the past are subcodes of a new synthesis. Roman and Greek columns provide a retro *mise-en-scène* . . . Signs of classical Oriental mythology recur. Chinese designs are revisited in neon lighting . . . All of Los Angeles . . . is of the order of hyperreal and simulation."

This same logic determines the characters' behavior: J. F. Sebastian (WILLIAM SANDERSON) quite literally makes artificial friends, almost as if he cannot stand the sight of human company. Tyrell (JOE TURKEL), the chair of the corporation that bears his name, has no feelings for anyone, particularly the replicants. To him everything—including the chess game where Batty outwits his creator—is simulated, providing an opportunity for further experiment. This continues a theme first explored in *Alien*, in which the Company pretends to show concern for their employees' welfare yet regards them as expendable in their relentless search for information concerning the alien's habits. The sense of simulation characterizes modes of discourse used in the film. English and Japanese words appear in advertisements on elevators and in the city, while the language spoken on the streets ("Cityspeak") is a polyglot combination of English, Japanese, German, "what have you" as Deckard puts it. As social systems are dissolved, so their characteristic languages are subject to a similar process of disintegration. Words are no longer used to communicate; rather, they are a means of filling an empty space. People pretend to talk to one another. Much of *Blade Runner*'s dialogue is composed either of brief exchanges or non sequiturs. The only way the characters can express themselves is through soliloquies—for example, Deckard's voiceovers (incorporated in the 1982 theatrical release but deleted from subsequent versions of the film) or Batty's long speeches at the end. Otherwise the dialogue resembles a continuous babble of noise in which sound assumes more significance than sense. This is evident in the scene where Deckard tries to find out Zhora's (JOANNA CASSIDY's) whereabouts by asking the bartender Taffey (Hy Pike). No one—least of all the viewers—can understand what he says.

Scott also emphasizes the notion of linguistic dislocation in the scene where Tyrell challenges Sebastian to a chess game. Sebastian is not actually in Tyrell's presence, but exchanges moves with his employer by radio. Neither of them can bear the idea of face-to-face communication. Such scenes might be considered a good example of heteroglossia—a postmodern mix of languages distinguished by diversity. Roswitha Mueller believes that this is designed to promote difference "in all of its forms . . . in a non-repressive environment." The problem is that the Los Angeles of *Blade Runner* does not promote difference; rather, it denies its inhabitants the privilege of exchanging views with one another in "a topsy-turvy world in which androids [replicants] appear to be human and humans like androids." In such a world, it is not surprising that Deckard should begin to consider the question of whether the replicants are indeed rabid dogs or the product of a simulated world described by Marilyn Gwaltney as one in which moral, legal, and linguistic standards no longer exist, nor any restraint in the use of deadly force.

The film can be understood as a quest for perfect sight, which in this sense means possessing the capacity to restore clear-headed thinking. The opening shot features a disembodied eye staring over the Los Angeles landscape. Reflected in this eye are lurid flames bursting from the top of buildings. This orb above, yet within, the fires of the world suggests a harmony that simply does not exist among the citizens, something they strive to recover. In the next scene we see the eyeball of Leon Kowalski (BRION JAMES) through the lens of the Voight-Kampf test. Holden (Morgan Paull) studies the sphere to ascertain whether Leon is a replicant or not. The assumption is this: the eye is an "I," a synecdoche of human beings, a numinous microcosm. If the eye/I is full of life, emotion, and vitality, then there might be some future hope for people (or replicants, for that matter).

The only character who can even approach the ideal eye/I is Batty. In his first appearance he visits the factory where the replicants' eyes are made. He finds Chew (JAMES HONG), an eye engineer. Although Batty is dedicated to prolonging his four-year mechanical life, he is also passionate about vision: "If only you could see what I've seen with your eyes." This line emphasizes what separates Batty from Deckard; at least until the film's final moments. Whereas Deckard vacillates between received opinions and immediate perceptions (whose validity he immediately doubts), Batty embraces his visual experiences, not as sites of skepticism but as something to be savored. During his visit to Chew, he quotes the following lines, slightly adapted from WILLIAM

BLAKE: "Fiery the angels fell,/ Deep thunder rolled round their shores,/ Burning with the fires of Orc." Batty regards himself as a rebel angel—an eternal rebel against the tyranny of the Los Angeles world. He might be a replicant, but according to Eric G. Wilson, his "inhuman mechanisms allow [him] . . . to benefit from self-awareness."

However, the fact that Batty possesses such clear-sightedness does not prevent him from suffering. Even though he is exuberant about his superiority to humans and other replicants, he is profoundly affected by the iniquities of his four-year existence. He can see terror as easily as joy: the tyrannies of Los Angeles shake him to the core. This provides the justification to rebel against Tyrell, his evil creator. Batty's quest is twofold: to find more life in hopes of overcoming his own mortality; and to rebel against the evil magus who fashions machines that serve as slaves and then die.

In the film's final scene, both Batty and Deckard undergo epiphanies. Deckard at last comes to realize the importance of the I/eye and to discover ways to heal the gaps in his soul. Meanwhile, Batty achieves aesthetic wisdom by learning how to play and to enjoy increasingly intense experiences for themselves. To enjoy this condition is to be in the world but not become involved in its corruption. This is evident as he stands on the roof of the Bradbury buildings, bearing in his hand a white dove (a symbol of the Holy Spirit). He stands above Deckard and reminds him of the realities of life in Los Angeles: "Quite an experience to live in fear, isn't it? This is what it means to be a slave." Batty grabs Deckard's arm and pulls him up on the roof; now baptized by Batty, Deckard sits at the side of his liberator, ready to begin his new life. Meanwhile Batty expires; as he does so, the clouds break and the dove flies off through them. He has passed on his unique insight to others; now his work has finished.

Blade Runner has attracted a vast amount of critical attention. Three book-length studies have appeared—one devoted to the making of the film by Sammon, the other two offering varied interpretations. Judith B. Kerman's *Retrofitting Blade Runner* focuses on "the texts and influences which converge in . . . *Blade Runner*, considering literary, filmic and technical [as well as thematic] issues." Scott Bukatman's monograph *Blade Runner* (1997) sees Scott's vision of a futuristic Los Angeles as "a nostalgic return . . . to the city as a *cinematic* environment, an industrial space poeticized and narrated by the camera." Nick Lacey's *Blade Runner* in the York Film Notes series gives a comprehensive guide to the film for students, focusing especially on background, narrative and form, style, ideology and cultural contexts. Most recently, Will Brooker's edited collection *The Blade Runner Experience* focuses on the film's continuing significance in popular culture.

Published studies of the film's cityscapes include W. A. Senior's "*Blade Runner* and Cyberpunk Visions of Humanity," and Roswitha Mueller's "The City and Its Other." Andrew Benjamin's "The Architecture of *Blade Runner*" looks at the designs from an architectural critic's perspective. Feminist interpretations of the film, concentrating in particular on the collapse of gender identities (providing a fruitful point of comparison with *Alien*), have been published by Elissa Marder and Kaja Silverman in a single issue of *Camera Obscura* (1991). Silverman in particular concludes that "the category of 'humanness' like those of 'masculinity' and 'whiteness' . . . [are] not an originary norm from which everything else derives, but rather a fiction created through the denial of the second-handedness of all subjectivity." Janet Bergstrom considers the film as a good example of androgyny—a world in which MASCULINITY and femininity no longer matter. By contrast, Valerie Su-Lin Wee believes that femaleness forms an essential part of *Blade Runner*, as the male director treats Pris's death "either as a means of controlling the evil and deviance she is made to represent, or a means of establishing male power, strength and superiority over female weakness, helplessness and inferiority." The philosophers Deborah Knight and George McKnight adopt a gender-free approach, arguing that the film evokes "complex philosophical questions about the relationship between mind and body, as well as the role played by memory, on the one hand, and the emotions and desires, on the other, in our understanding of human life." *Blade Runner*'s philosophical aspects have also been explored by Slavoj Žižek and Robert Pfaller. Robert Barringer views *Blade Runner* as an allegory of slavery: "[T]his is a film . . . in which the slaves are coded black, a film which flaunts its vision of a multi-ethnic metropolis," in which it is "desirable and politically feasible to construct a new race of slaves."

Blade Runner has also been cited as perhaps the exemplary mirror of the postmodern. However, this notion has been challenged by Marcus A. Doel and David B. Clarke, who believe the film should be viewed from an altogether different perspective, "in accordance with the principle of symbolic exchange," as articulated by Baudrillard.

Blade Runner's roots in FILM NOIR, as well as its literary antecedents, have been explored by David Desser, Susan Doll and Greg Fuller, Rachela Morrison and Mariacristina Cavecchi, and Nicoletta Vallorani. The last two authors draw an explicit parallel between *Blade Runner* and Shakespeare's *Tempest*, focusing in particular on the representation of a Prospero-like figure as a magus and scientist. More recently, Erling B. Holtsmark has cited *Blade Runner* as a good example of the Greek mythic pattern of katabasis—literally, "a going down, a descent, capturing the imagined physical orientation of the other world relative to this one."

The religious aspects of the film have been discussed by Sharon L. Gravett and Eric G. Wilson. Grevett believes that by telling the story of "humans versus replicants in relation to ancient Biblical tales, and by allowing the tugs and oppositions in these tales to come to the surface, the film engages its viewers, asking them the age-old question of what it is to be human." Giuliana Bruno and Vanin Begley adopt a diametrically opposing view: *Blade Runner* is not about humanity at all, but a postmodern text in which "symbols and narrative markers are mere stylistic adornments to the imagistic pastiche." Maybe it is no longer possible when analyzing the film "to speak of the protagonist and the subject, narrative and history."

The pedagogic aspects of teaching *Blade Runner* have been explored by Nick Peim, who believes that if it were to be introduced into the classroom, especially in British high schools, it might prompt discussion on "the exploration of textual identities and the consciousness of their institutional determinations . . . questions about the identity and proper orientation of the subject have very significant social and cultural effects in terms of public definitions of literacy and the determination of social destinies." David C. Ryan takes a look at the film, twenty-five years after its first release, and comes to the conclusion that its popularity with critics can be attributed to three things: its themes of enduring value; its ability to provoke contemplation of the link between memory, knowledge and identity; and its creation of images of dark, terrible beauty.

References

Nigel Andrews, "Blade Runner," *Financial Times*, 10 September 1982, 17; Robert Barringer, "Blade Runner: Skinjobs, Humans and Racial Coding," *Jump Cut* 41 (May 1997): 13–15, 119; Vanin Begley, "Blade Runner and the Postmodern," *Literature/Film Quarterly* 32, no.3 (October 2000): 186–92; Will Brooker, ed., *The Blade Runner Experience: The Legacy of a Science Fiction Classic* (London and New York: Wallflower Press, 2005); Giuliana Bruno, "Ramble City: Postmodernism and *Blade Runner*," in *Cultural Theory and Contemporary Science Fiction Cinema*, ed. Annette Kuhn (London: Verso, 1990), 187–88; Andrew Benjamin, "At Home with the Replicants: The Architecture of *Blade Runner*," *Architectural Design* 64, nos.11–12 (November 1994): 23–25; Janet Bergstrom, "Androids and Androgyny," *Camera Obscura* 15 (October 1988): 37–43; Scott Bukatman, *Blade Runner*, BFI Modern Classics (London: British Film Institute, 1997), 36; David Castell, "Inhuman Race," *Sunday Telegraph* (London), 12 September 1982, 30; Mariacristina Cavecchi and Nicoletta Vallorani, "Prospero's Offshoots: From the Library to the Screen," *Shakespeare Bulletin* 15, no.4 (October 1997): 35–37; David Desser, "*Blade Runner*, Science Fiction and Transcendence," *Literature/Film Quarterly* 13, no.3 (July 1985): 172–79; Marcus A. Doel and David B. Clarke, "From Ramble City to the Screening of the Eye: Blade Runner, Death and Symbolic Exchange," Working Paper 9/12 (School of Geography, University of Leeds, 1996); Susan Doll and Greg Faller, "*Blade Runner* and Genre: Film Noir and Science Fiction," *Literature/Film Quarterly*

15, no.2 (1986): 89–101; Sharon L. Gravett, "The Sacred and the Profane: Examining the Religious Subtext of Ridley Scott's *Blade Runner*," *Literature/Film Quarterly* 26, no.1 (1998): 38–45; Marilyn Gwaltney, "Androids as a Device for Reflection on Personhood," in *Retrofitting Blade Runner*, ed. Judith B. Kerman, 2nd ed. (Bowling Green: Bowling Green State University Popular Press, 1997), 33; David Harvey, *The Condition of Postmodernity: An Enquiry into the Origins of Cultural Change* (Oxford: Basil Blackwell Ltd., 1989); Erling B. Holtsmark, "The Katabasis Theme in Modern Cinema," in *Classical Myth and Culture in the Cinema*, ed. Martin M. Winkler (Oxford: Oxford University Press, 2001), 36; Tom Hutchinson, "A Shocking Home Truth: The Future Begins Here," *Mail on Sunday* (London), 12 September 1982, 27; Pauline Kael, "The Current Cinema: Before the Rain Must Fall," *New Yorker*, 12 July 1982, 85; Judith B. Kerman, "Introduction," *Retrofitting Blade Runner*, 2; Deborah Knight and George McKnight, "What Is It to Be Human?: *Blade Runner* and Dark City," in *The Philosophy of Science Fiction Film*, ed. Steven M. Sanders (Lexington: The University Press of Kentucky, 2008), 34; W. M. Kolb, "*Blade Runner*: An Annotated Bibliography," *Literature/Film Quarterly* 18, no.1 (1990): 19–64; William M. Kolb, "*Blade Runner*: The Director's Cut that Nearly Wasn't," *Perfect Vision* 6, no.23 (October 1994): 120–25; Nick Lacey, *Blade Runner* (London: York Press, 2000); Elissa Marder, "*Blade Runner's* Moving Still," *Camera Obscura* 27 (September 1991): 89–107; Rachela Morrison, "Casablanca Meets Star Wars: The Blakean Dialectics of *Blade Runner*," *Literature/Film Quarterly* 18, no.1 (1990): 2–11; Roswitha Mueller, "The City and Its Other," *Discourse* 24, no.2 (Spring 2002): 42–43; Nick Peim, "If Only You Could See What I've Seen with Your Eyes: *Blade Runner* and *La Symphonie Pastorale*," in *Classics in Film and Fiction*, ed. Deborah Cartmell, I. Q. Hunter, Heidi Kaye, and Imelda Whelehan (London and Sterling, VA: Pluto Press, 2000), 14–33; Robert Pfaller, "Negation and Its Reliabilities: An Empty Subject for Ideology?" in *Cogito and the Unconscious*, ed. Slavoj Žižek (Durham and London: Duke University Press, 1998), 225–46; Rolando J. Romero, "The Postmodern Hybrid: Do Aliens Dream of Alien Sheep"? *PostScript* 16, no.1 (1996): 41–52; David C. Ryan, "Dreams of Postmodernism and Thoughts of Mortality: A Twenty-Fifth Anniversary Retrospective of *Blade Runner*," *Senses of Cinema* 43 (2007): www.sensesofcinema .com/contents/07/43/blade-runner.html (accessed 2 August 2008); Paul M. Sammon, *Future Noir: The Making of Blade Runner*, 2nd ed. (London: Gollancz, 2007); Ridley Scott, quoted in David Aldridge, "*Blade Runner*: The Director's Cut," *Starburst*, December 1992, 12–13; Ridley Scott, quoted in Phil Edwards and Alan McKenzie, "Ridley Scott," *Starburst* 51 (November 1982): 24; Ridley Scott, quoted in Geoffrey Macnab, "The Knives Are Out," *The Independent* (London), 5 October 2007, 10–11; W. A. Senior, "*Blade Runner* and Cyberpunk: Visions of Humanity," *Film Criticism* 31, no.1 (Fall 1996): 7; Kaja Silverman, "Back to the Future," *Camera Obscura* 27 (September 1991): 109–31; Valerie Su-Lin Wee, "The Most Poetic Subject in the World: Observations on Death (Beautiful) Women and Representation in *Blade Runner*," *Kinema* 7

(April 1997): 71; Nigel Williams, "Morality with Special Effects," *Tribune*, 8 October 1982, 9; Eric G. Wilson, "Moviegoing and Golem-Making: The Case of *Blade Runner*," *Journal of Film and Video* 57, no.3 (Fall 2005): 36; Slavoj Žižek, *Tarrying with the Negative: Kant, Hegel and the Critique of Ideology* (Durham and London: Duke University Press, 1995).

Bibliography

W. M. Kolb's "*Blade Runner*: An Annotated Bibliography" contains a complete list of every article, review and interview published in the United States and Great Britain between 1982 and 1990. Brief comments on some of the entries give a guide to the themes and/or subjects covered.

Other bibliography includes: Brian Carr, "At the Thresholds of the 'Human' Race, Psychoanalysis and the Replication of Memory," *Cultural Critique* 39 (Spring 1998): 119–50; Joe Christopher, "On Future History as a Basic SF Literary Form," *Riverside Quarterly* 9, no.1 (August 1992): 26–31; Patrick Crogan, "Blade Runners: Speculations on Narrative and Interactivity," *South Atlantic Quarterly* 101, no.3 (Summer 2002): 639–57; Eric Daffron, "Double Trouble: The Self, the Social Order and the Trouble with Sympathy in the Romantic and Post-Modern Gothic," *Gothic Studies* 3, no.1 (2001): 75–83; Harlan Kennedy, "Twenty-First Century Nervous Breakdown," in *Ridley Scott Interviews*, ed. Laurence F. Knapp and Andrea F. Kulas (Jackson: University Press of Mississippi, 2005), 31–41; Keefer Kyle, "Knowledge and Mortality in *Blade Runner* and Genesis 2:3," *Journal of Religion and Film* 9, no.2 (October 2005): 35–43; Giancarlo Lombardi, "Virgil, Dante, *Blade Runner* and Italian Terrorism: The Concept of Pietas in *La Seconda Volta* and *La Mia Generazione*," *Romance Languages Annual* 11 (1999): 227–32; Marcin Mazurek, "Visualization as the Dominant Practice of Terminal Culture," in *Literature and Linguistics Vol.1*, ed. Zygmunt Mielczarek, Tadeusz Rachwal, and Dariusz Rindel (Czestochowa, Poland: Academic Papers of College of Foreign Languages, 2002), 93–105; Kevin McNamara, "*Blade Runner's* Post-Industrial Workspace," *Contemporary Literature* 38, no.3 (Fall 1997): 422–46; Robyn Morris, "Making Eyes: Colouring the Look in Larissa Lai's *When Fox is a Thousand* and Ridley Scott's *Blade Runner*," *Australian-Canadian Studies* 20, no.1 (2002): 75–98; Robyn Morris, "What Does It Mean to Be Human? Racing Monsters, Clones and Replicants," *Foundation: International Review of Science Fiction* 33, no. 91 (2004): 81–96; Gloria Pastorino, "The Death of the Author and the Power of Addiction in *Naked Lunch* and *Blade Runner*," in *Science Fiction, Critical Frontiers*, ed. Karen Sayer and John Moore (Basingstoke and New York: Macmillan Press Ltd., 2000), 100–115; Ann Pearson, "Apocalyptic Visions: Beyond Corporeality," *Journal of Religion and Film* 2, no.3 (December 1998), www.unomaha.edu/ jrf/apocalyp.htm (accessed 3 August 2008); Peter Ruppert, "*Blade Runner*: The Utopian Dialectics of Science Fiction Films," *Cineaste* 17, no.2 (1989): 8–13; Don Shay, *Blade Runner: The Inside Story* (London: Titan Books, 2000); Vernon Shetley and Alissa Ferguson, "Reflections in a Silver Eye: Lens and Mirror in *Blade Runner*," *Science*

Fiction Studies 28, no.1 (2001): 66–76; Jenna Tiiltsman, "If Only You Could See What I've Seen with Your Eyes: Destabilized Spectatorship and *Blade Runner*," *Cross-Currents* 54, no.1 (2004): 32–47; Kin Yuen Wong, "On the Edge of Spaces: *Blade Runner*, Ghost in the Shell and Hong Kong's Cityscape," *Science Fiction Studies* 27, no.1 (2000): 1–21; Lisa Yaszek, "Of Fossils and Androids: (Re-)Producing Sexual Identity in *Jurassic Park* and *Blade Runner*," *Journal of the Midwest Modern Language Association* 30, nos. 1–2 (Spring 1997): 52–62.

BLADE RUNNER: THE DIRECTOR'S CUT

US 1992 r/t 117 min col. The story of how the film was rereleased ten years later as the Director's Cut, and how that version differed from the other available versions, has been told in detail by William M. Kolb.

The major difference between the original film and the Director's Cut is that Deckard's (HARRISON FORD's) voiceovers have been dropped. After the introduction of Deckard at the sushi stand, there is no narration whatsoever. Scott also restores the unicorn shot as Deckard sits over the piano, dreaming of his past. This shot, showing a white unicorn coming towards the camera, ties in with a moment at the end of the film when the camera focuses on an aluminum foil unicorn as Deckard and Rachael leave Deckard's apartment. This unicorn is designed to confirm Deckard's status as a REPLICANT; it is an artificial memory implanted by the Tyrell Corporation—one to which Gaff (EDWARD JAMES OLMOS) is also privy, since it is he who makes the aluminum foil model. The Director's Cut does not show Batty gouging out Tyrell's (JOE TURKEL's) eyes, and shortens Pris's (DARYL HANNAH's) death scene. The film also drops the shots of the nail penetrating the back of Batty's (RUTGER HAUER's) hand during the final confrontation scene between Batty and Deckard. The film ends with the closing elevator doors; there is no coda of Deckard and Rachael driving in the country.

Reference

William M. Kolb, "*Blade Runner*: The Director's Cut That Nearly Wasn't," *Perfect Vision* 6, no.23 (October 1994): 120–25.

Bibliography

Blade Runner: The Director's Cut—Information Source Pack (London: British Film Institute Library and Information Services, 1994); Paul M. Sammon, "Do Androids Dream of Unicorns: The 7 Faces of *Blade Runner*," *Video Watchdog* 20 (November/ December 1993): 32–59; Geoff Mayer, "*Blade Runner*: The Director's Cut," *Metro Education* 9 (1 January 1997): 3–7.

BLADE RUNNER: THE FINAL CUT

US 2007 r/t 113 min col. The definitive version of *Blade Runner* released theatrically in late 2007 in theaters and subsequently as part of the five-disc *Blade Runner: Collector's Edition*. This version originated out of Scott's dissatisfaction

that the *BLADE RUNNER*: THE DIRECTOR'S CUT of 1992 did not represent his final statement on the film. Originally Scott and his DVD producer CHARLES DE LAUZIRIKA agreed to assemble a *Blade Runner* Special Edition DVD in 2001 for a 2002 release, but time (and the difficulty of obtaining rights from Warner Bros.) prevented the two of them from doing so.

The film came about from De Lauzirika's initiative: he assembled a list of visual and audio adjustments that he felt the director might like; Scott approved or rejected them, adding his own thoughts along the way. The film retained the ending of the Director's Cut, but made further alterations.

The major differences between the Final Cut and the other versions include: some reworked opening and closing credits; altering Bryant's (M. EMMET WALSH's) dialogue to indicate that there were only four REPLICANTS left for Deckard to track down, not five; revealing more details about the exterior of Deckard's apartment building and the interior of the apartment itself; new shots of Deckard's investigations into the whereabouts of the replicants; and a more violent death scene involving Batty (RUTGER HAUER) and Tyrell (JOE TURKEL). Pris (DARYL HANNAH) is shown breaking Deckard's nose and is eventually shot three times; the nail Batty puts into his hand during his final confrontation with Deckard can be seen emerging from the back of his hand; and the music heard over the end titles of the Final Cut is actually a new, VANGELIS-generated version of the original music. Other slight alterations were made to Zhora's (JOANNA CASSIDY's) death scene.

Reviews for the Final Cut were generally encouraging. The London *Times* observed that the film was "a far more bitter watch" than the original version, as it minimized the differences between Deckard and the replicants. The *New York Times* called it "darker, bleaker, more immersive." The DVD release includes commentaries by HAMPTON FANCHER, DAVID PEOPLES, MICHAEL DEELEY, SYD MEAD and DOUGLAS TRUMBULL, as well as Scott.

References

James Christopher, "*Blade Runner*: The Final Cut," *The Times*, 3 September 2007, 16; Fred Kaplan, "A Cult Classic Restored, Again," *New York Times*, 30 September 2007, www.nytimes.com/2007/09/30/ movies/30kapl.html (accessed 13 April 2008).

Bibliography

Paul M. Sammon, "The Final Cut," *Empire* (August 2007): 116–17; Paul M. Sammon, *Future Noir: The Making of Blade Runner*, 2nd ed. (London: Gollancz, 2007).

BLADE RUNNER NOVELS

Archie Goodwin scripted the comic book adaptation, *A Marvel Comics Super Special: Blade Runner*, published in September 1982. This adaptation was poorly received and widely ridiculed because of poor writing and misquoted dialogue taken from the film.

K. W. (Keith Wayne) Jeter, a friend of PHILIP K. DICK, has written three official, authorized *Blade Runner* novels that continue Rick Deckard's story, attempting to resolve many differences between *Blade Runner* and the source novel *Do Androids Dream of Electric Sheep? Blade Runner 2: The Edge of Human* (1995); *Blade Runner 3: Replicant Night* (1996); *Blade Runner 4: Eye and Talon* (2000).

Blade Runner co-writer DAVID PEOPLES wrote *Soldier* (1998), which is set in the same fictional universe. It features spinners; however, it remains an informal sequel, unapproved by the Blade Runner Partnership, which owns the *Blade Runner* universe rights.

Ridley Scott toyed with the idea of a sequel film, which would have been titled "Metropolis." However, the project was ultimately shelved due to rights issues. A script was also written for a proposed sequel entitled *Blade Runner Down*, which would have been based on K. W. Jeter's first *Blade Runner* sequel novel. At the 2007 Comic-Con, Scott again announced that he was considering a sequel to the film, although nothing more has been heard about it to date.

BLADE RUNNER VIDEO GAMES

Two games have been released based on the original film—one in 1985 for Commodore 64, ZX Spectrum and Amstrad computers. It was published by CRL Group Plc., and based on the music by VANGELIS. The 1997 video game *Blade Runner* was a point-and-click adventure game, developed by Westwood Studios and published by Virgin Interactive Entertainment.

Bibliography

Barry Atkins, "Replicating the *Blade Runner*," in *The Blade Runner Experience: The Legacy of a Science Fiction Classic*," ed. Will Brooker (London and New York: Wallflower Press, 2005), 79–92; Susana P. Tosca, "Implanted Memories: or the Illusion of Free Action," in *The Blade Runner Experience: The Legacy of a Science Fiction Classic*.

BLADE RUNNER: THE WORKPRINT VERSION

US 1991 col. r/t 112 min. On Friday, 27 September 1991, Santa Monica's NuArt Theater and San Francisco's Castro Theatre began a two-week run of what was then called "The *Blade Runner* Director's Cut." Audience reaction to this version was unprecedented; the film grossed $230,059 in Los Angeles alone.

This version was neither the 70mm "Director's Cut" screened in Los Angeles prior to the San Francisco engagement nor the version that eventually became the DIRECTOR'S CUT, released theatrically in 1992. It was actually a completely different version, a workprint, discovered by the preservationists Ron Haver and Robert A. Harris in 1991. This version has previously only been screened in Great Britain as a sneak preview; it was the shortest version of the film available at that time (112 min).

This workprint version differs quite substantially from the other versions of the film. The film begins with the words "Harrison Ford" sliding across the screen, accompanied by the sound of two knives being scraped together. This is quickly replaced with the words "Blade Runner" (also to the sound of scraping steel). The workprint dispenses with the explanation of the term REPLICANT, substituting instead an excerpt from a twenty-first-century dictionary, defining a replicant as being the end result of a series of artificially created human beings, a progression listed in the dictionary as "Robot, android, nexus."

The workprint omits the full-scale close-up of a gigantic blue eye as it surveys the city. After Leon (BRION JAMES) shoots Holden (Morgan Paull), all previous versions show the policeman crashing through an office wall. The workprint has Holden slumped over a computer, face resting on the keyboard. When Deckard is shown eating sushi in the street, the workprint includes an extra shot of his favorite dinner—jellied shrimp.

The workprint includes an extra audio track during Gaff's (EDWARD JAMES OLMOS's) and Deckard's (HARRISON FORD's) descent towards the Tyrell Pyramid: not one written by VANGELIS; rather, a Tower Control Voice guiding the spinner towards a landing.

As with the Director's Cut, the workprint omits all the voiceovers that were included in the film's original release. Instead it includes other sounds—notably the laughter of distant children when Deckard looks at a falsified photograph of Rachael (SEAN YOUNG) and her mother. This is a good move, because the moment has not been destroyed by Deckard's over-emphatic voiceover (from the original 1982 release): "Replicants weren't supposed to have feelings."

As Deckard plays a tune on the piano, the workprint substituted different Vangelis music throughout the scene. The unicorn sequence that appears in the Director's Cut is not in the workprint. Just before Deckard enters the nightclub where Zhora (JOANNA CASSIDY) works, the workprint includes a shot of two near-nude women wearing masks and gyrating in a capsule above the club's entrance.

Tyrell's death scene underwent significant changes in the workprint. The bloody sockets of Tyrell's eyes are visible, and an extra shot of the replicant owl is seen. When Batty begins to move towards the terrified Sebastian (WILLIAM SANDERSON) after the replicant has murdered Tyrell, the workprint inserts a few extra lines of dialogue: Batty says "Sorry, Sebastian" followed by "Come, come." The workprint ends with a shot of Sebastian whimpering as he tries to run out of Tyrell's apartment.

When Deckard enters the Bradbury Building, the workprint drops Vangelis's score altogether; instead, various temporary tracks are added. Just before Batty begins to pursue Deckard through the abandoned upper stories, he yells out "I'm coming to get you!" During the ensuing chase, the workprint incorporates temp tracks lifted from JERRY GOLDSMITH's score for *ALIEN*. As Batty dies, the workprint adds the only piece of voiceover narration throughout the entire film from Deckard: "I watched him [Batty] die all night. It was a long, slow thing, and he fought it all the way." The workprint then picks up the *Alien* music once again, as Deckard searches for Rachael in his apartment. Like the Director's Cut, the film concludes with the two of them closing the door and boarding the elevator. The workprint ends with the words, "This version copyright 1991 the Blade Runner Partnership. All rights reserved."

The workprint version was released commercially for the first time since 1991 as part of the five-disc *Blade Runner Collector's Edition* in 2007.

Bibliography

Paul M. Sammon, "Do Androids Dream of Unicorns? The 7 Faces of *Blade Runner*," *Video Watchdog* 20 (November/December 1993): 33–59; Paul M. Sammon, *Future Noir: The Making of Blade Runner*, 2nd ed. (London: Gollancz, 2007), 330–49.

BLAKE, HOWARD (1938–)

Blake began his career as a composer providing music for television commercials and British adventure series such as *The Avengers*. He met Ridley Scott for the first time in the late 1960s, when Scott was making commercials for RSA (Ridley Scott Associates).

Blake composed the music for *THE DUELLISTS*. In a commentary provided for the DVD release of the film, he recalled that he created three distinct types of music: dueling music, romantic music, and period music. The first of these has been rendered deliberately discordant, almost modernist in tone, designed to alert viewers to the inherent sense of danger in the sword fights between D'Hubert (KEITH CARRADINE) and Feraud (HARVEY KEITEL). The two men will always fight to the death. Blake's romantic music crops up during the love scenes between D'Hubert and Laura (DIANA QUICK). Such themes are tinged with sadness: however much D'Hubert might be devoted to his wife, he is nonetheless prepared to put his life on the line by fighting Feraud. The music emphasizes Laura's mood as she watches him preparing for battle. The period themes are designed to give the film an appropriate period feel—for example, the hurdy-gurdy music heard on the soundtrack as we watch D'Hubert in a tavern, or the Bach song sung by the castrato early on in the film.

Blake's music works to notable effect in the duel scenes. In the second scene, for instance, we hear snatches of what the composer describes in the commentary as "threat-music," played on a violin that sounds like a shiver of apprehension. When this is combined with the clash of the duelists' long swords on the soundtrack, we are made aware of just how dangerous the duels actually are. This is not a swashbuckling film, glorifying the arts of sword-fighting as did *The Three Musketeers* (1973); rather, Scott aims to show the reality of the duel, and thereby invite us to speculate on the validity of the code of honor that dominates D'Hubert's and Feraud's lives. Such scenes as this provide a good example of Scott's familiar layering technique—the desire (in PAUL M. SAMMON's words) to create "a dense, kaleidoscopic accretion of detail within every frame and set of a film."

Blake's music also appears to good effect in the film's final moments, which dissolves from the discordant, dueling music into the basic *Duellists* theme played on a flute and oboe, as Feraud walks away from D'Hubert into exile. The effect once again reminds viewers of the sheer pointlessness of the duels—all they have done is to render Feraud a pariah, condemned to a future of perpetual isolation.

References

Howard Blake, commentary to the 2003 release of *The Duellists* by Paramount DVD in the "Special Collector's Edition" (London: Paramount Home Entertainment, 2003); Paul M. Sammon, *Future Noir: The Making of* Blade Runner (London: Gollancz, 2007), 47.

BLAKE, WILLIAM (1757–1827)

William Blake was an English poet, painter, and printmaker. Largely unrecognized during his lifetime, Blake's work is today considered seminal and significant in the history of both poetry and the visual arts.

Ridley Scott's films contain numerous references—both explicit and implicit—to Blake's work. In *BLADE RUNNER* Roy Batty (RUTGER HAUER) quotes the following lines, slightly adapted: "Fiery the angels fell,/ Deep thunder rolled round their shores,/ Burning with the fires of Orc." Batty regards himself as a rebel angel—an eternal rebel against the tyranny of the LOS ANGELES world. He might be a REPLICANT, but his "inhuman mechanisms allow [him] . . . to benefit from self-awareness."

In *LEGEND* the unicorn theme (played at the end of the film) was recorded with vocals by Susanne Pawlitzki based on William Blake's poem, "The Angel," but was rejected in favor of a new version written by Jon Anderson. In the film there is an overt reference to Blake's poem "The Sick Rose" as Darkness (TIM CURRY) offers Lily (MIA SARA) a rose as an invitation to become his bride and forget about daylight forever.

According to cinematographer JOHN MATHIESON, Blake's paintings also provided Scott with an inspiration for HANNIBAL. There is also an explicit reference to Blake in a postcard chosen by Mason Verger (GARY OLDMAN) of "The Ghost of a Flea." This grotesque drawing of a naked man with a spinal column protruding, making him look part-human, part-animal, sums up Verger's conception of himself as a result of his assault by Hannibal Lecter (ANTHONY HOPKINS). This helps to explain why Verger harbors such a strong desire for revenge. STEVEN ZAILLIAN's original script has a print of Blake's "The Ancient of Days" hanging in Verger's mansion; but this was deleted from the finished film.

Bibliography

Alexis Harley, "America, a Prophecy: When Blake Meets *Blade Runner*," *Sydney Studies in English* 31 (2005): 61–76.

BLETHYN, BRENDA (1946–)

Born Brenda Ann Bottle in Ramsgate, Kent, United Kingdom. After twenty years on the British stage and television playing character roles, Brenda Blethyn came to prominence in the 1990s as Mrs. Jenkins in the adaptation of the Roald Dahl novel *The Witches* (1990). Cast as Cynthia Rose Purley in the Mike Leigh film *Secrets and Lies*, Blethyn received a British Academy Award and an Oscar nomination for her performance. In the next year she was nominated once again for her performance in *Little Voice*.

Cast as Louella Parsons, the acid-tongued gossip columnist in *RKO 281*, Blethyn relishes the chance to play someone who can wield power on behalf of her employer William Randolph Hearst (JAMES CROMWELL), secure in the knowledge that no one can stop her. Even the studio heads, notably Louis B. Mayer (DAVID SUCHET), have no defense against her, particularly when she threatens to expose their Jewish background to the Hollywood press. At one point she tells Mayer that if he does not work to have the film *Citizen Kane* banned from public exhibition, she will run down the street "like a screaming woman with her throat cut." Director BENJAMIN ROSS cuts to a close-up of her blowing cigarette smoke in the studio mogul's face, emphasizing her contempt for him.

BLOOD MERIDIAN

CORMAC MCCARTHY's 1985 Western novel following the story of a young cowboy who enlists with a group of rogue soldiers to massacre communities of Indians in Mexico. Scott has planned to adapt this novel ever since *KINGDOM OF HEAVEN*. He told the British film magazine *Empire* in November 2008, "It's an amazing book . . . But one of the difficulties is what do you say about it, because as an author he [McCarthy] doesn't have to give an answer to anything. He writes the book and says if you get it, you get it and if you don't, you don't. And therefore there are no answers at the end of the book." To date, production on the adaptation has not begun, even though the *Internet Movie Database* lists Todd Field as a possible director.

Reference

Jack Foley, "Sir Ridley Hints at *Blood Meridian*," *Empire* (20 November 2008), www.indielondon.co.uk/film/kingdom_heaven _scott_next.html (accessed 16 January 2009).

BLOOM, ORLANDO (1977–)

Born in Canterbury, United Kingdom, Bloom's first film was *The Lord of the Rings: The Fellowship of the Ring*, in which he played Legolas. He repeated the role in the other films in the trilogy.

Cast as Private Todd Blackburn in *BLACK HAWK DOWN*, Bloom gives a convincing performance as the youngest and greenest of the Rangers brought over to fight in Mogadishu. Before filming he had to attend a military boot camp in Georgia, with the emphasis placed on fighting strategy, the handling of firearms and explosives—the kind of training the actors in *G.I. JANE* had experienced seven years earlier. For Bloom the part called more for "reacting than acting," as he told his biographer Robert Steele. His role was a small one—Blackburn is eventually injured as he falls out of a helicopter—but nonetheless pivotal, as his accident causes a delay in the raid and thereby allows the Somalis to regroup and resist the American troops.

Scott cast him in the leading role of Balian in *KINGDOM OF HEAVEN*, a role very similar to those in his most recent films, notably *GLADIATOR*. In the book of the film, Scott describes Balian "a gifted and extraordinary man (or woman), though not one born to power, caught up in great events—a sympathetic character who gives audiences a place to focus their attention and emotions within a cinematic canvas of epic scope. Even more, a character who comes through hardship or tragedy to emerge as a real hero, someone who sets an example by taking a stand and refusing to be moved off it." Orlando Bloom went through a transformative journey of his own to portray Balian, involving considerable physical and vocal training. Bloom was quoted in the book of the film as saying that the character appealed to him on account of the "incredible arc" that he experiences, "starting out as a sort of reluctant hero and eventually becoming defender of Jerusalem."

Despite his extensive preparation, Bloom received lukewarm reviews for his performance. The *Boston Globe* likened him to someone "holding the fort for a genuine star who never arrives." Yet Bloom's Balian is never meant to be a stereotypical hero (resembling Russell Crowe in *Gladiator*). Ian Huffer's long article "New Man, Old Worlds; Rearticulating Masculinity in the Star Persona of Orlando Bloom" argues that Balian rejects the position of male/moral authority at the end of the film, and thereby reinforces the film's criticism of the violence which ultimately underpins this masculine ideal, suggesting that it is perhaps impossible to hold authority and be pious. The film ultimately conceives Balian as someone favoring kindness and negotiation rather than violence, yet also upholding the chivalric ideal of right action—possibly in the form of invasion or active defense—where necessary. This potentially contradictory combination of values reveals "the instability of masculinity as a category." On this view, *Kingdom of Heaven* demonstrates Scott's interest in new forms of MASCULINITY, also evident in *Black Hawk Down*.

References

Orlando Bloom, quoted in Robert Steele, *Orlando Bloom: Wherever It May Lead* (London: Plexus Publishing Ltd., 2004), 62; Ty Burr, "Historically and Heroically Challenged 'Kingdom' Fails to Conquer," *Boston Globe*, 6 May 2005, www.boston.com/movies/display?display=movie&id=5694 (accessed 15 January 2009); Ian Huffer, "New Man, Old Worlds: Re-articulating Masculinity in the Star Persona of Orlando Bloom," *Scope; An Online Journal of Film and TV Studies* 9 (October 2007), www.scope.nottingham.ac.uk/article.php?issue=9&id=956 (accessed 15 January 2009); Diana Landau, ed., *Kingdom of Heaven: The Ridley Scott Film and the History behind the Story* (London: Simon and Schuster Ltd., 2005), 16, 68.

Bibliography

"Bloom Saves Dog," *Film Review* 657 (June 2005): 22–23; Anwar Brett, "Heaven Can Wait," *Film Review Special #57* (May 2005): 6–12, 14–19, 22; Tom Fox, "Full Bloom," *Film Review* 654 (March 2005): 56–60, 62, 64–66.

THE BODY

The image of the body is most obviously evident in *ALIEN*. The face-hugger both subjugates and transforms the male body as it attaches itself to Kane (JOHN HURT). In the famous chest-buster scene, the male body is repositioned to correspond to the female body: the male mouth becomes the vagina, his chest the womb. The gender difference separating male from female is broken down, as all humanity is female (a womb) in the face of the alien.

The body imagery also resurfaces in the character of Ash (IAN HOLM), the android constructed by the Company to supervise the crew's activities. Ximeno Gallardo and C. Jason Smith describe him as completely feminized in the sense that he is "created, defined, controlled, and deprived of power . . . this . . . is represented by his grotesque, exposed, open body—a disgusting mass of white fluid and spaghetti-like entrails festooned with clear grape-sized modules." Parker's (YAPHET KOTTO's) revulsion at Ash's body suggests not only the corruption of the Company but also Parker's own potential feminization. By contrast, the alien—an object of Ash's consistent admiration—represents what Ash would like to be and also is the ultimate expression of the corporate body of the Company, "a well-oiled, amoral machine of flesh with a wonderful defense mechanism to ensure its survival and proliferation."

Alien represents an attack on the two-sex model, that there exists a specific set of characteristics known as "masculine" and "feminine." By doing so, it not only dramatizes male fears of women, but also shows that the body is unspeakably open; it can be used in different ways, as well as being perceived differently. By doing so the film explores "the monstrous Other" that exists outside rational definitions of gender.

Some critics have taken a different view and interpreted the film as an expression of male fears of MOTHERHOOD, as the alien body "progressively takes over more and more of the space previously occupied by the [largely male] crew, culminating in the *NOSTROMO* itself becoming host to the alien at the expense of the crew." In the same year Amy Taubin observed that Scott "played on anxieties set loose by issues of feminist and gay activism."

In *BLACK RAIN* there are at least two instances in which the male body is decapitated: Charlie Vincent (ANDY GARCIA) is ritually beheaded by Sato (YUSAKU MATSUDA) in revenge for having insulted the yakuza leader, and Sato himself undergoes the ancient ritual of yubitsume (slicing the joint of the little finger to atone for a mistake). The fact that such rituals are undertaken emotionlessly as part of Japanese custom suggests a lack of concern for the human body; like Ash in *Alien* it is perceived as "a disgusting mass" of blood and guts. *1492: CONQUEST OF PARADISE* contains a similar sequence, where Moxica (MICHAEL WINCOTT) cuts off the hand of an Indian—clearly Spaniards have scant concern for anyone they perceive as racially inferior to them. In *HANNIBAL* two other characters experience retributive justice from Hannibal Lecter, on account of their "free-range rudeness"—i.e., their corruption. Inspector Pazzi (GIANCARLO GIANNINI), who is hanged by the neck from a window of the Palazzo Vecchio in Florence while being disemboweled; and Krendler (RAY LIOTTA), who has his brain surgically removed and subsequently eats part of it fried in butter.

WHITE SQUALL takes an opposite view by celebrating the male body as the young crew lands on the Galapagos Islands, stripped to the waist. They are representatives of purity, of innocence; the complete antithesis of the Spanish colonists in *1492: CONQUEST OF PARADISE*. *THELMA & LOUISE* shows its protagonists operating within a world in which questions of gender identity are played out through the masculinization of the female body. Drawing on a long history of representations of male self-sufficiency, the film traces the characters' developing ability to handle a gun. Thelma (GEENA DAVIS) can barely bring herself to handle her gun, a gift from husband Darryl (CHRISTOPHER

McDONALD) at the beginning of the film—picking it up with an expression of distaste in a rather "girlish" fashion. As the narrative progresses, she acquires both physical coordination, which denotes self-possession, and the ability to shoot straight. When the two women shoot out the oil tanker, they happily compliment one another on their aim. In terms of the body, they have acquired the conventionally "masculine" characteristics that should prompt us to reflect on the gendered identity of the active heroine.

In *G.I. JANE*, the notion of the body and gender identity surfaces through the character of Jordan O'Neil (DEMI MOORE). Moore's work in the 1990s was characterized by a series of self-masquerades, transformative acts through which she managed to bring off a curiously paradoxical coup: like the obsessively self-transformative Madonna, disguising, masking, or completely making herself over only served to clarify Moore's star image, a singular sameness paradoxically constructed through the vacillations of physical difference. Moore's corporeal shape shifting was predicated on a peculiarly late twentieth-century notion of the body as a thing to be molded, worked on, and worked out, and which, through suitable customized transformations, was able to take her in a range of different generic directions. In the film she consciously masculinizes herself in a process that Linda Williams describes as "masculinity [in which] some of the qualities associated with masculinity are written *over* the muscular female body. 'Musculinity' indicates the way in which the signifiers of strength are not limited to male characters." Williams argues that this transformation is not confined to the character O'Neil but also applies to Moore herself as she tries to manipulate her star image: "The body of Demi Moore is a costume, a mask, a masquerade which conveys Jordan's development, but which Moore too carries through into all those [photo-ops] with Bruce and the kids, those chat show appearances . . . None of these faces, these voices, these actions, are real; only the products marketed by the illusions of genuineness are different."

The film is actually about "Jordan's (mythically American) war with her personal weakness . . . bodybuilding offers the possibility of self-creation, in which the intimate space of the body is produced as raw material to be worked on and worked over, ultimately for display on a public stage. The same might be said for Demi Moore herself . . . in the age of the muscular action heroine, hard work is no longer most visibly manifest in consumer rewards . . . 'hard work' must be demonstrated, enshrined, lived out *first* in the body." The Scott-produced film *IN HER SHOES* begins by reversing this image, as the camera lovingly focuses on CAMERON DIAZ's body in various stages of undress, apparently conforming to her star image as a sex-symbol. As the film unfolds, however, it soon emerges that this representation is actually part of her character Maggie's attempt to acquire

self-esteem. With no educational attainments to speak of and without a proper job, the only commodity Maggie has to secure self-advancement is her body. Maggie herself is aware of her existence as a prostitute in all but name when she demands of her sister Rose (TONI COLLETTE): "I want fifty bucks. That's the going rate, isn't it?" As the film unfolds, however, so Maggie gradually changes character: learning how to read poetry out loud and finding a suitable niche for herself as personal shopper to the elderly residents of her grandmother Ella's (SHIRLEY MACLAINE's) retirement home. The idea of the body is no longer a commodity for her but something to be elegantly clothed. This explains her willingness to choose a suitable wedding dress for her sister, because she is "good at this."

References

Carol Moore and Geoff Miles, "Explorations, Prosthetics, Sacrifice: Phantasies of the Maternal Body in the Alien Trilogy," *CineAction!* 30 (December 1992): 54–62; Ximeno Gallardo and C. Jason Smith, "Men, Women and an Alien Baby," *Alien Woman: The Making of Lieut. Ellen Ripley* (New York: Continuum, 2004), 51; Susannah Grant, "In Her Shoes Script" (transcribed from the DVD version of the film), www.script-o-rama.com/movie_scripts/i/in-her-shoes-script-transcript.html (accessed 17 January 2009), 28, 109; Yvonne Tasker, *Spectacular Bodies: Gender, Genre and the Action Cinema* (London: Routledge, 1993), 141; Amy Taubin, "Invading Bodies: *Alien 3* and the Trilogy," *Sight and Sound*, July 1992, 8–10; Linda Ruth Williams, "Ready for Action: *G.I. Jane*, Demi Moore's Body and the Female Combat Movie," in *Action and Adventure Cinema*, ed. Yvonne Tasker (London and New York: Routledge, 2004), 175, 181–82.

Bibliography

Thomas B. Byers, "Kissing Becky: Masculine Fears and Misogynist Moments in Science Fiction Films," *Arizona Quarterly* 45, no.3 (Autumn 1989): 77–95; Robert L. Cagle, "Auto-Eroticism: Narcissism, Fetishism and Consumer Culture," *Cinema Journal* 33, no.4 (Summer 1994): 23–33; Kim Gabbard and Glen O. Gabbard, "Phallic Women in the Contemporary Cinema," *American Imago* 50, no.4 (Winter 1993): 421–40; Kelly Hurley, "Reading Like an Alien: Posthuman Identity in Ridley Scott's *Alien* and David Cronenberg's *Rabid*," in *Posthuman Bodies*, ed. Judith Halberstam and Ira Livingston (Bloomington and Indianapolis: Indiana University Press, 1995), 203–24; Louise J. Kaplan, "Fits and Misfits: The Body of a Woman," *American Imago* 50, no.4 (1993): 457–80; Susan J. Napier, "Ghosts and Madness: The Technological Body," in *Liquid Metal: The Science Fiction Film Reader*, ed. Sean Redmond (London and New York: Wallflower Press, 2004), 203–15.

BODY OF LIES

US 2008 r/t 128 min col. *Production Companies*: De Line Pictures and Scott Free. *Producers*: Donald de Line and Ridley Scott. *Director*: Ridley Scott. *Writers*: William Monahan and Steven Zaillian (uncredited) from the book by David Ignatius.

Production Designer: Arthur Max. *Costume Designer:* Janty Yates. *Director of Photography:* Alexander Witt. *Music:* Marc Streitenfeld. *Cast:* Leonardo DiCaprio (*Roger Ferris*), Russell Crowe (*Ed Hoffman*), Mark Strong (*Hani*), Golshifteh Farahani (*Aisha*), Ali Suliman (*Omar Sadiki*), Alon Aboutbul (*Al-Saleem*), Simon McBurney (*Garland*).

The production originated in 2006 when Warner Bros. hired WILLIAM MONAHAN to adapt DAVID IGNATIUS's novel *Penetration* into a feature film. Ignatius, who covered the CIA and the Middle East for the *Wall Street Journal* before joining the *Washington Post*, had produced a quasi-documentary account of life in the front line during the "war on terror" in the Middle East. Scott evidently saw the book while still in galley form and offered the following observations: "It has an unusually incisive view into what actually happens up on the front lines, and the people at the front who make a difference." Co-producer DONALD DE LINE described the work in the film's production notes as "a well-crafted spy thriller about the kinds of people and levels of deception it takes to penetrate a country, a culture and, ultimately, the enemy. We really felt it had everything going for it in terms of a great movie plot." The script was eventually reworked by STEVEN ZAILLIAN, who removed many of the original subplots of Monahan's script and reworked many of the characters (even though he did not take screen credit).

LEONARDO DICAPRIO was formally cast in the lead role of Roger Ferris; RUSSELL CROWE agreed to costar once the script had been revised. The two of them had previously starred in *The Quick and the Dead* (1995). Filming took place in various locations—Washington, DC, Europe, and Morocco. Part of Capitol Hill was redressed to look like Amsterdam, while locations in Baltimore stood in for Manchester, England. Scott sought permission to film in Dubai, but permission was denied due to the script's potentially contentious subject matter. Scenes set in Jordan were filmed in Morocco, where Scott had previously worked on *GLADIATOR*, *BLACK HAWK DOWN*, and *KINGDOM OF HEAVEN*. DiCaprio was quoted in the production notes as saying that he found Morocco "a challenging filming experience . . . I love the people and the culture. The marketplace in Marrakesh is something that everyone in the world should see at least once, especially if they are big travelers. It's a phenomenal sight." The cast and crew spent nine weeks there, and filming wrapped up in December 2007.

Body of Lies received its premiere out of competition at the Venice Film Festival in September 2008, and was commercially released in the United States a month later. The British premiere took place in early November. Critical reaction was mixed, to say the least: Roger Ebert admired the two central performances but considered the film "sensationally implausible . . . Increasing numbers of thrillers seem to center on heroes who are masochists surrounded by sadists, and I'm growing weary of the horror!" The *San Francisco Chronicle* reviewer felt that Scott "pushes to create drama through sheer intensity, but it's like stirring an empty pot. There's nothing there." A. O. Scott in the *New York Times* was slightly less charitable: "it [the film] seems singularly untethered from anything like zeal, conviction or even curiosity." Nigel Andrews in the London *Financial Times* felt much the same: "Visually the film is so undistinguished it may be time for the maker of *Blade Runner* to be subjected to that film's Voigt-Kampff test, to determine whether the current owner of the name 'Ridley Scott' is real or a replicant." Roger Clarke in *Sight and Sound* seemed more kindly disposed: "*Body of Lies* is at least outward-looking and it's trying, through a veil of testosterone, to engage with real issues." Philip French identified the performance of MARK STRONG as Hani, the head of the Jordanian secret service, as the film's redeeming feature: "A man of honour, with perfect manners, impeccable taste in tailoring and an understanding of world politics, he's a countervailing moral and intellectual force to the crudity of Hoffman and the sentimental naivety of Ferris."

Just a week after the film's London opening, *The Guardian* reported with ill-disguised glee that *Body of Lies* had performed badly at the UK box office, taking only £1.5 million. This reflected a trend set at the American box office a month earlier, where the film had taken only $13.1 million on its opening weekend, with receipts far behind those of *Beverly Hills Chihuahua* and *Quarantine*. This led the *Guardian* writer to conclude that "Warners will now be reflecting that there may have been a mismatch between the material and what is believed to be a $90 million production budget, including two whopping 'full freight' salaries for stars DiCaprio and Crowe." By the time of the film's DVD release in February 2009, however, Jeff Giles pointed out in *DVD Review* that it had made a profit, chiefly due to overseas grosses.

In spite of Russell Crowe's disingenuous suggestion in an interview with the London *Daily Telegraph* that Scott is not "pushing any political agenda" but telling a story of "deception, seduction and abandonment," *Body of Lies* concerns itself specifically with the "war on terror." The opening sequence shows a terraced house in Manchester being blown up by suicide bombers threatened with capture by the SAS with considerable loss of life. Another attack on a crowded tourist area of Amsterdam leads to over seventy deaths. Scott is particularly concerned with reactions to the war on terror from the American and the Middle Eastern perspectives. For the CIA chief Ed Hoffman (Crowe) it represents nothing less than an attack on democracy: "These people [the terrorists] do not want to negotiate, not at all . . . They want every infidel converted or dead . . . We are an easy target." In his view every Middle Eastern male is potentially dangerous, so he has no time for "patience, Sidi, patience, and eat[ing] couscous with his family." This kind of casual racism causes frequent diplomatic headaches for agent Roger Ferris (DiCaprio), prompting him to observe at one point in Monahan's original script that Hoffman knows everything about how to win the "war on terror," but no idea how to put it into practice. With his fluency in Arabic, and his ability to pass as a native of that country in his long robes and wispy beard, Ferris appears the ideal mediator who can forge an alliance between the Arabs and the Americans. However, this proves nothing more than an illusion: Ferris tries and fails to set up a fake terrorist organization in order to capture the radical Islamic leader Al-Saleem (ALON ABOUTBUL), and by doing so double-crosses Hani, the head of the Jordanian Secret Service (MARK STRONG). Ferris underestimates the significance of Hani's words—"this is a part of the world where friendship matters. It can save your life"—and thereby fails to create an effective strategy to curtail the "war on terror." At the end of the film Al-Saleem suggests that the war is a just one, as he takes revenge on all those "non-believers"—especially the Americans—who have caused so much suffering in the world, particularly in detention centers like Guantanamo Bay. If *Kingdom of Heaven* explores the origins of the conflict between Christians and Muslims during the Crusades, *Body of Lies* shows that such conflicts remain unresolved nearly nine hundred years later.

Scott shows how the Americans' reliance on technology places them at a disadvantage in the "war on terror.' Like *Black Hawk Down* we see frequent sequences involving helicopters observing Ferris's activities on the ground or taking him to and from different locations. All the activities in the Middle East are beamed back to the CIA headquarters in Langley, Virginia, via screens of uplinked video, satellite television, and commercial news pictures, making it possible for Hoffman to direct Ferris via a Bluetooth link. However, all this equipment proves ineffective in the end: Al-Saleem's men use their vehicles to create a dust-cloud in the desert and thereby escape CIA surveillance as they bundle Ferris into a van and take him over the Jordanian border into Syria. Scott cuts back to CIA headquarters, where an employee asks Hoffman what he should do next. Hoffman does not reply, realizing (perhaps for the first time) that he is involved in a new form of conflict in which the enemy is frequently elusive. The only way of winning, as Hani observes later on, is through collaboration with other security services in on-the-ground operations.

While *Body of Lies* offers a vivid portrait of life in the war zone, its moral stance is still affected by COLONIALISM. Many sequences take place in the suburbs of the Jordanian capital Amman—a world of squalid streets, overcrowded housing and primitive transport that contrasts starkly with the shimmering concrete skyscrapers of downtown Amman or Abu Dhabi. Such representations imply that the Islamic world needs to develop further before it can match western standards of civilization. Scott substantiates this argument by showing how many Arabs still rely on primitive methods of punishment: the scenes where Al-Saleem breaks Ferris's fingers with a hammer are particularly brutal, recalling Alan Parker's *Midnight Express* (1978), in which another young American suffers at the hands of his captors. Even so-called "educated" Arabs like Hani believe that physical punishment is the best way of reinforcing one's authority. This is chillingly suggested in one sequence where Ferris is forced to witness what happens inside a prison cell. We do not see inside, but we can hear the unfortunate victim's screams.

On the other hand, Scott returns to the issue of the CIA and its perceived value in contemporary America—something also explored in *THE COMPANY*. Senior operatives like Hoffman are portrayed as careerists with little understanding of their responsibilities either to their staff or their country. For most of the time Hoffman directs Ferris on a Bluetooth link while taking his children to school, taking his son to the bathroom, or watching his daughter playing soccer. Compared to the smooth, immaculately dressed Hani, Hoffman lacks any diplomatic skill whatsoever—turning up for a meeting in a rumpled suit and trying to lay the law down for the Jordanian ("I would hate to have the president call His Majesty [the king of Jordan] and complain about this. We are all allies.") Hani brushes aside such threats by telling Hoffman that for the purposes of this meeting he is the king's representative, and casting doubts on Hoffman's competence as an agent ("You Americans, you are incapable of secrecy because you are a democracy.")

Hoffman is equally heavy-handed in his treatment of Ferris. While conceiving himself as one half of a double-act in a BUDDY MOVIE (he addresses Ferris throughout as "buddy"), Hoffman becomes more and more frustrated as the action unfolds. When Ferris turns down the chance to work alongside him in Langley, Hoffman accuses him of sacrificing his responsibility to the nation and consequently "giving up on America." Ferris responds coolly, "You be careful calling yourself an American. Have a safe flight home. Say hi to the wife and kids." Hoffman's concept of national identity is defined solely by his job: a cocooned environment communicating with the outside world via cell phones and satellite links and discouraging person-to-person communication. The film ends with Hoffman symbolically casting Ferris out of the organization by turning off the surveillance camera and murmuring "buddy's done" at the same time.

As with many of Scott's films—*THELMA & LOUISE*, *AMERICAN GANGSTER*—*Body of Lies* incorporates several shots of iconic CARS. They include the Mercedes and the

SUVs belonging to Hani and the American Embassy which speed through the streets of Amman or race along the Jordanian desert with a cloudless sky and bare mountain ranges in the background. However, they prove almost useless in a war zone. While they might look stylish, they are also an obvious target for potential attackers; by contrast, the used cars and dilapidated vans favored by the extremists provide an effective way of moving people around without attracting attention.

While *Body of Lies* ends happily with Ferris leaving the CIA and rejoining his Arab girlfriend Aisha (GOLSHIFTEH FARAHANI), it is perhaps the most pessimistic of Scott's FILMS AFTER 9/11. It suggests that the "war on terror" will never be won so long as a "body of lies" persists, preventing people of different cultures from collaborating with one another. Hani tells Ferris in no uncertain terms that he has "only one rule if we are to cooperate, my dear. Never lie to me." However, Ferris deliberately ignores that dictum as he tries and fails to create a fake terrorist network. Hani returns the favor by using Ferris as the fall guy to entrap Al-Saleem himself. The scheme nearly goes wrong, as Hani's forces rescue Ferris in the nick of time just before Al-Saleem kills him. Monahan's original script shows the two men—Ferris and Hani—at loggerheads, each blaming the other for their deceit. Hani sarcastically describes Ferris as a hero, but considers himself truly heroic, having captured Al-Saleem. The implication is obvious: both men put personal gain ahead of their responsibilities to their respective countries. The same also applies to people of the same culture: Hoffman never informs Ferris about the true nature of his plans, and thereby prevents the agent from undertaking his duties efficiently, or establishing effective communication with the Jordanians.

Body of Lies reveals the shortcomings of the so-called "New Patriotism" that emerged from *The Patriot* (2000), *We Were Soldiers* (2002), and *Black Hawk Down*. Frank J. Wetta and Martin A. Novelli argue that these films celebrate "the bond of brotherhood forged under fire." In *Body of Lies* that bond no longer exists; rather, it depicts a world that (as James Der Derian observes) is dominated by "a new imbalance of terror based on a mimetic fear and an asymmetrical willingness and capacity to destroy the other without the formalities of war."

James Castonguay's article "Conglomeration, New Media and the Cultural Production of the 'War on Terror'" suggests that films showing America involved in foreign conflicts enable spectators to "participate vicariously in the US imperial project as a mediated and exotic spectacle . . . the complicity between US media conglomerates, the government, and the military created a context of reception with limited possibilities for oppositional or politically progressive readings." This might be true for American audiences;

but box office figures show that films like *Body of Lies* were more popular outside, rather than inside, the United States. Perhaps some filmgoers constructed "oppositional or politically progressive readings." The implications of the so-called "war on terror" have been explored by Rosalind C. Morris, focusing in particular on how "the Woman Question and the Eastern Question came to substitute for one another, securing different patriarchies in their awful complicity and ensuring that technology of the highest and lowest sort be used for a war that neither declares itself nor imagines the possibility of its termination." In contrast, Catherine Elsworth's article for the *Daily Telegraph* argues that Hollywood misjudged the mood of the times, with films such as *Lions for Lambs*, *Rendition*, *In the Valley of Elah*, *Redacted*, *Grace Is Gone* (all 2007), and *Stop-Loss* (2008)—all of which took the wars in Iraq and Afghanistan as subjects—performing badly at the box office. She quotes one journalist who observes that "Hollywood and the left have generally misread this discontent [with the Bush administration] thinking there's a mandate for their trite Vietnam-era nostalgia for mass protest and Joan Baez specifying." Ridley Scott himself was quoted as saying in an interview with *Digital Spy* in late 2008 that many of the films flopped due to public anger over the war.

References

Nigel Andrews, "Impaired Vision and Blind Panic," *Financial Times*, 20 November 2008, www.ft.com/cms/s/2/e365e700-b648-11dd-89dd-0000779fd18c.html?nclick_check=1 (accessed 17 February 2009); Roger Clarke, "*Body of Lies*," *Sight and Sound*, December 2008, www.bfi.org.uk/sightandsound/review/4558 (accessed 17 February 2009); James Castonguay, "Conglomeration, New Media and the Cultural Production of the 'War on Terror,'" *Cinema Journal* 43, no.4 (Summer 2004): 106; James der Derian, "Imaging Terror: Logos, Pathos and Ethos," *Third World Quarterly* 26, no.1 (2005): 23; Roger Ebert, "*Body of Lies*," *Chicago Sun-Times*, 8 October 2008, http://rogerebert.suntimes.com/apps/pbcs.dll/article?AID=/20081008/REVIEWS/810089997/1023 (accessed 17 February 2009); Catherine Elsworth, "Hollywood Misreads Response to War on Terror," *Daily Telegraph*, 12 November 2007, www.telegraph.co.uk/culture/film/starsandstories/3669211/Hollywood-misreads-response-to-war-on-terror.html (accessed 19 February 2009); Philip French, "*Body of Lies*," *The Observer* (London), 23 November 2008, www.guardian.co.uk/film/2008/nov/23/body-of-lies-review (accessed 27 February 2009); Charles Gant, "Body of Lies Takes a Blow from My Best Friend's Girl," *The Guardian*, 25 November 2008, www.guardian.co.uk/film/filmblog/2008/nov/25/uk-box-office-body-of-lies (accessed 17 February 2009); Jeff Giles, "DVD Review: *Body of Lies*," http://popdose.com/dvd-review-body-of-lies/#more-12672 (accessed 19 February 2009); Mick LaSalle, "Muddled *Body of Lies*," *San Francisco Chronicle*, 10 October 2008, E1; Rosalind C. Morris, "Theses on the Questions of War:

History, Media, Terror," *Social Text* 20, no.3 (Fall 2002): 172; Martyn Palmer, "Russell Crowe: Why I had to Fatten up and Calm Down," *Daily Telegraph*, 6 November 2008, www.telegraph.co.uk/culture/film/3562948/Russell-Crowe-Why-I-had-to-fatten-up-and-calm-down.html (accessed 17 February 2009); *Production Notes: Body of Lies* (Los Angeles: Warner Bros. Entertainment, 2008), http://mix96tulsa.com/movies/notes/body-of-lies/note/4 (accessed 16 January 2009); Simon Reynolds, "Ridley Scott—*Body of Lies*," *Digital Spy*, 20 November 2008, www.digitalspy.co.uk/movies/a135416/ridley-scott-body-of-lies.html (accessed 19 February 2009); A. O. Scott, "Big Stars Wielding an Array of Accents, Fighting the War on Terrorism," *New York Times*, 10 October 2008, http://movies.nytimes.com/2008/10/10/movies/10lies.html?scp=2&sq=body%20of%20lies&st=cse (accessed 17 February 2009); Frank J. Wetta and Martin A. Novelli, "Now a Major Motion Picture: War Films and Hollywood's New Patriotism," *Journal of Military History* 67, no.3 (July 2003): 880.

BOLD AS BRASS

GB 1964 TV Series 6 × 25 min episodes b/w. *Production Company*: British Broadcasting Corporation. *Producer/ director*: Philip Barker. *Writers*: Ron Watson and David Climie. *Production Designer*: Ridley Scott. *Music*: Gordon Franks. *Cast*: Jimmy Edwards (*Ernie Briggs*), Beryl Reid (*Bessie Briggs*), Jill Hyem (*Peggy Briggs*), Ronnie Barker (*Mr. Oakroyd*).

The comic exploits of brass band-mad Ernie Briggs and his downtrodden wife Bessie. The series came out of a one-hour pilot (broadcast 28 November 1963) written by Douglas Moodie from an idea by Ron Watson. This six-part comedy ran from 4 April to 13 June 1964.

BOLOTIN, CRAIG (1954–)

Director and scriptwriter. Bolotin made his debut as a screenwriter with *No Small Affair* (1984) under the pseudonym of Charles Bolt. Other credits include one episode of *Miami Vice* (1986) and *Sapphire Man* (1988).

Bolotin was inspired to write *BLACK RAIN* after having visited Kobe, JAPAN, in 1987 and having witnessed at first-hand the large CARS driven by the yakuza, or Japanese gangsters. He also believed that the story of American-Japanese relations had a particular significance at a time when the two countries were not exactly getting along with one another. According to a documentary on the script issued with the film's DVD release in 2001, Warren Lewis was brought in to collaborate after Bolotin had written an outline. The first completed draft (dated November 1987) portrays Nick Conklin as a violent yet isolated police officer seeking brief solace with a succession of temporary girlfriends. Both he and Charlie become involved with the yakuza by accident while trying to arrest a member of the mafia in a New York bar. They are sent to Japan by their superior officer, Oliver (who harbors a particular resentment for Nick), on a mission to return the yakuza leader Kobo to his home country. Unfortunately they manage to lose him at Osaka airport, and try to find him once again accompanied by Inspector Ichiro Matsumoto—an overweight Japanese police officer with a penchant for Scotch whiskey. The three of them prove no match for Kobo's gang, and Charlie is eventually killed by Kobo, who pushes him in front of a subway train. Nick tries to find out what happened, but is served with a deportation order and told to leave the country within twenty-four hours. He escapes and pursues Kobo's girlfriend in the hope of finding further leads. Eventually he discovers that the best route to Kobo is to become acquainted with the elderly yakuza leader Sugai, and travels to the seaside resort of Beppu for that purpose. Kobo is eventually apprehended in a "love hotel" in Beppu and brought back by train to Osaka; however, he manages to escape and takes Nick's friend Joyce hostage in the process. The screenplay ends with a protracted gun battle in which Sugai loses his life, Joyce escapes, while Nick and Kobo fight one another on motorcycles. Badly wounded, Nick overpowers Kobo by slashing him with a Japanese sword. Eventually he returns to New York in triumph, accompanied by Matsumoto.

In addition to some name changes (Kobo becomes Sato and Matsumoto is changed into Masahiro), the final script portrays Nick somewhat differently: as a family man concerned for his two children's welfare, despite being divorced. The Italian-American plot-strand completely disappears: Nick is sent to Japan in an attempt to reestablish his reputation as an honest cop after having been found guilty of handling stolen money. Matsumoto/Masahiro is transformed into an unassuming personality obsessed with doing the right thing. The deportation order disappears altogether; instead, Nick is merely threatened with arrest if he should dare set foot in Japan again. Needless to say, Nick takes no notice and travels to Sugai's house, which is now located on the outskirts of Osaka. The final sequence takes place in a sake firm; ostensibly Sato and Sugai make peace, but Sato ends by stabbing Sugai in the hand and escaping. Joyce's role as a hostage is eliminated altogether. The ending remains roughly the same, except that Nick is seen departing for New York while Masahiro stays in Japan, having decided to renounce any loyalty to specific social groups and forge a new career on his own.

References

"*Black Rain*: The Script, The Cast," Special Feature included in the Special Collector's Edition DVD release of *Black Rain* (d. Laurent Bouzereau) (Los Angeles: Paramount Pictures, 2001); Craig Bolotin and Warren Lewis, "*Black Rain*: Draft Script" (November 1987), http://sky.ru/sfy.html?script=black_rain_ds (accessed 8 June 2008).

BOSCH, ROSELYNE

In the late 1980s Bosch was working as a journalist for the French news magazine *Le Point*. She went to Seville to do a piece on how Spain was planning to commemorate the five hundredth anniversary of Christopher Columbus's expedition. The more time she spent in the archives, the more she became enthralled, and the more she believed that his story should be transformed into a film. She wrote a précis of what was eventually to form the script, focusing on Columbus's many journeys—the existential as well as the maritime—as narrated by one of his illegitimate sons.

Bosch contacted fledgling film producer and distributor ALAIN GOLDMAN, who asked her to turn her ideas into a screenplay, and together they decided to make a film. Initially they planned it as a French venture but they found little support among French producers. They contacted Ridley Scott, who by chance had been planning a film about Columbus, and he agreed—so long as GÉRARD DEPARDIEU played the leading role.

Conflicts emerged between writer and director over the script. While Scott wanted to focus more on the plot, Bosch was more interested in preserving the ambiguities of Columbus's character while still emphasizing his heroic qualities. An epigraph attributed to Columbus (and included in the first draft copy of the script, dated 1991) makes this clear: "Nothing that results from human progress is achieved with unanimous consent. And those who are enlightened before the others are condemned to pursue that light in spite of others." Bosch's screenplay formed the basis of Robert Thurston's novelization of the film, which included several scenes not in the finished film—for example, an opening sequence involving Columbus's two sons Diego and Fernando, who discuss their father's contribution to posterity. Diego criticizes him for promising paradise and failing to deliver: "He made them [his crew] believe that all they'd have to do is to reach out for fruit, or bend for gold. He was a dreamer!" Fernando responds by calling him an idealist—and resolves to publish his father's memoirs. Diego petulantly responds, "I won't read it."

Bosch's finished screenplay was criticized by Vincent Canby of the *New York Times*, who observed that "only a very great writer could do justice to all the themes the Columbus story suggests. Ms. Bosch might be a very good researcher, but she's not a very great writer."

References

Roselyne Bosch, "Columbus," Unpub. script revised 4 May 1991 (Los Angeles: Percy Main Productions), 2; Vincent Canby, quoted in Paul Chutkow, *Depardieu: A Biography* (London: HarperCollins Publishers, 1994), 313; Robert Thurston, *1492: Conquest of Paradise Based on a Screenplay by Roselyne Bosch* (London: Penguin Books, 1992), 11.

BOTTIN, ROB (1959–)

Rob Bottin began his career as a special effects and makeup artist on films such as *The Fog* (1980) and *The Thing* (1982), both for John Carpenter.

For *LEGEND* Bottin transformed Darkness (TIM CURRY) into the quintessential horned demon by outfitting the actor with fluorescent contact lenses, two satyr-like furred and hoofed feet (which encased eighteen-inch-long, stilt-like extensions, to make Curry look taller), plus lightweight polystyrene horns measuring over three feet in length. The final touch was a dark scarlet makeup applied all over Curry's body. The effect was to make Darkness seem like a satyr—half-man, half-goat—an unearthly presence in an unearthly forest.

Miles Teves, who worked for Bottin as an illustrator on the production, recalled that Darkness was "a very bestial character—much more like a Minotaur" that could encourage the actor to develop his own performance without the need for animatronics. Not all of the characters in *Legend* had so much time lavished upon them. "Because we spent so long on Darkness and some of the other characters, when it came to the witch, Meg Mucklebones [ROBERT PICARDO], there was very little time left . . . Rob basically brought me a picture of the witch from Disney's *Snow White*, and said, 'This is what we're going to do—only more real and more extreme.' He liked the simple lines—the little apple cheeks, the bulgy eyes, and the way the chin hooked up to meet the nose. We really pulled that one off fast." Bottin believed that "the makeup [was] shocking in a fun way; it was like a childhood memory of *Eerie* and *Creepy* magazines."

References

Rob Bottin, quoted in Steve Biodrowski, "*Legend* Make-Up," *Cinefantastique* 15, no.5 (January 1986): 26; Rickard Rickitt, "Miles Teves—Character Designer," *Designing Movie Creatures: Discover the Best in the Business from the Best in the Business* (New York: Rotovision, 2006), www.graphics.com/modules.php?name=Sections&op=viewarticle&artid=501 (accessed 13 May 2008).

BOURDON, DIDIER (1959–)

Bourdon made his debut in an English language film in *A GOOD YEAR* as Francis Duflot. Screenwriter MARC KLEIN portrays the character in stereotypical fashion as an eccentric fond of red wine and dressed in a traditional black beret. However Bourdon makes something of the role, by portraying him as fundamentally fond of yet simultaneously repelled by Max Skinner (RUSSELL CROWE). Bourdon summed up their relationship thus in a preproduction interview: "They knew each other when they were younger. Their relationship is between friendship and mistrust." The two of them make a pact to clean up the château: Duflot spits into his palm and extends it to shake; Max spits an even bigger hock into his own palm; and the two of them shake, spit merging. They walk off in separate directions, describing one another in asides as a Frog tosspot and an English prick. Bourdon's climactic moment comes in the tennis match with Max: two middle-aged men huffing and puffing on a shabby court but playing as if their lives depended on it. Max eventually wins; and the two of them appraise one another; at last they are prepared to acknowledge each other as close friends. Crowe explained the origins of the tennis sequence thus: "[It] came about because Ridley is a great lover of the sport . . . He was bemoaning to me over a glass of red wine that we didn't have any battle sequences in the movie. That got me thinking. And we had the whole sequence set up by the tennis court, and a sequence playing tennis in flashback. And so I made the suggestion that perhaps we find a way of getting these two men to do battle on the clay court."

References

Marc Klein, "*A Good Year*: Screenplay" (Draft dated 5 September 2005), www.dailyscript.com/scripts/A-GOOD-YEAR-2.pdf (accessed 26 January 2009); *Pressbook: A Good Year* (Los Angeles: Twentieth Century-Fox Film Corporation, 2006), 7.

BOWDEN, MARK (1951–)

Journalist and author of *Doctor Dealer* and *Bringing the Heat*. Began his career at the *Philadelphia Inquirer*, and also wrote for magazines such as *Sports Illustrated*, *Playboy*, *Rolling Stone*, and *Parade*. Bowden wrote *Black Hawk Down* (1999), the original book from which Ridley Scott made his 2001 film of the same name. The book itself is a minute-by-minute account of the 1993 raid on Mogadishu, which took place against a background of increasing political instability in the country. Bowden's book began as a newspaper project and was eventually expanded into a book, based both on interviews with those involved and radio broadcasts produced at the time. Described at the time as "rip-roaring stuff, with one of the most gruesome battlefield wound treatments ever committed to paper," it was eminently suitable for filming.

When JERRY BRUCKHEIMER bought the film rights to *Black Hawk Down*, Bowden's contract stipulated that he write the first draft of the script: "I automatically assumed that the producers would throw out my script but at least I would still receive eighty thousand dollars for having done it." He spent three months writing the screenplay, and then KEN NOLAN was signed as primary scriptwriter. Bowden recalled that "the big discussion at the beginning of this project was how to focus the film. It was a process of narrowing down which characters and scenes we were going to use. Our first list of 'must-have' scenes and characters would have resulted in a seventeen-hour long film . . . Ridley decided to focus the film on the soldiers' experience." Bowden believed that the center of the film was the battle: "The key to good

filmmaking is storytelling and figuring out how to put it across. I always try to put myself into the shoes of the person I'm writing about to try and capture their feelings."

References

Mark Bowden, *Black Hawk Down* (London: Corgi Books, 2000); Mark Bowden, quoted in Joanna Sterkowicz, "Written Word versus Moving Image," *ScreenAfrica* 16 (April 2004): 34.

Bibliography

James Dobbins et al., *America's Role in Nation-Building: From Germany to Iraq* (Santa Monica, CA: Rand, 2003), 55–71.

BOWIE, DAVID (1947–)

Born David Burns in Brixton, south London. Bowie has for nearly five decades been involved in the music industry as a trendsetting singer and writer. He has also pursued an acting career in films such as *Merry Christmas Mr. Lawrence* (1983) and *THE HUNGER* (also 1983).

Bowie's performance in *The Hunger* (directed by TONY SCOTT) was described as competent, but tended to be lost in a film in which style triumphed over content. Bowie himself recalled in 1987 that he "felt very uncomfortable with that role . . . although . . . [he] loved being involved in a Tony Scott movie." In 1998–1999 Bowie was involved in *THE HUNGER* (TELEVISION), a Canadian-made horror anthology produced by Scott, based loosely on the concepts of the 1983 film. Bowie took over as host for the second series from TERENCE STAMP and played the starring role in the opening episode "Sanctuary," directed by Tony Scott. Here Bowie plays Julian Priest, a reclusive avant-garde artist focusing on macabre themes. An angry young man berates him with the words: "What does that mean, he's [Priest has] lost his art? Okay, I'll tell you what it means. Icons notwithstanding, it means you suck. You hung around too long, and look what happened—you created crap. Congratulations! You are the Fat Elvis!" In a series of ghoulish plot-twists, Priest regains his place at the cutting edge of modern art.

Bowie introduced the subsequent episodes in the character of Priest. Each sequence was photographed in a prison (and directed by Tony Scott), where the central character indulged in a series of bizarre activities, including taking an acid bath, feeding a mouse to a rattlesnake, or looking at a series of impassive faces on a bank of television screens. His comments focused in particular on people being true to their emotions, and the difficulties they experience in adjusting to life. His introduction to "Dream Sentinel" (Series 2, episode 3), sums up his view of life: "Facing death is easy, facing life is hard." Bowie does not give a great acting performance, but his eerie presence at the beginning and end of each episode is hard to ignore. As he himself observes in "The Perfect Couple" (Series 2, episode 22), viewers may want to "keep things out [including himself]," but this is ultimately an impossible task.

References

David Bowie, quoted in Nicholas Pegg, *The Complete David Bowie* (Richmond UK: Reynolds & Hearn Ltd., 2006), 561.

BOY ON BICYCLE

GB 1962 r/t 27 min b/w. *Production Company:* British Film Institute. *Producer/ Director/ Writer/ Director of Photography:* Ridley Scott. *Music:* John Barry. *Cast:* Tony Scott (*The Schoolboy*).

This black-and-white short film was made by Scott for sixty-five British pounds while still a student at the Royal College of Art. It records a day in the life of a young boy (TONY SCOTT) who deliberately misses school and sets off on his bicycle around the streets of Billingham, northeast England, ending up on the coast. He passes the time by taking in the sights, sounds, and smells around him and allowing his mind to wander on various subjects. Eventually it begins to rain; the boy takes shelter in a small hut, unexpectedly encounters a stranger and runs away on his bicycle into the distance.

This film records the thoughts, experiences, and emotions of a teenager growing up in early 1960s Britain. It begins with a long point-of-view shot of his bedroom, surveying the untidy mess of clothes, toys and other bric-a-brac littering the place. In the background we hear his mother and father (actually Scott's parents) telling him to come down to breakfast. He leaves for school as usual, but chooses to take the day off and explore his immediate surroundings. As he passes the school, he hears the students singing the familiar hymn "All Things Bright and Beautiful" and imagines just how dehumanizing school can be. He is no longer a person but rather "Scott, T"—a name on a register. He rides his bicycle along the quiet, deserted streets, passing the local fish-and-chips shop and pausing to buy something at the candy store before reaching the seaside. In the background we see the stark, forbidding towers of the Imperial Chemical Industries (ICI) plant at Billingham. The boy comments on what he observes through a stream of consciousness, combining immediate responses with childhood memories and imaginative speculation. Sometimes he recalls nursery rhymes or favorite books (Louisa M. Alcott's *Little Women* being one of them), or speculates on what life would be like for the boy in the Dutch folk-tale who puts his finger in a dyke to prevent flooding. When he gets to the little hut, certain objects he encounters stimulate further childhood memories—a tin of Lyle's Golden Syrup conjures up images of his mother and how angry she will be if he comes home late for tea, or his favorite teddy bear, or his grandparents (who are both deceased). The film ends with him cycling away into the distance; he is still free (at least for a limited period) to do as he wishes.

Boy and Bicycle focuses on CHILDHOOD, and how certain memories associated with it dominate the young boy's mind. Although he believes himself to be an adult, he is still very much tied to his parents' apron strings; he has to be home at a specific time or risk incurring their wrath. The film itself provides a fascinating social picture of northeast England in the early 1960s—a time when industry still flourished in the region and the local main street provided a focal point for the community, with family businesses still very much in evidence. The film was not released until 1965, by which time Scott had persuaded John Barry (the composer of the James Bond theme) to record a track, "Onward Christian Spacemen," for it.

The film includes images that would recur in Scott's later work: the boy on bicycle formed the subject for one of his most famous commercials for HOVIS BREAD, while the industrial landscape forms a backdrop for *BLADE RUNNER* and *BLACK RAIN*.

BRACCO, LORRAINE (1954–)

Born in New York, Bracco became a star in the 1970s as a model for the designer Jean-Paul Gautier. Her major break in films came in Ridley Scott's *SOMEONE TO WATCH OVER ME*.

As Mike Keegan's (TOM BERENGER's) wife Ellie, Bracco gives a feisty performance as someone refusing to conform to her husband's outmoded conception of gender roles. Far from seeking her husband's protection, she assumes a proactive role, going out to clean the family car while Mike sits at a table with a cup of coffee, or hitting him square in the nose when he insults her. As the daughter of a cop, Ellie knows the value of self-reliance. Although she and her husband are eventually reconciled, we are made well aware that she will not accept the roles imposed on her by a basically patriarchal partner: she is not in need of someone to watch over her. Lorraine Bracco's former husbands include HARVEY KEITEL and EDWARD JAMES OLMOS.

BRATT, BENJAMIN (1963–)

Born in San Francisco, Bratt made his name by playing Detective Rey Curtis in ninety-four episodes of the television series *Law & Order* (1994–1999).

Cast as Dr. Jeremy Stone in *THE ANDROMEDA STRAIN*, Bratt plays a brilliant scientist who has made a mess of his personal life. He is separated from his wife Lisa (Anna Galvin) and has a teenage son Lance (Michal Suchánek), who accuses him of using his work as an excuse to avoid responsibility for his family. In a sense Lance is right: we learn later on that he has had an affair with Dr. Angela Noyce (CHRISTA MILLER) which ended unhappily. Nonetheless

Stone redeems himself through a combination of dedication to his job and unflappability in the face of crisis. Even when the Andromeda virus has been released in the laboratory, he still finds the time to work out before devoting himself to his duties. The *New York Times* felt that Bratt's performance detracted from the overall effect of the production: "He looks dressed for a weekend in South Beach, and amid the film's urgent atmosphere, he adds all the tension of someone conducting a tax audit . . . Stone doesn't embody an interesting Crichtonesque paradox, the highly rational mind that makes poor moral choices. The film casts no judgments on his infidelity, portraying it as merely another aspect of his entitlement. His ex-wife at home is an irresponsible shrew." His role in many ways resembles that of Dallas (TOM SKERRITT) in *ALIEN*; the leader of a group of scientists and/or specialists faced with the responsibility of counteracting an invading force (the alien or the virus). Stone not only survives but also has the chance to speak out against those forces of capitalism that threaten the future of the entire planet.

Reference

Gina Bellafante, "Earth's End Is Near Again: Crichton's Brain Squad Is Back," *New York Times*, 26 May 2008, www.nytimes.com/2008/05/26/arts/television/26andro.html?_r=1&scp=1&sq=andromeda%20strain&st=cse (accessed 13 February 2009).

BRAUGHER, ANDRE (1962–)

Born in Chicago, Braugher has been associated with successful television series including *Homicide: Life on the Street* (1993–1998), and the Stephen King adaptation of *The Mist* (2007).

Cast as General George W. Mancheck in *THE ANDROMEDA STRAIN*, Braugher plays an officer of questionable motives who spends much of his time trying to cover up the story of how and why the Andromeda Strain came to be released in the first place. His behavior might seem outwardly respectable, but director MIKAEL SALOMON suggests that this is nothing more than a front. However, Mancheck meets a sticky end as he is eventually murdered by an unseen assailant (probably from the US MILITARY) for his part in causing the crisis. Braugher outlined his involvement in the film, and his role in particular, in an interview: "My interest in the entire project stems from my curiosity about how we were going to reconfigure this Andromeda Strain. Even before the script got to me I was intrigued by that idea. Mancheck, in his own way, is a misguided military figure who suddenly awakens to the extent and the depth of the danger of our situation and our unease with this Andromeda and what we've wrought." He was nominated for an Image Award for Outstanding Actor in a Television Movie, Mini-Series or Dramatic Special for this performance in 2009.

Reference

Ian Spelling, "Andre Braugher: The Andromeda Strain Interview," *Ugo.Com: Lifestyle for Games*, www.ugo.com/ugo/html/article/?id=18609 (accessed 15 February 2009).

BREMNER, EWEN (1971–)

Made his name in *Trainspotting* (1996), followed by roles in *The Acid House* (1998), and *Pearl Harbor* (2001).

Cast as Nelson in *BLACK HAWK DOWN*, Bremner has the chance to participate in some of the film's moments of semi-comic relief, as he and Twombly (Thomas Hardy) become detached from their company of Rangers and have to fend for themselves. Twombly resolves to go to the crash site; Nelson agrees but tells his friend not to fire his rifle too close to him as Nelson can "barely hear as it is." As soon as Nelson breaks his cover, however, enemy bullets start raining around him. An armed figure appears on the horizon; Twombly fires inches from Nelson's head to kill him; but ends up by deafening the unfortunate Nelson. Nelson rounds on his friend with a voice of thunder: "*What did I just tell you? I swear to God if you ever . . .* " In a later sequence Twombly is about to shoot what he thinks is another enemy soldier; but finds that it is actually a donkey that "briskly trots past." A little further down the block Yurek (Thomas Guiry) hears an unearthly sound: "clop, clop, clop." He prepares himself to fire—then he too discovers it is just the donkey patiently making his way home. Such sequences emphasize the fact that daily life in Mogadishu continues despite the conflict taking place.

Like most of his colleagues, however, Nelson remains dedicated to the task at hand. Although eventually separated from Twombly, he manages to survive. The two men reencounter one another at the Olympic Stadium; they embrace, secure in the knowledge that their mission has been completed.

Reference

Ken Nolan, *Black Hawk Down: The Shooting Script* (New York: Newmarket Press, 2002), 64, 76.

BRIDGES, JEFF (1949–)

Described once by the British critic Barry Norman as "a character actor trapped in the body of a leading man," which perhaps helps to explain why he has not become a major Hollywood star.

Cast as Captain Sheldon in *WHITE SQUALL*, Bridges's work was admired by Scott, who told Brian J. Robb that he was "one of the best actors in America . . . What's really remarkable about him is that Jeff always finds a unique character in each piece he does." Bridges spent some time with the real Captain Sheldon and discovered that he had "never completely rid himself of his guilt, especially about his wife. But he knew it was an existential happening, an act of nature. He had no control over it." In another interview with the London *Observer*, Bridges admitted that "Sheldon wasn't an emotional person. He was *very* emotional. What is interesting is how each of us manifests that. The filters are fascinating. I try to put emotion in all the roles and it leaks out of the characters in different ways." This proved especially interesting for an actor not normally accustomed to revealing his emotions on screen: "it [the role] surprised Bridges, an emotionally judicious man who seeks to contain his life in bound copies of his scripts. It is embarrassing, but also a privilege, to witness him . . . hit by a white squall of grief."

In the film Bridges portrays the captain as an essentially humane person who, while fond of his young crew, nonetheless remains determined to educate them. Although commending his performance for its sincerity, the *Washington Post* reviewer observed that he seemed to be "summoning the old *Sea Hunt* spirit of his [actor] father . . . knitting his brow convincingly and spouting such briny aphorisms as 'It takes discipline to make it out here!' and 'Where we go one, we go all' . . . a crewman sums up Bridges's character by saying, 'He's a real salt.'"

References

"Andrew Billen Talks to Jeff Bridges about Charisma, Conflict and Control," *Observer Review*, 28 April 1996, 28; Richard Leiby, "White Squall," *Washington Post*, 2 February 1996, www.washingtonpost .com/wpsrv/style/longterm/movies/videos/whitesquallpg13leiby _c0457a.htm (accessed 14 September 2008); Neil Norman, "Scott of the Caribbean," *Evening Standard*, 18 May 1995, 28; Barry Norman, "Give This Man an Oscar," *Radio Times*, 2–8 February 2002, 54; Brian J. Robb, *Ridley Scott* (Harpenden: Pocket Essentials, 2002), 68.

BROADBENT, JIM (1949–)

Lugubrious British character actor, who made his name in Great Britain in the 1970s and 1980s as part of the comedy team The National Theatre of Brent. In the 1990s his film career expanded, with leading roles in *Life Is Sweet* (1990), *Richard III* (1995), *The Borrowers* (1997), and *Topsy-Turvy* (1999) where he played W. S. Gilbert.

Cast as Desmond Morton in THE GATHERING STORM, Broadbent plays a dependable civil servant—one of the few trustworthy friends Winston Churchill (ALBERT FINNEY) possesses to advise him. Churchill doesn't always listen to Desmond, but Desmond is always there, and supports him even if it no longer seems feasible to do so. Broadbent himself described the character thus in an interview: "He was a great friend of Churchill's—he was a neighbour of his near Chartwell, and head of the industrial intelligence services—and in the story of the film he is instrumental in feeding Winston the true facts and figures about what Germany was up to." He also serves as a source of support to Churchill during his "Black Dog" periods of depression; as witnessed, for instance, when Morton goes to the pigpen at Chartwell

to persuade Churchill to come to lunch. Morton does not say much, but his reassuring presence encourages Churchill inside, where Morton tells him about a report from Britain's air attaché in Berlin alleging that Hitler is training over eight thousand pilots. This inspires Churchill to further action.

Reference

The Gathering Storm: Information Pack, issued 17 June 2002 (London: BBC, 2002), www.bbc.co.uk/pressoffice/pressreleases/stories/ 2002/06_june/17/gathering_storm_pack.pdf (accessed 24 December 2008), 12.

BROLIN, JOSH (1968–)

Noted character actor who made his film debut in *The Goonies* (1985). Other successes include *Hollow Man* (2000) and *NO COUNTRY FOR OLD MEN* (2007).

As the corrupt detective Trupo in AMERICAN GANGSTER, Brolin described himself in an interview with the British film magazine *Empire* as a "criminal with a badge" who personified the police corruption of the early 1970s. He recalled a conversation with a seasoned police officer who candidly told him that "All you had to tell a drug dealer was, 'All I have to do is shoot you, put the gun in your hand, and I'm gonna get a medal. That's it. It's that simple.' Back then, there weren't a lot of drug dealers or gangsters who killed cops, that was just off-limits; you didn't do it."

Trupo's appearance, as described in STEVEN ZAILLIAN's script, reveals his true nature; with his Zapata mustache and slicked-back hair, he is one of four officers reveling in his position as kingpin of his particular district. He comes up to Richie Roberts (RUSSELL CROWE), looks him straight in the eye, and threatens him in a menacing tone: "Now, never, ever, come into the city again unannounced. You come in to see a fuckin' Broadway show you call ahead to see if it's okay with me." He laughs and remarks to his friends: "What do we hate most? Isn't it the transgressions of others we fear we're capable of ourselves?" However, Trupo's reign of terror proves a short one, as Frank Lucas names him as one of the officers involved in the web of corruption dominating early 1970s NEW YORK. Eventually he has no other option than to commit suicide as an alternative to lifetime imprisonment.

References

"Brolin Point," *Empire* 224 (February 2008): 21; Steven Zaillian, "*American Gangster:* Final Shooting Script" (27 July 2006), www. roteirodecinema.com.br/scripts/files/american_gangster.htm (accessed 8 February 2009).

THE BROTHERS GRIMM

Jacob (1785–1863) and Wilhelm Grimm (1786–1859): German literary scholars, philologists, and editors of the famous collection of folktales. Some of them are sinister, some funny; others talk about love, compassion or revenge, greed, cruelty or kindness. Because of their sheer range and scope, they have become central to the western children's literary tradition. The tales transport readers to strange lands where birds and beasts deal with dwarves, giants, princesses, and peasants.

Ridley Scott acknowledged the influence of the Brothers Grimm in his screenplay for *LEGEND* (written in collaboration with WILLIAM HJORTSBERG). Not only does the story deal with dwarves and giants, but its main subject consists of a quest where a peasant rescues a beautiful princess from the evil Darkness's clutches.

Bibliography

Cay Dollerup, "Translation as a Creative Force in Literature: The Birth of the European Bourgeois Fairy-Tale," *Modern Language Review* 90, no.1 (January 1995): 94–102.

BROWN, JAMES (1933–2006)

The self-styled "Godfather of Soul" made a few appearances in films such as *Rocky IV* (1985) and *Blues Brothers 2000* (1998). He also guest-starred in one episode of *Miami Vice* (1987).

Cast as himself in *THE HIRE: BEAT THE DEVIL,* Brown does little acting, but his sheer physical presence in the film suggests excess. Although not a young man any more, his vitality impresses The Driver (CLIVE OWEN) to such an extent that the Driver even becomes willing to accompany him on a crazy car-chase with The Devil (GARY OLDMAN) down the Las Vegas streets. James Brown died of pneumonia on Christmas Day 2006.

THE BROWNING VERSION (1951)

GB 1951 r/t 90 min b/w. Cert PG. *Production Company:* Javelin Films. *Producer:* Teddy Baird. *Director:* Anthony Asquith. *Director of Photography:* Desmond Dickinson. *Writer:* Terence Rattigan from his stage play of the same name. *Production Designer:* Carmen Dillon. *Cast:* Michael Redgrave (*Andrew Crocker-Harris*), Jean Kent (*Millie Crocker-Harris*), Nigel Patrick (*Frank Hunter*), Wilfrid Hyde White (*Frobisher*), Ben Smith (*Taplow*), Ronald Howard (*Gilbert*).

Michael Redgrave gives the performance of his career in Anthony Asquith's adaptation of TERENCE RATTIGAN's unforgettable play. Redgrave portrays Andrew Crocker-Harris, an embittered, middle-aged schoolmaster who begins to feel that his life has been a failure. Diminished by poor health, a crumbling MARRIAGE, and the derision of his pupils, the once brilliant scholar is compelled to reexamine his life when a young student offers an unexpected gesture of kindness. A heartbreaking story of remorse and atone-ment, *The Browning Version* is a classic of British realism and the winner of best actor and best screenplay honors at the 1951 Cannes Film Festival. *The Browning Version* was one of Ridley Scott's favorite films, which he himself was slated to remake in the early 1990s. Eventually the responsibility as director passed to MIKE FIGGIS, with Scott as producer.

THE BROWNING VERSION (1994)

GB 1994 r/t 97 min col. *Production Company:* Percy Main. *Producers:* Mimi Polk Gitlin and Ridley Scott. *Director:* Mike Figgis. *Writer:* Ronald Harwood from an original play by Terence Rattigan. *Director of Photography:* Jean-Francois Rabin. *Production Design:* John Beard. *Music:* Mark Isham. *Cast:* Albert Finney (*Andrew Crocker-Harris*), Greta Scacchi (*Laura Crocker-Harris*), Michael Gambon (*Headmaster*), Matthew Modine (*Frank Hunter*), Julian Sands (*Tom Gilbert*), Ben Silverstone (*Taplow*), Bruce Myers (*Dr. Rafferty*).

The Browning Version was planned as part of a series of projects from Paramount British Pictures, the Hollywood major's London-based European production arm. The initiative was launched in June 1990; by 1992 it had only green-lighted one film, a remake of *Wuthering Heights* (1992) starring Ralph Fiennes and Juliette Binoche.

Originally Scott had wanted to direct this remake of TERENCE RATTIGAN's play himself, but he eventually passed the responsibility on to MIKE FIGGIS. The two of them decided to update the piece, which had been filmed as *THE BROWNING VERSION* (1951) by Anthony Asquith with Michael Redgrave in the title role. Figgis explained that he "had a real problem with period pieces . . . particularly in film. Radio and novels work fine, but the minute you put people in wigs, and using cars that are of the period, and perfect tea sets, all people do is wonder where you got it all from." They decided to update the piece to the mid-1990s, in the belief that "the public school system hasn't changed visually in any way—the codes are the same but the nuances are going to be completely different. In the original they're getting rid of [the central character] Crocker-Harris because he's an absolute duff. In this one they're moving him out because they're moving his subject out—the Classics are of less importance."

The script was written by RONALD HARWOOD, a playwright and screenwriter whose major successes included *The Dresser* (1983). He consciously updated Rattigan's text, incorporating a more explicit focus on the central relationship between Laura and Frank, while emphasizing the hardships of public school life—the bullying, the reliance on outmoded traditions, and the determination to suppress emotional involvement at all costs.

From the outset Figgis treated *The Browning Version* as a character piece, focusing less on the school environment and more on the protagonists' emotions. The pressbook quoted ALBERT FINNEY (playing the central character Crocker-Harris) as saying that he had seldom played a character "so isolated and stoic. It goes back to English good manners—that you're not supposed to show the world how you are, how you feel or express your emotions." GRETA SCACCHI (playing Laura Crocker-Harris) felt that Laura suffered as a result of Crocker-Harris's reticence: "To have spent so many years giving herself to all the requirements of that position [as a teacher's wife] and then to have it taken away so abruptly must feel like a terrible betrayal. This is a woman in need of tenderness, love and affection . . . she's not getting those things from her husband and hasn't for a long time. She's also being spurned by her lover. She's very vulnerable." BEN SILVERSTONE felt that the young boy Taplow cared for both Crocker-Harrises, as his own parents were divorced; they were surrogate parents for him. Principal photography commenced in the early summer of 1993 in Sherborne, Dorset at the historic public school, and wrapped three months later.

Reviews were mixed: Geoff Brown of the London *Times* was surprised that "the directors of *Alien* and *Stormy Monday* would aspire to such pedigree British fare." Although they produced a worthy film, it seemed to be little else other than "an exercise in widening one's portfolio, supplying the market with genteel fodder. You rarely feel they were motivated by fresh thoughts about the material." Geoffrey Macnab of *Sight and Sound* agreed, criticizing screenwriter Harwood for failing "to communicate what makes *The Browning Version* relevant to 1994, or to chart any of the social and political changes since it was first performed in 1948." He wondered why the film had been made in the first place, "if neither director, scriptwriter nor star had anything new to add to the innumerable *Browning Versions* that have gone before it" (even though there had only been one previous film version of the play). Geoff Andrew of *Time Out* believed the film's principal focus of interest lay in the characterizations, especially Finney's; his "quiet but overwhelmingly moving performance . . . lends the film an emotional truth its heritage trimmings hardly deserve."

Responding to the critics' comments, Figgis gave an interview to the London *Independent*, in which he accused them of misunderstanding his purposes: "My interest was less in the school, the boy and his teacher than on the failure of a marriage. It was not my intention to make him a cold-hearted teacher . . . He is simply out of time and misunderstood . . . So I put the relationship into the foreground. I don't care about the original in terms of reverence. I don't think what we did was out of character with the original. The boy's character also benefited from this change of emphasis." The film experienced problems with distribution in the United States, so much so that it made only $400,000 in the first year of its release.

From the film's beginning, we realize that we are back in the world of *THE DUELLISTS*, one dominated by tradition and eccentric codes of behavior. Anyone caught breaking the rules is put in "Cromwell's" (the school's euphemism for being punished); boys should not speak to the teachers once the bell has rung signaling the beginning of a lesson; the end-of-semester celebrations are marked by the annual cricket match between the first team and the Old Boys; the entire school meets for prize-giving; and the boys themselves are encouraged not to show their emotions, as this would be a sign of weakness on their part. Crocker-Harris is a living symbol of the school's ethos; nicknamed "the Hitler of the Lower Fifth," his "end-of-term treat" consists of having his students read the *Agamemnon* by Aeschylus out loud in Latin, even though none of them have the faintest clue what is going on. The fact that Greek and Latin continue to be taught in private schools is testament to the power of tradition. Frank Hunter (MATTHEW MODINE) might marvel at one point that, by walking around the school, "you feel the history, the tradition," but the film suggests that this is something potentially destructive, rather than beneficial, to the students' education.

The film uses visual devices to reemphasize this point. On several occasions Laura and Frank are shown riding their bicycles along winding country roads, with the green English fields in the background. This movement-image contrasts with the interior shots of the school, where staff walk sedately and senior students scold their juniors for running down the corridors. Crocker-Harris is frequently photographed from the inside, looking through a barred window at the fields outside: a classic prison-image characteristic of HERITAGE FILMS of the 1980s and 1990s.

In such a world, it is hardly surprising that boys and teachers alike grow up emotionally stunted. The boys themselves never experience a true CHILDHOOD, being bound to observe certain rules and conventions which so inhibit them that they are cruel to one another; for example, the older boy Trubshaw's (Oliver Milburn's) arbitrary bullying of Taplow in the showers (where he calls Taplow's mother a whore). Nor are the teachers of much help: Dr. Rafferty announces brusquely to the boy Buller (Walter Mickleth- wait) that Buller's parents will not be coming to the school for prize-giving and that Buller himself should take the train home. When Buller's face screws up with tears, Rafferty asks him the pointless question "Are you all right?" and pauses, until the boy recovers his sang-froid and replies "Yes, sir." In this kind of environment, manliness is achieved by suppressing one's emotions. Nor can the boys expect much sympathy from the headmaster Dr. Frobisher, who brusquely announces during the end-of-semester celebrations that he does not believe in "stuffing the boys" either with food or pastoral care.

The prime example of how the school's atmosphere can affect an individual can be found in Crocker-Harris himself, a once brilliant classical scholar who has learned to keep his emotions under wraps at all times. Even when the headmaster tells him that he will not receive a pension from the school on his retirement, Crocker-Harris's characteristic reaction is to nod his head and accept the decision, even if it will cause him considerable financial strain. When the idealistic teacher Tom Gilbert (JULIAN SANDS) asks him about his future career, Crocker-Harris responds by repeating the phrase—"My future career?"—and taking a long pause before finishing the discussion with the words, "Thank you." Even when he learns from Frank of his wife's infidelity, Crocker-Harris's mask of civility never drops; he admits that Laura and he "were incompatible from the moment we met" and thereby concludes that perhaps her adultery was inevitable.

In this film we are back in familiar Scott territory. The role of the emotions in determining human behavior has also been analyzed in *BLADE RUNNER*, as the REPLICANT Batty (RUTGER HAUER) turns out to be more human than Deckard even though he has been manufactured by Tyrell (JOE TURKEL). In the futuristic world of LOS ANGELES, emotions are not particularly significant—especially for beings with a limited four-year life span. Similarly, in *The Browning Version* human emotions are equally unimportant; what matters more is to maintain the school's finances and thereby ensure that long-established traditions survive. In a significant sequence, the headmaster is shown brushing aside a parent's complaints about the quality of the food as he seeks to cultivate the friendship of a rich Nigerian prince (Jotham Annan) in the hope of securing a substantial financial gift.

The Browning Version also parallels *Blade Runner* in its view of language, which is perceived not as a means of communication but as a way of filling the empty void. This is especially evident during the end-of-semester cricket match, where everyone congratulates the star all-rounder David Fletcher (David Lever) on his performance, whether they are interested in the game or not. While the school choir is shown performing a classical piece in the chapel, not one of the assembled company actually listens to them. The headmaster continues his social ritual of talking to affluent parents; two prominent old boys Newton and Trimmer (Stephen Mitchelson, David Pullan) offer financial assistance to Crocker-Harris; and the teachers gossip amongst themselves. It seems that silence is discouraged on the basis that it might prompt the characters to reflect on their personal inadequacies.

Figgis emphasizes this point through repeated close-ups of Laura's face, staring expressionlessly into the distance while everyone else continues to speak. She understands how life in the school has transformed her into an emotional cripple and led to the destruction of her marriage. The point is reemphasized in the film's climactic scene, when Fletcher delivers his farewell speech to the boys. Although highly adept at cricket, he can barely communicate except in a series of meaningless clichés.

However, unlike *Blade Runner*, *The Browning Version* offers some hope for the future in Crocker-Harris's climactic speech. Having spent his entire teaching career cultivating a mask of emotional indifference, he takes the opportunity to look back on his life. He moves down from the podium into the audience and apologizes to the boys for his failure to give them sympathy, encouragement or humanity. This is why everyone called him "the Hitler of the Lower Fifth." He admits that he had ideals when he first came to the school eighteen years before, but that he has now lost them; for this he begs the students' forgiveness. As he walks through the auditorium, the camera tracks him in medium close-up: here is a man desperately trying to acknowledge his inadequacies in public, perhaps for the first time. When he finishes, the audience applauds—hesitantly at first, but gradually gaining in enthusiasm as they realize exactly what he has done. The film ends with Crocker-Harris removing his academic gown as he watches Laura driving away in a minivan; symbolically this represents him throwing off the shackles of his previous life and looking forward to the future, even if it might seem uncertain.

The Browning Version returns once again to the question of LOVE VS. DUTY that runs through so many of Scott's films. In Crocker-Harris's case, the conflict simply does not arise; he has consciously suppressed any emotions and dedicated himself to the duty of teaching the Classics. Towards the end of the film he is shown standing outside the school with a stone statue in the background, an image that well expresses his state of mind. However, there are at least occasions upon which Crocker-Harris hints at the imaginative possibilities lurking beneath the surface. At one point he is shown reading the *Agamemnon* out loud to his class; his voice wraps itself round the Latin consonants, and, just for once, we see just how dramatic Aeschylus can be if performed by an enthusiast. The sequence is punctured by a bathetic climax, as the bell rings to signal the end of the lesson, Crocker-Harris falls silent and the students nervously offer their good wishes, consisting mostly of the two words "Bye, sir." Even in this restricted environment, where students and staff alike are restricted from expressing their feelings except in monosyllables, Crocker-Harris retains his love of literature. It is one of the tragedies of this film that he cannot communicate it to his students; the only way he can deal with this is to suppress his emotions and concentrate on his duties. Only when he delivers his retirement speech does Crocker-Harris have sufficient confidence to show his true personality—one which totally contradicts his reputation as "the Hitler of the Lower Fifth." One of the other nicknames he is given is that of "the Crock"—which either can refer to a crocodile or describe someone who has been injured (as in, he/she has been "crocked") in British English. This is precisely what has happened to Crocker-Harris; eighteen years in a public school has transformed him into an emotional cripple, obsessed with duty and incapable of love.

This *Browning Version* may have its anachronisms (some of the idioms—"cut along," meaning "off you go"—have long passed out of current British English usage), but it once again shows off Rattigan's ability to create dramas of narrowly reclaimed opportunity. His protagonists do not achieve much, but what they do achieve is worth keeping—for example, self-respect.

References
Geoff Andrew, "The Browning Version," *Time Out*, 2 November 1994, 68; Geoff Brown, "Rather a Browned-off Version," *The Times* (London), 27 October 1994, 37; Mike Figgis, interviewed by David Benedict, *The Independent*, 3 November 1994, 26; Mike Figgis, quoted in Anwar Brett, "Back to School," *What's on in London*, 26 October 1994, 31; Geoffrey Macnab, "The Browning Version," *Sight and Sound*, November 1994, 42; *Production Information: The Browning Version* (Los Angeles: Paramount Pictures, 1994), 4–5; "Profiles—Mike Figgis," *Empire*, November 1994, 56–57.

Bibliography
Brian Case, "Grave Browning," *Time Out*, 2 November 1994, 67.

BRUCKHEIMER, JERRY (1945–)
Born Jerome Leonard Bruckheimer in Detroit, Bruckheimer has enjoyed a long and successful career as a producer in films and television. His numerous successes include *TOP GUN* (1986), *Con Air* (1997), *Armageddon* (1998), and *Pearl Harbor* (2001).

Bruckheimer bought Mark Bowden's book *Black Hawk Down* for the film of the same name as a follow-up to *Pearl Harbor* (2001). He brought in Scott to direct, on the basis of his track record in war films, notably *G.I. JANE*. He had worked with Scott thirty years previously, when the two of them had collaborated on a tire commercial.

Bruckheimer had a close hands-on involvement with the making of the film. He insisted in an interview that the actors had to prepare meticulously for their roles by spending some time in US Army training camps: "[I]t was really important for the actors to actually become part of the military, even for a short time, if they were going to portray soldiers. We wanted actors to have respect for the military and understand the physical challenges that they go through. If you talk to any soldier who has been through a battle or a war, they'll tell you that the only thing that saved their lives was either the

man next to them, or their training." Bruckheimer also had to deal with the bureaucratic problems arising from the decision to film in Morocco. In the production notes he recalled that "even though we have a great relationship with the government, this was a much bigger operation than anything we had attempted before . . . We were talking about actual troop deployment." Eventually the problems were overcome, and Bruckheimer subsequently oversaw much of the filming: "it was an awesome sight to see . . . This isn't a movie where we're using a lot of computer-generated imagery. It's the real deal, and I've never seen anything quite like it. They [the crew and the pilots] did an amazing job."

James Clarke remarks that the film, when it opened, was considered by many to be "nothing less than a piece of American propaganda, the second such produced by Bruckheimer in 2001 [after *Pearl Harbor*]."

References
Jerry Bruckheimer, quoted in A. C. Parfitt, *Orlando Bloom: The Biography* (London: John Blake Publishing Ltd., 2004), 50; James Clarke, *Ridley Scott* (London: Virgin Books, 2002), 210, 219; "Production Notes: *Black Hawk Down*," in Ken Nolan, *Black Hawk Down: The Shooting Script* (New York: Newmarket Press, 2002), 172–73.

BRUNO, DYLAN (1972–)
Born in Milford, Connecticut, Bruno made his debut on the NBC series *High Sierra Search and Rescue* (1995) while working as a model for Calvin Klein. He made his film debut in *Naked Ambition* (1997).

Bruno has played agent Colby Granger in seventy-three episodes of *NUMB3RS* since 2005. A reliable presence within the FBI team, he had the chance to lead an investigation in "One Hour" (Series 3, Episode 17). A veteran of the war in Afghanistan, Granger brings some of his army training to the process of trying to solve crime in the series. His behavior seems impeccable, which made the revelation (at the end of Series 3) that he had apparently been spying for the Chinese seem all the more shocking. The occasion caused such consternation amongst fans of the series that they opened up a website, *Save Colby!*—dedicated to the character—which continues to this day, even if the character still remains in the series.

References
Save Colby! http://community.livejournal.com/savecolby (accessed 22 February 2009).

BUDDY MOVIES
In *SOMEONE TO WATCH OVER ME* and *BLACK RAIN*, Scott uses the convention of the buddy film to suggest the strength of male bonding and thereby reiterates the fact that there is something clearly definable as "masculine" behavior.

A buddy film is a film in which the central characters are two friends who appear together throughout the film. The buddy cop film is a popular sub-genre of the buddy film; this is especially evident in *Black Rain*, with the central characters Nick Conklin (MICHAEL DOUGLAS) and his sidekick Charlie Vincent (ANDY GARCIA). When Charlie meets a bloody end, Nick forms another bond with the Japanese police officer Masahiro (KEN TAKAKURA). As with other buddy cop films, *Black Rain* analyzes the friendship that exists (and develops) between the police officers. In a reassertion of MASCULINITY, Scott stresses the importance of loyalty towards one's buddy when logic (or outside forces) would demand otherwise. The same also applies in the reality series *AMERICAN FIGHTER PILOT*, where group loyalty ensures that the pilots remain a coherent fighting unit both in war and peacetime. *BLACK HAWK DOWN* elevates the notion of male bonding into a creed that determines the soldiers' lives. Hoot (ERIC BANA) sums up the Rangers' outlook succinctly in a short speech towards the end: "Why do you do it man? [fight in battle] Why? You some kind of war junkie? I won't say a god damned word. Why? Because they [outsiders] won't understand. They won't understand why we do it. They won't understand, it's about the men next to you . . . and that's it . . . that's all it is." In *AMERICAN GANGSTER—EXTENDED VERSION* Scott includes a new ending which shows the police officer Richie Roberts (RUSSELL CROWE) and the ex-drug dealer Frank Lucas (DENZEL WASHINGTON) walking down the streets of Harlem together. Once deadly enemies, they now try to help one another out. The same also applies to the two brothers, Don and Charlie Eppes (ROB MORROW, DAVID KRUMHOLTZ) in *NUMB3RS*; although they come from vastly different backgrounds, they always look out for one another.

If that sense of camaraderie is lost, then individual men often do not know how to act; this is the case with Melot (Henry Cavill) in *TRISTAN + ISOLDE*, who loses his two friends Simon (Leo Gregory) and Tristan (JAMES FRANCO) in battle, and who subsequently turns against his king in the hope of obtaining power. Needless to say, Melot is punished for his action, as Wicktred (MARK STRONG) stabs him to death.

The validity of male bonding is subject to intense scrutiny in *CLAY PIGEONS*. Earl (Gregory Sporleder) commits suicide in front of his best friend Clay (JOAQUIN PHOENIX), despite proclaiming that Clay is his best friend. The explanation, according to MATT HEALY's script, is simple: Clay has been sleeping with Earl's wife Amanda (GEORGINA CATES), and in Earl's view Clay has to pay for this: "I'm not saying with your life. But you got to do some time . . . I got it all figured out, Clay." Clay strikes up another friendship with Lester Long (VINCE VAUGHN), but finds himself unable to shake the other man off, even though

Long happens to be a serial killer. The friendship only ends when Long has no further use for him: Long hitches a lift with a man in a pickup truck carrying horses, bidding Clay a cheery farewell with the observation that perhaps "we'll do better next time." But perhaps there will be no "next time": the truck driver is actually Sheriff Mooney (SCOTT WILSON) in disguise, preparing to arrest Long for murder. The fragility of male bonding is also explored in *RKO 281*, where Orson Welles (LIEV SCHREIBER) cultivates a close friendship with screenwriter Herman Mankiewicz (JOHN MALKOVICH), but willfully omits his name from the finished script of *Citizen Kane*. The two of them are apparently reconciled as Welles tells a sentimental tale of his stormy relationship with his father; but screenwriter JOHN LOGAN makes us aware this is nothing more than a ploy designed to appeal to Mankiewicz's better nature: "his [Welles's] expression is one of 'Gotcha!'—even as his cheeks are still wet with tears." Welles has no close friends; everyone can be manipulated to serve his own interests. The same fate awaits the three college buddies in *THE COMPANY*—Jack (CHRIS O'DONNELL), Leo (ALESSANDRO NIVOLA), and Yevgeny (RORY COCHRANE). Their friendship is nothing more than an illusion: Yevgeny's education has been funded by the Soviet government so that he can successfully pass as an American during his career as a spy; Leo turns out to be a Soviet mole (codenamed Sasha) within the CIA; while Jack ultimately denounces Leo as a traitor. Similarly in *THE ASSASSINATION OF JESSE JAMES BY THE COWARD ROBERT FORD*, every member of the James gang suspects one another of treachery—and with good reason, as Robert Ford (CASEY AFFLECK) connives with his brother Charley (SAM ROCKWELL) to bring Jesse James (BRAD PITT) to justice and thereby claim a substantial reward. In *BODY OF LIES*, the whole convention of the buddy movie is turned on its head: Ed Hoffman (RUSSELL CROWE) uses the term simply to make his subordinate Roger Ferris (LEONARDO DICAPRIO) believe that the two of them are working for the CIA as a team. In truth, Hoffman pursues his own agenda and manipulates Ferris to carry it out.

The male bonding convention is given a feminist slant in *THELMA & LOUISE*. While the primary relationship in the film is between two women (SUSAN SARANDON, GEENA DAVIS), Scott suggests that their relationship is similar to that of the two cops in *Black Rain* in the sense that they empathize with one another. Louise, for instance, has always appreciated that Thelma was "a little crazy." Their relationship derives from friendship and trust, in contrast to the relationships between the two sexes, which are perpetually subject to misunderstanding and misinterpretation. The most extreme example of this occurs in the truck scene where the trucker (MARCO ST. JOHN) makes lewd gestures to the two women, gestures about which they later question him

("What's that supposed to mean, exactly?"). Such comments make no sense to him; in his view two women driving along on an open road must always be available. When he stops the truck, he takes off his wedding ring and grabs a couple of condoms, asking them as he does so whether they are "about ready to get serious." The humor of this scene derives from what he and the women understand by what it means to "get serious." More importantly, such moments underline the importance of same-sex relationships—as embodied in the buddy film—as a way of coping with the world.

WHERE THE MONEY IS depicts a similar relationship—only this time it involves Carol MacKay, a younger woman (LINDA FIORENTINO), and Henry Manning, an older man (PAUL NEWMAN), who describes himself as old enough to be her great-great-great-grandfather. There is nothing sexual here; rather, the two of them are bound by a shared desire to experience the world firsthand, to enjoy the thrill of robbing a security firm or a jeweler's shop. Like Thelma and Louise, they empathize with one another, and it is this empathy that keeps them together.

References

Matt Healy, *In Too Deep* (Draft Script dated 7 January 1997) (Beverly Hills, CA: Scott Free, 1997); John Logan, "Draft Script for *RKO 281*" (dated May 1, 1997), http://sfy.ru/sfy.html?script=rko218 (accessed 16 November 2008), 37; Ken Nolan, *Black Hawk Down: The Shooting Script* (New York: Newmarket Press, 2002), 126.

BURROUGHS, WILLIAM S. (1914–1997)

Author of the original text *BLADE RUNNER*, from which Scott borrowed the title for his film. *Blade Runner—A Movie* was published as a screenplay treatment wherein Burroughs explored the coming apocalyptic medical-care crisis, and the birth of a tenacious and inventive underground holistic medicine.

Burroughs himself suggested that the book was "about America. What America was and what America could be, and how those who try to stifle the American dream are defeated . . . about a city we all know and love, a city which has come to represent all cities. In the year 2014 New York, world center for underground medicine, is the most glamorous, the most dangerous, the most exotic, vital, far-out city the world has ever seen . . . this film is about a second chance for Billy the blade runner, and for all humanity." The framework remains much the same in Scott's film, even though it takes place in LOS ANGELES rather than NEW YORK. However the Burroughs text contains a racist element that does not exist in the film as he refers to "the niggers and the spics" kept on Medicare and thereby retaining sufficient strength to mug or cause harm to hapless middle-income white people.

Reference

William S. Burroughs, *Blade Runner (A Movie)* (Berkeley: Blue Wind Press, 1979), 3–5.

CAGE, NICOLAS (1964–)

Born Nicolas Coppola, the son of an academic. His uncle is Francis Coppola, director of the *Godfather* trilogy; his aunt is actress Talia Shire and his grandfather was composer Carmine Coppola. His mother, Joy Vogelsang, was a dancer.

Wanting to distance himself from the Coppola family and the baggage that brought with it to Hollywood, he changed his name to Cage, after a comic book hero. Cage established the reputation of being a versatile actor, with performances ranging from his Oscar-winning role in MIKE FIGGIS's *Leaving Las Vegas* (1995) to the name part in *Captain Corelli's Mandolin* (2001). In *MATCHSTICK MEN* he plays Roy Waller, a part reminiscent of his earlier role in *Honeymoon in Vegas*. Producer Steve Starkey described the part thus in a preproduction interview: "He has a whole catalogue of nervous tics. It takes an actor with a certain sensibility to do more with these compulsive mannerisms than just play them for laughs. Nicolas Cage has the comic instinct for that, but it's the vulnerability he brings to the character that makes you really feel for him, and I believe that's critical to the role." However, the part as written was not necessarily comic, but as Cage remarked, "we tried to present them in such a way that audiences could see the humor in it [by offering] . . . some very entertaining moments without mocking people who actually have these kinds of problems."

NICK AND TED GRIFFIN's script gives Cage plenty of opportunity to display his versatility. One sequence begins with Roy staring out of the window, coffee cup in hand, at the swimming pool outside. Suddenly this moment of serenity is violated as he espies two leaves floating on the water. He removes them with a long pole, rinses out his coffee mug, cleans the kitchen countertop, runs the faucet, and looks for his vial of pills. However, he accidentally knocks the vial into the sink and sends the pills scattering down the garbage disposal. Unable to recover any of them, he walks up and down the living room—only to discover that he has dirtied the rug. This prompts another flurry of activity, as he cleans the living room, bathroom, and all the exterior windows. The entire sequence lasts about two to three minutes, and is shot at speed, rather like a Keystone Cops film, emphasizing the comic aspects of Roy's behavior.

Cage understands the importance of the single gesture as a way of signaling Roy's character development. When he believes that Angela (ALISON LOHMAN) has shot Frechette (BRUCE McGILL), he tells her, "Sit tight, honey." He maintains eye contact with Angela—something he never could have contemplated earlier on. Angela returns unexpectedly into his life at the end of the film, as she and her boyfriend visit the carpet shop where Roy now works. Now it is she who cannot look at him; by contrast, Roy is a man at ease who talks to people directly without embarrassment.

References

Nick and Ted Griffin, "*Matchstick Men*: Shooting Draft" (14 October 2002), www.imsdb.com/scripts/Matchstick-Men.html (accessed 4 January 2009); *Production Information: Matchstick Men* (Los Angeles: Warner Bros. Pictures, 2003), 6–7.

Bibliography

Olivier de Bruyn, "Pourquoi on Sait Pas Qui T'Es?" *Premiere* (French ed.) 319 (September 2003): 94–97; Chris Hewitt, "Play: Ridley Scott: Q&A," *Empire* 177 (March 2004): 138; Ian Markham-Smith and Liz Hodgson, *Nicolas Cage, The Unauthorised Biography* (London: Blake Publishing Ltd., 2001); Rebecca Murray, "Nicolas Cage Plays a Con Artist in '*Matchstick Men*,'" *About.com* (September 2003), http://movies.about.com/cs/matchstickmen/a/matchnicolas.htm (accessed 7 August 2008).

CALLEY, JOHN (c. 1930–)

Producer and former president of Sony Pictures Entertainment (1996–2003). His credits include *Ice Station Zebra* (1969), and *Castle Keep* (1969) and more recently *Closer* (2004) and *The DaVinci Code* (2006). He had vetoed an early draft of *WHITE SQUALL* before the project was handed on to Ridley Scott. In 2006 Calley initiated the project to film *THE COMPANY* by contacting KEN NOLAN, who later introduced him to Scott. The two of them—Calley and Scott—acted as co-executive producers of the series.

CANUEL, ERIK (1964–)

Canuel directed three episodes of THE HUNGER: TELEVISION SERIES, including "Night Bloomer" (Series 2 episode 12). Subsequent work in television includes Big Wolf on Campus (1999–2002) and The Dead Zone (2007).

CAPSHAW, KATE (1953–)

Born Kathleen Sue Nail in Fort Worth, Texas. Capshaw made her debut in the daytime soap opera The Edge of Night (1981), and beat 120 actresses to secure the part of Wilhelmina ("Willie") Scott in Indiana Jones and the Temple of Doom (1984).

Cast as Joyce in BLACK RAIN, Capshaw had for the first time to play a tough-girl role, something she had hitherto not experienced in films. She also had to undergo a "radical appearance change," spending eight hours in a New York salon having her naturally brunette hair dyed seriously blond: "Blond women are a hot commodity in Japan . . . The concept for Kate in Black Rain is golden goddess. Virtually everything she appears in is gold." However, she fulfills a largely peripheral role in the film as an itinerant American living in Osaka who has acquired the language but still cannot appreciate the nuances of the local culture. She works at a local bar providing "comfort" for tired businesspeople. Her relationship with Nick Conklin (MICHAEL DOUGLAS) is a stormy one; she chides him for his lack of cultural sensitivity and provides him with minimal assistance in his search for the yakuza leader Sato (YUSAKU MATSUDA). However, CRAIG BOLOTIN and Warren Lewis's script has her undergoing a miraculous change of heart; by the film's end she is prepared to conduct a tentative love affair with Nick even though she is well aware it will not last.

As with other actresses (notably JOANNA CASSIDY in BLADE RUNNER), Scott does not seem particularly interested in Capshaw. Consequently, she gives a colorless performance, particularly when compared to the male protagonists. In the original script Joyce had a more substantial role, in which she is taken hostage by Kobo/Sato and held at gunpoint in exchange for Sato's freedom, but this sequence was taken out of the final version.

References

Kate Capshaw, interviewed in "Black Rain: The Script, The Cast," Special Feature included in the Special Collector's Edition DVD release of Black Rain (d. Laurent Bouzereau) (Los Angeles: Paramount Pictures, 2006); Jerry Lazar, "Going for the Gold," Premiere 2, no.11 (July 1989): 64.

CAPTIVE AUDIENCE PRODUCTIONS

This company was responsible for the visual effects in HANNIBAL, especially the silicone makeup for Mason Verger (GARY OLDMAN). Wes Wofford, key makeup artist, observed in an interview that "The whole film was reality-based. . . . And there was the technical aspect of Verger, trying to do the disfigured thing so Gary Oldman could come through it and not be covered up too much. He still has to look deformed. When you cut the face off, and subtract it, that's always a challenge." The company was also responsible for the animatronic model of RAY LIOTTA, used during the climactic scene when the character is seen eating his own brains.

References

Douglas Eby, "Captive Audience: Realizing the Gruesome Makeup Efx," Cinefantastique 32, No.6 (February 2001): 14.

CARHART, TIMOTHY (1953–)

Born in Washington, DC, Carhart made his film debut with small roles in Ghostbusters (1984), Witness (1985), and Working Girl (1988).

Cast as the drunken Harlan in THELMA & LOUISE, Carhart portrays a character who initially seems attractive and charming, but who expects a payoff at the end of the evening as he tries to rape Thelma (GEENA DAVIS). When she refuses, he reacts with disbelief; this is not how women should behave in a patriarchal world. He ignores her pleas to stop, so Louise (SUSAN SARANDON) shoots him; what she witnesses is very close to her own experiences of rape in Texas. The role of Harlan is a thankless one, but is nonetheless important to the film as an example of the kind of male behavior that the two women repudiate as they forge new identities for themselves.

CARNAHAN, JOE (1969–)

Graduated from Fairfield High School, California in 1987. Carnahan made his directorial debut with a low-budget thriller Blood, Guts, Bullets and Octane (1998). THE HIRE: "TICKER" was his major debut as a writer-director. In the "Director's Commentary" to the film, he recalled how he tried to keep the story fragmented in order to maintain the audience's interest. Although supposed to take place in an unspecified African country, the film was actually shot in northern California. He also likened the plot of the film to Hitchcock's North by Northwest (1959).

References

Joe Carnahan, Director's Commentary to the DVD release of The Hire: Ticker (Los Angeles, BMW of North America, 2003).

CARRADINE, KEITH (1949–)

Keith Carradine, the son of John Carradine and Sonia Sorel, got the break that launched his career while providing musical accompaniment for his late brother David during an audition for the Broadway musical Hair. The author and stars found Carradine to be more suited for the part, and he spent nearly a year on Broadway, eventually moving into the lead role of Claude (1969). He then landed the role of a young gunslinger in *A Gunfight* (1970) with Kirk Douglas and Johnny Cash, which was followed by Robert Altman's *McCabe and Mrs. Miller* (1971) with Warren Beatty, and the Altman classics *Thieves Like Us* (1974) and *Nashville* (1975).

Carradine was Ridley Scott's second choice for the role of Feraud in *THE DUELLISTS*, after STACY KEACH. At the time of filming, he was enjoying such success with the song "I'm Easy" (which resulted in a US tour) that it was uncertain until the last moment whether he could accept the part. Nonetheless, Carradine eventually played the role—and proved to be extremely competent. Scott recalled that the actor was especially good at horseback riding and also encouraged the director's two children—who played small parts in the film—to act naturally in front of the camera.

Carradine turns in a powerful performance as the aristocratic Feraud that contrasts starkly with the bullish HARVEY KEITEL as D'Hubert. Carradine is especially good later on in the film, when he realizes the futility of the duel and requests in vain to finish it with an apology rather than a fight to the death. His face twitches in close-up as he realizes that, in spite of the fact that he enjoys a prosperous life with an attractive spouse (CRISTINA RAINES) and children, he must satisfy the code of HONOR by continuing the combat. No one can explain why, but he is duty bound to do so. He stalks out of the right hand side of the frame, leaving D'Hubert's second (Arthur Dignam) staring after him in disbelief. The reviewer in *Variety* described Carradine's Feraud as "determined and a bit troubled but also caught up in this strange need of one to prove honor [D'Hubert] and the other [Feraud] slaking a twisted nature"—the "twisted nature" being one that feels obliged to satisfy the code of honor even though it seems perfectly ludicrous to do so. Following his role in this film, Carradine was dubbed "the thinking person's sex symbol."

References

"The Duellists," *Variety* (June 1977), www.variety.com/review/VE1117790602.html?categoryid=31&cs=1&p=0 (accessed 13 November 2007); Douglas Martin, "Can Keith Carradine Lasso the Essence of Will Rogers?" *New York Times*, 28 April 1991, B4; Ridley Scott, "Director's Commentary" to the 2000 release of *The Duellists* by Paramount DVD in the "Special Collector's Edition" (London: Paramount Home Entertainment, 2000).

CARROLL, GORDON (1928–2005)

Born Charles Gordon Carroll III; studied at Princeton University and worked in advertising before becoming a producer. His credits included Cool Hand Luke (1967) and *PAT GARRETT AND BILLY THE KID* (1973).

Carroll formed Brandywine Productions in association with DAVID GILER and WALTER HILL. The three of them made a list of candidates to direct *ALIEN* and came up with Scott as an idea. Scott had failed to raise capital for his next project *TRISTAN AND ISEULT*, so he agreed to direct the film. Carroll was closely involved in all aspects of the film. He also produced other films in the *Alien* series, as well as *ALIEN VS. PREDATOR*.

Bibliography

Gordon Carroll biography, www.twistytales.com/03_Gordon Carroll.pdf (accessed 1 March 2009).

CARS

Several Scott commercials celebrate certain brands of car, notably the NISSAN 300ZX TWIN TURBO. Iconic cars crop up in several Scott films. In *ADAM ADAMANT LIVES!* the eponymous hero drives a trademark Mini-Cooper (registration number AA 1000). There is the futuristic flying car that Harrison Ford uses in *BLADE RUNNER*, which hermetically seals him up from the DYSTOPIAN scene around him. Stephen Rowley suggests that the car distances him from the overcrowding, dirtiness, and crime that defines the film's nightmare world.

In *THELMA & LOUISE*, the 1966 Thunderbird the protagonists use is in itself a star of the film. Scott suggested in an interview with Paul M. Sammon that screenwriter CALLIE KHOURI "identified it as a car that's always represented a symbol of freedom, because the Thunderbird was one of the last great American cars . . . American automobiles used to have their own absolute singular identity that somehow reflected everything that was attractive about the United States." He revealed in the film's pressbook that he actually used five cars, one as the "principal" car, one as a backup, one as a camera car (in which sections were cut away to allow space for cameras and their operators, and two that were used as stunt vehicles. Marita Sturken observes that "the car . . . is the height of impracticability, a veritable road car meant to put its driver on display." Louise's (SUSAN SARANDON's) commitment to the car is evident—at one point she yells out to a few errant cows on the road, "Don't dent my car!" It is her one indulgence, and ultimately its conspicuousness is crucial to the story's end. The luxury cars of *BODY OF LIES*—including several SUVs and a Mercedes—fulfill a thematic purpose; although stylish in themselves, they are totally impractical for use in the teeming streets of the Jordanian capital Amman or in the desert separating Jordan from Syria.

AMERICAN GANGSTER uses iconic cars of the early 1970s, including a Lincoln Continental for the gangster Dominic Cattano (ARMAND ASSANTE) and a Shelby Mustang for the police officers Richie Roberts (RUSSELL

CROWE) and Javier Rivera (JOHN ORTIZ). In *WHERE THE MONEY IS*, the two central characters Henry Manning (PAUL NEWMAN) and Carol MacKay (LINDA FIORENTINO) make their escape from the pursuing police cars in a 1970s Mustang. This not only alludes to a similar chase sequence involving a Mustang in the 1968 film *Bullitt* but reminds us how much a classic car can become an expression of personal identity. The series *THE HIRE* was commissioned by BMW to advertise several of its luxury cars. The three episodes produced by Ridley and Tony Scott, "HOSTAGE," "TICKER," and "BEAT THE DEVIL," featured the BMW Z4 model.

References

Stephen Rowley, "False LA: *Blade Runner* and the Nightmare City," in *The Blade Runner Experience: The Legacy of a Science Fiction Classic*, ed. Will Brooker (London and New York: Wallflower Press, 2005), 204; *Pressbook: Thelma & Louise* (London: United International Pictures [UK], 1991), 7; Paul M. Sammon, *Ridley Scott Close-Up: The Making of His Movies* (New York: Thunder's Mouth Press, 1999), 108; Marita Sturken, *Thelma and Louise* (London: BFI Publishing, 2000), 27.

CARSON, JOHN (1927–)

Gravelly-voiced British actor, whose voice has often been compared to that of James Mason. Never a star, Carson has been involved in British films and television since 1952. In "THE LEAGUE OF UNCHARITABLE LADIES" he plays Randolph, a villain masquerading as a butler, who works at a ladies' club (The Gentlewoman's Charity League). Although apparently dedicated to peace and universal disarmament (the professed aim of the club), Randolph is actually employed by the Communists to eliminate as many British politicians as possible, and thereby undermine confidence in western democracy. Eventually he meets a sticky end as he is poisoned by Hope (Sheila Grant) while fighting a duel with Adam Adamant (GERALD HARPER).

Carson's Randolph is typical of the villains in the television series *ADAM ADAMANT LIVES!* most of whom were deliberately overplayed (in keeping with the light-hearted tone of the series). He acts in a camp manner, his mincing walk and fastidious gestures contrasting with the eponymous hero's gentlemanly gait. Randolph also has a speech impediment—being unable to pronounce the letter "r" properly—which also contrasts with Adam's exquisite vowels.

CARTWRIGHT, VERONICA (1949–)

Born in England, Cartwright spent much of her early career in US television series such as *Daniel Boone* (1964–66), as well as taking a leading role in Hitchcock's *The Birds* (1963).

Cast as Lambert in *ALIEN*, Cartwright had once been in the running for the role of Ripley (eventually played by SIGOURNEY WEAVER). She only learned she was being cast as a different character when she saw the name tag on the uniform that she was due to wear. Cartwright recalled in a 2004 interview that everything "on that *Alien* set, everything was connected. You walked down a hall and the first room you hit was the engine room, and out of that was a corridor that went to the place where we are, and from there to the hospital, and so on. Every single room was connected, you had to go through everything to get to it. It was very claustrophobic, because once you were in there, where could you go?" In such an atmosphere, it is not surprising that Lambert should become more and more hysterical as the film unfolds. We are not sure how she dies in the end; what we do know, however, is that she freezes to the spot, unable to move, as the alien moves towards her. This contrasts with the reaction of Ripley, who adopts a more proactive approach to resisting the alien.

References

John Millar, "Tough Little Son-of-a-Bitch," *Film Review Special* 53 (August 2004): 32; "The Voice of Reason," *Starlog* 359 (October 2007): 34.

CASSIDY, JOANNA (1945–)

Born Joanna Virginia Caskey in New Jersey, Cassidy began her career in television series such as *Mission: Impossible* and *Starsky and Hutch*.

BLADE RUNNER was her first major film role, as Zhora. According to PAUL M. SAMMON she felt that the character "was an independent—she didn't belong to anybody. Certainly not like Pris (DARYL HANNAH) was with Roy (RUTGER HAUER) . . . I really sympathized with them, those REPLICANTS." The role calls for Cassidy to display strength and dexterity as she deals with a huge python (which is supposed to be artificial). However, there is a strong suspicion that Scott presents her as an object of the male gaze, as she poses in the nude and subsequently takes a shower. This creates an interesting ambiguity in the film—although we are asked to sympathize with her as she runs through the streets in a futile attempt to escape from Deckard (HARRISON FORD), we also feel that she, running through the incessant rain in a skimpy bikini and clear plastic mackintosh, is being fetishized. This prompts us to ask whether Scott himself has any concern for the replicants or whether he, like Deckard at the beginning of the film, treats them as second-class citizens.

Cassidy has a leading role in one of the episodes of the first series of *THE HUNGER*—"The Other Woman." She plays an ambitious fashion designer who has a very public love affair with her boss (Nicholas Campbell). As someone determined to get what she wants both professionally and personally, she believes there should be "no holding back."

Eventually her ambition comes to nothing, as she and her boss are caught *in flagrante delicto* by the boss' wife, who shoots them both dead. However the fashion designer has the last laugh as the two of them are reunited "together in death." Cassidy does not have much to do other than to perform the obligatory sex scene and wear padded shoulders to signify her independent nature.

Reference

Paul M. Sammon, *Future Noir: The Making of Blade Runner*, 2nd ed. (London: Gollancz, 2007), 152.

CASSIDY, PATRICK (1956–)

Patrick Cassidy was born in Claremorris, County Mayo, Republic of Ireland. He is best known for works he has written for orchestra and choir based on Irish mythology. *The Children of Lir* remained at the top of the Irish classical charts for a full year. In addition to his concert work Cassidy has scored and collaborated on numerous films including *KING ARTHUR* (2004), *Che Guevara* (2005), and *Ashes and Snow* (2005). Cassidy also provided music for *HANNIBAL* and *KINGDOM OF HEAVEN*. The aria Cassidy wrote for *Hannibal*—'Vide Cor Meum'—was the only piece by a living composer on the Warner Classics 2006 compilation *The 40 Most Beautiful Arias*.

CATES, GEORGINA (1975–)

Born Clare Woodgate in London. Cates made her debut in British television series such as *2 Point 4 Children* (1992–1994) under her real name. She changed her name when she graduated to the big screen in films such as *An Awfully Big Adventure* (1994), *Stiff Upper Lips* (1996), and *Big City Blues* (1998).

Cates married Hollywood actor Skeet Ulrich and came to work in America. Although British-born, she apparently put her heart and soul into the auditions. Director DAVID DOBKIN recalls that "Georgina had such a European sensibility, which is what I love . . . And she just blew me away when I watched the casting tape back." Cates herself felt that Amanda "is someone who wants to get what she wants, and doesn't care how she gets it." However, "I thought she was, in some ways, a victim—the need she has to keep Clay is so strong, and I think that need makes her so completely obsessive to get what she wants that she becomes a victimizer." In another interview she relished the fact that she had the chance to "do practically everything you shouldn't do—as an actress and as a woman. I got to play The Guy: my character wants sex and that's all she cares about."

Cates makes the most of her limited appearances in the film. She comes across as an insatiable personality who is prepared to go to any lengths to keep Clay (JOAQUIN PHOENIX) for herself. In many ways she provides the focus

for the film's fundamentally misogynist tone: all women, Dobkin suggests, are either virgins or vamps. Cates falls into the second category.

References

Michael Atkinson, "Heavenly Cates," *Movieline*, August 1998, 16; Georgina Cates, David Dobkin, interviewed in "Production Notes: *Clay Pigeons*," included on the European DVD release of the film (Frankfurt: BY Internationale Medien und Film, 1998).

CHEADLE, DON (1964–)

Don Cheadle was born in Kansas City but moved throughout his childhood. He made his name at first in the television series *Fame* (1982). He was then cast in the John Irvin film *Hamburger Hill* (1987). He first became recognized in *Devil in a Blue Dress* (1995), which won him the Best Supporting Actor Award from the Los Angeles Film Critics.

Don Cheadle takes a leading role in *THE HIRE: "TICKER,"* where he plays a government agent trying to take a heart to an unnamed leader to prolong his life and thereby sustain democracy in his country.

CHESTNUT, MORRIS (1969–)

A tall, handsome, and versatile African-American actor, Morris Chestnut first came to be recognized by moviegoers starring as Ricky in *Boyz n the Hood* (1991). He later starred in the action flick *Under Siege 2: Dark Territory* (1995).

Cast as McCool in *G.I. JANE*, Chestnut gives a sympathetic performance as a person who understands the experience of discrimination. Thus he is one of the first to accept Jordan O'Neil (DEMI MOORE) as someone with the right to be treated on equal terms as the other male soldiers. DAVID TWOHY's script makes this clear: Jordan asks him "What about you, McCool? Any problem with the room assignment?" McCool (described in the script as "an imperturbable black lieutenant") simply ignores the question and quotes from the SEAL manuals: "It's not a job—it's an adventure." For him it doesn't matter whether Jordan is female or not; she is a soldier.

Reference

David Twohy, "*G.I. Jane*: First Draft" (6 August 1995) http:// sfy.ru/sfy.html?script=gi_jane (accessed 21 October 2008).

CHICK FLICKS

Genre associated with women, either as stars or directors. From its first big cycle of women's melodramas in the early 1980s, through the persistent stream of high-profile costume dramas and, in particular, the continuing triumph of new romantic comedy, female-orientated cycles have continued to flourish throughout the 1990s and into the twenty-first century (for example, *THELMA & LOUISE*). The widespread media phenomenon of the term "chick flick" is in itself evidence of the phenomenon. Furthermore, this trend has developed in conjunction with other female-oriented cultural forms such as CHICK LIT (the works of writers such as Jane Green, Freya North, and Helen Fielding) and chicks-television (*Ally McBeal, Sex and the City, Desperate Housewives*).

Examples of recent successful chick flicks include CURTIS HANSON's *IN HER SHOES*, produced by Ridley Scott, based on the novel by JENNIFER WEINER, is another good example of the genre. Roberta Garrett has discussed the birth of "POSTMODERN" chick flicks that move away from the domestic and maternal towards a consistent focus on the tension between traditional notions of femininity and female educational and career aspirations. Such films register the triumph of the liberal rather than the radical feminist vision of female empowerment. Although she does not discuss *In Her Shoes* directly, the film can be approached in this way.

Reference
Roberta Garrett, *Postmodern Chick Flicks: The Return of the Woman's Film* (Basingstoke and New York: Palgrave, 2007).

Bibliography
Jo Berry and Angie Errigo, *Chick Flicks: Movies Women Love* (London: Orion Books, 2004); Samantha Cook, *The Rough Guide to Chick Flicks* (London: Rough Guides Ltd., 2006); Brenda Cooper, "Chick Flicks as Feminist Texts: The Appropriation of the Male Gaze in *Thelma & Louise*," *Women's Studies in Communication* 23, no.3 (Fall 2000): 277–306.

CHICK LIT
A term used to denote genre fiction written for and marketed to young women, especially single, working women in their twenties and thirties. The genre's creation was spurred on, if not exactly created, by Sue Townsend's *Adrian Mole* diaries, originally published in Great Britain in the 1980s, which inspired Adele Lang's *Confessions of a Sociopathic Social Climber: The Katya Livingston Chronicles* in the mid-1990s. Later with the appearance of Helen Fielding's *Bridget Jones' Diary* and similar works; the genre continued to sell well in the 2000s, with chick lit titles topping bestseller lists and the creation of imprints devoted entirely to chick lit. JENNIFER WEINER's novel *In Her Shoes* is a good example of the genre; the book was later filmed by CURTIS HANSON and produced by Ridley Scott.

CHILDHOOD
Several Scott films deal with the subject of childhood. In *ALIEN*, the monstrous birth of the alien out of Kane's (JOHN HURT's) chest suggests that children can be somehow monstrous—especially if their parents are corrupt. By contrast, *LEGEND* shows how children can be extraordinarily resilient in the face of adversity: Jack (TOM CRUISE) manages to resist Darkness's (TIM CURRY's) attacks and emerge triumphant in the end. The same also applies to *ALL THE INVISIBLE CHILDREN*—"JONATHAN," where groups of children are shown getting on with their lives in the midst of devastation. Despite the lack of resources, they understand the significance of group identity, with each looking out for the other. *THE BROWNING VERSION* shows what happens when groups of children—especially boys—are placed in an unnatural, rule-bound environment where they have little chance to express themselves. They grow up inhibited, often incapable of expressing themselves except through violent means (e.g., bullying). Childhood can prove problematic even for the cleverest people; in *NUMB3RS* we are made well aware that Charlie Eppes (DAVID KRUMHOLTZ) had a difficult time, particularly during his teenage years when he attended the same classes as his elder brother Don (ROB MORROW), even though he was five years younger. Being a thirteen-year-old prodigy in college proved equally problematic for Charlie, as he had no time to develop emotionally. The same could apply to the teenage boy (TONY SCOTT) in Scott's early short film *BOY AND BICYCLE*—which perhaps helps to explain why he chooses to take a day off school and go riding instead around the streets near his home. He seems like a typical teenager of the early 1960s who seeks freedom from a traditional type of education (based on singing Christian hymns such as "Onward Christian Soldiers") yet remains subject to his parents' authority.

Those who try to be different from the herd such as Taplow (BEN SILVERSTONE) in *The Browning Version* are ostracized or dismissed as "sissies." The theme is continued in a different way in *MONKEY TROUBLE*, where Eva's (THORA BIRCH's) parents set an appalling behavioral example to their daughter. She only learns the true value of childhood once she establishes a life of her own by looking after the monkey. *IN HER SHOES* has the two central characters, Maggie and Ruth (CAMERON DIAZ, TONI COLLETTE), recalling the innocence of childhood when their mother was still alive; Maggie in particular still values the day her mother brought her a puppy (called Honey Bun) to look after. Although her father took it away from her (believing that neither his daughter nor their mother was capable of looking after it), Maggie never forgets the occasion and, in one sequence, tries to recreate the magic by borrowing a dog for herself and renaming it Honey Bun Two. *A GOOD YEAR* likewise represents childhood as a time of supreme happiness, as Young Max (FREDDIE HIGHMORE) enjoys his holidays in Uncle Henry's (ALBERT FINNEY's) château with no restrictions placed on him as to when to go to bed, or whether or not to drink alcohol.

CHRISTOPHER COLUMBUS

GB 1949 r/t 104 min col. *Production Company:* Gainsborough Pictures. *Producer:* A. Frank Bundy. *Director:* David MacDonald. *Writers:* Muriel Box, Sydney Box, and Cyril Roberts. *Director of Photography:* Stephen Dade. *Production Designer:* Maurice Carter. *Music:* Arthur Bliss. *Cast:* Fredric March (*Christopher Columbus*), Florence Eldridge (*Queen Isabella*), Linden Travers (*Beatriz de Paraza*), Francis L. Sullivan (*Francisco de Bobadilla*), Kathleen Ryan (*Beatriz*), Derek Bond (*Diego de Arana*), James Robertson Justice (*Martin Pinzon*).

This story focuses on Columbus's voyage, his struggles with the Royal Commission, the voyage, the discovery of San Salvador, the return to Spain, his journey to the country as Viceroy and his replacement as Viceroy by Bobadilla, the villain of the piece. The film ends with Columbus being forbidden to return to the New World and falling ill. On his deathbed he sees a vision of his companions on his voyage. They comfort him by foretelling that a mighty nation is destined to arise in the New World.

The film was conceived as a costume drama with "magnificent settings, rich draperies and intricate decoration. It brings you the glory of sunlight through stained glass, the arched perfection of a Renaissance ceiling, a myriad of gorgeous glowing colours. Here, in this great film, is all the grandeur and opulence of the court of Spain as only Technicolor can record it." The film was reviewed favorably even if it was not counted as one of March's best-known roles. *The Motion Picture Herald* described it as "most elaborately mounted," of particular interest to audiences, "even though few will find it completely satisfactory" on account of the fact that "almost two-thirds of the film [is] devoted to court scenes. An hour of running time passes before a ship is seen." Although there is no evidence to suggest that Ridley Scott saw this film, it is nonetheless based on the same plot—even though, as suggested in the *Motion Picture Herald* review, the focus here is more on the court scenes rather than discovering the New World (as in *1492: CONQUEST OF PARADISE*).

References

Pressbook, Christopher Columbus (London: The Rank Organization, 1949), 5; "The Product Digest," *Motion Picture Herald* 177, no.3 (15 October 1949): 49.

CHRISTOPHER COLUMBUS: THE DISCOVERY
(aka *CHRISTOPHER COLUMBUS*)

US 1992 r/t 121 min col. *Production Company:* Quinto Centenario. *Producers:* Alexander and Ilya Salkind. *Director:* John Glen. *Writers:* John Briley, Cary Bates, and Mario Puzo. *Director of Photography:* Alec Mills. *Production Designer:* Gil Parrondo. *Music:* Cliff Eidelman. *Cast:* Marlon Brando (*Grand Inquisitor Tomas de Torquemada*), Tom Selleck (*King Ferdinand*), Rachel Ward (*Queen Isabella*), Robert Davi (*Martin Alonso Pinzon*), Catherine Zeta-Jones (*Beatriz*), Oliver Cotton (*Harana*), Benicio del Toro (*King John of Portugal*), George Corraface (*Columbus*).

A rival film to *1492: CONQUEST OF PARADISE*, *Christopher Columbus: The Discovery* involved its producers Alexander and Ilya Salkind in a long legal battle. Originally they had engaged Scott to direct their film; but Scott left the production and joined producer ALAIN GOLDMAN on *1492*. As a result, Salkind unsuccessfully sued both Scott and Goldman in an attempt to stop the rival production.

The Salkinds' film went through endless troubles. George Pan Cosmatos was originally slated to direct; Timothy Dalton was due to play the title role, but left before the film's release. Marlon Brando wanted his name removed from the credits on account of the film's inaccurate portrayal of NATIVE PEOPLES. Local film workers in Malta, Spain and the Caribbean complained of non-payment. The film opened in September 1992 to largely negative reviews. *Time Out* called it "wretched in most respects," *The Guardian* called it "dead meat" and likened Brando's performance to "a giant beetle squirming painfully on a pin."

References

"Christopher Columbus—The Discovery," *The Guardian*, 10 September 1992, 28; "Christopher Columbus—The Discovery," *Time Out*, 9 September 1992, 61.

Bibliography

Brian Case, "Sales Talk," *Time Out* (London), 9 September 1992, 14–15; Charles Fleming, "Competing Columbus Pix Hit Rough Water," *Variety*, 22 April 1991, 3, 9.

CHURCHILL, SIR WINSTON SPENCER (1874–1965)

Winston Churchill was born on 30 November 1874 at Blenheim Palace in Oxfordshire, United Kingdom. In 1908 he entered the British Cabinet as president of the Board of Trade, becoming home secretary in 1910. The following year he became First Lord of the Admiralty. He held this post in the first months of World War I, but after the disastrous Dardanelles expedition, for which he was blamed, he resigned. From 1919 to 1921 he was secretary of state for war and air, and from 1924 to 1929 was Chancellor of the Exchequer. The next decade saw his "wilderness years," in which his opposition to Indian self-rule made him unpopular while his warnings about the rise of Nazi Germany and the need for British rearmament were ignored. This period is covered in the Ridley Scott-produced film *THE GATHERING STORM*. When war broke out in 1939, Churchill became First Lord of the Admiralty. In May 1940, Neville Chamberlain resigned as Prime Minister and Churchill took his place. His refusal to surrender to Nazi Germany inspired the country. In 1951, he became Prime Minister again. He resigned in 1955 but remained an MP until shortly before his death on 24 January 1965.

CLASS DIFFERENCES

The subject is fleetingly raised in *BLADE RUNNER* when Deckard describes the REPLICANTS, who are clearly members of an inferior social group. It is also central to *THE DUELLISTS*, where D'Hubert (KEITH CARRADINE) is an officer and a gentleman, whose manners, bearing, and education contrast violently with those of Feraud (HARVEY KEITEL). *SOMEONE TO WATCH OVER ME* contrasts Claire Gregory's (MIMI ROGERS's) world of privilege with the modest existence pursued by good cop Mike Keegan (TOM BERENGER). While the two worlds are shown colliding in the film's central love story, Scott also suggests that Mike and Claire can never be together. Their background, education, and sense of social morality prevent them from doing so. Such concern for social mores is perhaps uncharacteristic of mainstream Hollywood films but reflects Scott's status as an outsider commenting on 1980s American culture. A similar thematic preoccupation is evident in *1492: CONQUEST OF PARADISE*, where Columbus (GÉRARD DEPARDIEU) is always perceived as an outsider despite his achievements and despite his patronage from Queen Isabel (SIGOURNEY WEAVER). Robert Thurston's novelization of the screenplay has Sanchez reflecting thus: "This man [Columbus] has clearly forgotten his humble origins . . . Whence this newfound aristocratic manner? In reality, the man was just one step above the savages [in the New World] he was currently describing to his breathless audience, who seemed to adore him."

In *THELMA & LOUISE*, the topic is discussed from a female perspective. The film focuses on the limitations of class and gender identity and, beyond that, the possibilities for change. The only static image of the two women we see is the photo they snap at the beginning of their journey; grinning as they operate in a semiotic universe in which movement invariably means freedom. It is this static image which appeared in the advertisements and posters for the film. Lillian S. Robinson suggests that this image is "also the most working-class image of the two women that we get, precisely because it *is* such a static and posed vision of 'enjoyment.' The real point is, after all, that these women do not simply get away for a vacation. They get as far away as they can from the limits of their class and gender." Jane Collings reads this kind of liberation in a negative way; having escaped the requirements of their social class, "[they] are so misunderstood and so relentlessly pursued . . . [that] they must bow out entirely. They can be seen either to have killed themselves or, on a more textual level, to have left the film [and the society it portrays]."

References

Jane Collings, "The Hollywood Waitress: A Hard-Boiled Egg and the Salt of the Earth," in *The Hidden Foundation: Cinema and the Question of Class*, ed. David E. James and Rick Berg (Minneapolis and London: University of Minnesota Press, 1996), 271; Lillian S. Robinson, "Out of the Mine and into the Canyon: Working-class Feminism, Yesterday and Today," in *The Hidden Foundation: Cinema and the Question of Class*, ed. David E. James and Rick Berg (Minneapolis and London: University of Minnesota Press, 1996), 185; Robert Thurston, *1492: Conquest of Paradise Based on a Screenplay by Roselyne Bosch* (London: Penguin Books, 1992), 126–27.

Bibliography

Sean Redmond, "Purge! Class Pathology in *Blade Runner*," in *The Blade Runner Experience: The Legacy of a Science Fiction Classic*, ed. Will Brooker (London and New York: Wallflower Press, 2005), 173–90.

CLAY PIGEONS

Germany/ US 1998 r/t 104 min col. *Production Companies*: IMF Internationale Medien und Film GMBh & Co Produktions KG, Intermedia Films, Polygram Filmed Entertainment, and Scott Free. *Producers*: Ridley Scott, Chris Zarpas, Chris Dorr, Audrey Kelly, and Carrie Morrow. *Director*: David Dobkin. *Writer*: Matt Healy. *Director of Photography*: Eric Alan Edwards. *Production Designer*: Clark Hunter. *Music*: John Lurie. *Cast*: Joaquin Phoenix (*Clay Bidwell*), Vince Vaughn (*Lester Long*), Georgina Cates (*Amanda*), Scott Wilson (*Sheriff Mooney*), Janeane Garofalo (*Agent Shelby*), Vince Vieluf (*Deputy Barney*), Monica Moench (*Kimberly*).

The idea for *Clay Pigeons* began with screenwriter MATT HEALY, who according to the production notes wanted to write a film whose opening scene contained a *coup de théâtre* that "springs a surprise on the audience and at least one of the characters . . . From there, I was able to very quickly plot out the rest of the story." He entered the screenplay for a contest, which he eventually won, and from thence managed to obtain an agent from ICM (International Creative Management).

Clay Pigeons marked the screen debut of DAVID DOBKIN, who hitherto had only worked on commercials for RSA, Ridley Scott's commercial producing arm. SCOTT FREE, the company set up to produce films, bought the screenplay for him. Dobkin said in the production notes that he liked Healy's idea "because it breaks a lot of boundaries. It's at once very dark and very funny. It's a very risky film. When you're riding on the edge of what's socially acceptable, you often find the funniest stuff." In another interview with *Eye Weekly* he claimed to be inspired by the Coen Brothers—especially *FARGO* (1996), which "took a classic, rather shallow situation and turned it into something new . . . you always have a sense that these people [the characters] have rich, full interior lives, a true philosophical depth, even if they live in a little town, even if they talk differently from you or I."

Casting for the production was based on the assumption that, as the production could not afford to pay large salaries, the actors would participate because they liked the script. At least, this was JOAQUIN PHOENIX's view, according to the production notes, when he agreed to play Clay Bidwell: "I got on with him [Dobkin] immediately. His passion, his excitement about the film—suddenly I realised, 'Wow, this could be amazing.'" JANEANE GAROFALO concurred: "I remember thinking [the script] was weird, but I also felt it was important to have a strong lead character [FBI Agent Dale Shelby] in a movie where there's some violence against women. I felt that it was important that I participated, to try and take the edge off that." VINCE VAUGHN seized the opportunity to play a character who himself "plays different roles, different things, depending on what he wants from someone, or what he's after. He [Lester] is a man with no conscience. Nevertheless, Lester is a charmer—women love him, and men easily become his friends."

The script (originally titled "In Too Deep") went through a few changes before it reached the screen. Certain scenes were removed—for example, a short sequence involving Sheriff Mooney and his deputy Barney, where Barney is seen filling in a crossword puzzle; and a sequence where Mooney visits the local train station in search of Gloria and encounters two local staff—Tom, the station manager; and Max, the oldest resident of the town of Mercer. Both Tom and Max were deleted from the final script. Other deletions included a long telephone conversation between Clay and Amanda and another plot-driven scene in which Glen the bartender tells Clay that Shelby has been asking too many questions. The only major rewrite took place at the end, where director Dobkin created a new scene at a roadside café in which Clay and Lester meet up once again and Lester drinks a milk shake, followed by a final sequence which follows the outlines of the original script (where Lester goes off with a middle-aged man with a trailer carrying a horse) but transforms the man into a disguised Sheriff Mooney. Although not yet aware of it, Lester will be brought to justice: in the original script he just escapes into the distance. Dobkin also adds another scene where Clay gets into his car and hits the open road, having escaped at last from the SMALL-TOWN values of Mercer, Montana.

The six-week shoot took place on location in northern Utah. Apparently the shoot was a happy one, with the actors warming to playing opposite one another as they worked with Healy's screenplay: "'It was really a group effort,' GEORGINA CATES remembered in the production notes: . . . there were 'such different energies in there. Most of the time, a scene would be five different things, all going on at once.'" While filming took place, Dobkin worked hard to create an effective soundtrack: "Music is so much of a director's signature . . . Martin Scorsese was a huge influence for me." Phoenix observed again in the production notes that Dobkin "has a great sense of rhythm, with music and imagery combined. From the beginning of rehearsals, we would sit down and talk about a scene, and play different songs to launch the scene."

The film was released first at the Toronto Film Festival on 15 September 1998, with an American premiere a week later. As an independent film, it was released only on nineteen screens, and reviews were few and far between. The *Village Voice* hated it: "This is the kind of movie asinine enough to believe that the mere juxtaposition of sadistic violence and a jaunty tone on the soundtrack is, in itself, clever. That said, the main problem with *Clay Pigeons* isn't even questionable taste . . . the film has trouble establishing a tone, and gets progressively more flaccid." *Entertainment Weekly* observed that "every scene is powered by a cut from a soundtrack available from a CD bin near you. In other words, it's young-Hollywood-driven business as usual in this derivative, nasty, and ultimately empty drama." *Screen International* provided the one favorable review, commending Vaughn on his "nicely understated job as the goofy and frighteningly charismatic Lester." However the journal also noted—rightly as it turned out—that "the unusual tone and the absence of hot young stars will limit the film's theatrical potential." The film cost $8 million to produce; by November 1998 it had only grossed just over $1.7 million at the US box office. It was released five months later on DVD.

Despite its reception, *Clay Pigeons* remains a fascinating text incorporating direct references to Scott's earlier work. The opening scene involving Clay and his bosom buddy Earl (Gregory Sporleder) directly parodies the conventions of MASCULINITY in *WHITE SQUALL* and *G.I. JANE*. While both films celebrate the virtues of male bonding, in *Clay Pigeons* Earl decides to shoot himself, even though Clay is his best friend. Clay strikes up a friendship with Lester Long (VINCE VAUGHN), but finds himself ruthlessly exploited. Clay makes several futile attempts to escape, but Lester keeps close to him, protesting all the while that "after things die down, maybe we can get together . . . You meet a lot of people in life, Clay. But friendships like this are special." So special, in fact, that Lester tells Clay in no uncertain terms that if he dies, he will take Clay with him. The film incorporates a sequence where Clay disposes of Earl's body by driving Earl's truck to the edge of a cliff, jumping out at the vital moment and then watching the truck somersault down the hill before finally coming to rest and bursting into flames. The sequence directly calls to mind a similar moment at the end of *THELMA & LOUISE*, where the two women at last escape from patriarchal power. In *Clay*

Pigeons, however, Earl's death signals the beginning of Clay's troubles, as he is wrongfully accused of two murders and becomes involved with a serial killer.

Clay Pigeons incorporates a direct visual quotation from *ALIEN*, when Agent Shelby hits the play button on the video-recorder in her hotel room and watches the famous "chest-bursting" sequence in which the alien bursts out of Kane's (JOHN HURT's) stomach. Suddenly the picture goes to snow; a couple of seconds later a homemade video comes on showing graphic footage of Clay and Amanda having sex. The sequence is reshown in the sheriff's office as Shelby and Mooney ask Clay to describe his relationship with Amanda. As in *Alien*, Dobkin uses it to emphasize monstrosity; only this time it is explicitly identified with the female. Early on in Healy's script Amanda is described thus: "Amanda is white trash, but she's cute white trash." One character observes at one point that, while not wanting to speak ill of people, she can never understand why Earl married such a woman. When Amanda meets Clay in his bedroom following her husband's death, she tells him to "kick off those boots and come to Mama." By agreeing to be filmed while having sex, Clay willingly subjugates himself to this monstrous female's rule.

Such references create the impression that *Clay Pigeons* is fundamentally about misogyny. Lester congratulates Clay for having struck Amanda across the face: "you handled her right tonight . . . I guarantee she won't be so quick to open her mouth the next time." The script has Lester reaching into the water at Bear Lake to handle the corpse of a dead woman; and he remarks later on that he knows "how to handle women. Besides she [Amanda] really ain't a bad piece of ass." Having stabbed Amanda to death several times with a kitchen-knife, Lester tries to convince Clay that "I did the world a great service" by disposing of her: "She was vile . . . You should have heard some of the shit she was saying."

Dobkin makes great comic play out of the contrast between the SMALL TOWN values of Mercer, Montana, and the metropolitan values of Agent Shelby. Mercer is a sleepy place of 1,134 people (down from 1,135 after Earl's death), where life unfolds at a leisurely pace. The coroner is not around to identify Earl's body, being on holiday in Wyoming. When Agent Shelby accompanies the local police force into Amanda's house to identify the body, she has to reprimand Sheriff Mooney's assistant Barney (Vince Vieluf) for accidentally standing in a pool of Amanda's blood. Shelby subsequently asks Mooney why the room is so full of people—state police, the fire chief, and a couple of councilmen. Mooney replies truthfully: the fire chief came because he had done some police work before, while the councilmen just wanted to come. Exasperated at what she perceives as small-town inefficiency, Shelby just frowns and lamely requests that nobody touches anything.

Barney is well-meaning yet hopelessly inefficient, with a tendency to fall asleep at the wrong moments. He fails to hear Clay's cries for food; and when he does respond, he carries the tray right into Clay's cell, allowing Clay to escape and lock Barney in. Such behavior is contrasted with that of Agent Shelby, who describes herself as very good at her job and meticulously goes about her task of bringing the murderer to justice. Screenwriter Healy describes the clash between small-town and metropolitan values thus: "Agent Shelby and Mooney stare at each other; Agent Shelby startled at the sight of the small-town sheriff, and Mooney confounded by the prospect of a female FBI agent." The last sentence helps to explain why the script might be misogynist in tone: small-town males believe it is their right and privilege to assume patriarchal authority over women.

However, SMALL-TOWN values can also be approached positively. Mooney, having known Clay all his life, trusts Clay implicitly, and tells Shelby that Clay is not the kind of person likely to commit murder. When Lester proves the guilty party, Mooney's faith is vindicated. Mooney exploits the small-town resident's tendency to take people at face value: disguised as just another middle-aged man with a pickup truck, he offers Lester a lift, which the latter willingly accepts. Although we do not see it, we expect the sheriff to make a swift arrest.

Eric Alan Edwards's photography vividly captures the film's small-town setting; the lonely diners, isolated shops, and shabby garage where Clay earns a living as a mechanic. In the production notes Dobkin cited a pictorial influence of "Edward Hopper paintings—the lighting and the colours. The interiors in the daytimes are all lit from the windows and are never [light-] source driven. I thought, the brighter and punchier and more colourful the film is, the more it's going to create a unique and original mood . . . The daylight lets people get a little bit more comfortable." The soundtrack incorporates frequent examples of country music—a genre which, while appreciated by the locals, Agent Shelby positively abhors. At one point she is sitting in the bar while Pat Boone's "Why Baby Why" trills away on the radio. She frowns, and Lester responds: "Country's an acquired taste." However, Dobkin also suggests that, while there are definite social and cultural distinctions between metropolitan and small-town characters, they are all powerless in the face of the elements. This is evoked by frequent pans of the Montana landscape taken at various times of the day—dawn, sunset, nighttime—with the clouds scudding by. None of the characters have any control over their destinies; as in *WHITE SQUALL*, they are subject to the vagaries of an impersonal fate. At one point, when accused of Carol Pierce's murder, Clay exclaims: "This is crazy, Mooney, tell her [Shelby] that this is crazy." Shelby responds without a hint of irony: "Talk about coincidences. You find the body of one victim, you were sleeping with another, and you dated somebody else who's missing."

Clay Pigeons has attracted little comment since its original release. In a 2000 interview, Vince Vaughn made every effort to dissociate himself from his previous roles: "I'd like to make it clear that I don't want to be branded 'the serial killer guy.' I have no fascination with those guys . . . I've been that way [obsessive] with certain things, to a degree." Despite this, the review for the British magazine *Empire* observed that it has "been undeservedly on the shelf [since 1998]. The 'quirky' small-town crime comedy-drama has been overworked, but the rethink of Patricia Highsmith themes in a modern Western setting is fresh, funny and creepy."

References

David Dobkin, interviewed in *Eye Weekly* (1998) reproduced on the *Wikipedia* website, http://en.wikipedia.org/wiki/Clay_Pigeons (accessed 8 November 2008); John Hazelton, "Clay Pigeons," *Screen International* 1178 (2 October 1998): 29; Matt Healy, David Dobkin, Georgina Cates, Joaquin Phoenix, Janeane Garofalo, Vince Vaughn, interviewed in "Production Notes: *Clay Pigeons*," included on the European DVD release of the film (Frankfurt: BY Internationale Medien und Film, 1998); Matt Healy, *In Too Deep* (Draft Script dated 7 January 1997) (Beverly Hills, CA: Scott Free, 1997); Dennis Lim, "Clay Pigeons," *Village Voice*, 6 October 1998, 123; "Kim Newman's DVD DTV Dungeon," *Empire*, February 2006, 152; "No More Mr. Nasty Guy," *The Guardian: The Guide*, 16–22 September 2000, 13; Lisa Schwarzbaum, "Fowl Play," *Entertainment Weekly* 452 (2 October 1998): 45.

COBB, RON (1937–)

Cobb began his career as an animator and political cartoonist. His first film assignment was *Dark Star* (1974) directed by John Carpenter and written by DAN O'BANNON. He also worked (uncredited) as a creature designer on *Star Wars* (1977).

Cobb was hired by O'Bannon to work on *ALIEN* in collaboration with designer Chris Foss. Their work is clearly evident in the designs for the spaceship *NOSTROMO*, which went through several incarnations before Scott was satisfied with the final version. Paul Scanlon and Michael Gross's *The Book of Alien* shows how this process was completed. Cobb also designed the spaceship interiors; the spare, almost shabby structures revealing that this is a working craft chartered by the Company to bring the alien back for tests. The designer observed in an interview in 1979 that in such an environment "the crew . . . is almost empty as are the astronauts in [Kubrick's] *2001*."

References

Phil Edwards, "Ron Cobb on *Alien*," *Starburst* 16 (November 1979): 5–9; Paul Scanlon and Michael Gross, *The Book of Alien*, ed. Charles Lippincott (London: Star Books, 1979): 8–30.

COCHRANE, RORY (1972–)

Born in Syracuse, New York, Cochrane's first major film role was as Jeff Goldblum's son in *Fathers and Sons* (1992). Other films include *Dogtown* (1997) and *Right at Your Door* (2006).

Cast as Yevgeny Tsipin in *THE COMPANY*, Cochrane plays the role of a Yale University-educated Soviet spy passing as an American. Although he admires the American people and their way of life, Yevgeny "cannot ignore their faults or their shortcomings. Americans are trapped in a system which brings out the worst in them. They are raised to believe that democracy is the ideal, yet they turn a blind eye to the twenty-five million Americans that go to bed hungry every night." He prefers to work for a system believing "that all should be equal without poverty, crime, racist hatred, without all the things that make America the grotesque giant it is." However, Yevgeny's loyalty proves misplaced, as he discovers that the Soviet system in which he believes has consigned his Jewish girlfriend Azalia (Erika Marozsán) to a labor camp for nearly twenty years. Eventually Yevgeny returns permanently to the Soviet Union where he attempts to rebuild his life with her in spite of her sufferings.

COLD GUINNESS—IT'S NOT BAD—GOOD

GB 1974 Commercial r/t 30 sec col. *Production company*: RSA Films. *Director*: Ridley Scott.

The advertisement shown on British television opens with a young man (Robert Lindsay) standing in a pub; the landlord asks him "Guinness, sir?" The man takes the glass and drinks from it, repeating, "That's good, that's so, so good" over and over again. He finishes his beer and resumes the conversation with the landlord: "I could tell you, that was really, really . . . " The landlord interjects "Good?" Scott cuts to a close-up of the young man who responds: "Oh, it was much better than that," as he finishes his beer and wipes his mouth.

COLLETTE, TONI (1972–)

Australian actress who made her name in *Muriel's Wedding* (1994), followed by international hits such *The Hours* (2002).

Cast as Rose in the Ridley Scott-produced adaptation of the JENNIFER WEINER novel *IN HER SHOES*, Collette put on twenty-five pounds to increase her weight for the role. In an interview she explained that this was done to show how the character is not satisfied with herself despite having a successful career as a lawyer: "I think the most interesting thing about any story is when the character is confronted and goes through some kind of change. Being stagnant in life or at work is not too good . . . I don't think that Rose does choose between work and a life, actually. I think that what she chooses to do is to let go of the responsibility she feels for everybody else in her life and start taking care of herself. And leaving her job is kind of a bi-product of that." Rose resembles many characters in Scott films faced with the conflict between LOVE VS. DUTY. At first she throws herself into her work as a way of consciously forgetting about her personal life; but as the film unfolds she gradually comes to realize the importance of putting herself first. She leaves her job and takes on an ad hoc job, similar to those pursued by her sister Maggie (CAMERON DIAZ), as a freelance dog-walker. Although happy professionally, her personal life remains confused; she is so afraid of the dark that she cannot bear making love to Simon Stein (MARK FEUERSTEIN) unless the light is on. Rose only learns to trust people at the end of the film, when she is reconciled with Maggie and her grandmother Ella (SHIRLEY MACLAINE), and can trust in her sister to choose her wedding dress.

Collette was congratulated by Mike Goodridge in *Screen International* for her ability to "bring an audience to tears with just one look, and [she] does so on several occasions in CURTIS HANSON's *In Her Shoes*. As the smart, successful Rose who struggles with her weight problems, she commanded the screen—not an easy task when Cameron Diaz and Shirley MacLaine are among your co-stars."

References

Mike Goodridge, "Women on Top," *Screen International* 1528 (16–22 December 2005): 20; Rebecca Murray, "In Her Shoes," *about.com* 10 January 2005, http://movies.about.com/od/inhershoes/a/shoestc 100105.htm (accessed 8 August 2008).

COLONIALISM

The subject is raised in *BLADE RUNNER* in the treatment of the REPLICANTS. Brian Carr remarks that "the futurity implies by 2019 LOS ANGELES operates ritualistically through the past, particularly in the representational nexus of slavery, inhumanity, and the discursive possibilities by which the boundaries of the 'human' are imaginable." In *1492: THE CONQUEST OF PARADISE*, the subject is analyzed at length. Towards the beginning of the film the city of Grenada is shown being taken over by the Spaniards, who drive out the occupying Muslims into the wilderness. Robert Thurston's novelization of the screenplay explains: "It was one thing to defeat the [Islamic] opposition, but to openly deride their religion seemed unnecessary . . . 'These people built Granada, centuries ago,' Santangel said, sadly. 'It is a great victory over the Moors, Don Colón, and yet what a tragedy it is.'" A similar sequence appears in *WHITE SQUALL*, where the youthful crew lands on the Galapagos Islands, bare-chested, dressed in shorts and carrying spears. Chuck Gieg (SCOTT WOLF) observes that they were about to lay claim to the land as their own. Although their presence on the land is only temporary, they feel that they have matured sufficiently to consider themselves as following in Columbus's footsteps nearly four centuries earlier.

1492: The Conquest of Paradise reinforces colonialist assumptions: the Indians are presented either as strange or as objects of sexual desire. A dream sequence, included in the novelization but deleted from the film, makes this point clear: "Around a curve he [Columbus] came upon an Indian girl standing in the water. She was not at all embarrassed at being viewed by a man, even a clothed man. Columbus, suddenly barefoot, walked toward the girl, who in turn came toward him. She reached toward him and, hand in hand, they walked through the shallow waters together." Such tropes are characteristic of European (or American) cinema's reconstruction of the colonies. Graham Harper comments: "Film has for over a century promoted/encouraged a European view of beauty, an aesthetic sense, and how this had fed ideas about the uses of figurative and non-figurative images, dialogue, music and sounds, and all film's attendant aspects of movement, color and shape, carrying along with it at least some, if not a great many, elements of story, theme and subject."

In *G.I. JANE* the colonialist elements are more overt, as Scott represents the Libyan troops as animal-like, almost brutal, speaking their own language (which is not given the benefit of subtitles for non-Arabic speaking filmgoers). This foreshadows a similar portrayal of the Somalis in *BLACK HAWK DOWN*, who are consistently called "skinnies" by the American troops. Their basic inhumanity is underlined when Durant (Ron Eldard) is "kicked, spit on, uniform ripped at, [the] crowd trying to pull him apart." They even deny him the right to pick up a photograph of his family that falls from his grasp; one man stamps on his hand and kicks it away. The fact that the Somalis are shown to be brutal, but not the Americans, has led some critics to accuse the film of bias; in reality the American soldiers (like the United Nations peacekeepers) were equally guilty of cruelty and abuse. The same criticism could be leveled at *BODY OF LIES*, where the extremist leader Al-Saleem (ALON ABOUTBUL) is shown torturing Roger Ferris (LEONARDO DICAPRIO) in a sequence reminiscent of *Midnight Express* (1978).

In *KINGDOM OF HEAVEN* Scott portrays the Christian colonizers as barbaric, massacring innocent Muslim citizens in their quest to defeat Saladin (GHASSAN MASSOUD). However, the film suggests that tolerance between different races is possible so long as everyone respects each others' cultures. Saladin offers the Christians a safe passage out of Jerusalem—"every soul; the women, the children, the old, and all your knights and soldiers and your queen"—so long as he can have control of the city, once they have departed. He has been impressed by the example set by King Baldwin (EDWARD NORTON); as he remarks earlier on to Guy de Lusignan (MARTON CSOKAS): "A king does not kill a king. Were you not close enough to a great king to learn by his example?"

References

Brian Carr, "At the Thresholds of the 'Human': Race, Psychoanalysis and the Replication of Imperial Memory," *Cultural Critique* 39 (Spring 1998): 136; Graeme Harper, "They're a Weird Mob: European Cinema Beyond Europe," *Spectator* 23, no.2 (October 2003): 20; Ken Nolan, *Black Hawk Down: The Shooting Script* (New York: Newmarket Press, 2002), 90–91; Robert Thurston, *1492: Conquest of Paradise Based on a Screenplay by Roselyne Bosch* (London: Penguin Books, 1992), 48, 109.

Bibliography

Alberto Elena, "Spanish Colonial Cinema: Contours and Singularities," *Journal of Film Preservation* 63 (October 2001): 29–36.

COLUMBUS, CHRISTOPHER (1451–1506)

Columbus was an Italian navigator, colonizer, and explorer whose voyages across the Atlantic Ocean led to general European awareness of the American continents in the Western Hemisphere. His reputation has varied widely in recent years. For the British writer Max Faber, writing an unpublished screenplay about his life in 1938, he was a hero, who was "able to display his knowledge of the sea, and by a strange happening is able to distinguish himself through displaying precise action during a severe part of the expedition." He returns to Spain, having gathered sufficient proof of his discovery of the New World, and "is proclaimed a national hero and Pope Alexander VI lauded him in public and declared all lands a hundred miles west of the Azores to be discovered as crown property."

More recently, however, Columbus's reputation has been questioned. The writer Kirkpatrick Sale says that he never discovered a New World; "all [he] . . . ever found was half a world of nature's pleasures and nature's peoples that could be taken, and they took them, never knowing, never learning the true regenerative power there, and that opportunity was lost. Theirs was indeed a conquest of Paradise, but as is inevitable with any war against the world of nature, those who win will have lost—once again lost, and this time perhaps forever." Ridley Scott's *1492: CONQUEST OF PARADISE* follows Sale by presenting Columbus's voyage as a colonialist enterprise with very little result, except to show Columbus's obsessive nature. A historian in the British film journal *Empire* complained that Scott's interpretation only sustained "the trappings of historical veracity around yet another fictitious Columbus . . . The legacy of violence and treachery actually begun by Columbus is blamed on Moxica, a fictitious and frustrated noble who is supposed to have introduced the commonplace practice of amputating Indians' hands when they failed in their mission to fill a hawksbell with gold-dust . . . five hundred years on from this highly unequal exchange, we are being offered more of the same—the adventurer-as-hero in place of the true story of one man's impact on the course of history . . . On one point alone, the film hits the nail on the head, with the best line of the script being, 'There was always faith, hope and charity, but greater than any of these is banking.'"

References

Max Faber, "Christopher Columbus: An Original Film Story Based on His Early Life and His Voyage of Discovery to the West Indies and America," Unpub. script dated 2 June 1938, 1–3; Amanda Hopkinson, "Conquest of History?" *Empire*, November 1992, 90; Kirkpatrick Sale, *The Conquest of Paradise: Christopher Columbus and the Columbian Legacy* (London: Hodder and Stoughton, 1991), 370.

THE COMPANY

US 2007 TVM 3 × 95 min episodes col. *Production Companies*: Turner Network Television, Scott Free, Sony Pictures Television and John Calley Productions. *Executive Producers*: Ridley Scott, Tony Scott, Cary Brokaw, David W. Zucker, David A. Rosemont, and John Calley. *Producers*: Robert Bernachi, Jonas Bauer, Rola Bauer, Ron Binkowski, Tim Halkin, and Nick Witkowski. *Director*: Mikael Salomon. *Writer*: Ken Nolan from the book by Robert Littell. *Cinematography*: Ben Nott. *Production Design*: Marek Dobrowolski. *Music*: Jeff Beal. *Cast*: Chris O'Donnell (*Jack McCauliffe*), Alfred Molina (*Harvey Torriti/ The Sorcerer*), Michael Keaton (*James Angleton*), Tom Hollander (*Adrian Philby*), Alessandro Nivola (*Leo Kritzky*), Rory Cochrane (*Yevgeny Tsipin*).

A miniseries tracing the development of the CIA over a fifty-year period based on the best-selling *THE COMPANY* (NOVEL) by Robert Littell. The series came about when producer JOHN CALLEY contacted KEN NOLAN about writing a screenplay. Having collaborated with Scott on *BLACK HAWK DOWN*, Nolan brought him in on the project. The original plan was to film *The Company* for the cinema, but Sony Pictures balked at the potential cost, so Calley and Scott took it to TNT as a television miniseries. The three two-hour films were to be directed by different people (including Scott); but eventually it was agreed that MIKAEL SALOMON—whose television work included *The Grid* (2004)—would assume responsibility for the entire project. Salomon expressed considerable enthusiasm for the project, commenting in an interview that "being able to create it [the miniseries] as a six-hour limited series instead of a two-hour feature, as originally envisioned, allows us to go into much greater depth and detail. In many ways, television has assumed the role of independent cinema, and this is a great example. It's exciting drama that addresses essential Cold War questions of, 'What was it all about? What was achieved?'"

Filming took place in various locations, including Toronto (which stood in for scenes at Yale, New York, and Washington, DC), Budapest (the scene for the restaging of the Hungarian uprising, as well as providing the backdrop for sequences in Moscow and Tel Aviv), and Puerto Rico (which set the stage for the Bay of Pigs invasion in Cuba and Guatemala). The location work in Budapest took place during the commemoration of the fiftieth anniversary of the Hungarian Uprising in October 1956: co-producer David Rosemont commented that at this point filming "had a certain 'truth is stranger than fiction' ring to it . . . It affected several aspects of our production, not the least of which was securing locations and tank permits." Some of the sequences were quite dangerous to film: one involved the central character Jack McAuliffe (CHRIS O'DONNELL), and uprising leaders Arpad Zelk (Misel Maticevic) and Elizabet Nemeth (Natascha McElhone), fleeing from a pursuing tank, which was meant to burst straight through a tramcar. As O'Donnell and McElhone glanced back at the fast-closing tank, and then rushed ahead, the look of alarm on their faces was genuine. McElhone subsequently recalled that at this point the cast genuinely feared for their safety. Shooting took five months, from June 2006 onwards.

The series was screened on TNT on consecutive Sunday evenings, beginning on 5 August 2007. Reviewers were generally enthusiastic: The *New York Times* described it as "a look back in sorrow, but also in muffled fondness, at an era that by post-9/11 standards seems enviably unambiguous and navigable." Rather like George Clooney's film *Good Night and Good Luck* (2005), *The Company* recalled a period in American history "when the lines of battle were clearly drawn, and the enemy played by the same rules and was easy to spot." The series was likened to the BBC drama *TINKER TAILOR SOLDIER SPY* (1979) in its depicting of "the same shadowy netherworld" of spying. An online reviewer particularly liked MICHAEL KEATON's performance as James Angleton, "whether coldly interrogating a suspect or offering a rambling, seemingly deluded critique of the CIA as a mere shadow of its once shadowy self." Although the series "regularly overplays its mood music," it was nonetheless "an ambitious, accomplished and overall enthralling effort that saves its very best for those riveting closing hours [in Part 3]."

Although the story of the six-hour series is continuous, covering a period of four decades from the early 1950s to 1991, each of the three episodes focuses on different themes. The first concentrates on the so-called "Great Game," a term originally used to describe the rivalry between the British Empire and the Russian Empire in Central Asia. In Salomon's drama it refers to the rivalry between the CIA and the KGB for control of hearts and minds during the Cold War period. Jack McCauliffe (O'Donnell) describes it thus: "We [the Americans} are engaged in a life-or-death crisis with the Communists. When it's over, only one side will survive. I've been asked to join the battle." His superior Frank Wisner (Ted Atherton) employs similar language in his address to the fledgling CIA agents earlier on: "A very thin line of patrols mans the ramparts [in West Berlin]. We need men and women who are aggressive, willing to take risks, who can plunge into the unknown without worrying how to get back out."

To participate in this Great Game, agents on both sides are expected to be dedicated to their respective ideological causes (democracy or communism). The Soviet spy Yevgeny Tsipin (RORY COCHRANE) is informed in no uncertain terms by his superior Starik Zhilov (Ulrich Thomsen) that he should give up his Jewish girlfriend Azalia (Erika Marozsán) and devote himself to "Mother Russia." Only then will Yevgeny understand how men like his father, grandfather, and Starik himself have "spilled blood" on Yevgeny's behalf to ensure that he has had a good education at Yale University. Starik puts a stark choice between LOVE VS. DUTY for Yevgeny: a world of "simple domesticity with a woman who will never allow you to rise in the party ranks, or a life of changing the world." Needless to say, Yevgeny chooses the second option. If the KGB works in the cause of "Mother Russia," the CIA's agenda is dictated by Angleton, codenamed "Mother." As in *ALIEN*, individual self-determination is no longer important: every employee of the Company on the Russian and the American sides (the parallels between the two films here is deliberate) must subject themselves to the dictates of a higher authority.

To play the Great Game successfully, every agent must understand that nothing is what it seems to be. The CIA informant Lilli (Alexandra Maria Lara) actually turns out to be a Soviet agent, who supplies disinformation to Jack and Harvey Torriti (ALFRED MOLINA). The senior MI5 advisor Adrian Kim Philby (TOM HOLLANDER) likewise turns out to be working for the Soviets. At one point Jack narrowly escapes an attempt on his life by the Soviet agent Borisov (Hristo Mitzkov); he later discovers that it was nothing more than a charade designed to drive him closer to Lilli (and thereby reveal CIA secrets to the Russians). Early on in the episode we see Jack, Yevgeny, and Jack's future colleague Leo Kritzky (ALESSANDRO NIVOLA) completing their education at Yale. They are apparently inseparable members of a rowing team celebrating their success with beer and late-night talks. It is only later on that we discover that Yevgeny is on the Soviet payroll, while Kritzky, who adopts the codename Sacha, is a high-ranking mole within the CIA who passes on secrets to the Soviets. The idea of male bonding as the source of MASCULINITY—a theme common to several Scott films—is here reduced to a charade. A quotation from Lewis Carroll's *Alice in Wonderland*, used as a preface to this episode, sums up the world of the Great Game: "'How do you know I'm mad?' said Alice. 'You must be,' said the Cat, 'or you wouldn't have come here.'"

The second episode of *The Company* depicts two valiant if futile military conflicts—the Hungarian Uprising of 1956 and the Bay of Pigs invasion five years later. Both sequences depict freedom fighters seeking to liberate their respective countries. As things turn out, however, that support does not materialize and the Hungarian and Cuban rebels are ruthlessly crushed. As in *Black Hawk Down*, the focus of attention centers on a group of people left to fend for themselves against impossible odds—although they have been military assistance from the American government, it never materializes. The reason for this is chiefly self-interest: America did not want to be seen to be intervening in another country's affairs. Salomon's narrative concentrated on notions of HONOR—the Hungarian rebels fight for their honor against a Soviet regime determined to crush them while the Cubans remain dedicated to their cause, however futile it might be. Jack tries to restrain them, but the Cuban leader Roberto Escalona (Raoul Bova) tells him to leave: "We don't need America's help any more. Castro will capture you . . . He'll tell the world my men died for America, not for Cuba . . . Don't take away our dignity. It's the last thing we've got!" The CIA is equally concerned with sustaining its honor: Angleton tells Jack that one of the reasons it should not become involved in the Cuban crisis is that any action would "cripple the Company for years to come." However, the film suggests that perhaps the CIA sacrificed its honor in favor of long-term goals. Wisner delivers a passionate speech to that effect in the wake of the Hungarian crisis: "Everyone here in this room, hell, everyone in Washington itself is culpable in the deaths of these freedom fighters. We will, all of us, have blood on our hands."

Perhaps the agents should have learned from the example of Elisabet Nemet—an English woman dedicated to another country's political cause. Jack asks her why she remains on the field of battle, refusing to return home. Elisabet replies: "[Hungary] is my daughter's country. And I'll fight for her freedom, for her future so that she doesn't have to live in fear of imprisonment and torture. And I'll stand at her father's side to do that." Although the CIA agents remain equally committed to the cause of freedom, their involvement in the Great Game renders them unable to participate in such honorable causes. They are imprisoned by their work—a fact underlined throughout the second episode through visual imagery; for example, Jack looking through the doors of his cell while being interrogated by the Soviets.

The third episode focuses more directly on issues of identity, as indicated in the prefatory quotation from *Alice in Wonderland*: "Who am I, then? Tell me that first, and then, if I like being that person, I'll come up. If not, I'll stay down here till I'm somebody else." In the world of spying, there is no such thing as a stable identity. Kritzky is jailed on suspicion of being the CIA mole Sasha, but later released on account of insufficient evidence. He is given a hero's welcome back into the Company family and told that everyone

owes him a debt of gratitude. In response, he quotes JOHN MILTON's famous line "They only serve who also stand and wait" (from Sonnet XIX "When I consider how my Light is Spent"), suggesting that standing still and waiting for an order is just as important as obeying it. It would seem that Kritzky has reestablished his credentials as an ideal Company man, but in the end this proves nothing more than another illusion, as Kritzky explains that he became a double agent "because [he] believed in serving a country whose system of government offered the best hope for the future." Forced to live in the Soviet Union under an assumed name for his own safety, he discovers to his cost that the socialist ideal he fought for no longer exists, as Gorbachev makes strenuous efforts to democratize the nation. Philby likewise has to sacrifice his identity as a master spy supporting the Soviet cause; forced to spend the rest of his life in a shabby apartment in Moscow, shadowed twenty-four hours a day by Soviet minders who monitor his every move, his passionate commitment to communism and Marxism comes to naught. Although a dyed-in-the-wool English patriot, he can never return to his country. Yevgeny, for all his loyalty to the Soviet ideals, discovers that once his profession as a spy has been revealed, the KGB has no further use for him. All he can do is return to the Soviet Union and try to reconstruct his old identity as a lover and a gentleman with Azalia.

According to Angleton, people like Yevgeny, Philby, and Kritzky have only themselves to blame, having worked to implement the Soviet "master plan, feeding layer upon layer of disinformation to the wishful thinkers of the west to make them think we are winning the Cold War . . . [They] have made certain the world view of America has shifted from a beacon of hope and justice to a tyrannical, power-mad colonialist juggernaut." While this cynical view of the Cold War and its effects on AMERICANISM makes for good drama (as Angleton bids farewell to his CIA career), the film suggests that the spying game as a whole deprives its practitioners of the security of knowing who they are or what causes they are supposed to fight for. This is brought out in the film's final scene, in which Jack and Harvey are on the golf course looking back on their careers in the CIA. Jack asks: "[Do you] think we made a difference, Harvey? Any difference at all?" and Harvey responds confidently, "You and me, kid, we put our warm bodies on the firing line, and we turned them [the Soviets] back . . . Something like the Cold War has to have a moral, otherwise what was it all about?" Jack believes that "it was about the good guys beating the bad guys"; but asks, "Which side were we on, Harvey?" Harvey can only reply: "We won, didn't we?"—a statement that poses more questions than it answers. Did the Americans actually win the Cold War? And if so, what difference did it make to the world? Do the spies actually understand the distinctions between right and wrong, good and bad, or have they been the victims of a not-so-Great Game involving two monolithic organizations (the CIA and the KGB) committed to outwitting one another through illusion or disinformation?

The Company was one of a spate of films appearing in the early 2000s in the theater and on television with the CIA as its subject. Others included *Munich* (2005), *Syriana* (2005), *THE GOOD SHEPHERD* (2006), *638 Ways to Kill Castro* (TV documentary, 2006), and *Rendition* (2007). Scott was to take up the topic once again in *BODY OF LIES*. Matthew Alford and Robbie Graham's article in the London *Guardian* investigates the organization's involvement with films since Hitchcock's *Torn Curtain* in the mid-1960s. Frances Stonor Saunders looks at how the CIA secretly funded western culture as well as the non-Communist Left, to combat the Soviet cultural offensive. Daniel J. Leab's *Orwell Subverted: The CIA and the Filming of Animal Farm* analyzes how the organization tried to influence the making of the film in the mid-1950s. The effect of films dealing with the CIA on film audiences—referring especially to Oliver Stone's *JFK* (1991)—has been dealt with in a research study by Lisa D. Butler, Cheryl Koopman, and Philip G. Zimbardo. They conclude that many viewers' experience of watching the film led to "a significant decrease in . . . reported intentions to voice or make political contributions. A general helplessness is proposed to account for the increase in feelings of anger and hopelessness and the decrease in intentions to vote or make political contributions." It might be interesting to speculate as to how viewers might have reacted to *The Company* which, although released sixteen years later, nonetheless takes an equally critical look at the CIA's work over the past half-century.

References

Matthew Alford and Robbie Graham, "An Offer They Couldn't Refuse," *The Guardian*, 14 November 2008, www.guardian.co .uk/film/2008/nov/14/thriller-ridley-scott (accessed 3 February 2009); Ed Bark, "Miniseries Review: *The Company*," *National TV Reviews and News*, www.unclebarky.com/reviews_files/8c2eca3c96d 653249a6901a517efa49e-215.html (accessed 12 August 2008); Lisa D. Butler, Cheryl Koopman, Philip G. Zimbardo, "The Psychological Impact of Viewing the Film *JFK*: Emotions, Beliefs, and Political Behavioral Intention," *Political Psychology* 16, no.2 (1995): 237; Daniel J. Leab, *Orwell Subverted: The CIA and the Filming of Animal Farm* (Pennsylvania: Pennsylvania State University Press, 2007); *Production Notes: The Company*, www.tnt.tv/series/thecompany/ bts/ (accessed 12 August 2008); Frances Stonor Saunders, *Who Paid the Piper?: The CIA and the Cultural Cold War* (London: Granta Books, 1999); Alessandra Stanley, "Cloak and Dagger in All Its Charm," *New York Times*, 3 August 2007, www.nytimes.com/2007/ 08/03/arts/television/03comp.html?ref=arts (accessed August 12, 2008).

THE COMPANY (NOVEL)

A best-selling 2002 work by Robert Littell, recounting the history of the CIA over fifty years: agents fighting the "good fight" not only against foreign enemies but also against people within their own country. Spanning a fifty-year period in history from the Cold War and the Soviet invasion of Hungary to Afghanistan and the Gorbachev putsch, the novel tells the story of agents involved in double lives, contending with enemies that are amoral, elusive, and powerful. It also exposes the conflicts within the CIA itself. The novel was adapted in 2007 into a miniseries directed by MIKAEL SALOMON and produced by Scott.

CONRAD, JOSEPH (1857–1924)

Born in Berdyczow in the Ukraine of Polish parents, Jozef Teodor Konrad Korzeniowski joined the merchant navy and later became an able-bodied seaman in the British navy, eventually rising to the rank of captain. His first work, *Almayer's Folly*, appeared in 1895, the same year he adopted the pen name of Joseph Conrad. Numerous novels followed including *NOSTROMO* (1904), *The Secret Agent* (1907), and *Under Western Eyes* (1911). He also published numerous short stories including "THE DUEL" (1908). In May 1924 he declined an offer of a knighthood from the British Prime Minister Ramsay MacDonald. Two months later he died of a heart attack.

Conrad's works have also proved fitting subjects for adaptation. Apart from Ridley Scott's *THE DUELLISTS* (1977), adaptations have also appeared on film and television of *An Outcast of the Islands* (1952), *Lord Jim* (1965), and most recently *Heart of Darkness* (1994), *Victory* (1995), *Nostromo* (1996), and *The Secret Agent* (1997). Scott's interest in Conrad resurfaces in *WHITE SQUALL*, a tale which, although not based on a Conradian source, nonetheless shares Conrad's preoccupation with HONOR and loss of innocence. Orson Welles (LIEV SCHREIBER) is shown contemplating an adaptation of *Heart of Darkness* in *RKO 281* before the idea of *Citizen Kane* takes over his life.

Bibliography

Carola M. Kaplan, *Conrad in the Twenty-First Century: Contemporary Approaches and Perspectives* (New York: Routledge, 2005); Gene M. Moore, *Conrad on Film* (Cambridge: Cambridge University Press, 1997); Norman Page, *A Conrad Companion* (Basingstoke and London: Macmillan, 1996); Norman Sherry, *Joseph Conrad: The Critical Heritage* (London: Routledge and Kegan Paul, 1973).

CONTEMPORARY WAR FILMS

If war films produced in the three decades following World War II tended to concentrate on ideas of heroism, MASCULINITY and American supremacy—as embodied, for instance, in the use of John Wayne in *The Green Berets* (1969)—their descendants in the 1990s and 2000s had very different ideas. Examples of this include *Saving Private Ryan* (1998), *Pearl Harbor* (2001), and *BLACK HAWK DOWN*.

Philippa Gates observes that this new breed of war film creates an ideal of feminized masculinity: mostly the stars are younger actors who "embody the conflicting notions of masculinity that result from crisis—from physical and emotional vulnerability to *machismo* and violence." This might provoke them to act rashly, or to endanger their fellow-soldiers in combat. Whereas we might criticize them for not thinking sufficiently about their actions, the films actually ask us to forgive them, as their impulsiveness stems "from a desire to get the job done at any cost: in one moment the youth can be confident, even arrogant, about his abilities as a soldier (or a young man) and the next cry for his mother as he lies dying." Nonetheless, we have to admire their strength of character as they sacrifice themselves to serve their country. This is especially true of some of the young recruits in *Black Hawk Down*.

BODY OF LIES shows how such ideals no longer apply in the so-called "war on terror" in the Middle East, where neither the CIA nor their antagonists actually declare war on one another, and where it is very difficult to separate enemies from allies. In this kind of long-term conflict, there are no winners and losers, just victims.

Reference

Philippa Gates, "'Fighting the Good Fight': The Real and the Moral in the Contemporary Hollywood Combat Film," *Quarterly Review of Film and Video* 22, no.4 (October–December 2005): 302.

Bibliography

Lou Coatney, "Black Hawk Down," *American Historical Review* 107, no.4 (October 2002): 1338; Simon Dalby, "Warrior Geopolitics: *Black Hawk Down* and *Kingdom of Heaven*," *Political Geography* 27, no.4 (May 2008): 439–55; Michael Hammond, "Some Smothering Dreams: The Combat Film in Contemporary Hollywood," in *Genre and Contemporary Hollywood*, ed. Steve Neale, 62–76. London: British Film Institute, 2002; James I. Matray and Robert Brent Toplin, "*Black Hawk Down*," *Journal of American History* 89, no.3 (December 2002): 1176–77; Paolo Palladino, "On the Political Animal and the Return of a Just War," *Theory and Event* 8 no.2 (2005): 126–39; Marilyn B. Young, "In the Combat Zone," *Radical History Review* 85 (Winter 2003): 253–64.

CONTI, TOM (1941–)

Tom Conti made his name in television and the theater in *The Glittering Prizes* (BBC, 1976) and the original West End production of Brian Clark's play *Whose Life Is It Anyway* (1977).

In *THE DUELLISTS* he plays Dr. Jacquin, a confidante of D'Hubert (KEITH CARRADINE), whose function is largely to advance the plot. He informs us that Feraud (HARVEY KEITEL) is determined to win at all costs, and advises D'Hubert to pull rank (which would therefore oblige him not to fight). Conti's brief appearance ends with him playing *The Duellists'* theme on the flute. This sequence foreshadows the film's final scene, in which the same theme is heard on the soundtrack while Feraud stands alone, surveying the desolate landscape. The tune reminds us of the futility of the duel; for Feraud, it only leads to social ostracism.

CORNISH, ABBIE (1982–)

Born in New South Wales, Australia, Cornish came to Scott's attention while playing the lead role in Cate Shortland's *Somersault* (2004). Cast as Christie, the twenty-one-year-old illegitimate daughter of Uncle Henry (ALBERT FINNEY) in *A GOOD YEAR*, Cornish plays an innocent who, contrary to Max Skinner's (RUSSELL CROWE's) assumptions, has not come to the château to lay claim to it. Her sole purpose is to find out more about her father; something she discovers after reading his letters: "Everything I need to know about my dad is right here . . . right in front of me [*sweeps her hand across the estate*]. And if this place meant as much to him as I think it did, then you're [Max is] worse than I thought for even thinking about selling it."

Christie proves to be an innocent—so much so that Max refrains from making love to her, even though he would like to. Her one redeeming virtue is an encyclopedic knowledge of viniculture, which stands her in good stead when she inherits the château at the end and tries to upgrade its vines. Christie is also no fool; she knows that Max has forged the letter (ostensibly from Uncle Henry) naming her as the heir to the château. However she raises no objection, as she (like Max) has discovered something in him that she can relate to: that neither of them grew up with a proper mother and father.

Reference

Marc Klein, "*A Good Year*: Screenplay" (Draft dated 5 September 2005), www.dailyscript.com/scripts/A-GOOD-YEAR-2.pdf (accessed 26 January 2009), 78A.

COTILLARD, MARION (1975–)

Cotillard's early films include *Big Fish* (2003) and *A Very Long Engagement* (*Un Long Dimanche des Fiançialles*) (2004). Cast as Fanny in *A GOOD YEAR*, Cotillard comes across as a practical no-nonsense person refusing to succumb to Max Skinner's (RUSSELL CROWE's) blandishments. Even towards the end of the film, when the two of them have spent the night together and seem destined to fall in love, Fanny admits to him that she only gave in "because once you [Max] have done what you came here [to Provence] to do, you will not return. For us, there can be no future . . . there is safety in that, *n'est-ce pas?*" However, all is not what it seems: the men of the local village where she works view her as an object and congratulate Max for making her show her derrière. She once had a relationship with a soccer player; since then she will let no man near her. Duflot (DIDIER BOURDON) offers the following advice: "[R]ecall what Proust said: 'Leave pretty women to men without imagination.'" However, Max replies that he is a banker possessed of no imagination and continues his pursuit of her. Once he has left London for good and given himself to the château, Fanny trusts him sufficiently enough to forge a relationship; the final sequence shows the two of them in an embrace with Fanny teaching Max some basic spoken French.

Cotillard liked the role of Fanny; in the pressbook she asserted that the character was the catalyst for Max's change of heart: "he comes to understand what he really needs is right here at the chateau and in Provence." Fanny herself understood through the relationship that "she needs love, she definitely needs love. And she deserves it, too."

Reference

Pressbook: A Good Year (Los Angeles: Twentieth Century-Fox Film Corporation, 2006), 6.

CRIMESTOPPERS

GB 2003 Commercial r/t 42 sec col. *Production Company*: RSA Films. *Director*: Ridley Scott

Commercial for the British charity Crimestoppers, screened in theaters in the United Kingdom as part of their campaign "Crossing the Line." The company made two commercials—one rated 18 (the equivalent of a US R-rating); the other 12A (or PG-13), to be shown with the film *American Pie 3—The Wedding*. The commercials highlighted teenagers' relaxed attitudes to crime by showing a group of youths discussing it in an urban setting. One says, "Everybody does a bit of fucking around. But it don't mean we're bad." Another believes that individuals cannot change the situation: "Fuck it, how can we stop it? There's nothing we can do." The commercial aimed to show that teenagers can do something: if they witness a crime, they can report it anonymously to Crimestoppers.

CROMWELL, JAMES (1940–)

The son of director John Cromwell and actress Kay Johnson, Cromwell's early films included *Murder by Death* (1976). Thereafter he pursued a career as a character actor in films and television.

In *RKO 281* Cromwell portrays William Randolph Hearst as a bully who, like Orson Welles (LIEV SCHREIBER), is equally preoccupied with himself, at everyone else's expense. A tall, angular figure, Cromwell's Hearst "moves with a delicacy surprising for such a famously merciless man. Although the word ruthless does not begin to do justice to the press baron's animus, Hearst is endlessly polite and almost painfully soft-spoken." For most of the film, Hearst is content to show his power at any and every opportunity, for example threatening his employees such as Louella Parsons (BRENDA BLETHYN) with dismissal unless she brings him all the inside information about Welles's film. This kind of character has appeared frequently in Scott's work, notably Tyrell in *BLADE RUNNER*.

However, we do sympathize with Hearst at the end, particularly in a short scene in an elevator where he unexpectedly encounters Welles and observes, "What kind of sad future are we two making? A future where men will do anything to sell their newspapers and their movies? A future where no price is too high for fame and power? When we will all scratch each other to pieces just to be heard?" Although Hearst himself has been responsible for creating this kind of world, at least he understands the consequences of his actions—which is more than can be said of Welles, who shouts "*Charles Foster Kane would have accepted* [the invitation to watch the film]*!*" He has little or no understanding of the world outside; the film *is* his life.

Reference

John Logan, "Draft Script for *RKO 281*" (dated 1 May 1997), http://sfy.ru/sfy.html?script=rko218 (accessed 16 November 2008).

CRONENWETH, JORDAN (1935–1996)

Jordan Cronenweth's early career included films such as Billy Wilder's remake of *The Front Page* (1974), *Altered States* (1980), and *Cutter's Way* (1981).

In an interview first published in July 1982, Cronenweth emphasized the fact that "the style of the photography in *Citizen Kane* most closely approached the look he [Scott] wanted for *BLADE RUNNER*. This included high contrast, unusual camera angles and the use of shafts of light. This is especially evident, for instance, in the bright light shining from outside through the latticed windows of the Bradley Building as Deckard (HARRISON FORD) pursues Batty (RUTGER HAUER). Deckard turns away from the window, and we see a door barring his way, with a yellow light shining through its wooden bars. The entire sequence suggests that Deckard is somehow imprisoned; for all his determination to "retire" (i.e., kill) the REPLICANTS, he shares their fate in the sense that he cannot escape his destiny.

Cronenweth also took great care with the street scenes: "We used contrast, backlight, smoke and lightning . . . the streets were depicted as terribly overcrowded, giving the audience a future time frame to relate to. We had street scenes just packed with people . . . like ants. So we made them appear like ants—all the same . . . like going nowhere. Photographically, we kept them rather colorless."

The other key ingredient in the photography of *Blade Runner* was the use of shafts of light: "They were used for both advertising and crime control, much the way a prison is monitored by moving search lights. The shafts of light represent the invasion of privacy by a supervising force; a form of control. You are never sure who it is, but even in the darkened seclusion of your home, unless your pull your shades down, you are going to be disturbed at one time or another." This continues a theme first explored in *ALIEN* about the extent to which human beings are simply objects, subject to the authority of a higher power. Scott returned to the theme once again in his famous commercial for APPLE COMPUTERS (1984), based on George Orwell's *1984*.

Jordan Cronenweth won a BAFTA (British Academy Film Award) for his work on *Blade Runner*, which the critic PAUL M. SAMMON describes as "Vermeerish" in style with its "deep pools of darkness" and its "complicated palette." Cronenweth died in 1996 of Parkinson's Disease.

References

Herb A. Lightman and Richard Paterson, "Cinematography for *Blade Runner*," *American Cinematographer*, March 1999, 158, 161–62; Paul M. Sammon, interviewed in "Remembering Jordan Cronenweth" (d. Charles de Laurzirika), included in *Blade Runner: Collector's Edition* (Warner Bros. Entertainment and the Blade Runner Partnership, 2007), disc 4.

CROWE, RUSSELL (1964–)

Born in Wellington, New Zealand, Crowe made his name in CURTIS HANSON's *LA Confidential* (1997), an adaptation of the James Ellroy bestseller about the seamier side of 1950s LOS ANGELES.

Cast as Maximus in *GLADIATOR*, Crowe was just emerging from unknown quantity to rising star when he landed the role. In a publicity interview with the British film magazine *Empire*, he suggested that the part differed quite substantially from the kind of action hero associated with Stallone or Schwarzenegger: "To play a Roman general from both sides [leader and slave], so it's not just the Spartacus story, and it's not just *Ben Hur*, it's kind of both." In another interview published in the book *The Making of Gladiator*, he remarked that "Maximus goes from being a great general to being shackled and sold into slavery as a gladiator—a slight change in lifestyle . . . For a while then he lives only to stand in front of the new emperor and enact his revenge, but he is caught up in the political turmoil of the day and can't help but become involved. For want of a better expression, he is a good man."

Crowe and Scott fought constantly during filming, with Crowe arguing things from his character's point of view.

Their first argument centered on Maximus's accent. Since the script said he was from Spain, Crowe thought he should speak Spanish; but Scott thought otherwise. Scott also axed the love scenes between Crowe and actress Gianina Facio, who played Maximus's wife in the film. Despite the conflicts, Crowe apparently enjoyed the experience of working with Scott. His biographers Tim Ewbank and Stafford Hildred quote him as saying that "We all knew that we didn't have the complete narrative when we began but through a long process and lot of sleepless nights we found our story . . . Working with Ridley was like doing quantum physics with Picasso." Richard Rushton describes Crowe's performance as one that foregrounds virtues such as democracy, family values, mercy and honor, particularly in the final sequence: "All attention is paid to the body of Maximus as he is triumphantly carried from the Colosseum on the shoulders of the guards . . . [he] is graced with what the Greeks referred to as a 'beautiful death,' . . . Maximus's death brings to an end a journey that had been prefigured in the film's opening scene and alluded to many times throughout the film. His death sees him delivered into an Arcadian promised land where he is reunited with his wife and son. His 'beautiful death' ensures that his deeds and fame will live in the memory of the people of Rome who, we must presume, will reclaim Rome as a Republic."

Cast as Max Skinner in *A GOOD YEAR*, Crowe admitted in an interview with *Premiere* that both he and Scott faced "a completely different set of problems than we faced last time [on *Gladiator*]." Max was not a hero but someone who gradually acquired self-awareness: "He learns that things that he was taught when he was a younger man have great value . . . through his ambition, he has lost sight of the things that were really important and of the importance of the person who taught him those things." Crowe's performance is not exactly comic, though he does communicate a certain winsome charm—particularly when he understands the shortcomings of his life in London. After spending the night with Fanny (MARION COTILLARD), Max blithely states in MARC KLEIN's script that "nothing's preventing us from moving your café to Notting Hill," without thinking for a moment that Fanny might be perfectly happy in PROVENCE. Fanny rebukes him; and Max's tone becomes far less confident as he stops himself and hesitatingly admits, "This place . . . it doesn't fit my life." Fanny's response leaves him completely at a loss: "No Max, it [your life] doesn't fit this place." For the first time in years (ever since he was a child) Max understands that the vainglorious pursuit of money is not life's only option. He resembles a lost little boy as he stares at the camera "in a state of anxious turmoil" and subsequently sits on a bench at the edge of the tennis court, "depressed [and] contemplative." However, all turns out fine in the end, as Max gives up his job and takes on the role of château-owner, following in his Uncle Henry's (ALBERT FINNEY's) footsteps. Once again Max resembles a little boy as he sits on his front step, wearing a self-satisfied smile as he listens to Christie (ABBIE CORNISH) and Duflot (DIDIER BOURDON) arguing inside.

Crowe's next film for Scott, *AMERICAN GANGSTER*, had him playing Richie Roberts, the head of a special unit set up to purge the streets of NEW YORK of drugs in the early 1970s. In the production information Crowe described the character as fundamentally contradictory: "None of his real story has traditional elements—and he's not somebody you can easily categorize." Although scrupulously honest in his daily life—to such an extent that he turns in $1 million in stolen money rather than keeping it for himself (like his fellow officers)—Richie has strong connections to the Mafia through his friend Joey Sadano (Richie Coster). At one point Joey offers him the use of an expensive ski-hut in the Aspen mountains so long as Richie leaves the Mafia leader Dominic Cattano (ARMAND ASSANTE) alone. STEVEN ZAIL-LIAN's script reflects Richie's dilemma: "What Richie knows is that no matter what he does or says at this point he's got a problem." He rejects the offer—even if he realizes that it costs him his friendship with Joey.

One of Richie's main virtues in Crowe's performance is his persistence in the face of adversity—a quality also characteristic of Maximus in *Gladiator*. Even when faced with an aggressive attorney (Roger Bart), he doggedly maintains that "Frank Lucas is above the mafia in the dope business. I believe he . . . uses US military planes and personnel to bring pure number-four heroin into the United States." Such outlandish claims are rejected out of hand; but Richie resolutely maintains his convictions. This is what makes him so good at his job, as well as an intimidating opponent in the fight against organized crime. Despite his power and influence, Frank Lucas (DENZEL WASHINGTON) ends up being "worried . . . by this cop who doesn't take money sitting placidly in front of him . . . Frank has never been so frustrated by anyone in his life. He wants to work something out with Richie obviously, but can't figure out how." Frank has no choice but to pass on the names of his associates as well as all the police officers he has bribed, in return for a limited jail sentence.

For his next role in *BODY OF LIES*, Crowe had to put on fifty pounds to play the slovenly Ed Hoffman, director of the CIA's Near East Division. In the production notes DAVID IGNATIUS, the author of the original novel, claimed that Hoffman could multi-task with a ruthless efficiency and a sense of detachment totally foreign to a hands-on operative like Roger Ferris (LEONARDO DICAPRIO): "Ed Hoffman is cynical, tough, a man who was born to use other people . . . He doesn't care about the human cost of what he

does." In Crowe's performance Hoffman comes across as a boor—someone who willfully neglects his family as he talks incessantly on a Bluetooth link with Ferris. His view of the "war on terror" is uncomplicated (and fundamentally racist); if the Americans don't destroy the Muslims, then they will be destroyed themselves. No Arab can be trusted; and if any of them do help the Americans, they can be picked up and dispensed with at will. Diplomatic niceties are not for him; while walking to a meeting with Hani, the head of the Jordanian Secret Service (MARK STRONG), Hoffman quotes the golfing legend Sam Snead, who apparently said "if you're not thinking about pussy, you're not concentrating." All Hoffman cares about is his status within the CIA— "a results-oriented organization," as he claims. WILLIAM MONAHAN's original script has him making even more outrageous remarks, claiming (for instance) that the Muslims resemble the barbarians staring across the River Tiber at the ancient city of Rome. This provides a neat intertextual reference to *Gladiator*. The *San Francisco Chronicle* reviewer described him with justification as "some variety of fanatic, perhaps a particularly American variety, one whose faith in his own virtue is so complete that he could commit any atrocity with a clear conscience."

Not everyone liked Crowe's characterization, however; Roger Clarke in *Sight and Sound* described it as "one of his laziest . . . Crowe's take on the man, though occasionally amusing, is annoyingly opaque. Apart from the odd rant about the threat of an international caliphate, Crowe's determined underplaying of his character offers little clue to his soul or even, rather strangely, his motivations."

References

American Gangster: Production Information (Los Angeles: Universal Pictures, 2007), 6; *Body of Lies: Production Notes* (Los Angeles: Warner Bros., 2008), www.mix96tulsa.com/movies/notes/body-of-lies/note/4 (accessed 16 January 2009); Roger Clarke, "*Body of Lies*," *Sight and Sound*, December 2008, www.bfi.org.uk/sightandsound/review/4558 (accessed 17 February 2009); Tim Ewbank and Stafford Hildred, *Russell Crowe: The Biography* (London: Andre Deutsch, 2006), 174–75; Marc Klein, "*A Good Year*: Screenplay" (Draft dated 5 September 2005), www.dailyscript.com/scripts/A-GOOD-YEAR-2.pdf (accessed 26 January 2009); Diana Landau (ed.), *Gladiator: The Making of the Ridley Scott Epic* (Basingstoke and London: Boxtree, 2000), 53; Mick LaSalle, "Muddled *Body of Lies*," *San Francisco Chronicle*, 10 October 2008, E1; Martin Palmer, "Grrrrr," *Empire* 132 (June 2000): 78; Richard Rushton, "Narrative and Spectacle in *Gladiator*," *CineAction* 56 (September 2001): 40; "When It Comes to Acting . . . ," *Premiere*, November 2006, 72; Steven Zaillian, "*American Gangster*: Final Shooting Script," 27 July 2006, www.roteirodecinema.com.br/scripts/files/american_gangster.htm (accessed 8 February 2009).

Bibliography

James L. Dickerson, *Russell Crowe: The Unauthorized Biography* (New York: Schirmer Trade Books, 2003); "Interview: Russell Crowe," *Film Review* 676 (November 2006): 72–74; Russell Crowe interview by Rob Carnevale, www.indielondon.co.uk/Film-Review/a-good-year-russell-crowe-interview (accessed 8 August 2008); Christy Lytal, "A Crowe's Eye View," *Premiere* 20, no.3 (November 2006): 70–72, 107; James Mottram, "As the Crowe Flies," *Film Review* 676 (November 2006): 70–74; "News: *American Gangster*," *Empire* 214 (April 2007): 28–30; Martyn Palmer, "Original Gangsters," *Empire* 221 (November 2007): 114–24; Martyn Palmer, "Royal Flush," *Time Out* (London), 10–17 May 2000: 24; Martyn Palmer, "Russell Crowe: Why I Had to Fatten Up and Calm Down," *Daily Telegraph*, 6 November 2008, www.telegraph.co.uk/culture/film/3562948/Russell-Crowe-Why-I-had-to-fatten-up-and-calm-down.html (accessed 17 February 2009); Garth Pearce, "A Barbaric World . . ." *Total Film* 41 (June 2000): 46–55; "World Exclusive: *American Gangster*," *Empire* 214 (April 2007): 29.

CRUISE, TOM (1962–)

Born Thomas Cruise Mapother IV in Syracuse, New York, on 3 July 1962. The only son (among four children) of nomadic parents, young Tom developed an interest in acting and abandoned his plans of becoming a priest, dropped out of school, and at age eighteen headed for New York and a possible acting career. He made his film debut with a small part in Franco Zeffirelli's *Endless Love* (1981) and from the outset exhibited an undeniable box office appeal to both male and female audiences.

Cruise was cast as Jack o'the Green in *LEGEND* on the strength of his performances in *Taps* (1981) and *Risky Business* (1983). According to PAUL M. SAMMON Scott wanted him to become a beast-man, and screened Francois Truffaut's *L'ENFANT SAUVAGE* (1970) for the young actor, "to give Tom an idea of the feral quality I had in mind for Jack." Cruise's biographer Andrew Morton reports that Scott wanted Cruise to grow his hair and emulate the wolfish gestures of Truffaut's child, whom the director saw as a heroic force of nature.

The English crew apparently liked Cruise. In another biography by Ian Johnstone, the film's unit publicist Geoff Freeman recalls that the actor "was rather reluctant to go out and about too much as he had had to grow long hair . . . and felt self-conscious about it." Cruise does not have much to do in the film, apart from playing the role of a young attractive boy engaged on a quest, both to rescue the unicorns and to prove his own manhood. Like D'Hubert in *THE DUELLISTS*, he realizes that it is his duty to embark on the rescue mission, even if he is initially unwilling to do so. As in many Scott films, Jack has to choose between LOVE VS. DUTY, especially when he is seduced by the fairy Oona (ANNABELLE LANYON). She offers him the prospect of "fairy glamour" and to acquire a heart both "fearless and free." However, Jack resists such temptations, and eventually kills Meg Mucklebones (ROBERT PICARDO) to secure entry into Darkness's (TIM CURRY's) lair. This act eventually proves his strength, both to himself and the fairies. It is therefore quite logical that they should congratulate him, as he vanquishes all opponents to secure Lily's release.

Originally Scott was going to have Jack undergo even more tasks. In *LEGEND: THE DIRECTOR'S CUT* there is a reproduction of a storyboard which has Jack facing up to a two-headed giant named Abraxas, with each head having a different personality. One of the heads has a toothache, prompting Gump to pretend that Screwball is a tooth fairy, which distracts the giant while Jack locates Darkness's weapons. The scene was eventually deemed too expensive and too extraneous to produce.

Reviews of Cruise's performance were grudging at best. Morton quotes one who observed that Cruise seemed "so overwhelmed by sets and special effects that his character could be played by anybody." Apparently people laughed when he had to deliver lines such as "When I get to heaven I know just how the angels will sound." Cruise himself admitted that in the film he was "just another color in a Ridley Scott painting" and tends to dismiss the film as a bit of a joke.

References

Iain Johnstone, *Tom Cruise: All the World's a Stage* (London: Hodder and Stoughton, 2006), 101; Andrew Morton, *Tom Cruise: An Unauthorized Biography* (New York: St. Martin's Press, 2008), 73, 74–75, 80; Paul M. Sammon, *Ridley Scott Close-Up: The Making of his Movies* (New York: Thunder's Mouth Press, 1999), 80.

CRUSADER FILMS

Hollywood has frequently used the Crusades as a way of reinforcing western Christian values, especially during times of social and political turmoil. Paramount Pictures' *The Crusades* (1935) starring Loretta Young and Henry Wilcoxon and directed by Cecil B. DeMille, was planned as a follow-up to the tremendously successful *Cleopatra* (1934). The story tells of King Richard's efforts to reclaim the Holy Land from the Muslims. Initially Richard (Wilcoxon) embarks on the Crusade to escape his obligation to marry Alice of France (Katherine DeMille). Soon the love of the beautiful Barengaria (Young) helps to bring more noble motivations to the fore and rekindles Richard's belief in God. The film turned out to be a box office failure and for more than a decade DeMille concerned himself with elaborate versions of American history.

During the height of the McCarthy period Warner Bros. made *King Richard and the Crusaders* (1954), in which Richard

(George Sanders) drives out the heathen Saracens led by Saladin (Rex Harrison). Dissent leads to treachery among his allies and only the valiant Sir Kenneth of Scotland (Laurence Harvey) proves to be a loyal subject. Saladin falls in love with a Christian woman, Lady Edith (Virginia Mayo), which prompts Richard to try and win her back for the sake of his country's future. Despite the overt pro-western message, the film proved box office poison, although Max Steiner contributed an interesting score.

Other well-known films involving the crusades include *Ivanhoe* (1952), *The Lion in Winter* (1968), *Monty Python and the Holy Grail* (1975), and *A Knight's Tale* (2001). Carlo Ludovico's *The Mighty Crusaders* (1957) adapts Renaissance poet Torquato Tasso's epic *Jerusalem Delivered*, focusing on the exploits of Godfrey of Boulogne in the First Crusade. Anthony Mann's *El Cid* (1964) tells of the eponymous hero (Charlton Heston) who drives the Moors from eleventh-century Spain, while Andrei Tarkovsky's *ANDREI RUBLEV* (1966) depicts feudal wars through the life of the title character, a visionary icon painter. Scott professed an admiration for the latter film in the book accompanying the release of *KINGDOM OF HEAVEN*. Unlike most previous Crusader films, Scott's film adopts an even-handed approach to historical events by portraying the Muslims as fundamentally decent—unlike many of the Christian warriors who regard their opponents as "the enemies of God."

Reference

Diana Landau, ed., *Kingdom of Heaven: The Ridley Scott Film and the History behind the Story* (London: Simon and Schuster Ltd., 2005), 22.

CSOKAS, MARTON (1966–)

Born in New Zealand, Marton Csokas starred in the 1996 film *Broken English*, followed by a stint in *Xenia: Warrior Princess* (1997–98, 2000–2001). Other films included *The Lord of the Rings: The Return of the King* (2003) and *The Bourne Supremacy* (2004).

Cast as Guy de Lusignan in *KINGDOM OF HEAVEN*, Csokas portrays a ruthless power-seeker who will stop at nothing to achieve his ends. He has little regard for Balian, whom he believes to be an upstart bastard; indeed, Guy will not even deign to sit at table with him. Guy de Lusignan also despises Jerusalem, a place where he believes "there are no civilized rules." The irony of course is that it is Guy himself, a native of France, who has no "civilized rules" determining his behavior. He eventually suffers a humiliating defeat by Saladin (GHASSAN MASSOUD), while his wife leaves him and joins Balian (ORLANDO BLOOM) in the exodus from Jerusalem. In *KINGDOM OF HEAVEN*: THE DIRECTOR'S CUT Guy suffers further indignities, as he is released by Saladin (an act intended to humiliate Guy in the eyes of his for-

mer subjects) and subsequently challenges Balian to a duel. Once again Guy comes off second best, and he has to endure the further humiliation of being spared once again, this time by Balian.

CURRY, TIM (1946–)

Born in Cheshire, Tim Curry began his acting career in musicals such as *Hair*. He shot to fame as Frank 'N Furter in *The Rocky Horror Show* in London and New York, and subsequently in Jim Sharman's cult film *The Rocky Horror Picture Show* (1975). He became a noted actor on screen and on stage, playing a season at the Royal National Theatre, London and starring in the US tour of Noel Gay's musical *Me and My Girl*.

Scott cast him as Darkness in *LEGEND* on the strength of his performance in *The Rocky Horror Picture Show*. In his lifelike, moist red skin, with a mask allowing his emotions to register on his face (designed by makeup artist ROB BOTTIN), Curry's Darkness is a truly alarming personality. His booming voice echoes across the screen, even in his quietest speeches, and the aural effects added to the sound alter considerably with the tone of his delivery. This is especially evident in the way he commands Lily (MIA SARA) to sit with him at table in a demonic voice that demands respect.

Like Roy Batty (RUTGER HAUER) in *BLADE RUNNER*, Curry's Darkness is at once repellent yet powerfully attractive—for example, in the way he seduces Lily. A masked dancer dressed all in black moves round the terrified princess, and slowly, as the shadows of the danger's fingers creep across her face, Lily is drawn into the rhythm. The sequence reveals how Lily is gradually drawn into Darkness's trap. The next shot introduces an erotic dimension as the dancing figure moves across the frame, at first obscuring and then revealing Lily's enraptured features as she falls victim to the seduction.

Darkness casts his personality over the entire film as he describes issues relating both to the characters and the viewing audience: "The dreams of youth are the regrets of maturity. Dreams are my specialty. Through dreams I influence mankind." As they witness the action unfolding in front of them, viewers are drawn into the film's dream-world. Darkness realizes this; his lines have a particular significance in a world that places significance on youthful looks and rejects orthodox religious values. He will exploit people's self-interest and greed and thereby draw them into his sphere of influence. Darkness's final words demand our attention: "You think you have won. I am a part of you all. You can never defeat me. We are brothers eternal." The pronoun "we" refers to everyone, both on and off the screen.

In *LEGEND*: THE DIRECTOR'S CUT Darkness's character is developed further. The scene where he chats to his father (Mike Edmonds) about Lily is further amplified; the father advises him to "woo her . . . tempt her. Win her" and later to "make her one of us." Darkness becomes more of a satanic figure; he is not simply out to woo her, but seeks to convert her to his hellish faith. He will try anything to achieve his goal, including persuasion, flattery and temptation. At one point in the Director's Cut he tells Lily: "Judge me not too harshly, mistress. I invite you to share this supper. Look how sweet it is." The biblical echoes are obvious: Lily is being invited to her own Last Supper.

Curry's performance was not universally appreciated (one fan site likened his characterization to "a devil goat . . . another role that'll mark him a weirdo for life. Hasn't Tim learned anything from movies like *Star Wars*?"

References

"The Career of Tim Curry: Uncovering the Curse," www.x-entertainment.com/messages/477.html (accessed 8 May 2008).

CYBERPUNK

Ridley Scott's *BLADE RUNNER* appeared just two years before William Gibson's quintessential cyberpunk novel *Necromancer* (1984). Future urban nightmares form the settings of both works; technology permeates each, while the Frankensteinian theme of man experimenting with new forms provides the conflict and the philosophical dialectic that runs both through the film and the novel. *Blade Runner* asks questions characteristic of cyberpunk fiction such as: what does it mean to be human? What are the boundaries of humanity? How human or humane are human beings? How can one tell human beings from imitations? How human are REPLICANTS, androids or other artificially designed human forms?

Blade Runner blurs the line between human and machine, because no visual distinction between human and replicant exists. In the film the humans want to to kill the replicants in part because the replicants can integrate into society so well. Should the replicants rise up against the humans, humans wouldn't stand a chance against their genetically superior counterparts. The film also addresses the question of what it is to be a cyborg—a human being whose body has been taken over in whole or in part by electromechanical devices. What exactly is a cyborg? In basic terms, one could say that humans feel emotions while a cyborg doesn't. However, all of the cyborgs/replicants in *Blade Runner* have the capacity to feel emotions; sometimes they resemble trapped souls trying to escape.

Bibliography

The Cybercultures Reader, ed. David Bell and Barbara M. Kennedy (London and New York: Routledge, 2000); "Did *Blade Runner* Influence William Gibson When He Wrote His Cyberpunk Classic?" www.brmovie.com/FAQs/BR_FAQ_BR_Influence.htm (accessed 13 April 2008); William Fisher, "Of Living Machines and Living-Machines: *Blade Runner* and the Terminal Genre," *New Literary History* 20, no.1 (Autumn 1988): 187–98; "Information Database: The Cyberpunk Project," http://project.cyberpunk.ru/idb/bladerunner.html (accessed 13 April 2008); W. A. Senior, "Blade Runner and Cyberpunk Visions of Humanity," *Film Criticism* 21, no.1 (Fall 1996): 1–12; Steven Shaviro, "The Erotic Life of Machines," *Parallax* 25 (October–December 2002): 21–32; Wong Kin Yuen, "On the Edge of Spaces: *Blade Runner, Ghost in the Shell* and Hong Kong's Cityscape," in *Liquid Metal: The Science Fiction Film Reader*, ed. Sean Redmond (London and New York: Wallflower Press, 2004), 98–111.

DANTE (DANTE ALIGHIERI) (c. 1265–1321)

Durante degli Alighieri, commonly known as Dante Alighieri, was a Florentine poet of the Middle Ages. His central work, the *Divina Commedia*, is one of the greatest literary works composed in Italian language and a masterpiece of world literature. Hence he is known as the father of the Italian language.

Dante frequently wrote of courtly love—the kind of rituals of courtship that were characteristically taught to young boys of noble birth. They were taught to honor the Christian church, to respect women, and to devote their lives to the service of a lady. Such service was supposed to increase their abilities as warriors. Often a knight would worship his lady at a distance, never speaking to her and perhaps never even seeing her. Sometimes the courtly love inspired the lovers to great suffering as they fell in love with their beloved women, who seldom reciprocated.

HANNIBAL includes specific allusion to Dante's sonnets: Hannibal Lecter (ANTHONY HOPKINS) quotes both in Italian and English from the first sonnet in *La Vita Nuova*, and *The Inferno*. Such allusions emphasize the depth of his affection for Clarice Starling (JULIANNE MOORE), which is so great that he is prepared to cut his own hand off with a meat-cleaver at the end of the film to break the handcuffs joining him to Clarice and thereby ensure his escape from potential custody.

DAVIS, GEENA (1956–)

Born Virginia Elizabeth Davis in Wareham, Massachusetts. She entered New England College in New Hampshire and subsequently majored in drama at Boston University. Throughout the 1980s she made several important films, including *Tootsie* (1982), *The Fly* (1986), *Beetle Juice* (1988), and *The Accidental Tourist* (1988), for which she won an Oscar as Best Supporting Actress.

Evidently Davis heard that Scott was going to direct *THELMA & LOUISE* and asked to play the part of Thelma herself. At the beginning of the film, she comes across as a gawky, unfulfilled personality, who is unable to conform to the role of housewife imposed on her by her husband Darryl (CHRISTOPHER McDONALD). When offered the chance to escape from her life, she perceives it as little more than a holiday. As the action progresses, however, Thelma gradually transforms herself into a strong, independent woman—especially after her experiences with JD (BRAD PITT). Whereas once she was so unreliable that when counting her money she accidentally lets twenty dollars fly out of the window, she now assumes a leading role, forces Louise (SUSAN SARANDON) back on the road, and robs a grocery store for money. This scene is pivotal in the relationship between the two women, as Davis recalled: "Louise has never fallen apart before. It's pretty profound to see this happen. But I realize that one of us has not to fall apart, so this is the scene where I start taking control."

Davis herself was unaware of the impact her role would have on the film audience, especially in America. It was only when it opened in July 1991 that she became aware that "people would come up to me, saying 'it changed my life.' They would honk at me at stoplights and raise their fists and shout 'Whoo-hoo!'" Davis herself has embraced the feminist cause; like Thelma, she believed herself to be "on the same journey as the character I play . . . This is a movie about two women finding their power and taking responsibility for their lives and that's just what I am trying to do myself."

References

Simon Banner, "There Were Never Such Devoted Sisters," *You Magazine (Mail on Sunday)*, 14 July 1991, 32–33; Juliann Garey and Bronwen Hruska, "Road Worriers," *Premiere* 14 no.10 (June 2001): 84; Betsy Sharkey, "Ridley Scott Tries to Make It Personal," *New York Times*, 18 November 1990, Section 2, 24.

DAVIS, VIOLA (1965–)

Born in Saint Matthews, South Carolina, Davis has worked mainly in American television on series such as *City of Angels* (2000), *Century City* (2004), and *Traveler* (2007).

Cast as Dr. Charlene Barton, one of the scientists in *THE ANDROMEDA STRAIN*, Davis faces a conflict of LOVE VS. DUTY, as she is forced to leave her husband Sam (Adrian Holmes) with her son and spend all her days and nights in the laboratory Wildfire in a search for the antidote to the Andromeda Strain which threatens to engulf America. In a preproduction interview Davis said the experience of filming in a confined space helped her understand Barton's experiences: "We were in such close quarters that life mirrored art, art mirrored life. We started to find out what these scientists actually were really going through in the story, as actors in this small space that they had constructed up in Vancouver." Barton's experiences are much more painful than those of her colleagues, as members of the military take her husband hostage and force her to take samples of the virus for future research. Although the film ends happily with Charlene restored to her husband and the country apparently free of the Andromeda Strain, we know for a fact that it still exists. The final sequence shows an (unnamed) astronaut putting a canister of it away in an icebox. The implication is clear—as a result of the military's self-interest, America is still at risk of future infection, in spite of the scientists' efforts.

Reference

Fred Topel, "Viola Davis Talks About *Andromeda Strain*," *About .com: Hollywood Movies*, http://movies.about.com/od/interviews withactors/a/andromeda51208_4.htm (accessed 15 February 2009).

DE BONT, JAN (1943–)

Jan de Bont was born in the Netherlands to a Roman Catholic Dutch family on the 22 of October 1943. He has always had a creative mind and good mentality for camera techniques and soon got into film as a popular cinematographer. His major Hollywood breakthrough came with *Die Hard* (1988), and on the strength of this film he was engaged as director of photography on *BLACK RAIN*.

De Bont's greatest achievement in the film is his portrayal of the city of Osaka in JAPAN as a living hell, similar to the futuristic Los Angeles in *BLADE RUNNER*. This is not only evident in the exterior sequences—where the neon lights, anonymous buildings and endless stream of CARS suggest a DYSTOPIA where individuals have no power—but also in interior sequences such as a murder sequence, taking place in a bar. De Bont's camera tracks across the dimly lit room, focusing on the impassive-looking faces of the Japanese customers trying hard to enjoy their few moments of freedom. In the center of the frame stands Nick Conklin (MICHAEL DOUGLAS)—an aloof, lone figure trying to make sense of what is happening around him; no one seems in the least interested in the murder as they continue tossing back their overpriced champagne and taking advantage of the services offered by the so-called "hostesses." The whole scene resembles a living hell dedicated to hedonism where indifference and self-interest prevail.

Another memorable sequence—that is characteristic of De Bont's work in stylish action pieces and slick adventures—takes place in an iron foundry where Nick and Masahiro (KEN TAKAKURA) pursue Sato (YUSAKU MATSUDA) and his gang. The *mise-en-scène* is awash with red and orange colors; sparks fly in all directions; and smoke billows through the air. As in *LEGEND*, the characters appear to have fallen into Darkness's lair, an earthly place of torment threatening to engulf them in flames.

Bibliography

David Jon Wiener, "High Crime Culture Clash in *Black Rain*," *American Cinematographer* 70, no.9 (September 1989): 42–49.

DE GANAY, THIERRY (?–?)

Producer of *SOMEONE TO WATCH OVER ME*. De Ganay was drawn to the film (his first English-language film) on account of its subject, which he felt "completely corresponded with the tastes and special sensitivities of Ridley Scott. Howard Franklin manages to illustrate the persistence of the class system in the United States, but his interest and intentions are timeless." De Ganay reemphasized the point in another interview, saying that what really interested him was the subject of class division, especially in the United States, which tried to project a vision of classlessness to the world. He believed there were two worlds in the film—one of the police and the other of money.

References

Thierry de Ganay, interviewed in the pressbook for *Someone to Watch Over Me* (Burbank, CA: Columbia Pictures, 1987), 3; "Thierry de Ganay: Producteur Francais à Hollywood," *Le Film Français* 2187 (8 April 1988): 4.

Bibliography

Sarah Drouhaud, "Larry Clark Rejoint Lambert pour 'Un Beau Jour Pour Mourir,'" *Le Film Français* 2995 (13 June 2003): 8.

DE LAURENTIIS, DINO (1919–)

Born Agostino de Laurentiis in Torre Annunziata, Italy. De Laurentiis began as long ago as 1947 in Italy with *La Figlia del Capitano*; his Hollywood career took off in the early 1970s when he produced a string of hits including *Mandingo* (1975), *The Shootist* (1976), and the first remake of *King Kong* (also 1976). Following the success of *U-571* (2000), de Laurentiis went on to produce *HANNIBAL*, a film he believed was not a sequel to *THE SILENCE OF THE LAMBS* but rather "the second act of Hannibal Lecter's life . . . It is the life of Hannibal Lecter free from the prison as an intellectual man in Florence, in the middle of the culture. Even then Starling comes back in a different position." STEVEN ZAILLIAN's script emphasizes the significance of the location through stage directions: "*Florence—Day*. One of the most magnificent views in the world. Drifting across it, then down, reveals a piazza below." Later on he describes the interior of the Palazzo Vecchio thus: "It's under long-term restoration, scaffolding everywhere. A large assembly of men ranging in age from middle-aged to the Middle Ages, it seems, are gathered round a long twelfth-century table." Even Florence's inhabitants are part of its history. Bearing this in mind, it is not surprising that de Laurentiis should suggest that "[The city] is a character . . . next to Hannibal Lecter. It is not just a location. We gave it the atmosphere, the right lighting and the character comes out." De Laurentiis's association with the Hannibal franchise continued as he produced both *Red Dragon* (2002) and *Hannibal Rising* (2006).

References
Joe Mauceri, "Dino de Laurentiis: King of Producers," *Shivers* 88 (April 2001): 31–32; Steven Zaillian, "*Hannibal*: Screenplay Based on the Novel by Thomas Harris," Revision (9 February 2000), http://sfy.ru/sfy.html?script=hannibal2001 (accessed 15 December 2008), 29–30.

Bibliography
Roger Clarke, "Dino Takes a Bite out of Jody," *Evening Standard*, 15 February 2001, 30–31; Andrew Pulver, "Fellini Wouldn't Cut the Scene—So I Stole It," *The Guardian*, 1 June 1999, Section 2, 6–7; David Rooney, "Dino Night," *Variety*, 19–25 June 2000, 44, 54.

DE LAUZIRIKA, CHARLES (?–)
A graduate of University of Southern California School of Cinema and Television, de Lauzirika worked at Ridley Scott's company, SCOTT FREE Entertainment, for two years before becoming a DVD producer. He worked on producing the "Director's Cut" of *LEGEND*. De Lauzirika completed work as restoration producer on *BLADE RUNNER*: THE FINAL CUT and DVD producer on *Blade Runner* 5-disc *Collector's Edition*, *Twin Peaks* 10-Disc Definitive Gold Box Edition, and Scott's *AMERICAN GANGSTER*: 3-Disc Collector's Edition. He also produced documentaries about the making of *MATCHSTICK MEN*, *KINGDOM OF HEAVEN*, *NUMB3RS*, and *THE COMPANY*.

De Lauzirika was involved in the creation of *LEGEND*: THE DIRECTOR'S CUT (2002)—a job which, he admitted in an interview with *Film Score Monthly*, was enormously hard. Eventually he located two copies of the original 113-minute version of the film—one in Universal's vaults in London, the other in Los Angeles. The 2002 release was based on the Los Angeles print. The main difference in the Director's Cut, according to de Lauzirika (in another interview with Sean Murphy), was it felt "more whole and satisfying" compared to the original film (1985): "There's just more character development in general . . . [and] JERRY GOLDSMITH's score just works like gangbusters."

References
Sean Murphy, "Digital Bits interview with Charles de Lauzirika," *Legend: Frequently Asked Questions*, www.figmentfly.com/legend/different4k.html (accessed 25 April 2008); "Restoring *Legend*: An Interview with DVD Producer Charles de Lauzirika," *Film Score Monthly* 7, no.4 (May/June 2002): 15–16.

DE LINE, DONALD (?–)
Film producer, executive producer, and former studio head, whose credits include *Pretty Woman* (1990), *The Italian Job*, (2003), and *BODY OF LIES*.

Bibliography
"*Production Notes: Body of Lies*" (Los Angeles: Warner Bros. Entertainment, 2008), http://mix96tulsa.com/movies/notes/body-of-lies/note/4 (accessed 16 January 2009).

DEAKINS, ROGER (1949–)
Deakins began working as a still photographer before enrolling in Britain's National Film School in 1972. Among his credits are *Sid and Nancy* (1986), *A Beautiful Mind* (2001), and Vadim Perelman's *House of Sand and Fog* (2003).

As director of photography on *THE ASSASSINATION OF JESSE JAMES BY THE COWARD ROBERT FORD*, produced by Scott, Deakins tried to create a look both austere and sumptuous. His camera occasionally offers glimpses of life seen through the flawed and rippled glass that was typical of the time. In one scene, Robert Ford (CASEY AFFLECK) while a guest at the James household, intently and surreptitiously studies Jesse at his leisure in the yard through a back window. Deakins suggested that such sequences revealed "the transitory nature of reality." In another scene, during a nighttime train robbery, Jesse suddenly and dramatically appears from a billow of white steam, as if "emerging from another world, perhaps from hell . . . It's as if Jesse [BRAD PITT] is a ghost already." Another sequence showing the characters like specks against the vast landscape reveals "how humans are just a small part of nature, despite our feelings of importance."

Deakins also worked as director of photography on the Oscar-winning *NO COUNTRY FOR OLD MEN*.

References
"About the Production," http://party931.com/common/movies/notes/54706-1-full.html (accessed 12 August 2008); Stephen Pizzello and Jean Oppenheimer, "Western Destinies," *American Cinematographer* 88, no.10 (October 2007): 31–47.

DEE, RUBY (1924–)
Ruby Dee grew up and began her career as a member of the American Negro Theatre. She received her BA from Hunter College and later studied acting with Paul Mann, Lloyd

Richards, and Morris Carnovsky. Her film career began in 1950; since then, she has been featured in *A Raisin in the Sun* (1961), and Jules Dassin's *Up Tight!* (1968). In 1991, she was awarded an Emmy for her performance in *Decoration Day* (1990). With her actor husband Ossie Davis, she received the John F. Kennedy Center Honors in 2004.

Cast as Mama Lucas in *AMERICAN GANGSTER*, Dee revisited the place where she grew up; her experiences proved helpful insight for all with whom she worked. In the production information she observed that "The time of Frank Lucas that *American Gangster* is about doesn't seem as much of a film to me as it does more of a memory. Gangsters played a very important role in the life of the community, because they were part of the community. They controlled the rackets." As a child, she lived in an apartment building on 137th Street and 7th Avenue. Of that time, Dee recalled that "People who looked like Denzel [Washington] would come to the door in twos or threes, and they would give you a greeting and hand you a shopping bag. In there would be a turkey at Thanksgiving; at Christmas there would be toys." Only later in life would she learn that they weren't just helpful citizens; there was a "political connection to the gangster element."

Dee's major sequence in the film comes towards the end, when she berates her son for thinking about shooting a police officer. Such things are simply not honorable in terms of her beliefs; she cares neither about where he got his money nor whether he will continue in his life of crime, but she does not want to hear him lie to her. STEVEN ZAILLIAN's script says that "she's not pleading, but telling"— Frank, for his part, cannot look her in the eyes. Eventually Mama Lucas slaps him across the face; a final gesture of contempt signaling the breakdown of relations between mother and son.

References

American Gangster: Production Information (Los Angeles: Universal Pictures, 2007); Steven Zaillian, "*American Gangster:* Final Shooting Script" (27 July 2006), http://www.roteirodecinema.com .br/scripts/files/american_gangster.htm (accessed 8 February 2009).

Bibliography

Ossie Davis and Ruby Dee, *With Ossie and Ruby: In This Life Together* (New York: Harper Paperbacks, 2000).

DEELEY, MICHAEL (1932–)

Film producer whose major works include *The Italian Job* (1969), *The Man Who Fell to Earth* (1976), *The Deer Hunter* (1978), and *BLADE RUNNER*.

Michael Deeley read through HAMPTON FANCHER's initial treatment of the novel and agreed to produce it. He believed that the story was "a marvelous blending of a

thriller with a romance. There was also a dramatic moral problem at the heart of the [PHILIP K. DICK] book, the idea that this sanctioned executioner was become emotionally attracted to one he's supposed to kill. That aspect enormously appealed to me . . . what ultimately appealed to me on the project was Hampton Fancher's script . . . That sort of ultimately pulled in Ridley Scott, as well. And he's not an easy person to seduce by writing, I'll tell you."

The full story of Deeley's involvement in *Blade Runner,* and how he ultimately came to be removed from the film, has been told in his recent autobiography *Blade Runners, Deer Hunters, and Blowing the Bloody Doors Off: My Life in Cult Movies* (2008), described by Scott in his foreword as "an accurate and entertaining read."

References

Michael Deeley, *Blade Runners, Deer Hunters, and Blowing the Bloody Doors Off* (London: Faber and Faber, 2008), ix; Paul M. Sammon, *Future Noir: The Making of Blade Runner*, 2nd ed. (London: Gollancz, 2007), 34.

DELTA FORCE: BLACK HAWK DOWN

A first-person shooter video-game set during the United Nations intervention in the Somali civil war, with missions taking place primarily in the Jubba Valley and the Somali capital, Mogadishu, based both on the actual events in 1993 and on the Scott film of the same name.

The game was developed by NovaLogic and was released on Microsoft Windows on 24 March 2003, on Mac OS X on 21 June 2004, on the PlayStation 2 on 27 July 2005 and on the Xbox on 8 September 2006. It is the sixth game of the *Delta Force* series.

DEMME, JONATHAN (1944–)

Born Robert Jonathan Demme in Long Island. Early directorial efforts included *Crazy Mama* (1975) and *Fighting Mad* (1976), as well as episodes of the television series *Colombo*. His first major commercial success before *THE SILENCE OF THE LAMBS* was *Married to the Mob* (1988). For the first Harris adaptation Demme won the Oscar for Best Director.

Demme was originally slated to direct *HANNIBAL,* but walked out, claiming that he did not want to work on a sequel to the film. He might also have been disturbed by the violence of THOMAS HARRIS's original novel. Having taken over the direction of *Hannibal,* Scott was working on his first sequel; an ironic decision in view of the fact that he had refused to direct the sequel to *ALIEN,* which was eventually helmed by James Cameron. When asked in an interview how he felt about the fact that he had taken over Demme's version of the Hannibal saga, Scott replied defensively, "I don't know."

Reference
Jonathan Demme, quoted in Adam Smith, "Signed, Sealed, De-livered," *Empire* 141 (March 2001), 76.

DEPARDIEU, GÉRARD (1948–)

Gérard Depardieu started his acting career at the small traveling theatre Café de la Gare along with Patrick Dewaere and Miou-Miou. After minor roles in cinema, he at last got his chance in Bertrand Blier's *Les Valseuses* (1974). He made his English-language debut in Peter Weir's film *Green Card* (1990).

For his biographer Marianne Gray, Depardieu's leading role in *1492 CONQUEST OF PARADISE* represented a "make or break" chance for the actor to establish himself as in international star: "Depardieu describes Columbus as 'an Italian gypsy, who is also Jewish, who made journeys comparable to our conquering of space. He's often thought of as just a famous sailor but there's more to him than that. He took enormous risks, telling people the earth was round and keeping the Church happy by bringing in gold. He was driven by the gods and had a sacred faith, and then,' he adds shyly, 'you have the love story with Queen Isabella.'" Depardieu has in fact worked previously with one of the film's stars, SIGOURNEY WEAVER, on the film *Une Femme ou Deux* (*One Woman or Two*) (1985).

Depardieu did considerable research for the role, not only reading most of the recent biographies, but also listening to the opera by Darius Milhaud. His biographer Michel Mahéo believed that he brought a certain mystical, passionate presence to the film which was something unique. Scott admired what Depardieu did; in an interview with the British film magazine *Empire* he described the actor as "a true modern artiste, he can conjure dreams from something passionless and technical. He is able to go beyond the technique of the camera, and put it at the service of the imagination."

Depardieu summed up his role in the film thus in the *Empire* interview already cited: "[H]e was an artist as well as someone who had the temperament to convince people to follow him. It was as if a Mexican turned up at the White House and tried to sell a programme to go and discover Mars." His performance in the film is low key (at least by Depardieu's standards). He is someone who is not only obsessive in his quest to discover the new world, but also proud of his family. At times his obsession recalls Gregory Peck's Captain Ahab in the 1956 film *MOBY DICK*—a man prepared to sacrifice everything in search of his dream. Robert Thurston's novelization of the screenplay makes this clear: "[Columbus] was not quite human . . . had perhaps become mythic. Is that true, Columbus thought, or is it merely my conceited imagination? In making my exorbitant demands and then setting out on a voyage that made most ordinary men tremble with apprehension, am I placing myself in the same company with mythic beings?"

Depardieu's combination of aggressive MASCULINITY plus an open display of feminine qualities in the film is characteristic of the actor's star image, as Ginette Vincendeau remarks: "While in many ways Depardieu represents a traditional vision of aggressive French machismo . . . one of the most common descriptions of his screen image as well as his behaviour as a performer, to the extent that it has become a cliché, is that of his 'femininity'—. . . a fragile man, with a flaw in his personality, a very feminine character in the end . . . Ultimately though, this gender displacement does not entail changes in either casting patterns, or the values associated with femininity and masculinity, which are left at their most traditional (male = active, female = passive). This is in a sense consistent with the film's gender politics, which reinforce the idea of the aggressive, go-getting male leaving his spouse at home to look after the home while he goes off on his voyages. His partner Beatrix (ANGELA MOLINA) is presented as an object for our admiration, as she 'keeps' herself for her husband, in spite of the approaches of other men."

References
Marianne Gray, *Depardieu: A Biography* (London: Warner Books, 1991), 201; Michel Mahéo, *Gérard Depardieu: 25 Ans de Cinéma* (Lausanne, Éditions Favre, 1999), 154; Mark Salisbury, "In Nineteen Hundred and Ninety Two . . . ," *Empire*, November 1992, 84, 88; Robert Thurston, *1492: Conquest of Paradise Based on a Screenplay by Roselyne Bosch* (London: Penguin Books, 1992), 72; Ginette Vincendeau, *Stars and Stardom in French Cinema* (London and New York: Continuum, 2000), 227–29.

DIAL "M" FOR MURDER

GB 1962 TVM r/t 50 min b/w. *Production Company:* British Broadcasting Corporation. *Producer:* Alan Bridges. *Director/ Production Designer:* Ridley Scott. *Writer:* Frederick Knott. *Cast:* Diana Fairfax (*Sheila Wendice*), Richard Pasco (*Tony Wendice*), Barry Letts (*Max Halliday*), Leslie Sands (*Inspector Hubbard*).

A fifty-minute live television version broadcast in the *Sunday Night Play* slot of Frederick Knott's famous stage thriller that marked Ridley Scott's début as a television director for the BBC. Unfortunately the original broadcast has been lost.

DIAZ, CAMERON (1972–)

Blonde leading actress who enjoyed her first major success with *The Mask* (1994). Cast as Maggie in the Ridley Scott–produced film *IN HER SHOES*, Diaz at first seems as if she has been cast as an object of male desire, as the camera lovingly focuses on her half-naked BODY stretched out on the sofa. As the story unfolds, however, we discover that this image is something Maggie has constructed for herself to compensate for her crippling lack of self-esteem. Unlike her sister Rose (TONI COLLETTE), who enjoys an apparently successful career as a lawyer, Maggie suffers from dyslexia; the only thing she can rely upon to attract people's interest is her own body. At one point she narrowly escapes being assaulted by two hobos, who take her back to a parking lot and expect 'payment' for returning her car. While visiting her grandmother Ella (SHIRLEY MACLAINE) at the retirement residence, Maggie puts on her bikini and sunbathes by the pool, much to the enjoyment of the elderly residents. Diaz herself summed up this aspect of her role in a preproduction interview: "It was important to me to exploit that aspect of Maggie because that was really who she was. Her body was her tool. It was her instrument, it was how she got through the world the way that she had up until that point. For me it was important to be able to exploit that part of her. We could have gone further, definitely could have gone further, and we didn't. I could have actually been naked. I could have gone anywhere. I could have really worn skimpy stuff. I didn't really think any of her, other than the cleavage and the bikini, I didn't think that anything was really inappropriate. She wore jeans and it was winter and she was bundled up. And in Florida it was one little short skirt. But I didn't feel like she was . . . Everything she had fit into a garbage bag. Everything she owned fit into a garbage bag. She didn't have a lot of choices."

However, Maggie undergoes a complete change of character: not only does she acquire self-esteem (as a professor congratulates her on her ability to interpret the poem, Elizabeth Bishop's "One Art," that she has just read to him), but learns to care for the retirement home's residents. This is underlined in one sequence where she shows her sister around, beginning with the pharmacy and taking in the exercise pavilion and "The Bench" (where retired lawyers pass the time of day). Wherever she goes, everyone takes the time to acknowledge her as a valued member of their community. Diaz herself admitted that the role represented something of a departure for her as an actress: "To me, I thought it was really courageous and something that I'd like to portray for an audience."

Reference

Rebecca Murray, "Cameron Diaz Talks about Her Role in *In Her Shoes*" (29 September 2005), *About.com*, http://movies.about.com/od/inhershoes/a/inshoescd092905.htm (accessed 8 August 2008).

Bibliography

"Cameron Diaz: In Her Shoes and in the News," *Empire* 198 (December 2005): 83.

DIBENEDETTO, TONY (1944–)

Tony DiBenedetto's early films included *The Exterminator* (1980), *Deathtrap* (1982), and *Splash* (1984).

Cast as the cop T. J. in *SOMEONE TO WATCH OVER ME*, DiBenedetto emphasizes the importance of duty. Even though watching over Claire Gregory's (MIMI ROGERS's) apartment is boring, often tedious work, T. J. carries it out without demur. The fact that he is eventually shot by Venza's hired assassin (Harlan Cary Poe) shows how dangerous the job can be. Unlike Mike (TOM BERENGER), T. J. does not acknowledge his personal feelings; in fact, he is downright inarticulate ("Detective Keegan is . . . Mike . . . 'Michael' asked me to tell you [Claire] he's under the weather. . . . Yeah, just . . . bad gut. Y'know").

DICAPRIO, LEONARDO (1974–)

Born in Hollywood, Leonardo DiCaprio got his breakthrough part as Toby in *This Boy's Life* (1993), along with Robert De Niro and Ellen Barkin. His first major starring role was in *Romeo + Juliet* (1996), directed by Baz Luhrmann, followed by *Titanic* (1997).

Cast as Roger Ferris in *BODY OF LIES*, DiCaprio was quoted in the production notes as saying that the character was "well-versed in weapons training and hand-to-hand combat, but he's also a really intelligent, highly effective field agent who has immersed himself in Middle Eastern culture. He knows the language and the culture and respects the attitudes and customs of the people. He's become very skilled at forging relationships and infiltrating terrorist networks." For all his skills, however, there is a strong element of mimicry in DiCaprio's performance as he dons Arab robes and passes himself off as a native, while displaying his language skills. His characterization resembles that of Peter O'Toole in *LAWRENCE OF ARABIA*. For all his apparent sensitivities, he still describes the Jordanian Secret Service chief Hani's (MARK STRONG's) operation as a "fingernail factory"—suggesting that they are preoccupied with torture. This actually turns out to be true, but such statements are hardly likely to promote good diplomatic relations between America and its Arab allies. Like MICHAEL DOUGLAS in *BLACK RAIN*, DiCaprio plays the all-American hero—a tough, no-nonsense operator in a foreign context combining heroism with sensitivity (particularly to the Iranian nurse Aisha (GOLSHIFTEH FARAHANI).

Some critics liked DiCaprio's performance: Kenneth Turan in the Los Angeles Times saw his Ferris as "the CIA's ace on the ground . . . a caring, sensitive individual who values human life." However, A. O. Scott found the actor unconvincing, revealing "his commitment to full employment for dialect coaches . . . with some good old-boy inflections that are helpfully identified by Mr. Crowe's character as originating in North Carolina." Nick Curtis in the London *Evening Standard* felt sorry for DiCaprio who had to try to make sense of the film's "daft plot" with "nothing but a wispy beard to disguise his American features."

References

Body of Lies: Production Notes (Los Angeles: Warner Bros., 2008), www.mix96tulsa.com/movies/notes/body-of-lies/note/4 (accessed January 16, 2009); Nick Curtis, "*Body of Lies* Leaves You Feeling Cheated," *Evening Standard*, 7 November 2008, www.thisislondon .co.uk/film/review-23583655-details/Body+of+Lies+leaves+ you+feeling+cheated/review.do?reviewId=23583655 (accessed February 17,2009); A. O. Scott, "Big Stars Wielding an Array of Accents, Fighting the War on Terrorism," *New York Times*, 10 October 2008, http://movies.nytimes.com/2008/10/10/movies/10lies.html?scp=2& sq=body%20of%20lies&st=cse (accessed 17 February 2009); Kenneth Turan, "*Body of Lies*," *Los Angeles Times*, October 10, 2008. www.calendarlive.com/movies/cl-et-body-10-2008oct10,0, 708812.story (accessed 17 February 2009).

Bibliography

Xan Brooks, "Leonardo DiCaprio Is a Boy in a Man's World," *The Guardian*, 20 November 2008, www.guardian.co.uk/film/filmblog/ 2008/nov/20/leonardo-di-caprio (accessed 17 February 2009); Chrissy Iley, "Leonardo's Renaissance," *The Observer*, 2 November 2008, www.guardian.co.uk/film/2008/nov/02/leonardo-dicaprio- body-of-lies (accessed February 17, 2009); "Leonardo DiCaprio on Barack Obama's Election Victory," *Daily Telegraph*, 6 November 2008, www.telegraph.co.uk/culture/film/3562910/Leonardo-Di- Caprio-on-Barack-Obama%27s-election-victory.html (accessed 17 February 2009).

DICK, PHILIP K. (1928–1982)

Philip K. Dick grew up in Washington, DC, where he experienced firsthand the poverty of the Great Depression. He moved to California and entered Berkeley High School. He briefly attended the University of California at Berkeley in 1949, where he declared himself a philosophy major. It was at this time that he inherited the philosophical skepticism characteristic of his work. Early in the 1950s, perhaps as a result of his own association and his then-wife's acquaintance with Communist Party members on the Berkeley campus, Dick was approached by two FBI agents and recruited to spy on suspicious enemy agents at the University of Mexico. The extent of his responsibilities is unclear; but from that time onwards he became preoccupied with the paranoia, distrust, suspicion and repressive domestic surveillance characteristic of post-World War II America. Dick's first novel *Solar Lottery* appeared in 1955; in the same year a volume of short stories, *A Handful of Darkness*, was published in London. Thereafter he wrote prolifically until his untimely death in 1982.

Dick was primarily concerned with the question of what it is to be human, particularly in a world in which life seemed perpetually threatened by nuclear war. To emphasize this point, Dick stressed that human beings were not necessarily different from one another; the great and powerful had similar aspirations and abilities as an ordinary person. Storekeepers and shop clerks were just as likely as warlords and messiahs to be Dick's focus of attention. Dick's third major theme was war and devastation and his fear of it. This forms the subject of novels such as *DO ANDROIDS DREAM OF ELECTRIC SHEEP?* (adapted by Scott as *BLADE RUNNER*).

Dick had an ambivalent reaction to *Blade Runner*. He had completed a pamphlet "Notes on *Do Androids Dream of Electric Sheep?*" (1968) for filmmaker Bertram Berman, who had purchased an option on the novel, but this project came to nothing. Dick was initially skeptical about Scott's film; in a 1981 article he commented thus on an early version of the script: "It was terrific. It bore no relation to the book . . . What my story will become is one titanic lurid collision of androids being blown up, androids killing humans, general confusion and murder, all very exciting to watch. Makes my book seem dull by comparison." Dick's attitude changed, however, when Scott showed him twenty minutes of special effects footage; by early 1982 he told one interviewer that the opening sequence "is simply the most stupendous thing I have ever seen in the way of a film. It's simply unbelievable."

References

Philip K. Dick, "Universe Makers . . . and Breakers" (1981), in *The Shifting Realities of Philip K. Dick: Selected Literary and Philosophical Writings*, ed. Lawrence Smith (New York: Vintage Random, 1995), 104; Gwen Lee and Doris Elaine Sauter, Doris Elaine, eds., *What If Our World Is Their Heaven: The Final Conversations of Philip K. Dick* (Woodstock: The Overlook Press, 2000), 23.

Bibliography

Dominic Alessio, "Redemption, 'Race,' Religion, Reality and the Far-Right: Science Fiction Film Adaptations of Philip K. Dick," in *The Blade Runner Experience: The Legacy of a Science Fiction Classic*, ed. Will Brooker (London and New York: Wallflower Press, 2005), 59–79; Aaron Barlow, "Reel Toads and Imaginary Cities: Philip K. Dick, *Blade Runner* and the Contemporary Science Fiction Movie," in *The Blade Runner Experience: The Legacy of a Science Fiction Classic*, ed. Will Brooker, 43–59; "Philip K. Dick: *The Blade Runner* Interviews," Featurette included in Disc 4 of *Blade Runner: Collector's Edition* (Los Angeles: Warner Bros. Entertainment and the Blade Runner Partnership, 2007); Alison Landsberg, "Prosthetic Memory: *Total Recall* and *Blade Runner*," in *Liquid Metal: The Science Fiction Film Reader*, ed. Sean Redmond (London and New York: Wallflower Press, 2004), 239–48; Brian J. Robb, *Counterfeit Worlds: Philip K. Dick on Film* (London: Titan Books, 2006); Philip Strick, "The Age of the Replicant," *Sight and Sound*, July 1982, 168–72; Lawrence Sutin, *Divine Invasions: A Life of Philip K. Dick* (New York: Carol and Graf Avalon, 2005); Jason P. Vest, *Future Imperfect: Philip K. Dick at the Movies* (Westport, CT: Praeger Publishers, 2007).

DICKEN, ROGER

Specialist model-maker responsible for the "face-hugger" in *ALIEN* that attaches itself to Kane's (JOHN HURT's) face and makes the crew realize that they are dealing with a creature infinitely more dangerous than even the ferocity of its initial onslaught (on the deserted planet) had suggested. When efforts to pry the hugger from Kane's face prove unfruitful, Dallas (TOM SKERRITT) and Ash (IAN HOLM) mount a direct assault by attempting to amputate one of its fingers. At the first incision, however, a yellowish fluid oozes from the wound, incredibly corrosive, that eats through the floor within seconds. The face-hugger's appearance, according to Ridley Scott in an interview with Don Shay, was "enough to make audiences uncomfortable, which is what we wanted." More significantly, the fact that it covers the whole of Kane's face suggests that once he has been possessed by the alien, Kane no longer has the capacity for self-determination.

Reference

Don Shay, "Creating an Alien Ambience," in *Alien: The Special Effects*, ed. Don Shay and Bill Norton (London: Titan Books, 1997), 28.

DILLEY, LESLIE (?–)

Born in Wales, Leslie Dilley began his career by working on *The Saint* television series with Roger Moore. One of his first film assignments was Richard Lester's *The Three Musketeers* (1974); and he subsequently worked on the first *Star Wars* movie (1977).

Dilley's work on the Ridley Scott-produced film *MONKEY TROUBLE* is evident in his use of interior design, which contrasts the order of Amy's (MIMI ROGERS's) living room with the chaos of her daughter Eva's (THORA BIRCH's) room, which suggests how much the little girl has been neglected. Dilley also creates a suitably untidy interior for the gypsy Azro's (HARVEY KEITEL's) caravan, thereby drawing a parallel between his inability to look after his two "sons" (the monkey and his real son Peter) and Amy's difficulties of caring for her daughter. The film at one level is about the inadequacies of parenthood: Dilley's designs draw our attention to this.

Bibliography

Pat Jankiewicz, "Time Capsule: Leslie Dilley," *Starburst* 213 (May 1996): 58–61.

DO ANDROIDS DREAM OF ELECTRIC SHEEP?

PHILIP K. DICK's 1968 novel posits a religion—Mercerism—that allows Earth's inhabitants to extract some hope from their lives in the wake of a nuclear holocaust. *BLADE RUNNER*, Ridley Scott's version of the novel, retains the bleak, dark and depressing portrait of a futuristic society. However, it resituates the action not in San Francisco of 1992, but in LOS ANGELES of 2019. In this new world there has not been a world war and the city is certainly not deserted. On the contrary, it is teeming with people, all of whom seem to be soulless, acting according to prearranged ideas rather than thinking on their own. The film's center of attention is not on Isidore (who is eliminated altogether) but on Deckard (HARRISON FORD), who is changed from a freelance bounty hunter into a member of the state bureaucracy, despairing at what he sees. As he comes to love Rachael (SEAN YOUNG), Deckard undergoes a spiritual growth by ignoring the constraints of a society that objectifies and dehumanizes the androids (renamed REPLICANTS in the film). In both novel and film, Deckard becomes progressively uncertain about the replicants' inhumanity. This skepticism becomes more explicit in the novel when Deckard visits a police station staffed by androids and presided over by Inspector Garland. Garland reveals that both he (Garland) and Resch (the bounty hunter introduced to Deckard) are androids. Having encountered such people, Deckard begins to question whether the androids are as inhuman as he once assumed, and whether they should be "retired" (i.e., exterminated). Scott omits this sequence: Deckard experiences his awakening by means of a growing sexual attraction to Rachael. Scott also makes Rachael a more interesting character: a replicant who thinks she is human who eventually discovers she is a replicant. The film's ending is altered from the book, in which Deckard kills the three replicants before returning home to his wife. In the film, Batty (RUTGER HAUER) saves Deckard before dying; as he does so, he becomes the savior for *Blade Runner*'s immoral world. As he dies he releases a white dove which flies up and away from him—a clear allusion to the fact that Batty's soul now ascends heavenwards. This conclusion, while optimistic in one sense, also underlines the film's ambiguity; it is difficult to separate human beings from androids. This further emphasized in the 1992 DIRECTOR'S CUT of the film, when Deckard picks up an aluminum foil unicorn, referring us back to an earlier dream sequence (omitted from the original 1982 US theatrical release) when Deckard dreams about a unicorn running through a field. This implies that the cop Gaff (EDWARD JAMES OLMOS) has access to Deckard's implanted memories.

In general the film concentrates more on visual detail rather than plot (as in the novel). Perhaps this represents one of its shortcomings; in a 2007 documentary on the difference between the novel and film, screenwriter DAVID PEOPLES expressed the opinion that perhaps the film's narrative could have been sharper.

Reference

David Peoples, interviewed in "Sacrificial Sheep: Novel vs. Film," Featurette included in *Blade Runner: Collector's Edition* (Los Angeles:

Warner Bros. Entertainment and the Blade Runner Partnership, 2007), Disc 4.

Bibliography
Jason P. Vest, *Future Imperfect: Philip K. Dick at the Movies* (Westport, CT: Praeger Publishers, 2007).

DOBKIN, DAVID (1969–)

Born in Washington, DC, Dobkin made his name directing music videos for Elton John, John Lee Hooker, and Bryan Ferry.

The Ridley Scott-produced black comedy *CLAY PIGEONS* was his major feature film debut, following an episode of the television series *Love Street* (1995). Dobkin claimed he was drawn to MATT HEALY's script (originally titled "In Too Deep") as it was "at once very dark and very funny. It's a very risky film," taking place in a SMALL TOWN, a place he believed to be "really outrageous and interesting. There's something scarier about when things are isolated; they tend to become more extreme and more personified." The actors admired Dobkin's enthusiasm for the film: JOAQUIN PHOENIX was quoted in an interview as saying that the director "has a great sense of rhythm, with music and imagery combined." One such sequence could be seen in the sequence where Lester Long (VINCE VAUGHN) knifes Amanda (GEORGINA CATES) to death, which took place to the strains of Elvis Presley's "It's Now or Never" on the soundtrack. Not only did this sum up Long's state of mind, but the romantic nature of the song provides a savage counterpoint to what takes place on the screen.

Reference
David Dobkin, Joaquin Phoenix, interviewed in "Production Notes: *Clay Pigeons*," included on the European DVD release of the film (Frankfurt: BY Internationale Medien und Film, 1998).

Bibliography
"Clay Pigeons," Entry in *Wikipedia*, http://en.wikipedia.org/wiki/Clay_Pigeons (accessed 8 November 2008).

DOBROWLSKI, MAREK (?–)

Dobrowlski's films include *Last Action Hero* (1993) (Art Director), *The Craft* (1996) (Production Designer), and *Into the West* (Miniseries, 2005) (Production Designer).

As production designer for *THE COMPANY*, Dobrowlski created a world of shadows and dark corners appropriate to the world of spying. Filming took place in several locations, including Toronto and Budapest, a city which, according to Dobrowlski in the production notes, "presented logistical challenges, but . . . offered beautiful gleaming architecture and, right alongside it, some wonderfully old, rough-hewn structures with run-down alleys and decrepit courtyards that connote foreboding images of lurk-ing spies and intrigue. It's a wonderful backdrop for a Cold War battleground."

One sequence in particular was filmed in Vac Prison, a long-term detention center forty minutes outside the city. Built in the eighteenth century as a college for aristocrats, the building was turned into a prison a century later, and housed many political prisoners rounded up by the Hungarian secret police (AVH) during the period of Soviet rule. Dobrowlski and art director Laszlo Rajk found the experience of filming there a painful one: Rajk said in the production notes that "there were so many writers, anti-government leaders and intellectuals held in Vac that it was referred to as 'the best political union in the world.'" Scientists and academicians were so numerous in the prison that the Communist government relied on them to conduct research in physics and math and to translate English literature into Hungarian.

Reference
Production Notes: The Company, http://www.tnt.tv/series/thecompany/bts/ (accessed 12 August 2008).

DOCTOR WHO

Long-running British science fiction television series (1962–89) recently revived with great success. Some critics of Scott have claimed that he worked on the series in the mid-1960s, but Scott himself emphasizes that he had no connection with the series, other than to work with VERITY LAMBERT on *ADAM ADAMANT LIVES!* (Lambert herself was responsible for the famous police box in *Dr. Who*.)

Bibliography
"Director Ridley Scott Quizzed," *BBC News Forum*, 26 March 2001, http://news.bbc.co.uk/2/hi/talking_point/forum/1234177.stm (accessed 26 February 2009).

DOMINIK, ANDREW (1967–)

Born in New Zealand, Dominik worked in music and video production before making his first feature film *Chopper* (2000) starring ERIC BANA.

According to the production notes, when he read Ron Hansen's *THE ASSASSINATION OF JESSE JAMES BY THE COWARD ROBERT FORD* (NOVEL), he was intrigued by the characters—especially Robert Ford: "This was a portrait . . . I had never seen before . . . It gives you a sense of what that event might actually have been like for him—to shoot a man in his own house with Jesse's wife and children nearby and then to wait around for days with a brother who was completely unnerved, and try to deal with the enormity of public reaction. You see his anxiety, his neediness and his ambition and you think, 'That's probably what it was like.' That's what moved me about the book and what I wanted to capture on screen."

The film itself was part funded by BRAD PITT's own company Plan B and Ridley Scott's SCOTT FREE. It was eventually completed in November 2006, but release was delayed a year while the final cut was assembled. Evidently Dominik was removed from the production at this point.

The Assassination of Jesse James bears strong resemblances to earlier Westerns involving two characters; for example, Sam Peckinpah's *PAT GARRETT AND BILLY THE KID*, that tell of "violent, real-life criminal[s]." However, the film's visual style was very different, as Dominik explained to the British film magazine *Empire*: "We looked at a lot of old period photographs. You realise that the era [1882] didn't seem Western; it was more Dickens, more Victorian. It looked like *Oliver Twist*." In another interview with Paul Whittington Dominik explained further: "The story is set mainly in St. Joseph and Kansas City, which were big, rapidly expanding cities at that period, so it wasn't like the old frontier. Nobody wore cowboy hats, they wore homburgs and bowlers. So the idea of making a Dickensian Western was very appealing."

References

"About the Production," http://party931.com/common/movies/notes/54706-1-full.html (accessed 12 August 2008); Mark Salisbury, "Sticking to his Guns," *Time Out*, 7 November 2007, 61; The Assassination of Jesse James . . . By the Coward Robert Ford. Big Title, Big Ideas," *Empire* 220 (October 2007): 12–14; Paul Whittington, "The Big Interview: Andrew Dominik, *The Assassination of Jesse James*," *Irish Independent*, 30 November 2007, www.independent.ie/entertainment/day-and-night/the-big-interview-andrew-dominik-the-assassination-of-jesse-james-1233098.html (accessed 6 February 2009).

DOUGLAS, MICHAEL (1944–)

Born in New Brunswick, New Jersey, the son of Kirk and Diana Douglas, who divorced when he was six years old. His first real break came as Inspector Steve Keller in the television series *The Streets of San Francisco* (1972–1976), opposite Karl Malden. He left the show to produce *One Flew Over the Cuckoo's Nest* (1976). Perhaps his greatest success came in 1987, when he played Gordon Gekko in *Wall Street*, recently voted Number Twenty-Five in *Premiere* magazine's Twenty Greatest Movie Characters of All Time.

Douglas suggested in an interview published to the film's release that he was drawn to *BLACK RAIN* on account of its subject matter: "I felt . . . that there was something between us and Japan that was unresolved, that was a mixture of hostility and admiration on both sides—really confused . . . I thought . . . that this particular picture, as a cop-action picture, could explore some of the differences in customs and behavior—explore some of the hostilities that our two cultures and societies have for each other." Although

producing as well as starring in the film, Douglas did not travel to Japan for the location-scouting expeditions as he wanted to see the country with fresh eyes. In an interview accompanying the film's DVD release he recalled that he was also looking for an alternative to the unsympathetic roles he had played in *Wall Street* and *Fatal Attraction* (also 1987).

Douglas plays the central character Nick Conklin as a fundamentally good person, dedicated to his job, who has fallen prey to temptation by accepting bribes from the mafia. Scott suggested in an interview accompanying the DVD that this was inevitable, given the fact that he was paying alimony to his ex-wife and living on a subsistence salary. To atone for his guilt, he seeks to prove himself the best biker in town as he races along the banks of the Hudson River in NEW YORK. The fact that he wins in the end provides at least partial compensation for an unfulfilled existence in which he can see his children very infrequently, except to take them to school or offer them rides on the back of his bike.

Douglas's Nick rarely departs from the stereotype of a hard-bitten cop, similar to Mike Keller in *The Streets of San Francisco*. He swears at his Japanese counterparts when they fail to understand him and leaves himself open to ridicule when he complains that no one speaks "fucking English," only to find that Masahiro (KEN TAKAKURA) does indeed speak the language. However, Nick's obstinacy is also his greatest virtue as he refuses to be dissuaded from the task of catching the yakuza leader Sato (YUSAKU MATSUDA). His worst enemy is "the suits"—those bureaucrats who prevent him carrying out his duty by quoting the rulebook at him.

Nick undergoes something of a change of heart as he realizes that things can be accomplished more smoothly if he works with Masahiro rather than resenting him. He encourages his Japanese colleague not to think too much but to "grab [his] balls"—in other words, rely on spontaneity. Nick tries to eat noodles with chopsticks like the locals, despite finding it difficult. None of these scenes actually extend Douglas's range as an actor, but at least they show him portraying the character more sympathetically.

In the end, however, Nick remains a man's man, favoring the security of male bonding over female company and perpetually seeking to prove himself through violent means. This is especially true at the end when he seeks out and captures Sato at the sake factory. The film ends with Nick triumphantly leaving the country having acquired some understanding of local customs (he can now eat noodles with chopsticks). This seems somehow appropriate for Douglas's star persona during the late 1980s, which sought to move away from the *Wall Street* image of a tough, no-nonsense operator and instead combine heroism with sensitivity (hence his choice to star in comedies such as *The War of the Roses*).

Not all critics liked his performance. The British monthly *Film Review* took him to task for his "obvious desire to be Mel Gibson. He runs down the road with a gun, sports a mullet [haircut] more dangerous than the gang he's pursuing and behaves in a generally bad-ass way." However, Douglas told *Films and Filming* that he was pleased with the fact that "the movie has not only done incredible business in Japan, but all the reviews talk about it as an accurate portrayal of their country by foreigners. That's very important when you're making a film about somebody else's culture."

References
"Black Rain," *Film Review*, November 2000, 48; Donald Chase, "In *Black Rain*, East Meets West with a Bang! Bang!," *New York Times*, 17 September 1989, B7; Michael Douglas, interviewed in "*Black Rain*: The Script, The Cast," Special Feature included in the *Special Collector's Edition* DVD release of *Black Rain* (d. Laurent Bouzereau) (Los Angeles: Paramount Pictures, 2006); Jeff Hayward, "The Rain Man," *Films and Filming* 422 (December 1989): 26; Ridley Scott, interviewed in "*Black Rain*: The Making of the Film Part 1," Special Feature included in the *Special Collector's Edition* DVD release of *Black Rain* (d. Laurent Bouzereau) (Los Angeles: Paramount Pictures, 2006).

DUDLEY, ANNE (1956–)
Born Anne Jennifer Beckingham in Chatham, Great Britain. She was an original member of the 1980s rock band the Art of Noise. Her film and television scores include *The Crying Game* (1992), *The Full Monty* (1997), and *Bright Young Things* (2003). For *TRISTAN + ISOLDE* Anne Dudley had some big Wagner-shaped shoes to fill: rather than try to reproduce the nineteenth century rhythms, she returned instead to the story's Celtic origins. Reviewing her score for the trade journal *Music from the Movies*, Michael Beek wrote that "the music is broad and full of colour; the stylistic blending of classic orchestral devices, modernistic elements and Celtic hues help to bring the story to life and work well with the beautiful locations and the pretty faces of the romantic leads. [The score for] *Tristan + Isolde* is, in that sense then, aesthetically pleasing and while it doesn't really do anything too unexpected, I discover more to enjoy with each listen."

Reference
Michael Beek, "Tristan + Isolde," *Music From the Movies* 50–51 (October 2006): 96.

"THE DUEL"
1908 short story by Joseph Conrad. Based on actual events, Joseph Conrad's "The Duel" depicts the story of an absurd series of duels between two officers of Napoleon's army at first fought with swords; however, the conflict escalates into a dangerous obsession with HONOR and is finally settled with pistols. Conrad borrowed freely (consciously or uncon-sciously) from an 1848 *Harper's* article, though he claimed in his 1920 author's note to *A Set of Six* that he had found the story in a "ten-line paragraph" in a "small provincial paper in the South of France" and had to "invent" the plot himself. Conrad called the story of Feraud and D'Hubert "simply entertainment." Joseph Conrad and Ridley Scott compared their earliest work in fiction and film to adversarial conflicts, each using a metaphor common to his time— the pen as sword for Conrad, and the camera as gun for Scott. Conrad called the pen "the cold steel of our days" and constructed an epic simile for the scattered results of his early writing attempts, comparing the manuscript pages to the wounded on a battlefield. Scott's metaphor for filmmaking is apparent when he says that, when he was "shooting" his first feature film *THE DUELLISTS* based on "The Duel," he was thinking of it not as an art film but as a Western.

Scott's other films, especially *ALIEN*, *BLADE RUNNER*, and *THELMA & LOUISE* suggest that he was drawn to "The Duel" for two reasons. First, since its theme (the custom of dueling) was already an anachronism at the dawn of the twentieth century, Conrad was able to deal with dueling with the kind of detachment that seemed appropriate to Scott's sensibility. Second, dueling has formed a central theme in Scott's subsequent films. *The Duellists* emphasizes duality as it explores Conrad's motifs of the secret code. Nor does Scott leave Conrad behind after *The Duellists*. In *Alien*, for example, the spaceship is called the *NOSTROMO*. In *Blade Runner* dueling and duality is treated on an even larger scale as Scott shows how the positive aspects of the American Revolution had been transformed into the POSTMODERN nightmare of American corporate and technological tyranny. In *AMERICAN GANGSTER* the plot revolves around a duel of wits between Frank Lucas (DENZEL WASHINGTON) and Richie Roberts (RUSSELL CROWE).

Reference
Ridley Scott, quoted in *What's On in London*, 10 July 1991, 78.

THE DUELLISTS
GB 1977 r/t 100 min col. *Production Companies*: Enigma/National Film Finance Corporation (NFFC). *Producers*: David Puttnam and Ivor Powell. *Director*: Ridley Scott. *Writer*: Gerald Vaughan-Hughes from an original story "The Duel" by Joseph Conrad. *Director of Photography*: Frank Tidy. *Production Designer*: Ann Mollo. *Music*: Howard Blake. *Cast*: Keith Carradine (*D'Hubert*), Harvey Keitel (*Feraud*), Albert Finney (*Fouché*), Edward Fox (*Colonel*), Cristina Raines (*Adele*), Robert Stephens (*General Treillard*), Tom Conti (*Dr. Jacquin*), Diana Quick (*Laura*), Meg Wynn Owen (*Leonie*), Stacy Keach (*Narrator*).

The Duellists was Ridley Scott's second attempt to make a feature film after fifteen years of directing television commercials. He had previously worked with screenwriter GER-ALD VAUGHAN-HUGHES on a screenplay of the Gunpowder Plot (1605), but failed to find funding. He had written two screenplays himself—"Castle X" for THE BEE GEES, and "Ronnie and Leo," a heist movie with Michael York and Ernest Borgnine—neither of which were produced.

For *The Duellists* Scott secured the $900,000 budget from Paramount Pictures, but the studio was initially reluctant to give the go-ahead, especially as the weather was likely to hold up production. Eventually they relented on condition that Scott provided a completion bond; Scott offered himself as the bond and waived his director's fee. Filming began in September 1976 in the town of Sarlat in the Dordogne region of France and took fifty-six days.

The creative personnel had all worked with Scott during his career in advertising. Cinematographer FRANK TIDY had never made a film before. Filming began; after five days Scott, dissatisfied with the results, decided to operate the camera himself while instructing the actors at the same time, which helped him to focus more specifically on aspects of the *mise-en-scène*—specifically, sets, lighting, and positioning actors within the frame. This method of working helped Scott to establish his reputation as a pictorial director, someone who later on would be able to make epics like *GLADIATOR* or *KINGDOM OF HEAVEN*.

Unlike Joseph Conrad's original story "THE DUEL" (1908), Scott switches the focus of attention to the duels themselves. There are six in *The Duellists*, each escalating in terms of the danger of the weapon used: two are with rapiers; two with sabers; and two with pistols. In the first of these, Feraud is wounded, justly, because he has broken the code of HONOR by not providing seconds. In the second rapier duel, D'Hubert is wounded, again justly, because D'Hubert is fully aware of the absurdity and illegality of what is going on. In the third duel, fought with sabers, seconds are arranged but the duelists do not adhere to the rule of first blood, fighting to a standstill and falling into each other's arms at the end. The next saber duel is fought on horseback, and goes to D'Hubert; if only by luck rather than judgment.

Of the final pair of duels, fought with pistols, only the last is in Conrad's story. Scott adds another duel taking place in Russia during the retreat of Napoleon's army from Moscow. Neither the bitter cold nor the political ambitions of the ruler can deter Feraud from trying to complete his revenge. As the two men stand ready to fire at one another, a Cossack clad in skins (Richard Graydon) appears on horseback and mockingly laughs at the two men settling a point of honor in such treacherous conditions. Feraud responds by shooting the Cossack dead, while the other Cossacks in the background are shot by the other three balls in the two duelists' pistols. Ridiculous as they are, they are still good soldiers when they put their guns to proper use.

Richard Collins, in an illuminating article on the film, suggests that such moments focus our attention "on the ludicrous aspects of the adversaries' personal war." This is further emphasized by the photography; for example, the second duel scene is at dawn with the two characters pictured in a long shot against a brightening dawn sky, the trees and bushes towering above them. This suggests that the characters have been quite literally swallowed up by the landscape; their fight (which seems so important to them that they are prepared to keep it going on any and every occasion) appears tremendously insignificant. Life will go on, whether or not one of them perishes at the other's hands. Neither D'Hubert and Feraud are longer part of civilization any longer; rather, they resemble pygmies cast into the wilderness fighting for nothing in particular.

The fourth duel scene—fought on horseback with sabers—takes place once again at dawn. Here Scott takes great care with the *mise-en-scène* as the camera zooms in on D'Hubert's face, ominous music in the background. As he begins to ride towards Feraud, the action dissolves into a sequence of rapid cuts that show his state of mind as he prepares to fight. His life passes before him: his girlfriend, his past life as a soldier, a close-up of Feraud's face, and then back to D'Hubert's face. The camera cuts between two tracking shots of the two soldiers riding towards one another as the music gradually mounts to a crescendo of discordant violins. The scene ends with a shot of Feraud's ceremonial peaked cap crashing to the ground, and a close-up of D'Hubert's bloodied sword before showing D'Hubert on his horse jumping over a haystack and riding off into the distance. This moment, following the example of classic Westerns like John Ford's *The Searchers* (1956), clearly suggests that he is once again being swallowed up by the landscape. Although continuing to live the life of a soldier in Napoleon's army, he clearly prefers the wilderness.

The climactic duel scene shows the two protagonists quite literally merging with the landscape. All pretense of formality has been abandoned; this is a fight to the death. D'Hubert stands in front of a clump of tall pine trees without leaves, a wan sun glinting down on his pistols. Meanwhile, Feraud walks down a steep hill towards a lonely isolated wall, brushing some twigs out of the way as he does so. Nothing can be heard on the soundtrack except the sound of violin music (once again) and the crack of leaves and twigs as the two protagonists search for one another. Richard Collins is right in saying that the whole sequence is reminiscent of Fred Zinnemann's *High Noon* (1952). Again Scott employs another shot where Feraud is photographed against the vast background of the landscape, emphasizing his insignificance. The climax is shot as a series of intercut close-ups between the two men, pistols in hand, pointing them at one another: truly a Gunfight at the Paris Corral. The scene ends with Feraud being deluded into believing he has killed D'Hubert and running out of bullets; however, D'Hubert does not kill his unarmed adversary, preferring to let him live. The sequence is certainly dramatic, with the soundtrack helping to create an atmosphere of suspense; the audience quite literally does not know what will happen next. In thematic terms, however, it demonstrates how far the two protagonists have traveled from the world of civilization.

This may appear positive at first glance: now the characters can behave as they wish, without having to conform to any particular codes (especially the code of honor which determined their behavior throughout the preceding sequences). However, it also means that the two of them are totally isolated; they have nowhere to go to except back into the wilderness. This is emphasized in the film's final shot, which shows Feraud standing high on a hill, silhouetted against the landscape, watching the sun rise over the water stretching out in front of him. Truly he is a man alone; as Scott himself suggests (in the director's commentary to the DVD release), he is like Napoleon in exile, someone who overreached himself and paid the consequences for doing so. The Western hero may be alone and independent, but he is also isolated.

None of this exists in Conrad; but Scott deliberately incorporated such images to remind audiences of the parallels between *The Duellists* and the American western. The historical period might be different; but the themes remain similar. I suggest that this decision to reshape the material was a commercial one—a deliberate attempt to sustain Paramount Pictures's interest. The film was never going to receive more than art house distribution (it was only released in theaters in NEW YORK and LOS ANGELES), but it helped to launch Scott's Hollywood career. His next film, *ALIEN*, although made in Britain, was backed by Twentieth Century-Fox to the tune of $11 million, which suggests that his marketing ploy paid off.

The Duellists is not just a film designed for marketing purposes, however; it provides a good example of how Scott endeavored to incorporate cinematic techniques derived from advertisements into his narrative. Unlike the HERITAGE FILMS characteristic of directors such as Merchant-Ivory, which often employed long takes and close-ups to draw the viewers' attention to the historic locations and colorful costumes, Scott is more concerned with moving the narrative forward by means of sequences comprised of fast cuts. This is especially evident in the first duel sequence, where the camera alternates between behind-the-shoulder shots of the duelists, point of view shots from both of their perspectives, and shots with a hand-held camera swooping downwards towards the ground, emphasizing the violence of the conflict. The sequence itself lasts no more than one minute; but within that time we are made well aware of the fact that this is a fight to the death. It becomes a mini-story in itself. Scott was well versed in such techniques, having made over three hundred commercials before he began his career as a film director, including classics such as the advertisement for HOVIS BREAD (1973), which became so popular in Britain during the early 1970s that it spawned several sequels. His ability to tell a story in a short space of time proved invaluable in *The Duellists*, transforming Conrad's tale into a gripping epic by using the kind of shot-strategies which would subsequently become characteristic of the pop video, and which were were later incorporated into adaptations such as Baz Luhrmann's *Romeo + Juliet* (1996).

The Duellists was the British entry at the Cannes Film Festival of 1977, where it won the prize for Best Debut Film. It was marketed as a fresh look at a classic text, helmed by a producer, DAVID PUTTNAM, who according to the pressbook was "not the type to sit at a desk with a phone in his ear and his feet propped on the desk." Some reviewers responded enthusiastically: the London *Daily Express* felt that "the balance between visual appeal and human content is just about perfect." While the *Sunday Telegraph* reviewer enjoyed the photography, he felt that the film lacked "some deeper sense of the personal, social and historical seeds from which this bizarre enmity [between D'Hubert and Feraud] must spring . . . what we mainly retain is the impression of two clockwork antagonists." The *Monthly Film Bulletin* complained that the film "clearly betrays the dampening influence of television," by relying heavily on brief, static scenes comprised of close-ups. Despite the hard-working cast, the film proved once again "that Conrad does not translate to the screen too easily." Despite favorable reviews from critics such as Pauline Kael, the film did little or no business in America. Scott recalled in the "Director's Commentary" that Paramount made precisely seven prints for distribution.

Since its premiere *The Duellists* has received a goodly share of critical attention. A 1980 article "Conrad Dramatized" took issue with the *Monthly Film Bulletin* by arguing that Scott's adaptation was "cinematically effective," particularly at the end when Feraud is represented "as a symbol of the ultimate futility of Napoleon's military glory." Two years later the British critic Patrick Stoddart celebrated Scott's ability "to express specific moods and ideas" in visual terms; he "gets a lot more than a thousand words out of every picture." A decade later Charles Shiro Tashiro discussed the film's representation of the "two-faced ideal" characteristic of the eighteenth and early nineteenth century military: "one, bourgeois, austere, republican . . . repressive; two, aristocratic, military, flamboyant." Scott's film was even judged faithful to Conrad's text ("[he] establishes the visual qualities of *The Duellists* as the cinematic equivalent of Conrad's meditative tone"), which reveals how questions of fidelity frequently depend on individual perception. James Clarke called it "an essential Ridley Scott film, of economical and powerful storytelling . . . A quiet classic." Since then it has achieved cult status: Richard Collins remarks that "it set the themes and genre for Scott's later films, for here the heroes are most conspicuously defending, in good swashbuckler fashion, 'a point of honor,' and simply for its own sake."

References

Alan Brien, "The Duellists," *Sunday Telegraph*, 5 February 1978, 22; Ian Christie, "Fur Coat and Knickers Too," *Daily Express*, 4 February 1978, 13; James Clarke, *Ridley Scott* (London: Virgin Books Ltd., 2002), 28; Richard Collins, "Truth in Adversaries: Ridley Scott's *The Duellists* and Joseph Conrad's "The Duel," *Studies in the Humanities* (2000): 17–18; Roderick Davis, "Conrad Dramatized: *The Duellists*," *Literature/Film Quarterly* 8, no.2 (1980): 129; Pauline Kael, "The Current Cinema," *New Yorker*, 23 January 1978, 80; Tom Milne, "The Duellists," *Monthly Film Bulletin*, December 1977, 258; *Pressbook: The Duellists* (London: Paramount Pictures, 1977), 4; Ridley Scott, "Director's Commentary," to the 2003 release of *The Duellists* by Paramount DVD in the "Special Collector's Edition" (London: Paramount Home Entertainment, 2003); Allan Simmons, "Cinematic Fidelities in *The Rover* and *The Duellists*," in *Conrad on Film*, ed. Gene M. Moore (Cambridge: Cambridge University Press, 1997), 121; Patrick Stoddart, "Video Views," *Broadcast*, 17 May 1982, 21; Charles Shiro Tashiro, "The Bourgeois Gentleman and The Hussar," *The Spectator: University of Southern California Journal of Film and Television Criticism* 13, no.2 (Spring 1993): 39.

Bibliography

Donald Chase, "Ridley Scott Directs *The Duellists*," in *Ridley Scott Interviews*, ed. Laurence F. Knapp and Andrea F. Kulas (Jackson: University Press of Mississippi, 2005), 3–11; Brian J. Robb, *Ridley Scott* (Harpenden: Pocket Essentials, 2002).

DUNE

US 1984 r/t 137 min col. (original release). *Production Companies*: De Laurentiis. *Producer*: Raffaella De Laurentiis. *Director*: David Lynch. *Writer*: David Lynch, from the novel by Frank Herbert. *Director of Photography*: Freddie Francis. *Production Designer*: Anthony Masters. *Music*: Toto. *Cast*: Francesca Annis (*Lady Jessica*), Brad Dourif (*Piter De Vries*), José Ferrer (*Padishah Emperor Shaddam IV*), Linda Hunt (*Shadout Mapes*), Kyle MacLachlan (*Paul Usul Muad'Dib Atreides*), Virginia Madsen (*Princess Irulan*).

Frank Herbert's novel, first published in 1965, took a long time to reach the screen. Producer Arthur P. Jacobs took up an option on the novel in 1971, but died two years later. Subsequently a French consortium purchased the rights and announced that Chilean director Alejandro Jodorowsky would direct. Many of the talents who would later work on *ALIEN* were engaged, including H. R. GIGER, Chris Foss, and DAN O'BANNON. By late 1976 DINO DE LAUREN-

TIIS had purchased the rights and commissioned a script from Frank Herbert, which was later deemed unsuitable. Some two and a half years later he engaged Scott as director, following the success of *Alien*; work began at Pinewood Studios with Giger rehired to work on storyboards. After eight months the two men had created what they considered a workable script. By mid-1980 Scott had begun production, using a script created by Giger and Rudolph Wurlitzer; however, by September the project had been shut down, with script difficulties proving too difficult to overcome. Scott left the project, citing pressure of work and the recent death of his elder brother Frank as reasons for doing so.

Eventually David Lynch was hired to complete the project; following a great deal of preproduction difficulties, the film was eventually released on 3 December 1984 to indifferent reviews. Never one to mince words, Roger Ebert described it as "a real mess, an incomprehensible, ugly, unstructured, pointless excursion into the murkier realms of the one of the most confusing screenplays of all time."

References

Dune: Book to Screen Timeline, www.duneinfo.com/unseen/timeline .asp (accessed 25 February 2009); Roger Ebert, "Dune," http:// rogerebert.suntimes.com/apps/pbcs.dll/article?AID=/19840101/ REVIEWS/401010332/1023 (accessed 25 February 2009).

DUNN, KEVIN (1956–)

Studied drama at Illinois Wesleyan University and appeared on stage in Chicago as well as at the Williamstown Theatre Festival. Dunn made his film debut in 1988 as Agent Bird in *Mississippi Burning* (1988). Had supporting roles in *The Bonfire of the Vanities* (1990), *Hot Shots!* (1991), and *Chaplin* (1992).

Cast as Captain Méndez in *1492: CONQUEST OF PARADISE*, Dunn's role is to express the feelings of Columbus's (GÉRARD DEPARDIEU's) crew, as they spend endless years at sea without sight of land. He represents the skeptical voice that Columbus has to overcome if he is to have any chance of fulfilling his desires both to discover new territories and create new worlds. His role in the film is similar to that of Gaff (EDWARD JAMES OLMOS) in *BLADE RUNNER*. Despite the hardships involved, Méndez remains a supporter throughout—even if, at the end, he realizes that the mutiny of the Spaniards, led by Moxica (MICHAEL WINCOTT) results in the total collapse of the dream of creating a New World. Robert Thurston's novelization of the screenplay expresses Mendez's feelings succinctly: "Beside Columbus, Méndez started sobbing. Columbus realized suddenly that it was not just his world being destroyed, but the world of Méndez and the others, the loyal ones who had faith in his grand design. It was as if the design was being swept away by the current, too."

References
Robert Thurston, *1492: Conquest of Paradise Based on a Screenplay by Roselyne Bosch* (London: Penguin Books, 1992), 171.

DYSTOPIA

Scott is especially concerned to create a dystopian city in *BLADE RUNNER*. In an interview with Harlan Kennedy published at the time of the film's original release, he described it thus: "I think various groups are developing today—faction groups which are religious, social, whatever—and Punk . . . some louts . . . who developed their own little culture of protest . . . and I think the police force will become a kind of paramilitary . . . We're in a city which is in a state of overkill, of snarled-up energy, where you can no longer remove a building because it costs far more than constructing one in its place." What makes the society in *Blade Runner* so frightening is that it resembles our own. Just like *Neuromancer* and other CYBERPUNK dystopias, *Blade Runner* does not predict change, but escalation. Every negative tendency in our time has been amplified. In the Ridley Scott-produced film *THE LAST DEBATE*, director JOHN BADHAM applies the dystopian idea to contemporary American society. In a world dominated by the media, in which politics has become a branch of show business, no one cares any more for old-fashioned virtues such as loyalty and integrity. This is a world in which journalists take the electoral process in their own hands as they systematically destroy the Republican presidential candidate Richard Meredith's (Stephen Young's) chances of winning the election. Meredith storms off the stage yelling "Is this what America is? God is gonna punish you!" Sadly his prediction proves inaccurate: no god exists in this amoral world.

Scott creates another dystopian world in *LEGEND*, as Lily (MIA SARA) ignores Jack's (TOM CRUISE's) orders and ushers in a new ice age, where the forest is covered with a blanket of snow, human beings are frozen to death and the world is plunged into darkness. In this kind of atmosphere Darkness (TIM CURRY) can implement his campaign to deprive the world of all sunlight and thereby assume absolute power. *TRISTAN + ISOLDE* employs a similar design concept, as designer MARK GERAGHTY creates a world of the Dark Ages whose principal colors are black, gray, and off-white. Everything seems pale and washed out: no one wears bright clothes for fear of being considered an outsider. The only ray of light in an otherwise drab world is the central love affair between the two protagonists (JAMES FRANCO, SOPHIA MYLES).

In *BLACK RAIN* Scott returns to the theme of the decaying city with the portrayal of Osaka in JAPAN as a place of alienation, full of flashing lights and high-tech CARS, but simultaneously a threatening area where individuals such as Nick Conklin (MICHAEL DOUGLAS) and Charlie Vincent (ANDY GARCIA) are continually under threat from faceless gangs. However this film differs from *Blade Runner* in its portrayal of a dystopia. According to Andrew Milner, the earlier film suggests that in the futuristic LOS ANGELES it is no longer important whether men and women are "still actually human, no longer persuaded of our evolutionary superiority as a species" in cities comprised of "the mounting wreckage of a civilization nearly beyond repair." By contrast *Black Rain* restores our faith in humanity by showing the two policemen Nick and the Japanese police officer Masahiro (KEN TAKAKURA) bringing the yakuza leader Sato (YUSAKU MATSUDA) to justice and thereby ridding the city of gangland influence. This climactic moment to the film suggests that the dystopia can be improved so long as there are police officers with sufficient confidence to rely on their own instincts. No such redemption exists in the London of *A GOOD YEAR*; it is a place reserved for moneymakers who spend all their days staring at plasma screens with little concern for what happens in the outside world. The central character Max Skinner (RUSSELL CROWE) only discovers what life is like when he quits the city altogether and moves to PROVENCE. The same also applies to the Harlem of *AMERICAN GANGSTER*, which is so overrun with drug-pushers and corrupt police that no one has any sense of right and wrong any more.

References
Harlan Kennedy, "21st Century Nervous Breakdown," *Film Comment* 18, no.4 (July–August 1982): 64–68; Andrew Milner, "Darker Cities: Urban Dystopia and Science Fiction Cinema," *International Journal of Cultural Studies* 7, no.3 (Autumn 2004): 259–79.

Bibliography
Peter Brooker, "Imagining the Real: *Blade Runner* and the Discourses on the Postmetropolis," in *The Blade Runner Experience: The Legacy of a Science Fiction Classic*," ed. Will Brooker (London and New York: Wallflower Press, 2005), 213–25; Judith B. Kerman, "Technology and Politics in the *Blade Runner* Dystopia," in *Retrofitting Blade Runner*, ed. Judith B. Kerman, 2nd ed. (Bowling Green: Bowling Green State University Popular Press, 1997), 16–24; Brian Opie, "Android Textuality, or Finding a Toad in the Desert of America," in *Remembering Representation*, ed. Howard McNaughton (Christchurch: University of Canterbury, Department of English, 1993), 76–89; Michael Ryan and Douglas Kellner, "Technophobia/Dystopia," in *Liquid Metal: The Science Fiction Film Reader*, ed. Sean Redmond (London and New York: Wallflower Press, 2004), 48–56; Vivian Sobchack, "Cities on the Edge of Time: The Urban Science Fiction Film," in *Liquid Metal: The Science Fiction Film Reader*, ed. Redmond, 78–87; Brian Winston, "Tyrell's Owl: The Limits of the Technological Imagination in an Epoch of Hyperbolic Discourse," in *Theorizing Culture: An Interdisciplinary Critique after Postmodernism*, ed. Barbara Adam and Stuart Allen (London: UCL Press Ltd., 1995), 225–35.

EDEN ROC CHANEL No. 5 (1989)

GB c.1989 Commercial r/t 1 min col. *Production Company*: RSA Films. *Director*: Ridley Scott. *Cast*: Carole Bouquet.

This was the first Chanel No. 5 advertisement featuring the French actress Carole Bouquet. The featured music is Nina Simone's "My Baby Just Cares for Me." This advertisement suggests that the perfume makes the central character irresistible to men. Bouquet is shown kissing an old man and subsequently tantalizing a much younger man while sitting in the driver's seat of a bright red automobile. Eventually she meets the man of her dreams; the two of them come together into a kiss as the commercial fades to black. The action ends with a close-up of Bouquet saying "Share the fantasy. Chanel No. 5" with her hand on the bottle.

Another commercial demonstrating Scott's visual flair; there are long panning shots of a desert landscape (a precursor to *THELMA & LOUISE*) with Bouquet's car no more than a red speck at the center of the frame.

Reference

"Eden Roc Chanel No. 5," www.youtube.com/watch?v=C7Dq UpSHIb8 (accessed 4 February 2008).

EDEN ROC—CHANEL No. 5 (1990)

US c.1990 Commercial r/t 1 min col. *Production Company*: RSA Films. *Director*: Ridley Scott. *Cast*: Carole Bouquet.

Another commercial for Chanel, released soon after the first one featuring Carole Bouquet. Set on a gloriously sunny day beside a swimming pool, this advertisement focuses on Bouquet's body as well as her face as she takes a drink and sunbathes on a chaise lounge. A man walks towards her and kisses her; Bouquet throws her head back as if expecting the kiss. The commercial ends with a shot of Bouquet in close-up speaking the words "Share the fantasy. Chanel No. 5" as the camera cuts to a shot of the perfume bottle. As with the EDEN ROC CHANEL NO. 5 (1989) commercial, Scott makes clever use of unusual shots—for example, shots of the man's legs, or Bouquet's feet, to suggest the sensuality of the occasion.

EDUCATION

Some of Scott's films touch on the question of educating the young. In *MONKEY TROUBLE*, Eva (THORA BIRCH) has to make a presentation at school, using a pet or a younger family member. At first she cannot do this; as someone coming from a largely dysfunctional family, she lacks both the application and the talent. However, as the film progresses, she learns self-reliance and confidence through caring for the monkey, learns to confide in Christine the teacher (Andi Chapman), and realizes the importance of telling the truth. The school in this film is identified as a place where students can develop themselves both socially and intellectually.

The complete opposite is true of *THE BROWNING VERSION*. Set in a boys' private school in the rolling English hills, the film suggests that education has very little to do with growth or self-development and everything to do with creating generations of emotionally stunted young men committed to outdated ideals of MASCULINITY (being good at games, enduring punishments and not showing one's emotions). This ethos—if it can be described as such—dominates the teachers' behavior as much as the students': Crocker-Harris (ALBERT FINNEY) would far rather conceal his emotions rather than criticize the headmaster (MICHAEL GAMBON) for denying him a pension or slighting him by asking him to speak first at the prize-giving ceremony, though it is his right as senior teacher to speak last. The student Buller (Walter Micklethwait) quietly whimpers in a corner of his dormitory, having discovered that his parents cannot come to the end-of-term ceremonies. Another pupil tries to console him by saying, "Don't worry, you'll get used to it, believe me." Buller's response is succinct and to the point: "Fuck off." This is precisely director MIKE FIGGIS's point: why should young people have to "get used to" this kind of environment, where they are treated as human cannon fodder, and forced to learn archaic subjects such as Latin and Greek? Education should consist of a lot more—as Crocker-Harris admits in his climactic final speech in which he wishes he could have taught with sympathy, encouragement and humanity.

The same point recurs in *WHITE SQUALL*, where the parents of the teenage crew are shown to be either repressive or insensitive—for example, when Chuck Gieg's (SCOTT WOLF's) father Charles (Jordan Clarke) takes him clothes shopping immediately upon his return from the voyage in the belief that this will provide a suitable means for his son to forget the experience. Inevitably Chuck rebels by running out of the fitting-room and into the street, pursued by his father (who pauses to tell the store owner, "We'll be right back."). The true "fathers" in the film are the boys themselves and Captain Sheldon (JEFF BRIDGES). Sheldon occasionally might be extreme in his behavior—for example, when he forces the acrophobic Martin (RYAN PHILLIPPE) to climb the rigging—but he manages to create an atmosphere in which the boys can mature very quickly. At one point the English professor McCrea (JOHN SAVAGE) quotes from Kipling's poem "If . . ." which is all about the idea of acquiring maturity. Scott shows that the boys clearly understand the implications of these words. Gieg observes at the end that, "[We] shared his [Sheldon's] burden, the burden of sea-captains and fathers, the burden of men." By contrast, Gieg believes that when parents send their children away, "they want to keep their kids the same."

EJIOFOR, CHIWETEL (1974–)

Born in London, Ejiofor made his feature film debut in Steven Spielberg's *Amistad* (1997). A decade later he won a Golden Globe nomination for Best Performance by an Actor in a Motion Picture Musical or Comedy for *Kinky Boots* (2005). Recent stage work includes *Othello* in London (2007).

Cast as Huey, one of Frank Lucas's many brothers on *AMERICAN GANGSTER*, Ejiofor teamed up once again with DENZEL WASHINGTON, with whom he had already worked on *Inside Man* (2006). Unlike Frank, Huey is a flamboyant personality, fond of wearing expensive clothes and jewelry. This represents a threat to the stability of Frank's organization, which prides itself on wearing "expensive tailored suits" and persuading their partners to be "nicely dressed—not too much makeup." The main intention is to sustain a façade of respectability so that they do not get noticed by the police. By contrast, Huey's clothes are, in Frank's words, "a costume. With a sign on it that says Arrest Me . . . You wanna be Superfly? Go work for him, end up in a cell with him." Huey might be loyal to his brother, but his grandiosity eventually causes Frank's downfall. He shouts loudly on a pay phone, and by doing so unwittingly reveals the number of the flight bringing the latest shipment of heroin from Vietnam.

Reference

Steven Zaillian, "*American Gangster*: Final Shooting Script" (27 July 2006), www.roteirodecinema.com.br/scripts/files/american_gangster .htm (accessed 8 February 2009).

ELASTOPLAST AIRSTRIP PLASTERS

GB 1970 Commercial r/t 30 sec col. *Production Company*: RSA Films for J. Walter Thompson. *Director*: Ridley Scott.

A commercial demonstrating the versatility of Elastoplast adhesive bandages. A little girl does a ballet dance, bending her knees and putting her hands above her head to the tune of "I Am a Courtier Grave and Serious" from Gilbert and Sullivan's *The Gondoliers*. An adult female voice—presumably the ballet teacher—is heard on the soundtrack, telling us that Elastoplast is "waterproof, dirt proof and germproof. In fact, almost everything-proof. Yet it still breathes in air." Compared to later works such as McDOUGALLS PASTRY MIX or HOVIS BREAD, this commercial sells a product directly to the viewer without creating a mini-narrative. Many of the camera techniques used have their origins in B-Movies (recalling *ADAM ADAMANT LIVES!*), for example, the use of zoom out as the girl twirls round, her hands above her head.

ELLZEY, LISA (?–)

In 2007 Ellzey was a production executive at Twentieth Century-Fox. Previously, she was the president of SCOTT FREE Entertainment, the company owned by Ridley Scott and Tony Scott. She produced *TRISTAN & ISOLDE*, *IN HER SHOES*, *KINGDOM OF HEAVEN*, *A GOOD YEAR*, and *THE GATHERING STORM*. In 2002 she co-executive produced the reality television show *AFP—AMERICAN FIGHTER PILOT*. Ellzey began her career by producing the low-budget independent film *The Poison Tasters*, starring French Stewart, which premiered at the Cannes Film Festival in 1995. Between shooting the film and taking it to the festival, she worked at Creative Artists Agency for three years as an assistant in the Motion Pictures Literary department.

EXCALIBUR

GB/USA 1981 r/t 140 min col. *Production Company*: Orion Pictures Corporation. *Producer/Director*: John Boorman. *Writers*: Rospo Pallenberg and John Boorman, from *La Morte d'Arthur* by Thomas Malory. *Director of Photography*: Alex Thomson. *Music*: Trevor Jones. *Production Designer*: Anthony Pratt. *Cast*: Nigel Terry (*King Arthur*), Helen Mirren (*Morgana*), Nicholas Clay (*Lancelot*), Cherie Lunghi (*Guenevere*), Paul Geoffrey (*Perceval*), Nicol Williamson (*Merlin*), Robert Addie (*Mordred*).

A spirited account of the legend of King Arthur, which inspired DEAN GEORGARIS to write the screenplay for *TRISTAN + ISOLDE*.

FAISON, FRANKIE (1949–)

Born in Newport News, Virginia, Frankie Faison made his debut in the film *Permanent Vacation* (1980). In Michael Mann's *Manhunter* (1986), the first of the Hannibal Lecter films, Faison played Lieutenant Fisk; five years later he played the ward orderly Barney Matthews in *THE SILENCE OF THE LAMBS*. Repeating the role once again in *HANNIBAL*, Faison has a small part as someone who is eventually persuaded by Clarice Starling (JULIANNE MOORE) to refrain from selling Hannibal's (ANTHONY HOPKINS's) X-Ray and return it once again to its rightful place. If not, then he will be arrested on fraud charges. While Barney is right in claiming he is fundamentally "not a bad guy," he is an example of the institutional corruption that permeates the film. Faison reappears in the fourth Hannibal film *Red Dragon* (2002) in the same role.

Reference

Steven Zaillian, "*Hannibal*: Screenplay Based on the Novel by Thomas Harris," Revision (9 February 2000), http://sfy.ru/sfy.html?script=hannibal2001 (accessed 15 December 2008).

THE FALL OF THE ROMAN EMPIRE

USA 1964 r/t 188 min col. *Production Company*: Samuel Bronstein Productions. *Producer*: Samuel Bronston. *Director*: Anthony Mann. *Writers*: Ben Barzman, Basilio Franchina, and Philip Yordan. *Director of Photography*: Robert Krasker. *Music*: Dmitri Tiomkin. *Production Designers*: Veniero Colasanti and John Moore. *Cast*: Sophia Loren (*Lucilla*), Stephen Boyd (*Livius*), Alec Guinness (*Marcus Aurelius*), James Mason (*Timonides*), Christopher Plummer (*Commodus*), Mel Ferrer (*Cleander*), Anthony Quayle (*Verulus*), Omar Sharif (*Sohamus*).

Legendary Roman epic, whose plot was largely borrowed by DAVID FRANZONI and JOHN LOGAN for *GLADIATOR*. The film tells the story of a moment in history when Rome—the mightiest empire—paused on the crest of its glory before plunging into oblivion. Part of a cycle of epics Bronston produced; others included *El Cid* (1962), *55 Days at Peking* (1962), and *Circus World* (1963).

While condemned by reviewers at the time for its excessive length, *The Fall of the Roman Empire* contains many of the themes that would resurface in Scott's films, especially the emotional EDUCATION of the hero and the idea of tests (by joust or by fire) set against the backdrop of epic landscape. The film was also noticeable for the non-appearance of RICHARD HARRIS, who was due to play Commodus but walked out of the film before the cameras rolled. Eventually the role was played by Stephen Boyd. Harris played Commodus's father Marcus in *Gladiator*.

Bibliography

"The Rise and Fall of an Epic Production: The Making of the Film [*Fall of the Roman Empire*]," Documentary on the 2008 release of *Fall of the Roman Empire* (Los Angeles: Paramount Pictures, 2008).

FANCHER, HAMPTON (1938–)

Actor and screenplay writer. Fancher's career as an actor included supporting roles in television series such as *Gunsmoke*, *Rawhide*, *Perry Mason*, and *Bonanza*. *BLADE RUNNER* was his first major assignment as a writer.

The story of how the script evolved and how Fancher's role changed in the process of bringing PHILIP K. DICK's work to the screen has been recounted both by PAUL M. SAMMON and in the documentary *Dangerous Days: Making Blade Runner*, included in the five-disc *BLADE RUNNER: COLLECTOR'S EDITION* (2007). IVOR POWELL claimed in an interview that, while Fancher's original script had its virtues, DAVID PEOPLES was brought in to improve it because "Hampton was, quite frankly, exhausted after working on this for a year or two before we [Powell and Scott] came along . . . Hampton Fancher is a very romantic writer and in his original script the relationship between Deckard and Rach[a]el was much stronger and in the end she realises that there isn't much future for them because he's human and she's a REPLICANT. She is standing on the roof and he realises that she might be going to do something stupid and he rushes to her. He gets up on the roof and she's standing on the edge of the roof holding onto the *real* sheep that he's bought . . . A very powerful scene." On the other hand, Powell observed in a 1982 article that "there were some things in Fancher's script which were unacceptable. For instance, Deckard just arrives at Zhora's place without an explanation as to how he got there."

Fancher himself recalled in 1997, "At the end of 1980, I began to realise there was a slow process of involuntary addition and elimination going on in what was now called *Blade Runner* [a title Fancher had appropriated from WILLIAM S. BURROUGHS's 1979 book, *Blade Runner: A Movie*] through Ridley, who was jettisoning key concepts in my screenplay. That horrified me, and I became very vocal. I found out I'd been kicked off the picture in a Christmas party, when I picked up a Blade Runner script I'd never seen before with the name David Peoples on it. I thought, 'Who the fuck is that?'" However, Fancher eventually obtained a credit as co-author and executive producer on the film. In a 1999 interview Fancher recalled that he had originally believed that Rachael should have died at the end of the film, as Deckard shoots her: "They're [Deckard and Rachael] in love, and he's become kind of human through this . . . he becomes less of a machine through the ordeal of falling in love with her. She's smarter than he is and she's better than he is, and at the end, he kills her. And it's not an outright execution. It's elliptical. But you hear the shot, and you see where it took place, and you saw her face, and she wanted it, and it was an act of love." However, Fancher seemed to have reconciled himself to the fact that despite the sometimes-negative experiences in working on it, *Blade Runner* was a great film: "Everybody made that movie. It's not just one of us."

References

Jeffrey M. Anderson, "Interview with Hampton Fancher" (24 September 1999), *Combustible Celluloid Magazine*, www.combustible-celluloid.com/intfancher1.shtml (accessed 13 April 2008); Phil Edwards and Alan McKenzie, "The *Blade Runner* Chronicles: Ivor Powell," *Starburst* 50 (October 1982): 27–28; Paul M. Sammon, "Fear of a Bleak Planet," *Neon*, March 1997, 103; Paul M. Sammon, *Future Noir: The Making of Blade Runner*, 2nd ed. (London: Gollancz, 2007), 24–29, 36–38, 52–64; "Incept Date—1980: Screenwriting and Dealmaking," Disc 2 in *Blade Runner: Collector's Edition* (Los Angeles: Warner Bros. Entertainment and the Blade Runner Partnership, 2007).

FANDOM

Several of Scott's films have exercised considerable influence over popular culture, especially *ALIEN* and *BLADE RUNNER*. Not only have they spawned their own websites, fanzines, chat groups, but they have given rise to new versions of the films spread over the Internet. *Alien* (and the

three films in the sequence) spawned a series of comic books produced especially for the fans of the series.

The many versions of *BLADE RUNNER* that have appeared since 1982 have stimulated fandom even more. There have been three separate prints of the film—the original version, the DIRECTOR'S CUT, and the FINAL CUT—and since the early 1990s the *Blade Runner* cast and world have been taken up by novels (*Blade Runner* 2, 3, and 4) written by K. W. (Kevin Wayne) Jeter. One video game was released in 1985; Westwood Studios released another *Blade Runner* game in 1997.

Such materials have stimulated a whole host of fan sites which invite surfers to become part of the *Blade Runner* world, offer a series of incredibly detailed questions and answers based on the various versions of the film, and provide numerous opportunities for blogging and/or other commentary. Will Brooker comments that fan groups visiting such sites are stimulated by the film's introspective nature: "[The film] attracts a project based not so much around community but solitary dedication, and is as such something quite unique among the Internet fan groups described in academic study to date." By comparison, the *Alien* fans respond most to "'the buddies shooting the bull' mode . . . an online equivalent of the role-playing groups whose popularity peaked in the mid to late 1980s."

The same phenomenon is evident with *LEGEND*, which has become a cult film even though it flopped on its first release in 1985. As a result, perhaps, of the film's growing cult status (a *Legend* FAQ website was created and currently exists on www.figmentfly.com/legend/background1.html), Scott collaborated with his long-term video producer CHARLES DE LAUZIRIKA to produce an "Ultimate Edition" DVD of *Legend*, with a new 113-minute *LEGEND: THE DIRECTOR'S CUT*, including deleted scenes and interviews with some of the production's main personalities.

NUMB3RS has spawned numerous fansites online, notably Numb3rs.org, the Numb3rs Fan Club, everythingisnumb3rs.eponym.com, and the official website maintained by the producers CBS (www.cbs.com/primetime/numb3rs/).

Reference

Will Brooker, "Internet Fandom and the Continuing Narratives of *Star Wars*, *Blade Runner* and *Alien*," in *Alien Zone 2: The Spaces of Science Fiction Cinema*, ed. Annette Kuhn (London: Verso, 2000), 56, 70.

Bibliography:

Kerry Gough, "Translation Creativity and Alien Econ(c)omics," in *Film and Comic Books*, ed. Ian Gordon, Mark Jancovich, and Matthew P. McAllister (Jackson: University Press of Mississippi, 2007), 37–64; Christy Gray, "Originals and Copies: The Fans of Philip K. Dick, Blade Runner and K. W. Jeter," in *The Blade Runner Experience: The Legacy of a Science Fiction Classic*," ed. Will Brooker

(London and New York: Wallflower Press, 2005), 142–59; Jonathan Gray, "Scanning the Replicant Text," in *The Blade Runner Experience: The Legacy of a Science Fiction Classic*," 111–24; Matt Hills, "Academic Textual Poachers: Blade Runner as Cult Canonical Movie," in *The Blade Runner Experience: The Legacy of a Science Fiction Classic*, 124–42; Paul M. Sammon, *Future Noir: The Making of Blade Runner*, 2nd ed. (London: Gollancz, 2007).

FARAHANI, GOLSHIFTEH (1983–)

Daughter of the Iranian actor and theatre director Behzad Farahani and sister of noted actress Shaghayegh Farahani, Farahani began studying music and piano as a child. She was supposed to continue her education at the Vienna Conservatory in Austria but decided to pursue her acting career instead. Her film credits include *Niwemang/Half Moon* (2006), for which she won the Golden Sea Shell at the 2006 San Sebastian Film Festival.

Farahani made her English-language debut in *BODY OF LIES* as the nurse Aisha, who falls in love with Roger Ferris (LEONARDO DICAPRIO) but retains a commonsense understanding of the world around her. Although Ferris stays in Jordan and tries to continue the relationship, we are left in doubt as to whether it will flourish in a world where Ferris will always be a marked man, even if he has left the CIA.

In the production notes Scott commended Farahani for her "strength and dignity . . . The camera really loves her." The actress herself liked the role she was offered: "In the beginning, she [Aisha] finds Ferris interesting, but she doesn't take him seriously. When she discovers that he has a good heart, she lets herself get more involved. She is disarmed by his sincerity." However, their attraction is complicated by the conventions of her culture, which frowns upon men fraternizing with unmarried women, as Scott observed: "He [Ferris] can't even shake her hand because he knows that would be very bad for her." Nonetheless in DiCaprio's opinion "Ferris feels a very strong affinity for Aisha. He's very respectful of her culture and tradition, and he works at developing a relationship with her."

Reference

Production Notes: Body of Lies (Los Angeles: Warner Bros. Entertainment, 2008), http://mix96tulsa.com/movies/notes/body-of-lies/note/4 (accessed 16 January 2009).

FARGO

US 1996 r/t 98 min col. *Production Companies*: PolyGram Filmed Entertainment, Working Title Films and Gramercy Pictures. *Producers*: Tim Bevan, Joel and Ethan Coen. *Writers/Directors*: Joel and Ethan Coen. *Director of Photography*: Roger Deakins. *Music*: Carter Burwell. *Production Designer*: Rick Heinrichs. *Cast*: Frances McDormand (Marge Gunderson), William H. Macy (*Jerome "Jerry" Lundegaard*), Steve Buscemi (*Carl Showalter*), Peter Stormare (*Gaear Grimsrud*), Kristin Rudrüd (*Jean Lundegaard*), Harve Presnell (*Wade Gustafson*), Tony Denman (*Scotty Lundegaard*).

Jerry hires two men to kidnap his wife so he can get his rich father-in-law to pay the ransom of $1 million. Once the ransom is paid the kidnappers will get forty thousand dollars and Jerry will get the rest. That's the plan—but what happens is something totally different. Blood is shed when a cop and two innocent people are killed. Marge Gunderson is the police chief who investigates the murders. While she does so, Jerry gets involved in deeper problems, ranging from financial troubles to threats from the kidnappers.

Cult film set in SMALL TOWN America which by the admission of director DAVID DOBKIN served as the inspiration for the Ridley Scott-produced film *CLAY PIGEONS*.

FARR, DIANE (1969–)

Born in New York, Farr's credits include the television series *Like Family* (2003–2004) and *Rescue Me* (2004–2005). Farr played FBI agent Megan Reeves for sixty-three episodes in Series 2–4 (2005–2008) of *NUMB3RS*. Always a practical personality, Megan carries out her job to the best of her ability, even when faced with extreme danger; for example, in the episodes "Spree" and "Two Daughters" (Series 3, Episodes 1–2), in which she is held captive by a psychopathic woman, Crystal Hoyle (Kim Dickens). The two-part story ends with a shoot-out reminiscent of *THELMA & LOUISE*, where Crystal escapes from her FBI pursuers in her car and hits the open road, only to be shot in the head by Agent Ian Edgerton (Lou Diamond Phillips). Megan sustains an on again/off again relationship with the academic Larry Fleinhardt (PETER MACNICOL). While the two of them are obviously fond of one another, they can never make their love affair work. Eventually the two split up when Megan leaves the FBI to return to New York.

Bibliography

Michael Ausiello, "Diane Farr's Numbers Up," *TV Guide*, 25 March 2008, www.tvguide.com/news/Exclusive-Diane-Farrs-8105.aspx (accessed 22 February 2009).

FEMINISM

Several of Ridley Scott's films have engaged the issue of feminism. In *ALIEN*, for instance, Ripley's triumph can be perceived as utopian, fulfilling the fantasy that white, middle-class women can not only be accommodated into the world of work but also emerge victorious. However, her "victory" is somewhat lessened by the fact that, in stripping down to her underwear, she is also presented as sexually desirable. Critics have long disputed Ripley's role in the film: Chad Herrmann, for example, observes that while she defeats the alien, it is a "hollow victory . . . she saves only herself and a cat. She effectively loses everything, and she is lost herself: alone, drifting hopelessly through space, with the haunting memories of one dead father figure and four murdered children." Sasha Vojkovic celebrates Ripley's status as someone who matters: "the features that confirm her status as an outsider in the symbolic universe of the father, such as 'alien,' 'monster,' or 'synthetic humanoid,' if taken within a new, normative injunction, can become the features that matter. These features matter because they mark a deviance and difference from 'woman' as a universal category."

BLADE RUNNER has likewise caused considerable critical debate. While the film certainly contains strong women such as Zhora (JOANNA CASSIDY), there remains a sense in which Scott presents the female body voyeuristically, appealing to the male viewer. For example, why does Zhora have to strip naked in the shower, after she has finished her performance with the snake; and later on, why does she escape from Deckard through the Los Angeles streets clad only in her underwear and a plastic mackintosh? During the final conflict between Pris (DARYL HANNAH) and Deckard (HARRISON FORD), Pris takes Deckard's head between her legs and sticks her fingers in his nostrils: in visual terms this scene reminds us of the image of the "monstrous feminine" giving birth in *Alien*, when the creature appears out of Kane's stomach. Another monstrous female appears in *THE HIRE*: "HOSTAGE," when the company CEO, Linda Delacroix (Kathryn Morris), recovers from a kidnap attempt to confront her adversary Harry (Maury Chaykin), who has tried to kill himself and is now in the hospital. The sight of Linda standing in front of him, mockingly likening him to a moth who must now "embrace the flame" is enough to kill the unfortunate Harry.

As long ago as 1984 Douglas Keller, Flo Leibowitz, and Michael Ryan complained that Scott's work contained reactionary features: "It is especially regressive in its sexual politics." This view can certainly be defended in the light of Scott's subsequent work: television series like *THE HUNGER* are especially regressive in their stereotyped representation of gender roles. Similarly, in *TRISTAN + ISOLDE*, King Donnchadh (DAVID PATRICK O'HARA) treats his daughter Isolde (SOPHIA MYLES) as a commodity to be given as a reward to his favorite soldier Morholt (Graham Mullins). Feminist critics in the journal *Camera Obscura* tried to defend Scott's view of gender: Janet Bergstrom argued in 1988 that *Blade Runner* collapses gender distinctions, a point developed by Kaja Silverman three years later. Valerie Su-Lin Wee refutes these arguments; she believes that the film continually objectifies women "by the use of techniques such as slow motion, the manipulation of the soundtrack and the highly conscious, controlled construction of the images" (for example, in Zhora's death scene, where the camera focuses on her bloodied corpse).

Moreover Scott represents the woman as "a threatening, destructive aggressor, a representative of Otherness who must be eliminated so that order and stability can be restored." The same theme resurfaces in *LEGEND*, which draws on a tradition extensively analyzed by Julia Kristeva in which women are constructed as abject. Lily appears outwardly pure in her white dress, but is simultaneously portrayed as inwardly corrupt: "abjection is no longer exterior. It is permanent and comes from within." The division of pure/impure is transformed into one of inside/outside.

Although not directly concerned with feminist issues, *SOMEONE TO WATCH OVER ME* deals with the subject of gender roles. The title is significant—that "someone" entrusted with the responsibility of caring for others might be a male or female, depending on the context. Mike Keegan (TOM BERENGER) believes it is his duty as a man to watch over his family and Claire Gregory (MIMI ROGERS). However, as the action unfolds we see him neglecting his duty as he fails in love with Claire. Eventually the roles are reversed; it is Claire who volunteers to take care of Mike. Meanwhile, Mike's wife Ellie (LORRAINE BRACCO) takes on the role of protector once her husband moves out; she practices firing a shotgun, using an image of a man as a target. Unable to accept the idea of a man in her life, Ellie assumes the roles of both mother and father. Even though she is reconciled with Mike at the end of the film, we are uncertain as to whether the two of them will reassume their appointed roles, in spite of Mike's desire to start again. *Someone* might not suggest anything radical about gender constructions, but it returns to an issue previously explored in *Alien* of what constitutes "MASCULINE" and "feminine" behavior.

Following the premiere of *THELMA & LOUISE*, a syndicated piece published in the US in 1991 and reprinted by Shoma A. Chatterjee credited the film with the rebirth of feminism. The story began: "First, it was Thelma and Louise battling sexism across the southwest. Then it was Dr. Frances Conley blowing the whistle on harassment at Stanford University Medical School." In her view, *Thelma & Louise* was a film that focused attention once again on what the term "battle of the sexes" actually meant. She related the film to women's inferior status in the workplace and interviewed women who felt discriminated against because of their gender. Quoting a 1990 Department of Labor report, Chatterjee reported that women accounted for just 3 percent of senior managers and an overwhelming 84 percent of information and service jobs, similar to those held by Louise (SUSAN SARANDON).

The film was released at a time in the early 1990s when the second-wave feminism of the 1960s and 1970s had emerged from the 1980s in a fractured state. Not only was the whole concept of "MASCULINITY" and "femininity" in question (as Scott's earlier films had shown), but the rise of conservatism in the 1980s, in particular Reaganism and Thatcherism, had put feminist principles under the microscope. Central to many feminists at that time was the figure of the male-bashing feminist, who wanted to gain power by taking over men's roles. Much of the criticism of *Thelma & Louise* came from feminists who believed that the film showed precisely this: the two central characters choose to behave like men. Does feminism mean that women have the same right as men to hit the road, take delight in blowing up trucks, and rob convenience stores? Manohla Dargis wrote in the British journal *Sight and Sound* that "*Thelma & Louise* sells a kind of feminism brut, inarticulate and inchoate. Yet after more than ten years of Reagan, Bush and the murky chimera of post-feminism, how many can still speak the language of liberation with any assurance?"

However, such comments overlook the fact that Scott's film focuses less on violence per se than on the way in which there is no going back once one has killed, the remorse that emerges from having acted impulsively with a gun. In spite of Dargis's remarks, the film is actually not that violent—a woman robs a grocery store, a policeman is locked in the trunk of his car, a truck is blown up with no one in it. Moreover, such comments overlook the complexity of the film's ending, which might show the two characters driving to their deaths, or might also show them rejecting the patriarchy once and for all and entering a new world of bright lights and female bonding.

G.I. JANE can be seen as either an extension or a rebuttal of the ideas of *Thelma & Louise.* Whether or not the film can be considered "feminist" depends very much on whether one believes that women have to behave like men in order to be accepted on equal terms. There are certainly some overtly misogynist references in the script, ranging from the (unnamed) Flag Officer's observation that "No woman is going to last one week in a commando training course," to the scriptwriter's stage direction showing the recruits "glancing Jordan's way, cashing in on a cheap wet T-shirt contest," to the Commanding Officer Salem's (SCOTT WILSON's) observation that he resents Jordan O'Neil's (DEMI MOORE's) perfume, "however subtle it may be, competing with the aroma of my fine three-dollar-and-fifty-nine cent cigar, which I will happily put out this very instant if the phallic nature of it happens to offend your goddam fragile sensibilities." Even scriptwriter DAVID TWOHY observes later on that "at least the two of the guys in her [Jordan's] crew are blue-ribbon misogynists." The question is whether Jordan's deliberate shedding of her female identity—cutting her hair, her deliberate decision to share a room with the male soldiers, and her willing adoption of rituals such as drinking in a bar—represents a bid for feminine freedom or a willing submission to masculine rituals. The same ambiguity also applies to *HANNIBAL*: Clarice Starling (JULIANNE MOORE) is cer-

tainly a strong woman with a capacity to dominate her male colleagues, but our understanding of the character is very much influenced by JODIE FOSTER's performance in *SILENCE OF THE LAMBS*. Linda Mizejewski explains: "[The film shows] the more complex traits of this character: powerful, competent female authority, beauty without glamour; and a sexual attractiveness that excludes easy categorization . . . the sexuality of Starling . . . is more acceptable if read through Jodie Foster, whose persona makes some of these contradictions or unanswered opinions acceptable."

By contrast, *WHERE THE MONEY IS* rejects the opposition between MASCULINITY and femininity. Rather, it suggests that men and women alike should be free to play whatever roles they choose, without fear of peer pressure. Henry Manning (PAUL NEWMAN) plays a stroke victim, a gentleman, a religious zealot, and a tough guy with equal facility; his sidekick Carol MacKay becomes his surrogate mother, his partner in crime and a telephone operator. While the film has a wish-fulfilling ending—the two of them escape the clutches of the law to pursue their lives of crime—it nonetheless represents a step forward from the rather hackneyed conceptions of gender in *G.I. Jane*.

The Ridley Scott-produced *IN HER SHOES* can be seen as a post-feminist text, being characterized by an emphasis on neo-liberal feminine subjectivities (as personified by the two sisters Maggie (CAMERON DIAZ) and Rose (TONI COLLETTE) and their grandmother Ella (SHIRLEY MACLAINE). It also focuses on key discourses such as the notion of the BODY as the key source of identity for women—focusing in particular on the representation of Diaz on the screen; discourses of boldness, entitlement, and choice; and a belief in the integrity of women's worlds.

References

Janet Bergstrom, "Androids and Androgyny," *Camera Obscura* 15 (October 1988): 36–43; Shoma A. Chatterjee, "Two Women," *Deep Focus* 4, no. 2 (1992): 76; Manohla Dargis, "The Road to Freedom," *Sight and Sound*, July 1991, 18; Chad Herrmann, "Some Horrible Dream About (S)mothering: Sexuality, Gender and Family in the Alien Trilogy," *PostScript* 16, no.3 (1997): 38; Douglas Kellner, Flo Leibowitz, and Michael Ryan, "*Blade Runner*: A Diagnostic Critique," *Jump Cut* 29 (1984): 7; Julia Kristeva, *Powers of Horror: An Essay on Abjection*, trans. Leon S. Boudiez (New York: Columbia University Press, 1982), 113; Linda Mizejewski, "Stardom and Serial Fantasies: Thomas Harris' *Hannibal*," in *Keyframes: Popular Cinema and Cultural Studies*, ed. Matthew Tinkcom and Amy Villarejo (London and New York: Routledge, 2001), 165–66; Kaja Silverman, "Back to the Future," *Camera Obscura* 27 (September 1991): 109–31; David Twohy, "*G.I. Jane*: First Draft" (6 August 1995). Unpub. Screenplay, http://sfy.ru/sfy.html?script=gi_jane (accessed 21 October 2008); Sasha Vojkovic, "What Can She Know, Where Can She Go? Extraterritoriality and the Symbolic Universe in the

Alien Series," *New Review of Film and Television Studies* 1, no.1 (2003): 127; Valerie Su-Lin Wee, "The Most Poetic Subject in the World: Observations on Death, (Beautiful) Women and Representation in *Blade Runner*," *Kinema* 7 (April 1997): 70.

Bibliography

Judi Addelston, "Doing the Full Monty with Dick and Jane: Using the Phallus to Validate Marginalized Masculinities," *Journal of Men's Studies* 7, no.3 (Spring 1999): 337–52; Ellen Bishop, "Alien Subject/Alien Thought: The Female Subject in the *Aliens* Films," in *Critical Studies on the Feminist Subject*, ed. Giovanna Covi (Trento: Dipartimento di Scienze Filologiche e Storiche, 1997), 127–63; Patricia Ticineto Clough, "The 'Final Girl' in the Fictions of Science and Culture," *Stanford Humanities Review* 2, nos. 2–3 (1992): 57–69; Brenda Cooper, "Chick Flicks as Feminist Texts: The Appropriation of the Male Gaze in *Thelma & Louise*," *Women's Studies in Communication* 23, no.3 (Fall 2000): 277–306; Thomas Doherty, "Genre, Gender and the *Aliens* Trilogy," in *The Dread of Difference: Gender and the Horror Film*, ed. Barry Keith Grant (Austin: University of Texas Press, 1996), 181–99; Jessica Enevold, "The Daughters of *Thelma and Louise*: New Aesthetics of the Road," in *Gender, Genre and Identity in Women's Travel Writing*, ed. Kristi Siegel (New York: Peter Lang Publishing, Inc., 2004), 73–97; Linda Frost, "The Decentered Subject of Feminism: Postfeminism and *Thelma and Louise*," in *Rhetoric in an Antifoundational World: Language, Culture and Pedagogy*, ed. Michael Bernard-Donals and Richard R. Glejzer (New Haven and London: Yale University Press, 1998), 147–69; Rosalind Gill and Elena Herdieckeroff, "Rewriting the Romance: New Femininities in Chick Lit?" *Feminist Media Studies* 6, no.4 (2006): 487–504; Lynda Hart, "'Till Death Us Do Part: Impossible Spaces in *Thelma and Louise*," *Journal of the History of Sexuality* 4, no.3 (January 1994): 430–46; Ros Jennings, "Desire and Design—Ripley Undressed," in *Immortal, Invisible: Lesbians and the Moving Image*, ed. Tamsin Wilton (London and New York: Routledge, 1995), 193–206; Deborah Jermyn, "The Rachel Papers: In Search of *Blade Runner*'s Femme Fatale," in *The Blade Runner Experience: The Legacy of a Science Fiction Classic*, ed. Will Brooker (London and New York: Wallflower Press, 2005), 159–73; Barbara Johnson, "Lesbian Spectacles: Reading *Sula, Passing, Thelma and Louise*, and *The Accused*," in *Media Spectacles*, ed. Marjorie Garber, Jann Matlock, and Rebecca L. Walkowitz (New York and London: Routledge, 1993), 160–66; Louise J. Kaplan, "Fits and Misfits: The Body of a Woman." *American Image* 50, no. 4 (1995): 457–80; Kathleen Murphy, "Only Angels Have Wings," *Film Comment* 27, no.4 (July–August 1991); 26–29; Zhuang Qing, "Freedom in Residence: Feminism in *Thelma & Louise*," in *Re-reading America: Changes & Challenges*, ed. Zhong Weihe and Han Rui (Lockhampton, UK: Reardon Publishing, 2004), 227–37; Raphael Shargel, "Gender and Genre Bending," *New Leader* 80, no. 15 (22 September 1997): 20–21; Robert Torry, "Awakening to the Other: Feminism and the Ego Ideal in *Alien*," *Women's Studies: An Interdisciplinary Journal* 23, no.4 (1994): 343–63; Jason P. Vest, "Double Jeopardy: The Sexual Dynamics of *Blade Runner*," in *The Image of the Twentieth Century: Proceedings, 2000 Conference, Society for the Interdisciplinary Study of Social Imagery*, ed. Will Wright and Steven Kaplan (Pueblo, CO: University of Southern Colorado, 2001), 349–58; Jeffrey Walsh, "Elite Woman Warriors and Dog Soldiers: Gender Adaptations in Modern War Films," in *Gender and Warfare in the Twentieth Century: Textual Representations*, ed. Angela G. Smith (Manchester and New York: Manchester University Press, 2004), 195–216; Linda Williams, "Body Talk." *Sight and Sound* 7, no.11 (November 1997): 20–21.

FERRY, BRYAN (1945–)

Scott co-directed the video for the song "AVALON," released by Bryan Ferry and Roxy Music in 1982. Four years later Ferry sung the ballad "Is Your Love Strong Enough?" which plays over the end credits of *LEGEND*. Ferry collaborated with Scott on the production of the video/feature film trailer for the film, which featured Ferry singing the song while assuming "good and evil characteristics. There is also the screen [featured behind Ferry on the video] which is looking out at the room with a hand that seems to be reaching down to Bryan." Ferry liked working on the film's theme because he believed that the film "is a fantasy and has a mood to it—like my songs."

References

Rod Powell, "A Bit of a Legend," *Televisual*, May 1986, 42.

FEUERSTEIN, MARK (1971–)

Feuerstein's first major film was *Rules of Engagement* (2000). Cast in the largely secondary role of Simon Stein in *IN HER SHOES*, produced by Scott and directed by CURTIS HANSON, Feuerstein does not have to do much other than to give an understated performance. It is clear he doesn't understand his fiancée Rose, accusing her of "ping-ponging between comatose and homicidal," when her main problem consists of not being able to talk about her family tragedy—her mother's suicide when she was a child. Eventually Simon discovers what was wrong, and agrees to marry Rose—even though he understands that her sister will make his life a living hell. In a preproduction interview, Feuerstein claimed he accepted the role because he enjoyed playing "a guy who loves food, which is me. Playing a guy who is upfront and honest about what he feels. It was just a dream for me."

References

Susannah Grant, "*In Her Shoes* Script" (transcribed from the DVD version of the film), www.script-o-rama.com/movie_scripts/i/in-her-shoes-script-transcript.html (accessed 17 January 2009); Rebecca Murray, "In Her Shoes" (10 January 2005), *about.com*, http://movies.about.com/od/inhershoes/a/shoesmf100105.htm (accessed 8 August 2008).

FICHTNER, WILLIAM (1956–)

Born in 1956 on Long Island, New York, raised in Cheek-towaga, William Fichtner graduated from Maryvale High School in 1974. His first roles were in sitcoms like *Grace Under Fire* (1993). He has also been in films such as *Armageddon* (1998) and *The Perfect Storm* (2000).

Cast as Sanderson in *BLACK HAWK DOWN*, Fichtner was struck by the rigor of the training the actors had to endure before filming began. In a preproduction interview he recalled that: "They [the soldiers in the camps] took us out to this place in the woods, blew the door off the hinges, and said, 'Who's next? Go ahead, Bill.' It didn't take long to figure out that if the insurance company had any idea, I don't think we'd be doing this." On their final day in Fort Bragg, North Carolina, Fichtner (ERIC BANA) and other members of the cast received detailed instructions on the proper handling and operation of weapons used by the Delta Force in Somalia, as well as "breaching training" (entering locked or obstructed doorways or windows using explosives, and learning how to enter and clear a building of potential threats).

As a member of the Delta Force, Sanderson is committed to his duties—even if it brings him into conflict with the Rangers. As one point during the raid he encounters Steele (JASON ISAACS) and tells him that he is simply "doing [his] job! Look, we gotta get to that crash site! We gotta get on to that street and we gotta move! . . . give me some of your shooters and that'll get closer to the bird [i.e., the crashed Black Hawk helicopter]." Impressed, Steele agrees to Sanderson's demands.

References

William Fichtner, quoted in Fred Schruers, "The Way We War," *Premiere* 15, no.6 (February 2002): 53; Ken Nolan, *Black Hawk Down: The Shooting Script* (New York: Newmarket Press, 2002), 71.

FIGGIS, MIKE (1948–)

First film was *Stormy Monday* (1988), followed by *Internal Affairs* (1988). His film *Mr. Jones* (1993) experienced considerable difficulties obtaining a release.

Figgis was invited to direct *THE BROWNING VERSION* by producer Ridley Scott. In a 2003 interview he recalled that he "read the script, and it was a good piece of writing and a very good adaptation, it was set in England, which I liked the idea of. And it helped that Ridley was a director that I respected. . . ." In another interview published prior to the film's 1994 premiere he admitted that he "certainly had a lot of sympathy for Crocker-Harris's character and could relate to it and his constant humiliations . . . I needed a change of pace. If I had been playing a sort of hard rock, there's something very attractive about doing an album of Cole Porter standards, because they're brilliant. There's a

cruelty and a subtlety and a kind of sophistication to them which are open to interpretation."

Filming was apparently a pleasurable experience, according to Figgis in 2003: "We had an idyllic summer shooting the film in the most beautiful part of England. It's a strong piece of drama, and I thought Albert [Finney] was incredible." But what happened afterwards certainly wasn't: "I delivered the film. I knew that Ridley didn't like the film, and he made no bones about it when I saw it. He didn't like Finney's performance. He didn't like the way I directed it. So I kind of felt I was back in a very familiar territory in a way . . . I ended up back in LA with the film, because I had to show it to the studio. SHERRY LANSING from Paramount Pictures was there, and Ridley was there, along with some others . . . I was being somewhat shocked by what appeared to be their favorable reaction. I remember catching the word 'Oscar' and Sherry saying, 'It's just the most beautiful film. ALBERT FINNEY is going to get an Oscar. Everybody come to my office and we'll talk about this.' . . . It was kind of an odd situation because I knew Ridley didn't really like the film, and suddenly Sherry loved the film, you know. She was the head of Paramount!"

Compared to Figgis's other work, *The Browning Version* is something of an anachronism; one does not expect the director of a gritty contemporary work to helm an adaptation of a TERRENCE RATTIGAN play. Nonetheless, Figgis does a competent job with the material, as he focuses in particular on the four central characters in the play—Crocker-Harris (Finney), Laura (GRETA SCACCHI), Frank (MATTHEW MODINE), and Taplow (BEN SILVERSTONE). The subject matter might be very localized, even parochial (non-British audiences might find it difficult to respond to the material set in and around a British "public" school—even the name of which would confuse many American viewers), but the conflicts between the characters are readily accessible.

References

Robert J. Emery, *The Directors—Take Four* (New York: Allworth Press, 2003), 181–83; Howard Feinstein, "No Gravy in Browning," *The Guardian*, 20 October 1994, Section 2, 8.

FIGHTER PILOT

GB 1940 r/t 8 min b/w. *Production Companies*: Ministry of Information in association with British Movietone News. *Producer*: Gerald Sanger. *Director*: Raymond Perrin.

An attempt to cover the life of a fighter pilot in World War II, covering training, operations, sleep (if at all), take-off, flight and battle in the air against the German invaders. Ridley Scott covered similar material in his television series *AFP—AMERICAN FIGHTER PILOT*, but the impact sixty-two years later was minimal compared to the earlier British version.

FILM NOIR

This popular cinematic genre of the 1940s is characterized by a series of elements, notably low-key lighting, claustrophobic framing of character and scene, the use of heavy shadow, offbeat compositions and bizarre camera angles, and rain-soaked urban landscapes.

BLADE RUNNER consciously borrows from this tradition in its determination to depict a dark, value-bereft society in which the distinctions between right and wrong no longer exist. Ethical distinctions are as difficult to draw as the line between REPLICANTS and human beings. The film also suggests that human beings are powerless in this world; their life span has been predetermined, and such qualities as friendship or even person-to-person communication are no longer valued. Film noir became a popular genre immediately after the end of World War II, as filmmakers caught the atmosphere of insecurity existing amongst the American people, who had won the battle abroad, yet had come back to a country in which age-old moral certainties (and gender distinctions) no longer seemed important. Blade Runner suggests that the world of the early 1980s was experiencing similar conflicts of value.

SOMEONE TO WATCH OVER ME likewise incorporates film noir elements. New York City might be "the ultimate object of man's desire" but it is also a threatening place, where crooks like Venza (ANDREAS KATSULAS) can escape conviction and force a woman such as Claire Gregory (MIMI ROGERS) to be perpetually looking over her shoulder. Claire herself is portrayed as a classic femme fatale, an ice-cold beauty whose first appearance marks her out as "a special beauty and clearly someone very special." Despite her attractions, Claire remains a fundamentally lonely woman who is forced to give up the opportunity of personal happiness to ensure the future of Mike Keegan's (TOM BERENGER's) MARRIAGE. In the amoral world of film noir, no one can achieve happiness, friendship no longer exists, and love affairs are doomed to fail. This atmosphere is especially appropriate to Someone, whose soundtrack incorporates 1930s and 1940s standards such as the title song, Al Bowlly's "What More Can I Ask?" "Suspicious Minds," and "Cry."

James Maxfield's book The Fatal Woman situates THELMA & LOUISE in the film noir tradition, but argues that the film departs from generic expectations of the film by showing how the heroines' actions are justifiable. Maxfield deplores their deaths as a tragic waste after their triumphant battles against patriarchy. The Ridley Scott-produced film CLAY PIGEONS relocates the noir tradition in SMALL TOWNS; consequently, much of the dialogue takes place in daylight rather than darkness. Carol Reed's classic film noir THE THIRD MAN provided the inspiration for the settings in the war-torn city of Budapest during the Hungarian Uprising, as depicted in THE COMPANY.

Bibliography

Susan Doll and Greg Faller, "Blade Runner and Genre: Film Noir and Science Fiction," Literature/Film Quarterly 14, no.2 (1986): 89–101; W. Russel Gray, "Entropy, Energy, Empathy: Blade Runner and Detective Fiction," in Retrofitting Blade Runner, ed. Judith B. Kerman (Bowling Green: Bowling State University Popular Press, 2nd ed., 1997), 66–75; James Maxfield, The Fatal Woman: Sources of Male Anxiety in American Film Noir 1941–1991 (Cranfield, NJ: Associated University Presses, 1996); Isolde Standish, "Akira, Postmodernism and Resistance," in Liquid Metal: The Science Fiction Film Reader, ed. Sean Redmond (London and New York: Wallflower Press, 2004), 249–59; Slavoj Žižek, "The Thing That Thinks: The Kantian Background of the Noir Subject," in Shades of Noir: A Reader, ed. Joan Copjec (London and New York: Verso, 1993), 199–226.

FILMS AFTER 9/11

Several of Ridley Scott's most recent works make reference to the changed sociopolitical situation after 9/11.

While BLACK HAWK DOWN avoids any direct allusion to the tragedy (even though the idea was contemplated by the director and the producers), it nonetheless articulates a specific conception of American identity, based on fear of the Other. Like BLACK RAIN before it, the film represents non-Americans as unthinkingly brutal: such strategies, according to Trevor B. McCrisken and Andrew Pepper, were significant for the United States' efforts to recover its self-image. The film overlooked issues of "causation, morality and political significance and instead emphasized the individual courage and valor of American soldiers who managed to extricate themselves from a seemingly impossible situation." In the "Director's Commentary" to the 2004 DVD release, Scott recalled that he withdrew a title-card at the end of the film suggesting that the US withdrawal from Somalia paved the way for the 2001 terrorist attack. This was done to avoid upsetting the families of those soldiers who perished in the Somalian raid.

Despite this move, Black Hawk Down was a script the new government/Hollywood alliance deemed appropriate for the post-9/11 environment. Its original release was pushed forward to December 2001, and Sony Pictures sponsored a special screening at the White House attended by President George W. Bush and other members of his staff. Oliver North attended the Washington premiere. Copies were also flown out to boost morale among American troops in Afghanistan.

Although principal photography was completed on the reality series AMERICAN FIGHTER PILOT before 9/11, the producers incorporated direct references to the tragedy, once it was broadcast on CBS in 2002. Each episode begins with a montage sequence showing images of the disaster and the people associated with it—one of the planes crashing into the Twin Towers, the scene of devastation on the NEW YORK streets, and a close-up of Osama bin Laden—plus a shot of the Stars and Stripes. On the soundtrack a recording of President George W. Bush's speech can be heard, as he emphasizes America's strength and its willingness to fight for freedom. Throughout the series the three recruits—Mike Love, Marcus Gregory, and Todd Giggy—make reference to the disaster, and their determination to ensure that it never happens again, even if that means bombing Iraq. Made with the full assent of the Pentagon, the series was clearly designed to improve morale in the wake of 9/11. Sadly, the reviewers did not respond in the same way to the series; many of them found it boring and poorly shot. CBS canceled the show after only two of the scheduled seven episodes had been broadcast.

The remake of THE ANDROMEDA STRAIN shows what happens when governments do not pay sufficient heed to the threat from external forces that threaten to engulf the population. The Andromeda Strain virus itself might be seen as a symbol of terrorism, which can only be neutralized by everyone—citizens, scientists, the US MILITARY as well as governments—working together. The script also includes some overt references to the possible threat posed to America's stability by communist states such as North Korea.

While KINGDOM OF HEAVEN did not communicate such an overt political message, Scott was nonetheless careful to acknowledge in the introduction to the book of the film that "[as] we are now living in the post 9/11 world, Kingdom of Heaven will inevitably be looked at from that perspective. We did make some conscious choices about the values expressed through the story, beginning with the central situation of two leaders trying to serve their own people and their sense of mission, while exercising a degree of tolerance of the 'other.'" He continues the analysis in BODY OF LIES, by showing that the conflicts initiated during the Crusades persist to this day, creating a situation where there are no winners and losers, just victims. There seems no place for tolerance in a context where no one actually trusts one another, despite the Jordanian Secret Service chief Hani's (MARK STRONG's) exhortation to CIA agent Roger Ferris (LEONARDO DICAPRIO) that "this [i.e. the Middle East] is a part of the world where friendship matters. It can save your life." A similar discourse permeates certain episodes of NUMB3RS, particularly "When Worlds Collide" (Series 4, Episode 18).

References

Trevor B. McCrisken and Andrew Pepper, *American History and Contemporary Hollywood Film* (Edinburgh: Edinburgh University Press, 2005), 204; Ridley Scott, "Director's Commentary" to the 2-disc DVD release of *Black Hawk Down* (Los Angeles: Revolution Studios Distribution Company LLG & Jerry Bruckheimer, Inc.,

2004); Ridley Scott, "Introduction," in *Kingdom of Heaven: The Ridley Scott Film and the History Behind the Story*, ed. Diana Landau (London: Simon and Schuster Ltd., 2005), 8.

Bibliography

Robin Andersen, *A Century of Media, A Century of War* (New York: Peter Lang Publishing Inc., 2006); Wheeler Winston Dixon, ed., *Film and Television After 9/11* (Carbondale: Southern Illinois University Press, 2004); Nancy Lynch Street, "Stanley Kubrick and America's 'Strange Love' of War," in *War and Film in America: Historical and Critical Essays*, ed. Marilyn J. Matelski and Nancy Lynch Street (Jefferson, NC and London: McFarland and Co. [Publishers], 2003), 175–95.

THE FINEST HOURS

GB 1964 r/t 116 min b/w & color. *Production Companies*: Columbia Pictures Corporation and Le Vien International. *Producer*: Jack Le Vien (later Jack Levin). *Director*: Peter Baylis. *Writer*: Victor Wolfson from the book *The Second World War* by Winston Churchill. *Director of Photography*: Hone Glendinning. *Music*: Ron Grainer. *Cast*: Orson Welles (*Narrator*), George Baker, Faith Brook, David Healy, Patrick Wymark (*Voices*).

A life of Winston Churchill placing particular emphasis on his role in the years leading up to the outbreak of World War II, as well as his career as Prime Minister. The film's material anticipates much of that used in THE GATHERING STORM.

The director Jack le Vien (later known as Jack Levin) had worked with Churchill during his visits to the various battle fronts in World War II, where he organized press coverage. The film uses archive footage interspersed with Churchill's own words read by actors. Le Vien's aim, as expressed in the book of the film, was to "illustrate certain facets of his [Churchill's] life in a fresh candid and sometimes, perhaps, surprising way."

References

Jack le Vien and Peter Lewis, *The Finest Hours* (London: Corgi Books, 1964), 10.

FINNEY, ALBERT (1936–)

Albert Finney came to films after a distinguished theatrical start to his career. His first major role was Arthur Seaton in Karel Reisz's *Saturday Night and Sunday Morning* (1960). Finney plays a cameo role as Fouché, the chief of the secret police, in THE DUELLISTS. Ludicrously over-dressed in tight-fitting pants and braided jacket, he looks the very epitome of authority as he agrees to remove Feraud's (HARVEY KEITEL's) name from the list of officers to be tried for treason. However, we soon learn that he controls the soldiers' destinies as a way of saving himself; like the film's two main characters, his life is dictated by self-interest. This explains the presence of so much poverty in Scott's film: people seldom bother to work for the community at large.

In THE BROWNING VERSION (1994), produced by Scott and directed by MIKE FIGGIS, Finney plays Arthur Crocker-Harris, a classics teacher who (like Fouché) values self-interest above public duty. To prepare for the role, Finney watched a classics class at Sherborne School, Dorset, in southwest England; his apparent facility with Greek and Latin came courtesy of some teaching by an academic at Balliol College, Oxford. Finney claimed that he had "never played a part that's so isolated and stoic. It goes back to English good manners—that you are not supposed to show the world how you are, how you feel or to express your emotions . . . In this role, instead of showing the character's true feelings and intentions, I had to keep masking them." Crocker-Harris is a remote personality, unable to look his students in the eye while trying (and dismally failing) to compensate for his inadequacies by speaking in a sarcastic tone. Such failings are prompted by Crocker-Harris's belief that his life has been a failure. Once a brilliant classical scholar, he entered into an unhappy MARRIAGE while rotting away at a minor private school, ruthlessly exploited by his colleagues and a Machiavellian headmaster (MICHAEL GAMBON). Crocker-Harris's character is brilliantly suggested in Finney's performance, his face remaining expressionless as he stares at the ground or into the middle distance, as if experiencing a living death.

When the boy Taplow (BEN SILVERSTONE) gives him a present of the Robert Browning translation of Aeschylus's *Agamemnon* (the "Browning Version" of the film's title), Crocker-Harris can hardly control himself as he realizes that someone cares for him after all. His lips tremble and his body shakes with emotion as he puts a hand to his mouth and turns away from Taplow, mumbling that he has been "under rather a strain." In spite of everything, he has the capacity to change lives. This quality is reemphasized in the film's climax as Crocker-Harris stands before the entire school and apologizes for being a failure, for not committing himself to the task of training young minds. He begs the students' forgiveness and then walks out of the hall with his head held high. Although his future is far from secure (having been forced to leave the school because of ill health), Crocker-Harris has emerged from his cocoon of self-interest; it is not surprising that he should be applauded as he bids farewell.

Finney creates another study of self-interest as Winston Churchill in the Ridley Scott–produced television film THE GATHERING STORM (2002). In a preproduction interview Finney asserted that Churchill "had an extraordinary personality"—as manifested in a remarkable capacity for work. He was quite accustomed to working twenty hours a day, "and he expected them [his staff] to work extraordinary hours, as he did—they all adored him. They certainly seemed to tolerate it—he had people for a very long time, he was a fascinating man." Finney worked hard on recreating Churchill's speech patterns, although he stopped short of giving a direct impersonation: "I had to free it up so it was a creative act and not an imitative one. I had to have the essence of him, that was all . . . It doesn't worry me, people who have their idea of him have it anyway."

Described as "a self-serving opportunist," Finney's Churchill truly believes in his destiny to save England and the [British] Empire. One shot in *The Gathering Storm* recalls *The Duellists*, as he stands at the edge of the frame, with the glorious Kentish hills in the background illuminated by winter sunlight. Unlike the earlier film (which uses a similar shot to emphasize Feraud's alienation), *The Gathering Storm* stresses Churchill's intimate relationship to his country. Like Crocker-Harris, Churchill comes to understand the importance of relating to others. One sequence begins with him criticizing his wife Clemmie (VANESSA REDGRAVE) for accepting an offer to go on a foreign trip, even if that means leaving home and family. Clemmie responds by storming out of the room, upsetting a plate of sprouts as she does so. As a maid (Lyndsey Marshall) tries to clear them up, Churchill smiles sheepishly and explains that the vegetables were angry and fell to the ground of their own accord. While seeking not to lose face in front of the servants, he believes that something must be said, even if it is only a weak joke. Churchill goes upstairs and taps on Clemmie's door, using his pet name of "Mr. Pug" in an attempt to placate her. It is obvious that he is very much in love, even after twenty-six years of marriage. Churchill's attitude towards people is summed up in an epigraph to the film, taken from his VE Day speech of May 1945: "In all our long history, we have never seen a greater day than this. Everyone, man or woman, has done their best." Finney won the Best Actor Emmy award in 2002 for his performance.

In Scott's A GOOD YEAR (2005), Finney's Uncle Henry comes across as someone totally in control of himself. Having moved to FRANCE and taken on a vineyard, he discovers life's enduring virtues—sunshine, fresh air and good wine. At one point his associate Duflot (DIDIER BOURDON) describes him as "a man of secrets. A man of passions." Scott continually photographs him in soft-focus, his face illuminated by bright sunlight or the flicker of a candle—a technique recalling Scott's work in commercials such as HOVIS BREAD. By this method Scott emphasizes Henry's satisfaction with life's simple pleasures. Max (RUSSELL CROWE) remembers him with affection; when he was a boy he learned Henry's philosophy of life, which according to the film's pressbook "has mostly to do with wine in particular, but around that is a philosophy of enjoying life." Uncle Henry is contrasted with his nephew Max Skinner

(Crowe), a city slicker who gradually undergoes a process of self-discovery, something signaled by a change in the way Crowe delivers his lines. By the final sequence he reproduces Finney's slow, measured tones, suggesting that both men have now understood that happiness lies in the unchanging world of the château.

References

Quentin Falk, *Albert Finney in Character* (London: Robson Books, 2002), 195; *The Gathering Storm: Information Pack Issued 17 June 2002* (London: BBC, 2002), www.bbc.co.uk/pressoffice/pressreleases/stories/2002/06_june/17/gathering_storm_pack.pdf (accessed 24 December 2008); Marc Klein, "*A Good Year*: Screenplay" (Draft dated 5 September 2005), http://www.dailyscript.com/scripts/A-GOOD-YEAR-2.pdf (accessed 26 January 2009); *Pressbook: A Good Year* (Los Angeles: Twentieth Century-Fox Film Corporation, 2006), 3.

FIORENTINO, LINDA (1958–)

Made her name playing Bridget Gregory in *The Last Seduction* (1993), plus roles in *Men in Black* (1997) and *Dogma* (1999).

Interviewed by Bruce Kirkland while promoting her role as Carol MacKay in *WHERE THE MONEY IS*, Fiorentino claimed to find PAUL NEWMAN, her seventy-five-year-old leading man, very attractive: "He's about the only man I could think of that I would have sex with even if he were in his nineties. He is beautiful physically, but he has this internal beauty, too. It's endless. It's forever . . . His skin still looks soft and supple, his body is still trim and virile and those colour-blind, baby-blue eyes still pierce when people lock him in a gaze." This is certainly not the case in the film itself; whereas Carol certainly admires Henry Manning (Newman's character), the relationship is strictly platonic, based on mutual respect rather than sexual attraction.

Alexander Walker found the casting of Fiorentino in the film "a perfect match" for Newman: "Her resourcefulness answers his, feisty flash for flash: they perform a sort of venerable Butch and feminist Sundance." Anthony Quinn in *The Independent* admired her "comic touch that's very appealing indeed. It [this film] won't be a milestone in her career, but it won't do her any harm either."

References

Linda Fiorentino, quoted in *Daniel O'Brien, Paul Newman* (London: Faber and Faber Ltd., 2004), 296; Anthony Quinn, "The King of the Hustlers Pulls off One More Sting," *The Independent*, 6 October 2000, 10; Alexander Walker, "A Con, a Pro and a Caper to Treasure," *Evening Standard*, 5 October 2000, 29.

FODEN, TOM (?–)

British-born production designer who made his name with music video designs on "Closer" (Nine Inch Nails), "Scream" (Michael Jackson), "Bedtime Stories" (Madonna), and "Weird" (Hanson). Foden was engaged as designer on *MATCHSTICK MEN*, and was keen to exploit the LOS ANGELES locations to show Roy's (NICHOLAS CAGE's) idiosyncrasies of character. In a preproduction interview he stressed that Roy would have to live "in a spare and orderly environment," with much of the inspiration coming from "the paintings of John Register . . . His [Register's] use of strong afternoon sunlight and long shadows, combined with contemporary settings was an idea I thought could set the mood of the film. It provided a linear sectioning between order and disarray which really defines the character of Roy."

References

Production Information: Matchstick Men (Los Angeles: Warner Bros. Pictures, 2003), 14.

FORBIDDEN PLANET

US 1956 r/t 98 min col. *Production Company*: MGM. *Producer*: Nicholas Nayfack. *Director*: Fred M. Wilcox. *Writer*: Cyril Hume. *Director of Photography*: George J. Folsey. *Production Designers*: Cedric Gibbons and Arthur Lonergan. *Music*: Bebe and Louis Barron. *Cast*: Walter Pidgeon (*Dr. Morbius*), Anne Francis (*Altaira Morbius*), Leslie Nielsen (*Commander Adams*), Warren Stevens (*Lieut. "Doc" Ostrow*), Jack Kelly (*Lieut. Farman*), Richard Anderson (*Chief Quinn*), Earl Holliman (*Cook*), Robby the Robot (*Himself*).

The famous movie based on Shakespeare's *Tempest*. *ALIEN* contains numerous allusions to it—notably in the scene where the crew members investigate the deserted planet where they first encounter the beast. Both films also explore the consequences of human beings seeking to meddle with the unknowable.

Ridley Scott was interviewed about the film—and other classics that inspired him—in the 2005 TV documentary *Watch the Skies! Science Fiction, the 1950s and Us*. Written and produced by critic Richard Schickel, this documentary chronicles the history of science-fiction movies, from the silent era to the present. It is currently available on the two-disc fiftieth-anniversary DVD release of *Forbidden Planet*.

Given Scott's enthusiasm for science fiction, it came as rather a surprise to find that by 2007 he was prepared to state that the genre was all but dead: "There's nothing original. We've seen it all before. Been there. Done it."

Reference

Dalya Alberge, "Sci-fi Films Are as Dead as Westerns, Says Ridley Scott," *The Times* (London), 30 August 2007, 30.

FORD, HARRISON (1942–)

His father was Irish, his mother Russian-Jewish. He was a lackluster student at Maine Township High School East in

Park Ridge, Illinois (no athletic star, never above a C average). He became a star as Bob Falfa in George Lucas's *American Graffiti* (1973). Ford was not the first actor to be considered for the role of Deckard in *BLADE RUNNER*. Originally screenwriter HAMPTON FANCHER thought of Robert Mitchum—remembering, perhaps, that Mitchum had played Philip Marlowe in two recent remakes of *Farewell My Lovely* (1975) and *The Big Sleep* (1978). Other actors were also in the frame, notably Dustin Hoffman. Eventually Ford was engaged on the basis of his performance in *Star Wars* (1977). Producer MICHAEL DEELEY observed in 1981 that "Deckard's curious mixture of emerging sensitivity and hard-boiled bureaucracy would offer an excellent chance for Harrison [Ford]." Ford himself liked the "ambiguity" of the role: "He's [Deckard is] struggling with a job-oriented fear. That involves killing; shooting people is not something he likes to do. So although he might be a pretty good Blade Runner, Deckard's also a reluctant one." Scott observed in the pressbook for the film's original release that "Harrison possesses some of the laconic dourness of Bogey [Humphrey Bogart], but he's more ambivalent, more human. He's almost an antihero."

Ford's characterization focuses on Deckard's gradual discovery of human feeling—that quality separating a human being from a REPLICANT. This is brought out in the sequence where we see him slumped over the piano in his apartment. In the DIRECTOR'S CUT (1992), this shot is followed by a dissolve to a shot of a unicorn in a forest, galloping towards the camera, before returning to a close-up of Deckard. Both versions of the film then show a pan of a series of photographs on Deckard's piano; Deckard picks one up and analyzes it closely, to ascertain whether Rachael (SEAN YOUNG) is a replicant. This sequence shows Deckard's meticulous nature; like all good detectives, he investigates the evidence thoroughly. On the other hand, Rachael's memory clearly stimulates his imagination, prompting him to reflect on his past.

Deckard's growing self-awareness is stressed later on, when he turns towards Rachael at the piano and compliments her: "You play beautifully." This is followed by a two-shot where Deckard kisses her tentatively on the neck and moves towards her lips. Rachael runs away, pursued by Deckard who slams the door, takes her in his arms so that she cannot escape, and forcibly kisses her on the lips. Deckard's sudden release of pent-up emotion, born of frustration, is extremely powerful; he wants to show his love for Rachael, but cannot do so except through violent means.

In the end, however, Deckard does change; having seen off Batty (RUTGER HAUER), he returns to his apartment to find Rachael covered with a sheet. Thinking that she is dead, Deckard puts his face close to hers and bursts into tears. When she wakes up he murmurs "Do you love me?"

and she replies "I love you" without coercion. At last Deckard has discovered the kind of tenderness that enables him to sustain a relationship.

As the two of them leave the apartment, Deckard picks up an aluminum foil model of a unicorn while we hear the line "It's too bad she won't live, but then again, who does?" on the soundtrack. In the original theatrical version, this moment underlines Rachael's mortality; her love affair will inevitably be a short one, despite the fact that both of them escape the city for an edenic world of green fields. In the DIRECTOR'S CUT, the unicorn clearly refers us back to the earlier, dream-sequence one, suggesting that the memory has been implanted in Deckard's mind—and thus he (like Rachael) is a replicant.

In a documentary "Deck-a-Rep: the True Nature of Rick Deckard" included in the five-disc collector's edition of *Blade Runner*, Scott states quite categorically that Deckard is a replicant. Others are not so sure; in the same documentary Ford insists that Deckard is a human being, "an emotional representative" that viewers can identify with in a DYSTOPIAN world. It is not particularly important whether or not Deckard is a replicant; what matters more is Ford's performance as someone who "must shake off the troubles he's seen, the numbing shell, to get back in touch with his feelings. He becomes human again, thanks primarily to the replicants who are driven by love for one another to develop empathy."

Both PAUL M. SAMMON's *Future Noir* (on the making of the film) and the Collector's Edition suggest that Ford had his differences with Scott during the making of the film. Nonetheless, *Blade Runner* remains one of his signature performances in a career as a star which continues to this day.

References

Michael Deeley, Harrison Ford, quoted in Paul M. Sammon, *Future Noir: The Making of Blade Runner*, 2nd ed. (London: Gollancz, 2007), 88–89; Rita Kempley, "Blade Runner," *Washington Post*, 11 September 1992, A2; Ridley Scott, Harrison Ford, interviewed in "Deck-a-Rep: the True Nature of Rick Deckard," Documentary included in *Blade Runner: Collector's Edition* (Los Angeles: Warner Bros. Entertainment, Inc., and the Blade Runner Partnership, 2007).

Bibliography

Brad Duke, *Harrison Ford: The Films* (Jefferson, NC and London: McFarland & Company, Inc., 2005).

FORD, ROBERT (1862–1892)

An American OUTLAW who gained fame by killing JESSE JAMES in 1882. He was an idealistic and ambitious young man who had devoted his life to the hope of one day riding alongside his idol. He could never have imagined that history would ultimately mark him as the "the dirty little coward" who shot Jesse in the back. ANDREW DOMINIK, director of *THE ASSASSINATION OF JESSE JAMES BY THE COWARD ROBERT FORD*, described him thus: "Robert is a person who seems easily hurt. He might have imagined that if he was with Jesse James—more to the point, if he was Jesse James—it would be a kind of armor that would protect him [from censure] . . . A person imagines himself having a special connection to someone, then discovers it's not true, or it's not enough. Adoration turns to anger. I think Ford's feelings are always running side by side between the two emotions."

Ford was eventually assassinated in the small town of Creede by Edward O'Kelley in 1892. Ford's gravestone says "The Man That Shot Jesse James."

References

"About the Production" [The Assassination of Jesse James], http://party931.com/common/movies/notes/54706-1-full.html (accessed 12 August 2008).

FOSTER, JODIE (1962–)

Jodie Foster made her name as a child star in *Taxi Driver* (1976). She received two Oscars before she was thirty years old—one for *The Accused* (1988) and the other for *SILENCE OF THE LAMBS* (1991).

Originally slated to repeat her award-winning role as Clarice Starling in *HANNIBAL*, Foster eventually withdrew from the picture on account of the script, which she believed was too grisly and too far-fetched for her: "The original movie worked because people believed in Clarice's heroism. I won't play her with negative attributes she would never have." She was eventually replaced by JULIANNE MOORE. Nonetheless her presence in the film is very apparent, as Linda Mizejewski observes: "[Those] who imagine Foster as Starling in the new *Hannibal* have a vivid way to picture the more complex traits of this character: powerful, competent female authority, beauty without glamour; and a sexual attractiveness that excludes easy categorization . . . the sexuality of Starling . . . is more acceptable if read through Jodie Foster, whose persona makes some of these contradictions or unanswered opinions acceptable."

References

Jodie Foster, quoted in Adam Smith, "Signed, Sealed, De-livered," *Empire* 141 (March 2001): 73; Linda Mizejewski, "Stardom and Serial Fantasies: Thomas Harris's *Hannibal*," in *Keyframes: Popular Cinema and Cultural Studies*, ed. Matthew Tinkcom and Amy Villarejo (London and New York: Routledge, 2001), 165–66.

Bibliography

Boyd Farrow, "Food Fight." *Screen International* 1235 (19 November 1999): 27; Daniel Fierman, "Lamb Chops," *Entertainment Weekly* 521 (14 January 2000): 12–13; "Has Foster Killed Agent Starling?" *StarBurst* 259 (March 2000): 6; Karen Hollinger, *The Actress: Hollywood Acting and the Female Star* (New York and London: Routledge, 2006).

FOSTER'S QUEST

GB 2007 Commercial r/t 30 sec col. *Production Company*: RSA Films. *Director*: Ridley Scott.

This commercial, produced for RSA Asia, begins with a shot of the Australian outback at sunset, with the words "Sometime in the Future" appearing on screen. The action dissolves to an improvised shelter, where two farmers—one young, one old—watch a recording of two T-shirted women drinking Foster's lager by a beautiful blue sea. The young farm worker exclaims, "The amber nectar, eh?" to which the older man replies, "That was real special, son, like an angel crying on your tongue." On the soundtrack some sweet nostalgic music can be heard. The action cuts back to the younger man asking: "Could it be the inspiration for a more decent way of life?" The older man replies, "Nah—but it tastes good," as the music abruptly ceases. The older man continues: "Son—the time has come. Take the one machine that still works and go out and find it. Remember all I've taught you about urban survival!" The young man replies: "No worries. Always lay the soup spoon on the outside of the knife," as he gets into his truck and speeds off into the sunset. The old man exclaims approvingly, "That's my boy," as the words appear on screen "Will he find it? Is there anyone else out there?" "Whatever happened to computer dating?" The final shot shows a glass of Foster's with the words, "Search for the Amber Nectar."

This commercial makes fun of familiar film conventions, such as the young man leaving the country for the city in his truck, while suggesting that any activity other than going to find Foster's is ultimately futile. As with many of Scott's works, both as director or producer, the commercial deliberately foregrounds the landscape—in this case, the rolling Australian prairie.

1492: CONQUEST OF PARADISE

GB/France/Spain 1992 r/t 155 min col. *Production Companies*: Légende Enterprises, France 3 Cinéma, Due West, CYRK, with the participation of the French and Spanish Ministries of Culture. *Producers*: Alain Goldman and Ridley Scott. *Director*: Ridley Scott. *Writer*: Roselyne Bosch. *Director of Photography*: Adrian Biddle. *Production Designer*: Norris Spencer. *Music*: Vangelis. *Cast*: Gérard Depardieu (*Christopher Columbus*), Armand Assante (*Sanchez*), Sigourney Weaver (*Queen Isabel*), Angela Molina (*Beatrix*), Fernando Rey (*Marchena*), Michael Wincott (*Moxica*), Tcheky Karyo (*Pinzon*), Kevin Dunn (*Captain Mendez*), Frank Langella (*Santangel*), Mark Margolis (*Bobadilla*), Bercello Moya (*Utapan*).

After *BLACK RAIN* Scott told Ana Maria Bahiana that he was looking to do a period film, one that reconstructed period behavior and attitudes. The idea for *1492* came about when journalist ROSELYNE BOSCH was researching an article about the five-hundredth anniversary celebrations of the discovery of America to go into *La Pointe* magazine. She took her story to producer ALAIN GOLDMAN and they tried to find a suitable director. Scott was their fifth choice, after Francis Coppola, Roland Joffé, Oliver Stone, and DAVID PUTTNAM. Scott himself had been approached by the Salkind brothers to work on the rival Columbus film to be produced at the same time, which was eventually titled *CHRISTOPHER COLUMBUS: THE DISCOVERY*. This was not the first film to be made about Columbus: in 1949 the British director David MacDonald had made *CHRISTO-PHER COLUMBUS*, with Fredric March in the title role. It was not a success.

For the latest version, Scott's one condition was that GÉRARD DEPARDIEU be cast as Columbus; he told Amy Taubin that the French actor was one of the few possessing "the proper energy and outsized personality for the Columbus character . . . Gérard Depardieu is Columbus. He is an extremely passionate character driven almost purely by his intuition." Anjelica Huston was approached for the role of Queen Isabella but ultimately was unable to commit and so the part went to SIGOURNEY WEAVER. Several of the technical staff had worked with Scott before, including production designer NORRIS SPENCER, composer VANGE-LIS, cinematographer ADRIAN BIDDLE, and set decorator Ann Mollo (*LEGEND*).

However the choice of subject proved problematic with potential financial backers: production at Pinewood Studios in England was halted twice through lack of funds. None of the major Hollywood studios would touch the project, and Scott eventually financed the film by selling the distribution rights territory by territory. Scott himself admitted in an interview in the British film magazine *Empire* that "Columbus is going to be very unpopular. We're going to have every Indian society after us for racism. But his vision was very extreme—even more extreme than NASA's and more daunting. His crew believed he was going to sail to the edge of the world. The NASA people, at least, have their co-ordinates when they send up a mission."

Nonetheless, after several initial hiccups, shooting began on 2 December 1991 and continued for about eighty days. Exterior footage was shot in Spain, the Dominican Republic, and Costa Rica, the primary location for the New World part of the film because of its pristine beaches, islands, and jungles. Scott was enthusiastic about the project. He insisted in the *Empire* interview that he was not striving for historical recreation but to offer an "intelligent speculation on what really happened and who he [Columbus] really was, and at the end you make up your own mind. Was he a man finally ridden by guilt, or was he unaware of what he's really done?

Could he in fact have had a perspective on what he was doing at that particular time, given the fact that the norm was to burn twenty-nine heretics in a square in Seville or Madrid?"

However this enthusiasm was not shared by reviewers. Michael Sragow of the *New Yorker* called it "one huge objet d'non-art." J. Hoberman of the *Village Voice* went further, describing it as "a lumbering bear-hug of a movie, his worst since *Legend*. Impaled on the clichés of Roselyne Bosch's script, Scott hoists flags, rings bells, and flogs extras in vain. The more desperate the tumult, the more lifeless the wax museum." British reviewers were no less censorious: Kevin Jackson described the film as a "historical epic as rock video. The tropical storm that destroys Columbus's settlement is shot on eye-scorching strobes right out of *ALIEN*, and this is not the only moment which prompts comparison between the *Santa Maria* and the *NOSTROMO*." Jonathan Romney took a more ironic stance: "Everything is beautifully worn and weathered—the sails, the maps, the monks—but next to nothing happens, bar the year's most realistic on-screen garottings. The story . . . will be remembered for one lovely shot of mists parting, and for Depardieu solemnly telling Sigourney Weaver's Isabel, 'You're the only queen I know.'" The only dissenting voice came from the film magazine *Empire*, who complimented Scott on producing "a snapshot of history on a par with the best, the atmosphere of fear, dread and ignorance in medieval Spain being brilliantly recreated, and the sheer *vastness* of the undertaking . . . coming across . . . despite the irritating use of some coloured filters left over from *The Duellists*."

The film encountered problems even before it opened, as the producers battled with the Salkind brothers over the right to use the name Christopher Columbus in the title. Eventually producer Goldman emerged victorious, according to the *Hollywood Reporter*. However *1492* was a financial disaster at the box office: costing $44 million to make, it grossed only $7 million at the US box office.

Nonetheless the film is an interesting text, as it takes up and develops several of the themes raised in Scott's earlier work. CLASS DIFFERENCES become a major issue, as the foreign adventurer Columbus expects everyone, even the Spanish nobles, to work on building his city in the New World. Robert Thurston's novelized version of the screenplay makes this clear: "He [Moxica] wished he had not come to this godforsaken new world, especially to knuckle under the leadership of this damned rogue Columbus." Back in Spain, Sanchez and his fellow nobles experience similar feelings: "The last few days, in the company of the members of the court, he [Columbus] had begun to question his own ambition to be accepted in the higher realms of society. While they feted him and praised his discoveries, they continually seemed to sniff at his lower origins with their aristocratic noses." Moxica renders these prejudices explicit just before he dies: "You are nothing! . . . Your bastards will not inherit your titles! *We* are everything. We are immortal." "We" in this sense refers to the Spanish nobles who, as representatives of the Old World, consider themselves untouchable. The clash between Columbus and Moxica recalls that of *SOMEONE TO WATCH OVER ME*: while ostensibly contributing to the greater good of Spain, Columbus can never become one of the ruling elite. He will always remain the outsider, whose titles have been awarded rather than inherited.

The clash between Old and New Worlds is an interesting one. On the one hand Scott asks us in *1492* to believe that Columbus's world is one of possibility—despite the hardships involved, Columbus's desire to colonize new territories is identified as something positive. This is made clear right at the end, when Columbus is permitted by the queen to continue his voyages, and an end title-card informs us that he eventually discovered the Pacific Ocean, thus proving the adage that "Life has more imagination that we carry in our dreams." This stands in stark contrast to the Old World of medieval Spain, which is dominated by fear and suspicion and where crowds gather to watch heretics being burned at the stake. A failure to respect "the word of God" (in other words, the official view of Catholicism) inevitably leads to punishment. The Old World is also a violent world; at one point Moxica suspects an Indian of lying and punishes him by cutting off his hand with a sword. This scene recalls a similar sequence in *Black Rain*; like the Japanese in the earlier film, the Spanish have an extreme way of dealing with what they perceive as "dishonorable" behavior.

On the other hand, the New World proves equally unforgiving, as Columbus's efforts to create an ideal city come to nothing. The Spanish crew seek to leave this "godless place," while Brother Buyl (John Heffernan) observes that "no one wants a New World"—least of all the Indians, who eventually turn against the Spaniards. Ultimately the city is destroyed by a violent storm; the church—supposedly the symbol of Spanish "civilization"—is reduced to ruins, while insects are seen crawling over Columbus's prostrate body as he tries to come to terms with what has happened. At this point the New World resembles other *DYSTOPIAS* from Scott's films, notably that of *BLADE RUNNER*. Thurston's novelization describes Columbus's feelings thus: "[He] realized suddenly that it was not just his world being destroyed, but the world of Méndez and the others, the loyal ones who had faith in his grand design."

In complete contrast to *THELMA & LOUISE*, where the protagonists were both women and Scott seemed to be trying to reflect on established gender relations, *1492* follows *BLACK RAIN* and *Someone to Watch Over Me* by focusing on a male hero embarking on a voyage of self-discovery. Although in many ways a visionary in his desire to discover

new territories, Columbus has been tainted by Old World values; this is especially evident, for instance, in the way he hangs those members of his crew who have mutinied against him, in a sequence specifically designed to recall the earlier sequence in Spain when religious traitors are hanged and burned at the stake. Like the true imperialist, he sympathizes with yet refuses to acknowledge Indian values; the Indian servant Utapan (BERCELIO MOYA) accuses him quite rightly at one point of neglecting to learn the local language. Like Nick Conklin in *Black Rain*, Columbus refuses to embrace the values of the Other. The novelization sums up this moment succinctly: "In an automatic response, Columbus was going to ask Utapan to translate, but the Indian stepped backward into the shadows and seemed to vanish." The word "vanish" is significant here; it appears that Utapan does not exist in Columbus's mind as a living human being, but solely as a presence, a servant to carry out his wishes. When the Indian refuses to serve him, he is mentally expunged from Columbus's mind.

By contrast the women are depicted as largely passive. Columbus's partner Beatrix has a largely thankless role as the woman staying at home while the man she loves embarks on his travels. Her stoicism (as well as her modesty in refusing the advances of other men) is presented as something admirable: Columbus realizes only that such qualities are far more important than riches, titles, or social influence. He tells Beatrix: "Do you think I care? I'm a free man again. Riches don't make a man rich, they only make him busier . . . God, how much I've missed you." While Queen Isabella possesses the power to sanction Columbus's voyages and secure his release from prison later on, she is never seen as an active presence in the film. She either sits on her throne or moves within the confines of a darkened room. In the novelization of the film Sanchez (FRANK LANGELLA) at one point concludes that "Isabel romping seemed a remote possibility." The fact that she is played by Sigourney Weaver—whose role as an active female in *Alien* remains fresh in the mind—reveals how differently Scott approaches the issue of femaleness in *1492*.

Scott's film is shot through with COLONIALISM and colonialist imagery. While the Indians are presented as pacific, respectful of their environment and balanced in their economic practices, they are also objectified; the camera lingers lovingly over shots of naked women and men as they gather to welcome the Spanish. In a later sequence, an unnamed female servant moves in between Moxica and Pinzon (TCHÉKY KARYO), her breasts glistening in the sunlight. The camera cuts to close-ups of the two Spaniards eyeing her lustfully; Moxica says to Pinzon that he can have her whenever he wants. While the sequence is obviously designed to show the Spaniards' bestial nature, the fact that the camera tracks from one man's face to the other, while giving spectators a side-on shot of the woman's breasts, also suggests that she is being objectified to suit the male viewer's expectations.

Critical judgments on *1492* are few and far between. James Clarke's careful analysis in his book on Ridley Scott asserts that "the love of his family is what ultimately saves Columbus in this film." He notes the fact that, like many of Scott's films, *1492* centers on "the conflict between the wild and the civilized." As in *Legend*, "Scott invokes classic lost Eden, fallen Paradise associations, notably in the shot of the snake on a branch." While the film might not be one of the director's most memorable efforts, its concentration on the life of a hero and his dreams is reminiscent of *GLADIATOR*. The presence of Moxica as Columbus's *bête noire* anticipates Maximus (JOAQUIN PHOENIX) in the later film.

Richard A. Schwartz's *Films of Ridley Scott* argues that *1492* also anticipates *WHITE SQUALL* in its analysis of "the problems that arise when self-serving individuals in positions of power thwart the sincere efforts of those who do not enjoy power." Columbus is presented as a specifically 1990s hero in "a sympathetic, politically correct fashion that allows Scott to share with the revisionists his dismay over the exploitation and murder of the NATIVE PEOPLES, without diminishing the enormity of Columbus's achievement or the greatness of the man who changed the course of history, for better and for worse." The French critic Gilbert Salachas (writing in 1997) shared the same opinion: "Here Columbus is not a prophet, the precursor of modern times, but a simple seaman driven by his obsession . . . the film is not lyrical, but rather didactic [reserving its criticism] for the horrors of the Inquisition, the revolt of the Indians, the atrocities of the colonial conflict. This is not a 'pleasant history' . . . but a decisive moment, a bloody moment in time."

Peter Wollen takes an opposite view in one of the few academic articles devoted to the film. He argues that Ridley Scott's film "follows the lead of Kirkpatrick Sale's major revisionist book on *Columbus, The Conquest of Paradise: Christopher Columbus and the Columbian Legacy*, published in 1990 . . . Columbus is placed within a historical context that sees his arrival in the Americas as an epochal moment of culture clash, in which Columbus, as protagonist, is little more than the representative of already tainted European values." More contentiously, he identifies the whole film as an allegory of the director's struggles to get the film made in the first place: "The director is easily conceived of as a hero with a vision who finds it difficult to get funded, difficult to execute his or her dream and difficult to control the final product after it has finished. Indeed, in a way, this is the story of *Blade Runner*: the story of an adventure, a voyage, carried out by a perfectionist. . . whose work is distrusted and sabotaged and taken away from him, before the original, director's version is finally and triumphantly released. In this sense, *1492* falls into the tradition of *The Barefoot Contessa* or *The Big Knife* or even *The Player*—history refracted into Hollywood on Hollywood."

Wollen's views were taken up by David I. Grossvogel, who saw the film as an attempt "to turn the past into a vision of the present . . . instead of inviting the viewer to see it as an accurate historical moment, it directs the viewer to memories of other motion pictures set at that time." This point was expounded by an anonymous critic who identified Columbus as a male reincarnation of *Thelma & Louise*, "the forerunner, the archetype, of the new woman who sheds her boundaries, enters the updated caravel of the green Thunderbird and sails across the southwest, a mere symbol of the ocean solidified, the new literary text." On this view, Scott's film focuses once again on the search for freedom—both physical and emotional—that preoccupies males and females alike.

References

Ana Maria Bahiana, "*1492: Conquest of Paradise*: Ridley Scott," *Cinema Papers* 90 (October 1992): 33; James Clarke, *Ridley Scott* (London: Virgin Books Ltd., 2002), 142–44; "Geez Louise: Columbus Meets Thelma and Louise and the Ocean Is Still Bigger Than Any of Us Thought," *Women's Review of Books* 9, nos. 10–11 (July 1992): 13; David I. Grossvogel, *Didn't You Used to Be Depardieu? Film as Cultural Marker in France and Hollywood* (New York: Peter Lang Publishing Inc., 2002), 143; J. Hoberman, "1492," *Village Voice*, 20 October 1992, 53; *Hollywood Reporter*, 15 October 1991, 1, 82; Kevin Jackson, "Sailing the Ocean Blues," *The Independent*, 23 October 1992, 16; Jonathan Romney, "1492," *New Statesman Society*, 23 October 1992, 37; Gilbert Salachas, "1492, Christophe Colomb," *Télérama* 24 December 1997, 77; Richard A. Schwartz, *The Films of Ridley Scott* (Westport, CT and London: Praeger Publishers, 2001), 105, 109; Mark Salisbury, "In Nineteen Hundred and Ninety Two . . . ," *Empire*, November 1992, 83; Michael Sragow, *New Yorker*, 19 October 1992, 110; Amy Taubin, "The Film's Not About Rape. It's About Choices and Freedom," *Sight and Sound* 1, no.3 (July 1991): 19; Philip Thomas, "1492: Conquest of Paradise," *Empire*, November 1992, 24–25; Robert Thurston, *1492: Conquest of Paradise Based on a Screenplay by Roselyne Bosch* (London: Penguin Books, 1992), 127, 131, 147, 166, 170–71, 185; Peter Wollen, "Cinema's Conquistadors," *Sight and Sound* 2, no.7 (November 1992): 22–23.

Bibliography

Richard Alleva, "Goodby, Columbus—*1492: The Conquest of Paradise*," *Commonweal* 119 (20 November 1992): 20; Nancy Griffin, "Discovering Columbus," *Premiere* (US ed.), October 1992, 89–94; Jean-Pierre Lavoignat, "1492: Christophe Colomb de Ridley Scott," *Studio* 61 (May 1992): 64–73; Jean-Pierre Lavoignat and Laurent Tirard, "Christophe Colomb: Les Secrets," *Studio* 66 (October 1992): 71–79; Tom Shone, "He Came, He Saw, He Conquered," *Sunday Times*, 18 October 1992, Section 8, 13.

FOX, EDWARD (1937–)

The son of actress Angela Fox and agent Robin Fox, and grandson of the playwright Frederick Lonsdale, author of *The Last of Mrs. Cheyney*. Ridley Scott described him as a theater actor of the old school (even though he was only forty when he made *THE DUELLISTS*) who did not require too much direction.

Fox plays the cameo role of the colonel, who accuses D'Hubert (KEITH CARRADINE) of being disloyal to Emperor Napoleon. D'Hubert vehemently denies the accusation and suspects the charge of having originated from Feraud. The colonel returns to Feraud, who repeats the accusation, in spite of the fact that D'Hubert has spent some considerable time fighting in the emperor's cause. These two short scenes once again underline the futility of the quarrel; Feraud in particular cannot remember why it continues and has to invent trumped-up accusations in order to justify himself. Scott cuts to a close-up of the colonel looking to the right of the camera, as if unwilling to face up to what he already knows: that the two soldiers are actually fighting for nothing.

The colonel reappears in a later scene taking place after the fall of Napoleon. Both he and Feraud have fallen on hard times; Feraud has been arrested, while the colonel has been reduced to beggary outside a Paris café. The colonel rather bitterly accuses D'Hubert of being a "slippery fellow"—in other words, someone who sacrifices his integrity in favor of personal advancement. This is not necessarily true; but this sequence shows how rapidly French society changed at the end of Napoleon Bonaparte's reign.

Scott was particularly struck by Fox's performance in this scene; he described him as the perfect "tattered ex-aristocrat" striving to sustain his honor and pride, even though it was highly likely that he had turned to the bottle for solace.

References

Ridley Scott, "Director's Commentary," to the 2000 release of *The Duellists* by Paramount DVD in the "Special Collector's Edition" (London: Paramount Home Entertainment, 2000).

FRANCE

Ridley Scott first used France as a location for his films in *THE DUELLISTS*. According to the film's pressbook he and producer DAVID PUTTNAM sought historic sites "that have remained virtually unchanged since the early nineteenth century." They were found at Sarlat in the Dordogne, the birthplace of Fournier-Sarloveze (the original historical figure upon which JOSEPH CONRAD based his character Feraud in "THE DUEL"). The location filming not only situates the film in its appropriate historical context but suggests that the traditions of HONOR which determine the characters' behavior have become part of the local culture. This explains why D'Hubert and Feraud value them so highly; to reject them would be tantamount to rejecting France and everything it stands for—its architecture and its way of life.

At the beginning of *KINGDOM OF HEAVEN* the French locations are portrayed as stark and unforgiving—a suitable abode for a group of Christians who believe that "to kill an infidel is not murder. It is the path to heaven." Balian's (ORLANDO BLOOM's) wife commits suicide, then has her head cut off after her death in punishment for such a "blasphemous" act. However, when Balian returns to the country at the end of the film, it is now springtime, with the green hills in the background creating an edenic scene. His selfless act of leadership in leading the Christians out of the Holy Land has in a sense "redeemed" his community back home; this is reflected in the landscape.

Scott returned to France for *A GOOD YEAR* (2005). Filmed in PROVENCE, in the south of the country, close to where the director lived, the locations once again emphasize permanence—an aging chateau, farm buildings, vineyards producing an annual grape harvest to be turned into wine. In a documentary "A Good Life," produced to accompany the film's 2006 DVD release, Scott, ALBERT FINNEY, and the author PETER MAYLE (author of the original book upon which the film is based) extol the virtues of the region—its beauty, fertility, permanence, and above all its wine. Throughout the film Max Skinner (RUSSELL CROWE) gradually rediscovers such virtues and thereby matures as a person. The château (belonging to his uncle Henry) refuses to let him go; at the end he returns to live there. For Skinner the region is associated with freedom, pleasure and self-reliance—qualities he seldom appreciated since his CHILDHOOD.

References

"A Good Life," Documentary on the UK DVD release of *A Good Year* (Los Angeles, Twentieth Century-Fox Film Corporation and Dune Entertainment LLC, 2006); *Pressbook: The Duellists* (London: Paramount Pictures, 1977).

FRANCO, JAMES (1978–)

James Franco starred in *Spiderman* (2002) and *Spiderman 2* (2004), as well as James Dean in a television production about his life (2001). He was the first to be cast in the film of *TRISTAN + ISOLDE*; and it was chiefly due to his box-office potential that Twentieth Century-Fox agreed to back the film. Franco admitted in a preproduction interview that he believe Tristan to be "the classic tragic hero who becomes torn between loyalty to his king and the overpowering love he has for this woman . . . His tragedy consists of those two warring sides of loyalty." Franco's performance divided the critics: Carrie Hickey in the *Philadelphia Inquirer* likened him to "a biker boy with a broadsword;" while Wesley Morris in the *Boston Globe* believed that while the actor himself could be exhilarating, "here his jaw never stops quivering and his eyes stay welled up, advertising a breakdown that never comes." Tristan's reluctance to show his emotions is part of his make-up: while clearly attracted to Isolde, he also has to bear in mind his responsibilities as a warrior, who is responsible for ensuring the future health of his kingdom. Hence his insistence to Isolde (SOPHIA MYLES) that she must marry Marke (RUFUS SEWELL). Occasionally Tristan lets his mask drop—as for instance, when he castigates Isolde for "laughing at the market, holding hands [with Marke], a caress on the neck while he pours you wine." However, he comes to understand his responsibilities and sends Isolde away in a boat, telling her than "for all time, they [his people] will say that it was our love that brought down a kingdom. Remember us." He emerges triumphant from the battle to defend Marke's castle, cutting Wicktred's (MARK STRONG's) head off and displaying it in front of the drawbridge. Although he admits to Isolde that he does not "know if life is greater than death, but love was more than either," we realize that this can only be achieved once he has fulfilled his duty to Marke. Tristan is first and foremost a loyal soldier rather than a lover.

References

James Franco, quoted in *Production Notes: Tristan + Isolde* (Los Angeles: Twentieth Century-Fox, 2005), vii–viii; Reviews quoted on the *Metacritic.com* website, www.metacritic.com/film/titles/tristanandisolde (accessed 26 January 2009); "*Tristan + Isolde*. Written by Dean Georgaris, Transcript by Chani at tristanandisolde.net," www.imsdb.com/Movie%20Scripts/Tristan%20and%20Isolde%20Script.html (accessed 23 January 2009).

FRANKENSTEIN

Mary Shelley's trend-setting novel inspires several themes in *BLADE RUNNER*. Both share the satanic idea of confronting one's creator. Victor Frankenstein and Eldon Tyrell (JOE TURKEL) desire to give mankind a great gift, a technological innovation of great importance (i.e., the created human being) as Prometheus gave the revolution of fire to man in the myth.

In bestowing the gift of life, both Tyrell and Frankenstein take on godlike roles, while their creations fight against them. The monster in Shelley's novel philosophizes about his place in the world and his relationship to his God/creator. Similarly, Roy Batty (RUTGER HAUER) embarks on a quest to come to terms with his life and his relationship to God and other human beings. Both the monster and Batty identify themselves as separate from humankind, which rejects them. They feel ostracized; and this causes them to develop a hate for men and women. In *Frankenstein* the monster strikes back against the doctor's family and friends. In *Blade Runner* Batty strikes first at Chew, the manufacturer

of REPLICANT eyes (JAMES HONG), and then Sebastian (WILLIAM SANDERSON), the mini-creator who quite literally makes friends.

When the monster confronts the creator in both texts, it represents a conflict between self and other. In *Frankenstein* this conflict proves tragic; in *Blade Runner* this struggle is complicated, because Batty must not only confront Tyrell but also Deckard (HARRISON FORD). Batty is Deckard's other; as a result of Batty's death, the healing process takes place within Deckard. This contrasts with Shelley's work, where both self and other (the monster and creator) are sacrificed.

The conflicts between monster and creator also form part of two episodes of the first series of *THE HUNGER*. In "Room 17" a traveling sales representative (Curtis Armstrong) spends the night at a lonely motel and conjures up for himself an ideal woman who appears on the television screen and emerges from the screen into his room to fulfill all his sexual fantasies. Unfortunately she ends up by expecting something in return: Burt has to give her an expensive necklace. He obliges, but finds as a result that he loses both the woman and the necklace. In "A Matter of Style" a beautiful vampire (Isabelle Cyr) not only creates her ideal male protégé but educates him in the facts of life before he can become a dashing seducer of innocent young women.

Bibliography

Joe Abbott, "The 'Monster' Reconsidered: *Blade Runner's* Replicant as Romantic Hero," *Extrapolation* 34, no.4 (1993): 340–50; Jay Clayton, "Frankenstein's Futurity: Replicants and Robots," in *The Cambridge Companion to Mary Shelley*, ed. Esther Schor (Cambridge: Cambridge University Press, 2003), 84–99; David Desser, "The New Eve: The Influence of *Paradise Lost* and *Frankenstein* on *Blade Runner*," in *Retrofitting Blade Runner: Issues in Ridley Scott's* Blade Runner *and Philip K. Dick's* Do Androids Dream of Electric Sheep? ed. Judith B. Kerman, 2nd ed. (Bowling Green: Bowling Green State University Popular Press, 1997), 53–66; Robyn Morris, "'What Does It Mean to Be Human?' Racing Monsters, Replicants and Clones," *Foundation: International Review of Science Fiction* 33, no.91 (Summer 2004): 81–97.

FRANKLIN, HOWARD (?–)

Franklin wrote and directed the (now-cult) 1990s comedy *Quick Change* (1990), starring Bill Murray, GEENA DAVIS, and Jason Robards and *The Public Eye* (1992), a thinly veiled biography of the tabloid photographer, Weegee, starring Joe Pesci. His other screenplays include *SOMEONE TO WATCH OVER ME* directed by Scott. Franklin had little or no direct involvement in the making of *Someone to Watch Over Me*—as with many of his other films, Scott brought in other writers to refine it. They included Danilo Bach and David Seltzer.

Bibliography

"Someone to Watch Over Me," Script by Howard Franklin, Danilo Bach, and David Seltzer, dated 4 December 1986, http://www .imsdb.com/scripts/Someone-To-Watch-Over-Me.html (accessed 26 February 2009).

FRANZONI, DAVID (1947–)

Born in Vermont, Franzoni studied geology in college, while running a commercial company at the same time. Made his big-screen debut with *Jumpin' Jack Flash* (1986). Franzoni wrote the screenplay for *Amistad* (1995), on the strength of which he was given a three-picture deal with DreamWorks SKG. Having already seen *LEGEND*, which he believed to be "a brilliant film," Franzoni was more than happy to work with Scott.

His initial idea for *GLADIATOR* was to do a story set in the ancient Roman arena, a place that brought together the whole of Roman society, from the emperor and the senators down to the lower classes and slaves. Inspired by Daniel P. Mannix's novel *Those About to Die* (1958), republished in 2001 as *WAY OF THE GLADIATOR*, Franzoni produced a script about a central character Narcissus, who wins the war in Germania and is then shipped as a condemned prisoner to the Colosseum, where he becomes a huge popular success. A superstar gladiator sponsored by the Golden Pompeii Olive Oil Company, Narcissus ultimately strangles Commodius and sails off into the sunset with his wife and two daughters.

Jon Solomon's essay "*Gladiator* from Screenplay to Screen" discusses in detail the various changes Franzoni's screenplay underwent before it reached the screen. Franzoni envisioned the film as a tragedy reminiscent of *All Quiet on the Western Front*: "a grownup movie about war, death and life in Rome—the life of a gladiator." Apparently the film underwent numerous changes, not least in the final editing stage, where Scott transformed the film from an action film into a somber study of war: the film opens with Maximus's (RUSSELL CROWE's) vision of death as an endless field of wheat, a plant long associated with Proserpina, queen of the land of the dead. Maximus's speech to his soldiers before battle is now not about Roman politics, as Franzoni originally wrote it, but rather death and eternity: "If you find yourself alone, riding in green fields with the sun on your face, do not be troubled, for you are in Elysium, and you're already dead! Brothers, what we do in life echoes in eternity." Such semi-tragic endings are characteristic of Scott's work; notably *ALIEN, BLACK RAIN*, and *THELMA & LOUISE*.

Producer DOUGLAS WICK was enthusiastic about the screenplay in its various forms, on account of its "modern relevance. It was all about theater, about distraction—a way to control the populace." Later on other screenwriters collaborated on the project including JOHN LOGAN and WILLIAM NICHOLSON.

References

Christian Divine, "Word Warrior," *Creative Screenwriting* July/August 2000, 36; David Franzoni, Douglas Wick quoted in Diana Landau, ed., *Gladiator: The Making of the Ridley Scott Epic* (Basingstoke and London: Boxtree, 2000), 31; Jon Solomon, "*Gladiator* from Screenplay to Screen," in *Gladiator: Film and History*, ed. Martin M. Winkler (Malden, MA and Oxford: Blackwell Publishing Ltd., 2004), 1–16.

Bibliography

Joyce Annette Barnes, *Amistad* (prose version of Franzoni's screenplay) (Harlow, UK: Pearson Education Ltd., 1999); Richard Stayton, "Death & Wrestling," *Written By* 4, no.7 (August 2000): 30–53.

THE FRENCH CONNECTION

US 1973 r/t 104 min col. *Production Companies*: Schine-Moore Productions and D'Antoni Productions. *Producer*: Philip D'Antoni. *Director*: William Friedkin. *Writer*: Ernest Tidyman, based on the book by Robin Moore. *Director of Photography*: Owen Roizman. *Production Designer*: Ed Garzero. *Music*: Don Ellis. *Cast*: Gene Hackman (*Jimmy "Popeye" Doyle*), Fernando Rey (*Alain Charnier*), Roy Scheider (*Detective Buddy "Cloudy" Russo*).

Multi-Oscar award winning early 1970s crime thriller, told in documentary style, following the smashing of a major drug-trafficking operation. This film was an inspiration for Scott in *AMERICAN GANGSTER*. HARRIS SAVIDES, the director of photography on the later production, observed in an interview that "We [i.e., himself and Scott] didn't want to ape those films [like *The French Connection*] but I think their color palette is what evokes that period in people's minds—or helps to sell it . . . If this movie had the color and resolution of modern films, it wouldn't play as well."

Reference

Jay Holben, "Blood on the Streets," *American Cinematographer* 88, no.12 (December 2007): 49.

FRYE, E. MAX (?–)

A screenwriter born in Oregon and raised in Eugene, Frye wrote and directed the film *Amos and Andrew* (1993). He also wrote the screenplays for *Palmetto* (1996) and *WHERE THE MONEY IS* (2000).

Frye is best known for writing JONATHAN DEMME's *Something Wild* (1986). The story of a con and a militant black playwright, the movie was a lot funnier than it got credit for. As in *Where the Money Is*, the central characters are outcasts with no patience for the dullness of routine.

GALLAGHER, PETER (1955–)

Character actor, mostly in television, who appeared in adaptations such as *Long Day's Journey into Night* (1987), *The Caine Mutiny Court Martial* (1988), and *Bergerac* (1990) for the BBC.

Cast as Tom Chapman in *THE LAST DEBATE*, Gallagher offers a dependable performance as an investigative magazine reporter trying to find out how a Republican candidate's personal details were leaked to the panelists at a presidential debate. However, this apparent reliability is shown to be nothing more than a fraud; like the panelists he seeks to expose, he welcomes the cult of celebrity arising from the publication of his book on the scandal.

GAMBON, SIR MICHAEL (1940–)

Made his name at London's National Theatre under Sir Laurence Olivier. An actor more accustomed to theater and television in productions such as *The Singing Detective* (BBC, 1986), *Maigret* (ITV, 1993–1934).

Gambon originally played Crocker-Harris in *THE BROWNING VERSION* on the stage at Liverpool, northwest England. Cast as the headmaster in MIKE FIGGIS's 1994 film, Gambon brings out the callous side of the character—despite his outwardly charming nature, it is clear that he has no interest in the welfare of his staff or the boys in his school. He is far more interested in charming rich parents at the end-of-term cricket match, so as to ensure their continued financial support of his institution. Money matters to him, rather than people. This kind of character repeatedly crops up in Scott's films, whether he is director or producer; compare JOE TURKEL's Tyrell in *BLADE RUNNER*, who creates REPLICANTS to undertake the tasks once performed by human beings.

The headmaster's callousness is evident in the way he treats Crocker-Harris (ALBERT FINNEY). In one sequence, taking place during the cricket match between the school first team and the old boys, the two of them walk the grounds, both wearing panama hats—the very epitome of two English gentlemen enjoying themselves in summer. However, the subject under discussion is far from gentle-

manly: the headmaster is forcing Crocker-Harris to agree to speak first at the prize-giving ceremony, even though, as the senior teacher, he is duty bound to speak last. The headmaster's reasons are simple: if Crocker-Harris speaks before David Fletcher (David Lever), a popular young teacher who is also leaving the school, then the boys might not listen to what Lever has to say. The headmaster justifies his decision with a familiar cliché: "Nothing personal; boys will be boys." The irony of the situation is that the headmaster's decision is completely personal; he finds Crocker-Harris a bore and would much rather listen to Fletcher (even though, as it turns out, Fletcher has absolutely nothing worthwhile to say). Crocker-Harris has his revenge on the headmaster, however, as he pulls rank over Fletcher and chooses to speak last, giving a speech in which he admits his past failings as a teacher. The headmaster scowls at him; but in a school where tradition matters, there is absolutely nothing he can do.

GANGSTER FILMS

Gangster films have enjoyed something of a renaissance in the 1990s and early 2000s, with films such as *Pulp Fiction* (1994) proving especially popular. According to John McCarty, one reason for this could be "the anarchic appeal of the genre itself, which viewers find liberating, especially as the rules, regulations, and restrictions imposed by contemporary society increase. The antihero gangster—like his counterpart hero or villain in the Western—is not bound by fences. He goes where he wants, does what he wants, and takes no bull from anybody . . . Another reason is that in terms of great turmoil or change, people tend to look back to the way things were. In terms of entertainment, that means opting for the recognizable and familiar—genre forms that may be as old as time but still relevant, and thus reassuring." *AMERICAN GANGSTER* offers some of these pleasures in its portrayal of Frank Lucas (DENZEL WASHINGTON), a NEW YORK drug dealer who enjoys almost unlimited power as well as the adulation of celebrities past and present including Joe Louis and Muhammad Ali. The action is set in the early 1970s, in a New York which, although riddled with corruption, is nonetheless hedonistic—in stark contrast to the contemporary era. Moreover Scott and his designer ARTHUR MAX have gone to great lengths to recreate the period in loving historical detail; like many films involving the two of them, viewers are invited to enjoy the spectacle of what they see before them.

Reference

John McCarty, *Bullets over Hollywood: The American Gangster Picture from the Silents to "The Sopranos"* (Cambridge, MA: Da Capo Press, 2004), 7–8.

Bibliography

Fran Mason, *American Gangster Cinema From "Little Caesar" to "Pulp Fiction"* (Basingstoke: Palgrave Macmillan, 2002); Esther Sonnet and Peter Stanfield, "'Good Evening Gentlemen; Can I Check Your Hats Please: Masculinity, Dress, and the Retro Gangster Cycles of the 1990s," in *Mob Culture: Hidden Histories of the American Gangster Film*, ed. Lee Grieveson, Esther Sonnet, and Peter Stanfield (New Brunswick, NJ: Rutgers University Press, 2005), 173–85.

GARCIA, ANDY (1956–)

Born Andrés Arturo Garcia Menéndez in Havana, Cuba. Brian DePalma cast him as George Stone, the Italian cop accepted into Eliot Ness's (Kevin Costner's) famous band of law-enforcers in *The Untouchables* (1987).

Cast as another cop in *BLACK RAIN*, Garcia's Charlie Vincent projects a more sympathetic image when compared to his senior partner Nick Conklin (MICHAEL DOUGLAS). In a preproduction interview published in 1989, the actor saw the character as providing "a special kind of movement . . . [he] is responsible for motivating Michael Douglas through the last part of the movie." When Nick swears at his Japanese colleagues, it is Charlie who provides less offensive English translations. He warns Nick to go easy, particularly while communicating with Superintendent Ohashi (SHIGERU KOYAMA), who firmly believes that the two Americans should be "nothing more than interested observers" while the Japanese police go about their business of fighting crime. Charlie also understands the significance of HONOR; having heard Masahiro (KEN TAKAKURA) tell them that it is his honor to look after them while in JAPAN, Charlie says the same thing while persuading Masahiro to join him in singing "What I'd Say" at a karaoke bar. Such enthusiasm— coupled with his cultural sensitivity—encourages Masahiro to undertake "an incredibly alien and painful thing" (as Scott observed in an interview with Donald Chase). Garcia recalled in 2006 that much of the business in this scene had been improvised and was not in the original script.

However, Garcia's Charlie also suggests that this sensitivity is merely a façade. When Sato (YUSAKU MATSUDA) snatches his coat and escapes on his bike, Charlie loses his cool and chases after him, in his haste failing to realize that it is a trap. Eventually Charlie is led to an underground car park surrounded by metal grilles; escape is impossible. Sato and his gang surround the police officer, and Sato completes the *coup de grace* by beheading Charlie with a sword. The entire sequence reduces Charlie to a caged animal undergoing ritual slaughter. More significantly, this death scene shows the inherent dangers lurking within a foreign culture— especially for tourists unacquainted with rituals and honor killings. In many ways Masahiro is right when he tells Charlie and Nick that they should learn to "think less of yourselves and more of your group [including one's friends]. Try to work like the Japanese."

References

Donald Chase, "In *Black Rain*, East Meets West with a Bang! Bang!," *New York Times*, 17 September 1989, B7; Andy Garcia, interviewed in "*Black Rain*: The Making of the Film Part 1," Special Feature included in the *Special Collector's Edition* DVD release of *Black Rain* (d. Laurent Bouzereau) (Los Angeles: Paramount Pictures, 2006); Andy Garcia, quoted in Steve Pond, "Shot by Shot: Mischief Turns to Mayhem on an Osaka Street in Ridley Scott's *Black Rain*," *Premiere* 3, no.2 (October 1989): 107.

GARCIA, ERIC (1972–)

His debut novel *Anonymous Rex* (1999) introduced the human guised Velociraptor Vincent Rubio, a down-on-his-luck private investigator dealing with his partner's death. Two other novels in the series followed—the prequel *Casual Rex* (2001) and *Hot and Sweaty Rex* (2004). Also in 2004 he published *Cassandra French's Finishing School for Boys*, a parody of the CHICK LIT genre.

His novel *MATCHSTICK MEN* was published in 2002 and filmed by Scott a year later. Marilyn Stasio commended Garcia in the *New York Times Book Review* for creating a series of "con games (never tricks) [which] seem right for these guys, who use fast hands to make a living but depend on fast talk for their lives." The film rights for *Matchstick Men* had already been purchased by Warner Bros., almost as soon as it was published. Garcia liked the subject matter because "People are fascinated with con men like they're fascinated with mobsters—at least, the fictional kind . . . There's something mythical about them that draws us to them and makes want to watch them operate. Maybe it's the idea that they're using their wits to make a living while everyone else is accomplishing the same thing through toil and effort . . . I think the lifestyle appeals to us because the day may come when we get laid off or the mortgage is on the line and we'd like to imagine that, given the opportunity, we have the potential to make a quick buck the 'easy way'—if only we could do it." Although the film version, written by NICK AND TED GRIFFIN, departed from the novel, Garcia proclaimed himself satisfied by the project.

References

Production Information: Matchstick Men (Los Angeles: Warner Bros. Pictures, 2003), 3; Marilyn Stasio, "Killer Camp," *New York Times Book Review*, 29 December 2002, 29.

Bibliography

"An Interview with Eric Garcia," *Flash Fiction* website (March 2008), www.flashfictiononline.com/c20080302-interview-with-eric-garcia.html (accessed 7 January 2008); David Soyka, "A Conversation with Eric Garcia," *SF Site Interview* (March 2001), www.sfsite.com/06a/eg105.htm (accessed 7 January 2009).

GARNER, JAMES (1928–)

Born James Scott Bumgarner, the son of an Oklahoma carpet layer. Starred in two long-running television series *Maverick* (1957–1960) and *The Rockford Files* (1974–1980, 1995–1999).

Cast in the central role of Mike Howley in THE LAST DEBATE, Garner offers another study of an apparently dependable man impervious to the corruption around him and trying to look on the bright side of life. However, it is clear that he is as preoccupied with self-image as anyone else involved in the media, as he carefully cultivates the persona of a world-weary cynic apparently uninterested in party politics. As it turns out, however, Howley is actually a committed Democrat who deliberately smears the Republican candidate Richard Meredith (Stephen Young) on television so as to ensure that the Democrat governor Paul Greene (Bruce Gray) wins the presidential election. Once Howley's part in the conspiracy has been revealed, his reputation as a television pundit evaporates; the image has been destroyed, with nothing left underneath.

Bibliography

"James Garner," *Emmy* 26, no.3 (June 2004): 178–84.

GAROFALO, JANEANE (1964–)

Made her debut on *The Larry Sanders Show*, followed by appearances in *Now and Then* (1995) and *Copland* (1997). Normally provides comic relief in dramas. One such was the Ridley Scott-produced CLAY PIGEONS, a film she found "disappointing" despite her original enthusiasm for the script. In the film's production notes she was quoted as saying that she agreed to do it because she "felt it was important to have a strong lead character . . . in a movie where there's some violence against women. I felt that it was important that I participated, to try and take the edge off that." If that was her aim, then the finished film shows that she singularly failed to achieve it. Agent Shelby is portrayed as a hard-working FBI officer, whose shortcomings are consciously exposed by Lester Long (VINCE VAUGHN): "Underneath all that attitude, you really aren't that tough, are you?" In spite of her efforts, she fails to bring Lester to justice; it is left to the SMALL-TOWN Sheriff Mooney (SCOTT WILSON) to accomplish that task. The film places its female characters in secondary roles and refuses to allow them any opportunity to assert themselves.

According to one profile published in 2000, Garofalo considers herself as a down-to-earth comedian first and an actress second: "if I can be one of a handful of actresses that chooses not to participate in that kind of [celebrity] culture, then I feel like I'm doing something positive." This has meant that many of her roles have been character parts—for example, in *Dogma* (1999), *Wonderland* (2003), and *Stay* (2005). Garofalo also starred in *LAW DOGS*, a pilot for a CBS television show with Scott as executive producer.

References

Janeane Garofalo, interviewed in "Production Notes: *Clay Pigeons*," included on the European DVD release of the film (Frankfurt: BY Internationale Medien und Film, 1998); Martyn Palmer, "Janeane Garofalo: Actress/Comedienne," *Total Film*, January 2000, 28.

THE GATHERING STORM (1974)

GB/US 1974 TVM r/t 75 min col. *Production Companies*: British Broadcasting Corporation, Hallmark Hall of Fame Productions, and National Broadcasting Company (NBC). *Producers*: Jack Levin (Le Vien) and Andrew Osborn. *Director*: Herbert Wise. *Writer*: Colin Morris. *Production Designer*: Eileen Diss. *Music*: Camille Saint-Saëns. *Cast*: Richard Burton (*Winston Churchill*), Robert Hardy (*Von Ribbentrop*), Ian Bannen (*Hitler*), Robert Beatty (*Lord Beaverbrook*), Virginia McKenna (*Clementine Churchill*), Angharad Rees (*Sarah Churchill*), Lesley Dunlop (*Mary Churchill*).

An earlier version of the so-called "wilderness years" of WINSTON CHURCHILL, as depicted in the Ridley Scott-produced film THE GATHERING STORM (2002) directed by RICHARD LONCRAINE. One reviewer on amazon.com describes the film thus: "Richard Burton, thrilling to watch as Churchill, uses his stentorian voice and imposing presence to convey the heart of the man who, just before war was declared, had furiously exclaimed, 'We have sustained a total and unmitigated defeat without a war!' . . . The supporting cast is outstanding, with Virginia McKenna as the beautiful and supportive Clemmie Churchill, Robert Hardy as an appropriately smarmy von Ribbentrop, and Ian Bannen as the explosive Adolf Hitler . . . Filled with details about the political interactions which led to the declaration of war, including Neville Chamberlain's decline of an early offer of help from the United States, this is a memorable film which shows just how close Europe came to having national boundaries permanently changed."

Reference

Mary Whipple, "My Words Sink in the Sand in Which They Bury Their Heads" (10 September 2004), http://www.amazon.com/

Gathering-Storm-Richard-Burton/dp/6303425461 (accessed 27 December 2008).

THE GATHERING STORM (2002)

US/ GB 2002 TVM r/t 96 min col. *Production Companies*: HBO Films, BBC Films in association with Scott Free. *Producers*: Ridley Scott, Tony Scott, Frank Doelger, and David M. Thompson. *Director*: Richard Loncraine. *Writer*: Hugh Whitemore from a story by Larry Ramin and the book of the same name by Winston Churchill. *Director of Photography*: Peter Hannan. *Production Designer*: Luciana Arrighi. *Music*: Howard Goodall. *Cast*: Albert Finney (*Winston Churchill*), Vanessa Redgrave (*Clemmie Churchill*), Jim Broadbent (*Desmond Morton*), Linus Roache (*Ralph Wigram*), Derek Jacobi (*Stanley Baldwin*), Ronnie Barker (*Inches*), Tom Wilkinson (*Sir Robert Vansittart*).

The title had been used at least twice before in biographies about Churchill. In 1961 ABC had produced an episode "WINSTON CHURCHILL—THE GATHERING STORM" in the series *The Valiant Years*, focusing in particular on Churchill's wartime career; thirteen years later the BBC produced a drama *GATHERING STORM* about Churchill and Hitler, with Richard Burton in the title role. Another documentary, *THE FINEST HOURS*, released in cinemas in 1964, covered much the same ground.

This project (originally entitled "The Lonely War") originated from Scott himself, who, following the success of *RKO 281*, took the idea to HBO and then to the BBC. Scott explained in an interview, "Churchill strikes a note in my life because my father worked on Mulberry Harbour, which was the code name for the temporary concrete harbours which were towed across the Channel to make the D-Day landings in France possible . . . Dad used to reminisce about when he met Eisenhower, and how Churchill would pop in, in the late hours of the evening or night, siren-suited, carrying a cigar, when he'd obviously had a very good dinner." What really inspired Scott was the idea of making a film that "would be more about the personal side of Churchill rather than the public side, the speech-maker . . . It's interwoven in the process of his struggle and travails to make himself heard; his process of failure and then success runs parallel to the story of his relationship with [his wife] Clementine."

RICHARD LONCRAINE was invited to direct the film after his success with the HBO miniseries *Band of Brothers* (2001). Initially he was reluctant to take on the project, but when he discovered that ALBERT FINNEY was to play the title role, his viewpoint changed dramatically. The British dramatist HUGH WHITEMORE wrote the script; like Loncraine, he was quoted in the production notes as being initially skeptical of the idea, "because I was frightened of writing Churchill—how on earth do you go about making him a real person as opposed to a Madame Tussaud's repre-

sentation with a large cigar?" Loncraine liked his first draft, but worked with Whitemore to create a more effective piece of work—especially at the end, "because Churchill wasn't prime minister at the end of our movie. It was eighteen months later that he became prime minister. So getting the ending was quite a challenge." Eventually the two of them settled on showing Churchill sitting with his wife Clementine in a car and thanking her for "loving [him] in a way [he] thought [he]'d never be loved." The action then cuts to Churchill entering the Foreign Office, climbing the stairs and acknowledging the good wishes of a single soldier that "Winston is back." Loncraine shows him standing at the top of the stairs, cigar in mouth, and exclaiming with obvious pleasure, "Winston is back. And so he bloody well is!"

The casting of the film was essential to its success. Frank Doelger, producer for HBO, recalled in the production notes that he knew they "had the potential to attract a great cast with Hugh's powerful script but, at the time, I could not have dreamt that we'd get everyone we wanted." Finney agreed to play Churchill, while VANESSA REDGRAVE took on the role of his wife Clementine (Clemmie), as she felt a strong empathy with the character: "She [Clemmie] threw herself into politics with him [Churchill] and, although they later had children, she went through the vicissitudes of changing parties and his losing all position of any power whatsoever." The major supporting roles were played by JIM BROADBENT, LINUS ROACHE, and DEREK JACOBI. However, the greatest buzz of interest arose when RONNIE BARKER emerged from a self-imposed fourteen-year retirement to play the role of the butler Inches. He explained why in the production notes: "It's a very worthy film . . . That's the word I picked out as being a description of the film after reading the script—which is very good—and that's why I wanted to do it."

Filming took place at SHEPPERTON STUDIOS and at various locations in and around London, including Chartwell, Churchill's old home. Loncraine emphasized his intention in the production notes to include as many actual locations as possible, such as Fleet Street, the old center of the newspaper industry in London: "There's an amazing modern building [there] which was built in 1928, and our film is in 1932. So it was a four-year-old building when we see the movie. I [also] put in things like tube stations. You know subway, subway stations. So that you got a feeling of real life going on. Not just high society in pillared halls."

Although the film was co-financed by HBO, the producers were determined not to Americanize the material. David Thompson, head of BBC Films, insisted in an interview with Matthew Bell that the producers wanted to "maintain the integrity of a British approach to the project with a British director and writer. This is not a Hollywood take on Churchill."

According to the production notes, Mary Soames, Churchill's sole surviving daughter, who was in her eighties at the time of filming, visited the set and told Loncraine "with a twinkle in her eyes, 'I've seen all the [Churchill] imitators before, my dear.'" Loncraine continued filming and then showed her some of the rushes: "As the finished, she looked up at me and there were tears streaming down her cheeks and she said, 'It's my Papa, it's my Papa.'"

The film premiered on HBO in April 2002 to overwhelmingly favorable reviews. The BBC production notes enthusiastically quoted the *Washington Post*, which felt that "Albert Finney's portrayal of Churchill must be the best-ever done anywhere by anyone, with the exception of Churchill himself." The *Wall Street Journal* called it "television at its finest, a dramatization of one of the most inspiring episodes in the long extraordinary life of Winston Churchill." When *The Gathering Storm* premiered on the BBC two months later, Rob White wrote in *Sight and Sound* that "there's such warmth between Redgrave and Finney that their relationship as actors begins to eclipse their relationship as characters . . . Actors and television historians can do great justice to the past by stamping their personalities on it, interpreting it through vigorous argument, and so encouraging their audience to do the same." Albert Finney won the 2002 Emmy for Best Actor for his performance in the film.

As Scott suggested in the production notes, *The Gathering Storm* concentrates on Churchill's private life as a husband and father as well as his political struggles during the so-called "Wilderness Years" of the 1930s. He is portrayed as extravagant, perpetually in debt yet unwilling to give up on little pleasures such as eating Dundee cake for tea. Clemmie knows that he can be "a dreadful bully"—especially with the servants. When Inches tells him that one of his constituency workers is on the telephone, Churchill roars: "Inches, out! I'm in the middle of a letter." The butler doggedly stands his ground, provoking Churchill further: "Idiot! Have you no sensitivity? . . . God Almighty! Bloody hell!" The two men exchange insults ("You're very rude to me, Inches." / "You're very rude to me, sir") before Churchill storms out, claiming that he is justified in behaving like this, because he is "a great man." Inches mutters *sotto voce* that his employer is actually "a stupid old bugger."

On the other hand, Churchill can inspire great loyalty amongst his staff. While answering the phone, Inches and Churchill's secretary Violet Pearman, or "Mrs. P." (Celia Imrie), confer about his future: "Mr. Baldwin, or someone higher up, is trying to get him pushed out."/" . . . If they do kick him out, I shall never vote Tory again." Churchill reenters in a towering rage, quoting an anonymous poem: "Who is in charge of the clattering train?/ The axles creak and the couplings strain;/ The pace is hot, and the points are near,/ And sleep has deadened the driver's ear." He then storms out

of the room once more. Concerned for his future welfare, Mrs. P. and Inches suggest that "he'll be needing a glass of champagne."/ "Possibly two."

Churchill has a similar relationship with Clemmie. On the one hand he can be insufferably egotistical, as he criticizes her for going on vacation: "Clemmie, you have four children who require your love and support, not to mention a husband who has to work twenty hours a day to keep this household afloat . . . Don't you think it [the idea] might be construed as just a little selfish?" Incensed, Clemmie responds that she "put [his] . . . happiness before the children's happiness; before my happiness!" and throws a dish of Brussels sprouts at him. On another occasion Clemmie makes a vain attempt to reduce their domestic expenses; Churchill responds by asking her to look out of the window at the English landscape stretching as far as the eye can see: "And it's ours to look at and to cherish for the rest of our lives." (For "ours," read "mine.") However, Churchill possesses such zest for life that he can inspire those around him. During one of his depressive moods (which he characterizes as being attacked by the "Black Dog") Clemmie says to him, "Mr. Churchill needs me," he [Inches] said. And it's not just Inches, it's Mrs. P., the staff, your constituency workers, me, we're all the same. You have the ability to make people carry on, no matter what." Moreover, it is obvious that despite their domestic quarrels, Churchill and Clemmie remain very much attached to one another. Churchill thanks her for loving him in a way he thought he would never be loved, and they call each other pet names ("Mrs. Pussycat, Mr. Pug is very sorry. Pussycat, do let me in, Mr. Pug is very lonely out here. Mrs. Pussycat, please.").

Loncraine's film also focuses on Churchill's leisure interests—his fondness for keeping pigs, his painting, and his bricklaying. In the "Director's Commentary" to the film's DVD release, Loncraine suggests that Churchill was not particularly competent at bricklaying (despite Desmond Morton's (Jim Broadbent's) flattering comment that he is "getting pretty good at this"). But the film suggests that such pastimes provided an essential antidote to the stresses and strains of political life. In an early sequence, set in the mid 1930s, Churchill curtails his speech in the House of Commons about Indian self-government when he is shouted down by other Members of Parliament. The experience proves traumatic for him; he remarks rather bitterly to Morton that he possesses "no power [and] no prospect of power."

However, he emerges triumphant in the end, through a combination of innate cunning and consummate political skill. In one sequence Churchill is shown rehearsing his speech, even down to the pauses ("'We are entering a period of danger and anxiety.' Comma. 'Let us stop and see exactly . . .' No, scrub that. Bugger"); and subsequently delivering it in the House of Commons ("There is no doubt that the Germans are superior to us in the air at the present time"). This time no one interrupts him; he occupies center stage as he reveals the truth about German rearmament. From this moment on, Stanley Baldwin's (Derek Jacobi's) days as prime minister are numbered; it is only a matter of time before Churchill returns to the seat of government.

The film focuses to a large extent on characters faced with the conflict of LOVE VS. DUTY. Churchill is very much in love with Clemmie, but he also believes that it is his destiny to run the country. In an important exchange with Ralph Wigram (Linus Roache), he recalls a schoolboy fantasy in which he believed that "one day in the future, Britain will be in great danger, and it will fall to me to save London and the Empire." By doing this, he will follow the example set by his illustrious ancestor John Churchill, first Duke of Marlborough, who triumphed over the Franco-Bavarian forces at the Battle of Blenheim (1704). The importance of this conflict to Churchill is stressed in a fantasy sequence at the beginning of the film, as he witnesses Marlborough's (Tim Bentinck's) triumph.

Wigram faces a similar conflict as he agonizes about whether to pass on classified information about German rearmament to Churchill. Even when he does so, he wonders whether it is actually of any benefit to the country's future. Churchill responds with characteristic vehemence: "It's very important what you're doing, Ralph. You mustn't stop now, Ralph, KBO. Remember our motto, keep buggering on." Unlike Churchill, however, Ralph is a minor civil servant in the Foreign Office and therefore more vulnerable to pressure from the government. His wife Ava (Lena Headey) receives a visit one day from Ivo Pettifer (Hugh Bonneville), a senior civil servant, who advises her husband not see so much of Churchill. If he continues to do so, then "he might find himself being posted somewhere inconveniently distant, which would, of course, be difficult with regard to your son." By issuing such threats—especially to a young family with a mentally handicapped child—Pettifer shows how the British government at that time would deliberately exploit an individual's conscience to ensure that no one spoke out against official policy. While Lena believes that Pettifer has made "a tactical error" in threatening her family, the stress proves too much for Ralph, who commits suicide on Christmas Day. While the government tries to save itself by claiming that he died from a pulmonary hemorrhage, Churchill believes that Ralph committed an heroic act of self-sacrifice: "He saw all those dangers [to himself and his family] and was afraid of them. But he did what he did, in spite of his fear. No man can be braver than that." Such choices were essential to the war effort, to ensure that Britain knew what kind of military resources their enemies possessed, and could act accordingly. *The Gathering Storm* has been extensively discussed on the website of The Churchill Centre (www.winstonchurchill

.org). There are pages devoted to examining the parallels between the film and Churchill's book *THE GATHERING STORM: MEMOIRS*—the first volume of his massive history of World War II, which was first published in 1948. The film itself has been the subject of a magazine article in *Exposure* containing interviews with David Thompson, then-head of BBC Films, who describes the experience of working on the film thus: "What fascinated us was bringing a legend to life, warts and all . . . It's a portrait of an extremely strong man who also had a great deal of fragility . . . Churchill was struggling for money and to hang on to his wife." The film has also been extensively reviewed by Richard M. Langworth on the Churchill Centre website; he generally appreciates the film, but wonders why the writer and director chose to skip from 1936 (with Baldwin's retirement as Prime Minister) to 1939, and thereby omit the Munich crisis.

References

Matthew Bell, "Location Story: A Lonely War Brings Churchill Back to Life," *Broadcast B+*, 7 December 2001, 3; *The Gathering Storm: Information Pack Issued 17 June 2002* (London: BBC, 2002), www.bbc.co.uk/pressoffice/pressreleases/stories/2002/06_june/17/gathering_storm_pack.pdf (accessed 24 December 2008), 3–6, 10, 16; "*The Gathering Storm*: Transcript of the Screenplay by Hugh Whitemore," www.script-o-rama.com/novie_scripts/g/gathering storm-script-transcript.html (accessed 23 December 2008), "Interview with Richard Loncraine," *The Gathering Storm: Artist Interviews*, www.hbo.com/films/gatheringstorm/cmp/interviews .shtml (accessed 24 December 2008); Richard M. Langworth, "Review of Movie in *Finest Hour*," www.winstonchurchill.org/i4a/pages/index.cfm?pageid=443 (accessed 27 December 2008); Richard Loncraine and Frank Doelger, commentary to the 2003 DVD release of *The Gathering Storm* (Los Angeles: HBO Films, 2003); David Thompson, interviewed in "Out of the Wilderness," *Exposure* (Spring 2002): 22–23; Rob White, "The History Man," *Sight and Sound* 12, no.8 (August 2002): 7.

THE GATHERING STORM: MEMOIRS

The first volume in WINSTON CHURCHILL's massive history of World War II. In the preface to the first edition (1948), Churchill set forth his credo, of trying to be as fair as possible to everyone while remaining true to his essential beliefs, both of which provided the basis for the film's screenplay and ALBERT FINNEY's interpretation of the role: "I have adhered to my rule of never criticising any measure of war or policy after the event unless I had before expressed publicly or formally by opinion or warning about it . . . There was never a war more easy to stop than that which has just wrecked what was left of the world from the previous struggle . . . It is my earnest hope that pondering upon the past may give guidance in days to come, enable a new generation to repair some of the errors of former years, and thus govern, in accordance with the needs and glory of man, the awful unfolding sense of the future."

Reference

Winston S. Churchill, *The Second World War Vol.1: The Gathering Storm* (London: Cassell & Co., Ltd., 1949), ix–x.

GEORGARIS, DEAN (?–)

Early screenplays include *Lara Croft Tomb Raider: The Cradle of Life* (2003), *Paycheck,* and the remake of *The Manchurian Candidate* (also 2003). Georgaris wrote the script for *TRISTAN + ISOLDE* in 1998 as a writing sample: Ridley Scott bought it and finally put it into production after seven years. He had conducted considerably research, not only investigating the TRISTAN AND ISOLDA myth but looking at how it had been reinvented in works by A. E. HOUSMAN as well as in other TRISTAN AND ISOLDE FILMS. In an interview published to mark the film's release, Georgaris admitted that the first draft of the script was "very similar to other movies like it that we'd seen [for example, John Boorman's *EXCALIBUR* (1981)]. That I'd written the dialogue to be a little Shakespearean, and it was all a little flowery . . . The most challenging [part of the script], and ultimately the most rewarding, were the scenes between Tristan and Isolde from when she's married to when she has the affair with Tristan . . . They had a level of sophistication, particularly Tristan, in dealing with their feelings. But the whole point of this was that Tristan's never been in love. He should react the way I reacted when I was fifteen and had my heart broken. It's challenging because every person watching your movie has been in the situation where they've been in love, or wanted something, and haven't been able to have it."

In the commentary to the 2007 DVD release of the film, Georgaris reveals that his screenplay had been severely shortened during filming, with much of the characters' dialogue being replaced by close-ups. Another major change was to remove any sense of anger between Tristan and Isolde (SOPHIA MYLES)—even though the two of them can rarely be together. Even when Tristan brought Isolde to England to marry Marke (RUFUS SEWELL), he did not seem either angry or resentful; rather, he accepted the political realities of the situation. Another alteration was the introduction of the sequence where Marke offers Tristan and Isolde their freedom after having discovered the affair between them. This seemed a logical move—Marke needs Tristan to help him defeat the marauding Irish forces. Georgaris incorporated one direct allusion to Excalibur, during the tournament when King Donnchadh (DAVID PATRICK O'HARA) permits Tristan's (JAMES FRANCO's) opponent to be given a new sword, so that he can continue the joust. The phrase "allow it" represents Georgaris's homage to Boorman.

The screenplay received mixed reviews. *Variety* described it as "solid," giving director KEVIN REYNOLDS the chance to provide "brisk pacing and straightforward storytelling." Conversely, the *San Francisco Chronicle* felt that Reynolds and Georgaris took "a story of mad passion and made the participants into bland, reasonable people, thus blunting the intensity of their attraction—and its [the story's] fascination for an audience . . . everything connected with the lovers, who are the point of the movie, is either ordinary or unwittingly funny."

References

Dean Georgaris, Commentary to the 2006 DVD release of *Tristan + Isolde* (Los Angeles: Twentieth Century-Fox Home Entertainment, 2006); Mick LaSalle, "An Ancient Tale of Love, Longing—and a Spot of Beefcake," *San Francisco Chronicle*, 13 January 2006, www.sfgate.com/cgi-bin/article.cgi?f=/c/a/2006/01/13/DDGHSGLAKI21.DTL (accessed 26 January 2009); Joe Leydon, "*Tristan + Isolde*," *Variety*, 12 January 2006, www.variety.com/review/VE1117929236.html?categoryid=31&cs=1&p=0 (accessed 26 January 2009); "*Tristan & Isolde*: Screenplay by Dean Georgaris," *Creative Screenwriting* 13, no.1 (2006): 32; "*Tristan + Isolde*. Written by Dean Georgaris. Transcript by Chani at tristanandisolde.net," www.imsdb.com/Movie%20Scripts/Tristan%20and%20Isolde%20Script.html (accessed 23 January 2009).

GERAGHTY, MARK (?–)

Production designer on *Welcome to Sarajevo* (1997), *Dancing at Lughnasa* (1998), and *The Count of Monte Cristo* (2002), directed by KEVIN REYNOLDS.

Engaged as designer on *TRISTAN + ISOLDE*, Geraghty tried to create an imaginary world of the Dark Ages, where the colors reflected the political uncertainties of the times—all blacks, grays, and drab tones. Rather than opting for historical accuracy, Geraghty created a world "which in fact does not exist . . . So we looked to marry the best of Ireland and the best of the Czech Republic into this fabricated, imaginary place." For the castle of King Donnchadh (DAVID PATRICK O'HARA), both he and director Reynolds "went for a Celtic influence, because we were very sure that was there . . . for anything that was set in England, we drew more upon the Roman influence."

Reference

Mark Geraghty, Kevin Reynolds, quoted in *Production Notes: Tristan + Isolde* (Los Angeles: Twentieth Century-Fox, 2005), ix.

GETTY, BALTHAZAR (1975–)

Grandson of J. Paul Getty, who came to prominence in an adaptation of Henry James's *The Turn of the Screw* in the *Nightmare Classics* series for television (1989). In *WHITE SQUALL* Getty plays a similar role, that of a teenage boy cast out of his comfortable suburban home and embarking on a voyage of self-discovery on the *Albatross*. As Tod Johnstone, Getty gives a creditable performance as someone learning self-reliance and taking responsibility for his fellow crew members. His climactic moment comes in the final scene, when he is being cross-examined by coastguard Sanders (Zeljko Ivanek). Although determined to protect everyone at all costs, he eventually breaks down in the face of insistent questioning and admits that he disobeyed Captain Sheldon's (JEFF BRIDGES's) orders because he was scared. Even though his father stands up and roars, "That's not true, Tod!" it is clear that the young man's evidence has thrown Sheldon a lifeline; the captain was not responsible for the ship's sinking.

Getty also has a leading role in an episode from the first series of *THE HUNGER* (TELEVISION)—"The Swords," directed by TONY SCOTT. He plays a drug addict forced by his father to leave New York and come to live in London, where he attends a cosmetics conference. He falls in love with a beautiful young woman (Amanda Ryan), a member of a magic act who spends her evenings in clubs having swords stuck into her. Unfortunately she cannot cope with the emotional trauma of her affair (having spent much of her past life serving others) and she kills herself. Getty has a faceless role as a fundamentally decent man lacking the ability to understand women. Her death is his tragedy as much as hers.

GIANNINI, GIANCARLO (1942–)

He was born in La Spezia, Italy. Giannini made his big-screen debut in *Libido* (1965), a Freudian psychological thriller. He also starred as a Jewish musician arrested by the Nazis in *Lili Marleen* (1981). Giannini has also played numerous supporting roles in Hollywood productions, such as *HANNIBAL*, where he played Inspector Pazzi. The inspector is a good example of someone devoted to his job—like Clarice Starling (JULIANNE MOORE)—who is corrupted by the desire for money. Hence he contacts the FBI and informs them about Hannibal Lecter's (ANTHONY HOPKINS's) whereabouts. As one of his fellow detectives remarks in STEVEN ZAILLIAN's script, Pazzi is driven by the desire to please his "pretty young wife with the ever-open beak." Hannibal readily understands what Pazzi has done, and taunts him with the idea of retribution. Like his illustrious ancestor, Pazzi ends up being disemboweled and hanged with a noose round his neck from the window of the Palazzo Vecchio.

Reference

Steven Zaillian, "*Hannibal*: Screenplay Based on the Novel by Thomas Harris," *Revision* (9 February 2000), http://sfy.ru/sfy.html?script=hannibal2001 (accessed 15 December 2008).

GIEG, CHUCK (1943–)

Gieg was born in Bryn Mawr, Pennsylvania, but grew up in towns across the country because of his father's work in Washington, DC. He was in high school in Wilton, Connecticut, when, in 1960, he flew to Bermuda to join the crew of the Brigantine *Albatross* as part of his studies of celestial navigation and marine science. During its twelve-thousand-mile trip, the *Albatross* spent two months in the Galapagos Islands, then traveled through the Caribbean and up the coast of Central America. On that arm of the voyage the crew awoke one morning surrounded by American war ships and found out they were en route to Cuba for the Bay of Pigs invasion. The boat continued along to the Yucatan, but about half way back to Bermuda it was struck by an invisible "downburst," a column of warm air that rises, then cools and drops at a high speed to the surface. The impact of that white squall, named thus because it cannot be detected, sank the boat and took the lives of five crew members trapped below deck and another man who died while cutting the lifeboats free. Gieg spent his senior year in Wilton writing a book about the adventure entitled *The Last Voyage of the Albatross*.

After a flurry of initial activity, all the survivors were keen to move on and were given room to do so. Gieg only came to prominence once again when he acted as consultant on the film *WHITE SQUALL*, a fictionalized account of the disaster. Interviewed by *The Guardian* at the time of its release, Gieg recalled that he managed to track down the real Captain Sheldon (played by JEFF BRIDGES in the film): "He is now seventy years old and runs a small mail-order company from his home in Connecticut . . . after the film's American release, in February [1996], other survivors started to make themselves known . . . One, the real-life model for crew member Shay, offered a 'principled objection' . . . [However,] at the Albatross reunion which Gieg has organised for later in year, old memories will be exchanged . . . The scene he finds most moving . . . [is] the final scene."

Gieg took on many jobs, including carpentry, running a mini-cab firm, and most recently running his accounting office. He toured Europe to publicize the film through press interviews, and then returned to Nantucket where he still lives.

Reference

Robert Yates, "It was 35 Years Ago Today," *Guardian Section* 2, 2 May 1996, 10–11.

Bibliography

Chuck Gieg and Felix Sutton, *The Last Voyage of the Albatross* (New York: Duell Sloane Pierce, 1962); Mary Lancaster, "Meet Your Neighbor," *The Nantucket Independent Online*, 5 March 2008, www.nantucketindependent.com/news/2008/0305/other_news/005.html (accessed 14 September 2008).

GIGER, H. R. (1940–)

Giger was the first designer responsible for all aspects of the *ALIEN* landscape and the alien itself. The *NOSTROMO* was designed by RON COBB. Scott wanted two different designers with different approaches.

The creature in *Alien,* when we first encounter it, appears to be the opposite gender of what it turns out to be. Its first appearance is in the form of a face-hugger attaching itself to Kane (JOHN HURT), its proboscis thrust down his throat. When it exits from Kane's stomach it resembles a large penis with teeth. The fully grown alien has several phallic attachments, including a tail; it is also capable of fertilizing its victims, cocooning them, and transforming them into eggs. This is evident in the scene (omitted from the 1979 release but restored in *ALIEN: THE DIRECTOR'S CUT*) where Dallas (TOM SKERRITT) is shown cocooned in an underground cellar.

But these masculine attributes pale beside the recurring gynecological imagery evident in Giger's designs. For example, the abandoned spaceship has a vagina-shaped entrance as well as a moist, organic interior in which the eggs are housed. This is where we first meet the alien, its cylindrical shafts and membrane-like walls suggesting a pathologist's view of the female anatomy. Such designs indicate the male fear of the dark continent of female sexuality which, like the alien, seems to spring from nowhere and threatens to smother anyone in its wake.

Giger's diary on the making of *Alien* records the fact that many people found his designs repulsive; there was considerable debate over what the alien should look like: "Behind every film monster I always see a human being, well or less well disguised; they give me no shock at all." Scott relied for its shock effect on showing the escalating mouth and tongue opening, with the aggressive double rows of teeth. Giger's artwork played an instrumental role in the director's vision. From the outset, it was Giger's unique vision, a blend of nightmare surrealism with industrial design, that seemed to lift *Alien* out of the conventional, his creations shaping and challenging its production values. *Alien* is a perfect example of an image-driven film.

Giger's real accomplishment has to do with changing our idea of the alien in relation to its environment and with rethinking the look of technology. He challenged viewers to think about outer space in new ways, and thereby—according to Joe Doense and Les Paul Robley— "immersed us in a systematically alien environment, an entire implicit ecology, confronting us with a spaceship at once so vast and so strange-looking that it subverted our comfortable distinctions between biology and machinery, our expectations of mechanical forms with implicitly clear functions, and with a creature that threatened us from without and from within."

Giger was engaged to work with Scott on the adaptation of Frank Herbert's *DUNE,* but withdrew from the production when Scott quit.

References
Joe Doense and Les Paul Robley, "An Interview with the Artist H. R. Giger," *Cinefantastique* 18, no.4 (May 1988): 28; H. R. Giger, *Giger's Alien: Film Design* (London: Titan Books, 1989), 58.

Bibliography
Mark Patrick Carducci and Glenn Lovell, "Making *Alien*: Behind the Scenes," *Cinefantastique* 9, no.1 (October 1979): 10–39; "Alien," *Movie* (February–March 2001): 69; Dan Scapperotti, "Species 2: Designer H. R. Giger," *Cinefantastique* 30, no.1 (May 1998): 28–31.

G.I. JANE (1951)

US 1951 r/t 62 min b/w. *Production Company*: Murray Productions Inc. *Producer*: Murray Lerner. *Director*: Reginald Le Borg. *Writer*: Jan Jeffries (aka Harry Blankfort) from a story by Murray Lerner. *Director of Photography*: Jack Greenhalgh. *Production Designer*: F. Paul Sylos. *Music*: Walter Greene. *Cast*: Jean Porter (*Jan*), Tom Neal (*Tim*), Iris Adrian (*Lt. Adrian*), Jimmie Dodd (*Tennessee*), Jimmie Lloyd (*Lt. Bradford*), Jeanne Mahoney (*Hilda*), Mara Lynn (*Pilsnick*).

The story of a party of GIs attempting to fraternize with a group of WAC (Women's Auxiliary Corps). Television producer Tim Rawlings is called up and sent to a remote army camp. He makes a bet that he will be able to introduce some girls into the camp, and after considerable maneuvering, he arranges matters so that Lieutenant Bradford is transferred to Alaska and a company of WACs arrives in his place. Lieutenant Adrian makes an effort to keep her girls away from the soldiers, and she has scarcely relented when authority drives to dispatch the WACs to their proper destination. It is then revealed that the experience was a dream—Rawlings is still a television producer.

There is no evidence that Scott saw this B-movie musical before producing his own version of *G.I. JANE,* but the subject matter remains roughly similar. Clearly attitudes had not changed in the four decades separating the two films.

G.I. JANE (1997)

US 1997 r/t 125 min col. *Production Companies*: Caravan Pictures, First Independent Films, Hollywood Pictures, Largo Entertainment, Moving Pictures, Scott Free, and Trap-Two-Zero Productions, Inc. *Producers*: Ridley Scott, Roger Birnbaum, Demi Moore, and Suzanne Todd. *Director*: Ridley Scott. *Writers*: Danielle Alexandra and David Twohy. *Director of Photography*: Hugh Johnson. *Production Designer*: Arthur Max. *Music*: Trevor Jones. *Cast*: Demi Moore (*Jordan*), Viggo Mortensen (*Master Chief*), Anne Bancroft (*Lillian DeHaven*), Jason Beghe (*Royce*), Daniel von Hargen (*Theodore Hayes*), John Michael Higgins (*Chief of Staff*).

G.I. Jane came about as a result of the initiative of screenwriter Danielle Alexandra, who had heard that DEMI MOORE was looking for a physically formidable role that she could sink her teeth into. In a biography of Moore, Alexandra was quoted as saying, "Even before I sold the project and wrote the screenplay, there was never any question that anyone other than Demi would play the role of O'Neill. I believe she was the only actress credible enough and capable of handling the physical and emotional ride. I thought of the personal and physical strength that she has as an individual, a survivor, a woman, an achiever, an actress."

Evidently Moore was very excited by the project, as it presented her with the opportunity to deal with a topical subject. She was quoted by her biographer as saying, "What *G.I. Jane* afforded me was the opportunity to deal not only with the enormous physical demands of the action genre, but also to be involved with something that had real substance." The subject of women in the armed forces was a contentious one which had been on the political agenda ever since the mid-1970s and formed part of the *G.I. JANE* BACKGROUND.

Moore took the project to Scott, who apparently loved it—not only did he think it was a suitable vehicle for the actress, but he was also intrigued by the idea of dealing with a US MILITARY film, something he had not hitherto attempted: "I was drawn to the military subculture it [the film] took place in. I also liked the fact that Jane's subject matter was so provocative. A woman entering combat training in a very rarefied area of the military, and how she fares against the obstacles placed in her way, seemed a challenging topic." Scott would return to the military theme in later films such as *BLACK HAWK DOWN*.

The topic of women's roles in the American military was particularly contentious at that time. The Navy was being scrutinized for its handling of the Tailhook scandal (wherein a group of female Naval pilots-in-training had accused their male counterparts of sexual harassment). Just a week before shooting on the film began, another scandal broke over a young woman experiencing problems trying to enter the Citadel, an all-male military academy in Charleston, South Carolina. The film's American release in August 1997 came at the end of a week that saw the first women cadets take their places on the "Rat Line," a ritual of "character-building" abuse that kick-starts training at the infamously brutal Virginia Military Institute. At the same time, *The Guardian* reported that the military had to deal with several cases of what was diplomatically described as "unlawful command influence," entwining rape and rank and the violent abuse of female recruits.

Scott's version of *G.I. Jane* was not the first film to deal with the topic of women in the military. An earlier film *G.I. JANE* (1951), a B-movie with music, focused on how a group of GIs tried to fraternize with members of the WAC (Women's Army Corps), but failed to do so as a result of strict bureaucratic rules.

Alexandra's script was rewritten by DAVID TWOHY, who had previously worked on the HARRISON FORD version of *The Fugitive* (1993). Many scenes which were originally filmed were eventually cut from the final print—for example, an opening sequence showing Moore practicing a winter sport called luge, which, according to Scott, was designed to portray her "as being so physically capable that she was almost Olympics material." Another scene that did not make the final cut showed Moore showering with the male recruits: Scott believed this directed the audience's attention away from the main point of the sequence, which "involved her promotion, not . . . showering with men." The ending was also completely rewritten; in Twohy's original script Moore's character (O'Neil) rejoins the SEAL course, and Urgayle takes her back into combat training. The action shifts to a helicopter sequence, where a chopper Urgayle uses accidentally loses power and crashes into the sea. O'Neil manages to rescue Urgayle and, while doing so, questions his authority: "Sir, let me suggest you stop giving orders and start doing exactly what I say, because that's the only way we're all getting out of here." Scott claimed he was uncomfortable with this sequence for two reasons—first, it seemed redundant, as "we'd already seen how good she [O'Neil] was on the course"; and second, he wanted to show what the SEALS really did for a living. He therefore created an entirely new ending set in Libya (actually filmed near Santa Barbara, California), in which O'Neil engages in real combat and rescues Urgayle. Scott actually filmed two *dénouements* to this sequence: one showing O'Neil and Urgayle being picked up by a helicopter and flown out of Libya; the other showing O'Neil being killed by a stray bullet and dying on the floor of the helicopter next to the chief. Apparently preview audiences did not respond to the second ending, so Scott let O'Neil live and eventually receive the Navy Cross medal from Urgayle, something that in the director's view "signified both his [Urgayle's] respect for O'Neil's perseverance and abilities and Urgayle's gratitude for her pulling him out of a lethal situation. So it was a nice wrap-up."

Filming took place mostly on location in Washington, DC, and Florida. The Pentagon declined to cooperate with Scott—despite the fact that Moore had telephoned the White House and tried to use her political connections to persuade President Clinton to allow the production company access to a real training facility. Consequently, Scott made use of a compound in northern Florida which had once been used by the Navy and was now the property of the National Guard. Filming *G.I. Jane* proved a grueling experience: military technical adviser Harry Humphries told Moore's biographer, "we tried to show the Special Forces training and the skills, including weapons-handling, that are taught in the training. We encapsulated a seventeen-week course into two weeks, so those actors were harassed to hell." Producer ROGER BIRNBAUM agreed: "The role that Demi played was extremely demanding, one of the most challenging roles I think any actor, regardless of whether they are a man or a woman, has probably had to go through. But she is extraordinary. She put her whole heart and soul into this, and she was there every single moment for this film."

Despite Moore's efforts, the release of the film was delayed (according to the *Sunday Times*) on account of the fact that America had "lost its appetite" for the actress. When it was eventually screened, the *Evening Standard* reported that the Southern Baptist church had condemned it because it contained too much swearing. Another newspaper report claimed that the film "devastated Washington" by portraying the government as "a sink of hedonism, a miserable contrast to being a SEAL."

The reaction from reviewers was equally extreme. Alexander Walker of the *Evening Standard* saw it as "a vindication of gender fascism . . . that should shame any civilized viewers, of whatever sex. This isn't about exalting female equality; it's about extinguishing it." The columnist Taki in the *Sunday Times* believed that "not one second of the film is even remotely true." By contrast, Amy Taubin in the *Village Voice* saw the film as "a genuinely feminist depiction of a woman who pushes gender to the edge." Other reviewers noted the parallels between *G.I. Jane* and earlier Scott films such as *ALIEN* and *THELMA & LOUISE*: Tom Shone of the *Sunday Times* wondered "whether Scott's most feminist film wasn't the one he made before he got feminism: *Alien*, in which Lieutenant Ellen Ripley soldiered her way to survival with quiet, unfussy grace." Robert M. Payne in *Sight and Sound* thought differently: "I can't help wondering if between them [Scott and Moore] they intentionally used the line [i.e., the plot]—in some small way—to turn the tables on the society that sent Thelma and Louise to their deaths."

The film grossed $48 million at the US box office, which according to figures issued on *The Numbers* website meant that the film just about recovered its costs.

The film's perceived endorsement of FEMINISM depends very much on how one interprets Jordan's deliberate shedding of her female identity and adoption of masculine rituals of behavior. Her hair-cutting can be interpreted in terms of the Medusa-myth: Medusa was originally a beautiful young woman whose crowning glory was her magnificent hair. She was raped by Neptune in the Temple of Athena; Athena was outraged at her sacred temple being violated and punished Medusa by turning her beautiful tresses into snakes and giving her the destructive power to turn anyone who looked directly at her into stone. The myth has been interpreted as expressive of the subjugation of women's bodies and enslavement of their spirit by a violent and oppressive male-oriented culture. By cutting her hair Jordan symbolically rejects this oppression and strikes out on her own. Her exclamation "suck my dick!" confirms the success of her venture; now she can compete with her male colleagues on equal terms. They realize this, and greet her exclamation with an enthusiastic cheer.

On the other hand, the film contains scenes of excessive violence, as Jordan is tortured by Chief Urgayle in the belief that such treatment will transform her into a "proper" soldier: "I am saving your life, O'Neil. You may not know it, but I do. You're an inferior soldier, a bad officer, and I don't want you learning that inconvenient truth when you're stuck in a muddy bomb crater behind enemy lines and don't know how the fuck to get out." In an interview with the *Daily Telegraph* published prior to the film's London opening, Scott was asked whether he thought the sight of a woman being viciously beaten "quite squared with anyone's idea of entertainment." While citing examples of women being treated badly in the US Army, he "would not discuss the unease of audiences faced with such violence." This led the interviewer to conclude that "if he is not a misogynist or a chauvinist, where's the evidence?" The scene as filmed suggests that O'Neil willingly subjugates herself to male authority in order to earn their respect, which suggests that she endorses rather than rejects the Medusa-myth.

Tom Shone drew a parallel between Urgayle's treatment of Jordan and Deckard's treatment of Zhora (JOANNA CASSIDY) in *BLADE RUNNER*: "As scenarios to justify near-rape go, I thought that [scene between Deckard and Zhora] couldn't be bettered . . . Until I saw *G.I. Jane*, that is, and heard Moore's drill instructor . . . shouting, 'Are you ready for the next evolution?' and realised that she was the next evolution—an acting REPLICANT in excelsis, who could be put through the mill with similar impunity."

One sequence of *G.I. Jane* takes place at sea, where Urgayle punctured Jordan's dinghy and taunts her: "Your boat just hit razor corral. What do you do now?" The crew tries to save their sinking boat, but Jordan is left in the water. This recalls the disaster that befalls the *Albatross* in *WHITE SQUALL*, in which some of the boys perish while the survivors are left to fend for themselves in a makeshift boat. Scott invites us to reflect on the power of the sea, which can swallow up human beings in minutes. Only those with sufficient determination or strength of character—like Jordan or Captain Sheldon (JEFF BRIDGES)—can survive. *G.I. Jane* and *White Squall* are also linked by the presence of the ship's bell; in the earlier film it symbolizes group solidarity among the *Albatross*' crew, while in *G.I. Jane* it fulfills precisely the opposite function. If anyone wants to leave the group undergoing military training, all they have to do is to ring it three times.

G.I. Jane is one of the first of Scott's films to comment openly on American politics. In his view the government in Washington is impossibly corrupt, concerned not with individuals but with their own self-preservation. Even Senator DeHaven (ANNE BANCROFT) admits that the whole idea of having a woman undergoing military training was nothing more than a charade in which "there's more to be gained from the fight than the victory." She has little or no time for Jordan—even though Jordan protests that she was glad of the opportunity to prove herself. Eventually Jordan threatens to expose DeHaven as a fraud—something which the Senator obviously resents ("Don't play politics with me, little darlin'. You'll be up way past your bedtime.") but can do nothing about. Eventually she is forced to let Jordan return to her training. Scott admitted to Sammon that he "always liked the political element in Jane's script, because [he] felt it gave the story another realistic shading. I mean, on a certain level, O'Neil is being used by the system. Certainly by DeHaven, who seems to support this idea of women in the military but really doesn't . . . DeHaven is engaged in a subterfuge from the beginning."

Unfortunately the film's political case is weakened by its inherent COLONIALISM, most obviously apparent in DeHaven's scornful observation that, if Jordan were to complete her training, she would spend her life "squat-pissing in some third-world jungle." The end of the film shows her not in some "third-world jungle" but in Libya fighting a brutal army which seems intent on exterminating every American soldier they encounter. The sequences are dramatically filmed with a hand-held camera, creating the kind documentary "feel" associated with Scott's later military films such as *BLACK HAWK DOWN*. On the other hand, the Libyan troops speak their own language without the benefit of subtitles: Scott did not think it important that we should understand what they say. As in *BLACK RAIN* this sequence appeals to the (western) audience's xenophobic instincts, with the American soldiers—led by Jordan—as the good guys escaping from their Muslim enemies.

The cultural distinctions between the two nations is reinforced at the end, when Jordan is shown reading some poems left by Urgayle, including "Self Pity" by D. H. Lawrence. Scott suggested to Sammon that such works revealed "something surprising about this guy [Urgayle] . . . that there was another side to his character that you wouldn't expect." At the same time, the use of Lawrence's poem emphasizes the cultural distance between the American troops and the "savage" Libyan forces.

Critics have generally condemned the film both for its portrayal of gender relationships and its central performances. While James Clarke identifies it as "something of a sequel to *Thelma & Louise*, with its female protagonist and, maybe even more importantly, its placing of a woman at the heart of a man's world," he also describes it as "absolutely the worst film Scott has ever made." Judi Addleston concentrates on its representation of gender: "As the penis is the main marker for MASCULINITY, as soon as Jordan claims one for herself, she becomes, in effect, a man. No longer do the men make passes at her, for she is no longer a sexual object for them." More recently Jeffrey Walsh asserts that the film "unintentionally defeats its own ostensibly feminist thesis . . . O'Neil cannot, the film suggests, be naturalised as a man without first subjugating her identity as a female. This confirms patriarchy as the working ideology of the state by demanding that a woman soldier must not only possess commensurate physical attributes to a man but also reconfigure herself as culturally masculine."

References

Judi Addelston, "Doing the Full Monty with Dick and Jane: Using the Phallus to Validate Marginalized Masculinities," *Journal of Men's Studies* 7, no.3 (Spring 1999): 348; Danielle Alexandra, quoted in Nigel Goodall, *Demi Moore: The Biography* (Edinburgh and London: Mainstream Publishing, 2000), 163; James Clarke, *Ridley Scott* (London: Virgin Books Ltd., 2002), 170; *Evening Standard*, 20 August 1997, 22; David Gritten, "Call This Entertainment?" *Daily Telegraph*, 13 November 1997, 28; D. H. Lawrence, "Self-Pity," www.poemhunter.com/poem/self-pity/ (accessed 21 October 2008); *The Numbers: G.I. Jane*, www.the-numbers.com/movies/1997/GIJNE.php (accessed 22 October 2008); Robert M. Payne, "Head for the Border," *Sight and Sound*, 8, no.1 (January 1998): 64; Ridley Scott, quoted in Paul M. Sammon, "Joining the Club: Ridley Scott on *G.I. Jane*," in *Ridley Scott Interviews*, ed. Laurence F. Knapp and Andrea F. Kulas (Jackson, University Press of Mississippi, 2005), 135, 142, 148, 155, 163; Tom Shone, "A Coarse Assault," *Sunday Times*, 16 November 1997, Section 11, 7; *Sunday Times* (London), 18 May 1997, Section 10, 11; Taki, "Hell Bent with G.I. Jane," *Sunday Times*, 24 August 1997, Section 4, 2; Amy Taubin, "Dicks and Jane," *Village Voice*, 26 August 1997, 73; David Twohy, "*G.I. Jane*: First Draft" (6 August 1995)," http://sfy.ru/sfy.html?script=gi_jane (accessed 21 October 2008); Ed Vulliamy, "Take it Like a Man," *The Guardian*, 26 August 1997, Section 2, 2–3; Alexander Walker, "The War on Womanhood," *Evening Standard*, 30 June 1997, 9; Jeffrey Walsh, "Elite Woman Warriors and Dog Soldiers: Gender Adaptations in Modern War Films," in *Gender and Warfare in the Twentieth Century: Textual Representations*, ed. Angela G. Smith (Manchester and New York: Manchester University Press, 2004), 204.

Bibliography

Krista Donaldson, "Is It Time for G.I. Jane?" *Off Our Backs* 35, nos. 11–12 (November–December 2005): 32–36; Lesley O'Toole, "General Scott on Parade," *The Times*, 29 October 1997, 41; Adam Smith, "Action: What Has Become of Ridley Scott?" *Empire* 102 (December 1997): 110–18; Erica Wagner, "Great Scott—" *Times Metro*, 8–14 November 1997, 6, 8.

G.I. JANE BACKGROUND

The subject of women in the US MILITARY had been on the agenda ever since World War II. A position booklet *Women and the Military*, published in the late 1970s by The Brookings Institution in Washington, DC, argued that "Two powerful social forces are in collision: the push for women's equal rights is in conflict with deeply rooted traditions that question the propriety of women under arms . . . And despite two opportunities to interpret and clarify the 'national will'—during the debates on the Equal Rights Amendment and the proposal to admit women to attend the nation's military academies—the question remains unresolved."

Until 1976, leadership opportunities were closed to women because they were not admitted to the military academies. From the first co-ed commencement in 1980, women's graduation rates have been comparable to those of men, and the percentage of women who fail to finish for academic reasons has consistently been significantly lower. However, established attitudes amongst the higher echelons of the military have proved difficult to shift. A 2005 book recommended that "the concerns regarding job performance must be addressed in a way that links testing standards to necessary skills and enhances the credibility of female personnel with male colleagues and subordinates." The book also suggested the creation of strategies to educate "both women and men on harassment policy," and a reform of the military services so that they could adopt "a strong institutional commitment to the successful integration of women into combat roles." It would seem that individual stories of success such as that of Jordan O'Neil in *G.I. JANE* were still comparatively rare.

References

"Women and the Military," quoted in Martin Binkin and Shirley J. Bach, *Women and the Military* (Washington, DC: The Brookings Institution, 1977), 110–11; Sara L. Zeigler and Gregory G. Gunderson, *Moving Beyond G.I. Jane: Women and the US Military* (Lanham MD: University Press of America, 2005), 107–8.

GILER, DAVID (?–)

Born in New York City, David Giler was educated in California. His early career consisted of writing scripts for television programs like *Kraft Suspense Theater* and *The Man from UNCLE*. Giler worked with WALTER HILL in rewriting the script for *ALIEN*. In a 1979 interview he told Mark Patrick Carducci and Glenn Lovell that "we changed all the dialogue. Every word of it. Nothing is left of [Dan] O'Bannon's draft. Not a word of the dialogue is left in the film." Whether this is true or not is debatable: at that time Giler was involved in a legal wrangle over screen credit, and relations between himself and O'Bannon were strained, to say the

least. Giler told John Millar that he was responsible for engaging Ridley Scott as director: "I was looking at all he had done, all his commercials . . . You had to have that willingness to pay attention to details and not all directors have that." According to Carducci and Lovell, Giler was also responsible for the removal of the cocoon sequence involving Dallas—which was restored in *ALIEN*—THE DIRECTOR'S CUT (2003)—on the grounds that "it interfered with the pacing of the film. It looked terrible, awful."

Like Hill, Giler co-produced all the films in the ALIEN QUADRILOGY as well as the two *ALIEN VS. PREDATOR* works.

References

Mark Patrick Carducci and Glenn Lovell, "Making *Alien*: Behind the Scenes," *Cinefantastique* 9, no.1 (October 1979): 19; John Millar, "Tough Little Son of a Bitch," *Film Review Special* 53 (August 2004): 17.

GLADIATOR

US 2000 r/t 149 min col. *Production Companies*: Dreamworks LLC and Universal Studios in association with Scott Free. *Producers*: Ridley Scott, Douglas Wick, David Franzoni, and Branko Lustig. *Director*: Ridley Scott. *Writers*: David Franzoni, John Logan and William Nicholson from a story by David Franzoni. *Director of Photography*: John Mathieson. *Production Designer*: Arthur Max. *Music*: Hans Zimmer and Lisa Gerrard. *Cast*: Russell Crowe (*Maximus*), Joaquin Phoenix (*Commodus*), Connie Nielsen (*Lucilla*), Oliver Reed (*Proximo*), Richard Harris (*Marcus Aurelius*), Derek Jacobi (*Gracchus*), Djimon Hounsou (*Juba*), David Schofield (*Falco*), John Shrapnel (*Gaius*), David Hemmings (*Cassius*).

The film came about after DAVID FRANZONI approached the producers DreamWorks SKG with a story about gladiators in Ancient Rome. His script was apparently inspired by a book about gladiators called *Those About to Die* (reissued as *THE WAY OF THE GLADIATOR*) by Daniel P. Maddix, as well as the story of Commodus as written in the *Augustan Histories*. In the original script dated 4 April 1998 the main character was named Narcissus, after the gladiator who eventually killed the emperor Commodus, and the story was upbeat and ironic in tone: Narcissus manages to escape from Rome with both his wife and child. Eventually Franzoni's script was refined by screenwriter JOHN LOGAN, who had previously worked on *RKO 281*.

DreamWorks agreed to finance the project in association with Universal Studios, and overseen by two executive producers, Walter Parkes and Laurie MacDonald, together with line producer DOUGLAS WICK, who was enthusiastic about the project, so long as it differed from previous ANCIENT EPICS set in Rome, such as *Ben Hur* (1959) or *Cleopatra* (1963).

To secure Scott's services, the producers put before him a copy of Jean-Léon Gerome's 1872 painting *Pollice Verso* (Thumbs Down), a view of the Colosseum showing a gladiator with his foot on his fallen opponent's throat, looking up to the assembled crowd and giving the gesture that condemns his opponent to death. Scott was impressed: "That image spoke to me of the Roman Empire in all its glory and wickedness . . . Because what I love to do—apart from getting a good script and making movies—where I enjoy myself most, I think, is creating worlds." Scott welcomed the chance to return to his first historical film since *WHITE SQUALL*: "With history, your challenge, really, is to see how accurate you can be. It's to do with research and choosing the right people: the right production designer, the right costume designer, the right armorer, and so on. And of course you have to do massive research."

Evidently Mel Gibson was approached for the leading role, but turned it down, feeling the part was too reminiscent of *Braveheart* (1993). Instead, Scott looked for actors who weren't necessarily box-office draws but who could convey the personalities and relationships in the story. RUSSELL CROWE at that time was just beginning to emerge as a Hollywood name; the same applied to JOAQUIN PHOENIX and CONNIE NIELSEN. The main actors were supported by a cast of (mostly British and Irish) actors including RICHARD HARRIS, DEREK JACOBI, and OLIVER REED, with DAVID HEMMINGS in a small role. Said Scott: "These [actors] are of a generation that experienced some of the earlier epics firsthand, particularly Richard . . . It was a thrill for me to have an opportunity to work with them, and all the more interesting to revisit the genre with them."

Filming was a lengthy and painful process, taking in Malta, Morocco, as well as Great Britain. The process was complicated by the fact that on 2 May 1999, with about three weeks of shooting remaining, Oliver Reed died in Malta of apparent heart failure. His role was all but complete—however a few crucial scenes remained to be shot. Scott overcame the problem by reorganizing three shots of Reed's close-ups from three different scenes, and using a body double walking up to the camera, standing and talking. Scott finally created a computer-generated image of Reed's head, and put it on the body.

Perhaps the most noteworthy aspect of the film was the use of such computer-generated visual effects—the first time they had been used in a Roman epic. The most important tasks consisted of showing the might of the Roman army for the Germania battle and how technologically advanced it was; to arrange pyrotechnic effects for the climax; and to create realistic carnage by means of prosthetics and digital work. Aylish Wood observes that such effects were designed "to support the action of the human characters . . . to

enhance the illusion of a carefully constructed reality . . . As a tale of tragedy and revenge, the spectacle in *Gladiator* is in keeping with the epic films of the 1950s and 1960s, with a particular emphasis on scale."

Reviews were largely favorable. Andrew O'Hagan called it "a terrifically embroiling movie . . . a very good cowboy picture . . . [with] more clear-cut storytelling of the old-fashioned kind." Alexander Walker judged the film "a whopping success: the essence of all Roman epics"; Leslie Felperin wrote in *Sight and Sound* that "it's . . . the best film Ridley Scott has made . . . the quintessential big-budget studio product that's smarter than it looks, a fiendishly arduous logistical feat that clicks together like a well-tailored suit of armour." Other critics did not like the film at all: an anonymous critic wrote in 2002 that the film "fails to convince on every level . . . Director Ridley Scott's attitude towards the fight scenes is similar to that of the US Army in Afghanistan—fond of remote, state-of-the-art gadgetry but squeamish when it comes to hand-to-hand combat." Such comments foreshadowed those for *BLACK HAWK DOWN* (released in 2001). Sean Macaulay in *The Times* noted that Crowe "remains the glum, principled, laconic wounded hero throughout. He is as monotone as Rambo, another purveyor of 'hell' with a clearly token reluctance to shed blood."

Gladiator was a huge hit, taking over $400 million at the United States box office and winning the Oscar as Best Picture of the Year, as well as Best Actor for Russell Crowe and best Costume Design, Sound and Visual Effects. The film also won the Best Film award at the British Academy Awards and the Golden Globes, while Crowe won the Actor of the Year award from the London Critics Circle. A sequel to the film ("GLADIATOR 2") was proposed, with a script by Nick Cave (*The Proposition* [2006]), but to date nothing has yet materialized. James Russell argues that *Gladiator*'s financial success can be attributed to the rapid expansion of the DVD market: "This market, and the overseas theatrical box office, formed the economic foundation against which one can chart the revival of the American film epic . . . Empires will fall. Heroes will rise. Suicidal acts of commitment will abound." The film was first released on DVD on 20 November 2000, and has since been realized in several different extended and special editions. The three-disc *GLADIATOR: EXTENDED SPECIAL EDITION* was released in August 2005, including seventeen minutes of new footage, plus bonus features on the making of the film, storyboards, galleries and other extras.

Gladiator focuses on several themes characteristic of Scott's work. The code of HONOR is extremely important—particularly in battle. At the beginning of the film the Roman troops prepare for battle with the German forces with the cry "strength and honor"—which is repeated by Maximus (Russell Crowe), Valerius (John Quinn), and Quintus (Tomas

Arana). The slaves utter the same cry as they prepare to battle with the Praetorian guards while Maximus plans his escape. The phrase underlines the strength of male bonding and the sense of MASCULINITY amongst Maximus's forces, as well as showing how everyone is prepared to sacrifice individuality in pursuit of a noble cause. Scott contrasts this behavior with that of Commodus (Joaquin Phoenix), whose determination to hold on to power drives him to commit "dishonorable" acts. These include stabbing Maximus with a knife immediately before the two of them are due to fight to the death in the Colosseum, in the hope of obtaining an unfair advantage; and then ordering Quintus to "conceal the wound." Commodus's trickery brings scant reward, however, as he is eventually overcome by Maximus's "strength and determination."

Scott spends considerable time and energy focusing on the ritualistic aspects of the gladiator's life. Every battle they fight in the Colosseum should begin and end with a salute to the emperor. Maximus is well aware of this, but refuses to observe official protocol. Despite being a slave, he turns his back on Commodus in a very public display of contempt, despite the fact that he has been instructed not to. On the other hand, Maximus begins every fight by picking up a handful of dirt from the ground and rubbing it in his hands. This not only indicates his willingness to fight, but (according to Franzoni and Logan's screenplay) symbolizes "the honor of being a man" who considers himself intimately connected to the land. The significance of this ritual is reemphasized at the end of the film when Juba (DJIMON HOUNSOU) is shown burying the figurines of Maximus's wife and son at the place where Maximus died. At last the three of them have achieved their dream of returning to the earth that bore them.

Other rituals help the gladiators to win their duels, often against impossible odds. In their duel against the Legionnaires of Scipio Africanus, all they have is their swords, while their opponents encircle them in chariots with sharp knives affixed to the wheels. However the gladiators emerge victorious chiefly by forming a phalanx and fighting "as one." Maximus's orders continually stress the need to "hold as one" and form a "single column." Not only does this emphasize the need for soldiers to suppress their individuality for the greater good, but it shows how battles are won and lost through good technique. Gladiators are not born to fight; just like the soldiers in *THE DUELLISTS*, they must continually refine their skills on the training ground.

Gladiator also focuses on the personal sacrifices Roman soldiers experience while serving their country. As with many of Scott's heroes, Maximus suffers a conflict of LOVE VS. DUTY. He wishes to return to home after vanquishing the Germans, but the decision lies entirely with Marcus (RICHARD HARRIS) and Commodus. Neither ruler seems

particularly willing to let him go: Marcus offers him the governorship of Rome, in the belief that only Maximus can "give power back to the people . . . and end the corruption that has crippled it." Commodus asks for Maximus's continued loyalty by extending his hand; Maximus rejects it; and is immediately arrested by Quintus on the charge of insubordination. While Maximus successfully escapes execution, and hastens home to see his family, he finds to his horror that they have already been murdered by the Praetorian guards. His professional travails prevent him from fulfilling his role as a father. The same also applies to Marcus, who, although a great general has also been a poor parent to Commodus and Lucilla. He asks Lucilla at one point to "pretend that you are a loving daughter and I a good father," to which Lucilla replies, "This is a pleasant fiction, isn't it?" The same issue crops up again soon afterwards, when Commodus tells his father that "none of my virtues were on your list [of priorities]. Even then it was as if you didn't want me for your son . . . All I ever wanted to do was to live up to you, Caesar, Father." Marcus kneels in front of his son to beg forgiveness for his shortcomings; and Commodus smothers him to death. In the commentary to the Extended Special Edition, Scott justifies Commodus's action by suggesting that he could not forgive his father for what had happened in the past: maybe Marcus actually deserved this kind of punishment for neglecting his family.

At the same time, the film suggests that public duty is extremely important to ensure the survival of the Roman state. Commodus tells Maximus, "Rome salutes you and I embrace you as a brother" for defeating the German army. Maximus observes later on that he will "always serve Rome" through good and bad times. By doing so he follows Marcus's example; despite his shortcomings as a father, the old emperor "had a dream that was Rome" and strove throughout his life to realize it. His son harbors similar ambitions, but they are inspired not by a sense of public duty but a desire for self-glorification: "I will give the people a vision and they will love me for it. They [the people] will soon forget the tedious sermonizing of a few dry old men [the Senate]. I will give them the greatest vision of their lives." However such ambitions, if cleverly publicized, can prove extremely seductive for the people, as Gracchus (Derek Jacobi) rather cynically suggests: "I think he [Commodus] knows what Rome is. Rome is the mob. He will conjure magic for them and they will be distracted . . . He will give them death, and they will love him for it." The only person who can save the city is Maximus, the "savior of Rome" who dedicates himself to fulfilling Marcus's dying wish of returning the city's government to the people.

Given the scale of his task, it is perhaps not surprising that Maximus should place public duty above family loyalties. At the end of the film, when he has finally killed Commodus, he asks Quintus to free his troops, reinstate Gracchus as head of the Senate and thereby restore "the dream that was Rome, it shall be realized." Lucilla recognizes the gladiator's achievements: "Is Rome worth one good man's life? We believed it once. Make us believe it again. He was a soldier of Rome. Honor him."

Despite its epic qualities, designed to show off the sheer scale of the city of Rome, *Gladiator* ultimately communicates a pessimistic message: death is infinitely preferable to living in a world dominated by treachery and self-interest. Maximus makes this point early on, in a stirring address to his troops before the battle with the Germans: "If you find yourself alone riding in green fields with the sun on your face, do not be troubled, for you are in Elysium and you're already dead!!" When he has been captured by the Praetorian guards, and is about to be executed, he asks them: "At least give me a clean death—a soldier's death." In a later sequence Maximus opens a leather pouch handed to him by Cicero (Tommy Flanagan) containing figurines of his deceased wife and son. Juba (Djimon Hounsou) asks "Can they hear you?" to which Maximus replies: "Oh, yes . . . I tell him [my son] I will see him again soon, and to keep his heels down when he's riding his horse." Eventually the gladiator achieves his wish during his climactic duel with Commodus as he sees the gate to his home, followed by a wheat field and a long straight road, with his wife and son waiting at the end of it. At last he can leave the physical world and rejoin his family in death. Lucilla is clearly aware of this, as she shuts his eyes for the last time as she murmurs, "You are home."

Critics have commented extensively on *Gladiator* since its release in 2000. Martin M. Winkler's anthology *Gladiator: Film and History* (2004) offers a selection of viewpoints. Winkler himself relates the film to earlier Hollywood epics such as *Ben Hur* (1959) and *THE FALL OF THE ROMAN EMPIRE* (1964), focusing in particular on Scott's desire to reanimate the past for a modern audience. The next three essays, all written by classical scholars, criticize the film for its lack of fidelity to Roman history. Allen M. Ward berates the screenwriters for their want of "intellectual discipline and respect for the historical record. Poetic license is not a carte blanche for the wholescale disregard of historical facts in historical fiction or films." In similar vein, Kathleen M. Coleman asks whether it might not be possible to forge a "[s]ophisticated collaboration between film and director and historical consultant." On the basis of *Gladiator*, apparently the answer is a definite no. Arthur M. Eckstein concludes rather obviously that "the goals of historians and the goals of those who read essays by historians are not the same as the goals of Hollywood." The film is all about "visual and dramatic pleasures" which are fundamentally distinct from "the truth [about Roman history]."

In contrast, David S. Potter feels that the film's action sequences "draw a modern audience into the emotions of an ancient Roman crowd . . . he [Scott] succeeds, as no one else has succeeded, in bringing the experience of spectatorship alive." Richard Rushton begs to differ; in a 2001 article he argues that "the spectacle no longer wishes to draw attention to itself . . . the spectacle and special effects have merged with and become indistinguishable from the remainder of the *mise-en-scène*."

Another section in the Winkler anthology focuses on the film's resonance in contemporary America. Arthur J. Pomeroy, perhaps rightly, believes that Scott is offering "his own conservative vision of the past. Maximus's heroic sacrifice provides an escape from tyranny and mob rule and allows a return to aristocratic rule balanced by popular acceptance." This idea of escaping tyranny surfaced in the director's earlier work, notably *BLACK RAIN*. Monica S. Cyrino argues that the film is an allegory of contemporary American politics, suggesting, "that there are serious risks inherent in unchecked executive leadership. It argues in favor of a government marked by respect for republican principles and tempered by constitutional representation." Such messages later resurface in *KINGDOM OF HEAVEN*.

The charge of conservatism within the film has also been expressed by James R. Keller, who argues that the film "both affirms and undermines the complaints of Family Values advocates about violence in American entertainment. Ostensibly the film sermonizes about the potential corruption of young and old by violent entertainment and blames the proliferation of such diversions on poor political leadership." At the same time the film shows the kind of violence for which Ridley Scott has become "notorious" (in *Black Rain*, *BLACK HAWK DOWN* and *BLADE RUNNER*): "The director is, of course, attempting to draw a parallel between American and Roman blood lust and to show that the violence in our entertainment is a reflection, not the cause, of violence in America." At the same time "such entertainment can have redeeming social virtues by reinforcing normative American values regarding masculinity, democracy, fraternity, and paternity . . . it [the film] demonizes those who do not live up to normative gender codes . . . the family bigots are always more preoccupied with the corruptive potential of sex and gender than they are with violence."

Returning to the Winkler anthology on the film, Peter W. Rose feels that the film's politics reflect "the director's cynical self-congratulation about the power of the medium he controls and manipulates." In a globalized Hollywood, political messages assume little importance: money matters. In his book *Cartographic Cinema* Tom Conley comes to a similar conclusion: "*Gladiator* . . . became part of an 'empire' of cinematic control whose ultimate projection is one of a worldwide circulation of itself . . . [It] is meshed with other maps, mostly of strategic agencies of advertising and entertainment, but its cartographies open an interpretive space in which the ends of cinema, mapping and globalization are shown interrelated."

Other critics have tried to place *Gladiator* within the tradition of Hollywood representations of Ancient Rome, stretching back to the early years of the twentieth century. Sandra R. Joshel, Margaret Mahmud, and Maria Wyke's introduction to the collection *Imperial Projections* (2001) argues that such representations are so pervasive that "most Americans and Europeans . . . receive their principal contact with the ancient world through popular culture . . . television programs purporting to present the 'real' Rome use clips from Hollywood's historical epics to bring ancient Rome to life." Such films are usually profitable at the box office: James Russell argues that "*Gladiator* was an example of the profit-oriented, collaborative filmmaking [using historical subjects] that tends to dominate mainstream film production in Hollywood." Audiences responded favorably to the kind of material showing "an idealistic, politically motivated entertainer [i.e., Scott] bending the confines of his chosen medium in an attempt to affect the lives of audiences . . . *Gladiator* seemed to argue that historical epics were desperately needed in contemporary film culture, despite perceived economic risks attached to the form."

The film *Gladiator* has been the subject of a parody by Cleolinda Jones in her book *Movies in Fifteen Minutes*.

References

Kathleen M. Coleman, "The Pedant Goes to Hollywood: The Role of the Historical Consultant," in *Gladiator: Film and History*, ed. Martin M. Winkler (Malden, MA and Oxford: Blackwell Publishing Ltd., 2004), 52; Tom Conley, *Cartographic Cinema* (Minneapolis: University of Minnesota Press, 2007), 206; Monica S. Cyrino, "*Gladiator* and Contemporary American Society," in *Gladiator: Film and History*, 148; Arthur M. Eckstein, "Commodus and the Limits of the Roman Empire," in *Gladiator: Film and History*, 72; Leslie Felperin, "Decline and Brawl," *Sight and Sound*, June 2000, 35; David Franzoni, "Gladiator: First Draft (revised 4 April 1998)," www.hundland.com/scripts/Gladiator_FirstDraft.txt (accessed 28 July 2008); David Franzoni, "Gladiator: Second Draft (revised 22 October 1998), www.hundland.com/scripts/Gladiator_SecondDraft.txt (accessed 28 July 2008); "*Gladiator* by David Franzoni, revised by John Logan, Transcribed from the film," http://sfy.ru/sfy/html?script=gladiator_ts (accessed 29 November 2008); Cleolinda Jones, *Movies in Fifteen Minutes* (London: Gollancz, 2005); Sandra R. Joshel, Margaret Mahmud and Maria Wyke, "Introduction," in *Imperial Projections: Ancient Rome in Modern Popular Culture*, ed. Sandra M. Joshel, Margaret Mahmud, and Donald T. McGuire Jr. (Baltimore and London: The Johns Hopkins University Press, 2001), 1–22; James R. Keller, *Queer (Un)friendly Film and Television* (Jefferson, NC and London: McFarland and Co.[Publishers], 2002), 95–96; Sean Macaulay, "Gladiator," *The Times*, 8 May 2000, 20–21; Andrew O'Hagan, "Move Over, Ben Hur," *Daily Telegraph*, 12 May 2000, 21; Arthur J. Pomeroy, "The Vision of a Fascist Rome in *Gladiator*," in *Gladiator: Film and History*, 123; Peter W. Rose, "The Politics of *Gladiator*," in *Gladiator: Film and History*, 172; David S. Potter, "Gladiators and Blood Sport," in *Gladiator: Film and History*, 86; "The Reaper," "Sacred Cows: *Gladiator*," *Uncut* 62 (July 2002): 24; Richard Rushton, "Narrative and Spectacle in *Gladiator*," *CineAction* 56 (September 2001): 40; James Russell, *The Historical Epic and Contemporary Hollywood: From Dances With Wolves to Gladiator* (New York and London: The Continuum International Publishing Group Inc., 2007), 180–81; Ridley Scott, "Director's Commentary" to the Extended Special Edition of *Gladiator* (Los Angeles: Universal Studios, 2005); Ridley Scott, quoted in Diana Landau, ed., *Gladiator: The Making of the Ridley Scott Epic* (Basingstoke and London: Boxtree, 2000), 26, 28, 50; Alexander Walker, "Thumbs Up for Russell," *Evening Standard*, 11 May 2000, 29–30; Allen M. Ward, "*Gladiator* in Historical Perspective," in *Gladiator: Film and History*, 31–45; Martin M. Winkler, "*Gladiator* and the Traditions of Historical Cinema," in *Gladiator: Film and History*, 16–31; Aylish Wood, "Timescapes in Particular Cinema: Crossing the Great Divide of Spectacle Versus Narrative," *Screen* 43, no.4 (Winter 2002): 378–79.

Bibliography

David Bigorgne, "De L'Histoire de la Fable: *Gladiator* ou le Retour du Péplum-Opéra," *CinémAction* 112 (June 2004): 50–65; Rory Carroll, "Better Than the Real Thing," *The Guardian*, 5 May 2000, 10–11; Julian Champkin, "The Gladiator Fights Again," *Daily Mail Weekend*, 6 May 2000, 18–20; Vilashini Cooppan, "The Ruins of Empire: The National Politics of America's Return to Rome," in *Postcolonial Studies and Beyond*, ed. Ania Loomba, Suvir Kaul, Matti Bunzl, Antoinette Burton, and Jed Esty (Durham and London: Duke University Press, 2005), 80–100; Monica Silveira Cyrino, *Big-Screen Rome* (Malden, MA and Oxford: Blackwell Publishing, 2005), 207–57; Brant Drewery, "Veni, Vidi, VT," *Creation* (June 2000): 12–15; Martin Fradley, "Maximus Melodramaticus: Masculinity, Masochism and White Male Paranoia in Contemporary Hollywood Cinema," in *Action and Adventure Cinema*, ed. Yvonne Tasker (London and New York: Routledge, 2004), 235–51; Debra Kaufman, "Wam!net Eases Transatlantic Production," *American Cinematographer* 81, no.5 (May 2000): 40; Alex Lewin, "Rome Wasn't Filmed in a Day," *Premiere* 13, no.8 (May 2000): 43–46; Kevin H. Martin, "A Cut Above," *Cinefex* 82 (July 2000): 14–31; John Millar, "Blade Runner," *Film Review* 594 (June 2000): 62–67; John Millar, "Gladiator," *Film Review Special* #51 (2004): 6065; Mark Morris, "Empire Strikes Back," *Observer Screen* 23 (April 2000): 2–3; Garth Pearce, "A Barbaric World ..." *Total Film* 41 (June 2000): 46–55; Hilary Radner, "Hollywood Redux: All About My Mother and Gladiator," in *The End of Cinema as We Know It: American Film in the Nineties*, ed. Jon Lewis (New York and London: New York University Press, 2001), 72–83; Stephen Rebello, "The Real Fight Club," *Movieline* 11, no.8 (May 2000): 68–73; Damian Sutton, "Inside the 'Black Box:' From Jacques-Louis David to Ridley Scott," in *Screen*

Methods: Comparative Readings in Film Studies, ed. Jacqueline Furby and Karen Randall (London and New York: Wallflower Press, 2005), 72–83; T. P. Wiseman, "Gladiator and the Myths of Rome," *History Today* 55, no.4 (April 2005): 37–43.

GLADIATOR: EXTENDED SPECIAL EDITION

US 2005 r/t 164 min col. A rerelease of the original 2000 film, including seventeen minutes of extra material (which hitherto had only been available on previous DVD releases as deleted scenes). The extra material includes the following: after the battle scene at the beginning of the film, Maximus (RUSSELL CROWE) walks through the Roman camp surveying his wounded troops; Proximo (OLIVER REED) instructs Maximus not to kill the other gladiators so quickly and to provide entertainment for the crowd; Lucilla (CONNIE NIELSEN) meets with several members of the Senate in secret at Gracchus's (DEREK JACOBI's) residence as they complain about Commodus's (JOAQUIN PHOENIX's) poor leadership; after learning that Maximus is alive, Commodus goes to a dark room filled with busts of previous Roman leaders. He picks up a sword and begins to strike his father's bust before tearfully hugging and kissing it; Commodus presides over the execution of two Praetorian guards who have been accused of withholding information from Commodus about Maximus's whereabouts; as Proximo drinks some wine, two spies are seen in the background (they have been employed by Commodus to discover the possible plot to overthrow him).

GLADIATOR—A HERO WILL RISE

Novelization of the screenplay written by DAVID FRANZONI and JOHN LOGAN for *GLADIATOR*, written by Dewey Gram and published by Onyx in the US and Penguin Books (in Great Britain) in 2000.

The novel follows the basic outline of the screenplay, even down to the characters' speeches. It is advertised thus: "Fighting for his life and his honour, Maximus soon becomes one of the most feared gladiators in the empire. But when his enemy Commodus orders a great gladiator spectacle in Rome, Maximus's struggle for survival becomes a fight for revenge . . . revealing that the one power stronger than that of the emperor is the will of the people." Penguin Books also published a 1,700-word adaptation of the novel (by Annette Keen), designed for learners of English.

References

Annette Keen, *Gladiator: A Hero Will Rise* (London: Pearson Education Ltd., 2000); Dewey Gram, *Gladiator: A Hero Will Rise* (London: Penguin Books, 2000).

"GLADIATOR 2"

The screenplay for the as-yet-unproduced sequel to *GLADIATOR*, written by Nick Cave. It was conceived as an anti-war film, in which Maximus (RUSSELL CROWE) comes back to life as the eternal warrior. The final scene takes place in Vietnam. A detailed summary of the story is now accessible online at http://goneelsewhere.wordpress.com/2008/04/15/gladiator-2-script-review/.

GLEESON, BRENDAN (1955–)

Born in Dublin, Gleeson began his career as a teacher before turning to acting and making his film debut in *The Field* (1990). Cast as Reynald de Chatillon in *KINGDOM OF HEAVEN*, Gleeson has a largely minor role as a bloodthirsty Christian who admits that killing Muslims is "what [he] do[es]." With his red hair and bushy red beard, he looks a fearsome sight—the very epitome of an aggressive warrior. He ultimately meets an untimely end as Saladin (GHASSAN MASSOUD) slits his throat for daring to sip a glass of water intended for Guy De Lusignan (MARTON CSOKAS). As well as murdering innocent Muslim citizens, Reynald has compounded his felony by committing a social faux pas. In Saladin's view he deserves to die. In *KINGDOM OF HEAVEN*: THE DIRECTOR'S CUT Reynald meets an even more grisly fate; he is decapitated.

Gleeson's subsequent highlights include portraying WINSTON CHURCHILL in the recent film *Into the Storm* (2009), the Scott-produced sequel to *THE GATHERING STORM*.

GOLDMAN, ALAIN (1961–)

Producer of *1492: CONQUEST OF PARADISE*. Formerly worked in the studio system, but worked hard to raise the independent finances for the film by preselling the foreign rights to different countries, as well as relying on finance from the American studio Paramount Pictures and from the French company Antenne 2. Paramount contributed 20 percent of the total budget of $45 million in exchange for the North American rights, thanks to Scott's friendship with STANLEY R. JAFFE; while Antenne 2 contributed just about 15 percent. According to Jean-Pierre Lavoignat and Laurent Tirard, it was Goldman's idea to raise finance this way so that the production would be totally independent. Iceland was one of the first, followed by France, then Great Britain, and then America. The projected budget was set at $45 million; Todd Coleman estimates that the eventual cost was about $2 million more.

References

Todd Coleman, "How Columbus Discovered Europe," *Premiere* (US ed.), November 1992, 64; Jean-Pierre Lavoignat and Laurent Tirard, "Christophe Colomb: Les Secrets," *Studio* 66 (October 1992): 71–79.

Bibliography

Marie-Claude Arbaudie, "1492: Christophe Colomb," *Le Film Français* No. 2422 (2 October 1992): 9–10.

GOLDSMITH, JERRY (1929–2004)

Goldsmith began his career in television with music for series such as *Gunsmoke, The Man from UNCLE* and *Dr. Kildare.* He subsequently worked on films such as *ALIEN*, for which there were at least three different scores recorded: the original score composed by Goldsmith himself; the music track composed by TERRY RAWLINGS to give Scott flexibility during the film's editing difficulties; and the music used by Scott for the film's original release (1979). All three versions of the score were included on the ALIEN QUADRILOGY boxed set.

Goldsmith's music reflects the film's underlying mood with its use of bleak orchestrations, most notably in the higher woodwinds, oscillating string-textures and bizarre, sometimes savage sounds, especially from the brass section, which his arranger Arthur Morton built from the orchestral palette with various modern compositional techniques. Goldsmith also composed a main theme in the romantic style that barely appears in the finished film. A short passage from Mozart's "Eine Kleine Nachtmusik" plays during the scene in which Dallas (TOM SKERRITT) spends some time alone relaxing in the shuttle *Narcissus.* Scott and editor Terry Rawlings became quite attached to several of the preexisting cues that they had used for the temporary score while editing the film; as a result Goldsmith's score was combined with a temp score, and the final minutes of the first movement of Howard Hanson's Symphony No. 2 ("Romantic"), which replaced Goldsmith's music for the film's concluding moments of the film's showdown.

Over the years several bootlegged copies of Goldsmith's score appeared on the market, among them a Spanish two-CD release with all used and unused cues, including the retained temp score, and an archive bootleg that also included alternate takes from the recording sessions. On 15 November 2007 Intrada Records released the complete score to the film with additional alternate score tracks and the original LP-program in a two-CD set. In 1980 Goldsmith's film music for *Alien* received nominations for the Golden Globe Award (Best Original Film Score).

On the strength of Goldsmith's contribution to *Alien*, he was asked to provide an eighty-minute score for *LEGEND*, a work the composer later described as "one of the best soundtracks I've ever done." However, Goldsmith's score was replaced by a more modern-sounding track from the German synthesizer band TANGERINE DREAM after MCA's chief executive Sidney Sheinberg demanded that the film should be rendered more commercial prior to its American release. Goldsmith was particularly incensed by the change and never worked with Ridley Scott again. Goldsmith's score (restored to the film in *LEGEND*: THE DIRECTOR'S CUT) was naturalistic in style, designed to complement the fairytale elements of the story. He made use of a full symphony orchestra, which resulted in a score that combined well with Scott's memorable use of images. If Scott was inspired by French filmmakers such as Truffaut (*L'ENFANT SAUVAGE*), so Goldsmith was moved by composers such as Debussy and Ravel. Goldsmith acknowledged that the waltz accompanying Lily's (MIA SARA's) seduction by Darkness (TIM CURRY) was definitely influenced by Ravel's "La Valse." The score contained character motifs—for example an erratic sound cutting in and out at the beginning signaling Blix's (ALICE PLAYTEN's) entrance. Andy Dursin wrote that the Goldsmith score "gives *Legend* a lyrical sense of grandeur that was completely missing from the Tangerine Dream score."

References

Andy Dursin, "Legend Resurrected," *Film Score Monthly* 7, no.4 (May/June 2002): 14; Jerry Goldsmith, quoted in Matthew Aitken, "LEGEND: Ridley Scott (The Remnants of a Masterpiece)," http://www.figmentfly.com/legend/different4i.html (accessed 25 April 2008).

THE GOOD SHEPHERD

US 2006 r/t 167 min col. *Production Companies*: Universal Pictures, Morgan Creek Productions, Tribeca Productions and American Zoetrope. *Producers*: Robert de Niro, James G. Robinson and Jane Rosenthal. Director: Robert de Niro. *Writer*: Eric Roth. *Director of Photography*: Robert Richardson. *Production Designer*: Jeannine Oppewall. *Music*: Bruce Fowler and Marcelo Zarvos. *Cast*: Matt Damon (*Edward Wilson*), Angelina Jolie (*Margaret "Clover" Russell*), Alec Baldwin (*Sam Murach*), Billy Crudup (*Arch Cummings*), Robert de Niro (*Bill Sullivan*), Michael Gambon (*Dr. Fredericks*), William Hurt (*Philip Allen*).

The tumultuous early history of the CIA as viewed through one man's life. Edward Wilson (Matt Damon) is a morally upright young man who values honor and discretion, qualities that help him to be recruited for a career in the organization. While working there, his ideals gradually turn to suspicion, influenced by the Cold War paranoia present within the office. Eventually, he becomes an influential veteran operative, while his distrust of everyone around him increases.

The subject of this film is very similar to that of the Ridley Scott-produced miniseries *THE COMPANY*, released a year later. Damon's character is a fictionalized portrait of James Jesus Angleton, played by MICHAEL KEATON in the miniseries.

A GOOD YEAR

USA/GB 2006 r/t 118 min col. *Production Companies*: Fox 2000 Pictures and Scott Free. *Producer/Director*: Ridley Scott. *Writer*: Marc Klein, based on the book by Peter Mayle. *Director of Photography*: Philippe Le Sourd. *Production Designer*:

Sonja Klaus. *Music:* Marc Streitenfeld. *Cast:* Russell Crowe (*Max Skinner*), Albert Finney (*Uncle Henry*), Marion Cotillard (*Fanny Chenal*), Abbie Cornish (*Christie Roberts*), Didier Bourdon (*Francis Duflot*, Tom Hollander (*Charlie Wills*), Freddie Highmore (*Young Max*).

The film (and the book by PETER MAYLE that preceded it) was inspired by a story published in *The Times* of Hugh Ryman, a young British entrepreneur who moved to FRANCE when his father sold the family stationery business. He had studied winemaking in Bordeaux and in the centers of Yquem and Latour. With a combination of sheer energy and the latest technology, Ryman had created a successful business producing mid-price wines appealing to all consumers.

In an interview with Jack Foley, Scott claimed that he and Mayle—both of whom have houses in PROVENCE— were swapping stories about their experiences in the country one New Year's Eve. Scott called Mayle the next day and suggested that "'What we were talking about would be a good book,' and he said, 'Yes, it would.' So I said, 'You write the book and I'll do the movie.' It was quick, only about four years ago." Mayle's book (also called *A Good Year*) appeared in 2004 and quickly became a best-seller. Scott commissioned MARC KLEIN to write the screenplay.

According to the Foley interview, casting was a two-tiered affair. Having worked with RUSSELL CROWE on *GLADIATOR*, Scott had established a close personal and professional relationship with him. The two met in Hollywood, where Scott "spouted on about this [film] and [Crowe later] called me and said, 'You know, that stuck with me. It might be quite a nice thing to explore.'" Once Crowe's participation was assured, financing the film became much easier—even though Twentieth Century-Fox executives were a little skeptical about Scott and Crowe working on a comedy. Scott eventually convinced the studio that *A Good Year* was not just a comedy but "a romantic dramedy . . . driven by really good characters in situations that they get put into that for the most part, are amusing." In terms of style, the film was planned very much like *MATCHSTICK MEN*.

Scott cast two French actors, MARION COTILLARD (Fanny) and DIDIER BOURDON (Duflot) in major roles. FREDDIE HIGHMORE was engaged to play the young Max; according to the pressbook he built up a good relationship with Crowe: "Russell said to him, 'Hi Freddie, I'm going to be Max.' Freddie says, 'Yes, I know.' Russell says, 'Maybe we should get together' Freddie says, 'Why?' and Russell says, 'Well, you're going to be acting, I'm going to be acting, don't you think it would be useful?' and he said, 'I don't think so.' That was it." ALBERT FINNEY agreed to play Uncle Henry (who was only referred to in Mayle's book, but had been transformed into a major character in Klein's screenplay). *A Good Year* was his fourth film with Scott as director or producer—the other three being *THE DUELLISTS*, *THE BROWNING VERSION*, and *THE GATHERING STORM*.

Filming took place in autumn 2005 in an area close to Scott's house in Provence. Choosing a location for Uncle Henry's Château La Siroque proved difficult: Scott looked at almost a dozen locations in the area between Rousillon and Bonnieux, before coming back to the first one, La Canorgue, which according to the pressbook had "[a] spectacular view looking out over the Luberon, and the magical dusk light that bathes the main house in the late afternoon."

The film opened in late 2006 to lukewarm reviews. Despite the success of *Matchstick Men*, critics seemed unwilling (or unable) to acknowledge that Scott could direct comedy. *The Times* objected to his use of "broad cultural stereotypes," while *Sight and Sound* felt that "'jolly' is not a word one associates with Scott. His forte lies in the vivid realisation of spectacular, violent worlds . . . *A Good Year*, though tastefully photographed, comes to embody one character's closing prediction (denied by Max) of what life in the chateau will be: an attractive prospect but ultimately enervating." Other reviewers felt that Crowe had been fundamentally miscast in a comic role: "[He] doesn't have the chops to convince as a devil-may-care English wit . . . Crowe enters the story as an insufferably self-satisfied boor—and departs it unchanged." The *Empire* reviewer felt that the combination of Scott and Crowe was just too weighty for the material: "There's a forced jauntiness, a sense of careful calculation whizzing away behind the comedy beats, from Crowe's intense pratfalls as Max to escape a derelict swimming pool, to his plummy exclamations of 'bollocks' at every available opportunity." The *Sunday Telegraph* treated the film as "de luxe eye candy, beautifully shot and adequately acted, and mildly refreshing in the way that Max remains, if not nearly as horrid as he was in London, then certainly far from a saint." *The Guardian* described with ill-disguised glee how *A Good Year* has been received in France: "The newspaper *Libération* . . . accused Scott of leaving no cliché unturned and of pandering to British middle-class fantasies of life in France . . . We also have to mention the pitiful performance of Russell Crowe, supposedly playing a witty and laid-back person, when the Australian actor is better known for his cantankerous temperament than for his notoriously non-existent comic abilities."

A Good Year opened to poor box-office receipts; on the opening weekend in America, it took only $3.7 million, and by January 2007 its total gross was $7.5 million. The estimated cost of making the film was $35 million. As Scott suggested later in 2007, however, perhaps the critics were less than fair in their evaluation: "[W]ith *A Good Year* we really got beaten up. A journalist told me how much he liked it, and I said, 'Really? Did you write about it?' and he said, 'No.' That says it all."

The film's plot focuses the contrast between the high-tech world of the City of London and the more leisurely pace of life in Provence. Klein's script describes the Lawton Brothers' Office Building (where Max works) thus: "A three-story glass and concrete box at the top end of Threadneedle Street." Inside "a platoon of young, Savile Row-draped bond traders sit at their desks." In this money-obsessed world, no one cares about the view outside; they are solely concerned about "the plasma screens that broadcast business reports from all over the world." Max's well-appointed apartment is "shrouded in a gloomy soup of drizzle and fog"—although "sleek, modern [and] expensively appointed," its glass walls "give the impression that the place is literally floating in the foggy dawn sky." The overwhelming image is one of dislocation: Max works and lives in concrete boxes, sealed off from the outside world. In one of the few exterior sequences set in London, Max observes the rain-washed streets around Piccadilly Circus, thronged with people rushing from place to place with little time to stop and think. Such images of DYSTOPIA recall earlier films—notably the futuristic world of Los Angeles in *BLADE RUNNER* and late 1980s Osaka in *BLACK RAIN*.

Life in Uncle Henry's château and its environs can be best summed up by the lyrics of the Noël Coward song "A Room with a View," which plays on the soundtrack as Max looks around Henry's book-lined study ("A room with a view, and you,/ And no one to hurry us/ No one to worry us . . ."). Provence is identified with lasting values; the sunshine, the "pinwheel of colors in the sky" at sunset, and "a stunning view of the vineyard and the Luberon valley." This is the perfect place where Henry "can keep busy doing so little and enjoy it so much"; whose inhabitants work not to make money but to identify themselves with nature: "there's a magnificent poetry in his [Duflot's] devotion to each and every grape." Fanny's life as a bistro-owner transforms her into "an iridescent Provençal beauty," whose complexion matches the sky. Scott's imagery recalls *The Duellists* and *KINGDOM OF HEAVEN*, in which France is associated with lasting values unchanged for centuries.

With Max identified with the dog-eat-dog world of the City, it is not surprising that his uncle should have chosen not leave the château to him: "[H]e worried about what you [Max] had become. 'My nephew is selfish,' he used to say. 'How can I give La Siroque to a man who can't even appreciate the simple pleasures in life?'" As the film unfolds, so Max's point of view alters. He successfully prevents the sale of the château by forging a letter in his uncle's hand, specifying that it should be left to his illegitimate daughter Christie Roberts (ABBIE CORNISH). Meanwhile Max visits his boss Sir Nigel (Kenneth Cranham) and notices a reproduction of a Van Gogh painting on the wall of a rolling Provençal landscape with exquisite swirls of color and texture. At this moment he understands the importance of the French countryside, which should be experienced at first-hand rather than through a reproduction. He gives up his job and follows his uncle's example in pursuing a life of leisure. Rather than wearing Armani suits, he dons comfortable clothes, with his "shirt-top opened . . . [looking] a helluva lot like Henry."

CHILDHOOD is conceived in *A Good Year* as a time when boys and girls learn their most important lessons about life. In a series of flashbacks young Max learns the significance of the Provençal wine industry, which to Henry represents "nothing more than the art of bottling truth . . . wine will always whisper into your mouth with complete, unabashed honesty, every time you take a sip." In another sequence where Henry beats young Max at tennis, Max learns that "the act of losing . . . can elicit great wisdom ... not the least of which is how much more enjoyable it is to win." More importantly Max learns the value of companionship: Henry treats him as an equal—as seen, for instance, when young Max bowls the perfect off-cutter, or fast pitch, to dismiss (strike out) his uncle in a game of indoor cricket. Henry remarks at one point that "you're a genius, Maximilian. You could be me." This represents the opposite side of the coin to the view of childhood expressed in *THE BROWNING VERSION*, where young boys are brought up to suppress their instincts in a single-sex private school. The older Max only comes to understand the value of his past experiences when he puts the drunken Christy to bed: "God, I loved being here with him [Henry]. No bedtime, no chores, and best of all, no squabbling adults. I never told him, but those summers saved my childhood." Christy wishes him good night ("Thanks a million, Max-a-million") and Max pulls up with a start: "No one has ever called me that, except Uncle Henry."

Once Max embraces the Provençal life, his childhood memories come flooding back. In a final flashback the ten-year-old Fanny (described even then as "gorgeous and a bit dangerous") swims across the pool towards him and gives him his first kiss. Thus it seems somehow fitting that the two of them are reunited at the end of the film.

In contrast to *BLACK HAWK DOWN* and *AMERICAN FIGHTER PILOT*, both of which support the idea of the nuclear family, *A Good Year* suggests that the idea of belonging is more significant. Max's "family" at the château not only includes Fanny but Duflot, Ludivine (Isabelle Candelier), and Christie. Duflot in particular mourns Henry's passing; he admits to Max that "we became very close . . . Almost like father and son." Needless to say Max at this point does not understand in the least what the old man means. However when Christie tells him that her childhood was similar to his own (both of them grew up without parents), and they are still in a sense searching for security, Max's attitude begins to change. At length he admits to Fanny that Henry was the only person he had ever loved, and that he could not work out why he stopped coming to the château. The attractions of the château are summed up in the final sequence, where Max sits on the edge of the wall watching the gypsy-pickers do their work and listening to Christie and Duflot arguing about the best way to cut the stems. Fanny and Madame Duflot enter the frame, placing lunch on the table, adjusting flowers and uncorking wine. Klein's screenplay acknowledges that while La Siroque might be "just a tiny piece of *terroir* in a very big world," it is inhabited by a close-knit community.

A Good Year charts the characters' progress towards mutual understanding. At first they are prisoners of their cultural preconceptions: Fanny believes that Max's taste in food extends solely to McDonald's or fish and chips; Max describes Duflot as a French tosspot and Duflot in turn thinks of Max as an English prick. As the action unfolds, so their attitudes begin to change; this is chiefly signaled by their behavior during meals. Max and Fanny go out one evening and share a delicate display of food spread on a white cloth. Duflot invites Max and Christie to an elaborate dinner including thrush paté, eggplant purée, headless larks and civet of wild boar. Fueled with liberal quantities of wine and *Marc de Provence*, the guests gradually lose their inhibitions and start to enjoy one another's company. With its array of bizarre food, the meal itself recalls a similar sequence in *HANNIBAL*, where the eponymous hero (ANTHONY HOPKINS) fries Krendler's (RAY LIOTTA's) brains in butter. Whereas Hannibal treats the occasion as a performance, showing off his culinary skills as well as his cannibalistic inclinations, the Duflot's dinner in *A Good Year* brings people together. Although ending somewhat abruptly, as Christie exits in a drunken stupor vowing to find her way back to the château, the meal shows how people of different cultural backgrounds can interact with one another if they are prepared to indulge in a little give and take. Max understands Christie's motives for coming to the château in the first place; and finds out about the mysterious *Le Coin Perdu* wine; Duflot begins to comprehend Max's businesslike view of life; while Duflot's elderly father (Jacques Herlin) realizes the importance of listening to the vines rather following his son's inebriated rambling. The occasion foreshadows the final sequence when Duflot admits to Max that he loves this "mad person" Christie, while Max volunteers to "soften up" the intransigent French wine authorities through a mixture of flattery and charm.

To date, no critical articles have appeared on the film. A copy of extracts from the screenplay with photographs of Provence by Rico Torres appeared in 2006. Peter Mayle's work has been widely published in a variety of editions too numerous to mention here; but the best introduction to Provençal culture and how it shapes writers can be found in Richard Aldington's *Introduction to Mistral* (1960).

References

Dalya Alberge, "The Times Story of French Sour Grapes That Turned into a Film," *The Times*, 3 October 2006, 5; Richard Aldington, *Introduction to Mistral* (Carbondale: Southern Illinois University Press, 1960); Patrick Fahy, "A Good Year," *Sight and Sound*, 16, no.12 (December 2006): 55; Jack Foley, "Ridley Scott Talks about *A Good Year*," www.indielondon.co.uk/Film-Review/a-good-year-ridley-scott-interview (accessed 8 August 2008); "A Good Year," *The Times 2*, 26 October 1006, 16; Dan Jolin, "A Good Year," *Empire* 209 (November 2006): 38; Marc Klein, "*A Good Year*: Screenplay" (Draft dated 5 September 2005), www.dailyscript.com/scripts/A-GOOD-YEAR-2.pdf (accessed 26 January 2009); Marc Klein and Rico Torres, *A Good Year: Portrait of the Film Based on the Novel by Peter Mayle* (New York: Newmarket Press, 2006); Will Lawrence, "My Scraps with Russell Crowe," *Daily Telegraph*, 2 November 2007, 32; *Pressbook: A Good Year* (Los Angeles: Twentieth Century-Fox Film Corporation, 2006), 8; Anthony Quinn, "A Good Year," *Independent Arts and Books Review*, 27 October 2006, 8; Catherine Shoard, "A Good Year," *Sunday Telegraph*, 29 October 2006, 27; Kim Willsher, "A Good Year? It's No Vintage Scott, Say French Critics," *The Guardian*, 4 January 2007, 17.

Bibliography

Derek Malcolm, "Russell Crowe Is an Unlikely Englishman Abroad in a Ridley Scott Rom-com That Paints a Rose-Tainted Vision of Rural France," *Evening Standard*, 26 October 2006, 41; Ridley Scott, "Ripe on the Vine," *Fade In* 9, no.3 (October 2006): 48–53; James Cameron Wilson, "A Good Year," *Film Review* 676 (November 2006): 104.

GOODALL, CAROLINE (1959–)

Debuted in British television series such as *Rumpole of the Bailey* (1988) and the Australian-made *Ring of Scorpio* (1990). Goodall observed in 1994 that she was continually asked to play "the wife"—"the kind of women . . . who, yes, happen to be married and happen to have children, but who actually *do* something." It was perhaps on the strength of this ability that she was cast in *WHITE SQUALL*. She plays a supporting role as someone perfectly capable of competing with men when it comes to working on the *Albatross*. To the teenage crew members, she appears as an object of lust—at one point March (DAVID LASCHER) observes that "she looks pretty good in her all-together for being thirty . . . I look down into the skylight above Skipper's cabin and there she was, peelin' down." Alice Sheldon herself does not know the meaning of fear—after having helped steady the ship during a storm, she observes that she "cheated death again." Alice also has a playful side—when left alone with her husband in Panama, while the boys enjoy themselves at a party with the Dutch schoolgirls, she dances with him and recalls the time when Sheldon asked her for her hand in MAR-RIAGE "on the deck of the Yankee . . . We weren't much older than they were." Screenwriter TODD ROBINSON comments in the script: "She's sixteen again. There's something about him [Sheldon] that still makes her blush." Sadly she does not survive the white squall—despite her heroic efforts to escape, she is imprisoned in a cabin as the ship sinks.

Goodall's performance was commended by the *Sight and Sound* reviewer: "The sight of Jeff Bridges watching helplessly as Caroline Goodall is sealed up in a watery tomb is shattering because we have come to know and believe in their characters . . . Bridges is ideally cast as the grumpy, salty dog [Sheldon] with a heart of gold, but Goodall essays Dr. Alice Sheldon with equal conviction. Amidst all the on-screen chaos, the couple's final lingering look delivers a weighty dramatic punch."

References
Mark Kermode, "White Squall," *Sight and Sound*, May 1996, 64; "Profiles: Caroline Goodall," *Empire*, April 1995, 52; Todd Robinson, *White Squall: Revised First Draft* (dated 31 October 1994), http://sfy.ru/sfy.html?script=white_squall (accessed 8 September 2008), 78.

Bibliography
Hilary Kingsley, "Know the Face but Can't Place the Name," *TV Times* (London), 1 May 1999, 14–15.

GOODING, CUBA, JR. (1968–)
Born in the Bronx, Cuba Gooding Jr. made his film debut in John Singleton's 1991 hit *Boyz in the Hood*. He won an Oscar as Best Supporting Actor for his role in *Jerry Maguire* (1996).

Cast as Nicky Barnes, the main rival to Frank Lucas (DENZEL WASHINGTON) in the heroin trade in *AMERICAN GANGSTER*, Gooding played the part of a real-life character who wanted all that Lucas had and more, once appearing on the cover of the *New York Times Magazine*, asserting that he was "Mr. Untouchable." In the production information Gooding described Barnes as one of "the true celebrities. Today we have sports celebrities like the Mets and the Yankees or actors, but back then you had the drug dealers. They were the ones that were directly connected to the inner city and the people." Nicky Barnes is clearly conceived as the visual opposite to Frank Lucas. If Lucas, in his sober tailored suits, prefers restraint in behavior and dress (so as not to draw attention), Barnes wears wide collars and flared trousers characteristic of early 1970s popular fashion. He keeps a club where he cavorts with naked girls and which, according to STEVEN ZAILLIAN's script, resembles a set from a blaxploitation film. Nicky dislikes Frank's tone, particularly where issues of "trademark infringement" are concerned: "Catch me? Insist? Infringement? I don't like these words as much as please—thank you—sorry to bother you, Nicky. These are better words to use [when] you come to my place without an invitation." Frank does not respond, but we understand from his expression how much he despises his rival. Nicky "nods, Fine, okay, but it's more like a warning." Each drug baron has his own patch, and woe betide anyone who seeks to encroach upon it.

References
American Gangster: Production Information (Los Angeles: Universal Pictures, 2007), 6; Steven Zaillian, "*American Gangster*: Final Shooting Script" (27 July 2006), www.roteirodecinema.com.br/scripts/files/american_gangster.htm (accessed 8 February 2009), 82–84.

GORTON, ASSHETON (1930–)
Assheton Gorton began his career in television, turning later to films such as *Get Carter* (1971) and *The French Lieutenant's Woman* (1981).

For *LEGEND*, Scott in collaboration with Gorton at first explored locations in northern California's famous redwood forest, with an eye towards making it the primary filming site. Later, however, they chose to build an artificial forest on the world's largest sound stage, the so-called "007 stage" at Pinewood Studios. Dozens of live trees, a running book, a bear, numerous shrubs, horses, bees, flowers, small animals and a ten-foot-deep pond were spread across the stage. The set took sixteen weeks to create. Scott told PAUL M. SAMMON that "the general design . . . was based on a huge forest set that had been built for *Siegfried*, the Fritz Lang film . . . for a scene where Siegfried kills a dragon." For Gorton himself, speaking in a documentary about the making of the film, the forest symbolized life, death and nature—a wilderness where the characters embarked on a voyage of self-discovery. It was one of those "big archetypal stories which give enormous scope for the art department." His sources of inspiration included baroque architecture, Fransese's prison paintings and WILLIAM BLAKE.

The set also contained some "floating fluff" (actually cut-up duck down), as Scott wanted to suggest (according to a preproduction article of 1986) "a real forest during the spring, [where] there are usually things floating through the air all the time . . . Against the backlight, it looked like we had millions of seeds floating through the forest." For the winter scenes, fifteen hundred icicles were added to the set. Varying in length from one foot to eight feet, they were made of resin and hot wax to achieve the proper texture. The special effects team, under supervisor NICK ALLDER, also supplied tons of artificial snow in the process of "winterizing" the forest set. The forest set is but one of several major sets designed by Gorton for the film. Another is the gigantic kitchen at the bottom of Darkness's subterranean castle. Constructed on a mammoth scale and populated with giant demon cooks, it appears even bigger against the tiny bodies of the goblins appearing throughout the film. The castle's great hall is another spectacular set, which includes Darkness's huge and menacing throne. Among its other features: ominous jet-black columns, twenty-five feet high and nine feet in diameter; a gigantic black marble banquet table; and a massive fireplace adorned with fantastic sculptures.

Other important sets include an ancient tomb, heaped with gems and treasures and containing the corpse of a knight clad in gold chain mail and lying on a golden dais, his bejeweled sword on his chest; the Great Tree, where an inner tree sits transfixed by a curved bronze horn; and the woodcarver's cottage at the edge of the forest. Vincent Canby of the *New York Times* observed that Gorton was "the film's real auteur . . . [he] appears to have pigged out in the studio's carpenter's shop. He's created a series of fancy, plastic sets that keep the eye busier than the eye or the heart." The film's publicity made much of the sets: the production notes claimed that: "[I]t should come as no surprise, given Scott's reputation, that *Legend* is a visual feast. Indeed, production designer Assheton Gorton's sets are among the most elaborate ever constructed for a motion picture, pulsating with style and imagination."

References
Vincent Canby, "Legend," *New York Times*, 18 April 1986, D4; Assheton Gorton, interviewed in "The Making of *Legend*" (2002 documentary directed by J. M. Kenny), included on *Legend: The Ultimate DVD* (Los Angeles: Universal Studios, 2002); Production Notes: *Legend* (Los Angeles: Universal Pictures, 1986), http://www.figmentfly.com/legend/background3.html (accessed 13 May 2008); "Set Pieces," *AIP & Co* 71 (Jan/Feb 1986): 17; Ridley Scott, quoted in Paul M. Sammon, *Ridley Scott Close-Up: The Making of His Movies* (New York: Thunder's Mouth Press, 1999), 79–80.

Bibliography
"Légende," *L'Écran Fantastique* 60 (September 1985): 23–25; John Russell Taylor, *Anatomy of a Television Play* (London: Weidenfeld and Nicolson, 1962).

GOTHIC HORROR
Valdine Clemens claims that *ALIEN* constitutes a good example of Gothic horror. The only genuine Gothic aspects of Ridley Scott's work, as both producer and director, can be seen in the television series *THE HUNGER*. A good example of this can be seen in "The Lighthouse," an episode from the first series based on a story by Edgar Allan Poe. The story concerns a man with a broken heart (Bruce Davison) who decides to retire from the world by running an isolated lighthouse. Tormented by dreams of his lover Monica, he conjures up an ideal woman—symbolically known as Angelica (Simone Elise-Girard)—and the two of them make love. Eventually reality intrudes and the woman turns into a piece

of seaweed. The man encounters the lighthouse owner, strangles him in a fit of madness, drowns the old man in the sea, and then walks to his death in the same way. As he does so, director Darrell Wasyk intercuts between close-ups of the man and images of Angelica stretching before him, to emphasize the fact that he has symbolically been "possessed" by her. The episode ends with the host (TERENCE STAMP) intoning "love wounds, maims, even kills, but its absence—anything is better than that." *THE HIRE*: "BEAT THE DEVIL" contains some Gothic elements, as JAMES BROWN visits The Devil (GARY OLDMAN) in the hope of renewing his pact for maintaining eternal youth.

Yvonne Tasker penetratingly explores the ways in which *THE SILENCE OF THE LAMBS* and *HANNIBAL* develop the Gothic horror genre. She argues that the main difference between both films and their closest cinematic, television-based, and literary cousins is the heroine's relation to male-centered institutions. Though Clarice Starling (JODIE FOSTER, JULIANNE MOORE) is clearly working toward advancement in a male world, Tasker finds her far less tied to the opinions of any one man. Starling's quest for success and identity is ultimately personal, not defined within patriarchy. Her motivation is "clear and direct . . . [in *Silence* the director does not] simply allow Clarice Starling her autonomy; it is positively celebrated."

References
Valdine Clemens, *The Return of the Repressed: Gothic Horror from The Castle of Orlando to Alien* (New York: State University of New York Press, 1999), 24–25; Yvonne Tasker, *Silence of the Lambs*, BFI Classics (London: British Film Institute, 2002), 21.

W. R. GRACE DEFICIT TRIALS
US 1986 Commercial r/t 1 min col. *Production Company*: RSA Films for W. R. Grace. *Director*: Ridley Scott.

Set in 2017, this commercial features a little boy prosecuting people in the 1980s in "The Deficit Trials," condemning people for their irresponsibility. A young boy quizzes a time-traveler (looking very much like Roy Batty in *BLADE RUNNER*), accusing him of contributing to a National Debt in the US in 1986 of 2 trillion dollars. The camera suggests the suffering that this debt has caused through repeated pans of a group of paupers of various ages who are witnessing the trial taking place. The irony of the situation is further emphasized through a shot of a tattered white flag with the words "the republic," "the nation," and "equality for all." Clearly the commercial suggests that people during the 1980s took very little heed of these fundamental principles of American democracy. The time-traveler asks pathetically: "Are you ever going to forgive us?" A voice-over informs us, "At W. R. Grace, we want all of us [i.e., the people] to stay one step ahead of a changing world."

This commercial caused a good deal of controversy when it was first released in 1986. Although broadcast on 150 independent television stations throughout the country, it was deemed too controversial and too one-sided for inclusion on the big three networks. NBC's vice-president Rick Gitter remarked, "It's [the commercial is] too well done. It expresses a view that budget cuts are a moral imperative." Which was exactly the point: J. Peter Grace, the company chairman, served as head of President Reagan's commission on Waste and Inefficiency in Government.

Bibliography

"American Notes: Advertising," *Time*, 24 January 2001, 22.

GRANT, SUSANNAH (1963–)

American screenwriter and director who wrote the screenplays for major hits including *Erin Brockovich* (2000), for which she received an Oscar nomination. After her nomination, Grant adapted JENNIFER WEINER's novel *IN HER SHOES* (2005), produced by Scott. Grant seemed the right kind of person for the task, as she was preoccupied with her own image—claiming to have spent a sizable portion of her youth convinced that she might someday become the princess that she read about in so many stories. Her adaptation surprised those expecting a shallow romantic comedy, given its multilayered characterizations, intelligent dialogue, and sensitive lead portrayals.

Reference

Susannah Grant—The Dialogue—Learning from the Masters, (DVD 2005).

GRAZER, BRIAN (1951–)

Producer of *AMERICAN GANGSTER*, Grazer has been making movies and television programs for more than twenty-five years. His films include *Splash* (1984), *Apollo 13* (1995), and *The Da Vinci Code* (2006).

For *American Gangster* Grazer read MARK JACOBSON's article in *New York* magazine and immediately optioned the project for his company, Imagine Entertainment. Initially the film was to be directed by Antoine Fuqua with DENZEL WASHINGTON and Benicio del Toro in the leading roles; but Universal Pictures withdrew funding for budgetary reasons. Eventually the film was made by Scott with a script written by STEVEN ZAILLIAN. In the production notes, Grazer admitted that he was "fascinated by the cautionary tale of a man [Frank Lucas] with the dream of corporate America who found a way to make a deal with individuals in Southeast Asia that could lead him to the highest grade of heroin . . . [and] import it in body bags of US soldiers traveling from Vietnam back into America . . . I thought that was a remarkable, inescapable and interesting idea."

References

American Gangster: Production Information (Los Angeles: Universal Pictures, 2007), 3.

THE GREAT TEXAS DYNAMITE CHASE (aka DYNAMITE WOMEN)

USA 1976 r/t 90 min col. *Production Companies:* Yasny Talking Pictures and New World Pictures. *Producer:* David Irving. *Writer/Director:* Michael Pressman. *Director of Photography:* Jamie Anderson. *Production Designer:* Russell J. Smith. *Music:* Craig Safan. *Cast:* Claudia Jennings (*Candy Morgan*), Tara Stroheimer (*Pam Morgan*), Jocelyn Jones (*Ellie-Jo Turner*), Miles Watkins (*Boyfriend*), Nancy Bleier (*Carol*).

A source-film for *THELMA & LOUISE* that features two women who rob banks, seduce men, show off their bodies and finally escape to South Africa. Intended as a soft-porn film (with a tagline of "They'll steal your heart . . . and rob your bank!"), it a good example of mid-1970s sexploitation. *Variety* commented that the film provides "kicks for the ozoner crowd and tongue-in-cheek humor for the more sophisticated."

Reference

"The Great Texas Dynamite Chase," *Variety*, 18 June 1976, 3.

GREEN, EVA (1980–)

Born Eva Gaëlle Green in Paris. She made a remarkable debut in Bernardo Bertolucci's *The Dreamers* (2003), after considerable theater experience in France. On the strength of this performance, Jeena Jay, the casting director of *KINGDOM OF HEAVEN* told Diana Landau that she was perfect for the role of Sibylla, wife of King Baldwin IV (EDWARD NORTON) in a film "where there are no [other] significant female roles—so she is carrying a great deal. And she carries it off beautifully."

In a preproduction interview Green asserted that, far from showing Muslim people in a bad light, the film "says that war is futile and that people will find love irrespective of race. The title itself described Jerusalem as somewhere where all races live together harmoniously." Green told *Film Review* that she was aware of the issues underlying the film: "[I] went to the Arab Institute in Paris because I wanted to be aware of both sides of the argument. And I hope and pray this film will do good rather than bad."

In the original version of the film Green's Sibylla is portrayed as someone with both a private and a public face. In public she is every inch a queen; in private she is someone who tries to turn every situation to her own advantage. Balian (ORLANDO BLOOM) turns down her husband's request to marry her; once Balian has died, Sibylla responds by taking Guy de Lusignan (MARTON CSOKAS) for a husband even though she is well aware of his anti-Muslim views. Eventually she regrets what she has done; and tries to atone for it by cutting her hair and acting as a part-time nurse for the wounded in the defense of Jerusalem. By doing this she rejects the teaching of the Bible as set forth in I Corinthians 11:15: "But if a woman have long hair, it is a glory to her; for her hair is given her for a covering." The film ends with her casting off the regal role completely, and joining the exodus of citizens from Jerusalem.

In *KINGDOM OF HEAVEN*: THE DIRECTOR'S CUT Sibylla is portrayed as much more of a corrupt princess who quite openly continues her affair with Balian. Guy does not object; he is only interested in her for political reasons. Stephanie Zacharek commended her for showing "a measure of cool that defies her surroundings: She doesn't quite know what to do with her character's stilted dialogue, but she carries herself so regally that you barely notice."

References

Lorien Haynes, "*Kingdom of Heaven*: All About Eva," *Film Review* 657 (June 2005): 52–53; Diana Landau ed., *Kingdom of Heaven: The Ridley Scott Film and the History behind the Story* (London: Simon and Schuster Ltd., 2005), 69; Stephanie Zacharek, "*Kingdom of Heaven*," *Salon.com* 6 May 2005, http://dir.salon.com/story/ent/movies/review/2005/05/06/kingdom/index.html (accessed 9 January 2009).

GREGSON-WILLIAMS, HARRY (1961–)

Made his name in British films such as *The Borrowers* (1997), *Whatever Happened to Harold Smith* (1999), and *Chicken Run* (2000). He provided an atmospheric score for *Sanctuary*, the first episode in the second series of *THE HUNGER*: TELEVISION, which only serves to emphasize the eeriness of Julian Priest's (DAVID BOWIE's) world.

He also composed the aggressively minded score for *AMERICAN FIGHTER PILOT* (2002) and for the Tony Scott-directed short *THE HIRE*: "BEAT THE DEVIL" (2002) produced by Ridley Scott.

For *KINGDOM OF HEAVEN* Gregson-Williams chose to move away from the musical styles characteristic of HANS ZIMMER in *GLADIATOR*. Rather, his score incorporates Eastern influences—incorporating music played by Turkish musicians—and early music with Bach influences. The *Music from the Movies* reviewer described Gregson-Williams's score thus: "Veering somewhere between a liturgical mass and a medieval symphony, this is a fine development of the Eastern work . . . it's an earnest accomplished piece with an appeal that grows with each listening."

Reference

Nick Joy, "Kingdom of Heaven," *Music from the Movies* 45/46 (September/October 2005): 110–11.

Bibliography

Jeff Bond, "Harry King of Scots," *Film Score Magazine* 10, no.3 (May/June 2005): 12–13.

GRIFFIN, NICK (?–) and TED (1970–)

Born Nicholas and Theodore Griffin in Pasadena, California. They co-wrote *MATCHSTICK MEN*—their first official collaboration. The experience proved interesting: Ted Griffin admitted in a preproduction interview that the two of them wrote best "by not being in the same room. If we were in the same room we'd just start tearing at each other like a couple of kids in the back of a station wagon on a long road trip." Nick prepared for the project by speaking with two FBI agents on the subject of con men: "It's not as far-fetched or antiquated as people might believe."

They were quoted in the production information as liking the book on account of its story: "It's primarily the story of a man coming to terms with himself through meeting his daughter and the relationship that develops between them. The con scenario is essential but secondary . . . These characters still exist and they're still running the same old games, but they have also branched out lately to include the Internet and telemarketing."

The first draft of the script had been written before Scott was engaged as director. It went through several changes before shooting finished. Certain sequences were deleted: for example, a scene involving Roy (NICOLAS CAGE) where he encounters a young mother; the mother hands her baby to Roy, who becomes so enamored of the experience that he resolves to call his ex-wife Heather (Melora Walters). This sequence was judged too sentimental for a comedy which tries its best to take an unsentimental look at its three central characters' lives.

Another deleted scene took place in the supermarket, where the fourteen-year-old Angela (ALISON LOHMAN) takes some cartons of beer and places them in the trolley. Other scenes were rewritten, such as the con involving the lady in the launderette (Beth Grant), which originally showed Angela keeping the three hundred dollars. In the finished film Roy persuades her to give it back to the lady. Both of these alterations emphasized Roy's underlying moral sense—in spite of being a conman, he does not like taking advantage of anyone weaker than himself; nor does he approve of the idea of underage drinking. This underlines a point made early on in the finished script, which shows Roy conning a potential customer via the telephone, and though his voice may be grinning, his eyes betray him; he doesn't enjoy it.

Scott also created new scenes for the finished film—for example, one where Frank (SAM ROCKWELL) is shown talking on a headset in his car telling Frank about the sudden change of plan involving Frechette (BRUCE McGILL). The original script describes Frank as "stressed"; the film shows that, far from being stressed, Frank takes things very calmly. This provides yet another indication that all is not what it seems. Frank carried out the next stage in his elaborate con designed to fleece Roy of his savings.

The script was described by one reviewer as competent, but "without a great deal told about the various scams that the conmen use against their unsuspecting dupes . . . Unfortunately, for me, I saw what was coming fairly early on and it was a matter of movie run time before I was proved correct. This transparency in the story took things down a notch . . ."

References
Robin Clifford, "Matchstick Men," www.reelingreviews.com/matchstickmen.htm (accessed 9 January 2009); Nick and Ted Griffin, "*Matchstick Men*: Shooting Draft" (14 October 2002), www.imsdb.com/scripts/Matchstick-Men.html (accessed 4 January 2009); *Production Information: Matchstick Men* (Los Angeles: Warner Bros. Pictures, 2003), 3–4.

Bibliography
"The Dialogue: An Interview with Ted Griffin (2006)," www.youtube.com/watch?v=k6wdoHGXcPI (accessed 9 January 2009).

GRIFFITH, MELANIE (1957–)
Born in New York City, the daughter of actress Tippi Hedren, Griffith shot to stardom in the title role of *Working Girl* (1988), a box-office hit for which she received an Oscar nomination as Best Actress and won the Golden Globe Award as Best Actress in a Comedy. She won strong reviews in independent films like *Another Day in Paradise* (1997), which helped her obtain the role of Marion Davies in *RKO 281*. Described in JOHN LOGAN's script as "a shimmering and lively presence, [who] can still charm and captivate with almost effortless grace," Griffith's Davies bears strong resemblances to the actress herself, who struggled throughout the 1980s and 1990s with drugs and other related problems.

One of her most poignant scenes comes late on in the film, where she is shown dancing with William Randolph Hearst (JAMES CROMWELL) in the ballroom at Xanadu. Director BENJAMIN ROSS's camera tracks through deserted rooms, now shorn of all their furniture and expensive antiques, and finally focuses on the two of them alone. On the soundtrack Bunny Berigan's poignant song "I Can't Get Started" can be heard, whose lyrics in a sense sum up Hearst's and Davies's relationship: "I've got a house, a show place, [but] still I can't get started with you/ 'Cause you're so supreme . . . And I scheme just for the sight of you, baby, what good does it do?" Davies knows she and Hearst will never have a happy life, but she cannot leave him. Against all odds she actually *loves* him; and love is a rare commodity in early 1940s Hollywood. Her line—"I started out as a golddigger, ya know, but goddam if I didn't fall in love with the guy"—seems especially poignant.

Reference
John Logan, "Draft Script for *RKO 281*" (dated 1 May 1997), http://sfy.ru/sfy.html?script=rko218 (accessed 16 November 2008), 12.

GUINNESS—PLOUGHMAN
GB 1979 Commercial r/t 30 sec col. *Production Company*: RSA Films for J. Walter Thompson. *Director*: Ridley Scott.

This commercial opens with a close-up of a bottle opener, and a top being removed from a bottle, then cuts to a shot of a plough being lowered onto hay. Scott cuts back to a close-up of bread being cut (recalling the HOVIS BREAD advertisement) then to a shot of a cold Guinness being poured into a glass. The action switches to an exterior shot of the plough being operated in a field, followed by a close-up of cheese being cut and the Guinness glass being filled. Scott cuts back to a shot of the ploughman finishing his work and getting out of the cabin; then back to a shot of the complete ploughman's lunch—bread, cheese, tomatoes, onion, and Guinness. The Guinness is handed over to a pair of hands emerging from the left of the frame. The advertisement finishes with a dissolve to a shot of the ploughman sitting at a table in the pub, flanked by two of his friends, sipping the beer and beginning to eat. The slogan is heard in voiceover: "If you want to know how good a bottle of Guinness is, ask a ploughman."

GUINNESS—WHAT'S MY LINE
(aka GOOD FOR YOU)
GB 1975 Commercial r/t 30 sec col. *Production Company*: RSA Films for J. Walter Thompson. *Director*: Ridley Scott.

A commercial showing how Guinness can relax people. It begins with a shot of two young men in a pub drinking their beer, while all around them the other patrons seem to be under stress. A man is shown playing a fruit machine; two women drunkenly gossip with one another; another man upsets a chair in his excitement; and a secretary drums her fingers on the table as she waits for her companion to fetch a drink. The soundtrack emphasizes the pressure these customers experience with specific sounds: the man plays the fruit machine to the sound of a factory drill; the woman drums her fingers to the sound of a typewriter. Meanwhile the two men drink their beer calmly and silently. On the soundtrack a voice tells us, "After work, there are some people who relax" and enjoy "the first, slow rewarding taste" of the beer, rather than continuing to work.

This is another commercial demonstrating Scott's interest in telling a story while selling a product. As in *BLADE RUNNER*, many of the people in the pub are portrayed as dehumanized—so wrapped up in their working lives that they have lost the capacity to think for themselves. It is only when they relax that they can become human once again.

HALF HOUR STORY: "ROBERT"

GB 1967 TVM r/t 30 min b/w. *Production Company:* Rediffusion. *Producer:* Stella Richman. *Director:* Ridley Scott. *Writer:* Jeremy Paul from an original story by Stanley Ellin. *Cast:* Angela Baddeley (*Miss Gildea*), Frank Windsor (*Mr. Harkness*), Suzanne Neve (*Miss Reardon*), Robert Langley (*Robert*).

A contribution to Independent Television's weekly anthology series of single dramas, about the relationship between a school mistress and one of her pupils; an eleven-year-old boy named Robert, whose inattentive behavior in class belies a manipulative and malevolent nature. This was episode 12 (out of 29) in the first series, broadcast live on 2 August 1967. The series ran from 16 May to 30 September 1967. *Half Hour Story* ran three seasons until 29 July 1968, with a total of thirty-seven episodes.

HAMPTON, TIM (?–)

Production Manager on British films such as *The Ruling Class* (1973) and *Superman* (1978). Associate Producer on *Monty Python's Life of Brian* (1979). Hampton co-produced *LEGEND*, being particularly responsible for the filming at Pinewood Studios.

HANNAH, DARYL (1960–)

Born and raised in Chicago, Daryl Hannah attended the University of Southern California, and made her debut as Pam in Brian DePalma's *The Fury* (1978).

Cast as Pris in *BLADE RUNNER*, Hannah portrays the character as someone young, naïve, almost like a four-year-old child in her reliance on Batty (RUTGER HAUER), who never has the capacity to relax with Sebastian (WILLIAM SANDERSON). According to PAUL M. SAMMON she is simply "working on a deadline." Likened in one of the production's scripts to "a savage doll with a bleached white face and black ringed eyes," she sniffs Sebastian like a cat stalking its prey; her eyes glow, reminding us that she is a REPLICANT. When she hears that Zhora (JOANNA CASSIDY) and Leon (BRION JAMES) have been "retired" (i.e., killed

off) she idly twirls the torso of a broken doll between her fingers, reminding us that despite her strength she is as expendable as them.

In a scene with strong sexual overtones, Pris scissor-grips Deckard's (HARRISON FORD's) head between her thighs and forces him on to his back. Visually speaking, he resembles the monstrous child of the replicant emerging from her body, rather like the creature emerging from Kane's (JOHN HURT's) stomach in *ALIEN*. This underlines the inherent corruption of the *Blade Runner* world—in a society where replicants assume the responsibilities once undertaken by human beings, "natural" births no longer exist. Pris jams her fingers into Deckard's nostrils and lifts his head off the floor, causing his nose to bleed. She moves across the room and cartwheels towards Deckard for her final assault, but Deckard kills her with his gun.

In PHILIP K. DICK's original novel, Rachael and Pris are identical types, making it difficult for Deckard to kill Pris. Scott thought it would be unworkable to have the two look alike. However, he does allow Pris an honorable death, as Batty puts her tongue back in her mouth and kisses her. In a later sequence, the grief-stricken Batty touches the wound in her stomach and then his lips, retracing the spot where Pris touched him when they last met. This moment, according to Scott (interviewed in the *New York Times* prior to the film's American opening), provides the "trigger" for Batty to take revenge on all those people—Deckard included—who seek to curtail the replicants' lives.

References

Glenn Collins, "Blade Runner," *New York Times*, 30 June 1982, C19; Hampton Fancher and David Peoples, "Blade Runner," Unpublished script dated 23 February 1981, now in the British Film Institute, London; Paul M. Sammon, *Future Noir: The Making of Blade Runner*, 2nd ed. (London: Gollancz, 2007), 140.

HANNAN, PETER (1941–)

Australian-born cinematographer whose work includes *The Meaning of Life* (1983), *Withnail and I* (1987), and *Not Without My Daughter* (1991).

As cinematographer on the Ridley Scott-produced film *THE GATHERING STORM*, Hannan worked with director RICHARD LONCRAINE to produce a film which moved away from a picture-postcard image of England in the 1930s to a more realistic depiction. In an interview with Matthew Bell he recalled, "It's been dark and miserable [filming *The Gathering Storm*] and the only scene we have in the sun is scripted for rain. It used to be that this was one of the best times to shoot . . . We were allowed to shoot at Chartwell and one of the reasons we were there was to be able to see outside but we haven't been able to because of the weather. It has an extraordinary dining room with almost three sides of glass looking out over a wonderful valley . . . It's meant to be bright and sunny; that's the reason the Churchills were there and it even comes up in the script. He bought the house because he particularly loved the view. We've provided artificial sun, filters endlessly on and off, and basically got away with murder." Loncraine explained his aims in an interview: "I was very anxious that we should not have a film that was all about regal buildings and historical buildings . . . not just high society in pillared halls . . . Opening out the movie. Giving it more air."

References

Matthew Bell, "Location Story: A Lonely War Brings Churchill Back to Life," *Broadcast B+*, 7 December 2001, 3; "Interview with Richard Loncraine," *The Gathering Storm: Artist Interviews*, www.hbo.com/films/gatheringstorm/cmp/interviews.shtml (Accessed 24 December 2008).

HANNIBAL

US 2001 r/t 132 min col. *Production Companies*: Metro-Goldwyn-Mayer Pictures, Inc., Universal Studios, and Scott Free. *Producer*: Dino de Laurentiis. *Director*: Ridley Scott. *Writers*: David Mamet and Stephen Zaillian from the novel *Hannibal* by Thomas Harris. *Director of Photography*: John Mathieson. *Production Designer*: Norris Spencer. *Music*: Hans Zimmer. *Cast*: Anthony Hopkins (*Hannibal Lecter*), Julianne Moore (*Clarice Starling*), Ray Liotta (*Paul Krendler*), Gary Oldman (*Mason Verger*), Frankie R. Faison (*Nurse Barney*), Giancarlo Giannini (*Insp. Renaldo Pazzi*), Francesca Neri (*Allegra Pazzi*), Zeljko Ivanek (*Dr. Cordell Doemling*).

The idea for making *Hannibal*, a sequel to the money-spinning *THE SILENCE OF THE LAMBS*, was mentioned throughout the 1990s. JODIE FOSTER felt that director JONATHAN DEMME's film had equaled author THOMAS HARRIS's achievement of blending the popular with the cerebral: "I loved *Silence*. It's a movie that's stuck with me . . . It's both very complex and very literary, and at the same time great entertainment." ANTHONY HOPKINS likewise spoke enthusiastically of playing Hannibal Lecter once again and reuniting with Foster and Demme: "However, we must wait for the author Tom Harris to finish the story. You cannot rush him." Having passed on the film rights to *The Silence of the Lambs*, producer DINO DE LAURENTIIS did not intend to let the third installment in the Hannibal saga elude him. In May 1999, media reports claimed that he was close to buying the film rights for a reported $9 million, reportedly the biggest book-to-film deal ever. Eventually he came to an agreement with Universal Pictures to make the film, but Metro-Goldwyn Mayer claimed that it held all rights to Jodie Foster's character Clarice Starling, purchased from Orion Pictures when the latter went bankrupt. Industry insiders predicted a major bidding war for the rights, de Laurentiis and Universal going head-to-head with MGM. In the event, however, the parties settled on a co-production: MGM would distribute *Hannibal* in North America and Canada, while Universal handled the overseas markets.

Thomas Harris's sequel finally appeared in June 1999, becoming the fastest-selling hardback fiction work of all time in the United Kingdom. Most reviewers welcomed it, but there were certain dissenters who objected to the rambling plot, the graphic violence, and the finale. At the same time, Demme announced that he would not be directing the film version, in the belief that "irresponsible violent screen images could influence aggressive male behaviour, going out and performing real violence against other people." Daniel O'Brien speculates that Demme also was wary of working with De Laurentiis, as the producer was not known for granting his directors full creative control over their work. TED TALLY, the screenwriter of *Silence*, also refused to work on the sequel. De Laurentiis's first choice to replace Demme was Scott, who had previously worked with the producer on an adaptation of Frank Herbert's *DUNE* (1984)—even though Scott himself had left the project, to be replaced by David Lynch. Unlike Demme, Scott loved the book, finding Hannibal Lecter "a very charming character" and resolving to inject the sequel with the kind of humor that was conspicuously absent from *Silence*: "I shall be very disappointed if I hear that people aren't smiling. When they're not screaming." Ridley Scott recruited key members of his *GLADIATOR* crew for the new project, including director of photography JOHN MATHIESON, film editor PIETRO SCALIA, composers Klaus Badelt and HANS ZIMMER, and costume designer JANTY YATES.

However, there remained problems over casting: Foster still did not like the book. Harris agreed to supply a less repulsive ending for the film version, replacing the cannibalistic original. However even the new ending could not convince her to repeat her role: "The original movie worked because people believed in Clarice's heroism. I won't play her with negative attributes she would never have." Eventually she passed on the role, concentrating instead on a new directorial project *Flora Plum*. De Laurentiis claimed in an interview that he didn't really want Foster at all: "I don't believe Judy [sic] Foster from day one was right when I read the book."

Hopkins was furious because he had committed himself to the part and Universal was already over budget. The studio apparently considered abandoning the project, but the success of *Gladiator* assured them that Hannibal could work without Foster on board. Scott interviewed various leading ladies, including Gillian Anderson and Cate Blanchett, before settling on JULIANNE MOORE, whom he believed brought "a sharp intelligence and intensity" to the role of Clarice, even if she lacked Foster's "fan expectations of toughness and sexual enigma." Finally convinced that the new Lecter film would not be a "tawdry follow-up" to *Silence*, Hopkins finally signed on for a fee of $15 million plus a share in the profits. The third lead part of Mason Verger was filled by GARY OLDMAN, with other roles played by RAY LIOTTA, GIANCARLO GIANNINI, and FRANCESCA NERI.

The screenplay was originally written by DAVID MAMET, but STEVEN ZAILLIAN was brought in later on to go through the Harris novel and the Mamet screenplay, deciding which characters and story details would have to be changed, rearranged, or dropped altogether. In collaboration with Harris, he produced a new ending, in which Lecter and Clarice did not go off together. Despite the changes, Zaillian still felt that Hannibal was primarily a kind of "bizarre love story." Scott told Douglas Eby that he was satisfied with the finished product: "This has been a rather good experience. The problem with the book . . . is distilling long form into shorter form . . . and I think we've managed to do that . . . Only those who ask for it; only, as Hannibal puts it, the 'free-range rude' get retribution. So those who find their own comeuppance, certainly deserve it."

Budgeted at a healthy $87 million, *Hannibal* was filmed in Florence, ITALY; Richmond, Virginia; Washington, DC; and Asheville, North Carolina. The shoot was largely uneventful, but at the post-production stage Orion Pictures threatened legal action, claiming all rights to the Hannibal Lecter character traits in *The Silence of the Lambs* film that were not in Harris's original book. If Hopkins reused any of his distinctive such as the reference to eating a human being "with fava beans and a nice chianti," Orion would sue Universal and MGM. Rather than risk a lengthy expensive court case that might delay *Hannibal*'s release, MGM made cuts to the finished film.

Philip L. Simpson suggests that the various controversies over casting—which did not end once filming had finished, as Gary Oldman refused to take screen credit—served mainly to increase interest level in the finished product. As with many of Scott's films, the reviewers were divided. While Sean Macaulay described the effect as "strangely haunting,"

Mark Wilson of *The Independent* observed that while the film "might make a play for the high moral ground as a meditation on taste . . . it can't make up for a hollowness at its centre." Alexander Walker of the *Evening Standard* observed that the director's "pacing, editing and photography are all impeccably attuned to keeping your nerves on edge and the sick bag handy." Hopkins's performance generated similarly diverse opinions: Will Self thought it "cartoon-like," while J. Hoberman likened it to "a sinister Truman Capote—portly and soigné, peeking coyly from beneath his trademark Panama hat" and Peter Bradshaw of *The Guardian* described Hopkins's performance as "a show-stopping turn at the centre of the picture."

The film was a huge hit both in America and Great Britain, more than doubling its original budget by August 2001. It also inspired a cult of fashion: Alison Roberts in the *Evening Standard* reported that Hannibal's style was so chic so as to resemble anything on the cover of *Gentleman's Quarterly*.

Hannibal returns to the theme of the maverick law enforcement officer explored in earlier Scott films such as *SOMEONE TO WATCH OVER ME* and *BLACK RAIN*. Like Mike Keegan (TOM BERENGER) in *Someone*, Clarice Starling considers herself a model professional, concerned to stamp her authority over her male colleagues. When Officer Bolton (Terry Serpico) tells her that he is in charge of the drug raid at the fish market, Starling replies icily, "You're here . . . because our mayor wants to appear tough on drugs, especially after his own cocaine conviction . . . I'd appreciate if you took a step or two back, you're in my light." Bolton responds weakly, "You got a smart mouth, lady." In another sequence deleted from the finished film she threatens the nurse, Barney (FRANKIE FAISON), with the full force of the law unless he returns the stolen X-ray of Hannibal's broken arm: "[Your] reward is I don't have my friend the postal inspector nail you on *Use of the Mails to Defraud*, you don't get ten years, and you don't come out with a janitor's job." However, this devotion to duty comes at a price, as it renders her incapable of experiencing a personal life. Hannibal is well aware of her plight: "You fell in love with the bureau—with The Institution [the FBI]—only to discover, after giving it everything, that it doesn't love you. That is resents you, more than the husband and children you gave up to it ever would." Clarice's professionalism proves futile in the end, as her department suspends her without pay for incompetence and orders her to clear her desk. Scott shows her returning home with a cardboard box full of mementoes of her working life—ornaments, stationery and the like. She has nothing left to remind her of her service to the FBI except these few belongings.

Unlike Starling, the other members of the Bureau are portrayed as corrupt, ever ready to take bribes or manipulate the law according to their own ends. Agent Krendler (Ray Liotta) is more than willing to accept Mason Verger's (Gary Oldman's) forged postcard (allegedly written by Hannibal to Clarice) as evidence in the case against Clarice, in return for a five hundred thousand dollar bribe. Although Clarice publicly reveals Krendler's motives ("[he] is in collusion with him [Verger] and wants the FBI's effort against Dr. Lecter to work for Mr. Verger"), no one listens to her. Assistant Director Noonan (Francis Guinan) threatens her instead: "You'll be entitled to full reinstatement without prejudice—if you don't do—or say—something in the meantime that would make that impossible." Krendler consciously prevents Clarice from pursuing this course of action by commending her on television as "one of the best agents we have . . . I would be very surprised if the accusations [against her] turn out to be true." If she were to make her accusations public, it would reflect badly on her, not the Bureau. Like the two presidential candidates in THE LAST DEBATE, Krendler understands the importance of sustaining a reliable public image, even if it means consciously manipulating the media.

Like Krendler, the Italian police officer Renaldo Pazzi (Giancarlo Giannini) becomes a victim of corruption as he accepts a financial reward in return for passing on information to the FBI about Hannibal's whereabouts, in spite of his concern for his "so-called reputation." He writes down the telephone numbers in pen on the back of his hand and dials them. Once the deed has been done, Pazzi is shown scrubbing his hands "like Lady Macbeth, trying to get the stain of the phone numbers off his skin, the black ink clouding the water pooling in the sink before going down the drain." However much he might try, he can never rid himself of the sin he has committed.

On this view, Hannibal's determination to kill Pazzi and Krendler can be seen as justified; like the avenging angel, he sees his task as ridding the world of the "free-range rude"— those people lacking a proper understanding of the differences between right and wrong. He reminds Pazzi of his ancestor, who was hanged outside the Palazzo Vecchio in Florence for having killed Giuliano de Medici. During his lecture in the Palazzo, Hannibal espies Pazzi in the background and shows a slide of Judas Iscariot on the doors of the cathedral, hanging with his bowels falling out, as St. Luke the physician described him in the Acts of the Apostles. It comes as no surprise to find Pazzi being put to death in similar fashion, as he is tied to a lectern and hanged out of a window of the Palazzo, his bowels spilling out onto the ground below. In a macabre parody of the Last Supper, Krendler—another Judas-figure—is served part of his own brain, lightly fried in butter.

Throughout the film Scott contrasts the new world of America with the old world of Renaissance Europe. This is sustained not only visually—with the modern buildings of

Washington, DC, set against the Florentine architecture (described in the script as "one of the most magnificent views in the world")—but also in terms of value-systems. America is equated with superficiality, a world of casual affairs where sexism runs rife and where true friendship between men and women no longer exists. Krendler has no respect either for his wife or for his colleagues, repeatedly describing Starling as a piece of "cornpone country pussy." Nonetheless, he would be more than willing to enjoy a one-night stand with her. This world depends first and foremost on money; those who possess it can enjoy almost unlimited freedom. Mason Verger boasts at one point that he has "immunity from the US Attorney . . . immunity from the DA in Owings Mills . . . [and] immunity from the Risen Jesus and no one beats the Riz."

The world of Europe, as portrayed in the film, is one where the past never goes away: Pazzi is haunted by the misdeeds of his ancestor. Even at the opera house he witnesses a performance of the "Vide Cor Meum" (composed especially for the film by PATRICK CASSIDY), which symbolically reenacts the murder of Giuliano de Medici. Europe is also identified with permanence—as shown, for instance, in the perfume on Hannibal's letter to Clarice, comprised of Tennessee lavender, mountain sage, fleece, and ambergris (a whale product ensuring that the smell stays fresh for years). The same also applies to Hannibal's love for Clarice, which is likened throughout to DANTE ALIGHIERI's enduring affair with Beatrice Portinari. In a long speech to Pazzi's wife Allegra (Francesca Neri), Hannibal quotes from a sonnet written by Dante in which he experiences a disturbing dream in which "My lady lay asleep wrapped in a veil. He [the poet] woke her then, and, trembling and obedient, she ate that burning heart out of his hand." Incredulous, Allegra asks whether it is possible that a man could become so obsessed with a woman; Hannibal responds that anyone "might feel a stab of hunger for her [and] find nourishment in the very sight of her." The violence of the imagery here foreshadows the sequence at the end of the film, when Hannibal cuts his own hand off with a meat cleaver, so as to free himself from being handcuffed to Clarice. His love for her is so enduring that he is prepared to mutilate himself rather than cause harm to her.

The fact that the two will remain together eternally is also suggested in the final shot of Clarice, who stands at the boat dock in her evening gown watching Hannibal's distant signal—fireworks, the traditional film code of consummation—from another shore.

There have been numerous critical evaluations of the film. Linda Mizejewski admires Clarice's stoicism—even though she is badly treated by the FBI, she refuses "to go over, to turn outlaw." She concentrates on the ways in which the actors have in a sense determined the audience's responses to the characters: Jodie Foster's screen persona informs Clarice to such an extent that it shapes the way in which the character has been written in both the novel and film versions of *Hannibal*: "Though the novel's focus is Hannibal Lecter, its treatment of Clarice reveals repeated themes of stardom; the public image of this character, its interrogation, and its incitement to discover its private counterpart constitute a powerful subtext." Philip L. Simpson expresses a similar view, by arguing that "*Hannibal* is a horror event film . . . [with] a plethora of style but only an echo of substance . . . If the horror event movie is designed to soothe the consumer with pleasant reiterations of a loved and familiar formula given a certain ironic distance, *Hannibal* succeeds on those terms." He does not see any significance in the Dante references, other than a "rather obvious and spectacular application of . . . poetic justice to the 'free range' greedy and rude, such as Pazzi and Krendler." In similar vein, Ernest Mathijs argues that "those responsible for establishing *Hannibal* as horror (producers, marketers, critics, fans) have, consciously or not, been building upon a reference frame that has been in development since *The Silence of the Lambs* (hereafter *SOTL*). This reference frame focuses on the film's main character, Hannibal Lecter, and his function as the quintessential monster in/of culture. The presentation of this character as the kind of "cultural thing" that horror films have always dealt with, has not only guaranteed the ancillary labeling of *Hannibal* as horror."

David Schmid contrasts the novel and the film versions in detail, and concludes that the film is a good example of a "subversive adaptation": "It is the film's subversion of Harris's novel that makes the film superior and this superiority is especially clear when we consider how the filmic Hannibal represents Lecter's violence."

References

Peter Bradshaw, "Take Me to the Liver," *The Guardian*, 16 February 2001, 12–13; Jonathan Demme, quoted in Daniel O'Brien, *The Hannibal Files: The Unauthorised Guide to the Hannibal Lecter Trilogy* (Richmond, Surrey: Reynolds & Hearn Ltd., 2001), 139; Dino de Laurentiis, quoted in *The Hannibal Files*, 148; Douglas Eby, "Ridley Scott: The Director on Adapting the Thomas Harris Novel," *Cinefantastique* 32, no.6 (February 2001): 15; Jodie Foster, quoted in *The Hannibal Files*, 137; J. Hoberman, "Appetites for Destruction," *Village Voice*, 13 February 2001, 127; Anthony Hopkins, quoted in *The Hannibal Files*, 137; Sean Macaulay, "What's Eating You?" *The Times*, 5 February 2001, Section 2, 21; Ernest Mathijs, "The 'Wonderfully Scary Monster' and the International Reception of Horror: Ridley Scott's *Hannibal* (2001)," *Kinoscope* 2, no.19 (2 December 2002): www.kinoeye.org/02/19/mathijs19.php (accessed 3 August 2008); Linda Mizejewski, "Stardom and Serial Fantasies: Thomas Harris' *Hannibal*," in *Keyframes: Popular Cinema and Cultural Studies*, ed. Matthew Tinkcom and Amy Villarejo (London

and New York: Routledge, 2001), 161; Daniel O'Brien, *The Hannibal Files*, 143, 147, 151; Alison Roberts, "Lecter: Style to Die For," *Evening Standard*, 16 February 2001, 30–31; David Schmid, "The Kindest Cut of All: Adapting Thomas Harris' *Hannibal*," *Literature/Film Quarterly* 35, no.1 (2007): 7; Ridley Scott, quoted in *The Hannibal Files*, 143; Ridley Scott, quoted in Linda Mizejewski, *Hardboiled and High Heeled: The Woman Detective in Popular Culture* (London and New York: Routledge, 2004), 193; Will Self, "Hannibal," *Independent on Sunday Culture*, 11 February 2001, 1–2; Philip L. Simpson, "The Horror 'Event' Movie: *The Mummy, Hannibal* and *Signs*," in *Horror Film: Creating and Marketing Fear*, ed. Steffen Hantke (Jackson: University Press of Mississippi, 2005), 92; Alexander Walker, "Hannibal's Second Bite," *Evening Standard*, 6 February 2001, 8; Mark Wilson, "Lecter's Bloody Second Course has a Hollow Centre," *The Independent*, 6 February 2001, 9; Steven Zaillian, "*Hannibal*: Screenplay Based on the Novel by Thomas Harris," Revision (9 February 2000), http://sfy.ru/sfy.html?script=hannibal2001 (accessed 15 December 2008).

Bibliography

Douglas Bankston, "A Pound of Flesh," *American Cinematographer* 82, no.2 (February 2001): 36–49; Jill Bernstein, "Eat Drink Man Woman," *Premiere* 14, no.6 (February 2001): 59–61, 106–7; Andrew Collins, "He's Back," *Observer Screen*, 16 May 1999, 2–3; Barbara Creed, "Freud's Worst Nightmare: Dining with Dr. Hannibal Lecter," in *Horror Film and Psychoanalysis: Freud's Worst Nightmare* (Cambridge: Cambridge University Press, 2004), 199–202; Nikki Finke, "A Tough Act to Swallow," *The Guardian* 8 June 1999, Section 2: 10–11; Leigh Joyce Harding, "A Dangerous Woman and a Man's Brain: Mina Harker, Clarice Starling and the Empowerment of the Gothic Heroine in Novel and Film," *West Virginia University Philological Papers* 49 (2002–2003): 30–37; John Hiscock, "For Grisly, Call Ridley," *Daily Telegraph*, 18 April 2000, 26; John Hiscock, "Grisly Second Bite at the Lecter Story," *Daily Telegraph*, 2 February 2001, 25; Russell Lissau, "Hannibal," *Cinefantastique* 32, no.2 (August 2000): 6–7; Jenny McCartney and Olga Craig, "Mad, Bad . . . But Very Very Loveable," *Sunday Telegraph Focus*, 18 February 2001, 21; Mark Monahan, "Lecter Gets His Teeth into Florence," *Daily Telegraph Arts*, 20 May 2000, A6; Mick McKeown and Mark Stowell-Smith, "The Comforts of Evil: Dangerous Personalities in High-Security Hospitals and the Horror Film," in *Forensic Psychiatry: Influences of Evil*, ed. Tom Mason (Totowa, NJ: Humana Press, 2006), 109–35; Mark Morris, "Pleased to Eat You," *Observer Review*, 4 February 2001, 9; Gary Oldman, "Annus Hannibalis," *Time Out*, 14–21 February 2001, 24, 26; Alun Palmer, "£15m. for Hopkins as He Agrees to the Sequel of the Lambs," *Daily Mail*, 30 September 1999, 27; Paul M. Sammon, "Feeding Hannibal," *Fangoria* 200 (March 2001): 34–39; David Sexton, "Why We Will Always Be Frightened—" *Evening Standard*, 16 February 2001, 13; Adam Smith, "Signed, Sealed, De-livered," *Empire* 141 (March 2001): 70–76; Charles Whitehouse, "Hannibal Magnetism," *Sight and Sound* 11, no.1 (January 2001): 4–5.

HANSON, CURTIS (1945-)

Began his career as director and scriptwriter on films such as *The Hand That Rocks the Cradle* (1992) and *The River Wild* (1994). Engaged by Ridley Scott as director for *IN HER SHOES*, Hanson admitted in a preproduction interview that he "decided to make this movie for the same reason that I made my last four movies which is that I responded emotionally—to the characters and to the themes. The fact that these three characters were all women was exciting and different for me. As a movie-goer, it was also exciting because I've loved many female-driven films in the past. I loved the opportunity to work with three actors who would be necessary to get good performances from . . . It's like working on a political campaign where you're working so hard with people all toward a common goal. Outsiders, no matter how close they are to you, really can't be a part of it. That's what it was like with this movie, which was so much of a personal movie for everyone involved with it."

Hanson's emphasis on character is complemented by a strong visual imagination. As well as using the paintings of John Register to suggest loneliness, he uses the black-and-white photographs of Weegee (the pseudonym of Arthur Fellig [1899–1968]) of smiling children taken at movie theaters during the 1940s to emphasize the importance of the past for both main characters, Maggie (CAMERON DIAZ) and Rose (TONI COLLETTE). At one point Rose loses her temper and slams Maggie into the wall; the camera focuses on Maggie's tear-stained face, flanked by the photographs. Neither sister had ever managed to overcome the trauma of losing their mother Caroline, who committed suicide when Maggie was just six years old.

Hanson encourages his cast to play against type. SHIRLEY MACLAINE is normally associated with flamboyant roles; in this film she plays someone who registers emotional hurt through a single gesture—for example, a look away from the camera. This achievement was noted in another article published in *The Guardian* prior to the film's opening: "Hanson has an ability to get actors to play against audience expectations. [He believes that] people can and do change, often for the better. Things change. If I didn't believe in that I wouldn't see the point. In any of it."

References

Brad Balfour, "Curtis Hanson: The Director Steps into a Woman's World," PopEntertainment.com (15 October 2005), www.popentertainment.com/curtishanson.htm (accessed 8 August 2008); Ben Marshall, "If the Shoe Fits, Film It," *Guardian Guide*, 19 November 2005, 8–10.

HARMER, JULIET (1943–)

Juliet Harmer made her name playing Georgina Jones in *ADAM ADAMANT LIVES!* She was not the original choice for the role: Ann Holloway played it in the never-broadcast pilot episode, but was considered "not quite sixties enough" by producer VERITY LAMBERT. Lambert wanted someone more boyish, so that she could satisfy the requirements of BBC Head of Drama Sydney Newman, who had originally conceived the role for a male actor.

Harmer's performance as Georgina can best be described as feisty. Although willing to follow Adam on his various adventures, she seldom listens to anything he says to her. Whenever he orders her to stay at home and keep out of danger, we can be sure that she will do precisely the opposite. Georgina was a typical 1960s girl—a fun-loving, happy-go-lucky personality seeking new experiences. In "THE LEAGUE OF UNCHARITABLE LADIES," directed by Scott, her curiosity puts her in peril as she is hypnotized by the evil butler Randolph (JOHN CARSON) and instructed to kill Adam with a poisoned flag (the kind one receives after having given money to charity). Needless to say, Adam escapes in the end.

Despite her self-willed nature, Georgina can never leave Adam's side. One of her favorite catchphrases, appearing at the end of several episodes, is "Wait for me!" as she runs out of the frame in hot pursuit of her companion.

Reference

Verity Lambert, interviewed in *This Man Is the One* (documentary marking the 40th anniversary of *Adam Adamant Lives!* (London: BBC Worldwide, 2006).

HARPER, GERALD (1929–)

Suave leading actor, the star of two long-running television series—*ADAM ADAMANT LIVES!* (1966-1967) and *Hadleigh* (1968, 1969–1976).

Born in London and trained at the Royal Academy of Dramatic Art, Harper made his film debut in 1956 and appeared as a supporting actor in many British films over the next decade. At the time he was offered the leading role in *Adam Adamant Lives!* he was due to appear on Broadway, but the producers released him from his contract.

Harper plays Adam Adamant as a perfect English gentleman. Always polite—even to his enemies—he invariably finishes his exchanges with the phrase "Your servant, sir." He treats women with respect, even those who cause harm to him. Like Roger Moore (a near-contemporary who also made his name during the 1960s in a television adventure series—*The Saint*), Harper is the master of the throwaway look, the ironically raised eyebrow denoting surprise or displeasure, especially when confronted with an aspect of contemporary life that he dislikes.

Harper's Adam is not afraid of a fight: many episodes of *Adam Adamant Lives!* contain levels of violence that might seem unacceptable by today's standards. In Scott's

"THE LEAGUE OF UNCHARITABLE LADIES," Adam has a violent sword fight with Randolph (JOHN CARSON) that only comes to an end when Randolph is poisoned by Hope (Sheila Grant). The episode ends with Adam smiling broadly and congratulating Georgina (JULIET HARMER) on her "devious femininity" in being able to penetrate the ladies' club and discover exactly what is happening inside. Adam might never understand the concept of a liberated woman, but he has to accept the fact that they have the power to act on their own initiative. Hence the rare show of emotion towards Georgina.

HARRIS, RICHARD (1931–2002)

Born in Limerick, Ireland, Harris made his film debut in a comedy *Alive and Kicking* (1958). He shot to stardom as a result of playing the leading role in an adaptation of David Storey's *This Sporting Life* (1963).

Harris was originally signed to play Commodus in *THE FALL OF THE ROMAN EMPIRE* (1964) but left the cast after a dispute with the director Anthony Mann. The part was eventually played by Christopher Plummer. Like OLIVER REED, Harris's reputation was as much dependent on his off-screen antics as much as his film performances. Both men had a reputation for being hard-drinking womanizers. By the late 1990s, Harris's movie career had declined; apart from a leading role in *The Field* (1989), he had scarcely featured in many films. Scott cast him in *GLADIATOR* as Marcus, a character whom Harris described in the book of the film as "a man in crisis, wrestling with demons. He was a scholar and a philosopher, but he spent sixteen of his twenty years as emperor fighting battles and spilling blood to expand the empire. Now nearing the end, he comes to realize that his life has been a fraud, and that he has actually ruined his children—especially Commodus." Although once a great leader, he now understands that he paid insufficient attention to domestic concerns. When Maximus (RUSSELL CROWE) describes his family life in the film, focusing in particular on his vineyards with "grapes on the south slopes, olives to the north [and] . . . ponies play[ing] near the house," Marcus responds somewhat enviously "I envy you, Maximus. It is a good home." However, Marcus cannot allow Maximus to fulfill his dream of returning home; on the contrary, he offers the general the position of protector of Rome. This decision underlines Marcus's inability to understand people; if he really did, he would have realized that Maximus would never accept the position. Marcus is eventually smothered to death by Commodus, who cannot accept the fact that his faults as a son were entirely attributable to his father's failings.

Harris gives a restrained performance, which seems quite at odds with his off-screen reputation.

References

"*Gladiator* by David Franzoni, revised by John Logan," Transcribed from the film, http://sfy.ru/sfy/html?script=gladiator_ts (accessed 29 November 2008); Richard Harris, quoted in Diana Landau, ed., *Gladiator: The Making of the Ridley Scott Epic* (Basingstoke and London: Boxtree, 2000), 59.

HARRIS, THOMAS (1940–)

A native of Mississippi, Thomas Harris began his writing career covering crime in the United States and Mexico, and was a reporter and editor for the Associated Press in New York City. His first novel *Black Sunday* appeared in 1976, followed by *Red Dragon* (1981), *THE SILENCE OF THE LAMBS* (1988), and *HANNIBAL* (1999). The last of these was filmed by Scott two years later.

After the success of *The Silence of the Lambs*, both as a book and film, Harris admitted that he "dreaded doing *Hannibal*, dreaded the personal wear and tear, dreaded the choices I would have to watch, feared for Starling. In the end I let them go, as you must let characters go, let Dr. Lecter and Clarice Starling decide events according to their natures. There is a certain amount of courtesy involved."

Hannibal centers on the efforts of a former Lecter victim, the paralyzed and faceless multi-millionaire meat-packing magnate Mason Verger, to enlist the aid of corrupt Italian cops, snuff-film makers, pig trainers, and sleazy Justice Department official Paul Krendler in capturing Lecter and then feeding him alive to a herd of swine. When the novel was first published, it attracted considerable criticism—especially the climax, which places Starling and Lecter in a mutually cannibalistic and romantic union. Philip L. Simpson reports that many readers from the general public expressed almost apoplectic levels of outrage. The novelist Will Self has argued that whereas in *Red Dragon* and *Silence of the Lambs* "Harris never compromised his creation's fictional integrity by attempting to explain his behaviour or his motivations," in *Hannibal* this compromise begins when, for the first time, "Harris takes his reader into the hidden depths of Lecter's mind by the somewhat contrived means of the 'memory palace.'" Another critic, Linda Mizejewski, argued that Harris's ending transforms Clarice "into elegance, myth and romance . . . Left behind are those women colleagues at the FBI for whom Clarice was 'kind of special.' Left behind also are disappointed readers like me, to whom Clarice was also 'kind of special,' the courageous rescuer of another woman and once embodied by JODIE FOSTER."

Almost as soon as planning for the film version of *Hannibal* had begun, it was felt that Harris's conclusion, which featured Hannibal and Clarice in an apparently consensual sexual relationship, would simply have to be dropped. Screenwriter STEVEN ZAILLIAN kept the two of them apart, dropped the references to Lecter's memory palace, and omitted any mention of the trauma occasioned by the death of Lecter's sister. According to David Schmid, this new version ensured that Hannibal remained a mystery, a man without a past, a monster rather than a victim, who murders partly for retributive justice and partly to indulge his flair for the dramatic.

References

Thomas Harris, "Foreword to a Fatal Interview," in *The Hannibal Lecter Omnibus* (London: William Heinemann, 2000), ix–x; Linda Mizejewski, *Hardboiled and High Heeled: The Woman Detective in Popular Culture* (London and New York: Routledge, 2004), 191–92. David Schmid, "The Kindest Cut of All: Adapting Thomas Harris' *Hannibal*," *Literature/Film Quarterly* 35, no.1 (2007): 394; Will Self, quoted in Schmid, "The Kindest Cut of All: Adapting Thomas Harris' *Hannibal*," 393; Philip L. Simpson, "Gothic Romance and Killer Couples in *Black Sunday* and *Hannibal*," in *Dissecting Hannibal Lecter: Essays on the Novels of Thomas Harris*, ed. Benjamin Szumskyj (Jefferson, NC and London: McFarland & Company Inc., 2008), 50.

Bibliography

Neil McDonald, "Dr. Lecter, I Presume," *Quadrant* 45, no.4 (April 2001): 59–62; Jack Morgan, *The Biology of Horror: Gothic Literature and Film* (Carbondale and Edwardsville: Southern Illinois University Press, 2002).

HARTNETT, JOSH (1978–)

Hartnett came to prominence in the teen horror crossover film *The Faculty*, directed by Robert Rodriguez (1999). Also cast in a lead role in *Pearl Harbor* (2001) produced by JERRY BRUCKHEIMER. On the strength of this performance, Bruckheimer cast him in *BLACK HAWK DOWN*. The *Pearl Harbor* director of the latter film, Michael Bay, had shown Hartnett parts of the *Black Hawk Down* script; Jerry Bruckheimer was the producer of both films.

Hartnett's character was based on real-life army staff sergeant Matt Eversmann. At the time of the raid (1993) Eversmann was twenty-six years old, with five years experience of the US MILITARY. He was in charge of a group of twelve men known as a "chalk." Hartnett met Eversmann at the US Army War College, where Eversmann worked as a teacher. At one point during the making of the film, Hartnett said to one of his biographers that "we couldn't have any food . . . the people of Morocco [where *Black Hawk Down* was made] are so poor that having the food would have caused great fights from people trying to steal it . . . It made me feel terrible. But think about how bad some people have it in this world. You feel like this stupid fat cat . . . We had the same haircuts as the US military, but I didn't get much outward hatred from the locals. You still felt a bit like the ignorant white man coming in and wrecking everything for everyone else." The experience of the film was apparently

an eye-opener: "Ridley is such a masterful world-maker, catching these details—like the man near the beginning of the film, praying with the AK (Kalashnikov rifle) at his side. This suddenly brings you into the world that we're in."

Hartnett's character is perhaps the one most changed by the experience of the war. At the beginning he comes across as someone who genuinely believes that American intervention in Somalia is justified on the grounds that (according to KEN NOLAN's script) "we can either help, or we can sit back and watch the country destroy itself on CNN . . . I think I was trained to make a difference." By the end of the film, however, Eversmann understands that the main purpose of fighting a battle is to learn how to survive and to look out for one's fellow soldiers. The true heroes are not those who "make a difference" but those like Smith (Charlie Hofheimer) who perish in the task of fighting for their country. The script underlines this point in a stage direction: "Eversmann, needing to make a final connection, touches Smith's chest . . . a hero's heart . . . another somebody who didn't ask to be a hero." The experience of war has changed Eversmann completely: "there are other wounds [in his expression], the kind you can't see at first glance . . . a soldier who's been in combat . . . a look in a young man's eyes . . . a look that makes you stop and take a deeper look."

In an earlier version of the film, Eversmann introduced the action with a voice-over, describing the Somalian civil war in detail. However, Scott dispensed with this, preferring instead to make the spectators focus on the images of destruction—a lonely truck driving through ravaged countryside, bodies strewn everywhere, another body wrapped in a sheet being carried away, another man covering a dead person's face.

References

Josh Hartnett, quoted in Lorelei Laun, *Josh Hartnett: American Hero* (New York: Simon and Schuster, 2002), 44, 76; Ken Nolan, *Black Hawk Down: The Shooting Script* (New York: Newmarket Press, 2002), 18, 127.

HARWOOD, RONALD (1935–)

Harwood began life as an actor in the touring theater working for the British actor Sir Donald Wolfit before turning to playwriting. In the 1980s his play *The Dresser* was a critical and popular success in the West End of London, on Broadway, and in the cinema, with ALBERT FINNEY in the title role. Harwood adapted TERENCE RATTIGAN's play *THE BROWNING VERSION* for the 1994 film. While updating the action to the modern era, Harwood nonetheless tried to stay close to Rattigan's original intentions in terms of characterization. He added new scenes—for example, a storyline where Taplow (BEN SILVERSTONE) is taunted about his parents' divorce.

Harwood believed this was important, as he liked to "write about people who feel rather than about people who think. The characters I create [or adapt] seem to be able to laugh and cry with great facility. That is not only because I myself laugh and cry with great facility but also because I perceive the world as being unbearably funny and unbearably sad."

Reference

Ronald Harwood, "Introduction," *Plays 2* (London: Faber and Faber Ltd., 1995), viii.

HAUER, RUTGER (1944–)

Rutger Hauer studied theater in Amsterdam and worked in Basle, Switzerland. His first major film role was in Paul Verhoeven's *Turkish Delight* (1973); subsequently, he had roles in the same director's *Spetters* (1980) and *Soldaat van Oranje/Soldier of Fortune* (1977), in which he played a World War II resistance fighter. It was the latter film that convinced to sign him as Batty for *BLADE RUNNER*.

In a 2007 interview with Dan Jolin, Hauer insisted that Batty was "a hero in disguise," whose humanity contrasts with Deckard's (HARRISON FORD's) often brutal behavior. Both men seek to kill their enemies, although only one of Batty's kills occurs on screen—a subtle skewing of our sympathy on Scott's part. Both, too, have a romance with a mannequin-like woman; but compare Batty's playful language with Pris (DARYL HANNAH) with Deckard's clumsily forced love scene with Rachael (SEAN YOUNG). Batty has a sense of humor and a "poetic sense."

Batty is characterized as a quasi-divine figure; after killing Tyrell (JOE TURKEL), we see him descending in an elevator, looking up at the stars, the heavens ebbing away from him. On another occasion in Chew's (JAMES HONG's) eye works, Batty recites lines from WILLIAM BLAKE's "America: A Prophecy": "Fiery the angels fell . . . " Clearly Batty represents a fallen angel seeking redemption—something he achieves right at the end, when he and Deckard meet on the roof. Batty assumes the moral high ground, taunting Deckard for firing on an unarmed assailant and shouting "I thought you were supposed to be good. Aren't you the good man?" By the time Batty rescues Deckard from the roof, the high ground has been secured: Because life is important above all else, no matter what, Batty saves the life of someone who killed Pris, the woman he loved. Batty tells Deckard in his dying moments: "I've seen things you wouldn't believe. Attack ships on fire off the shoulder of Orion. I watched C-beams glitter in the dark near the Tannhauser gate. All those moments will be lost in time, like tears in rain. Time . . . to die."

Hauer recalled in the Jolin interview that these lines seemed significant to him as they revealed Batty's concern to "make his mark on existence . . . And that he can say in a small way to this so-called real world hero [Deckard] 'Boy, you've just been trying to escape and escape—you've never stepped up to the plate. How unwarrior like.' And the robot in the final scene, by dying, sort of shows Deckard what a *real* man is made of."

The final scene ends with a telling moment as Batty lets the dove go; and as he does so, grabs Deckard's wrist and murmurs, "Ah, kinship!" In a split second the two of them are united; they might both be REPLICANTS or human beings. If the latter is true, then Batty is certainly more human than Deckard (as the Tyrell Corporation motto informs us).

Batty has received a largely sympathetic reception from the film's critics. Leonard G. Heldreth wrote in 1991 that "Roy Batty, the replicant . . . at the end believed like a man." PAUL M. SAMMON quotes PHILIP K. DICK, who felt the final confrontation was "a wonderful moving sequence," helping to transform his novel "into a beautiful symmetrical reinforcement of my original." In his autobiography *All Those Moments* (2007), Hauer wrote that Batty was the greatest role of his career: "I knew after seeing it that I had done a good job. As time goes on and people keep responding to it in such a positive way, it reinforces my instinct that this is a great movie—one that is beautiful, dark, wicked, poetic, exotic and beautiful."

References

Rutger Hauer and Patrick Quinlan, *All Those Moments: Stories of Heroes, Villains, Replicants and Blade Runners* (New York: Harper Entertainment, 2007), 134–35; Leonard G. Heldreth, "The Cutting Edges of *Blade Runner*," in *Retrofitting Blade Runner*, ed. Judith B. Kerman, 2nd ed. (Bowling Green: Bowling Green State University Press, 1997), 40–52; Dan Jolin, "The Prodigal Son," *Empire*, August 2007, 114–15; Paul M. Sammon, "The Making of *Blade Runner*," *Cinefantastique* 12, nos.5–6 (July 1982): 26.

Bibliography

Christine Holmlund, "Rutger Hauer: The Netherlands' Paul Newman," in *Action and Adventure Cinema*, ed. Yvonne Tasker (London and New York: Routledge, 2004), 287–88.

HEALY, MATT (?–)

Also writes under the name Matthew L. Healy. Born in Trenton, New Jersey, Healy majored in journalism at the University of Colorado at Boulder. He then went on to work as a graphic designer for various newspapers.

The screenplay for *CLAY PIGEONS* (originally titled "In Too Deep") won him a prize in the Writer's Network screenplay contest. He was signed by a major agency, ICM (International Creative Management) and sold his script to Scott Free.

Healy revealed in the production notes that the inspiration for his screenplay had come from the novels of Elmore Leonard, who puts SMALL TOWN characters in urban environments, but Healy wanted to "switch that, and be faster-paced. Often, small-town movies go at a snail's pace, and I liked the idea of things happening pretty quick in this town [of Mercer, Montana]. The people don't have to be slow-witted, just because they live in a small town. Since I grew up in a small town, I guess I should want that." Healy wanted his film to be a "daylight noir . . . To put noir in a small town, almost by its very nature, it has to have a very different feel." Despite quirky performances from leading actors JOAQUIN PHOENIX and VINCE VAUGHN, the film was not a success, taking only $1.7 million in the first two months of its US release in September 1998. Since then, Healy has not been credited with writing any further screenplays.

Reference

Matt Healy, interviewed in "Production Notes: *Clay Pigeons*," included on the European DVD release of the film (Frankfurt: BY Internationale Medien und Film, 1998).

HEMMINGS, DAVID (1941–2003)

Born in Surrey, United Kingdom, Hemmings began as a child actor in *Billy Bunter of Greyfriars School* (1952) and *The Rainbow Jacket* (1954). He became an iconic figure of the 1960s after starring in Antonioni's *Blow-Up* (1966); this was followed by roles in *Camelot* (1967) and *The Charge of the Light Brigade* a year later.

Hemmings later turned to directing in films and American television, only returning to the screen for cameo roles such as the master of ceremonies Cassius in *GLADIATOR*, where he plays the role in a blond wig.

HERITAGE FILMS

A term first coined in the 1980s to describe a genre of adaptations of classic novels. The genre is exemplified by the work of the Merchant-Ivory production team in bringing adaptations of the novels of E. M. Forster to the screen. The heritage film has been the subject of intense debate since the 1980s and has been criticized by some for its commodification of the past—for its perceived tendency to present British culture and history in a prettified and conservative package.

Since the early 1990s there has been a move away from the heritage film towards adaptations of literary novels by a number of directors who have worked in other genres and have brought a fresh vision to the costume film. Perhaps the first to take this approach was Martin Scorsese, whose *The Age of Innocence*, adapted from the novel by Edith Wharton, was widely praised as a cinematic triumph.

Scott's period dramas such as *THE DUELLISTS* have differed from heritage films in the sense that they have not focused on the landscape or on glorifying the past. Rather, they demonstrate Scott's ability to create a *mise-en-scène* using fast cuts rather than long panning shots, reflecting his background in advertising.

THE BROWNING VERSION is perhaps Scott's closest approximation to a heritage film. Set in a private school in the rolling English countryside, the film includes a fair share of shots of the verdant landscape and the quaint, rustic quality of the village nearby. There are cobbled streets, a second-hand bookshop, and a village shop with an apartment above where Frank Hunter (MATTHEW MODINE) lives, and where Laura Crocker-Harris (GRETA SCACCHI) pays frequent visits. The landscape fulfills an important function in this film; set in contrast to the prison-like surroundings of the school, it offers a vision of freedom for students and teachers alike. Nonetheless the film has a certain picture-postcard quality, creating a vision of England as a place of perpetual sunshine and unchanging tradition designed to appeal to the American market.

HIGGINS, JOHN MICHAEL (1963–)

Early work includes appearances in the television series *Miami Vice* (1988), *Cybill* (1996), and *Seinfeld* (1997). Cast as the chief of staff working under Senator DeHaven (ANNE BANCROFT) in *G.I. JANE*, Higgins's performance is worth noting for two reasons: first, his willing acceptance of a woman as his superior, which contrasts with the attitude of the military faced with Jordan O'Neil's (DEMI MOORE's) presence at the SEAL training camp; and second, because he can tell anyone exactly what the senator thinks. As Scott observed in an interview with PAUL M. SAMMON, chiefs of staff are never just "secretaries . . . They're much more than that." To understand their point of view is to understand what senators also think.

Reference

Ridley Scott, quoted in Paul M. Sammon, "Joining the Club: Ridley Scott on *GI Jane*," in *Ridley Scott Interviews*, ed. Laurence F. Knapp and Andrea F. Kulas (Jackson: University Press of Mississippi, 2005), 144.

HIGHMORE, FREDDIE (1992–)

Made his debut as a child actor in *Five Children and It* (2004), followed by Tim Burton's remake of *Charlie and the Chocolate Factory* (2005). As Young Max in *A GOOD YEAR*, Highmore's characterization is almost completely antithetical to that of BEN SILVERSTONE in *THE BROWNING VERSION* (Scott's previous film with a male child actor in a leading role). Silverstone's Taplow is a model of reticence, a product of an English public school placing emphasis on repressing the emotions and observing group hierarchies. Highmore's Max is an individual—someone more than willing to cheat at chess if it means that he can beat his uncle Henry (ALBERT FINNEY). On the other hand, Young Max enjoys a happy CHILDHOOD at the château—one where he is treated as an equal by his uncle and where he could enjoy illicit pastimes such as drinking alcohol. In the film's pressbook Highmore described the intended effect of his character on audiences: "I think . . . [they] will come out with memories of their childhood after seeing this film . . . The film will make you look back on the things that have happened in your own life. Young Max didn't know at the time how important the lessons were that Uncle Henry was giving him. But, as he got older and comes back to visit this place, he realizes how important they have been in making him grow up."

Reference

Pressbook: A Good Year (Los Angeles: Twentieth Century-Fox Film Corporation, 2006), 3.

HIGHSMITH, PATRICIA (1921–1995)

American author known for her psychological thrillers, which have led to more than two dozen film adaptations. *Strangers on a Train* has been adapted for the screen three times, notably by Alfred Hitchcock in 1951. The basic plot of this story, with two young men operating on the edge of the law, provides the inspiration for the Ridley Scott-produced black comedy *CLAY PIGEONS*. The protagonists in many of Highsmith's novels are either morally compromised by circumstance or actively flouting the law. Many of her antiheroes, often emotionally unstable young men, commit murder in fits of passion or simply to extricate themselves from a bad situation. The same could be said for Lester Long (VINCE VAUGHN), the lead character in *Clay Pigeons*, a mass murderer of young women who escapes justice through sheer force of character. He seems an outwardly personable man—until, that is, he is faced with situations beyond his control. He is also a misogynist, which helps to explain why he abuses women ("Some people need killing. Amanda needed it more than most. She was vile.")

Reference

Matt Healy, *In Too Deep* (Draft Script dated 7 January 1997) (Beverly Hills, CA: Scott Free, 1997), 70.

HILL, WALTER (1942–)

After working in construction and oil fields, Walter Hill made his name in Hollywood with his first screenplay *Hickey and Boggs* (1972), starring Robert Culp and Bill Cosby. In partnership with DAVID GILER and GORDON CARROLL, Hill formed Brandywine Productions, which optioned DAN O'BANNON and RON SHUSETT's original script for *ALIEN* in early 1977. The first draft, according to Hill in an interview with Mark Patrick Carducci and Glenn Lovell, was "poorly written. It had a 'Jesus, gadzooks' quality and no differentiation in characters." Hill rewrote the screenplay very quickly. He kept a lot of O'Bannon's original material, which would later be cut—the alien ransacking the ship's food store, an attempt to poison the ship with gas. Hill added a note of discord by having the characters not like one another very much, and transformed the dialogue into terse, staccato sentences. He also included a sex scene between Ripley and Dallas. This new draft was presented to Twentieth Century-Fox, with Hill slated to direct.

Eventually Hill withdrew as director and engaged Ridley Scott instead. However Hill continued to work on the script. The spaceship's name was changed from the *Snark* into the *NOSTROMO*, a mining vessel owned by the Company (a reference to JOSEPH CONRAD's use of the same term in *Heart of Darkness*). The talking computer was rechristened "Mother"; two of the main characters became female; and Ripley became the new hero of the piece, whose toughness and courage would help her escape the alien's clutches.

Despite the extent of the changes, Hill did not receive a writing credit; to do so he would have had to alter 65-70 percent of the filmed material. Hill later worked on David Fincher and Vincent Ward's script for *Alien*[3]. He also co-produced the other two sequels in the ALIEN QUADRILOGY—*Aliens* (1986) and *Alien Resurrection* (1997)—as well as the two *ALIEN vs. PREDATOR* films.

Reference

Mark Patrick Carducci and Glenn Lovell, "Making *Alien*: Behind the Scenes," *Cinefantastique* 9, no.1 (October 1979): 16.

THE HIRE

USA 2002 8 × 8 min episodes col. *Production Companies*: Fallon Worldwide and RSA in association with BMW Films. *Executive Producers*: Ridley Scott, Tony Scott, David Fincher. *Producers*: David Mitchell, Robyn Boardman, Aristides (Tony) McGarry, Robert van der Weteringe Buys, Tapas Blank, Leon Corcos. *Directors*: Tony Scott, John Woo, Joe Carnahan, John Frankenheimer, Guy Ritchie, Ang Lee, Kar Wai Wong, Alejandro González Iñárritu. *Cast*: Clive Owen (*The Driver*).

In 2000, after doing some research, BMW decided to find a new way to advertise their CARS for the sake of advertising. They determined that their customers were, on average, middle-aged married males making $150,000 per year. They also determined that a majority of their customers chose what kind of a car they wanted to buy only after using the Internet. As a result of this, Jim McDowell, BMW's

North American VP of marketing, came up with an idea to create a fast-paced, high-class, ultra-glossy way of showcasing their automobiles: a series of short films with a central, recurring character, The Driver (CLIVE OWEN), who drove a BMW, and feature them on the Internet.

The first season was overseen by Fallon Worldwide, the advertising agency, with David Fincher as producer. The films produced included *Ambush* (directed by John Frankenheimer), *Chosen* (directed by Ang Lee), *The Follow* (directed by Wong Kar-Wai), *Star* (directed by Guy Ritchie), and *Powder Keg* (directed by Alejandro González Iñárittu). After the series began, BMW saw their 2001 sales figures go up by 12 percent and the films were viewed over twelve million times on the Internet. The films proved so popular that the company issued a DVD for customers who visited their dealerships. *Vanity Fair* also distributed a disc, but without *The Follow* on it; this was due to a dispute with the actor Forrest Whittaker, who agreed to take an unbilled part in the film so long as it was only shown on the Internet. The films were reviewed by the *New York Times*, which praised BMW for creating work designed for "discerning movie watchers."

The second season opened in October 2002 with RSA and Ridley and TONY SCOTT as producers. To encourage the audience's interest it was promoted with the following slogan: "You are about to get extremely familiar with the edge of your seat." The second season opened with a dark action/comedy piece by Tony Scott called "BEAT THE DEVIL." The movie (shot in Scott's trademark pseudo-psychedelic style) featured JAMES BROWN enlisting The Driver to take him to Vegas to rework a decades-old deal he made with the devil which evidently gave Brown his "fame and fortune." Some differences were evident. Whereas the first season was serious and subdued with tiny bursts of action and comedy, the second season was mostly lighthearted. JOHN WOO and JOE CARNAHAN were hired to direct "HOSTAGE" and "TICKER," respectively. The other main difference was that, instead of showcasing several different BMW cars (as in the first season), the only car showcased was the then-new BMW Z4 Roadster.

To celebrate the premiere of the second season, BMW staged a celebration at the Arclight Cinema in Hollywood on 17 October 2002, just a week before the movie's Internet debut. The party, co-hosted by *Vanity Fair*, also served as a charity/benefit for the homeless. A month after the premiere of "Beat the Devil," the satellite channel DirecTV began airing the entire series in half-hour loops. Four issues of *THE HIRE*: COMIC BOOK were also produced, the last of these appearing in 2005.

On 21 October 2005, BMW stopped distribution of *The Hire* on DVD and removed all eight films from the BMW Films website just four years after the first film debuted. The official reason given was one of expense. However there might be other reasons: Jim McDowell, who had been responsible for the project in the first place, left the company, while BMW split from its longtime advertising partner Fallon Worldwide. The series had been viewed over one hundred million times on the website, and changed the way in which cars were advertised. Nissan produced another short film in 2002 advertising the newly produced 350Z, directed by John Bruno, a protégé of James Cameron.

Reference

Elvis Mitchell, "Honk if You've Seen These Online Films," *New York Times*, 26 June 2001, http://query.nytimes.com/gst/fullpage.html?res=9504E0DB1030F935A15755C0A9679C8B63&scp=1&sq=the%20hire%20BMW&st=cse (accessed 4 January 2009).

THE HIRE: "BEAT THE DEVIL"

US 2002 r/t 9 min col. *Production Company*: RSA. *Executive Producers*: Ridley Scott, Tony Scott, and Jules Daly. *Producer*: David Mitchell. *Director*: Tony Scott. *Writers*: David Carter, Greg Hahn, and Vincent Ngo, based on an original concept by David Fincher. *Director of Photography*: Paul Cameron. *Production Designer*: Ken Davis. *Music*: Harry Gregson-Williams. *Cast*: Clive Owen (*The Driver*), James Brown (*Himself*), Gary Oldman (*The Devil*), Marilyn Manson (*Himself*), Tony Wilson (*Young James Brown*).

The Driver is hired to escort JAMES BROWN to a meeting with The Devil. Brown once sold his soul in exchange for fame and fortune; in late middle age, he seeks to renegotiate his deal. The Devil will not agree and Brown challenges him to a car race over the Nevada landscape. "Darkness is death's ignorance and The Devil's time," says James Brown.

This short contains numerous references to other films: The Devil peels eggs with his long fingernails, referencing/stealing from Robert De Niro's turn as Satan in Alan Parker's *Angel Heart* (1987). The shot at the beginning of the film, set in 1954 with a young James Brown getting out of the car in the desert, recalls a similar shot in *THELMA & LOUISE*. More importantly, The Devil here calls himself the Prince of Darkness, which recalls Darkness in *LEGEND*, who—like The Devil here—draws victims into temptation, whether willingly or unwillingly. "Beat the Devil" also contains distinct echoes of Scott's "Sanctuary" in the television series *THE HUNGER*, with GARY OLDMAN (as The Devil) speaking in a voice very reminiscent of DAVID BOWIE, tempting James Brown to renew his pact. In the "Director's Commentary" to the film, Scott acknowledges that his characterization of Oldman was inspired by Mick Jagger's role in the film *PERFORMANCE*, as well as the Robert Johnson song "Cross Road."

Thematically speaking, the film is very reminiscent of many of the episodes in *The Hunger*, with Brown seeking perpetual youth and challenging The Devil to a driving contest in Las Vegas. Scott shows the two driving faster and faster, until The Driver manages to maneuver his BMW across a railway line in front of a passing train. The Devil is too slow to follow; and crashes into the train. The moral is a familiar one: taking anything to excess inevitably causes destruction. "Beat the Devil" ends with a neat joke as The Devil is shown in his lair, when suddenly there is a knock on the door. His neighbor asks him to keep quiet, as he is trying to read—the neighbor is played by rock musician MARILYN MANSON, who is normally associated with loud music.

Reference

Tony Scott, "Director's Commentary" to the DVD of *The Hire* (Los Angeles: BMW of North America, 2003).

THE HIRE: COMIC BOOK

During the last quarter of 2004, BMW in association with Dark Horse Comics decided to produce a six-issue comic book series, based on "The Driver," the main character in the film series *THE HIRE*. The books were written by Kurt Busiek, Bruce Campbell, Katsuhiro Otomo, and Mark Waid, as well as other comic book talent. Four books were produced, including *Scandal* by Matt Wagner, and *Precious Cargo* by Bruce Campbell and Kilian Plunkett. The last book *Tycoon*, appeared in December 2005.

Bibliography

"BMW's The Driver to Get Comic Book Series," *Motor Trend*, 30 July 2004, www.motortrend.com/auto_news/112_040730_hire-comics/index.html (accessed 4 January 2009).

THE HIRE: "HOSTAGE"

US 2002 r/t 9 min col. *Production Company*: RSA. *Executive Producers*: Ridley Scott, Tony Scott, and Jules Daly. *Producer*: Tony McGarry. *Director*: John Woo. *Writers*: David Carter, Greg Hahn, and Vincent Nye. *Director of Photography*: Jeffrey Kimball. *Production Designer*: Deborah Evans. *Music*: Steve Jablonsky. *Cast*: Clive Owen (*The Driver*), Kathryn Morris (*Linda Delacroix*), Maury Chaykin (*Harry*).

The Driver is hired to deliver ransom money for Linda, a distinguished CEO who has been kidnapped and hidden in the trunk of her employee Harry's car. When the exchange has been completed, Harry provides a phone number instead of the hostage. The Driver is faced with a race against time before her battery—and her air supply—runs out.

An epic tale of the elements, arising from Harry's obvious resentment of the fact that Linda has broken up their relationship. Harry seeks to destroy the ransom money by fire, and drown Linda in the water. He likens himself to a butterfly and his victim to a moth, gradually coming too close to the fire. However the tables are turned once the FBI storms his apartment and his plan founders. Harry shoots himself; Linda is rescued by The Driver in the nick of time. Eventually Harry dies in hospital, with Linda telling him that their relationship was "just sex" and that she is the butterfly and he the moth.

The film is full of echoes of other Ridley Scott films. The fact that the FBI has to help The Driver in this raid reminds us of the opening sequence of *HANNIBAL* when Clarice Starling (JULIANNE MOORE) and her colleagues make an abortive attempt to catch a known drug dealer. A reference in the film to The Driver as the "knight in shining armor" reminds us of ORLANDO BLOOM's Balian in *KINGDOM OF HEAVEN*. However, The Driver proves ineffective as a modern-day knight, as Linda eventually gets her revenge on Harry by visiting his hospital ward and presiding over his death. She becomes the kind of predatory female—like Pris in *BLADE RUNNER*—who poses a perpetual threat to male security.

Director JOHN WOO tells the story through rapid intercutting and suitably dramatic music. In many cases the exterior shots of San Francisco recall similar shots set in New York in *BLACK RAIN*, with The Driver's BMW car whizzing underneath bridges and crossing the seafront at high speed.

THE HIRE: "TICKER"

US 2002 r/t 9 min col. *Production Company*: RSA. *Executive Producers*: Ridley Scott, Tony Scott, David Fincher, and Jules Daly. *Producer*: Leon Corcos. *Director*: Joe Carnahan. *Writer*: Joe Carnahan from a story by Joe Sweet. *Director of Photography*: Mauro Fiore. *Production Designer*: Missy Stewart. *Music*: Clint Mansell. *Cast*: Clive Owen (*The Driver*), Don Cheadle (*Government Agent*), F. Murray Abraham (*Foreign Dignitary*).

Political espionage, dramatic tension, and suspense come together in this thriller involving the delivery of a new heart to an (unnamed) political leader who is the only man to sustain democracy in the country. The Driver is involved in taking the agent to deliver the heart to the hospital.

"What is the life of one man worth?" One reviewer remarked that "this question runs through [the film] . . . Dynamically directed with a lavish budget, this is both a snippet from a lost action movie and a boy's toys corporate noir." Like *THE HIRE*: "BEAT THE DEVIL," it is set in a lonely landscape.

"Ticker's" resemblances to *BLACK HAWK DOWN* prove almost uncanny, as The Driver is pursued by a helicopter which tries to shoot him down. Eventually he manages to create a smokescreen of exhaust fumes so that the helicopter cannot see where he is. As a result the helicopter crashes into a railway bridge in a sequence very reminiscent of the crash-sequences in *Black Hawk Down*. The Government Agent (DON CHEADLE) is someone obsessed with duty—in this case, rescuing the heart from the hands of an enemy faction and ensuring it reaches the hospital to pro-long the life of a great dictator, one who has kept peace in the country for many years. Both films are set in African ter-ritories, which are dominated by factional in-fighting: in "Ticker" one group seeks to steal the dictator's heart in order to secure power, and it is Cheadle's responsibility to recover it. Like the soldiers in *Black Hawk Down*, he undertakes his task in the hope that order might be restored as a result of his actions. However, "Ticker" neatly reverses the plot of *Black Hawk Down*, being concerned with the restoration rather than the loss of human life.

Reference

The Hire: Ticker review, www.channel4.com/film/reviews/film .jsp?id=133197, (accessed 7 August 2008).

HIRSCH, JUDD (1935–)

Veteran stage, film, and television actor whose successes include *Taxi* (1978–1983) and *Dear John* (1988–1992).

Cast as Alan Eppes in *NUMB3RS*, Hirsch provides a sense of authority, not only as the patriarch of the family who helps the two sons—Don (ROB MORROW) and Char-lie (DAVID KRUMHOLTZ)—run their lives, in spite of their faults, but also as someone offering a source of stability in an often cruel world. Although the character has had occa-sional romances, notably with Charlie's boss Mildred Finch (Kathy Najimy) in Series 3, he remains resolutely single, determined to honor the memory of his late wife.

A journalist from the magazine *Emmy* visited the set in Series 1 in May 2005, and observed that Hirsch "brings a wise, well-honed delivery to his lines. He knows subtext. He knows absurdity. He knows how to crack up the crew." Hirsch was especially good at suggesting the father-son rela-tionship between himself and Charlie: "The father-son rela-tionship . . . is especially sweet, given that the violence on the show . . . doesn't directly affect their characters. If anything, there seems to be an almost comedic subtext to their inter-actions, as the elder Eppes struggles to understand the con-cepts put forward by Charlie."

Reference

Kathleen O'Steen, "Math Blaster," *Emmy* 27, no.3 (May 2005): 179, 185.

HJORTSBERG, WILLIAM (1941–)

William Hjortsberg made his reputation as a novelist rather than a screenwriter with works such as *Gray Matter* (1971) and *Tales and Fables* (1985), as well as the book *Symbiogra-phy* (1973).

It was on the strength of Hjortsberg's reputation as a mythmaker that Scott engaged him to write the screenplay of *LEGEND*. Hjortsberg claimed in an interview that his only reference for the script was *Fairies*, a picture book by Brian Froud and Alan Lee. This process of creating the script was a difficult one, with Hjortsberg writing fifteen drafts; however, the fundamental idea remained the same through-out, which is what sustained the scriptwriter's morale.

The original script had its good points, but at times the ideas were simply borrowed from classical mythology with-out actually integrating them into the story. In one scene where Jack takes Lily to see the unicorns, there is a snake that poisons the water so that it is no longer fit to drink until the unicorn purifies it with his horn. In another scene the virgin Lily encourages the unicorn to place his head in her lap. At this point she opens her dress and breast-feeds the animal in a moment reminiscent of "the Madonna and her infant Jesus." Such overtly Christian images did not seem appropriate for a family film, and were quickly dis-pensed with.

Hjortsberg's script turned Lily into an animal after committing the "sin" of leading the dark hunter to the uni-corns, with no attempt made by Jack to stop her. This alludes to the hunter myth, in which the maiden is cast as the hunter's accomplice; in Hjortsberg's original script the hunter provides a prototype for what would eventually become Darkness. Following the killing of the unicorn, Lily (now transformed into a half-human, half-animal) is cap-tured and taken to the demon's castle, where she is subject to various forms of violent torture until she agrees to have violent sex with him. Such scenes were immediately deleted—much to Hjortsberg's disappointment, as he recalled in a 1987 interview. Scott worked with Hjortsberg to rewrite the script so that a final shooting script was ready on 10 March 1984.

Hjortsberg's script was further changed prior to its original release—most likely without the screenwriter's participation—as Scott worked with the then-president of Universal Studios, Sidney Sheinberg, to render the film suit-able for release.

References

William Hjortsberg, interviewed by Dan Scapperotti, *Cinefantas-tique*, July 1987, 23; William Hjortsberg, "Legend Making," Intro-duction to *Legend of Darkness* (2002), www.figmentfly.com/ legend/script2.html (accessed 26 May 2008); William Hjortsberg, "Legend" (dated 10 March 1984), www.figmentfly.com/legend/ script3b.html (accessed 13 May 2008); William Hjortsberg, "Leg-end" (dated 25 September 1984), www.figmentfly.com/legend/ script3c.html (accessed 13 May 2008)

HOBBS, WILLIAM (1939–)

Fight director in both films and the theater. Early film cred-its include *Othello* (1965), *The Three Musketeers* (1973), and its sequel *The Four Musketeers* (1974).

Hobbs worked closely with Scott on the duel sequences in *THE DUELLISTS*. One of the best takes place in a stable, with D'Hubert and Feraud stripped to their undershirts and covered in blood. The duel is made up of a series of sword-strokes, the two soldiers using heavy weapons to smite one another to the ground, interspersed with wrestling sequences. It rises in intensity as the two of them become increasingly exhausted; they glare at one another as they puff out their cheeks and struggle to maintain balance. Covered in blood and surface wounds, they wrestle one more time and fall to the floor, exhausted.

Scott shoots the scene in a series of fast cuts, reminiscent of his work in advertisements, especially McDOUGALL'S PASTRY MIX. The fight resembles a kind of ballet in which the two duelists observe certain set conventions of sword-play. This reveals the extent to which form assumes more importance than content: neither participant really understands why they are fighting, but if they do fight, they must do so according to accepted rituals.

HOLLANDER, TOM (1967–)

Cambridge University-educated actor whose films include *Gosford Park* (2001) and Joe Wright's version of *Pride and Prejudice* (2005). Cast as Max Skinner's (RUSSELL CROWE's) estate agent buddy Charlie Willis in *A GOOD YEAR*, Hollander seems a typical representative of money-obsessed London in which surface impressions count for everything. In a film about good wines, he embarks on a pretentious tasting ritual in a London wine-bar, describing the wine's "polyphenolics" and its "magnificent hues of brick red indicating a mature Bordeaux." In truth Charlie has no idea who he is; like a chameleon, he tried to adapt himself to any and every occasion, but only succeeds in appearing more and more incongruous. While visiting Max's château, he wears a double-breasted blazer, pale gray flannels and a Panama hat; the typical attire of an Englishman abroad. The fact that it is completely inappropriate for a hot autumn day seems to have escaped him. Charlie confidently expects Max's rural idyll to come to a swift end: "And then, after months of eating, drinking, sleeping, and bonking, what have you got to look forward to? Boredom!" This speech only demonstrates how little he understands his best friend's desire for something more fulfilling than just making money.

In *THE COMPANY*, Hollander is faced with the problem of portraying a real-life character, Harold Adrian Russell ("Kim") Philby (1912–1988), a senior-ranking officer within MI5 who defected in the mid-1960s. Philby felt no love for his native country: "To betray you must first belong . . . I have never belonged." Rarely seen in public once he had moved to Moscow, Philby enjoyed all the privileges of a favored bureaucrat, including an apartment in the capital and a dacha, and never once regretted his decision: "I want

to be buried in the Soviet Union, a country which I have considered to be my own since the 1930s," he said shortly before his death. In *The Company*, screenwriter KEN NOLAN has taken certain liberties with the character. Philby is portrayed as an exceptionally clever person whose ability lies in carrying out Churchill's dictum of being able to evaluate contradictory information. However, when he is told by Yevgeny (RORY COCHRANE) that he must go "home" to the Soviet Union, Philby observes, "Russia is not my home. England is my home." He subsequently spends the rest of his life in an apartment, largely forgotten by the Soviet authorities. One shot, showing him wistfully gazing out of the window at the streets below, suggests his basic isolation and that perhaps playing the Great Game had not been such fun after all.

References

William A. Henry, Ann Blackman, and Frank Melville, "Espionage No Regrets: Kim Philby 1912–1988," *Time* 23 May 1988, www.time.com/time/magazine/article/0,9171,967442-1,00.html (accessed 3 February 2009; Marc Klein, "*A Good Year*: Screenplay" (Draft dated 5 September 2005), www.dailyscript.com/scripts/A-GOOD-YEAR-2.pdf (accessed 26 January 2009).

HOLM, IAN (1931–)

Ian Holm made his name in the theater as a member of the Royal Shakespeare Company at Stratford-on-Avon, England, both as a Shakespearean actor and a star in modern productions such as Harold Pinter's *The Homecoming* (1965).

When cast as Ash in *ALIEN* (1979), Holm had left the stage for three years following an attack of stage fright. "That was a very good film," he recalled in an interview published on a Web page devoted to his work. "Because it was made in 1979, I would have done anything then . . . I certainly had no idea it was going to become one of the great celebrated pieces of cinema." Holm had fond memories of working with SIGOURNEY WEAVER in her breakthrough film: "That was very strange. I can't to this day think why I got cast in that. I was one of the first people to be cast and then it was very interesting because I could see half way through the film the emphasis changed and there was the birth of a star in Sigourney. You could almost sense it. It wasn't just the underwear scene . . . I could just tell she was going to go on to big things. She's also a very nice lady. It was also an extraordinary experience working with someone as tough as Ridley Scott."

At first we are invited to sympathize with Ash, who appears to be a voice of reason on the *NOSTROMO* as the crew gradually becomes increasingly unable to cope with the presence of the alien on the craft. However, Scott has deliberately lulled us into a sense of false security: we discover that Ash is an android, deliberately placed on the craft by the

Company to spy on the crew's activities. He might be a voice of reason, but he is also dangerous.

Ash's most famous scene is that in which he tries to kill Ripley by stuffing a rolled-up magazine down her throat—a classic case of male attempts to dominate the female, both physically and sexually. He then has his head knocked off and then is reprogrammed by Ripley to help the crew defeat the alien. Ian Holm has also provided voice-overs for numerous commercials, including HOVIS BREAD.

Reference

Roger Crow, "Ian Holm Page," www.fortunecity.com/lavendar/sydenham/306/holm.html (accessed 15 March 2008).

HONG, JAMES (1929–)

One of the most prolific Asian-American actors on screen and television, James Hong made his debut in the mid-1950s in an uncredited role in *Love Is a Many-Splendored Thing* (1955). He graduated to television, playing Charlie Chan and appearing in many other series (*The Man from UNCLE, Hawaii Five-O,* and *Kung Fu*).

Cast as Chew in *BLADE RUNNER,* Hong plays the character as "a brilliant scientist who was on the edge of senility," someone who according to PAUL M. SAMMON is "constantly inventing all these gadgets to help him stay in the refrigerator . . . he can't bear the thought of leaving his eyeballs . . . any longer than he has to." He also speaks Chinese rather than English, which no one can understand, underlining the fact that no one communicates with one another in the film. The fact that Chew makes eyes is in itself ironic: while helping the REPLICANTS to see better, Chew actually sees nothing of the world around him, preferring to remain in his laboratory with only machines for company.

Reference

Paul M. Sammon, *Future Noir: The Making of Blade Runner,* 2nd ed. (London: Gollancz, 2007), 132–33.

HONOR

The code of honor governs the characters' behavior in *THE DUELLISTS.* It is what inspired D'Hubert (HARVEY KEITEL) to continue fighting with Feraud (KEITH CARRADINE), even when it no longer seems logical to do so. Scott shows how such codes transform the characters, rendering them oblivious to anything else. What seems a "reasonable" course of action (to forget about the duel after so many years) does not seem so to those who live by a code of honor. D'Hubert's motives are at once absurd (why should anyone behave like this?) yet noble; he is such an "honorable" man that he cannot let the matter drop.

In *BLACK RAIN* Scott returns to the theme, albeit with an orientalist slant. This time it is the Japanese characters

such as Sato (YUTSAKU MATSUDA) whose belief in honor is such that if someone fails to keep a promise, their only punishment is death. At the beginning of the film Sato ritually slays a rival yakuza leader in a NEW YORK bar by slitting his throat, wiping the knife clean after he has finished. Scott suggests that this code is barbaric, particularly in an ostensibly "civilized" country like the United States. This is conveyed somewhat obviously in a chase sequence involving Sato and New York police officer Nick Conklin (MICHAEL DOUGLAS) taking place in a slaughterhouse. In Sato's system of values, human beings are no better than animals killed for food. The scene where Sato cuts his finger off is another manifestation of this code; when confronted with Sugai (TOMISABURO WAKAYAMA), Sato has to mutilate himself in order not to lose face.

However, the Japanese code of honor has its positive side, especially for police officers like Masahiro (KEN TAKAKURA). They understand the difference between right and wrong, while remaining on the right side of the law. If they should veer from this path, then they dishonor themselves, their colleagues, and their families. On this view Nick is a "dishonorable" man, since he has previously accepted bribes from the Mafia. Timothy P. Hofmeister relates this code of honor to the myth of Achilles. *KINGDOM OF HEAVEN* operates according to equally strict codes of honor: the knights should always try to pursue a course of right action, and kings should always communicate with kings. When Reynald de Chatillon (BRENDAN GLEESON) tastes a cup of water intended for Guy de Lusignan (MARTON CSOKAS), Saladin (GHASSAN MASSOUD) slits his throat; in Saladin's view Reynald has committed a dishonorable act. The code of honor also underpins Saladin's decision to let Guy go free rather than killing him in *KINGDOM OF HEAVEN: THE DIRECTOR'S CUT*; this is perceived as humiliating for the French king. The same notion reappears in *TRISTAN + ISOLDE,* as King Marke insists that the British must fight against the Irish King Donnchadh (DAVID PATRICK O'HARA). To do nothing would be fatal for Marke's reputation as a ruler: he would "lose face in front of the other [British] tribes."

In *GLADIATOR* the code of honor is important—particularly in combat. At the beginning of the film the Roman troops prepare for battle with the German forces with the cry "strength and honor," which is repeated by Maximus (RUSSELL CROWE), Valerius (John Quinn), and Quintus (Tomas Arana). The slaves utter the same cry as they prepare to battle with the Praetorian guards, while Maximus plans his escape. The same view of honor provides the inspiration for the Hungarian and Cuban rebels in *THE COMPANY*—even though they are well aware that their task is futile. The motley crew of students, idealists and freedom fighters are no match for the Soviet tanks during the Hungarian Uprising of 1956, but as the leader Arpad Zelik (Misel Maticevic) suggests, they have to fight for their country. Director MIKAEL SALOMON's camera tracks across row upon row of admiring faces in Zelik's audience as they listen to his rousing speeches. The uprising is brutally crushed, which prompts the CIA operative Frank Wisner (Ted Atherton) to criticize his country and his leaders for their dishonorable behavior: "We offer damn pious phrases from [President] Eisenhower—'The heart of America goes out to the people of Hungary.' We told these people to rise up and break free of their communist chains, now we're turning our backs on them!" The Cuban freedom fighters suffer similar treatment during the Bay of Pigs invasion.

HANNIBAL deals with the theme of personal honor—particularly concerning Clarice Starling. Mason Verger (GARY OLDMAN) refers to her botched attempt to catch a drug-dealer as her "recent dishonor"—rightly understanding that Clarice acted according to established FBI procedure but received no recognition for it. In the dog-eat-dog world of contemporary America, notions of honor simply do not exist.

References

"*Gladiator* by David Franzoni, revised by John Logan," Transcribed from the film, http://sfy.ru/sfy/html?script=gladiator_ts (accessed 29 November 2008); Timothy P. Hofmeister, "Achillean Love and Honor in Ridley Scott's *Black Rain*," *Classical and Modern Literature* 13, no.1 (Fall 1992): 45–51; "*Tristan + Isolde* written by Dean Georgaris, Transcript by Chani at tristanandisolde.net," www.imsdb.com/Movie%20Scripts/Tristan%20and%20Isolde%20Script.html (accessed 23 January 2009); Steven Zaillian, "*Hannibal*: Screenplay Based on the Novel by Thomas Harris," Revision (9 February 2000), http://sfy.ru/sfy.html?script=hannibal2001(accessed 15 December 2008).

HOPKINS, ANTHONY (1937–)

Born Philip Anthony Hopkins in Port Talbot, Wales. Hopkins established himself as a member of the National Theatre of Great Britain under Sir Laurence Olivier, before he made his screen debut with *The Lion in Winter* (1968).

Hopkins received the script for *SILENCE OF THE LAMBS* in August 1989, when he was playing on the London stage. The film catapulted him into the superstar bracket; while the effect of his performance on popular culture was immense. The producer DINO DE LAURENTIIS's wife Martha reported once that she had a conversation with THOMAS HARRIS, author of *Silence*, who reported that he "had just had the strangest call from Anthony Hopkins, and I trembled because I didn't know what to say. I had to hang up real fast because this is Hannibal Lecter talking to me on the phone!"

When Hopkins was offered the chance to repeat the role in *HANNIBAL*, he readily accepted. He told his biographer

Quentin Falk that he "read it [the novel] in three sittings. I just loved the density of the story and characters. I liked the fact that it not only takes place ten years later but it was written ten years later and therefore it feels like something that's totally distinct from its predecessor . . . I've never been afraid of doing a sequel. I've just not had that combination of great material and talent that might have compelled me to do one before." However, matters proved problematic when JODIE FOSTER, Hopkins's co-star in *Silence*, refused to play in the sequel on account of its excessive violence. Hopkins was apparently unhappy with this decision, but was eventually placated when JULIANNE MOORE agreed to play the role instead: "[W]hen her name was mentioned, my immediate reaction was 'for my money, I think she's the perfect one for this part.'"

In this second installment of the saga, Hopkins plays the role of Hannibal with lip-smacking relish. He emphasized to Falk that he had "a feel for him [the character.] You put on the clothes, the funny hat or whatever and in comes this great actor [Giancarlo] Giannini [as Inspector Pazzi] and he's already in character so very nervous. He's got such a wonderful face, with all that fear in it . . . I suppose people are fascinated by the dark side of life . . . there's certainly plenty of it around . . . Some of the most colourful characters in classical literature—Iago, Richard III, Faust—have those qualities. They're so brilliant. They have no uncertainty. That's what makes them charismatic: they're always in control."

In *Hannibal*, as opposed to *Silence of the Lambs*, Hopkins combines a love of language with an innate capacity for violence. He takes a particular delight in telling Clarice in a voiceover that "this new assignment [i.e., catching him]" is not her choice: "Rather, it is part of 'the bargain.'" Each word is delivered precisely, placing full weight on the consonants. Hannibal is also a romantic—someone who understands the emotion behind DANTE ALIGHIERI's sonnet, as he speaks it first in Italian and subsequently translates it into English: "*Io fei gibetto a me de le mie case.* I—I make my own house be my gallows." STEVEN ZAILLIAN's script emphasizes the emotion behind these lines ("*Fell's normally composed face pains as he recites from memory Dante's words of the agonal Pier della Vigna.*") Despite this, we are never allowed to forget that Hannibal is also a serial killer, who abruptly drops the polite façade and announces his intentions to Pazzi (GIANCARLO GIANNINI) in a chilling phrase: "I must confess to you I'm giving serious thought to eating your wife."

Linda Mizejewski observes that Hopkins's presence was essential to the film's box-office success: "[He] provides a number of stabilizing star qualities for a slippery character who is both criminal and hero in this book . . . His ability to embody both class . . . and camp, both monstrosity and human depth, offers a coherent image for the Dr. Lecter of *Hannibal.*"

References

Quentin Falk, *Anthony Hopkins: The Biography* (London: Virgin Books Ltd., 2004), 243, 244, 245–47; Martha di Laurentiis, quoted in "Anthony Hopkins—à la Carte," *Film Review* 623 (October 2002): 35; Linda Mizejewski, "Stardom and Serial Fantasies: Thomas Harris' *Hannibal*," in *Keyframes: Popular Cinema and Cultural Studies*, ed. Matthew Tinkcom and Amy Villarejo (London and New York: Routledge, 2001), 168; Steven Zaillian, "*Hannibal*: Screenplay Based on the Novel by Thomas Harris," Revision (9 February 2000), http://sfy.ru/sfy.html?script=hannibal2001 (accessed 15 December 2008).

Bibliography

Douglas Eby, "Anthony Hopkins: The Oscar-winner on His Return as Hannibal," *Cinefantastique* 32, no.6 (February 2001): 10; Dann Gire, "Anthony Hopkins on Hannibal Lecter," *Cinefantastique* 23, nos. 2–3 (October 1992): 108–9; John Hiscock, "Lecter's Easy for Me To Play," *Daily Telegraph*, 7 October 2002: 21; Rod Lurie, "Doctor Lecter Will See You Now," *Empire* 24 (June 1991): 64–74; Joe Mauceri, "Hopkins on Hannibal," *Shivers* 86 (February 2001): 10–13; Martyn Palmer, "Empathy with the Very Devil," *The Times*, 6 February 2001, Section 2, 16–17; Cindy Pearlman, "His Just Desserts," *Premiere* 5, no.11 (July 1992): 17; John Reading, "Here Be Dragons," *Film Review Special* #42 (October 2002): 6–11; Ian Spelling, "The Lecter Circuit," *Fangoria* 218 (November 2002): 54–57; Sally Weale, "I Can't Take It Seriously. It Makes Me Laugh," *The Guardian*, 12 February 2001, Section 2, 12–13.

"THE HOT ZONE"

Still-born adaptation of a Richard Preston article, "Crisis in the Hot Zone." Published in October 1992, the article dealt with the superhuman efforts of the two USAMRID (US Army Medical Research Institute of Infectious Diseases) virologists to contain an outbreak of the virus Ebola, which had not only traveled from Africa to the eastern seaboard of America, but has also transferred from monkeys to humans. This became the basis for a projected film, whose script was originally written by James V. Hart. Scott agreed to direct in January 1994, at which point Hart suddenly found himself off the project. Scott brought in Tom Topor to rewrite the script, but called Hart back later. Robert Redford was slated to star; he brought in two further scriptwriters, Richard Friedenberg and later Paul Attanasio. JODIE FOSTER was briefly associated with the project, but withdrew; Redford followed soon afterwards. Meanwhile another film, *Outbreak* (released 1995), went into production, with much the same subject matter. Eventually Twentieth Century-Fox pulled the plug on "The Hot Zone" in August 1994. Scott tried to set up the production elsewhere, but found no takers. Apparently the projected budget ($40–50 million) scared the studios away, especially when there was a similar film (*Outbreak*) in the works.

Since then there have been rumors that the film of "Crisis in the Hot Zone" will be produced, but nothing has materialized as yet. *THE ANDROMEDA STRAIN*, produced by Scott in 2008, deal with similar subject matter. A copy of Hart's script dated 9 October 1993 can be accessed at www.hundland.org/scripts/HotZone.txt.

Bibliography

David Hughes, *Tales from Development Hell: Hollywood Film-Making the Hard Way* (London: Titan Books, 2004), 166–92.

HOUNSOU, DJIMON (1964–)

Came to Paris from Benin at the age of thirteen, couldn't find a job and ended as a vagrant, sleeping under bridges and rummaging in trash cans for food. Hounsou made his major feature film debut as the slave Juba in *GLADIATOR*.

The role calls for Hounsou to prove himself a good fighter, especially in the initial scenes where the slaves are being tested as potential gladiators in front of Proximo (OLIVER REED). The actor himself described the character thus in the book of the film: "Juba is a very skillful fighter, which enables him to stay alive physically, but he knows a way to stay alive mentally and spiritually as well. In his mind, he is with his people; his loved ones are there, waiting for him." Some of his most effective sequences take place with Maximus (RUSSELL CROWE), most notably one on the rooftop of Proximo's camp, where the two of them discuss their families. Juba imagines what his wife is doing: "[She] is preparing the food. My daughter is carrying water from the river." He hopes to see them again one day, but doubts if he ever will: "I will die soon. They will not die for many years. I will have to wait." This sums up the loneliness of the gladiator's life; like Maximus, Juba has no control over his destiny. He remains at the Romans' beck and call, to fight whenever they require it. In this kind of a world, it is not surprising that both he and Maximus yearn for death.

References

"*Gladiator* by David Franzoni, revised by John Logan," Transcribed from the film, http://sfy.ru/sfy/html?script=gladiator_ts (accessed 29 November 2008); Djimon Hounsou, quoted in Diana Landau, ed., *Gladiator: The Making of the Ridley Scott Epic* (Basingstoke and London: Boxtree, 2000), 58.

HOUSMAN, A. E. (1859–1936)

British poet whose most famous sequence of poems "A Shropshire Lad" refers at one point to the inevitability of death in a clear allusion to TRISTAN AND ISOLDE. Housman's sequence helped to popularize the myth in early twentieth-century Britain, providing the inspiration for DEAN GEORGARIS to write the screenplay for *TRISTAN + ISOLDE*, produced by Scott. The reference comes in the seventh poem of the sequence, in which a voice tells the speaker to lie down, and tells him of the futility of continually rising every day.

Reference

A. E. Housman, "A Shropshire Lad," Poem VII in *The Collected Poems of A. E. Housman* (London: Jonathan Cape, 1945), 18–19.

HOVIS BREAD

GB 1973 Commercial r/t 29 sec col. *Production Company*: RSA for Collett Dickenson Pearce and Partners. *Director*: Ridley Scott. *Music*: Antonin Dvorak. *Cast*: Carl Barlow (*The Boy*).

With the second movement of Dvorak's *New World Symphony* as a musical accompaniment, a little boy comes up a hill on a bicycle. Dressed in the clothes of the late 1920s or early 1930s, he is clearly a delivery boy coming to the end of his round. On the soundtrack an old man can be heard reminiscing that the climb uphill was "like taking bread to the top of the world." The boy delivers the bread and coasts downhill back to the baker's shop—as he does so, the old man informs us on the soundtrack, "I knew the baker'd have the kettle on and doorsteps of hot Hovis ready." The action dissolves to an interior shot of the baker's shop, as the baker puts the bread out and pours some tea. The old man tells us that the baker would say "get it [the Hovis bread] inside you, boy. You'll be going up that hill as fast as you come down." Scott ends the commercial with a close-up of the Hovis loaf, while another voice-over tells us that the bread is "as good for you today as it's always been."

A justifiably famous commercial, recently voted the all-time favorite of British television viewers. Only twenty-nine seconds long, it manages to evoke a mood of nostalgia of a simple, more innocent past. Although ostensibly set in the north of England (the old man speaks with a slight Yorkshire accent) it was actually shot in Shaftesbury, Dorset, southwest England). It confirms the truth of Scott's observation that the narrative structure of commercials demands as much care and attention as any film. The use of lighting to create dramatic effect suggests similar techniques in *THE DUELLISTS*, especially the use of light and shade in the baker's shop, which recalls the third duel scene in Scott's film. IAN HOLM provides the voice at the end of the commercial.

Reference

Ridley Scott, interviewed in "The Making of the Apple Commercial, 1984," www.youtube.com/watch?v=AD2Xs0Spj_8 (accessed 4 February 2008).

HUBBERT, CORK (1952–2003)

Real name Carl Hubbert. Born in Pendleton, Oregon, Hubbert made his debut in television series such as *Magnum PI*

(1981). As Brown Tom in *LEGEND*, Hubbert has an impish make-up, reminiscent of one of Disney's seven dwarfs. This is perhaps no coincidence, as Scott sought to create a fairy-tale drawing upon famous sources to render it accessible to the widest possible audience.

THE HUNGER (FILM)

GB 1983 r/t 100 min col. *Production Companies*: Metro Goldwyn-Mayer and Peerlord Ltd. *Producer*: Richard Shepherd. *Director*: Tony Scott. *Writers*: Ivan Davis and Michael Thomas from the novel by Whitley Streiber. *Director of Photography*: Steven Goldblatt. *Production Designer*: Brian Morris. *Music*: Michel Rubini and Denny Jaeger. *Cast*: Catherine Deneuve (*Miriam Blalock*), David Bowie (*John Blalock*), Susan Sarandon (*Dr. Sarah Roberts*), Cliff de Young (*Tom Haver*), Beth Ehlers (*Alice Cavender*), Dan Hedaya (*Lt. Allegrezza*), Rufus Collings (*Charlie Humphries*).

Cult horror film of the 1980s, setting the vampire story in the modern culture of death: the punk era. It is in that world of ubiquitous strobe lights and pink hair, black leather and body piercing, nihilism and anonymous sex, that Miriam and John hunt. In this world, even human life is disposable. The two of them kill their dates for the evening then throw them out in trash bags. SUSAN SARANDON has a supporting role as a doctor who becomes involved with Miriam; they make love and exchange blood, and soon Sarah herself becomes a vampire, devouring Tom Haver.

The Hunger was denounced at the time by John Simon as having an "utter lack of sense . . . Wan horror, limp sex, and minimal narrative are doused with every sort of visual opulence and chic." One of DAVID BOWIE's recent biographers agrees, calling it "an ill-conceived piece of sub-vampiric dross, with lesbian undertones." Apparently Bowie liked Sarandon, whom he described as "pure dynamite" but fails to empathize with her "radical feminist agenda." Despite the reviews, *The Hunger* not only became a considerable financial success, but spawned a television series (also known as *THE HUNGER*, produced by Tony and Ridley Scott, that ran for two seasons in the early 1990s).

References

Christopher Sandford, *Bowie: Loving the Alien* (London: Warner Books, 1997), 201; John Simon, quoted in John Kenneth Muir, *Horror Films of the 1980s* (Jefferson, NC and London: McFarland & Company Inc., Publishers, 2007), 323.

THE HUNGER (NOVEL)

Written by Whitley Streiber and originally published in 1980, this novel served as the basis for both Tony Scott's 1983 film and the 1997–2000 television series. The "hunger" in the novel is for blood, as the two main characters Miriam and Sarah become vampires. The novel focuses on the link between vampirism and sexuality, a connection brought out also in the film and television versions.

THE HUNGER (TELEVISION)

US 1997–1998, 1999–2000 TV series, 44 × 30 min episodes col. *Production Companies*: The Movie Network, Scott Free and Telescene Film Group Productions. *Producers*: Chris Burt, Jeff Fazio, Ridley Scott, and Tony Scott. *Directors*: Russell Mulcahy (six episodes), Darrell Wasyk (five episodes), Erik Canuel (three episodes), Daniel Grou (three episodes), Tony Scott (two episodes), Jeff Fazio (two episodes), Alain Desrochers (two episodes). *Writers*: Gerald Wexler (ten episodes), Bruce M. Smith (eight episodes), Terry Curtis Fox (five episodes), David J. Schow (five episodes), Gemma Files (four episodes), Mark Nelson (three episodes), Graham Masterton (three episodes), Marianne Ackerman (two episodes), Harlan Ellison (two episodes), Craig Miller (two episodes), Poppy Z. Bate (two episodes). *Directors of Photography*: François Protat (six episodes), Bernard Couture (four episodes), Pierre Gill (three episodes), John Mathieson. *Production Designers*: Sylvain Gingras (twenty-two episodes), Michel Proulx (four episodes), Tom Foden. *Music*: Benoît Juras (eighteen episodes), F. M. Le Sieur (seven episodes). *Cast*: Terence Stamp (*Host*: first series), David Bowie (*Host*: second series).

Two series of horror films, lasting twenty-four minutes, inspired by Tony Scott's 1983 film of the same name. Both ran for twenty-two episodes each. Each episode was based on a self-contained story introduced by the hosts—TERENCE STAMP (in the first series) and DAVID BOWIE (the second series). Stories focused on the themes of self-destruction and obsession, with a strong erotic component (one of the main attractions of Showtime products). Popular themes for the series included cannibalism, vampirism, sex and poison.

Some of the episodes in the opening season were directed by TONY SCOTT and Ridley Scott's son JAKE SCOTT. This was Tony Scott's first venture into television directing; in a prebroadcast interview he described the thirty-minute format as "very immediate," providing opportunities for "a fresh look, fresh energy and fresh pacing." Ridley Scott believed that the series would prove attractive to audiences in the wake of the success of science fiction films such as *Independence Day* (1996), so long as it was suitably structured: "Any fantasy . . . is only powerful and only really functions well if the creator has set up parameters, and within those parameters are the elements of the truth for that story. Science fiction gives the director, the artists, and the writer a stage upon which anything can go—providing you stay within the bounds of the walls that you set for yourself before you set out."

Scott described *The Hunger* in an interview with *Cinefantastique* as "a facet of fantasy. It isn't science in this instance. It's psychological, sexual fantasy. It's 'hunger'—the association of the word 'hunger' is also 'yearning.' Put together, hunger and yearning have a different, slightly sinister undertone. That's the series." Tony Scott added that the episodes would provide "a wholly different look at vampires—not vampires with teeth . . . these characters come through as being otherworldly or mortal beings. We try to make them as credible and as real-life as possible."

Filmed largely in Canada, the series was deliberately small-scale both in terms of casting and production values. Although not well received at the time, both series have subsequently acquired a cult following, being released on DVD in 2002 and 2003. A list of episodes with plot summaries follows:

Series 1

1. "The Swords" (broadcast 20 July 1997). *Director*: Tony Scott. *Cast*: BALTHAZAR GETTY. A lonely young American becomes infatuated with a showgirl whose body seems not to suffer any pain when she is stabbed with swords. However, their love affair changes everything.
2. "Marriage à Trois" (broadcast 20 July 1997). *Director*: Jake Scott. *Director of Photography*: JOHN MATHIESON. *Cast*: Lena Headey, Daniel Craig. A disabled woman runs a lascivious household with a young man and a nurse.
3. "Necros" (broadcast 20 July 1997). *Director*: RUSSELL MULCAHY. *Cast*: Philip Casnoff. A man falls for a deadly combination of a beautiful woman and her elderly companion.
4. "The Face of Helene Bournouw" (broadcast 27 February 1998). *Director*: Richard Cuipka. *Cast*: Stephen McHattie. A woman in a red overcoat causes many people to commit suicide.
5. "But at My Back, I Always Hear" (broadcast 31 August 1997). *Director*: Patricia Rozema. *Cast*: Michael Gross. A university professor is tormented by a female student.
6. "Footsteps" (broadcast 27 March 1998). *Director*: Jimmy Kaufman. *Cast*: Sofia Shinas. A vampire-woman searches for male victims and eventually meets a fellow vampire.
7. "Red Light" (broadcast 21 September 1997). *Director*: Christian Dugury. *Cast*: Lilliana Komorowska. A photographer obsessively snaps one of his female victims.
8. "Room 17" (broadcast 10 August 1997). *Director*: ERIK CANUEL. *Cast*: Curtis Armstrong. A traveling sales representative encounters his ideal woman on the television screen.
9. "The Secret Shih Tan" (broadcast 27 July 1997). *Director*: Russell Mulcahy. *Cast*: Jason Scott-Lee. An upwardly mobile chef serves up a human being as a special dish.

10. "The Other Woman" (broadcast 20 March 1998). *Director*: George Mihalka. *Cast*: JOANNA CASSIDY. A top female fashion designer falls for her married boss.

11. "Clarimonde" (broadcast 20 March 1998). *Director*: Tom Dey. *Cast*: David Lahaye, Audrey Benoît. A celibate priest is tempted by the thoughts of an ideal woman.

12. "Bridal Suite" (broadcast 3 August 1997). *Director*: Erik Canuel. *Cast*: Sally Kirkland, Colin Ferguson. A young married couple spends a night at a lonely inn. After a night of passionate lovemaking the groom disappears.

13. "The Sloan Men" (broadcast 28 September 1997). *Director*: Darrell Wasyk. *Cast*: Margot Kidder, Clare Sims. A newly wed woman discovers that her husband and father-in-law have magical powers over her.

14. "Plain Brown Envelope" (broadcast 6 March 1998). *Director*: Michel David. *Cast*: Jesse Borrego. A hitchhiker encounters a man whose truck is full of sex-aids.

15. "A Matter of Style" (broadcast 26 October 1997). *Director*: John Hamilton. *Cast*: Chad Lowe, Isabelle Cya. A vampire educates her protégé in the black arts.

16. "Anais" (broadcast 17 August 1997). *Director*: Darrell Wasyk. *Cast*: Nick Mancuso, Rebecca Dewey. An architect finds that all his drawings include a beautiful girl who fulfills all his sexual fantasies.

17. "I'm Dangerous Tonight" (broadcast 21 September 1997). *Director*: Russell Mulcahy. *Cast*: Esai Morales, Marie-Josee Croze. A young fashion designer causes mayhem while wearing a red dress.

18. "Fly by Night" (broadcast 31 January 1998). *Director*: Pierre Dalpé. *Cast*: Giancarlo Esposito, Kim Feeney. A war veteran encounters a vampire while spending the night in a mental hospital.

19. "No Radio" (broadcast 24 August 1997). *Director*: Howard Rodman. *Cast*: Amanda de Cadenet, Bruce Ramsay. Extra-marital lovers indulge in a complex series of role-plays.

20. "The Lighthouse" (broadcast 20 February 1998). *Director*: Darrell Wasyk from a story by Edgar Allan Poe. *Cast*: Bruce Davidson. A man with a broken heart tries and fails to find solace in an isolated lighthouse.

21. "A River of Night's Dreaming" (broadcast 6 February 1998). *Director*: John Warwicker. *Cast*: Ann Turkel, Marni Thompson. A female jailbird finds herself in a mysterious convent-like institution.

22. "Hidebound" (broadcast 23 January 1998). *Director*: Jeff Fazio. *Cast*: Brooke Smith, Paul Hopkins. A student taking a part-time job as a security guard meets an evil spirit in a lonely building.

Series 2

1. "Sanctuary" (broadcast 10 September 1999). *Director*: Tony Scott. *Cast*: David Bowie, Tony Calabretta. A crazed artist conducts bizarre experiments on a detective working for one of his rivals.

2. "Skin Deep" (broadcast 10 September 1999). *Director*: LUKE SCOTT. *Cast*: Sarain Boylan, Kim Feeney. A young woman falls in love with a lesbian dancer.

3. "The Dream Sentinel" (broadcast 10 September 1999). *Director*: Chris Hartwill. *Cast*: Eric Roberts, Alice Poon. A lap-dancer is haunted by the ghost of a previous lover.

4. "Wrath of God" (broadcast 9 January 2000). *Director*: Russell Mulcahy. *Cast*: Anthony Michael Hall, Carl Bernard. An angel dedicated to eradicating evil torments an apartment block.

5. "Nunc Dimittis" (broadcast 10 October 1999). *Director*: Russell Mulcahy. *Cast*: David Warner, Marini Orsini. An elderly retainer looks for a young hoodlum to take his place in a princess household.

6. "The Seductress" (broadcast 13 February 2000). *Director*: Alain Desrochers. *Cast*: William Katt, Rachel Hayward. A middle-aged female novelist seduces a young boy and suffers as a result.

7. "Brass" (broadcast 21 November 1999). *Director*: Jeff Fazio. *Cast*: Polly Shannon, Jesse Todd. A middle-aged man is tormented by a witch.

8. "Approaching Desdemona "(broadcast 6 February 2000). *Director*: Jason Hreno. *Cast*: William McNamara, Marie-Josée Colburn. A man falls in love with an ideal woman who emerges from his computer screen.

9. "Week Woman" (broadcast 17 October 1999). *Director*: Daniel Grou. *Cast*: Brooke Smith, David La Haye. A French artist marries a lesbian but finds he has got more than he expects.

10. "Triangle in Steel" (broadcast 14 September 1999). *Director*: Adrian Moat. *Cast*: Richard Robtaille, Victoria Sanchez. A man working on a bridge in a remote area falls in love with a a member of the NATIVE PEOPLES with unfortunate results.

11. "The Falling Man" (broadcast 27 February 2000). *Director*: Daniel Grou. *Cast*: A. Martinez, Maria Bertrand. An architect falls in love with a young artist.

12. "Night Bloomer" (broadcast 24 October 1999). *Director*: Erik Canuel. *Cast*: Glenn Plummer, Renée Madeline Le Guerrier. An ambitious executive and an unscrupulous scientist create a poisonous plant.

13. "The Suction Method" (broadcast 5 March 2000). *Director*: Darrell Wasyk. *Cast*: Fisher Stevens, Valérie Valois. An unusual view of carpet cleaning in suburban America.

14. "I'm Very Dangerous Tonight" (never broadcast). *Director*: Alain Desrochers. *Cast*: Paul Hopkins. A husband buys his wife a red dress, which transforms her into a deadly force.

15. "Replacements" (broadcast 28 November 1999). *Director*: Bruce M. Smith. *Cast*: Andreas Apergis, Pascale Devigne. A childless husband is menaced by vampires.

16. "And She Laughed" (broadcast 3 October 1999). *Director*: Jean Beaudin. *Cast*: Jennifer Beals, Ben Bass. A young academic living alone is menaced by a mysterious intruder.

17. "The Sacred Fire" (broadcast 3 January 2000). *Director*: Russell Mulcahy. *Cast*: Kim Huffman, James Marshall. A Good Samaritan meets a psychopathic schoolmate after many years.

18. "The Diarist" (broadcast 31 October 1999). *Director*: Alain Desrochers. *Cast*: Lisa Ann Hadley, Ian M. Watson. A young woman uses witchcraft to take revenge on her ex-lover.

19. "Double" (never broadcast). *Director*: John L'Écuyer. *Cast*: Lori Petty. A woman meets her doppelganger who tries to kill her.

20. "Bottle of Smoke" (broadcast 16 January 2000). *Director*: Jean Beaudin. *Cast*: Cathy Moriarty, Soo Gray. A woman visiting Morocco in the 1940s inherits a bottle with a genie in it.

21. "Sin Seer" (broadcast 7 November 1999). *Director*: Daniel Grou. *Cast*: Brad Dourif, Nancy-Ann Michaud. A psychopath predicts the future.

22. "The Perfect Couple" (broadcast 23 January 2000). *Director*: Darrell Wasyk. *Cast*: Bruce Dinsmore, Marie-Josée Colburn. A happy husband and wife are plagued by a mysterious presence.

Despite the producers' claims that the series would be "fresh" and "credible," the first series of *The Hunger* is actually very predictable; each episode follows a familiar pattern, with the protagonists suffering in one way or another, being involved in the obligatory sex scene and eventually being destroyed or destroying someone else. The characters conform to fairly predictable gender stereotypes (women are either victims or rapacious whores) while the photography is generally influenced by rock video conventions, with rapid cuts and colorful imagery.

Nonetheless, there are some aspects of the series that are worth commenting on. In "The Secret Shih Tan" (Series 1, Episode 9) a megalomaniac socialite Hugo (Kenneth Welsh) asks an upwardly mobile Chinese restaurant chef to cook him a meal according to the dictates laid down in the secret *Shih Tan*; a book of forbidden knowledge known only to the Chinese. When the chef objects, Hugo threatens to close his restaurant down. Eventually the chef agrees, even though he has to serve human flesh as part of the meal. The *Shih Tan* rules dictate that the flesh must be female, and must be taken at the point of orgasm. The chef duly makes love to Hugo's beautiful female sidekick, but kills Hugo and cooks

him instead. Director Russell Mulcahy's emphasis on the violence associated with oriental ritual recalls similar scenes in *BLACK RAIN*.

Kim Feeney's performance in "Fly By Night" (Series 1, Episode 18) as a war veteran in charge of a platoon, whose leadership abilities are called into question when one of her soldiers is accidentally blown up, anticipates DEMI MOORE's characterization in *G.I. JANE*. Both women are slim, almost man-like in appearance, fond of showing off their muscles and ready to fight with men at any and every opportunity. In "Fly By Night" the soldier is eventually driven mad with guilt, sells her soul to a vampire (Giancarlo Esposito), and decides to "leave nothing living" in pursuit of "eternal life."

The best episodes in the series are the first two—"The Swords" and "Marriage à Trois." Both of them were filmed in England. The first, directed by Tony Scott concerns a young woman (Amanda Ryan) who forms part of a specialty act where she is stabbed with sharp-edged swords and apparently feels no pain. She encounters a young American (Balthazar Getty) and falls in love, releasing a flood of emotion within her. Unable to cope with this, she no longer remains impervious to the swords, and dies on stage. Like Rachael in *BLADE RUNNER*, the young woman led a REPLICANT-like existence until the man comes along. The entire episode is photographed in a series of bright colors, mirroring the turbulence within her mind.

"Marriage à Trois," photographed by John Mathieson also foregrounds the bright colors of an old, disabled woman's (Karen Black's) bedroom—the bright red curtains concealing the windows, the shiny brown linoleum on the floor. She spends her life on morphine, which encourages her to dream almost incessantly of sex. Her fantasies are encouraged by a priapic nurse (Lena Headey) who regularly takes the old woman's junkie companion (Daniel Craig) to bed. At length fantasy and reality become inseparable; the old woman brainwashes the nurse into killing the young man and advertising for a new male companion/sex-slave. The episode ends with the woman saying "good help is so hard to find"; the word "help" here is deliberately ambiguous. In a pre-Bond role, Daniel Craig does not have to do much other than show off his supple body.

The second series seems preoccupied with predatory women: in "Nunc Dimittis" (Series 2, Episode 5) a young man meets a beautiful princess (Marini Orsini) and finds himself possessed by her dreams. Later on he becomes one of her sacrificial victims, as she drinks his blood and takes him on as her new servant. In "Brass" the male central character's girlfriend (Polly Shannon) turns out to be a witch trying to protect him from evil spirits. "Approaching Desdemona" (Episode 8) recalls "Room 17" (Series 1, Episode 8) in its portrayal of an ideal woman living in a computer screen, who eventually swallows up the male central character. "Week

Woman" (Episode 9) returns to the theme of bondage, as the lesbian lover of the male protagonist (Brooke Smith) ties him up and burns him on the chest with an iron. The female protagonist of "The Falling Man" (Episode 11) eventually persuades the male architect to jump to his death off a skyscraper. "The Suction Method" (Episode 13, one of the best in the series) recycles the plot of "Approaching Desdemona" by having the male central character swallowed up by beautiful girl who transforms into a carpet cleaning machine. "And She Laughed" (Episode 16) imagines a familiar situation with a young woman menaced by an unseen male character peering through the letterbox; she eventually gets her revenge by repeatedly stabbing him to death. "The Diarist" (Episode 18) likewise explores the theme of revenge, as a jilted female lover uses witchcraft in an attempt to kill her exboyfriend. Such characterizations might help to attract viewers; but they cast doubt on Scott's reputation as someone interested in exploring gender constructions.

As in the first series, there is a preoccupation with the distinction between "reality" and "illusion." The computerized woman in "Approaching Desdemona" is so "real" to the central character that she eventually takes over his life. In "Replacements" (Episode 15) a woman unable to have children opts for a "replacement" child—which eventually turns out to be a deadly predator (recalling the creature in *ALIEN*). "The Perfect Couple" (Episode 22) depicts the central characters as robots whose hearts and minds are controlled by a mysterious character (Noel Burton)—recalling Tyrell in *Blade Runner*. This theme is continually reiterated in the host Julian Priest's (David Bowie's) introductions to each episode: human beings should try to distinguish between the artificial and the tangible, if they wish to survive in this world.

More interestingly, several episodes in the second series of *The Hunger* seem to have been inspired by *Alien*. In "Night Bloomer" (Episode 12) the male central character is attacked by a predatory plant in a sequence very reminiscent of the face-hugging moment where Kane (JOHN HURT) discovers the alien for the first time. The same could also be said for the climactic moment in "And She Laughed," where the male protagonist is swallowed up face first by a carpetcleaning machine. In "Bottle of Smoke" (Episode 20) the references to Scott's film are more explicit as the heroine willingly allows herself to be possessed by a (male) genie but is simultaneously warned not to permit it to "grow inside

your body." Sadly, she fails to heed the advice, and the genie can now roam free, even when the woman has died. Julian Priest returns to the same theme in his closing remarks to "The Perfect Couple," when he describes MARRIAGE as a kind of prison in which people try to bury their differences. They never go away, however, but rather "grow inside you until [they] absorb you completely, [and] all you are left with is the hate."

The Hunger was nominated for an Emmy in 1998 for Outstanding Main Title Design. Bernard Couture won Canadian Society of Cinematographers Award in 2000 for his work on "Sanctuary" (Series 2, Episode 1).

Reference

Frank Barron, "*The Hunger*: Showtime's Adult Horror," *Cinefantastique* 28, no.12 (June 1997): 7.

HURT, JOHN (1940–)

Born in Derbyshire, England, John Hurt made his name in television and theater before making his name in the Independent Television (ITV) production of *The Naked Civil Servant* (1975) and the BBC's *I Claudius* a year later. He worked with Scott on some of his early commercials, including voiceovers for MOTHER'S PRIDE.

Hurt took over the role of Kane in *ALIEN* after Jon Finch, Scott's original choice, became ill. He portrays the character as a typical Company man, dedicated to his work and not particularly worried about anything else. He searches the alien planet for new forms of life; but eventually pays for his inquisitiveness as the alien invades his body.

Hurt's most famous scene is the famous "chestbusting" sequence, one which according to the psychologist Raj Persaud has "entered Western consciousness" in the last twenty-five years. Persaud argues that this is because viewers are fascinated with "the idea of things bursting out of other things and separating the goodness from the badness is very appealing. To choose a rather gross example, when you burst a [pimple], you've removed all the badness and the sense of bursting is enjoyable. That's what Scott [and Hurt] is playing on, that notion of a clean break."

Hurt sportingly reprised this sequence in Mel Brooks's spoof film *Spaceballs* (1987).

Reference

Raj Persaud, "Mind Games," *Empire*, September 1994, 68.

I

I AM LEGEND

US 2007 r/t 101 min col. *Production Companies*: Warner Bros. Pictures, Village Roadshow Pictures, Overbrook Entertainment, 3 Arts Entertainment, Heyday Films, Original Film. *Producers*: Akiva Goldsman, David Heyman, James Lassiter, and Neal Moritz. *Director*: Francis Lawrence. *Writers*: Mark Protosevich and Akiva Goldman from the novel by Richard Matheson and the screenplay by John William Corrington and Joyce Corrington. *Director of Photography*: Andrew Lesnie. *Production Designer*: Naomi Shohan. *Music*: James Newton Howard. *Cast*: Will Smith (*Robert Neville*), Alice Braga (*Anna*), Darrell Foster (*Mike*), Dash Mihok (*Alpha Male*).

Adaptation of a novel by Richard Matheson, already filmed as *The Last Man on Earth* (1960) and *The Omega Man* (1970). Scott intended to film the work immediately after *G.I. JANE* in 1997, with a script by Mark Protosevich and revised by JOHN LOGAN. The script was sent to Scott by way of Warner Bros. and Arnold Schwarzenegger. Scott told Paul M. SAMMON that he immediately accepted on the grounds that he wanted to work with the actor and because the book itself "contained a fascinating idea. That man's [the hero's] arrogance in dealing with genetics and disease and success with research had backfired on him and resulted in a mutated, airborne virus that had gotten loose and couldn't be controlled."

The project was going to be set in Los Angeles, and Scott and Logan worked on the script. However, the project was abandoned by Warner Bros., chiefly due to the projected size of the budget. Scott claimed that this was due to the studio's experience of recent box-office failures such as *WATERWORLD*. He also experienced problems with the script and with the design of the monsters. He "did want the vampires [in the film] to look monstrous, but we had difficulty with making them look monstrous without humanizing them . . . So we let that one go."

The film was eventually made in 2007 and grossed $77,211,321 on its opening weekend in 3,606 theaters, averaging $21,412 per venue, and placing it at the top of the box office. The film was the sixth-highest grossing movie of 2007, and as of July 2008 stands as the forty-second highest grossing film ever at the American box office.

Reference

Ridley Scott, quoted in Paul M. Sammon, "Joining the Club: Ridley Scott on *G.I. Jane*," in *Ridley Scott Interviews*, ed. Laurence F. Knapp and Andrea F. Kulas (Jackson: University Press of Mississippi, 2005), 169–71.

Bibliography

David Hughes, *The Greatest Sci-Fi Movies Never Made*, rev. ed. (London: Titan Books, 2008), 125–46; "I am Legend by John Logan," Script dated 8 September 1997, www.fortunecity.com/tattooine/clarke/38/scripts/IAmLegend.txt (accessed 28 February 2009).

IGNATIUS, DAVID (1950–)

Armenian-American journalist and columnist for the *Washington Post*. His 2006 novel *Penetration*, about the adventures of a CIA man Roger Ferris in Europe and the Middle East, served as the source for *BODY OF LIES*.

Scott was quoted in the film's production notes as saying that the novel "has an unusually incisive view into what actually happens up on the front lines, and the people at the front who make a difference." Ignatius himself recalled that the novel came about because he saw the spy business as "a lot like journalism. It's about identifying people who know things, gaining their trust, and then getting them to cross a line and tell you things they might not want to initially." It was this visceral, down-and-dirty look into the real lives of intelligence operatives that especially intrigued Scott: "I liked the idea of exploring the contrasts between the man on the ground and the man at the helm."

Penetration was re-released as *Body of Lies*, once Warner Bros. had acquired the film rights, in 2007.

Reference

"*Production Notes: Body of Lies*" (Los Angeles: Warner Bros. Entertainment, 2008), http://mix96tulsa.com/movies/notes/body-of-lies/note/4 (accessed January 16, 2009)

THE INFORMER: "NO FURTHER QUESTIONS"

GB 1967 TVM r/t 60 min b/w. *Production Company*: Rediffusion (ITV). *Producer*: Stella Richman. *Director*: Ridley Scott. *Writer*: Peter Wildeblood, based on characters created by Geoffrey Bellman and John Whitney. *Cast*: Ian Hendry (*Alex Lambert*), Neil Hallett (*Det. Sgt. Piper*), Jean Marsh (*Sylvia Parrish*), John Fraser (*Nicky Loach*), Ursula Howells (*Lady Tregunter*).

An episode from the second series (Episode 8) broadcast on Independent Television in Great Britain on 6 November 1967. When a blackmailer threatens a famous judge, and that judge happens to be the one who disbarred Alex Lambert from his profession, the informer has no hesitation in nailing the crooks. *The Informer* ran for two seasons from 1966 to 1967, with twenty-one programs in total, and starred Ian Hendry, who had previously made his name in *The Avengers*. "No Further Questions" was the only episode to be directed by Scott.

THE INFORMER: "YOUR SECRETS ARE SAFE WITH US, MR. LAMBERT"

GB 1967 TVM r/t 60 min b/w. *Production Company*: Rediffusion (ITV). *Executive Producer*: Stella Richman. *Producer*: John Whitney. *Director*: Ridley Scott. *Writer*: John Tyler, based on characters created by Geoffrey Bellman and John Whitney. *Production Designer*: Frank Nerini. *Cast*: Ian Hendry (*Alex Lambert*), Heather Sears (*Helen Lambert*), Neil Hallett (*Det. Sgt. Piper*), Jean Marsh (*Sylvia Parrish*), Peter Copley (*Richard Edwards*).

Two private detectives turn out to be planning a jewelry raid on their "clients." Unfortunately for them, they attract the attention of the Informer . . . . Another episode in the second series (Episode 8) of the popular television series. Unfortunately no copy of the program has been released.

IN HER SHOES

US/ Germany 2005 r/t 125 min col. *Production Companies*: Fox 2000 Pictures, Scott Free, Deuce Three Productions, Kumar Mobiliengesellschaft mbH & Co. Projekt Nr.3 KG. *Producers*: Ridley Scott, Carol Fenelon, Lisa Ellzey, and Curtis Hanson. *Director*: Curtis Hanson. *Writer*: Susannah Grant, from the novel by Jennifer Weiner. *Director of Photography*: Terry Stacey. *Production Designer*: Philip J. Bartell. *Production Designer*: Dan Davis. *Music*: Mark Isham. *Cast*: Cameron Diaz (*Maggie*), Mark Feuerstein (*Simon Stein*), Toni Collette (*Rose*), Shirley MacLaine (*Ella Hirsch*), Jerry Adler (*Lewis Feldman*), Norman Lloyd (*The Professor*), Brooke Smith (*Amy*).

This adaptation by SUSANNAH GRANT of JENNIFER WEINER's CHICK LIT novel was developed by Ridley Scott's company, SCOTT FREE in association with Fox 2000. CURTIS HANSON was engaged to direct and Carol Fenelon

to produce. The three principal roles were cast one by one: CAMERON DIAZ agreed first, followed by TONI COLLETTE (who put on an extra twenty-five pounds for the role of Rose), and lastly SHIRLEY MACLAINE, playing against type in the role of Ella. Hanson recalled in a preproduction interview that he began by telling the actress that she was "big in every way that's wrong for this part. This part is somebody who's quiet and hiding. You have this talent and this personality that you have exploited so well over the decades . . . Ultimately, she knew that she was being challenged . . . Once she felt that she could trust me, she craved this opportunity."

The film was shot in Philadelphia, Los Angeles, and Florida during one month in May 2004 on a tight budget. On its US release in October 2005, the reviews were generally favorable: *Empire* noted that, while the film provided yet another contribution to "the post-Bridget [Jones] chick-lit phenomenon . . . [Hanson] isn't afraid to pay tribute to the significance of human emotions, however apparently small, and the subtleties of evolving, maturing relationships." Lorien Haynes in *Film Review* discovered "[a] depth to the cinematography, and a realism [in the film], and that's true of the performances too." Released in Great Britain a month later, *In Her Shoes* attracted equally enthusiastic reviews: Jessica Winter in *Sight and Sound* noted the multiple symbolism of the shoe as "instrument of betrayal; link to the past; index of stability (a broken heel forestalls a broken engagement); and binge object—Rose has a closetful of pricey, barely worn footwear."

In Her Shoes takes up where *THELMA & LOUISE* left off in its link between shoes and female identity. The earlier film includes a sequence where Louise (SUSAN SARANDON) packs a pair of shoes in a plastic bag in preparation for her journey; in Hanson's film Rose has a cupboard full of shoes that she never wears. She explains to her sister Maggie (Diaz) that when she feels bad, she likes to treat herself: "shoes always fit." However, she possesses such low self-esteem that she never plucks up the courage to wear them in public. Maggie is shocked: "Shoes like this should not be locked in a closet. They should be living a life of scandal and passion, getting screwed in an alleyway by a billionaire, while his frigid wife waits in the limo thinking that he just went back in the bar to get his cellphone." Even when Rose actually wears a pair of her shoes, when she attends her friend Jim Danvers's (Richard Burgi's) engagement party, she finds that one of the heels has broken. This mishap sums up her existence, as well as foreshadowing her broken engagement to Simon Stein (MARK FEUERSTEIN).

While Maggie seems perfectly at ease wearing her sister's shoes (which might suggest a certain confidence), director Hanson shows this is nothing more than an illusion; like her sister she considers herself a failure, unable either to hold down a job or sustain a relationship for any length of time. This is emphasized in a sequence where she auditions as an MTV "VJ." The (unseen) executive asks her to read the autocue, "look into the camera, and give it that, that personality." Although stunningly attired, Maggie cannot show her real personality on account of her dyslexia. Needless to say, the company decides not to hire her. Other characters experience similar image problems: Mrs. Lefkewitz (Francine Beers), a guest at the retirement home where Ella lives, who returns in depression from a visit to the local shopping mall: "[It] is for young people, people with teeth . . . You know what I saw today? . . . Pants with 'Juicy' written across the heinie. I'm gonna wear that?"

Hanson suggests that the only way to overcome such inhibitions is to be true to oneself—in metaphorical terms, to wear one's own clothing (including shoes) and be comfortable with it. As the action unfolds, Maggie's self-esteem gradually increases as she learns to care for others, who respond by caring for her. This is achieved in several ways: by reading poetry out loud to the retired professor (Norman Lloyd); or by advising Mrs. Lefkewitz on the right kind of clothing to wear for her son's wedding. Maggie herself cares little for her appearance—as shown when she walks towards the camera in a supermarket wearing overalls and sneakers. Rose's transformation is signaled as she walks confidently up the aisle, accompanied by her father Michael (Ken Howard), wearing a pair of expensive shoes (lent to her for the occasion by Ella). All the old inhibitions have evaporated; she now possesses the courage to wear what she pleases in public. Hanson suggests this by means of a close-up that begins at her feet and then tracks upwards to her silk wedding dress and her bouquet of flowers, and ends with a medium close-up of her smiling face. This is followed by a point-of-view shot of Maggie, Ella and Simon all looking at her admiringly as she walks towards them.

In Her Shoes is also about overcoming loneliness, both mental and physical. Both Rose and Maggie are prisoners of their respective existences: Rose devotes all her energies to her job as a lawyer (to avoid thinking about herself), while Maggie picks up men and gets drunk most nights. Even when they get together, they fail to connect with one another. This is emphasized in a scene at a late-night diner, which begins with the two of them held in a two-shot as they laugh and joke with each other. When Rose asks the server "Are you hiring?" the mood abruptly changes, as her sister objects to the idea of working "the graveyard shift serving pancakes to cops and whores and drunks." When Rose insists that "there's a whole world of commerce out there that has nothing to do with sex," Maggie flounces out in a huff. The latter part of this sequence comprises a series of close-ups of each sister at the edge of the frame, flanked by empty seats, emphasizing their alienation from one another.

Following the example of designer TOM FODEN in *MATCHSTICK MEN*, Hanson reinforces this theme by means of the paintings of John Register, which hang on the walls of Rose's and Ella's houses. In a documentary accompanying the DVD release of *In Her Shoes*, Hansen justified his design concept by explaining how Register's work eliminates people together, creating images that draw attention to the void as well as emphasizing the twin themes of loneliness and alienation.

All three protagonists—Rose, Maggie, and Ella—suffer in this way because they cannot reconcile themselves to the loss of Caroline—Ella's daughter and the sisters' mother. They pretend that it never happened at all. However, when Ella shows the sisters a photograph album full of fading images, the truth gradually emerges: Caroline was a wonderful mother to her children, but experienced mental health problems. Ella wanted to keep her daughter on medication, and judged that her relationship with her husband Michael was "far too passionate for her to handle." Michael wanted to put Caroline away on the grounds that she was "unfit" to look after children. With no means to resist either of them, Caroline had committed suicide by driving her car into a tree. Hanson stages one of these revelatory scenes—involving the two sisters—in front of a bathroom mirror. As they speak, both Rose and Maggie look into it, suggesting that they are at last coming to terms with themselves and their shared CHILDHOOD.

In Her Shoes follows earlier Scott work—as director and producer—by focusing on the idea of parenthood. As in *MONKEY TROUBLE*, several characters prove bad parents: Ella appears "bossy, self-righteous, [and] nosy about things that weren't her business"; Michael wants Caroline to be hospitalized and later decided to cut Ella out of his family's life in the belief that they "were better off without her;" while his second wife Sydelle (Candice Azzara) dotes on her daughter Marcia (Jackie Geary), but pays scant attention to her stepdaughters. Even when she does stage an engagement party, Sydelle humiliates Rose by criticizing her love of books, her inability to sustain a romance, and her fondness for food. Thus it is not surprising that Rose should ask: "Why is she giving me this party? She hates me. Someone else should do it, somebody who l-loves me, someone who looks at me and say[s] 'all of this is nothing more than the happiness you deserve.'" The only person who unreservedly loved her children was Caroline. Maggie remembers that "she was special, different from other moms. She used to surprise us. One time I opened up my lunch box and there was a tiara inside." On another day she dressed her children in their best party dresses and took them to Lord and Taylor, the specialist department store in NEW YORK, in a vain attempt to sell fudge to them. The fudge ended up being spilt over the jewelry counter, but Rose recalls that "oh, God, she [Caroline] was beautiful" as she promised to buy presents for her daughters. Such memories prompt Ella into wishing that she had kept her big mouth shut sufficiently to hear what her daughter wanted out of life. The only unselfish "parent" in the film—understood, in this sense, as someone who dotes on others without expecting anything in return—is Maggie, who reads poetry to the professor, even though she is not very good at it. Just how much he appreciates it is revealed after his death, when his grandson (David Shatraw) tells Maggie that the professor talked about her "just a little" immediately before he passed away.

In Her Shoes sustains Scott's penchant for including direct literary quotations in the script. In *BLADE RUNNER*, Batty (RUTGER HAUER) quotes directly from WILLIAM BLAKE; in *In Her Shoes* Maggie reads "One Art" by Elizabeth Bishop to the professor, and quotes from e.e.cummings's "i carry your heart with me" in the final scene. Both poems are used to emphasize the importance of families loving one another as a way of insuring themselves against loneliness. Simon's father (Alan Blumenfeld) makes the point in his toast to Rose and Simon: "We're all blessed to be part of your happiness. Your love bonds not just your two hearts, but the hearts of two families."

So far there have been no scholarly essays devoted to *In Her Shoes*, but plenty has appeared on the CHICK LIT genre. Suzanne Ferris and Mallory Young's anthology (2005) contains several good examples. Katarzyna Smycznska looks at discourses of identity in the genre, focusing in particular on *Bridget Jones' Diary*. Caroline J. Smith argues that many authors working within chick lit provide complicated representations of women, designed to challenge existing stereotypes as well as provoke new conceptions of femininity.

References

Liz Beardsworth, "In Her Shoes," *Empire* 198 (December 2005): 48; Brad Balfour, "Curtis Hanson: The Director Steps into a Woman's World," PopEntertainment.com (15 October 2005), www.popentertainment.com/curtishanson.htm (accessed 8 August 2008); Suzanne Ferris and Mallory Young, eds., *Chick Lit: The New Women's Fiction* (New York and London: Routledge, 2005); Susannah Grant, "*In Her Shoes* Script" (transcribed from the DVD version of the film), www.script-o-rama.com/movie_scripts/i/in-her-shoes-script-transcript.html (accessed 17 January 2009); Lorien Haynes, "*In Her Shoes*: Grown Up Chick Flick," *Film Review* 664 (December 2005): 97; Caroline J. Smith, *Cosmopolitan Culture and Consumerism in Chick Lit* (London and New York: Routledge, 2007); Katarzyna Smyczynska, *The World According to Bridget Jones: Discourses of Identity in ChickLit Fictions* (New York: Peter Lang Publishing. 2007); Jessica Winter, "In Her Shoes," *Sight and Sound* 15, no.12 (December 2005): 57.

Bibliography

Kelly Borgeson, "Sophie de Rakoff," *Premiere*, October 2005, 105; "*In Her Shoes*: Fall Movie Preview," *Premiere*, September 2005, 78;

Ben Marshall, "If the Shoe Fits, Film It," *Guardian Guide*, 19 November 2005, 8–10; "Take One: First Look: In her Shoes." *Premiere*, March 2005, 36.

INVASION OF THE BODY SNATCHERS

US 1956 r/t 80 min b/w. *Production Company*: Walter Wanger Productions. *Producer*: Walter Wanger. *Director*: Don Siegel. *Writers*: Daniel Mainwaring and Richard Collins (uncredited), from a *Collier's Magazine* serial by Jack Finney. *Director of Photography*: Ellsworth Fredericks. *Production Designer*: Joseph Kish. *Cast*: Kevin McCarthy (*Dr. Miles J. Bennell*), Dana Wynter (*Becky Driscoll*), Larry Gates (*Dr. Dan ("Danny") Kauffman*), King Donovan (*Jack Belicec*), Carolyn Jones (*Teddy Belicec*), Ralph Dumke (*Police Chief Nick Grivett*).

Don Siegel's classic sci-fi film of the mid 1950s resembles *ALIEN* in its concern for what might happen if an alien transforms itself into a human being. Such films, according to Joseph Chien, "subvert human form and behavior—make of them something unknown." When the alien becomes the human being, it has the potential to destroy human society. It is no longer the "other" but has become part of the self. Ridley Scott himself suggested in one interview that the alien's next manifestation might be in human form. On the other hand, the alien is also identified as something that violates the human body. It uses people not as templates—as in *Invasion of the Body Snatchers*—but as a living incubator. The process of implantation involves entrance through the mouth, and exit through violent means—the stomach.

Reference

Joseph Chien, "Containing Horror: the *Alien* Trilogy and the Abject," *Focus Magazine* 14 (April 1994): 11.

IRONS, JEREMY (1948–)

Made his name on screen with *The French Lieutenant's Woman* (1981) and the television adaptation of *Brideshead Revisited* (1983). Later successes include *Lolita* (1997) and *Being Julia* (2004).

Irons's role of Tiberias in *KINGDOM OF HEAVEN* is remarkably faithful to his historical model, Raymond of Tripoli. In scene after scene, he parries the moves of the bloodthirsty Reynald and the ambitious Guy; at the end, when all is lost, he retreats to the island of Cyprus—as did Raymond. According to the book of the film, Irons's no-nonsense work ethic won admiration from all the other cast and crew, as did his willingness to modulate his own powerful acting style as needed to balance his scenes with the younger leads. Irons admired the film immensely; in a preproduction interview with the British magazine *Empire* he described it as "spectacle; it's emotional; what he's [Scott has] captured is fantastic . . . This is historical 'faction' come of age."

His role in the film is similar to that of Crassus (DEREK JACOBI) in *GLADIATOR*—someone who understands the hero's motives, yet is lacking sufficient moral or physical strength to support him. When deciding to pull out of Jerusalem, Tiberias admits that he misunderstood the situation: "First I thought we [the Christians] were fighting for God. Then I realized we were fighting for wealth and land. I was ashamed."

References
"Kingdom of Heaven," *Empire*, May 2005, 84; Diana Landau, ed., *Kingdom of Heaven: The Ridley Scott Film and the History behind the Story* (London: Simon and Schuster Ltd., 2005), 73.

ISAACS, JASON (1963–)
Born in Liverpool, United Kingdom, Isaacs made his name in films such as *Event Horizon* (1997), *Armageddon* (1998), and most notably as a sadistic British officer in Mel Gibson's *The Patriot* (2000).

As Steele in *BLACK HAWK DOWN*, Isaacs plays a Ranger who is initially skeptical of the Delta Force. In KEN NOLAN's script he tells them: "You D-Boys are a bunch of undistinguished cowboys. Let me tell you something, soldier. When we get on the five yard line, you're gonna need my Rangers . . . It's rough out there." He also demands absolute loyalty from those under him: when he sees Pilla (Danny Hoch) making fun of him in front of the troops, Steele grabs him in a headlock and growls: "If I ever see you undermine me again, you'll be cleaning latrines with your tongue until you can't taste the difference between shit and French fries. Is that clear?" On the other hand, Steele does possess redeeming virtues, such as a paternalistic concern for the welfare of those under him. At one point Sanderson (WILLIAM FICHTNER) urges him to move his men out of a filthy stable which is under attack from enemy forces. Steele replies in a livid tone, "We are combat ineffective. We've got too many dang wounded to move . . . [We'll] treat the wounded, and we'll wait for the convoy." In a sequence deleted from the original release, but restored in *BLACK HAWK DOWN: EXTENDED CUT*, Steele is shown walking around the Olympic stadium with a look of horror as he surveys the dying and wounded soldiers around him. Even though he is battle-hardened, he never expected the campaign to end like this. Nonetheless, Steele remains convinced that he has done his duty—following the example of the real Rangers who were involved in the Somalian campaign. Isaacs suggested in an interview with A. C. Parfitt that "[E]very single one of them said that their first instinct, after learning about the crashed Black Hawks, was to get out there to the site and bring back every single one of their brothers . . . The Rangers were fighting for the guy on their left, and the guy on their right." In another interview with the British magazine *Premiere* Isaacs admired "the bravery and the passion that they [the Rangers] show for each other—nothing to do with what they are fighting for—it does take your breath away. And it makes you misty-eyed."

References
Jason Isaacs, quoted in A. C. Parfitt, *Orlando Bloom: The Biography* (London: John Blake Publishing Ltd., 2004), 50; Jason Isaacs, quoted in Fred Schruers, "The Way We War," *Premiere* 15, no.6 (February 2002): 85; Ken Nolan, *Black Hawk Down: The Shooting Script* (New York: Newmarket Press, 2002), 14, 17, 70–71.

ISHAM, MARK (1951–)
Made his name on films such as *Billy Bathgate* (1991), *Little Man Tate* (1991), and *A River Runs Through It* (1992).

Brought in at the last minute to do the score for *THE BROWNING VERSION*, Isham immediately became the subject of a dispute between director MIKE FIGGIS, producer Ridley Scott, and executive producer SHERRY LANSING. Figgis recalled that "it became clear from our conversation she [Lansing] had absolutely no idea that I was a musician and that I had something to do with the score . . . I was promptly fired as the composer and Mark Isham was brought in to redo the score . . . The theme that I wrote for Albert Finney became the theme for *Leaving Las Vegas*, a much-lauded musical score . . . I really felt that music was the key to Albert Finney's character." Such disputes had occurred in previous Scott films, most notably *LEGEND*, where the original JERRY GOLDSMITH score was replaced by one written by TANGERINE DREAM.

Isham's score for the film is based on swirling violins, which reach a crescendo in the final sequence, as the camera tracks backwards from Crocker-Harris's (ALBERT FINNEY's) face and surveys the school in relation to the landscape. The music suggests that the old teacher has discovered some kind of freedom, now that he has cast off his academic gowns and left the school.

Isham has also worked on other films by Ridley Scott, providing jaunty scores for *WHERE THE MONEY IS* and *IN HER SHOES*.

Reference
Mike Figgis, quoted in Robert J. Emery, *The Directors—Take Four* (New York: Allworth Press, 2003), 182–83.

IZDIAK, SLAWOMIR (1945–)
Born in Katowice, Poland, Slawomir Izdiak made his name photographing Kieslowski's *Trois Couleurs: Bleu* (1993). Other credits include *The Last September* (1999) and *Proof of Life* (2000).

Scott recalled in the "Director's Commentary" to the film's DVD release that Izdiak was initially somewhat daunted by the sheer scale of *BLACK HAWK DOWN* (having previously worked on small-scale productions). How-ever, Izdiak soon attuned himself to the task in hand. One of his major strategies was to employ a bold and often daring use of color. Izdiak recalled in an interview that "Ridley mentioned that the film should make spectators sick to their stomachs and . . . I was trying to find inspiration in the color of vomit . . . First, it helped spectators identify the different topography in the film; the military base is monochromatically greenish, the town in the first battle scene is orange-green, and the command center was lit somewhat theatrically with a dominant blue that corresponded with the color of the monitors."

Izdiak's colors also lent authority to the visuals. On the night scenes, for example, his decision to use green tones was made because "bluish night would have appeared too aggressive, and every cut would have made us conscious of the conventionality of that night color. Secondly, 'TV nights,' like those presented on CNN, are almost always greenish, so we automatically associate that color with authentic events."

In Izdiak's view what differentiated *Black Hawk Down* from other CONTEMPORARY WAR FILMS was its sheer variety of colors: "We incorporated a wide variety of methods. We shot with a complete lack of cinematic patterns, but our method was to shoot as dynamically and densely as we could. Ridley's main philosophy was to use every means possible to achieve that goal."

References

Slawomir Izdiak, interviewed in Christopher Probst, "Screen Gems," *American Cinematographer* 83, no.6 (June 2002): 84–86; Ridley Scott, "Director's Commentary" to the two-disc DVD release of *Black Hawk Down* (Los Angeles: Revolution Studios Distribution Company LLG & Jerry Bruckheimer, Inc., 2004).

JACOBI, DEREK (1939–)

Began his career at Birmingham Repertory Theatre and London's National Theatre. Jacobi made his name in Jack Pulman's adaptation of Robert Graves's novels—*I Claudius* (BBC, 1976).

Like MICHAEL GAMBON, Jacobi's film career has been largely confined to supporting roles. In *GLADIATOR* he plays Gracchus, the senator who is determined to end the corrupt reign of Commodus (JOAQUIN PHOENIX), even at the risk of his own life. In a newspaper interview with *The Times* published before the film's opening, he contrasted work on the screen epic with that of *I Claudius*: whereas the BBC production was small-scale in concept, "the size and scale of this set [on *GLADIATOR*] is just jaw-dropping . . . we could be sitting here having gone $20 million over budget."

As the British Prime Minister Stanley Baldwin in *THE GATHERING STORM*, Jacobi contrasts both physically and vocally with Winston Churchill (ALBERT FINNEY). Baldwin is a slight, almost diminutive figure with a calm, measured way of speaking; Churchill is a rotund, splenetic man with a love of rhetoric. The real Baldwin was a bluff, plain-speaking personality; in the film, however, he is portrayed as shortsighted, a willing dupe of those interested in minimizing the threat of Nazism to Britain's future stability. Jacobi himself argued in a preproduction interview that Baldwin was "the one who wanted negotiations to continue, he was the pacifist and refused to see that war was coming. I don't think that makes him a villain, I think that makes him a bit short-sighted . . . He just backed the wrong horse." Baldwin's point of view is aptly summed up in a short scene taking place in the bathroom at the House of Commons. While believing that war is inevitable, he nonetheless tells Churchill that he is also right: "I have done everything in my power to preserve peace, and I would do the same all over again. Bloodshed, sorrow, irreparable loss—that's what I've been trying to prevent." Such wrong-headed strategies only serve to prove the rightness of Churchill's cause.

References

The Gathering Storm: Information Pack issued 17 June 2002 (London: BBC, 2002), www.bbc.co.uk/pressoffice/pressreleases/stories/2002/06 _june/17/gathering_storm_pack.pdf (accessed 24 December 2008), 19; "*The Gathering Storm*: Transcript of the Screenplay by Hugh Whitemore," www.script-o-rama.com/novie_scripts/g/gatheringstorm -script-transcript.html, (accessed 23 December 2008); Martyn Palmer, "Revisiting the Grandeur That Was Rome," *The Times*, 27 April 2000, 22–23.

JACOBSON, MARK (1948–)

Mark Jacobson achieved fame in the 1970s while writing for *Village Voice*, most notably for an account of life in the Chinatown Shadows Gang. He later wrote for *New York Magazine*. His account of an encounter with the former drug-dealer Frank Lucas, published in 2000, formed the basis for *AMERICAN GANGSTER*. Jacobson pictured him thus at the height of his fame during the 1970s: "Residing in a swank apartment in Riverdale . . . and running his heroin business out of a suite at the Regency Hotel on Park Avenue, Lucas owned several cars. He had a Rolls, a Mercedes, a Stingray, and a 427 four-on-the-floor muscle job he'd once tipped out at 160 miles per hour." Had he not been pushing an illegal, deadly substance new to the United States at that time, Lucas would surely have been celebrated as one of the keenest businesspeople of the early 1970s for his family-run enterprise. Jacobson's article was republished in a book *American Gangster and Other Tales of New York* in 2007.

Reference

Mark Jacobson, *American Gangster and Other Tales of New York* (London: Atlantic Books, 2007), 3–4.

Bibliography

"Mark Jacobson Archive: *New York Magazine*," http://nymag.com/ nymag/author_393/ (accessed 12 February 2009).

JAFFE, STANLEY R. (1940–)

American producer and director. Credits as producer include *Kramer vs. Kramer* (1979), *Taps* (1981), and *Fatal Attraction* (1987).

In 1984 he joined SHERRY LANSING to form the independent production company Jaffe-Lansing. *BLACK RAIN* was one of their earliest films after *Fatal Attraction* and *The Accused* (1988). They considered numerous directors for the film, and engaged Scott after MICHAEL DOUGLAS expressed enthusiasm for working with the director. Although the film eventually made a profit, the experience of working on it was not an entirely happy one: Jaffe stated in an interview published in *Premiere* magazine prior to its US release that "they [the Japanese] don't shoot movies exactly the way we do . . . But I've got total control here [in the US] and it's cheaper." When asked about the total budget, Jaffe brusquely responded "None of your business . . . It's an expensive movie, but not overly expensive. We're very proud of this picture."

Scott's relationship with Jaffe could not have been severely affected, however, as Jaffe was responsible for committing 25 percent of the total budget for *1492: CONQUEST OF PARADISE*.

References
Stanley R. Jaffe, interviewed in "*Black Rain*: The Script, The Cast," Special Feature included in the *Special Collector's Edition* DVD release of *Black Rain* (d. Laurent Bouzereau) (Los Angeles: Paramount Pictures, 2006); Kim Masters, "'Rain' Man," *Premiere* 2, no.9 (May 1989): 22.

JAMES, BRION (1945–1999)
Brion James began his career in the theater, graduating to small parts in television series such as *Gunsmoke* and *The Rockford Files*.

As Leon in *BLADE RUNNER*, James evokes considerably sympathy amongst viewers as he stares in horror at the dead Zhora (JOANNA CASSIDY) who has just been "retired" (i.e., eliminated) by Deckard (HARRISON FORD). James told PAUL M. SAMMON that he was muttering under his breath "He [Deckard] must die, he must die . . . Even though we were these rogue androids [REPLICANTS] and knew that the police were hunting us—that's how Leon knows Deckard's a Blade Runner at that point—Zhora's death really had me distressed . . . once again, you could see how much feeling these replicants had."

Reference
Paul M. Sammon, *Future Noir: The Making of Blade Runner*, 2nd ed. (London: Gollancz, 2007), 159.

JAMES, JESSE (1847–1882)
Jesse James was an OUTLAW in the state of Missouri and the most famous member of the James-Younger Gang. After his death, he became a legendary figure of the American West. JESSE JAMES ON SCREEN has always been a popular subject, but often the characterizations are romantic, overlooking the fact that his robberies enriched only himself and his gang. Andrew Dominik's *THE ASSASSINATION OF JESSE JAMES BY THE COWARD ROBERT FORD*, produced by Scott, offers a more balanced portrait of James as a legendary figure who nonetheless leads a very isolated existence.

Bibliography
"About the Production," http://party931.com/common/movies/notes/54706-1-full.html (accessed 12 August 2008).

JAPAN
In *BLACK RAIN* Scott's representation of the city of Osaka resembles that of the futuristic Los Angeles in *BLADE RUNNER*. We are introduced to the city through a panning shot of the skyline at dawn, the sun glowing like an orb in the background. Scott cuts to a shot of the teeming streets, a mass of brightly colored lights, rain-washed sidewalks and CARS careering along at high speed. No one appears to be going anywhere specific, but rather moving aimlessly, pausing briefly at one of the ramshackle restaurants to eat a bowl of noodles.

Later on Scott represents Osaka as a threatening place; the neon lights still flash on and off, but the streets are eerily deserted, as if all the citizens had decided to hibernate for the winter. As Nick Conklin (MICHAEL DOUGLAS) and Charlie Vincent (ANDY GARCIA) return to their hotel, they are menaced by a gang of leather-clad bikers (followers of the yakuza leader Sato [YUSAKU MATSUDA]). No police officers are around to restrain them; it is as if the streets have been abandoned to the forces of lawlessness. Superintendent Ohashi (SHIGERU KOYAMA) insists that the Japanese police—and their New York guests—should observe the correct procedure in carrying out their duties. Scott's vision of Osaka clearly indicates how they fail to perform even the most basic task of sustaining law and order.

In an interview with Jonathan Romney, published prior to the film's London opening in January 1990, Scott admitted that *Black Rain* was "a problematic film to make at a time when American distrust of Japan is running high—what with the recent bad blood over proposed trade embargoes and Sony's recent takeover of the Columbia empire." This led to accusations that the film was catering to American cultural paranoia. The theme was developed in a long article by Pat Dowell, who argued that "Nick Conklin's hysterically threatening brush with Japan is the nightmare, not of being bested, but of being transformed: that 'we' [the Americans] will become 'them.' It used to happen to women and children . . . but in *Black Rain* it is a grownup white man who is vulnerable. Nick Conklin, in every sense of the phrase, goes to Japan to save face."

References

Pat Dowell, "*Black Rain*: Hollywood Goes Japan Bashing," *Cineaste* 17, no.3 (1990): 10; Jonathan Romney, "Made in Japan," *City Limits* (London), 25 January 1990, 11.

Bibliography

Suzanne Moore, "Sun Rises in the East," *New Statesman Society*, 2 February, 1990, 44; Jacob Raz and Arnold E. Raz, "'America' Meets 'Japan': A Journey for Real between Two Imaginaries," *Theory, Culture and Society* 13, no.3 (August 1996): 153–78; Kin Yuen Wong, "On the Edge of Spaces: *Blade Runner*, Ghost in the Shell and Hong Kong's Cityscape," *Science Fiction Studies* 27, no.1 (2000): 1–21.

JESSE JAMES ON SCREEN

Jesse James has always been a popular subject for the cinema. The *Internet Movie Database* lists seventy-one films and television productions since 1921, from early silent productions such as *Jesse James Under the Black Flag* (1921) and *Jesse James as the Outlaw* (also 1921), both starring Jesse James Jr., to THE ASSASSINATION OF JESSE JAMES BY THE COWARD ROBERT FORD (2007) and most recently *Jesse James: The True Story* (2007).

Famous performances in the role include Tyrone Power in the 1939 Twentieth Century-Fox film of the same name; Roy Rogers in *Jesse James at Bay* (1941); Audie Murphy in *Kansas Raiders* (1950); James Dean in a television film *The Capture of Jesse James* (1953); and Robert Wagner in *The True Story of Jesse James* (1957), directed by Nicholas Ray. More recently, James has been played by James Keach in *The Long Riders* directed by WALTER HILL (1980); Rob Lowe in *Frank and Jesse* (1994); Colin Farrell in *American Outlaws* (2001); and BRAD PITT in THE ASSASSINATION OF JESSE JAMES BY THE COWARD ROBERT FORD (2007).

JOFFIN, JON (1963-)

American cinematographer whose credits include *The X-Files* (1996–1997) and *Masters of Horror* (2005–2007). Joffin's work for the remake of THE ANDROMEDA STRAIN shows traces of *The X-Files* in its use of washed-out colors and quick cutting to suggest the atmosphere of paranoia in America as the country is swept by an apparently incurable virus—the Andromeda Strain. One reviewer wrote that the visual style emphasizing paranoia is "justified" in this adaptation which includes "kidnappings, blackmailings, assassinations, plots within plots, all carried out by faceless men in uniform at the direction of shadowy government puppet masters. In the end, the team itself is not immune to betrayal from within."

Reference

Sarah Stegall, "Encoding Humanity," *SF Scope* (May 2008), http://sfscope.com/2008/05/encoding-humanitya-review-of-t.html (accessed February 14, 2009).

JOHNSON, BRIAN (1940-)

Johnson's credits as a special effects supervisor include *Space 1999* (ATV, 1975–1976) and *Revenge of the Pink Panther* (1978).

Johnson's principal work on *ALIEN* was on the legendary chestbuster sequence, famously filmed without the actors' prior knowledge, so that their reactions to what happened were entirely genuine. To achieve the desired effect, Johnson and his team employed a series of pumps that pushed the creature upwards, while others held Kane (JOHN HURT) under the table. The blood was also pumped upwards, combined with fresh pieces of offal. Ridley Scott recalled that this sequence not only showed the alien birth, but emphasized the extent to which it can possess and destroy human beings. He also explored this theme in *ADAM ADAMANT LIVES!* and would develop it in *BLADE RUNNER* and *THE ANDROMEDA STRAIN*.

Bibliography

Don Shay, "Creating an Alien Ambience," in *Alien: The Special Effects*, ed. Don Shay and Bill Norton (London: Titan Books, 1997), 6–44.

JOHNSON, HUGH (?-)

Johnson served as FRANK TIDY's camera assistant on *THE DUELLISTS*, shot the second unit sequences for *1492: CONQUEST OF PARADISE*, and was slated to shoot "THE HOT ZONE," based on the best-selling book, but the project disintegrated before a script could be finalized.

As Scott's director of photography on *WHITE SQUALL*, interviewed prior to the production, Johnson admitted that he had "basically been brought up in the 'School of Scotts' So in a way it's not very difficult to photograph for Ridley because I know what he likes, and I like the same things. . . ." Although initially reluctant to film another sea story after *1492*, Johnson eventually agreed on account of the fact that the film was "not a Ridley Scott showpiece where everything is visually perfect. The movie is about young boys at sea, it's about what happens. The photography isn't waiting for this beautiful or magic light; it's very natural in an acrid way . . . We wanted to shoot in hard light, in the weather we had, so you had the feeling of heat and warmth around the film. It's quite raw, really, especially during the boat sequences."

Despite Johnson's comments, the film nonetheless confirms Scott's ability to create memorable images on the screen. One of these occurs when the boys visit the Galapagos Islands for the first time, and they are shown as mere specks on a vast landscape—latter-day colonists discovering land (and their true selves) for the first time. As Sheldon (JEFF BRIDGES) observes, they are "claiming their place in the world."

Johnson later worked on *G.I. JANE*, where he and Scott tried to achieve a color and shooting style that according to PAUL M. SAMMON would reflect the "severe, very spartan" lives of the SEALs. This might have been the intention, but the film also suggests Scott's technique in *BLACK HAWK DOWN*, especially in the final battle sequence, where the sense of individual emotional involvement, especially of Jordan (DEMI MOORE), is replaced with an equally powerful sensation—the experience of combat. By using a handheld camera together with several zooms, Johnson and Scott draw the viewer into the action; like Jordan's group, we are willing to put our lives at risk. Scott himself admitted this was part of his desire to achieve "something more documentary-like" in the film.

References

David E. Williams, "Stormy Weather," *American Cinematographer* 77, no.2 (February 1996): 36–37; Todd Robinson, *White Squall: Revised First Draft* (unpub. script, dated 31 October 1994), http://sfy.ru/sfy.html?script=white_squall (accessed 8 September 2008); Hugh Johnson, Ridley Scott, quoted in Paul M. Sammon, "Joining the Club: Ridley Scott on *G.I. Jane*," in *Ridley Scott Interviews*, ed. Laurence F. Knapp and Andrea F. Kulas (Jackson, University Press of Mississippi, 2005), 138, 163.

JONES, TREVOR (1949–)

Born in South Africa, Jones made his debut writing scores for British films such as *Time Bandits* and *EXCALIBUR* (both 1981).

For *G.I. JANE* Jones's score includes one moment, when Jordan (DEMI MOORE) reports for duty; a meaty piece, militaristic in its overall sound, stirring yet tense and exciting. Another piece for the opening section shows the camera panning upwards over a river (recalling *BLACK RAIN*)

and to a building where a meeting takes place. In Peter Holm's view the music is somewhat dark and foreboding, the principal part of the work being performed by five French horns, supported by strings.

The music for the film was likened by music critic John Mansell to that of HANS ZIMMER, but nonetheless "highly percussive and rhythmic giving a strong military feeling . . . Since Jones has not 'overcooked' the score with action music that keeps hitting the listener's face, the true adrenaline pumping peaks of the score can become much more notable and enjoyable." Scott told PAUL M. SAMMON that there was about ninety-eight minutes of music in the film including Jones's score plus songs by Chrissie Hynde of The Pretenders, one of which is playing on a radio during the seminal scene when Jordan shaves her head. Scott observed that "[he] always thought if O'Neil could sing, her voice would be the voice of Chrissie Hynde."

References

Peter Holm, "Trevor Jones: *G.I. Jane*," *Music from the Movies* 23 (Spring 1999): 25; John Mansell, "*G.I. Jane*: The Sessions," *Legend* 23 (Spring 1997): 59–60; Ridley Scott, quoted in Paul M. Sammon, "Joining the Club: Ridley Scott on *G.I. Jane*," In *Ridley Scott Interviews*, ed. Laurence F. Knapp and Andrea F. Kulas (Jackson, University Press of Mississippi, 2005), 164.

Bibliography

Thomas Glorieux, "*G.I. Jane*: Pompous Music Sounds like Media Ventures, Go Jones for That," http://users.telenet.be/soundtrack-fm/Reviews/Trevor_Jones/gi_jane/gi_jane.htm (accessed 25 October 2008).

K

KAMEN, MICHAEL (1948–2003)

One of the leading film composers of the late twentieth century, with scores for over seventy movies and television shows—including the *Lethal Weapon* (1987–1998) and *Die Hard* (1988–1995) series.

Although not his best work, Kamen's score for *SOMEONE TO WATCH OVER ME* blends music by Antonio Vivaldi and Leo Delibes's *Lakme* into the soundtrack, both to emphasize Claire Gregory's (MIMI ROGERS's) social status and to draw attention to her loneliness. Richard Younger remarks that Kamen's score, coupled with the title song (played at various points throughout the film) "relate[s] to the principal characters . . . who are all in need of protection . . . Aside from their mere entertainment value, songs have proven to be a powerful element in the rich art of film noir."

Reference
Richard Younger, "Song in Contemporary Film Noir," *Films in Review* 45, nos.7/8 (July/August 1994): 48–49.

KANIEVSKA, MAREK (1952–)

British director, mostly known for his television work in the early 1980s such as *Muck and Brass* (BBC, 1982). Made his film debut with the cinema version of Julian Mitchell's play *Another Country* (1984), followed by an adaptation of Brett Easton Ellis's *Less Than Zero* (1987). Kanievksa made his reputation by directing commercials for Ridley Scott's company RSA, for example Pernod, Renault 5, and GUINNESS Extra.

Ridley Scott hired him to direct *WHERE THE MONEY IS*. A small, nondescript film set in California but filmed on location in Canada, it is directed with tact rather than flair, allowing the three main performers PAUL NEWMAN, LINDA FIORENTINO, and DERMOT MULRONEY to shine.

Bibliography
Brian Davis, "Commercial Breaks," *Sunday Telegraph Magazine*, 17 December 1984, 42–44.

KARYO, TCHÉKY (1953–)

Nominated for a César Award for his starring role in *La Balance* (1982), Karyo received the prestigious Jean Gabin Prize in 1986 in recognition of his talent.

Cast in the role of the shipbuilder Pinzón in *1492: CONQUEST OF PARADISE*, Karyo does not have much to do other than to look outraged once he discovers that Columbus has misled the crew. Columbus had no way of knowing, of course, just how far the Indies were from Spain, but when asked he fudged an answer, betraying the trust of his favored crew. Robert Thurston's novelization of the screenplay sums up Pinzón's mood: "Aboard a rowboat, Pinzón made his way toward the flagship. His lips were tightly together, his jaw clenched . . . He was plainly primed for an argument, but Columbus raised his hand and told him they would confer in his cabin."

Reference
Robert Thurston, *1492: Conquest of Paradise Based on a Screenplay by Roselyne Bosch* (London: Penguin Books, 1992), 85.

KATSULAS, ANDREAS (1946–2006)

Born Andrew C. Katsulas in St. Louis, Missouri, Andreas received a Master's Degree in Theater Arts from Indiana University. During a hiatus from the stage, a part in Michael Cimino's *The Sicilian* (1987) brought Andreas to Los Angeles, after which he was immediately cast as Joey Venza in Ridley Scott's *SOMEONE TO WATCH OVER ME*. The role of Venza is a traditional thuggish role as a villain. Kastulas does not have to do more other than to appear menacing. Although outwardly well dressed in a conservatively cut European pinstripe suit, Venza likes to assume authority over everyone, particularly women. He is certainly attracted to Claire (MIMI ROGERS) but he treats her as a plaything. This contrasts starkly with the central character Mike (TOM BERENGER), whose sensitivity to women eventually puts his MARRIAGE at risk.

KEACH, STACY (1941–)

Stacy Keach made his name in television before breaking into films in the early 1970s. His roles included the title role in *Luther* (1973) and *Conduct Unbecoming* (1975). As the narrator in *THE DUELLISTS*, Keach has the responsibility of delivering Conrad's original lines. His presence lends a certain weight to the film, by emphasizing its literary origins. This technique is also evident in other classical adaptations of the time such as *BARRY LYNDON*.

KEATON, MICHAEL (1951–)

Born Michael Douglas in Pittsburgh, Pennsylvania. Early successes included *Beetle Juice* (1988), *Batman* (1989), and *Batman Returns* (1992). More recently Keaton has moved into television films such as *Live from Baghdad* (TVM, 2002) and *The Last Time* (2007).

In *THE COMPANY* Keaton was faced with the challenge of portraying a real-life character, James Jesus Angleton (1917–1987) the former Deputy Director of the CIA and master spy-hunter, who was also the guardian of the MJ Majestic Twelve (MJ-12) project disclosing classified subjects such as extraterrestrial life forms and their technologies. He was described by one of his colleagues as "truly a bit of a lunatic. He fancied himself as a serious poet. He was half-Mexican (via his mother), very tall and gangly, a raconteur who could stay up all night talking. In fact, he fairly well destroyed the CIA single-handedly because of his paranoia. He put a security system in place that ensures even today that CIA people work in a bubble, isolated from the way the world works." Robert De Niro's film *THE GOOD SHEPHERD* (2006) is loosely based on his life, with Matt Damon in the title role.

Keaton admitted in an interview with *TV Zone* that portraying the character was "massively complex, and the work was, in some ways, for me, more difficult because it's the antithesis of what I normally do." He gives the character certain characteristic gestures—for example, emphasizing a point with a wave of his cigarette. In Keaton's performance, Angleton is portrayed as meticulous in his attention to detail—putting together apparently disparate pieces of evidence to build up a picture of his enemies in a "very delicate game." He believes that people need "the patience of a saint for counterintelligence." However, Angleton's persistence is vindicated, as he eventually uncovers Yevgeny's (RORY COCHRANE's) real identity and correctly identifies the mole within the CIA as Leo Kritzky (ALESSANDRO NIVOLA).

References
Vincent Graff, "Know Your Enemy," *Radio Times*, 24–30 (November 2007): 26–29; "The Company of Wolves," *TV Zone* 219 (September 2007): 58.

Bibliography
Timothy S. Cooper, "James Jesus Angleton—Deputy Director of Counter-Intelligence and Guardian of the CIA's Greatest Secret" (3

April 2000). www.rense.com/politics6/secret.htm (accessed 3 February 2009).

KEITEL, HARVEY (1939–)

Born in Brooklyn, Keitel won the male lead in the college film production *Who's That Knocking at My Door?* (1967), directed by Martin Scorsese. He subsequently appeared in *Mean Streets* (1973) and *Alice Doesn't Live Here Anymore* (1974).

He was cast as Feraud in *THE DUELLISTS* after holding out for two months. According to his "Director's Commentary," Scott eventually persuaded him with the promise of "food, France and cigars." Keitel had a role which in both the original story and the film appears slightly one-dimensional. The actor himself admitted this in a 1978 interview. Nonetheless, Keitel makes the best of his opportunities. When D'Hubert (KEITH CARRADINE) first brings him news of his arrest, Feraud is in the salon of Madame de Lionne (Jenny Runacre). Keitel demonstrates his character's common origins and lack of finesse by the way he sits and scowls among the fashionable people around him—particularly when forced to listen to a countertenor. But this is the early nineteenth century, when it is possible for people of humble rank to rise up the social scale without the benefit of power and/or influence. Hence Feraud takes a pride in wearing the *Légion d'Honneur*, a medal awarded for bravery. For Charles Shiro Tashuro, Keitel's Feraud represents "the destructive energies of the [French] Revolution . . . He is both the Terror and the Eighteenth Brumaire, yet with neither the revolutionary ideals of the former, nor the talents for rationalized organization of the latter."

On the other hand, Keitel's Feraud is intensely ferocious and implacable—the kind of person who will fight on any pretext, even when placed under arrest for dueling with a civilian. Pages of JOSEPH CONRAD's description are neatly summed up in a sequence when Feraud, exiled to the provinces, a splenetic figure in a black greatcoat, stares out a small dog trotting behind a farmhouse as though he would compete with it for a place in the road, and cut its head off if the occasion required. In serving Napoleon and the cause of war so passionately, Feraud embodies what Conrad describes as "the fixity of savage purpose" that men alone are capable of displaying.

According to Susan Knobloch, by the time Keitel made *THELMA & LOUISE*, he had acquired the screen persona of "a working-class tough guy usually on the wrong side of the law, with much more use for and understanding of the men in his life than the women—even as questions eat away at him about how to define, defend, enjoy and withstand his and others' masculinity." However, Scott cast him against type as Hal Slocombe, a good cop trying to bridge the different discursive spaces between men and women. Screenwriter CALLIE KHOURI described him thus: "Here was a guy who was really trying to help them [Thelma and Louise], really trying to see past their actions into what was motivating them. He really wanted to save them. I could go on about this, but the fact is I wasn't writing a treatise, I was writing an outlaw movie, so I wasn't necessarily interested in making blanket statements about men or women."

Slocombe is genuinely concerned about the two women, who seeks to know what they are thinking ("I swear, Louise, I almost feel like I know you"). However, this apparently attractive quality also renders him potentially the most dangerous threat to Thelma and Louise's freedom. By convincing Louise (SUSAN SARANDON) into believing that he can help her, he might be able to catch them. On the other hand, Slocombe's sympathy alienates him from his FBI colleagues. When he yells at his senior officer Max (Stephen Tobolowsky) "How long are these women gonna be fucked over?" he is portrayed as a hysterical man rather than a competent police officer. In gender terms, he has become too feminized for an aggressively masculine vocation. Scott here returns to a theme explored in earlier films such as SOMEONE TO WATCH OVER ME and BLACK RAIN about what makes a good police officer; whether they should concern themselves with people's feelings or confine themselves to the job of arresting (or controlling) them.

Keitel played the lead role of Azro the gypsy in the Ridley Scott-produced comedy MONKEY TROUBLE, directed by FRANCO AMURRI. The actor confessed to his biographer Marshall Fine that he made the film for his daughter's benefit: "When I told my daughter Stella I'm making a movie with a monkey, I can't describe to you the look on her face. She turned her head to me and broke into a grin and said, 'Daaaddy.' That was worth everything . . . It's for children and it discusses an ethic and it's a beautiful story, a children's fairy tale." In the pressbook Amurri claimed that "Harvey has waited years for an opportunity to be in a comedy . . . From the beginning, it was clear that he enjoyed this chance to be seen in a different light." Scott commented: "Though Harvey hasn't done a lot of comedy, he has a great sense of humor which has been under-utilized on film."

A slight tale of Eva, a young girl (THORA BIRCH) finding a monkey who has run away from Azro, a gypsy (Keitel), the film makes little demands on the actor's capabilities. Using an outrageous Italian-American accent, Keitel creates a caricature villain's role, complete with gold teeth and wavy hair. He meets his just deserts in the film's final moments, as he is forced to choose between being beaten up by two heavies working for the local Mafia (who have been badly let down by his false promises), or facing arrest for kidnapping Eva. He goes down on his knees in mock prayer, whining "Please don't hurt me!" and then kisses the policeman's feet in gratitude for saving him from a well-deserved beating. Roger Ebert of the *Chicago Sun-Times* criticized both the

actor and the filmmaker for reinforcing "all kinds of negative stereotypes" about gypsies through this characterization.

Harvey Keitel has never graduated to stardom, but has always proved a reliable if somewhat daunting character-actor. In a 2003 interview one journalist described him as someone who "defies expectations" who, in spite of his reputation for playing tough guys, "displays a sensitivity and reserve—an almost old-school politeness—that takes you by surprise." He was once married to LORRAINE BRACCO, who played Ellie Keegan in Scott's *SOMEONE TO WATCH OVER ME*.

References

Stuart Byron, "The Keitel Method," *Film Comment* 14, no.1 (January/February 1978): 39; Allegra Donn, "Harvey Keitel—Renaissance Man," *The Times*, 22 November 2003, 22; Roger Ebert, "Monkey Trouble," *Chicago Sun-Times*, 18 March 1994, http://rogerebert.suntimes.com/apps/pbcs.dll/article?AID=/19940318/REVIEWS/403180304/1023 (accessed 26 February 2008); Harvey Keitel, quoted in Marshall Fine, *Harvey Keitel: The Art of Darkness* (London: HarperCollins, 1997), 227; Callie Khouri, interviewed by Bernie Cook in *Thelma & Louise Live! The Cultural Afterlife of an American Film* (Austin: University of Texas Press, 2007), 176–77; Susan Knobloch, "Interplaying Identities: Acting and the Building Blocks of Character in *Thelma & Louise*," in *Thelma & Louise Live!*, ed. Bernie Cook, 100; *Pressbook, Monkey Trouble* (London: Entertainment Film Distributors, 1994), 13; Ridley Scott, "Director's Commentary," to the 2003 release of *The Duellists* by Paramount DVD in the "Special Collector's Edition"; Charles Shiro Tashiro, "The Bourgeois Gentleman and The Hussar," *The Spectator: University of Southern California Journal of Film and Television Criticism* 13, no.2 (Spring 1993): 38.

Bibliography

Jack Hunter, ed., *Harvey Keitel: Movie Top Ten* (London: Creation Books International, 1999).

KHOURI, CALLIE (1957–)

Born in San Antonio, Texas, Khouri attended Purdue University to study acting and drama, before relocating to Los Angeles. She subsequently worked at Propaganda Films (a Los Angeles-based music video production house) working on rock videos for Alice Cooper and Robert Cray before turning to screenwriting.

In an interview with David Konow, Khouri recalled that she hit upon the idea for *THELMA & LOUISE* one night as she sat outside her house: "I was pulling up in front of my house at 3:30 in the morning after an awful rock video shoot. I was producing music videos at the time. A day on a music video is twenty-four hours, so I was probably in my twenty-seventh hour. It kind of came to me . . . From where I was sitting, in the world I was working in at the time, anything that was centrally or mainly focused on women would have been out of the question . . . But, honestly, I thought the idea was so good I didn't really ask myself too many questions about why no one else had done it."

Khouri took the script to producer MIMI POLK, executive vice-president of PERCY MAIN (Ridley Scott's feature film development company), who passed it on to Scott: "At first he [Scott] didn't want to direct it himself, he was just going to produce it . . . I was trying to direct it myself . . . At that time, I figured I could probably direct it for three million dollars. I didn't have any reason not to attempt it . . . I wrote it to be a low-budget film . . . So Mimi [Polk] got it, and she asked if I would let Ridley read it. I was reluctant only in that I was so embarrassed to let a real director read anything I had written. But he read it, he liked it, he responded to it very strongly and we started having meetings . . . We essentially shot the first draft. The only work we really did was to combine a few scenes. The script was 136 pages and we had to get it down."

In the Konow interview Khouri proclaimed herself surprised by the reaction to the film, especially in America: "A lot of people were powerfully affected by it. I think mainly it had the same effect on women that other outlaw movies had on men, in that it validates that there's a side of your personality that exists outside of the social expectations, and it acknowledges you as larger than the perimeters by which you're expected to live . . . I certainly didn't set out to change the way that people conducted themselves . . . I just tell what I hope will be a powerful, moving story that will be entertaining." However, she did not consider the film particularly violent, despite what some reviewers said: "I think if you talk to pretty much any woman who's ever driven down a road, she's going to tell you that's just about as common an occurrence as you could imagine [for males to shout sexist remarks from a truck] . . . The thing that blows my mind is that a lot of people remember Thelma and Louise killing that character, when they didn't lay a finger on him. That kind of surprised me too . . . To me, it was fairly tame."

Khouri won an for her script Oscar in 1992, for Best Screenplay Written Directly for the Screen.

Reference

David Konow, "Sisters Are Doin' It for Themselves" (Interview with Callie Khouri), *Creative Screenwriting* 8, no.5 (September 2001): 53–58, 67.

Bibliography

Ana Maria Bahiana, "Scripting *Thelma & Louise*: Callie Khouri," *Cinema Papers* 85 (November 1991): 32–36; Deborah Chiel, *Something to Talk About: A Novel Based on the Screenplay by Callie Khouri* (New York: Signet Books, 1995); Bernie Cook, "Interview with Callie Khouri, December 19, 2002," in *Thelma & Louise Live! The Cultural Afterlife of an American Film*, ed. Bernie Cook (Austin: University of Texas Press, 2007), 168–91; Syd Field, "The Phenom-enon of *Thelma & Louise*: Callie Khouri," in *Four Screenplays: Studies in the American Screenplay* (New York: Dell Publishing, 1994), 1–77; Lizzie Francke, *Script Girls: Women Screenwriters in Hollywood* (London: BFI Publishing, 1994), 129–32; "Gary & Callie: Callie Khouri and Gary Ross Converse about Adapting *Seabiscuit*, Writing *Thelma & Louise*, and the Art of Directing Your Own Script." *Written by* 7, no.10 (December 2003): 40–46.

KIM, DANIEL DAE (1968–)

Born in Pusan, South Korea, Daniel Dae Kim has made his name playing Jin Kwon in *Lost* (2004–2009).

Cast as Dr. Tsi Chou in *THE ANDROMEDA STRAIN*, Kim plays a defector from the People's Republic of China who becomes the target of racist insults, most notably from Major Bill Keane (RICKY SCHRODER). However, director MIKAEL SALOMON shows that such insults are unjustified: Dr. Chou is not only committed to solving the problem of how to prevent the Andromeda Strain spreading but has turned his back on his Communist past. This is emphasized through a flashback sequence where he is shown ruing the moment when, as a young doctor back in China, he helped to release a deadly virus that killed several innocent citizens. Such moments emphasize the film's anti-Communist stance—also emphasized in the frequent references to North Korea as a rogue state which might have released the Andromeda Strain in its campaign against the Americans.

Kim's role in the film was criticized by the *Boston Globe* reviewer, who noted that, although the actor "speaks in fluent English here, the poor guy barely gets to utter a line of dialogue that isn't exposition."

Reference

Joanna Weiss, "Doomsday Plot of 'Andromeda' Stands the Test of Time," *Boston Globe* May 26, 2008, http://www.boston.com/ae/tv/articles/2008/05/26/doomsday_plot_of_andromeda_stan (accessed February 13, 2009).

KING ARTHUR

US 2004 r/t 126 min col. *Production Companies*: Touchstone Pictures, Jerry Bruckheimer Productions, Green Hills Productions and World 2000 Entertainment. *Producer*: Jerry Bruckheimer. *Director*: Antoine Fuqua. *Writer*: David Franzoni. *Director of Photography*: Slawomir Idziak. *Production Designer*: Dan Weil. *Music*: Hans Zimmer. *Cast*: Clive Owen (Arthur), Ioan Gruffudd (Lancelot), Mads Mikkelsen (Tristan), Keira Knightley (Guinevere), Stephen Dillane (Merlin), Hugh Dancy (Galahad).

Medieval epic, released two years before *TRISTAN + ISOLDE* that covers much the same ground. The visual style is much the same as that created by *Tristan*'s designer MARK GERAGHTY. Many of the creative personnel involved in *King Arthur*—DAVID FRANZONI, HANS ZIMMER, SLAWOMIR

IDZIAK—were involved in Scott's films. The cast also includes CLIVE OWEN and Ioan Gruffudd, who were in THE HIRE and *BLACK HAWK DOWN* respectively.

Bibliography

Susan Aronstein, *Hollywood Knights: Arthurian Cinema and the Politics of Nostalgia* (Basingstoke and New York: Palgrave, 2005), 191–215.

KINGDOM OF HEAVEN

US/GB/Spain/Germany 2005 r/t 145 min col. *Production Companies*: Twentieth Century-Fox Film Corporation, Scott Free, Cahoca Productions, Dritte Babelsburg Film, and Inside Track 3. *Producer/Director*: Ridley Scott. *Writer*: William Monahan. *Director of Photography*: John Mathieson. *Production Designer*: Arthur Max. *Music*: Harry Gregson-Williams. *Cast*: Orlando Bloom (*Balian*), Eva Green (*Princess Sibylla*), Jeremy Irons (*Tiberias*), David Thewlis (*Hospitaler*), Liam Neeson (*Godfrey of Ibelin*), Ghassan Massoud (*Saladin*), Brendan Gleeson (*Reynald de Chatillon*).

The production sprang into life as Ridley Scott's idea. He told Twentieth Century-Fox that he wanted to make a picture involving knights: "These figures have always given us great opportunities to tell stories that carry the attributes of a hero. And one of the most important is that the character carries with him his own degrees of fairness, faithfulness, and chivalry. What it's really about is right action." From knights to the Crusades was but a short step: "The Crusades spanned over two hundred years and gave rise to so many astounding stories—besides all the cinematic possibilities of the Holy Land setting and the clash of culture between Europe and the East. It was the obvious target."

Scott asked LIZA ELLZEY, president of SCOTT FREE in Los Angeles, to find a story and a writer; she read a screenplay called "TRIPOLI" by WILLIAM MONAHAN, which told of a political/military struggle between two cultures. Scott accepted the idea and sold it to Twentieth Century-Fox but the project was shelved due to casting difficulties. In the book of the film Scott claimed that "Tripoli" shared certain characteristics with *Kingdom of Heaven*: "It was a very interesting script: again a historical tale and very political—set on the Barbary Coast of North Africa in 1803, at the time of Thomas Jefferson. It was romantic but well documented, carefully and beautifully seen, as only a good historian or great journalist could do." Eventually the "Tripoli" script was shelved, and Scott and Monahan created *Kingdom of Heaven*; both realized that the basic material, which had been employed so many times in other CRUSADER FILMS, would assume a different meaning for audiences in the post-9/11 world.

Scott himself explained in the introduction to the book of the film that he wanted to make a film about peacemak-

ers, "beginning with the central situation of two leaders trying to serve their own people and their sense of mission, while exercising a degree of tolerance of the 'other.'" His model was David Lean's *LAWRENCE OF ARABIA*—which contained "a strong personal story within the big frame." Scott wanted *Kingdom of Heaven* to interpret the Crusades "from the Muslims' point of view as well [as the Christians'] . . . The Crusades were a sometimes glorious, often tragic, and world-shaping series of events that are still having an impact on events today. I hope that in opening a cinematic window on that time, we're doing a job that good drama is meant to do; to excite our emotions, stir our souls, and make us think, all at once."

Casting was accomplished in several stages. ORLANDO BLOOM was cast as Balian after an intensive search process. He had had a small role in *BLACK HAWK DOWN* as Blackburn; since then his largest roles to date, in the *Lord of the Rings* trilogy (2001, 2002, 2005), *Pirates of the Caribbean: The Curse of the Black Pearl* (2003) and *Troy* (2004) had not demanded the kind of multi-layered performance he was expected to deliver in *Kingdom of Heaven*. Other actors agreed to work for Scott on account of the "Ridley factor"—they admired his work so much that they went to great lengths to accommodate themselves. JEREMY IRONS and LIAM NEESON were two such performers. Sibylla was played by the young French actress EVA GREEN, whose previous major role had been in Bernardo Bertolucci's *The Dreamers* (aka *I sognatori* (2003)). Saladin was played by GHASSAN MASSOUD, a star of the stage and film in Syria.

Filming was completed in Spain and Morocco and wrapped up in June 2004; but a long road lay ahead; over a year of postproduction before the picture finally opened in May 2005. CGI technology was used to create the crowd scenes—of the Saracens attacking Jerusalem—as well as creating digital sets. As with many of Scott's previous films, *Kingdom of Heaven* encountered problems with the studio executives. The director's initial version ran to 194 minutes, but Twentieth Century-Fox's head Tom Rothman ordered the film to be cut in the belief that audiences would not be attracted to a three-and-a-half-hour film. Consequently the film was cut down to 145 minutes.

Even before *Kingdom of Heaven* was released, it had provoked controversy. During the filming in Morocco, more than a dozen death threats were issued, forcing King Mohammed V to offer a thousand soldiers to guard the set in the Sahara. Moderate politicians in the country accused the film of being part of an American propaganda campaign for legitimacy in the crusade against the Arab world—a reference to President George W. Bush's spontaneous use of the word "crusade" when launching his "war on terror" after 9/11. As early as January 2004, Charlotte Edwardes published an article in the London *Daily Telegraph* consisting almost entirely of denunciations from academics such as Jonathan Riley-Smith (Cambridge University) and Jonathan Philips (University of London). Riley-Smith was quoted as saying that the plot was "absolute balls . . . It's Osama Bin Laden's view of history. It will fuel the Islamic fundamentalists." Philips believed that by venerating Saladin, Scott was "following both Saddam Hussein and Hafez Ahmed, the former Syrian dictator." In an article published a year later, Riley-Smith elaborated on his opinions: "Where they [the filmmakers] could have created fictional characters they have opted for real historical personalities whom they have distorted ruthlessly. The characters and careers of the hero, her lover, her husband, the king and Saladin have been remanufactured to suit the needs of the script. *Kingdom of Heaven* will feed the preconceptions of the Arab nationalists and Islamists."

The film drew similar responses in America: when Sharon Waxman of the *New York Times* showed the script to Islamic and other religious scholars, she received some extreme reactions. Laila al-Qatami, a spokeswoman for the Anti-Arab Discrimination Committee in Washington, was quoted as saying that "there's a lot of rhetoric . . . with prominent figures talking about Islam being incompatible with Christianity and American values. This kind of movie may reinforce that theme in the discourse." Khaled Abou el-Fadl, a professor of law at UCLA, was quoted as saying that "this movie teaches people to hate Muslims . . . There is a stereotype of the Muslim as constantly stupid, retarded, backward, unable to think in complex forms."

In another interview el-Fadl protested that the film depicted Islam as "practically insane, reflecting nothing of the tolerance, historically, shown by Muslims to Jews and Christians; the film attributes that characteristic to the Christians . . . the movie makes no allusion to the fact the Crusaders butchered Jews and Arab Christians in horrendous numbers."

Two reviewers tried to counter these early criticisms. David Poland in *Hot Button* (12 August 2004) criticized Waxman for trying to stir up the kind of controversies that dogged Martin Scorsese's film *The Passion of the Christ* (1988): "What really disturbs me in this [Waxman's] story is seeing the *New York Times* chasing controversy that has not been created by political groups . . . it is the news organization leading the groups to the controversy in this case." Two months later Richard Corliss in *Time* magazine quoted Scott as saying that he was unmoved by the controversy: "'I was brought up on Ingmar Bergman,' he says, 'and in *The Seventh Seal* and *The Virgin Spring*, he brilliantly touched on areas where you can talk about religion without any discomfort.'"

Scott himself offered contradictory comments in preproduction interviews. In the Waxman article he was quoted as saying that "[The film] adopts a Boy Scout ethic. It talks about using your heart and your head, being ethical. How can you argue with that? There's no stomping on the Koran, none of that." But in another interview quoted in Arthur Lindley's article "Once, Present and Future Kings" Scott said: "The knight was the cowboy of the era. He carried with him degrees of fairness, faith and chivalry . . . Right action is what it is really all about."

Despite the controversy in the press, the film's release went ahead as planned in May 2005. As ever with Scott's films, the reviews were mixed: Derek Malcolm in the *Evening Standard* described the film as "a rather upmarket epic, trying to see both sides of the argument, while giving us as much blood and thunder as possible on the way. The result is undoubtedly better than *Troy* or *Alexander* . . . [but] *Gladiator* this is not." Peter Bradshaw in *The Guardian* felt that "everything about it [the film] looks glib and naïve, and Muslim audiences might well have mixed feelings about this fictional good guy crusader, congratulating himself on doing the right thing at all times." By contrast John Millar in *Film Review* felt that "The old master [Scott] hasn't disappointed with this sprawling, compelling and complex epic of the Crusades in which you can taste the dust of battle and the dust of death." The *Sight and Sound* reviewer sensibly remarked that "few should seriously be offended by a film whose simple message is 'We are the World,' though fundamentalists of all stripes will no doubt open their shirts and close their eyes for the blow." The review also sensed that "this would-be epic feels, at more than two hours, like a romp reduced from a naturally more thoughtful work." This perhaps helps to explain why Scott rereleased a longer version of the film a year later as *KINGDOM OF HEAVEN*: THE DIRECTOR'S CUT.

Kingdom of Heaven cost $130 million to make; by August 2005 it had only made just over $47 million at the American box office. However the worldwide receipts of $152 million by June 2005 helped to bring the film into profit. Robert Fisk's article "Why Ridley Scott's Story of the Crusades Struck Such a Chord in a Lebanese Cinema" explains why.

Kingdom of Heaven suggests that the best way to avoid armed conflict is through tolerance. Godfrey de Ibelin (Liam Neeson) tells Balian (Orlando Bloom) that he should embark on a crusade to establish "a kingdom of conscience [in Jerusalem], a kingdom of heaven [in which] there is peace between Christian and Muslim." In a stirring prebattle speech, Balian asks the Christians to decide "which is more holy. The [city] wall? The mosque? The sepulcher? Who has claim? No one has claim! All have claim!" Early on in the film Balian defeats Imad, Saladin's right-hand man (ALEXANDER SIDDIG), but lets him go in the belief that to kill him in cold blood would be a dishonorable thing to do. Imad returns the favor later on when Balian is defeated outside the walls of Jerusalem. In the film's climax, Balian and Saladin agree a truce, in which Saladin offers the Christians safe passage to the sea in return for Balian giving up Jerusalem. The exodus from the city is shown in a series of long shots, with the Christians in a line protected by Saladin's troops. Balian begins by riding his horse, but dismounts soon afterwards to join his people in the belief that true tolerance depends on ignoring social as well as religious differences.

Opposing Balian and Saladin are Christian zealots such as the priest (Michael Sheen), who confidently asserts towards the beginning of the film that "to kill an infidel [a non-Christian] is not murder. It is the path to heaven." Tiberias (Jeremy Irons) remarks despairingly on the ways in which "fanatics from Europe . . . [and] Templar bastards" come to Jerusalem in search of a fight—for example, Reynald de Chatillon (BRENDAN GLEESON), who believes that it is his divinely appointed duty to kill as many Muslims as possible. Guy de Lusignan (MARTON CSOKAS) denounces all Muslims as enemies of God and humiliates Tiberias in public for advocating peace rather than military action. The Hospitaler (DAVID THEWLIS) observes in despair that he has witnessed "the lunacy of fanatics of every denomination" supposedly carrying out the will of God. True holiness, he believes, consists of "right action and courage on behalf of those who cannot defend themselves."

Critics denounced the film for its distortion of history: one on the *Christian Broadcasting Network* website warned that the neo-liberal message of tolerance overlooked the fact that "when Mohammed couldn't get everyone to accept Islam he started killing people. That's built into the very fabric of his faith. So Saladin was a ruthless killer. The Muslims were a conquering army." The Director's Cut includes a documentary "The Scholars Speak," which defends Scott's interpretation: he uses past events to comment on the present. *Kingdom of Heaven* is another example of the FILMS AFTER 9/11, one that suggests peace can only be achieved through tolerance and acknowledgment of cultural differences. Balian and Saladin's truce shows how the kind of ethnic conflicts leading to unnecessary loss of life (including the American campaign in Somalia that forms the subject of *BLACK HAWK DOWN*)—can be brought to an end. It is only by means of such strategies that people's "safety and freedom"—whether in the medieval or the contemporary worlds—can be preserved.

The resemblances between *Kingdom of Heaven* and Scott's earlier films are obvious. In *GLADIATOR* Maximus's (RUSSELL CROWE's) loss of his family spurs him on to return to Rome and wreak revenge on Commodus (JOAQUIN PHOENIX). In *Kingdom of Heaven*, Balian loses his wife and suffers the indignity of having her head cut off by the priest as a punishment for her "blasphemy." This experience makes him aware of the importance of creating a more tolerant world, through either peaceful or aggressive means.

Balian's father Godfrey resembles Marcus Aurelius (RICHARD HARRIS) in *Gladiator*: while both of them have neglected their paternal duties, they are nonetheless loved and respected by their respective armies. Godfrey's view of the soldier's life is very similar to that practiced by the American troops in *Black Hawk Down*: "Be brave and upright that God may love thee. Speak the truth always, even if it leads to your death. Safeguard the helpless and do no wrong . . . [and] protect the people." Following his father's example, Balian concerns himself with everyone's welfare—not only his fellow soldiers, but the women and children immured within the city walls. Although a widower himself, he remains perpetually aware of his larger "family" responsibilities.

Scott makes use of PATRICK CASSIDY's choral piece "Vide Cor Meum" to show how the past exerts a profound influence over the present in both *HANNIBAL* and *Kingdom of Heaven*. In the early part of *Hannibal*, the music accompanies the stage performance of the murder of Giuliano de Medici by one of Inspector Pazzi's (GIANCARLO GIANNINI's) ancestors. In *Kingdom of Heaven* the same piece resurfaces in a sequence where Sibylla (Eva Green) marries Guy de Lusignan almost as soon as her husband King Baldwin (EDWARD NORTON) has passed away. Before long she comes to regret what she has done; just like Pazzi, she is haunted by past memories.

Although not directly described as such in the script, Balian's life is governed by a strict code of HONOR, which might be more precisely defined as a belief in fair play as well as trusting in one's own faith. King Baldwin reminds him that "even when those who rule you be kings or men of power, your soul is in your keeping alone." This is what persuades Balian to reject Sibylla's offer of MARRIAGE. Even when the Patriarch (Jon Finch) tells him that it is "God's will" for Balian to quit the city rather than defending it against Saladin, Balian responds that "God will understand, my lord. If he doesn't, then he is not God and we need not worry." A concern for personal safety rather than the welfare of his people represents a dishonor both to himself and to God. Hamid Dabashi suggests that the film follows earlier Scott work such as *THELMA & LOUISE* in tracing the development of a protagonist (or protagonists), who begin the films by being "bereft of faith and conclude with the restoration of that faith and its attendant hope."

The landscape plays an important part in reinforcing the film's principal themes. At the beginning Balian is shown eking out a living in a small French village set amongst harsh, unforgiving hills. The ambience recalls the enchanted world of *LEGEND*—a DYSTOPIAN scene where the sun rarely shines, whose inhabitants condemn Balian's widow to burn in hell for taking her own life. This scene contrasts starkly with the desert landscape outside the city of Jerusalem: through the repeated use of aerial shots showing the vast, barren landscape stretching as far as the eye can see, Scott transforms it into a wilderness—Balian's site of personal and emotional self-discovery. Having ensured the Christians' safe passage out of the city, Balian returns to FRANCE: now the landscape has been transformed into a sunlit world of green hills and fields, with cattle grazing peacefully in the distance. Whereas Jerusalem was once his Kingdom of Heaven, now he believes that "God [can] do with it as he wills." Balian embraces Mother Nature instead—as demonstrated in a close-up during the film's final moments as he caresses a spring flower.

Criticism of *Kingdom of Heaven* has focused on its treatment of religious issues. Kavel L. Afrasiabi believes that despite its plea for tolerance, the film "originates from the standpoint of Christianity." Nonetheless it constitutes "a welcome cinematic rebuff to proponents of the 'clash of civilizations' theory" by criticizing "the narcissistic West that is reflected in the ultimate disenchantment of the lead hero; the specificity of his experience is simultaneously instructional, vexing, and open-ended, and is inextricably linked to a strong distaste for stereotyping or mythologisation." Arthur Lindley likens the film to "the kind of 1950s liberal melodrama represented by *Twelve Angry Men*" that "displaces the conflict between Christians and Muslims into one between the tolerant of both sides and the fanatical in ways that clearly reflect the priorities of 2005 more than the relations of 1187." In an essay on *Kingdom of Heaven, Black Hawk Down* and *Gladiator*, Simon Dalby argues that *Kingdom of Heaven* is explicitly pro-western in terms of religious and political views: "The professional Western warrior . . . is a key figure of the post-September 11th era, physically securing the west, and simultaneously securing its identity as the repository of virtue against barbaric threats to civilization." This observation would seem to take a dim view of the film's ending. Kathleen Biddick concentrates on the film's representation of medieval history, focusing in particular on the significance of the First Crusade. She takes a more balanced approach, however, than the medieval historian Thomas F. Madden, who describes "the story as poor and the history is worse . . . Lasting peace, thought, would be better served by candidly facing the truths of our shared past, however politically incorrect those might be."

References

Kaveh L. Afrasiabi, "Persians and Greeks: Hollywood and the Clash of Civilisations," *Global Dialogue* 9, nos. 1–2 (Winter/Spring 2007): 97–98; Kathleen Biddick, "Unbinding the Flesh in the Time That Remains," *GLQ: A Journal of Lesbian and Gay Studies* 13, nos. 2–3 (2007): 197–225; Peter Bradshaw, "Holy Terror," *Guardian Review,* 6 May 2005, 16–17; "Church History: Thoughts on *The Kingdom of Heaven*—a Discussion with Ted Baehr," *Christian Broadcasting Network* (2005), www.cbn.com/spirituallife/ChurchAndMinistry/ ChurchHistory/Crusades_BaehrKOHThoughts.aspx (accessed 13 January 2009); Richard Corliss, "Ridley Scott's 1001 Arabian Knights," *Time*, 3 October 2004, www.time.com/time/covers/ 1101041011/nextentertainment.html (accessed 12 January 2009); Hamid Dabashi, "Warriors of Faith," *Sight and Sound* 15, no. 5 (May 2005): 27; Simon Dalby, "Warrior Geopolitics: *Gladiator, Black Hawk Down* and the *Kingdom of Heaven,*" *Political Geography* 27, no.4 (2008): 439; Charlotte Edwardes, "Ridley Scott's New Film 'Panders to Osama Bin Laden,'" *Daily Telegraph*, 17 January 2004, www.telegraph.co.uk/news/worldnews/northamerica/usa/1452000/ Ridley-Scotts-new-Crusades-film-panders-to-Osama-bin-Laden.html (accessed 13 January 2009); Khaled Abou el-Fadl, quoted in Steve O'Hagan, "Kingdom Under Siege: Will the Religious Backlash Start Here?" *Empire*, April 2005, 79; Robert Fisk, "Why Ridley Scott's Story of The Crusades Struck Such a Chord in a Lebanese Cinema," *Robert Fisk's Z-Space Page* (20 June 2005), www.zmag.org/znet/viewArticle/6012 (accessed 15 January 2009); Nick James, "Kingdom of Heaven," *Sight and Sound* 15, no.6 (June 2005): 64–65; Arthur Lindley, "Once, Present, and Future Kings: *Kingdom of Heaven* and the Multitemporality of Medieval Film," in *Race, Class and Gender in 'Medieval' Cinema*, ed. Lynn T. Romney and Tison Pugh (New York and Basingstoke: Palgrave, 2007), 19, 23; Thomas F. Madden, "Onward PC Soldiers: Ridley Scott's *Kingdom of Heaven,*" *National Review*, 27 May 2005, www.national review.com/comment/madden200505270751.asp (accessed 15 January 2009); Derek Malcolm, "Holy War of the Worlds," *Evening Standard*, 5 May 2005, 29; John Millar, "Kingdom of Heaven," *Film Review* 657 (June 2005): 115; David Poland, "Ain't It the New York Times?" *Hot Button*, 12 August 2004, www.thehotbutton.com/ today/hot.button/2004_thb/040812_thu.html (accessed 12 January 2009); Jonathan Riley-Smith, "Truth Is the First Victim," *The Times Screen*, 5 May 2005, 12–13; Ridley Scott, "Introduction," Diana Landau, ed., *Kingdom of Heaven: The Ridley Scott Film and the History Behind the Story* (London: Simon and Schuster Ltd., 2005), 8–11; Ridley Scott, quoted in Landau, *Kingdom of Heaven*, 22–23; Ridley Scott, quoted in Lindley, "Once, Present, and Future Kings," 26; Ridley Scott, quoted in Sharon Waxman, "Film on Crusades Could Become Hollywood's Next Battleground," *New York Times*, 12 August 2004, www.nytimes.com/ads/remnant/network redirect-leaderboard.html (accessed 13 January 2009); Waxman, "Film on Crusades."

Bibliography

"The Knight Who Says No," *Film Review* 662 (October 2005): 114; Cahal Milmo, "A Wound That Has Lasted 900 Years," *The Independent* 3 May 2005, 12–13; *Movie Details: Online Press Office: Kingdom of Heaven* (Los Angeles, Twentieth-Century Fox, 2005); Steve O'Hagan, "To Thy Kingdom Come," *Empire* 28 April 2005, 74–83; Ridley Scott, "When Worlds Collide," *The Guardian Review,* 29 April 2005, 7.

KINGDOM OF HEAVEN—THE DIRECTOR'S CUT

US/GB/Spain/Germany 2006 r/t 194 min col. Revised version of the 2005 film *KINGDOM OF HEAVEN*.

This four-disc set restores a subplot involving Baldwin V, the young son of Jerusalem princess Sibylla (EVA GREEN)—which was the subject of heated debate prior to the film's original release. The new version also gives more prominence to EDWARD NORTON (uncredited as Baldwin IV) and the priest (Michael Sheen). Released as part of a DVD in September 2006 which included extras such as commentary from Scott, screenwriter WILLIAM MONAHAN and ORLANDO BLOOM, as well as technical and production information on the production. There are also several feature-length documentaries: "Kingdom of Hope: The Making of Kingdom of Heaven," and "Kingdom of Heaven: Production Design Primer," "Production Morocco," "Post-Production," and "Release."

Other major alterations include: Godfrey (LIAM NEESON) is shown to be not only the father of Balian but the younger brother of the village lord (Robert Pugh) who believes that Godfrey is looking for his own son to be Godfrey's heir in Ibelin. It is this lord's son and heir who assails Godfrey in the forest.

The plot revolves around the firstborn son's right to exclusive inheritance: this is what apparently drove Godfrey to the Holy Land and the priest's desire to humiliate Balian. Baldwin IV is shown refusing the last sacrament from Patriarch Heraclius.

Balian fights a climactic duel with Guy de Lusignan (MARTON CSOKAS) near the end of the film, after Jerusalem is surrendered and Guy has been released by Saladin (GHASSAN MASSOUD).

The Director's Cut includes an extra scene with Balian discussing the current political situation with the Hospitaller (DAVID THEWLIS) in the desert, which includes Balian's line "I go to pray."

The new version suggests that Balian has fought in several battles in the past, which has rendered him a skilled fighter.

In an interview about the Director's Cut, Scott placed particular emphasis on the scenes involving Baldwin V: "One of the most important additions is the Princess Sibylla, who is the sister to Baldwin the Leper King, played by Eva Green . . . Now when Baldwin IV died, and the boy is coronated [*sic*], Princess Sibylla would be the consult to the young king, that was the advisor. The boy died within ten months, history says. History also says the possibility that the boy had died of leprosy. Now you don't die of leprosy in ten months. Leprosy is insidious and it takes a long time. History also says that the mother may have murdered her child. So you look at that, and you think, 'Well, wait a minute. Why would a mother let her child grow to seven or eight years old, knowing full well that her brother is very liable to die at anytime of leprosy? Why would she murder her son for power when she could have had him done away with before or earlier, or better still, not had a child? If there was no child, she would have had to find a man and go to throne.' So we address the possibility of leprosy, because leprosy was quite common in those days. If he got leprosy, then it could be argued that it was an act of tremendous love, so it was an act of euthanasia."

Reviews of the *Director's Cut*—especially in the trade press—were uniformly good: James Berardinelli of *Reelviews* thought that the film had been transformed from a run-of-the-mill historical film into "a breathtaking epic . . . It is the film Scott envisioned, and one that is worthy of the résumé of a director with many remarkable titles to his name." Likewise Brian Tallerico of the *Ugo.com* website believed that the film "will stand next to Ridley Scott's other great works as a truly impressive piece of filmmaking."

References

James Berardinelli, "*Kingdom of Heaven*: Director's Cut," *Reelviews .net*, www.reelviews.net/movies/k/kingdom_heaven_directors.html (accessed 15 January 2009; Ridley Scott interviewed by Reg Seeton, www.ugo.com/channels/dvd/features/tristanandisolde/interview2.asp (accessed 8 August 2008); Brian Tallerico, "*Kingdom of Heaven*: 4-disc Director's Cut DVD," *Ugo.com*, www.ugo.com/channels/dvd/features/tristanandisolde/kingdomdvdreview.asp (accessed 15 January 2009).

Bibliography

"*Kingdom of Heaven*: Director's Cut," *Sight and Sound* 16, no.10 (October 2006): 89.

KLAUS, SONJA (?–)

Set decorator on *KINGDOM OF HEAVEN*, Klaus became production designer for *A GOOD YEAR*. Her main task was to try and give the Provençal locations a 'lived-in" feel—especially Uncle Henry's (ALBERT FINNEY's) château. According to the pressbook, Scott's first words to her were: "'We're just going to hang out in the south of France and throw a few props around . . . Oh, and by the way, there's a tennis court. I think we might have to change the swimming pool, or build another swimming pool for all the stunts." Apart from such changes—the most difficult of which was building the new swimming pool, Klaus and her team also "landscaped the ground, putting in statutory and ornamentation. Inside, the whole point was to have this slightly dilapidated, lived-in, comfortable feeling—a feeling of shabby chic . . . cluttery, lived-in and homey. We wanted the place to feel as if one was staying with [a] favorite uncle or . . . favorite aunt."

Reference

Pressbook: A Good Year (Los Angeles: Twentieth Century-Fox), 9.

KLEIN, MARC (?–)

Klein wrote the screenplay for *Serendipity* (2001) and was subsequently engaged by Scott to work on *A GOOD YEAR*. Klein visited the South of FRANCE for research and getting a flavor of the area and collaborated with PETER MAYLE, author of the original book (also entitled *A Good Year*) on the background to the screenplay.

In a preproduction interview with Nancy Hendrickson Klein explained the changes he introduced: "There was a very cute element to the book and there were some cute characters but I felt, structurally, it needed a lot of work. The conflict and the romance needed to be amped up . . . There were two ideas I pitched in that initial meeting that Ridley really responded to . . . The first had to do with Max Skinner [RUSSELL CROWE] who, in the book, is a low-level bond trader . . . Ridley said, 'I think we should turn our character into a reluctant hero.' That's when the inversion of the character started. I said I thought he should be an extraordinarily successful bond trader so, when the telegram comes, it's actually a nuisance. He doesn't want to go to France, and when he does, it's to sell the place." The second major departure from the book Klein suggested to Scott involved Uncle Henry [ALBERT FINNEY]: "He's only mentioned once or twice in passing in the book. And I felt like it would be an extraordinary opportunity to bring in a really funny, almost hippie-like character in flashbacks."

Klein's first draft screenplay (dated 29 April 2005) portrayed Max unsympathetically as a xenophobe—someone who describes the French as "[a] lazy, arrogant lot" and who contemptuously admits that he has no clue of what many of them are talking about. The screenwriter himself shows little sympathy for his material: in one of his stage directions he refers to some "shitty French rap music coming from a radio." There are other elements of barely concealed racism—for example, the inclusion of some Saudi Arabians, interested in buying Uncle Henry's château, who are parodied both by Max and by the lawyer Mlle. Auret. The revised version, written six months later, renders Max a more sympathetic character and calls Auret by her first name, Nathalie. According to Scott such changes transformed the story into "a jolly romp . . . embedded in the lifestyle of Provence. For the movie, I found that the mechanism of the story needed to be adjusted a bit, to turn up the volume on the character of Max, who needed to learn an important life lesson."

References

Nancy Hendrickson, "*A Good Year*: Screenplay by Marc Klein based on the novel by Peter Mayle," *Creative Screenwriting* 13, no.6 (November 2006): 33; Marc Klein, "*A Good Year*: A Screenplay by Marc Klein" (29 April 2005), http://www.dailyscript.com/scripts/A-GOOD-YEAR.pdf (accessed 29 January 2009); Ridley Scott, quoted in *Pressbook: A Good Year* (Los Angeles: Twentieth Century-Fox Film Corporation, 2006), 3.

KOTTO, YAPHET (1937–)

His film debut was in 1963 in an uncredited role in *4 For Texas*, but his first big break came in *Nothing but a Man* in 1964. Kotto portrayed Idi Amin Dada in the 1977 television film *Raid on Entebbe*. He also starred as an auto worker alongside Richard Pryor and HARVEY KEITEL in the 1978 critical hit *Blue Collar*.

Cast as Parker in *ALIEN*, Kotto gives a convincing performance as a bluff, no-nonsense crew member, whose method of dealing with intruders—violence first, asking questions later—proves no match for the alien. Tom Fallows writes: "For his role . . . he also applied a method approach. The tough talking, hard-as-nails mechanic was a powerhouse, a man of action, and Kotto refused to believe that the slick black alien creature could kill him. He was fired up and would corner director Ridley Scott everyday and bark: 'I'm gonna kill it, man. There's no way it can kill me.' Indeed, there is a scene in the film were Lambert, his shipmate aboard the *NOSTROMO*, is trapped by the alien and Parker stands his ground and will not leave her to die. He can't get a clear shot with his flamethrower and screams for her to run. But she is paralysed with a fear and so he tosses his weapon aside and lunges with his [bare] hands. The creature's skin is like armour, it towers above even Kotto and it bleeds acid. But Kotto is so intense, so powerful and so ferocious that for a second, a fraction of time, we believe that this man could tear the creature apart. This performance was all Kotto."

Reference

Tom Fallows, "Cult Actors #4: Yaphet Kotto," *Obsessed with Film*, www.obsessedwithfilm.com/specials/cult-movie-actors-4-yaphet-kotto.php (accessed 27 February 2009).

KOYAMA, SHIGERU (1929–)

Japanese character actor who made his debut in 1958. *BLACK RAIN* marked his debut in a non-Japanese film. As Superintendent Ohashi Koyama he is the epitome of inflexible authority—someone who resents the presence of American police officers on his patch, and who expects them to know their place as "foreigners, nothing more than interested observers." Initially it seems that he does not know English—providing an excuse for Nick Conklin (MICHAEL DOUGLAS) to issue a volley of racist slurs—but this proves nothing more than a façade, designed to put the Americans in their place. Ohashi's concern for authority is accompanied by an unwillingness to make decisions: when Nick asks him whether the yakuza leader Sato (YUKAKU MATSUDA) can be apprehended, Ohashi replies noncommittally "it's possible." He has been brought up to deal with police affairs in a culture-specific manner, and no amount of hectoring from Nick will persuade him to change his ways.

Ohashi reappears throughout the film, frequently in confrontations involving Nick and Masahiro (KEN TAKAKURA). One takes place after the two officers have unsuccessfully chased Sato through an iron foundry but allowed him to escape on his motorbike. Ohashi appears, and the camera focuses on Masahiro's guilty countenance as he realizes that he will inevitably suffer for countermanding his superior officer's orders. In the end the superintendent is forced to acknowledge the two officers' efforts in bringing the yakuza leader to justice. He sullenly presents the two of them with rising sun medals; not one flicker of emotion passes over his features. This ritual is simply part of his daily duties.

KRUMHOLTZ, DAVID (1978–)

Born in New York, Krumholtz starred in films such as *The Santa Clause* (1994), *Santa Clause 2* (2003), and *Ray* (2004).

Since 2005 Krumholtz has achieved considerable stardom as Charlie Eppes in the television series *NUMB3RS*, portraying a mathematical genius who has gradually matured over the years. He began as someone so wrapped up in his academic work that he had little time for anything else; by the end of the fourth series he was able to sustain a long-term relationship with his colleague (and former graduate student), Amita Ramanujan (NAVI RAWAT).

Although Krumholtz never went to college, he has achieved the apparently impossible task of making math look cool. In an interview with the *New York Times*, he admitted that his uncanny facility with the language of math won him the part over about a hundred other actors. As a result Krumholtz was invited to several math conventions: "'I knew after the pilot that if this thing went it would be the best thing I'd ever done . . . And that it had the chance to influence people.'"

Working in *Numb3rs* also reunited him with JUDD HIRSCH, who had given him his first break at thirteen years old in the Broadway production of Herb Gardner's *Conversations with my Father*: "He [Hirsch] gave me my career . . . He gave me my life . . . I'm not too confident about how I would have turned out otherwise, to be honest."

Reference

Sean Mitchell, "David Krumholtz in *Numb3rs*: He Talks the Talk So Viewers Think He Figures the Figures," *New York Times*, June 25, 2006, www.nytimes.com/2006/06/25/arts/television/25mitc.html?_r=1&scp=2&sq=david%20krumholtz&st=cse (accessed 22 February 2009).

LAMBERT, VERITY (1935–2007)

One of British television's most versatile producers. Lambert began her career with ABC Television, part of the Independent Television network in the early 1960s, working with Sydney Newman. When he moved across to the BBC, Lambert followed. She was given her first job as producer on the highly successful series *DOCTOR WHO*.

ADAM ADAMANT LIVES! (1966–1967) was her second major series as producer. Although female producers were few and far between at that time—especially within the BBC—Lambert stamped her authority on the series. GERALD HARPER, who played Adam, described her as "feisty"— someone who would stand little nonsense on set in her determination to get the series finished on schedule. Lambert made every effort to give new, untried directors the chance to work on the series. One of these was Ridley Scott, who hitherto had very limited experience of working in television; he was better known as a designer. Scott directed three episodes, only one of which survives in the BBC archives ("THE LEAGUE OF UNCHARITABLE LADIES"). He certainly built up his reputation as a result of the series: the makeup artist Jo Young recalled that he was the first director she had seen to make use of a storyboard.

Adam Adamant Lives! ended after two seasons. Lambert recalled that despite its obvious advantages (a suave leading man, for example), the series never quite fulfilled its stated objective of satirizing 1960s mores. If it had done, then perhaps it might have attracted more substantial ratings.

Reference

Gerald Harper, Verity Lambert, Jo Young, interviewed in the BBC documentary *This Man is the One*, produced to celebrate the 40th anniversary of *Adam Adamant Lives!* (London: BBC Worldwide, 2006).

LANG, ROCKY (?–)

The son of producer Jennings Lang and actress Monica Lewis. Early productions included episodes of the television series *Remington Steele* (1985–1986) and *Race for Glory* (1989) as writer/producer.

As producer on the film *WHITE SQUALL*, Lang recalled that the process of creating the film was a painful one. Scriptwriter TODD ROBINSON "wrote about five drafts of the script before he was fully satisfied . . . When we had the script ready to go, we thought we were in great shape . . . because we had a script that everyone loved [at MGM] from the senior VPs right on down the line. We also thought [producer] JOHN CALLEY would really respond to it, especially since he's a master yachtsman himself. But for whatever reason, still not clear to us today, he didn't want to pull the trigger on it." Eventually Lang and Robinson showed the script to Ridley Scott, who agreed to do it, provided he could alter the script. The two men agreed so long as the story was kept in period and the voiceover narration of CHUCK GIEG would be retained. There was also the problem of finance: "Ridley wanted control of the picture and didn't want a studio telling him what he could and couldn't do . . . So we started a series of negotiations with Largo, Morgan Creek, Spelling and some other companies for foreign money, and the foreign dollars were put in place for domestic distribution. Sixty per cent of the budget was brought into the deal based on Ridley's name and reputation in Europe."

Reference

"*White Squall*: Director Ridley Scott and Producer Rocky Lang Reveal the Inside Story behind Their New Adventure Film," *Film and Video* 13, no.1 (January 1996): 10, 12, 104.

LANGELLA, FRANK (1938–)

A stage and screen actor of extreme versatility, Frank Langella won acclaim on the New York stage in *Seascape* and followed it up with the title role in the Edward Gorey production of *Dracula*. He repeated the role for the screen in *Dracula* (1979) and became an international star. Over the years he has done occasional films but prefers to concentrate on his first love, the legitimate theater.

Cast in the comparatively minor role of Luis de Santángel in *1492: CONQUEST OF PARADISE*, Langella acts as Columbus's (GÉRARD DEPARDIEU's) faithful ally, endeavoring to keep him from embarrassing himself. Robert

Thurston's novelization of the screenplay makes this clear: "Santángel . . . observed Columbus's fencing ineptitude with some amusement. This was, after all, a man who was opening new worlds; he did not have to learn to open small wounds."

Reference

Robert Thurston, *1492: Conquest of Paradise Based on a Screenplay by Roselyne Bosch* (London: Penguin Books, 1992), 130.

LANGFORD, RICHARD E. (1925–)

Former academic and teacher who was the real English teacher on the ill-fated voyage of the *Albatross* in 1962, which formed the basis for the film *WHITE SQUALL*.

Langford published his reminiscences in *White Squall: The Last Voyage of Albatross* (2001). The book is basically a travelogue of all the places visited by the ship on its voyage leading up to the disaster which resulted in the loss of six of its crew members. However, it contains a vivid account of the voyage and its purpose which, in Langford's words, was to provide the opportunity for teenage boys "to find out who they were, to become real people. Some shed their childish ways and turned into young men before the voyage ended. Others had to wait until *Albatross* slipped beneath the waves before they understood that no one lives forever, that every day and every experience is invaluable, that selfishness and egoism are wasteful vanities that in the end come to nothing."

In Langford's account, Captain Sheldon is represented as a disciplinarian, but with a genuine concern for his young crew, especially at a time of disaster. Before he swims to safety, he makes sure that "a couple of the weaker boys [climbed onto] the raft, and the rest of us got busy on the longboat." At this point Langford reflects on Sheldon's loss: "Skipper had lost his ship, his home and his wife, all within a few minutes. Years of hard work and preparation, years of dreams and anticipation, all were a mile beneath us on the bottom of the sea." Yet Sheldon himself "acted just as a ship captain should; he took command immediately, and we all worked together to empty the longboat. He was calm and sure, and he said nothing about his heavy personal loss."

In the end, Langford, like Sheldon, realizes that the experience is one for which "no one can blame the sea; the sea is neutral . . . I awaken to the real world and understand anew that some of us get through a lifetime and some of us just do not get a chance to try. It is simply the way things are." Yet the experience proved valuable, enabling him to learn something about himself: "If one is going to find out who he is, then he must get outside the protective personality of who he thinks he is or who he has been pretending to be."

Reference

Richard E. Langford, *White Squall: The Last Voyage of Albatross* (Harrisburg, PA: Bristol Fashion Publications, 2001), 22, 102–3, 116–17.

LANSING, SHERRY (1944–)

Born Sherry Lee Heimann in Chicago. After appearing in the films *Loving* (1970) and *Rio Lobo* (1970), Lansing switched to the production side. In 1984 she joined STANLEY R. JAFFE to form the independent production company Jaffe-Lansing.

Following successes such as *Fatal Attraction* (1987) and *The Accused* (1988), Lansing recalled that MICHAEL DOUGLAS asked Jaffe-Lansing Productions to produce *BLACK RAIN*. Lansing herself liked the project, on account of its characterization. She engaged Scott after the original director, Paul Verhoeven, dropped out. Interviewed in the production information brochure for the film, she suggested that the film showed "how far fear and often hatred can come from a lack of understanding. The relationship between the characters played by Michael Douglas and Ken Takakura parallels the wariness with which people of different countries often regard each other." She adopted a generally hands-off approach during filming; but once the rough cut had been assembled, she evidently cut out at least thirty minutes to bring the film's running time down to a more audience-friendly length (120 minutes). Lansing later became head of Paramount Pictures' Motion Picture Group, and was responsible for green-lighting the production of *THE BROWNING VERSION*.

Reference

Sherry Lansing, interviewed in "*Black Rain*: The Script, The Cast," Special Feature included in the *Special Collector's Edition* DVD release of *Black Rain* (d. Laurent Bouzereau) (Los Angeles: Paramount Pictures, 2006).

LANYON, ANNABELLE (1960–)

Born 4 October 1960 in Greenwich, London, Annabelle Lanyon made her name in British television drama series such as *The Brothers* (1974–1975), *The Flockton Flyer* (1977) and *Nanny* (1981–1982).

Cast as Oona in *LEGEND*, Lanyon very much resembles Tinker Bell in J. M. Barrie's *Peter Pan* as she buzzes round Jack (TOM CRUISE) like a firefly; clearly attracted to him. However, this fairy is not as benevolent as she first seems: when she offers Jack the promise of eternal life, it is in exchange for his love. Jack rejects the offer—much to Oona's disgust—vowing instead to remain true to Lily (MIA SARA) until he finds her once again.

In *LEGEND*: THE DIRECTOR'S CUT Oona's role is further expanded; she taunts Jack for being a mortal, while at the same time revealing her loneliness as she flits around the prison cell in the Great Tree, desperately hoping that Jack will accept her offer. When she is refused, all she can do is to carry out Gump's (DAVID BENNENT's) orders as he snaps his fingers and bids her give him the key to the prison door. In an important sequence later on, Oona is shown wandering around the Great Tree looking very much like Lily (who is searching for a means of escape). In visual terms this resemblance is deliberate: both girls are willing to sacrifice anyone in pursuit of their self-interested desires. Perhaps mortals are not that much different from fairies after all.

LASCHER, DAVID (1972–)

Early work was confined to television in forty-four episodes of *Hey Dude* (1989–1991), *Roseanne* (1991) and *Beverly Hills 90210* (1991–1992).

Lascher made his major film debut in *WHITE SQUALL* as Robert March, a bully who is eventually discovered to have feet of clay. Although a strong, virile young man, he has a chronic inferiority complex where his academic work is concerned; the only way he manages to secure a place on board the *Albatross* is to falsify his credentials. When faced with his exams, he tries to cheat; but eventually the other crew members come to his support and help him overcome his difficulties. When March passes his exams he observes to Chuck Gieg (SCOTT WOLF) that Gieg is "the glue. You're the thing that holds everybody around you together. You're strong, you listen and you see things in people the rest of us can't. It's a gift." March looks at Gieg, holding his exam as Gieg observes in a voiceover that "for the first time we felt safe, capable, sure of who we are and where we were going."

Reference

Todd Robinson, *White Squall: Revised First Draft* (unpub. script, dated 31 October 1994), http://sfy.ru/sfy.html?script=white_squall (accessed 8 September 2008).

THE LAST DEBATE

US 2000 TVM r/t 90 min col. *Production Companies*: Paramount Network Television Productions, Scott Free and Showtime Networks. *Executive Producers*: Ridley Scott, Tony Scott, and Diane Minter Lewis. *Producer*: John Maas. *Director*: John Badham. *Writer*: Jon Maas, from the book *The Last Debate* by Jim Lehrer. *Director of Photography*: Norayr Kasper. *Production Designer*: Eric Fraser. *Music*: Arthur B. Rubinstein. *Cast*: James Garner (*Mike Howley*), Peter Gallagher (*Tom Chapman*), Audra McDonald (*Barbara Manning*), Donna Murphy (*Joan Naylor*), Henry Ramirez (*Mark Sanchez*), Bruce Gray (*Governor Paul L. Greene*), John Badham (*Don Beard*).

One of Scott's lesser known projects—a television film, based on *THE LAST DEBATE* (NOVEL) by PBS news jour-

nalist JIM LEHRER and broadcast on the cable network Showtime. The narrative begins two weeks before the presidential elections, during which most US voters will have to choose between morality crusader-Republican Richard Meredith (Stephen Young) and Democratic Governor Paul Greene (Bruce Gray). Popular political columnist Mike Howley (JAMES GARNER) has been chosen to moderate the debate, and he's to be assisted in his task by three co-panelists, magazine writer Barbara Manning (AUDRA McDONALD), right wing reporter Henry Ramirez (MARCO SANCHEZ), and television anchorwoman Joan Naylor (DONNA MURPHY). Shortly before the debate, Howley receives some damaging info about one of the candidates, and he and his team decide to air this dirty laundry during the live debate. As a result of this incident, the Democrat wins by a landslide and the four journalists become instant celebrities. Enter Tom Chapman (PETER GALLAGHER), a clever investigative magazine reporter trying to find out how the information about the Republican candidate was leaked to the debate panelists.

The Last Debate follows in the tradition of films such as *NETWORK* (1976) and *WAG THE DOG* (1997) in satirizing the ways in which the media manipulates public opinion. It has obviously been inspired by the Bill Clinton/Monica Lewinsky scandal of 1998, in which the president publicly admitted that he had behaved improperly and asked for the American people's compassion. Their response vindicated his decision—as his wife Hillary reported in her memoirs: "The president's job approval was holding steadily throughout the crisis. A solid majority of about 60 percent also said that Congress should not begin impeachment proceedings, that Bill should not resign and that the explicit details [of the affair] in the Starr report were 'inappropriate.'" In *The Last Debate* the Republican candidate Meredith is publicly accused of physical violence towards his wife, daughter and other female employees, which makes a mockery of his commitment (expressed in his campaign video) to family values. Despite his protestations of innocence, his prospects of winning the presidency are ruined. While Meredith's behavior is certainly reprehensible, he does not deserve to be the victim of "journalistic terrorism," in which the four panelists "take the electoral process in their own hands" (as Tom Chapman aptly observes). However, perhaps this is the inevitable consequence of a media-dominated world in which moral or ethical standards have been abandoned.

Image now counts for everything—as shown, for instance, in a sequence prior to the televised debate in which the two presidential candidates are shown in close-up staring pensively at the ground. Once the director gives them their cue, they immediately assume fixed smiles and stride out on to the stage to face the viewing public. The debate itself takes place at a hotel in Williamsburg, Virginia, whose staff are all decked out in colonial costumes—long coats, breeches and curly white wigs—in a deliberate attempt to create a historical image for prospective guests. The media personnel behave according to similar logic, telling the presidential candidates how to respond to specific questions and what gestures to use.

The Last Debate is punctuated throughout by split-screen sequences where up to six real-life pundits and party activists offer their comments as if they were appearing on television. They include Democratic strategist Paul Begala, David Brooks (*The Weekly Standard*), Albert R. Hunt, GOP pollster Frank Luntz, Robert D. Novak (*The Chicago Sun-Times*), and James Warren (*The Chicago Tribune*). This represents a conscious attempt on director JOHN BADHAM's part to dissolve the distinction between "fiction" and "reality," neither of which assume much importance in an image-obsessed world. We cannot understand a word of what the pundits say, as they all speak at once in a desperate attempt to hook the viewers' attention. But again, this is of little importance; far more important is that they should look presentable in front of the camera. This vindicates former ABC anchor Ted Koppel's sardonic comment, included as a preface to the film: "'Mr. Koppel, what advice would you give to young people entering a career in journalism?'/ *Koppel*: 'Get a good make-up man.'"

The cult of celebrity is also of paramount significance. The long-serving network news anchor Don Beard (John Badham) is summarily dismissed and replaced by Joan Naylor, one of the four panelists involved in pillorying Meredith. Two other panelists, Barbara Manning and Henry Ramirez, are teamed up as a double-act in a Sunday morning talk show slot entitled *Hank and Barb*. Although politically at opposite ends of the spectrum (Barbara is a Democrat; Henry is a Republican), they set aside their differences and play the parts of two lovers perpetually at war with one another. In the network executives' view, this is the best way to attract high ratings. Chapman (Peter Gallagher) himself appears to be above this as he embarks on a relentless crusade to uncover the truth about that fateful last debate—but even he succumbs to the lure of celebrity; he signs a lucrative book deal with Simon and Schuster and appears on cable television.

In this self-obsessed world the views of ordinary people count for nothing; they simply exist to be manipulated by the media. Chapman frequently quotes opinion polls describing the panelists' "heroism" in exposing Meredith's shady past. In one of the film's wittiest moments, Beard quotes from another poll revealing that, while Governor Greene has clearly emerged as the winner in the presidential election, the people would much prefer to see Clint Eastwood or Rosie O'Donnell in the role. When Chapman pro-

claims, "we can't allow the American people to forget about the story," we realize that he is simply using the phrase to justify his actions.

Chapman's entire life operates according to similar logic. At one point Chapman challenges the security boss Sidney Robert Mulvane (Lawrence Dane) to reveal who passed on the information to Howley about Meredith's past. Mulvane declines on the basis that, as a man of HONOR, he thinks it is inappropriate to do so. Chapman responds in kind by saying that Mulvane is in fact being dishonorable by withholding the truth from him. It is evident that the journalist has no understanding of what the term actually means, as he admits in a voice-over: "Honor wasn't worth arguing about. The story needed an ending."

The Last Debate posits a cynical view of AMERICAN-ISM. In Badham's view, the emphasis on individualism has declined into narcissism—a preoccupation with self rather than upholding basic community values such as integrity, reliability and honor. As with Commodus (JOAQUIN PHOENIX) in *GLADIATOR*, the protagonists try to exploit a society governed by the media and for the media, in which conventional wisdom has been turned to "guacamole" (as Chapman aptly observes). Some politicians actively enjoy this kind of life: Charles Rangel, the Democrat member of Congress for New York at that time, appears as himself in the film expressing thanks for being involved in "this great show." As the credits roll, the sound of Ethel Merman singing "There's No Business Like Show Business" can be heard on the soundtrack—a fitting comment on contemporary American politics. As Neal Gabler observes in his 1998 book *Life: The Movie*, anyone who seeks similar celebrity should "get involved in a sex scandal, run for office, marry a billionaire, or just be weirder than anyone else. You don't have to audition because talent is no longer a prerequisite for celebrity. Yes, your fame may be fleeting but your infomercial will live forever. For, this is America, otherwise known as 'The Republic of Entertainment.'"

Reviewing the film on its first broadcast on 5 November 2000, *Variety* commended it for "moving along at a nice pace, revealing bits and pieces about the way journalists make their little deals with the devil. There are clever bits about TV executives offering a cheesy Sunday-morning TV show to Ramirez and Manning."

References

Hillary Clinton, *Living History* (New York: Scribner, 2003), 710; Neal Gabler, *Life: The Movie* (New York: Random House, 1998), 3; Ramin Zahed, "The Last Debate," *Variety*, 7 November 2000, 33.

THE LAST DEBATE (NOVEL)

Book by JIM LEHRER that forms the basis for the Ridley Scott-produced film of the same name.

The tale is told by magazine reporter Thomas Chapman, who notes that he has adopted the narrative form called "Journalism as Novel." While the extensive media critique is not as penetrating as one might hope, Lehrer's experience and inside knowledge allow him to point out some thought-provoking assumptions in the contemporary media, and his story is a gripping one.

LAW DOGS

US 2007 TVM r/t 60 min col. *Production Companies*: CBS Paramount Domestic Television and Scott Free. *Executive Producers*: Ridley Scott, Tony Scott, David W. Zucker, and Barry Schindel. *Director*: Adam Bernstein. *Writer*: Barry Schindel. *Director of Photography*: Michael Trim. *Production Designer*: Maxine Shepard. *Cast*: Janeane Garofalo (*Gloria Fontaine*), Josh Cooke (*Matt Harper*).

A pilot for a follow-up series to *NUMB3RS* by BARRY SCHINDEL, a revamped version of "Law Dogs," his 2003 pilot for NBC. This was conceived as an ensemble drama following the private lives and cases of a team of public defenders with JANEANE GAROFALO in the leading role. Garofolo played the quirky, sassy head of the public defender's office, bearing the scars of having made it in what is essentially a man's world. To date nothing has emerged from this pilot.

Reference

Nellie Andreeva, "Garofalo on Case for CBS Pilot," *The Hollywood Reporter*, 20 December 2006, 3.

LAWRENCE OF ARABIA

GB 1962 r/t 216 min col. *Production Companies*: Horizon Pictures and Columbia Pictures Corporation. *Producer*: Sam Spiegel. *Director*: David Lean. *Writers*: Robert Bolt and Michael Wilson from the book *Seven Pillars of Wisdom* by T. E. Lawrence. *Director of Photography*: F. A. Young. *Production Designer*: John Box. *Music*: Maurice Jarre. *Cast*: Peter O'Toole (*Lawrence of Arabia*), Alec Guinness (*Prince Faisal*), Anthony Quinn (*Auda abu Tayi*), Jack Hawkins (*General Allenby*), Omar Sharif (*Sherif Ali*), Jose Ferrer (*Turkish Bey*), Anthony Quayle (*Col. Brighton*).

This multi-Oscar winning epic inspired WILLIAM MONAHAN to write the script for *KINGDOM OF HEAVEN*. However, there are several differences between the two films: in an interview with *Creative Screenwriting* Monahan admitted that his screenplay stressed the common ground between Christians and Muslims; in particular his central character Balian (ORLANDO BLOOM) finds himself "transformed by the Middle East, and one thing he'd discovered was that Muslims were human beings." In Lean's film Lawrence (Peter O'Toole) underwent the same process; but at the same time felt only hate towards the Turks (who were also Muslims)

for their oppression of the Arabs. Monahan transforms Balian into "a guy who is made a knight and takes it very seriously throughout the rest of the story." However, the finished film—at least in its original release—rendered this transformation somewhat perfunctory. This led a contributor to *Creative Screenwriting* to conclude that Balian "lacks the grandeur of the great epic heroes [such as Lean's T. E. Lawrence]." In Scott's defense, it must be said that Balian is a different kind of hero: whereas O'Toole's Lawrence is a hero for the Cold War period, battling to preserve western values of democracy and fair-mindedness against a threatening enemy (whether it be the Turks or the Russians), Balian searches for more peaceful solutions, where people of different faiths can co-exist rather than fight with one another. This explains his willingness to forge a truce with Saladin (GHASSAN MASSOUD).

Kingdom of Heaven also follows the example set by *Lawrence of Arabia* in its representation of large, sweeping landscapes—especially in the desert sequences. One online reviewer believed that JOHN MATHIESON's stunning photography of the "jaw-dropping combat sequences" more than compensated for any shortcomings in the plot.

References

"*Kingdom of Heaven*: Screenplay by William Monahan, Final Shooting Script, Dated May 25, 2004," *Creative Screenwriting* 12, no.3 (2005): 25; "'Nix,' *Kingdom of Heaven* (2005): Movie Review," www.beyondhollywood.com/kingdom-of-heaven-2005-movie-review/ (accessed 15 January 2009).

"THE LEAGUE OF UNCHARITABLE LADIES"

GB 1966 TVM r/t 50 min b/w. *Production Company*: British Broadcasting Corporation. *Producer*: Verity Lambert. *Director*: Ridley Scott. *Writer*: John Pennington. *Production Designer*: Mary Rae. *Music*: David Lee. *Cast*: Gerald Harper (*Adam Adamant*), Juliet Harmer (*Georgina Jones*), Jack May (*William P. Simms*), Amelia Bayntun (*Charity*), Joyce Carpenter (*Mrs. Tudor*), John Carson (*Randolph*), Sheila Grant (*Hope*), Jean Gregory (*Mrs. Lightfoot*), Lucy Griffiths (*Faith*), Eve Gross (*Abstinence*), Geraldine Moffat (*Prudence*), Joan Paton (*Mrs. Jarrot*), Gerald Sim (*Jarrot*), Larry Noble (*Harry Marshall*).

"The League of Uncharitable Ladies" is the only surviving episode of *ADAM ADAMANT LIVES!* to be directed by Ridley Scott. It was broadcast on 22 September 1966 (Series 1, Episode 13). The other two episodes he helmed—The Resurrectionists" (Series 2, Episode 11) and "Death Begins at Seventy" (Season 2, Episode 8)—have both been wiped from the BBC archives.

Harry Marshall (Larry Noble), an important member of the security forces, mysteriously dies in a London park, apparently of a heart attack. His colleague Jarrot (Gerald

Sim) receives an invitation to meet his own death at ten o'clock the next day. Adam traces the source of this invitation to the Gentlewoman's Charity League, a ladies' club dedicated to peace and nuclear disarmament. Every new member—all of them married to prominent politicians—undergoes an initiation ceremony, during which they are hypnotized. They subsequently poison their husbands upon receiving the appropriate stimulus by means of a telephone call. Although ostensibly a ladies' club, the brains behind the operation is the butler, Randolph (JOHN CARSON), who has been contracted by the Communists to dispose of the politicians and thereby undermine public confidence in western governments. The three women in charge of the club, Faith, Hope, and Charity (Amanda Bayntun, Sheila Grant, Lucy Griffiths) eventually discover that Randolph has duped them. Adam comes to the rescue by invading the club, rescuing Georgina and ensuring that no further harm will come to the hapless members. Randolph meets his death in a similar way as the unfortunate politicians, as Hope poisons him.

As with all episodes of *Adam Adamant Lives!* "The League of Uncharitable Ladies" was shot very quickly in the studios with occasional filmed inserts. Directors had very little time to plan set-ups; rather, they relied on the kind of techniques—close-ups, two-shots and brief pans—developed in the low-budget B-movies of previous decades (most of which were equally rapidly filmed). In spite of such limitations, Ridley Scott manages to create some memorable sequences. At the beginning, when Harry is poisoned, Scott includes several point-of-view shots, as the camera swirls around and around in circles, suggesting Harry's gradual loss of consciousness. Scott achieves a similar effect later on, when Jarrot meets a similar fate. The camera zooms towards Mrs. Jarrot's (Joan Paton's) face—so close, in fact, that the image becomes blurred—and then the screen momentarily fades to black.

Scott makes ingenious use of his London location. Adam travels from his house to the club in his trademark Mini-Cooper (registration number AA 1000); the landmarks flash by in a series of rapid shots—Horse Guards Parade, Piccadilly Circus—clearly indicating that Adam enjoys driving fast CARS around the streets. Such images also suggest that "Swinging London" of 1966 is a place where life proceeds at a breathless pace.

Certain themes are raised in "The League of Uncharitable Ladies" that crop up in Scott's feature films. The members of the ladies' club—including Georgina—are reduced to robots which can be made to believe and do anything Randolph wishes. (Faith, Hope, and Charity believe they are fighting for world peace and disarmament.) He admits that he can "implant" suggestions in their minds, which can be subsequently stimulated by means of a telephone call. This notion of "implanting" is taken to a horrific extreme in *ALIEN*, where the alien implants itself in Kane's (JOHN HURT's) body. This issue of controlling people's minds is especially significant in *BLADE RUNNER*: we never really know whether the central character Deckard (HARRISON FORD) is a REPLICANT or not.

"The League of Uncharitable Ladies" makes some significant points about gender construction. As an Edwardian gentleman, Adam firmly believes that women should be seen and not heard; as in other episodes of the series, he urges Georgina to stay at home and not involve herself in potentially dangerous situations. The same also applies to Mrs. Jarrott, who is expected to fulfill her role as housewife and not worry about her husband's business affairs. However, this episode shows several women challenging such stereotypes. Georgina resolutely refuses to heed Adam's advice, while Randolph's sidekick Prudence (Geraldine Moffat) is a strong-willed personality employing a wide range of strategies to bring men—including Adam—under her control. Moreover, the club members are transformed from passive figures into murderesses. As in *Alien*, Scott uses the fantasy framework to explore issues of femininity. In the final scene, however, the episode reveals a failure of nerve, as the male characters reassert their dominant roles. Randolph dismisses Charity (and her fellow club members) as misguided old maids for daring to challenge his authority. Meanwhile Georgina is left to run after Adam, crying "Wait for me!" In spite of her aspirations, she will always remain his sidekick.

Critical reaction to the series on its premiere in 1966 was mixed, to say the least. The most charitable view was expressed by the *Sunday Times*, which described it as "worth watching," even if it seemed like a poor imitation of *The Avengers*. For a time the series featured as a cartoon strip in the British boys' comic *Hotspur*; a TV annual, featuring stories based on the series, appeared later in the year. Brian J. Robb's 2002 survey of Ridley Scott's career compliments the director on his use of "fluid movement" and "shaky, hand-held techniques" in "The League of Uncharitable Ladies," but suggests that his innovations were compromised by the need to "get the story told and concluded." James Chapman's longer study of the series claims that "the unusual camera angles and occasional blurring of focus" had a disconcerting effect on viewers, "that creates a slightly unworldly feel." He believes that the series had a significant influence on later time-travel adventures—for example, the *Austin Powers* trilogy, where the eponymous hero was once again faced with the difficulty of living out of his own time.

References

"Adam Adamant Lives!" *Sunday Times*, 26 June 1966, 36; James Chapman, *Saints and Avengers: British Adventure Series of the 1960s* (London and New York: I. B. Tauris Publishers, 2002), 140, 155; Brian J. Robb, *Ridley Scott: The Pocket Essentials* (Harpenden, UK: Pocket Essentials, 2002), 17.

LEGEND

US/GB 1985 r/t 89 min (original US release), 94 min (European release) col. *Production Companies:* Embassy International Pictures, Legend Production Company, Twentieth Century-Fox and Universal Pictures. *Producers:* Arnon Milchan and Tim Hampton. *Director:* Ridley Scott. *Writer:* William Hjortsberg. *Director of Photography:* Alex Thomson. *Production Designer:* Assheton Gorton. *Music:* Jerry Goldsmith and Tangerine Dream. *Cast:* Tom Cruise (*Jack*), Mia Sara (*Princess Lily*), Tim Curry (*Darkness*), David Bennent (*Honeythorn Gump*), Alice Playten (*Blix*), Billy Barty (*Screwball*), Cork Hubbert (*Brown Tom*), Peter O'Farrell (*Pox*), Robert Picardo (*Meg Mucklebones*), Annabelle Lanyon (*Oona*).

The troubled production history of this film has been recounted by PAUL M. SAMMON and Geoffrey M. Wright in his online article "Unnecessary Destruction." "The setting for *Legend* is timeless . . . It is not a film of the future, or of the past. It is not even a story of now. The conflict between darkness has been with us since the creation . . . and will remain with us through eternity." So said Ridley Scott in the production notes to his fourth film, the genesis of which came in the early 1980s, when the director expressed a wish to produce a medieval fantasy that "would lie somewhere between Cocteau's *LA BELLE ET LA BÊTE* (1946) . . . and the Hollywood version of *A Midsummer Night's Dream* (1935)." Scott told Sammon that he wanted to make something "a little lighter" after *BLADE RUNNER* and *ALIEN*—something that "children and everybody else could go to." He read a book called *Symbiography* (1973), written by WILLIAM HJORTSBERG, a poet and novelist; and commissioned him to write a screenplay tentatively called "Legend of Darkness."

According to James Olsen, the script went through fifteen rewrites before Scott was satisfied, involving not only the writer but other creative talents such as storyboard artist Martin Asbury. Financing was provided by Universal Pictures and Twentieth Century-Fox; under the terms of the agreement, Universal retained *Legend*'s North American distribution rights, while Fox held the overseas rights (excluding those of the United Kingdom). The budget was set at $25 million.

Shooting took place at Pinewood Studios in England. The entire forest setting was built by designer ASSHETON GORTON on the studio's largest stage (also used for the James Bond films); its total dimensions stretched to 2,721,600 cubic feet. Filming lasted twenty-one weeks; and was interrupted at the end by a huge fire on 27 June 1984 when the entire stage burned to the ground, taking the forest set along with it. Ridley Scott explained to Sammon that his "biggest headache was that after the fire I still had three weeks of Forest filming left to do, and no Forest left to do it. But Assheton Gorton had got ahead in building his other sets, so we were able to make those work overtime."

Legend's bad luck continued into its preview phase in Orange County, California, where audiences apparently rejected the film outright. Scott himself claimed in a 2002 documentary "The Making of *Legend*" that some of them were under the influence of hard drugs during the performance. When the time came to release the film in the United States, Sidney Sheinberg, the president of MCA, the parent company of Universal Studios at that time, decided that *Legend* needed some work to make it "better"—in other words, more marketable. Scott worked with Sheinberg to re-edit the film to emphasize the action elements and love story over the larger issue of saving the world.

Legend was slated to be released in American theaters in June 1985, but Universal canceled and rescheduled the date for November 1985. At this time the film was released in Great Britain, with a score by JERRY GOLDSMITH and a running time of ninety-four minutes. The producers had high hopes for the film, not only as a piece of entertainment, but as an educational resource. A study guide was prepared by Ian Wall for high school students, focusing both on the film's structural elements and on themes such as good vs. evil or heroes and heroines. Reviewers expressed qualified enthusiasm: Alexander Walker of the *Evening Standard* called the film "a triumph of decorative form over thinness of substance," while David Castell of the *Sunday Telegraph* felt that "a troubled production" had found "the happiest of endings." A *Sunday Times* profile, published to accompany the film's opening, congratulated Scott on his ability to "tailor a film to suit a target audience." However, the film failed to attract substantial audiences, so Universal postponed the American opening once again. The film was reduced to eighty-nine minutes and the Goldsmith score replaced by a more rock-oriented score from TANGERINE DREAM. One associate of Scott's was quoted by Pat H. Broeske as saying, "Perhaps American teenagers don't have imaginations. They have had difficulty relating to our picture . . . I think it's sad that they find it so difficult to enter a world of fairies and elves and all." Evidently there was no target audience in the United States as there had been in Great Britain.

By May 1986 Universal had still not released the film, in the belief that audiences would not accept TOM CRUISE's long hair. When Cruise made *Legend*, he was not yet a star; but by early 1986 he had shot to fame with *TOP GUN*. Nonetheless the spring release of *Legend* went ahead as planned, the eighty-nine-minute version which Scott described to Alan Jones as "much simpler," designed for audiences brought up on "sub-par montages all day long which makes them impatient . . . It's a sad fact of life but you are obliged to take note of that. You would be a fool not to." Sadly, the new version sank without trace, critics largely dismissing it as empty and characterless with a weak storyline. Vincent Canby of the *New York Times* described it thus: "[A] slapdash amalgam of Old Testament, King Arthur, 'The Lord of the Rings,' and any number of comic books . . . Mr. Cruise goes through all this nonsense gamely, as if it were an initiation into a fraternity he wants very much to join." Richard Corliss of *Time* magazine called the film "as simple as a bedtime tale." The British sci-fi fanzine *Starburst* expressed disappointment at the film from a director from whom they expected "nothing short of perfection in terms of originality and style . . . There are no actors in his film with any particular presence on the screen, so that the whole thing appears lop-sided in favour of the baddies, and no one gives a cuss who rescues the unicorns."

Box-office returns were equally disappointing, with only $4.2 million taken on the film's opening weekend (its total cost eventually spiraled to $30 million). Nonetheless the film received an Oscar nomination for Best Make-Up Design (for ROB BOTTIN), as well as three BAFTA nominations (British Academy of Film and Television Arts) for Best Costume Design, Best Make-Up Artist and Best Special Visual Effects (for NICK ALLDER).

In March 1989, Universal re-edited the film for syndicated television on its "Universal Debut Network"—a slightly extended version of the original theatrical release with the Tangerine Dream score. In March 1990, the film was released on laserdisc in Japan with the Goldsmith score and a running time of ninety-one minutes. As a result, perhaps, of the film's growing cult status, Scott collaborated with his long-term video producer CHARLES DE LAUZIRIKA to produce an "Ultimate Edition" DVD of *Legend*, with a new 113-minute *LEGEND*: THE DIRECTOR'S CUT plus deleted scenes and interviews with some of the production's main personalities. Universal released this DVD on 21 May 2002.

The finished version of the film draws on diverse sources, combining elements of classical European folktales (such as those collected by the BROTHERS GRIMM) and Judeo-Christian myth. But *Legend* is undoubtedly a fairy tale. The film contains several elements characteristic of the genre, such as fairy folk like Brown Tom (CORK HUBBERT), Screwball (BILLY BARTY), and Gump (DAVID BENNENT), as well as certain plot conventions. There is also the convention of showing Jack as incorruptible throughout: clearly, resilience is a characteristic of CHILDHOOD. However, there is a thread of evil running throughout the film which sets it apart from other fairy tales of princesses and heroes and culminates in the final battle between good and evil. The film establishes a balance between the sinister and the sentimental by means of cinematic resources—lighting, sound, set design, montage, and costume. Gorton's forest setting offers the opportunity to contrast the beauty of the green landscape with a dark, ominous uncertainty. On the other hand, Scott deliberately draws upon generic stereotypes to suggest that evil—as personified by Darkness (TIM CURRY)—is more exciting than good. Lily (MIA SARA) sings to the unicorns, a moment which according to Matthew Aitken seems "so terribly clichéd that Scott causes the 'beauty' of the scene to lapse into a somewhat removed sensibility." By contrast, Darkness embodies the classic form of Satan, an angel of death who never goes away. Even though Jack destroys him at the end, Darkness's words resonate throughout the film: "You think you have won. What is light without dark? I am a part of you all. You can never defeat me. We [all human beings] are brothers eternal."

As with *Blade Runner*, *Legend* seems to have been influenced by the work of JOHN MILTON, especially *Paradise Lost*. Darkness's lair resembles a hell on earth, with its endless passages, dungeons, and ever-present fire that threatens to engulf Jack and his companions as they try to recover the unicorn. Darkness seduces Lily and forces her into a macabre dance of death with a bewitched gown: this empty garment (animated by Darkness) chills the girl's heart, after magically wrapping itself around her body. When the dance finishes, Lily has been transformed into a diabolic figure complete with black lip-gloss. This transformation of the heroine from an innocent into a monstrous-female reveals Scott's concern with the issue of FEMINISM. Milton's work also influences the film's basic premise, as Darkness plots his revenge against humankind by depriving the world of natural light. This aspect of the film was emphasized in the trailer for the 1985 American release, which had Darkness exclaiming "There can be no heaven without hell, no light without . . . *me*!!" accompanied by the tagline, "There may never be another dawn." The idea of an evil genius threatening to take over the world crops up in Scott's earlier work—for example, "THE LEAGUE OF UNCHARITABLE LADIES."

Lily's transgressive act of touching the unicorns—even though Jack expressly forbids her—not only invests *Legend* with further Biblical echoes, but also ushers in a new ice age where the world freezes over and everything is laid to waste. Even the music box in Nell's (Tina Martin's) cottage, which once played a merry tune while showing a young courting couple, now only plays discordant notes. Gump observes quite accurately that Lily has "upset the order of the universe." The barren landscape of the frozen forest recalls the deserted planet visited by the crew in *Alien*, while the notion of a world in turmoil is evoked in the DYSTOPIA that is Los Angeles in *BLADE RUNNER*. The settings might be different, but the worlds are equally hellish. Scott used the same unicorn shots in both *Legend* and *BLADE RUNNER*: THE DIRECTOR'S CUT (1992).

Other shots in *Legend* echo *Blade Runner*, even though they are used differently. A rising sun appears at the end of *Legend*, signaling the dawn of a new day and the close of

Darkness's reign of terror. In *Blade Runner* the same shot appears as a backdrop to Tyrell's (JOE TURKEL's) office, when Deckard (HARRISON FORD) encounters Rachael (SEAN YOUNG) for the first time. In this film the sunlight is contrasted with the artificiality of Tyrell's world and the people living in it. Sunlight regularly appears in Scott's commercials to signify an ideal world, notably in the 1970s commercial for RADIANT WASHING POWDER.

Critical material on *Legend* has been scanty at best since the film's original release in 1985. The FAQ website contains essays on "The Remnants of a Masterpiece" as well as a guide to the extra footage in *Legend: The Director's Cut*, a history of the *Legend* DVD, a guide to the four available versions of the film (American release, European release, the Universal television version and the Director's Cut), and essays on "What's Wrong with the Picture" and "The Lost Films of Ridley Scott." Paul M. Sammon's *Ridley Scott Close-Up* contains an essay on the film, talking about its troubled production history but containing minimal analysis. Richard A. Schwartz's analysis in *The Films of Ridley Scott* concentrates on "the interconnectedness of good and evil," something "consistent with ancient Greek mythology, Eastern philosophy, and modern notions of a universe built on paradox and complementarity rather than Christianity." Mikel J. Koven's essay "Folklore Studies and Popular Film and Television" surveys the existing popular literature on the topic, and some of the films (*Legend* included) that take up folklore topics. Juliette Wood's "Filming Fairies" quotes a reviewer who described the film as "cloyingly self-conscious" and concludes that "the film did not live up to expectations" (the author does not define exactly what such expectations are). Carole Auroet's "Legend de Ridley Scott: Un Patchwork Culturel," an essay (in French) in *Contes et Legends à L'écran* tries to rehabilitate the film by situating it in the tradition of European folklore, Scott having drawn on various traditions in an attempt to revitalize them for contemporary filmgoers.

More general essays covering the themes explored by *Legend* include Kerstin Westerlund-Shands's "Female Fatality in the Movies" (1993). Arthur Lindley situates *Legend* in the context of medieval films, with a more detailed analysis of *KINGDOM OF HEAVEN*.

References

Matthew Aitken, "*Legend*: Ridley Scott (The Remnants of a Masterpiece?)," *Legend: Frequently Asked Questions*, www.figmentfly.com/legend/different4i.html (accessed 25 April 2008); Carole Aurouet, "*Legend* de Ridley Scott: Un Patchwork Culturel," in *Contes et Légendes a L'écran*, Cinem-Action Condé-sur-Noireau, CinemAction no.116 (Paris: Corlet Librarie 2005): 218–27; Pat H. Broeske, "The Late, Late Show," *Stills* 24 (February 1986): 13; Gordon Burn, "Daring to Be Cute," *Sunday Times*, 24 November 1985,

56; Vincent Canby, "The Screen: Ridley Scott's 'Legend,'" *New York Times*, 18 April 1986, C2; David Castell, "*Legend*," *Sunday Telegraph* (London), 1 December 1985, 14; Richard Corliss, "Legend," *Time*, 12 May 1986, 98; "It's Only a Movie," *Starburst* 8, no.6 (February 1986): 39; Mikel J. Koven, "Folklore Studies and Popular Films on Television: A Necessary Critical Survey," *Journal of American Folklore*, Spring 2003, 176–95; Arthur Lindley, "Once, Present and Future Kings: Kingdom of Heaven and the Multitemporality of Medieval Film," in *Race, Class and Gender in Medieval Cinema*, ed. Lynn T. Ramey and Tison Pugh (New York: Palgrave Macmillan 2007), 16–29; Sean Murphy, "History of the *Legend* DVD," www.figmentfly.com/legend.different4k.html (accessed 25 April 2008); James Olsen, "Script Drawing," *Starburst* 8, no.3 (November 1985): 18–23; Paul M. Sammon, *Ridley Scott Close-Up: The Making of His Movies* (New York: Thunder's Mouth Press, 1999), 76–85; Richard A. Schwartz, *The Films of Ridley Scott* (Westport, CT: Praeger Publishers, 2001), 57; Ridley Scott, interviewed in Alan Jones, "*Legend*," *Cinefantastique* 15, no.5 (January 1986): 27; Ridley Scott, interviewed in "The Making of *Legend*" (2002 documentary directed by J. M. Kenny) included on *Legend: The Ultimate DVD* (Los Angeles: Universal Studios, 2002); Ridley Scott, Production Notes on *Legend: The Ultimate DVD* (Los Angeles: Universal Studios, 2002); Alexander Walker, "Legend," *Evening Standard*, 27 August 1985, 22; Ian Wall, *Ridley Scott's Legend: A Study Guide* (London, Twentieth Century-Fox Film Co. Ltd., 1985); Kerstin Westerlund-Shands, "Female Fatality in the Movies," *Moderna Sprak* 87, no.2 (1993): 113–20; "What are the Differences Between the Four Confirmed Versions of *Legend*?" www.figmentfly.com/legend/different3.html (accessed 25 April 2008); "What is the Extra Footage in the *Legend* Director's Cut?" www.figmentfly.com/legend/different4c.html (accessed 25 April 2008); Juliette Wood, "Filming Fairies: Popular Film, Audience Response and Meaning in Contemporary Fairy Lore," *Folklore* 117 (December 2006): 279–96; Geoff Wright, "Legend: What's Wrong with the Picture?" www.figmentfly.com/legend/different4a.html (accessed 25 April 2008); Geoffrey M. Wright, "Unnecessary Destruction: The Lost Films of Ridley Scott," *Legend: Frequently Asked Questions*, www.figmentfly.com/legend/different4j.html (accessed 25 April 2008).

Bibliography

James Clarke, *Ridley Scott* (London: Virgin Books Ltd., 2002), 83–97; Brian J. Robb, *Ridley Scott* (Harpenden: Pocket Essentials, 2002), 41–48.

LEGEND: THE DIRECTOR'S CUT
GB/US 2002 r/t 113 min col.

This version (restored by CHARLES DE LAUZIRIKA) reconstructed the film in as close a form as possible to the original version, produced prior to the cuts forced on Scott by Universal Pictures in 1985. It allows for greater character development, accompanied by the JERRY GOLDSMITH score. There is much more emphasis on setting—for example, extra shots of the forest landscape and a greater focus on the sounds of the birds in the trees. Lily (MIA SARA) sings several new songs reflecting her state of mind at various points in the action; one of these she uses to attract, and subsequently calm, a unicorn. There is one noticeable break in the action (occasioned by a lack of suitable footage) when Lily escapes from Blix (ALICE PLAYTEN) and Brown Tom (CORK HUBBERT) tries to stand up to the goblins' arrows.

The plot centers more on Jack's (TOM CRUISE'S) need to prove himself by rescuing Lily and destroying Darkness (TIM CURRY). Every obstacle he encounters becomes a test of his ability; rather like Hercules, he has to overcome a variety of perils. In his fight with Meg Mucklebones (ROBERT PICARDO) Jack has firstly to distract her by using his shield as a mirror while he fumbles with his sword. When he cuts off her head, his line "I did it!" makes more sense than in the 1985 version, as he nearly loses his life in the process. Later on, in a distinct allusion to the folktale "Jack the Giant-Killer," Jack is shown vanquishing Blunder (Kiran Shah), much to his companions' delight. Jack's final test—kissing Lily and rescuing her from the spell imposed on her by Darkness—is described thus by Gump (DAVID BEN-NENT): "Look what we've been through. Look where we are. It is the greatest lesson we have learned. Only you can solve this riddle."

The Director's Cut devotes more attention to the female characters. Lily now seems more willful—someone who does not accept Jack at the end, even though he vows to be there for her always. Only time will tell if their relationship will prosper. Oona (ANNABELLE LANYON) becomes a lonely figure, as willful as Lily, who suffers the consequences of overreaching herself when she is rebuffed by Jack. All she can look forward to is a life of isolation. There is also a new sequence in which Scott intercuts medium close-ups of Lily and Oona trying to escape from the Great Tree. Neither can see the other, but it is clear that the director wants us to understand the similarities between the two. Both value self-interest above anything else and suffer as a result.

The Director's Cut also places more emphasis on the unicorns, who are seen at the end wandering about the forest. While they remain free, the world will be safe from corruption.

Goldsmith's rich, tuneful score gives the film an operatic quality—every action now seems almost elemental. Jack undertakes his challenges to save the world from Darkness; Darkness, on the other hand, seeks to ensnare willing victims by offering them unlimited wealth—provided, of course, that they renounce the enjoyment of natural light.

Bibliography

Andy Dursin, "*Legend* Resurrected," *Film Score Monthly* 7, no.4 (May/June 2002): 13–15; Sean Murphy, "What Is the Extra Footage in the *Legend* Director's Cut?" *Legend: Frequently Asked Questions*, www.figmentfly.com/legend/different4c.html (accessed 25 April 2008); "What are the Differences between the Four Confirmed Versions of *Legend*?" *Legend: Frequently Asked Questions*, www.figmentfly.com/legend/different3.html (accessed 25 April 2008).

LEHRER, JIM (1934–)

Commentator, journalist and the author of the book *THE LAST DEBATE*, from which Ridley Scott produced his 2000 TV movie of the same name.

Lehrer has always been interested in presidential affairs (the subject of the film). The *New York Sun* once criticized him for offering "softballs" in the form of questions to candidates. Lehrer brushed such criticisms aside, claiming that he is nothing more than an "old-fashioned purist . . . I really do believe the more information, the more points of view, however crazy they may be to some people, the better off we are in a democratic society. Let everybody speak and let everybody have a voice and let's assume everybody is just as smart as we are and can figure it out and sort through it."

Reference

Jim Lehrer quoted in Andrew Billen, "This Election Is News. If you Want Entertainment, Go to the Circus," *The Times Section 2*, 2 November 2004, 6–7.

L'ENFANT SAUVAGE

France 1970 r/t 83 min b/w. *Production Companies*: Les Films du Carrosse and Les Productions Artistes Associés. *Producer*: Marcel Bebert. *Director*: François Truffaut. *Writers*: François Truffaut and Jean Gruault, from the novel *Mémoires et Rapport sur Victor de l'Aveyron* by Jean Itard. *Director of Photography*: Nestor Almendros. *Production Designer*: Jean Mandaroux. *Cast*: Jean-Pierre Cargot (*Victor, enfant sauvage*), François Truffaut (*Le Dr. Jean Itard*), Francoise Seigner (*Madame Guerin*), Jean Dasté (*Professor Philippe Pinel*).

1798: in a forest, some country people catch a wild child who cannot read, write, or speak. Dr. Itard is interested in the child and starts to educate him; everyone thinks he will fail, but after a great deal of effort, the doctor achieves results. Truffaut's film based its premise on the classic Enlightenment distinction between "reason" and "nature" by showing the so-called "reasonable" citizens treating Victor as something to be derided rather than understood. Like the Elephant Man in David Lynch's film of the same name (1979), Victor is made a subject for public exhibition. Even when he is taken in by Dr. Itard, and supposedly given "sympathetic" treatment, Itard always pretends that he can understand the boy's feelings. What the doctor cannot recognize is that, to be truly free, Victor should be released once again into the wild: something that can never happen, or the doctor will have failed in his task to "humanize" him. Through this film Truffaut satirizes the notion of the Noble Savage; in his view it is nothing but another form of colonization, both physical and emotional.

Scott uses *L'Enfant Sauvage* as the basis for Jack's (TOM CRUISE's) characterization in *LEGEND*. Although Jack is an educated person, many of his body movements—especially at the beginning of the film—have been inspired by Truffaut's work. However, Scott approaches the notion of colonization in a positive light: Jack, the wild child, is "humanized" when he encounters Princess Lily (MIA SARA). The wild child theme recurs once more in *WHITE SQUALL* when Captain Sheldon (JEFF BRIDGES) lets the boys go ashore and they put face paint on and run up the hillside. On the boat, Sheldon's wife Alice (CAROLINE GOODALL) asks, "What are they doing?" to which Sheldon replies, "Claiming their place in the world." "Like Darwin himself we would see blessed nature," Chuck Gieg (SCOTT WOLF) narrates as the boys go running on the island barechested, while a tribal drumbeat can be heard on the soundtrack. "I finally understood Homer," claims Gieg. "The journey's the thing."

LE SOURD, PHILIPPE (?–)

A GOOD YEAR was his first English language film as director of photography. The film portrays a golden vision of PROVENCE as a world of perpetual sunshine, verdant landscapes and merriment. RUSSELL CROWE, who played Max Skinner, admitted that having to live in this world for two months was not hard work: "I loved waking up in Provence." However, the critic Kenneth Turan complained that, while the photography of the film was gorgeous, "something vital is missing in this all-too-leisurely film . . . a romantic comedy made by individuals with no special feeling for the genre who stretch a half hour's worth of story to nearly two hours."

Reference

Kenneth Turan, "A Good Year," *Los Angeles Times*, 10 November 2006, www.latimes.com/entertainment/news/movies/cl-et-good10nov10, 1,5187991.story (accessed 30 January 2009).

LIOTTA, RAY (1954–)

Liotta specializes in playing psychopathic characters who hide behind a cultivated charm. This helps explain why he was cast as Paul Krendler in *HANNIBAL*, the enemy of the eponymous central character (ANTHONY HOPKINS). Liotta himself described the character as someone who "has the opportunity and the know-how to make [Starling's (JULIANNE MOORE's)] life miserable . . . so that's what he does." A seventy-thousand-dollar animatronic dummy of Liotta was created for the final scene, which shows him eating his own brains: "They had all kinds of wires and things,

levers they're pushing, opening the mouth." Liotta had his head shaved for the role, and enjoyed playing someone who's "filled with drugs yet is still awake while all this is happening. I think people will definitely remember this scene . . . If anything, it's more explicit than in the book."

Liotta's Krendler is an unsavory character who takes pleasure in harassing Clarice and taunting her with offensive, sexist remarks. Even when he has been lobotomized at the end of the film, he still imagines her as "an office girl. Can you type and file? Can you take dictation? Take this down: Washington is full of cornpone country pussy." However, Krendler is not as clever as he thinks; when Mason Verger (GARY OLDMAN) offers him a $500,000 bribe to accept a forged postcard (allegedly written by Hannibal to Clarice), Krendler responds, "I'm not sure I understand." Screenwriter STEVEN ZAILLIAN sums up Verger's reaction thus: "*[He] sighs. Maybe he's making a terrible mistake. Maybe Krendler is just too stupid to be of any real use to him.*" In Hannibal's view, Krendler deserves everything he gets—including eating his own brains fried in butter: "Paul certainly won't miss this—the prefrontal lobe is the seat of manners."

References

Ray Liotta, quoted in Jill Bernstein, "Eat Drink Man Woman," *Premiere* 14, no.6 (February 2001): 107; Steven Zaillian, "*Hannibal*: Screenplay Based on the Novel by Thomas Harris," Revision (9 February 2000), http://sfy.ru/sfy.html?script=hannibal2001 (accessed 15 December 2008).

Bibliography

Charles Gant, "Looking Good, Fella," *Times Play*, 9–14 February 2003, 5.

LOGAN, JOHN (1961–)

Chicago-born playwright and screenwriter who his first major success on stage with *Never the Sinner* (1990) which premiered in London in 1990 and received its first American performance five years later.

Logan started working with Scott on the abortive *I AM LEGEND* project in 1997, working on a script based on Richard Matheson's 1954 novel. He recalled in an interview that he went through six drafts in the space of five months: "It was the most intensive work I've ever done in my life, and it was absolutely thrilling, because we were going in, reinventing, and making very brave choices." However, Logan was removed from the project at Warner Brothers' insistence and replaced by screenwriter Mark Protosevich. The project was eventually canceled in March 1998.

However Logan's collaboration with Scott on the script of *RKO 281* actually did make it to the screen, but only after considerable negotiation. The script was first created in

1997, at a time when the major studios were interested in the project. But negotiations faltered; a reticence to make a period film *about* a film, coupled with Ridley Scott's own demands, pulled the plug on a big-budget, big-screen film. Logan was put off the project until HBO stepped in to finance the project in collaboration with the BBC.

The original script was heavily altered to suit the requirements of a $10 million budget, rather than the $30 million originally planned. Whole scenes were removed; for example, an opening scene showing a woman (Orson Welles's mother) telling her young son, "You must have a dream. A great dream worthy of you." Several sequences showing the making of *Citizen Kane* were removed—for example, one where Welles is shown cajoling his actors (including Agnes Moorehead and Dorothy Commingore, both of whose roles were cut from the finished film) into showing their emotions more directly on the screen. Another deleted sequence shows an FBI agent coming to question Herman Mankiewicz about Welles's alleged Communist affiliations, plus a short, rather nostalgic moment where Welles and George Schaefer watch the Tara set from *Gone With the Wind* being razed to the ground. Logan also removed another sequence: Welles, in a nightclub celebrating the Children's Milk Fund Benefit, performs a jaunty song-and-dance version of the song "Disgustingly Rich" with Rita Hayworth in front of the studio bosses, including Louis B. Mayer. Clearly this is designed to show Welles's contempt for Hollywood, even while he attempts to make a living there. The Hayworth role was cut from the finished film. Logan also cut out another short exchange between Welles, Mankiewicz and the cinematographer Gregg Toland, in which they discuss the projected version of the life of Jesus Christ. Mankiewicz remarks meaningfully that a good scene might perhaps involve John the Baptist who "pulls your [Welles's] head out of the water and says, 'Look up, and behold your destiny.'" Needless to say, Welles ignores the insult and asks instead whether the scene is from one of the gospels. Finally, Logan removed another scene towards the end of the script showing Hearst's treasures being auctioned off to a crowd of eager bidders.

Logan was brought in to refine the script of *GLADIATOR*, which was originally written by DAVID FRANZONI. He changed the name of the central character and added the murder of Maxmius's (RUSSELL CROWE's) family, as well as Commodus's (JOAQUIN PHOENIX's) unhealthy interest in his sister and her son and a failed senatorial conspiracy against the emperor. In 2002 he was quoted in an interview as saying that he would be beginning work on the sequel to *Gladiator*. "It's doing very well and it's going to be really exciting." However, nothing concrete has emerged to date.

References

Ethan James, "CC Report! John Logan Talks 'Gladiator 2,'" *Cinema Confidential* 12 February 2002, www.cinecon.com/news.php?id=0212024 (accessed 6 December 2008); John Logan, "Draft Script for *RKO 281*" (dated 1 May 1997), http://sfy.ru/sfy.html?script=rko218 (accessed 16 November 2008); John Logan, quoted in David Hughes, *The Greatest Sci-Fi Movies Never Made*, rev. ed. (London: Titan Books, 2008), 137.

LOHMAN, ALISON (1979–)

Early roles include *Alex in Wonder* (2001) and *White Oleander* (2002). Cast as the fourteen-year-old Angela in *MATCHSTICK MEN*, Lohman described her role thus in a preproduction interview: "At first she thinks he's [Roy] a little dorky, the way he dresses and the way he keeps blinking; she's not sure what to make of him . . . But the more time she spends with him the more she likes him. I think she gets a kick out of him. He makes her laugh." Sean Bailey, one of the film's producers, offered further thoughts: "This is what kids dream about. It's exciting, like something they've seen in movies . . . there's a lot of pride in it, too, regardless of [Roy's] own conflicted feelings about his work, the truth is he's good at it and in some way I think he wants to show her what he can do."

As a twenty-something playing a fourteen-year-old, Lohman tried to recapture what she described as the childish look: "There's something in their eyes, between age ten and fifteen I think, it's just that sort of 'anything is possible' [look] . . . For me it's all about dreaming. What does she look like when she walks? What's the look in her eye? It's not about, 'Oh, on this move, I'm going to put my arm like that.' It's just the whole spirit, so that any way that I would move would be right."

That "look" as Lohman describes it, is most evident during the scene where Angela persuades Roy to involve her in one of his scams. Unable to contemplate the thought of listening to more of her love life, Roy gives in and promises to "show [her] one thing." Angela's reaction is typical of a wide-eyed fourteen-year-old: "She nearly jumps for joy. Kisses him on the cheek, getting toothpaste on her face, then skips down the hall . . . she's already frolicking into the living-room." In a scene reminiscent of Ryan and Tatum O'Neal's double-act in Peter Bogdanovich's *PAPER MOON* (1973), Roy and Angela embark on a con in the launderette, with Angela playing the innocent girl and Roy the passerby who just happens to be reading a newspaper. The two of them undertake their roles perfectly—so much so that Roy exclaims to Dr. Klein (BRUCE ALTMAN) that "she [Angela] took right to it. She even helped me, this fourteen-year-old girl, working these people with me . . . I really liked it. It was the best time we've had together."

In the "Director's Commentary" to the 2004 DVD release of the film, Scott emphasizes the fact that Angela treated the idea of playing Roy's daughter as a part of Frank's con; once she had finished, she would receive a cut of Roy's savings in payment. As the film develops, however, Angela becomes more and more attached to the older man. When she returns—albeit briefly—to his life as a nineteen-year-old, with a boyfriend in tow, dressed in dark glasses and cut-off jeans, she asks him whether he wants to know her real name. Roy replies, "I know your name," which prompts Angela to smile and issue the parting shot: "I'll see ya, Dad." The two of them might never meet again; but it is clear that they enjoyed their relationship, as it helped both of them to discover something about themselves.

References

Nick and Ted Griffin, "*Matchstick Men*: Shooting Draft" (14 October 2002), www.imsdb.com/scripts/Matchstick-Men.html (accessed 4 January 2009); Rebecca Murray, "'Matchstick Men's Impressive Young Talent, Alison Lohman," *About.com Interview* (September 2003), http://movies.about.com/cs/matchstickmen/a/matchlohman .htm (accessed 7 August 2008); *Production Information Matchstick Men* (Los Angeles: Warner Bros. Pictures, 2003), 10, 12; Ridley Scott, "Director's Commentary" to the 2004 DVD release of *Matchstick Men* (London: Warner Home Video UK, 2004).

LONCRAINE, RICHARD (1946–)

Began his career in television on *Play for Today* before making his debut with *Brimstone and Treacle* (1982). He then became associated with successful films such as *The Missionary* (1981) and *Richard III* (1995).

As director for the Ridley Scott-produced television drama *THE GATHERING STORM*, Loncraine was initially reluctant to do the project, as he thought that "Churchill was a kind of a one note samba really. And this is my ignorance as I found out, because it's been an amazing learning curve." He believed that "with a film about Churchill as with, say, Shakespeare, you have to ask yourself how you can make it into an entertaining, accessible story and not just for people who are only interested in modern history . . . Churchill was a bully we needed at the time to fight Hitler. He was also funny, kind, generous, loved music hall songs and was a great raconteur. Yes, he could be rude, aggressive and moody too. I think he was a complete madman in the best sense of the word, and certainly obsessed with power."

Loncraine found the experience of filming somewhat problematic: "Shooting period stuff in London is a nightmare. All the buildings are clean so Angus Bickerton, who's doing our visual effects, is having to do wire frame work to put dirt on them. Although it may be marginally better now, England has never been a film friendly country."

However, the experience of filming had its unexpected benefits: "We were filming in an old abandoned empty house outside London. I was there very early one morning . . . and I found the props table in the corner where the propmen had been cutting out pictures of Churchill—of the real Churchill for reference, for what his clothes were like . . . I found this picture of Churchill, which I thought absolutely captured the quality and the look and the way that I thought this man should be . . . I realized that I had picked out a picture of Albert Finney . . . I guess I had been living with the man, but it was mixed up with pictures of the real Churchill."

References

"Interview with Richard Loncraine," *The Gathering Storm: Artist Interviews,* www.hbo.com/films/gatheringstorm/cmp/interviews .shtml (accessed 24 December 2008); Richard Loncraine, quoted in "Out of the Wilderness," *Exposure,* Spring 2002, 22–23.

LOS ANGELES

The city of Los Angeles features most famously in *BLADE RUNNER*, where Scott creates a futuristic vision of the city as a DYSTOPIA, largely deprived of humanity and dominated by technology. In *MONKEY TROUBLE* and *MATCHSTICK MEN* Scott's vision is far less pessimistic. *Monkey Trouble* creates a world of perpetual sunshine in which people spend much of their leisure time walking, riding, skateboarding or enjoying the sideshows on offer. However, there is an undercurrent of menace: the gypsy Azro (HARVEY KEITEL) and his monkey rob people of their money; later on Azro is seen pursuing the little girl Eva (THORA BIRCH) in a desperate attempt to recover his monkey. Although we have no idea what will happen to her, we are sure that she is in danger. *MATCHSTICK MEN* contrasts the bright California sunshine and the neat suburban houses with the dingy interior of Roy Waller's (NICOLAS CAGE's) house. This emphasizes Roy's reclusive nature; he believes he has agoraphobia, but in reality it is entirely due to an unwillingness to engage with life. Each episode of *NUMB3RS* is set in Los Angeles—a city of perpetual sunshine and towering skyscrapers, yet, both downtown and the suburbs, a hotbed of crime requiring the FBI agents' constant attention.

Bibliography

Stephen Rowley, "False LA: *Blade Runner* and the Nightmare City," in *The Blade Runner Experience: The Legacy of a Science Fiction Classic,* ed. Will Brooker (London and New York: Wallflower Press, 2005), 203–13.

LOVE VS. DUTY

A major theme explored in Ridley Scott's films. In *THE DUELLISTS* D'Hubert (KEITH CARRADINE) often ignores his wife and family in his obsession with fulfilling the requirements placed on him by the code of honor, which requires him to fight repeated duels with Feraud (HARVEY KEITEL). The same thing appears in the Ridley Scott-produced film *THE BROWNING VERSION*, where Crocker-Harris's dedication to the duty of being a public school teacher renders him insensitive to his wife Laura's (GRETA SCACCHI's) desires, as well as to the emotional needs of the boys he teaches. Eventually given the nickame "the Hitler of the Lower Fifth," he seems dedicated to humiliating the boys he works with, either by making fun of them or forcing them to speak in front of the class. However, he comes to learn the error of his ways, admitting in a climactic speech at the end of the film that he has failed to teach with sympathy, encouragement or humanity. Duty has overwhelmed his basic goodness of heart. Maximus (RUSSELL CROWE) is also faced with a similar dilemma in *GLADIATOR*—one which leads to tragic consequences, as his loyalty to the Roman army prevents him from looking after his family. As a result they are easy prey for the Praetorian guards, who come unexpectedly to their farmhouse and hang them. In DAVID FRANZONI's script Maximus's reaction, when he arrives home too late to rescue them, is predictable: "He falls to his knees, crying in disbelief and anguish. He manages to stand up and comes closer, tenderly touching his wife's feet, caressing them as though to comfort her. He falls to the ground and passes out from the grief." It is only when he has avenged their death by killing Commodus (JOAQUIN PHOENIX) and returning Rome to the people that he can rejoin them in death.

In *SOMEONE TO WATCH OVER ME*, Mike Keegan (TOM BERENGER) encounters a similar conflict, as he is faced with the question of whether to abandon home, family and a secure job in favor of a love affair with Claire Gregory (MIMI ROGERS). Scott certainly sympathizes with him—in the final sequence of the original script Mike and Claire stare at one another, "not knowing quite what to say." However, the director makes clear Mike has no choice in the end; he has to return to his family and maintain the proper distance from Claire, to say good-bye. Other police officers are faced with the same choice: Richie Roberts (RUSSELL CROWE) in *AMERICAN GANGSTER* sees his wife Laurie and son Michael move to Las Vegas while he continues the fight against the drug barons in New York, while Don Eppes (ROB MORROW) in *NUMB3RS* is so committed to his work that he finds it incapable to sustain a lasting relationship. In *TRISTAN + ISOLDE* the two eponymous central characters (JAMES FRANCO, SOPHIA MYLES) are unable to meet due to their commitments to King Marke (RUFUS SEWELL). Isolde asks at one point in the script: "If we lived in a place without duty . . . would you be with me?" Tristan can give only one answer:

"That place does not exist." *BLACK RAIN* explores a similar conflict through the main protagonist Nick Conklin (MICHAEL DOUGLAS) and his Japanese counterpart Masahiro (KEN TAKAKURA). Nick's family life has been destroyed due to obsession with his work; Masahiro believes that duty prevails over everything else. If police officers forget this then, in Masahiro's view, they render themselves open to dishonor. Such dedication is satirized by the yakuza leader Sato (Kobo in the original script): "A couple of thousand years they've [Japanese workers] been bound by these little rules. Looking in. Always afraid. Ugly little lives . . ." The reverse is true of the Scott-produced film *IN HER SHOES*. Maggie (TONI COLLETTE), a successful lawyer, leaves her job, admitting to her fiancé Simon (MARK FEUERSTEIN) that she only pursued a workaholic life out of a fear of "what would happen to me without those people [her colleagues] to please and those tasks to get done. Like . . . maybe . . . those were the things holding me together, and without them I'd fall apart." Instead she pursues an itinerant existence as a freelance dog-walker, working as and when she pleases.

Other protagonists face more extreme choices. In *G.I. JANE* Jordan O'Neil (DEMI MOORE) sacrifices her relationship with her boyfriend Royce (JASON BEGHE) in pursuit of her dream of completing her military training at the SEAL camp. The soldiers in *BLACK HAWK DOWN* face a similar dilemma: Shughart (Johnny Strong) tries to exchange a few words with his wife prior to the raid on Mogadishu, but cannot sufficient time to talk to her. All he can say is "I'm missing you. I love you, baby" and put the satellite phone down. Shughart's wife rushes to answer, but is too late.

No such doubts affect the three recruits in the reality show *AMERICAN FIGHTER PILOT*; they believe it is their duty to complete their training to take on the responsibility of protecting America from further attack in the post-9/11 era. The same applies to DON CHEADLE's Government Agent in *THE HIRE*: "TICKER," who risks life and limb to rescue a replacement heart from the hands of an enemy faction in an unnamed African country so that it can be given to the existing ruler. Only then will peace be restored to the nation. Russell Crowe's Ed Hoffman makes a similar decision in *BODY OF LIES*, talking incessantly to his subordinate Roger Ferris (LEONARDO DICAPRIO), even while taking his young son Timmy (Chase Edmunds) to the bathroom. However, his obsession with work does not make him a better operative; on the contrary, it renders him even more self-absorbed and unable to see the bigger picture of diplomatic relations between America and Jordan.

Sometimes characters have no choice; they have to sacrifice their personal lives in the line of duty. This is certainly the case with the Soviet spy Yevgeny Tsipin in *THE COMPANY*, who is told in no uncertain terms to sacrifice his Jewish girlfriend Azalia Ivanova (Erika Marozsán) and commit himself to "Mother Russia." If he does not, he will never have the chance to change the world. In *THE GATHERING STORM*, Ralph Wigram (LINUS ROACHE) kills himself after having illegally passed on classified information about German rearmament to Winston Churchill (ALBERT FINNEY). Although the action was prompted by the best of motives (to ensure his country's future security), Wigram cannot endure the strain it causes both himself and his family.

In other films, employees are forced to submit to the will of their superiors, even when they know that the wrong decision has been made. In *ALIEN* Ripley (SIGOURNEY WEAVER) decides not to let the infected Kane (JOHN HURT) back into the *NOSTROMO*, as it violates Company rules. Dallas (TOM SKERRITT) overrules her, arguing that Kane is one of the crew and therefore entitled to the same treatment as the others. However, Dallas's decision proves fatal, as it ultimately leads to the corruption of the spaceship. Clarice Starling (JULIANNE MOORE) suffers a similar experience in *HANNIBAL*. Despite her devotion to the job, she is ultimately forced to submit to the will of her corrupt boss Krendler (RAY LIOTTA). Hannibal Lecter (ANTHONY HOPKINS) suggests that her devotion to the FBI has been futile: "You serve the idea of order, Clarice—they don't. You believe in the oath you took—they don't. You feel it's your duty to protect the sheep—they don't. They don't like you because they're not like you. They're weak and unruly and believe in nothing." Clarice's only solution—which she discovers by the end of the film—is to act according to her own instincts, rather than those of her employers.

Other films put forward the opposite view—that personal relationships are far more important than job satisfaction. In *BLADE RUNNER* Deckard (HARRISON FORD) gradually discovers that the REPLICANTS—whom he is supposed to destroy—have feelings of their own. This is especially evident during his exchanges with Rachael (SEAN YOUNG), in which he asks questions while Rachael acknowledges her love for him. Deckard has learned through bitter experience that emotions are far more important than duty to one's profession. This provides a pretext for the happy ending (to the 1982 United States theatrical version of the film), where Deckard and Rachael fly away from the city to a verdant landscape. In the Ridley Scott-produced comedy *MONKEY TROUBLE* the dedicated police officer Peter (CHRISTOPHER McDONALD) remains dedicated to his job, even to the extent of interrogating his stepdaughter Eva (THORA BIRCH) on suspicion of harboring stolen goods. At the end of the film, however, he realizes the importance of family life; he overcomes his initial reluctance to allow Eva to keep a pet (on account of his allergy to animal fur) and gives his permission. She has proved herself capable of being a good parent to Dodger the monkey; it is Peter's responsibility to follow her example.

References

Craig Bolotin and Warren Lewis, "*Black Rain*: Draft Script" (November 1987), http://sfy.ru/sfy.html?script=black_rain_ds (accessed 8 June 2008); Howard Franklin, Danilo Bach and David Seltzer, "Someone to Watch Over Me" (revised 4 December 1986) (Los Angeles: Columbia Pictures Corporation, 1987); *Gladiator* by David Franzoni, revised by John Logan," http://sfy.ru/sfy/html?script=gladiator_ts (accessed 29 November 2008); Susannah Grant, "*In Her Shoes* Script," www.script-o-rama.com/movie_scripts/i/in-her-shoes-script-transcript.html (accessed 17 January 2009); Ken Nolan, *Black Hawk Down: The Shooting Script* (New York: Newmarket Press, 2002), 30; "*Tristan + Isolde*. Written by Dean Georgaris," www.imsdb.com/Movie%20Scripts/Tristan%20and%20Isolde%20Script.html (accessed 23 January 2009); Steven Zaillian, "*Hannibal*: Screenplay Based on the Novel by Thomas Harris," Revision (9 February 2000), http://sfy.ru/sfy.html?script=hannibal2001(accessed 15 December 2008).

LUSTIG, BRANKO (1932–)

Executive producer on *GLADIATOR, HANNIBAL, BLACK HAWK DOWN, KINGDOM OF HEAVEN, A GOOD YEAR*, and *AMERICAN GANGSTER*.

Croatian-born Lustig began his film career in Europe, in Italian and Yugoslavian cinema, before moving to America and Germany in the early 1970s where he made *Fiddler on the Roof* (1971) and *Tin Drum* (1979). He subsequently worked on the mega-miniseries *The Winds of War* and *War and Remembrance* for American television. He helped Steven Spielberg produce *Schindler's List* in 1993, winning an Oscar in the process. It was Spielberg who recommended him to Scott when the latter was seeking help with multi-location work on *Gladiator*. For his work on this film, Lustig received his second Oscar.

On *Black Hawk Down* Lustig worked hard to try and smooth the production process, so that the crew could film in Morocco: "I had some guarantees . . . that we could film there . . . The king and his ministers reacted positively . . . feeling that it was about an historical event and was in no way slanted against Muslims. They not only agreed to allow us to film there, but also put up a great deal of Moroccan military materiel, from tanks to Humvees and helicopters, at our disposal."

On *Kingdom of Heaven* Lustig had to cope with a spiraling budget which ballooned to $130 million. He also had to work with Scott on frequent changes to WILLIAM MONAHAN's script. As in *Black Hawk Down*, Lustig had to work in Morocco, a place he liked because he believed "the people are very open, very honest. And when you've worked fifty years in movies, you know who is honest or not . . . I know the king. I always have great support from him. I have guarantees from him about safety."

References
"A Lust for Life," *Screen International* 1503 (3–9 June 2005), 8; "Production Notes: *Black Hawk Down*," repr. in Ken Nolan, *Black Hawk Down: The Shooting Script* (New York: Newmarket Press, 2002), 159–60.

LUV ICE CREAM: LYONS MAID
GB 1969 Commercial r/t 30 sec b/w. *Production Company*: RSA Films. *Director*: Ridley Scott. *Cast*: David Bowie.

Black-and-white commercial shot at 7 Eccleston Square in London on 22 January 1969. The product was launched in England on 12 May 1969; it was an ice-cream bar covered mostly in chocolate and hundreds-and-thousands ("sprinkles") and costing 9d (4.5p). DAVID BOWIE appeared in the commercial with the band Mint. The soundtrack contained the following music and spoken dialogue:

> Luv, Luv, Luv
> Let me give it all to you
> Let me know that someday you'll do the same for me
> Luv, Luv, Luv
> Now from Lyons Maid. Everybody needs it [spoken]
> Luv, Luv, Luv
> The pop ice cream. Nine pence [spoken]

Bibliography
"David Bowie in *The Image* 1967 short film/ *Luv Ice Cream Spot* with Ridley Scott and Alan Hawkshaw," http://pan2fla.blogspot.com/2005/11/david-bowie-in-image-1967-short.html (accessed 17 February 2009).

MACLAINE, SHIRLEY (1934–)

Born Shirley MacLaine Beatty in Richmond, Virginia, the sister of Warren Beatty. MacLaine's long career began with *The Trouble with Harry* (1954) and has included an Oscar-winning performance in *Terms of Endearment* (1983). MacLaine was unexpectedly cast in the Ridley Scott-produced film *IN HER SHOES*. Apparently director CURTIS HANSON was reluctant to do so, at least in the beginning: "The thought of Shirley occurred early on, but I dismissed it, cos she is such a powerful, big, big, presence . . . I could see that she felt challenged. She is someone who responds to a challenge. She has that defiance. And look at the movie—she's brilliant." As Ella, MacLaine gives a low-key performance most notable for its gestures which might seem insignificant but convey a wealth of emotion. When she first speaks to Maggie (CAMERON DIAZ) on the telephone, she listens to the opening phrase: "Did you have a daughter called Caroline?" After a pause lasting a second or two she responds hurriedly "Yes," in a vain attempt to cover up her guilty feelings. Her next lines ("Well, we've been having wonderful weather. I'm glad you called") represent an attempt to recover the situation. On another occasion Lewis Feldman (Jerry Adler) pecks her on the cheek as he leaves her house; surprised and shocked by the gesture, all Ella can do is to laugh nervously and reply "Yeah." Since her husband's death, no one has ever paid any attention to her, and this comes as a complete surprise. MacLaine described the film as "the story of a family that overcomes real dramatic disaster . . . That's why I did this movie and why Curtis wanted to move in and see what happens."

References

Susannah Grant, "*In Her Shoes* Script" (transcribed from the DVD version of the film), www.script-o-rama.com/movie_scripts/i/in-her-shoes-script-transcript.html (accessed 17 January 2009); Shirley MacLaine interview by Ray Dademo, www.thecinema-source.com/celebrity/interviews/Shirley-MacLaine-chick-flick-My-Ass-interview-195-0.html, (accessed 8 August 2008); Ben Marshall, "If the Shoe Fits, Film It," *Guardian Guide*, 19 November 2005, 8–10.

Bibliography

Ginny Dougory, "One Touch Kooky," *Times Magazine*, 5 November 2005, 22–29.

MacNICOL, PETER (1954–)

Born in Dallas, MacNicol's films include *Dragonslayer* (1981), *Sophie's Choice* (1982), and *Addams Family Values* (1993). Television includes *Chicago Hope* (1994–1998), *Ally McBeal* (1997–2002), and *24* (2007–2008).

Cast as Dr. Larry Fleinhardt in *NUMB3RS*, MacNicol portrays a brilliant academic who cannot sustain an effective personal life. Although attracted to Agent Megan Reeves (DIANE FARR), his relationship with her ends up going nowhere. Fleinhardt cannot even find a proper place to live: sometimes he finds improvised sleeping quarters at Caltech; other times, he moves in with the Eppes family. In Series 3 he is shown spending some time in a monastery, ostensibly in the hope of discovering life's purpose, but in reality as a way of retreating from a life he finds particularly unsatisfying. Fleinhardt's one redeeming feature is his academic ability, which renders him a perfect foil for Charlie Eppes (DAVID KRUMHOLTZ) in solving his various criminal cases.

MacNicol described his role thus in a 2005 interview: "This character is very mysterious . . . He's a little bit Yoda, a little bit (physicist) Richard Feynman, a little bit Dr. Watson. It was probably the third in a series of people (I've portrayed) who I would call a wise fool."

Reference

M. McDaniel, "Will New Show Sustain Viewers after Premiere?" *Houston Chronicle*, January 20, 2005, www.petermacnicolonline.com/numb3rs1.html (accessed February 22, 2009).

MADSEN, MICHAEL (1958–)

Born in Chicago, Madsen learned his craft at the Steppenwolf Theatre, where he worked with JOHN MALKOVICH, one of the company's founders. He had just played an associate of the rock band chronicled in *The Doors* (1991) when *THELMA & LOUISE* gave him the chance to play Jimmy, a brooding musician who apparently cares for his girlfriend Louise (SUSAN SARANDON).

However, this proves nothing more than an illusion. When Louise calls Jimmy to ask if he loves her, the pause at the end of the line is palpable. On his end, he takes the cigarette out of his mouth and, after what seems an age, replies "Yeah." This is the moment when Louise finally realizes that she has to live life on her own: Jimmy might offer roses, further protestations of love, and even an engagement ring, but he has no further place in her life. He makes every effort to speak the way Louise might like him to, but she just wonders whether he has taken "a pill that makes you say all the right stuff." Try as he might, he can never understand her language or her way of thinking.

In CALLIE KHOURI's original script, Jimmy comes across as a more sympathetic character who professes his love for Louise and persuades her to act out a fake MARRIAGE ceremony in which they vow "to have and to hold for the rest of the night, through richness and poorness and breakfast at the coffee shop until your plane leaves or it gets light, whichever comes first." Such scenes give a sense of hope for Louise to continue her relationship.

References

Callie Khouri, quoted in Marita Sturken, *Thelma and Louise* (London: BFI Publishing, 2000), 46.

MALICK, TERRENCE (1943–)

A maverick director of classic westerns and ROAD MOVIES, whose work includes *Badlands* (1973), *Days of Heaven* (1978), *The Thin Red Line* (1998), and *A New World* (2005). Malick is chiefly known for his concentration on landscape and atmosphere, often at the expense of the plot. His work was frequently invoked by reviewers of *THE ASSASSINATION OF JESSE JAMES BY THE COWARD ROBERT FORD*, whose 160-minute running time allows for plenty of concentration on atmosphere and location by cinematographer ROGER DEAKINS. Deakins acknowledged in an interview with Stephen Pizzello and Jean Oppenheimer that director ANDREW DOMINIK had been inspired by Malick's *Days of Heaven.*

Reference

Stephen Pizzello and Jean Oppenheimer, "Western Destinies," *American Cinematographer*, vol. 88, no.10 (October 2007): 37.

MALKOVICH, JOHN (1953–)

Born in Christopher, Illinois, Malkovich joined Chicago's Steppenwolf Theatre in 1976, making his New York debut seven years later in SAM SHEPARD's *True West*.

Cast as Herman Mankowitz in *RKO 281*, Malkovich makes the best of his opportunities to play a "wonderful wreck of a human being, forty-three years old, but looking considerably older, he is short and squat and bitter. A compulsive gambler and drinker, Mank still glimmers with wry humor but is equally wicked and corrosive." Despite his shortcomings, Mankiewicz is still a talented person, who resents the offhand treatment he receives from Welles (LIEV SCHREIBER). His most effective scene occurs early on film, when he learns that Welles has removed his name from the *Citizen Kane* script. As he sees Welles pulling into the drive and climbing out of his car, Mankiewicz takes a final swig of scotch and flings the typewritten copy of the script in the younger man's face, calling him as "selfish fuck" as he does so. Although Welles responds in kind by telling Mankiewicz that he took "350 pages of drunken rambling and . . . made a movie out of them," the screenwriter stands firm. Welles turns round and slams the door; Mankiewicz leans against it and murmurs, "I hope you choke on it. I hope it kills you." In this short sequence Malkovich captures the essence of the character—a talented artist who in spite of possessing more creative talent is nonetheless doomed to play second fiddle to Welles.

Reference

John Logan, "Draft Script for *RKO 281*" (dated 1 May 1997), http://sfy.ru/sfy.html?script=rko218 (accessed 16 November 2008).

MAMET, DAVID (1947–)

Mamet's film career began with the screenplay for the remake of *The Postman Always Rings Twice* (1981). He made his directorial debut with *House of Games* (1987), which he also wrote.

Mamet was initially hired to write the script of *HANNIBAL*, replacing TED TALLY (scriptwriter of *THE SILENCE OF THE LAMBS*), who had declined to adapt the sequel. However, his version of the script was deemed unsatisfactory by Scott, who felt it lacked any real narrative drive and failed to develop the crucial relationship between Hannibal Lecter and Clarice Starling, instead devoting too much time to supporting characters Mason Verger and Rinaldo Pazzi. According to David Orr, Mamet's version was "uninspired [and] shoddy," his "terse-staccato dialogue" proving grating rather than gripping. Mamet's script was significantly rewritten by STEVEN ZAILLIAN.

Reference

David Orr, "Script-review: *Hannibal*," *Creative Screenwriting* 8, no.2 (March/April 2001): 31.

MANSON, MARILYN (1969–)

Born Brian Hugh Warner in Canton, Ohio. Lead singer of his eponymous heavy-metal band; his stage name is formed from the names of Marilyn Monroe and the mass murderer Charles Manson.

Manson made his film debut in 1997 in David Lynch's *Lost Highway*, and took a guest role in *THE HIRE*: "BEAT THE DEVIL" as a neighbor of The Devil (GARY OLDMAN) who appears at his door, irritably asking The Devil to turn his music down.

MARGOLIS, MARK (1939–)

Born in Philadelphia, Margolis attended Temple University, before making his debut in television series like *Kojak* (1977) and an uncredited role in *Dressed to Kill* (1980).

Cast as Francisco de Bobadilla in *1492: CONQUEST OF PARADISE*, Margolis's role is largely symbolic. His face remains motionless; but his stately bearing and haughty manner are typical of Spanish nobles. It is clear that he will eventually take over from Columbus (GÉRARD DEPARDIEU) as governor of the Indies; he is just the kind of arch-imperialist whom the Spanish require to maintain authority over the Indians. However, it is clear that he is Columbus's intellectual inferior. Robert Thurston's novelization of the screenplay makes this clear: "How could he [Columbus] forget such a face, renowned not only for its ugliness but for its habitual expression of meanness and stupidity?"

Reference

Robert Thurston, *1492: Conquest of Paradise Based on a Screenplay by Roselyne Bosch* (London: Penguin Books, 1992), 177.

MARRIAGE

Several of Scott's films focus on the issue of marriage. In *SOMEONE TO WATCH OVER ME* the marriage between Mike Keegan (TOM BERENGER) and his wife Ellie (LORRAINE BRACCO) is put under almost intolerable strain by Mike's commitment to the job of protecting Claire Gregory (MIMI ROGERS). Nick Conklin (MICHAEL DOUGLAS) has experienced much the same thing in *BLACK RAIN*, his dedication to duty having led to the breakup of his marriage and restricted access to his children. Scott suggests that marriage causes untold suffering—especially if the partners are unsuited to one another. In the Scott-produced *IN HER SHOES*, Michael Feller (Ken Howard) contracts two unsuitable marriages: his first, to Caroline, ends in tragedy when Caroline commits suicide (after Michael has threatened to hospitalize her in the belief that she is unsuitable to look after her daughters); in his second marriage he plays second fiddle to Sydelle (Candice Azzara), who dotes on her daughter Marcia (Jackie Geary) and consciously neglects her step-daughters. In *THELMA & LOUISE*, Darryl (CHRISTOPHER McDONALD) treats his wife Thelma (GEENA DAVIS) like a child, by expecting her to cook, clean, and wait for him to return home when he chooses. It therefore comes as no surprise to find Thelma willingly accepting Louise's (SUSAN SARANDON's) offer to escape from the Arkansas life that

restricts them. The only true "marriage" comes at the end of the film, when the two women drive off the cliff into a world unfettered by patriarchal relations. Regarding whether their union is based on sexuality or friendship, Scott leaves viewers to make their own decisions. The same pessimistic view of male/female relationships within marriage also surfaces in *WHERE THE MONEY IS*, where Wayne MacKay (DERMOT MULRONEY) continually expects his wife Carol (LINDA FIORENTINO) to return to "normal"—in other words, accept a subordinate role within the marriage partnership. The fact that she refuses this makes him all the more concerned to reinforce the patriarchal order.

In *THE HUNGER* marriage is treated as a symbolic prison, inhibiting the (male) central characters' freedom of action. In the first-series episode "But at My Back I Always Hear" (Series 1, Episode 5), a respectably married university professor (Michael Gross) forms part of a student's (Karen Elkin's) sexual fantasy. Although determined to remain loyal to his wife and young child, it is clear that he is attracted to her. Eventually he is driven insane, as he tries and fails to escape the memory of the student (who commits suicide as a result of a broken heart). In "Room 17" (Series 1, Episode 8) a sales representative (Curtis Armstrong) escapes his nagging wife and enjoys the pleasure of an ideal woman who emerges from the television set in his motel room. However he comes to grief, the woman eventually stealing a necklace from him and disappearing into the television, never to return. "The Other Woman" (Series 1, Episode 10) ends with a jealous wife catching her husband and his lover *in flagrante delicto* and shooting them both dead. "Bridal Suite" (Series 1, Episode 12) begins with a happily married couple spending their wedding night in a lonely inn, but ends with the young man (Colin Ferguson) being transformed into ectoplasm—a punishment for his serial unfaithfulness. "The Sloan Men" (Series 1, Episode 13) are sex-obsessed; they regard marriage simply as a convenience, and literally and physically entrap any woman they encounter. The same applies to the protagonist in "Anais" (Series 1, Episode 16) (Nick Mancuso) who fantasizes about a young woman while working in Montréal. However, he meets a sticky end at the hands of her boyfriend and two of his acquaintances.

By contrast, in *THE GATHERING STORM* the marriage between Winston Churchill (ALBERT FINNEY) and Clemmie (VANESSA REDGRAVE) provides the foundation for Churchill's success as a politician. Clemmie tells him that "all these years I've put up with the miseries of political life, because I believe in you, and somehow I survived." Churchill is well aware of this, especially when Clemmie goes away on holiday and he is forced to fend for himself. In one of his letters to her (delivered in voice-over) he wishes that she had been around to deal with domestic problems involving his daughter Diana (Nancy Carroll): "I dealt with the situation very clumsily, I'm afraid. I wished profoundly that you'd been there to offer comfort and advice." Once she returns, Churchill is so overjoyed that he runs straight through the fish-pond at Chartwell in order to welcome her, exclaiming "Out of my way!" to his butler Inches (RONNIE BARKER) as he does so. In *AMERICAN FIGHTER PILOT* the three recruits—Mike Love, Marcus Gregory, and Todd Giggy—all believe in the institution of marriage as the foundation of a stable society, with gender roles clearly defined. Husbands are the breadwinners, while wives stay at home and provide a source of support both for their spouses and children. The same ideology underpins the ending of *MATCHSTICK MEN*: Roy Waller (NICOLAS CAGE) at last discovers stability in his life as he marries the supermarket check-out girl Kathy (Sheila Kelley) and has a child of his own. Kathy stays at home while he takes a job as a carpet salesperson. NICK AND TED GRIFFIN's script shows how happy the two of them are: "She rubs his head: nice job, then kisses him, and he kisses back—and when they break, she whispers sweetly in his ear, and he smiles even more. He looks down to lay his palm gently on her belly." Sometimes marriages survive even the biggest challenges: Zee James (MARY-LOUISE PARKER) still loves her husband Jesse (BRAD PITT), despite the fact that he leads the life of an OUTLAW in *THE ASSASSINATION OF JESSE JAMES BY THE COWARD ROBERT FORD*. When Jessie dies, she is the first to run to his side and cradle his head in her arms.

References

"*The Gathering Storm*: Transcript of the Screenplay by Hugh Whitemore," www.script-o-rama.com/novie_scripts/g/gathering storm-script-transcript.html (accessed 23 December 2008); Nick and Ted Griffin, "*Matchstick Men*: Shooting Draft" (14 October 2002), www.imsdb.com/scripts/Matchstick-Men.html (accessed 4 January 2009).

MARRIAGE LINES

GB 1963–1966 TV series 44 × 30 min episodes b/w. *Production Company*: British Broadcasting Corporation. *Producer*: Graeme Muir. *Directors*: Ridley Scott (amongst others). *Writer*: Richard Waring. *Music*: Dennis Wilson. *Cast*: Richard Briers (*George Starling*), Prunella Scales (*Kate Starling*).

A successful sitcom running for five series during the 1960s. Ridley Scott was responsible for directing one episode (Series 1, Episode 6, "The Old Flame") broadcast on 20 September 1963. The other members of the cast included Katy Wild, Sally Bazely, and Richard Carpenter. This episode concerned George being invited to a party with his wife, at which an ex-girlfriend of his was also present.

MASCULINITY

Several of Scott's films celebrate masculinity—for example in the sequence at the end of *WHITE SQUALL* when Gieg

(SCOTT WOLF) observes that "[We] shared his [Captain Sheldon's] burden, the burden of sea-captains and fathers, the burden of men." Masculinity is posited as an ideal in the reality series *AMERICAN FIGHTER PILOT*, where the chief instructor Robert "Shark" Garland suggests that "faith in God, your love of your family and then your country, an opportunity to defend your country, one nation under God, is the highest calling that a man can have." In *TRISTAN + ISOLDE* masculinity helps the British kingdom to survive, with Tristan (JAMES FRANCO) acting both literally and figuratively as King Marke's (RUFUS SEWELL's) right hand to ensure political stability.

In *G.I. JANE* Chief Urgayle (VIGGO MORTENSEN) beats up Jordan O'Neil (DEMI MOORE) in the belief that she will never be able to penetrate the masculine world. DAVID TWOHY's script has him saying scornfully to those watching him, "Who's gonna be chivalrous and stop this abuse? What, you want to see her get mauled?" He subsequently turns on O'Neil; as she is a woman she is inevitably "an inferior soldier [as compared to the men], a bad officer, and I don't want you learning that inconvenient truth when you're stuck in a muddy bomb crater behind enemy lines and don't know how the fuck to get out. You get out now, O'Neil. Seek life elsewhere. And if you can't do it in front of us, do it behind my back." In *GLADIATOR* Maximus (RUSSELL CROWE) becomes an ideal ego for male spectators by actively controlling the progression of the plot. He encourages us to identify with him, both through the situations in which he is involved and the way he effortlessly overcomes them. The critic Andrew Lindemann Malone observes that: "Ridley Scott . . . realized that, if you are going to name your gladiator Maximus and have him defeat four tigers and a man who outweighs him by about a hundred pounds as one of his lesser exploits, you need a real man to play the gladiator. [Russell] Crowe . . . is that man. He covers all the normal testosterone bases: he's pumped, handsome, takes no prisoners, and really knows how to stare people down . . . But he also has that indefinable presence, that essence of effortless masculinity, which lets everyone in the film and in the audience know that there is just no way anyone is going to stop him from doing whatever he wants to do." The film also extols the virtues of male bonding involving Maximus and Juba (DJIMON HOUNSOU).

Some characters are faced with a stark choice—for example, the spy Yevgeny (RORY COCHRANE) in *THE COMPANY*, who is told in no uncertain terms to commit himself to his chosen career and give up his Jewish girlfriend Azalia (Erika Marozsán). He has to "be a soldier and a man." According to his Soviet paymasters, the question is a simple one; if he opts for family life, he will be considered "unmanly." Huey (CHIWETEL EJIOFOR) faces a similar choice in *AMERICAN GANGSTER*; if he continues to wear ostentatious clothes, then his brother Frank will think of him as a girl rather than a man.

BLACK HAWK DOWN posits a more sympathetic model of masculinity, combining strength with compassion. Although the soldiers remain committed to their objective of capturing General Aidid, they are also concerned for one another's welfare. Several sequences show them tending the wounded, or consoling the dying—even when they know that there is no longer any hope. Eversmann (JOSH HART-NETT) tells Smith (Charlie Hofheimer) that the convoy is coming to rescue them; all Smith has to do is to "hold out just for a little bit." Later on the dying Ruiz (Enrique Murciano) asks Steele (JASON ISAACS) whether the Americans are "going after" the Somalis, and if so, he wants to be included. Steele responds by putting his hand on Ruiz's face and saying in a soft voice: "Now you get some rest now." The same also applies to KINGDOM OF HEAVEN, where Scott exploits ORLANDO BLOOM's star persona to suggest that the true hero is someone combining intelligence with a concern for others. He might be a good fighter, but he is only doing so "for the people, their safety and freedom." Imad (ALEXANDER SIDDIG) recognizes Balian's achievements: "If God does not love you, how could you have done all the things that you have done?" This aspect of the film has been analyzed in detail by Ian Huffer.

References

Ian Huffer, "'New Man,' Old Worlds: Re-articulating Masculinity in the Star Persona of Orlando Bloom," Scope: An Online Journal of Film and TV Studies 9 (October 2007): www.scope.nottingham.ac .uk/article.php?issue=9&id=956 (accessed 15 January 2009); Andrew Lindemann Malone, "Gladiator," Internet Playpen, www .spam-o-matic.org/movies/action/gladiator.html (accessed 5 December 2008); Ken Nolan, Black Hawk Down: The Shooting Script (New York: Newmarket Press, 2002); David Twohy, "G.I. Jane: First Draft" (6 August 1995), http://sfy.ru/sfy.html?script=gi_jane (accessed 21 October 2008)

Bibliography

Martin Fradley, "Maximus Melodramaticus: Masculinity, Masochism and White Male Paranoia in Contemporary Hollywood Cinema," in Action and Adventure Cinema, ed. Yvonne Tasker (London and New York: Routledge, 2004), 235–51; Joanne Jones, "It's a Fine Line Between Pleasure and Pain: Representations of Masculinity in Gladiator," Australian Screen Education 1 (July 2006): 18–21; Gio Messner, "Fractured Identity: Masculinity and Male Spectatorship in Gladiator," http://camswonks.blogs.com/cinesthesia/2004/ 12/messner_on_male.html (accessed 6 December 2008).

MASSOUD, GHASSAN (1958–)

Born in Damascus, Ghassan Massoud has worked extensively in the theater, as well as appearing in the Syrian film Dhilal al Sammt (aka Shadow of Silence [2006]).

Cast as Saladin in KINGDOM OF HEAVEN, Massoud confessed in the book of the film that the experience was "very, very special . . . as it would be for any actor from our country." He identified with the character, as he believed that Saladin was an important figure for the Arab world: "First of all, he is a statesman. Second, he is a man of war, the winner in many battles . . . We know that he is a good leader; he is charismatic. He knows how to make policy. If we can show all these parts of him, I think we can make a good impact with audiences in West and East."

Massoud's portrayal of Saladin emphasizes his humane side—someone who, unlike the Christians of the past, will never massacre his enemies just for the sake of it. He respects other religions—as shown in one sequence where he respectfully places a fallen cross back on the table after it had fallen during the three-day siege of Jerusalem. Robert Fisk reported that audiences in Beirut rose to their feet and applauded ecstatically during this scene. At the same time, Saladin remains a man of HONOR, who expects his enemies to conform to certain behavioral standards. He offers Guy de Lusignan (MARTON CSOKAS) a glass of water; fearing that it might be poisoned, Guy gives it to Reynald de Chatillon (BRENDAN GLEESON) to taste. Enraged, Saladin cuts Reynald's throat, explaining that the only reason why he does not do the same to Guy is that "a king does not kill a king. Were you not close enough to a great king [Baldwin IV (EDWARD NORTON)] to learn by his example?" In KINGDOM OF HEAVEN: THE DIRECTOR'S CUT Saladin decapitates Reynald, as a way of demonstrating how he punishes those who reject his hospitality. Saladin is also convinced of his own abilities as a soldier: when his right-hand man Imad (ALEXANDER SIDDIG) questions his military decision, Saladin responds, "When I am not king, I quake for Islam."

Predictably, some critics focused on the way in which screenwriter WILLIAM MONAHAN had altered historical fact in his portrayal of Saladin. Peter Hammond of Frontline Fellowship argued that "the film has uncritically accepted, and embellished, the legends about Saladin beyond what the historical record would support . . . Far from being the magnanimous victor depicted in modern legends and this film, Saladin was a ruthless general who . . . demanded that every man, women and child in Jerusalem pay a ransom for his or her freedom or face the grim prospect of . . . slavery. In order to save the lives and liberty of the poor people who could not afford the heavy ransom demanded by Saladin, Balian paid out of his own resources the ransom required for those who could not afford it." On the other hand, another reviewer believed that Massoud's "extraordinary" performance constituted "the closest representation of an actual historical figure in the film."

References

Robert Fisk, "*Kingdom of Heaven*: Why Ridley Scott's Story of the Crusades Struck Such a Chord in a Lebanese Cinema," *Z-Space*, 20 June 2005, www.zmag.org/znet/viewArticle/6012 (accessed 15 January 2009); Peter Hammond, "*Kingdom of Heaven*: Hollywood's Crusade Against History," *Frontline Fellowship* (2005), www.frontline.org.za/news/kingdom_heaven_review.htm (accessed 15 January 2009); Diana Landau, ed., *Kingdom of Heaven: The Ridley Scott Film and the History behind the Story* (London: Simon and Schuster Ltd., 2005), 75; Melissa Snell, "*Kingdom of Heaven*," http://historymedren.about.com/od/crusades/fr/kingdomofheaven.htm (accessed 15 January 2009).

MATCHSTICK MEN

US/GB 2003 r/t 116 min col. *Production Companies*: Warner Bros. Pictures, ImageMovers, Scott Free, LivePlanet, and HorsePower Entertainment. *Executive Producer*: Robert Zemeckis. *Producers*: Jack Rapke, Sean Bailey, Ted Griffin, Ridley Scott, and Steve Starkey. *Director*: Ridley Scott. *Writers*: Nicholas and Ted Griffin from the book by Eric Garcia. *Director of Photography*: John Mathieson. *Production Designer*: Tom Foden. *Music*: Hans Zimmer. *Cast*: Nicolas Cage (*Roy Walter*), Sam Rockwell (*Frank Mercer*), Alison Lohman (*Angela*), Bruce Altman (*Dr. Harris Klein*), Bruce McGill (*Chuck Frechette*).

The original novel *Matchstick Men* was published in 2003 by ERIC GARCIA to enthusiastic reviews, and the film rights were almost immediately purchased by Warner Brothers. Originally the film version was due to be directed by ROBERT ZEMECKIS, but he eventually passed on the project, and it was offered to Scott. In the Director's Commentary to the DVD release of the film, Scott recalled that he took on the project chiefly because he had never done anything like this before. He also had the time to take on the project while preparing for "TRIPOLI," from a screenplay by WILLIAM MONAHAN, which later became *KINGDOM OF HEAVEN*.

Scott liked *Matchstick Men* as it was not only a comedy, but "also somewhat of a moral tale, which is all the more interesting because it's filled with characters practicing very bad behavior . . . Their saving grace might be that their victims are people who are themselves seeking a fast buck or doing things they shouldn't be doing, so it's a case of them getting caught with their trousers down." He might not have directed a comedy like this before, but he had produced *WHERE THE MONEY IS* in 2000, whose plot was roughly similar—an aging crook Henry Manning (PAUL NEWMAN) teaches an aspiring hustler Carol (LINDA FIORENTINO) how to stage the Big Con. The crime goes wrong, but the experience proves so life-changing for Carol that she leaves her staid husband Wayne (DERMOT MULRONEY) and joins up with Henry in a life of crime. *Match-*

stick Men also recalls *THELMA & LOUISE*, both in its use of Californian locations and in the way the film focuses on character rather than action.

Casting was a straightforward affair, with NICOLAS CAGE and SAM ROCKWELL playing the leading duo of Roy and Frank. Scott looked around for someone to play the fourteen-year-old Angela and eventually came up with twenty-three-year-old ALISON LOHMAN. Lohman herself recalled that the role was "all about dreaming. What does she look like when she [Angela] walks? What's the look in her eye? It's not about, 'Oh, on this move, I'm going to put my arm like that.' It's just the whole spirit, so that any way that I would move would be right."

Filming took place at various locations in and around Los Angeles, including the Anaheim Convention Center (which doubled as the airport). The shoot was brisk, to say the least (15 July–31 August 2002)—partly because Scott had a limited schedule and partly because the director believed that that the comedy could only be sustained if each scene was filmed with fewer takes, and at a faster-than-normal pace. He told Tim Lammers that "comedy is very difficult to do, but in a funny kind of way, if you have it on paper, then speed is essential . . . It's like telling that funny joke—it's only really funny once. I think to keep things fresh, you also have to do things swift and decisive. If you cast your film right, chances are the actors are going to get it right in two or three takes." In the production information, Scott claimed that he responded to Roy Waller's character, as he had a lot of traits in common with him, "and [I] began to identify with him more as the project progressed, which I found surprising at first and then really amusing." However, he told Lammers that it was important to sustain Roy's comic timing to make him believable to the audience: "I didn't want to make him sad. I wanted to be sympathetic, always, of course, and humorous, ideally. So when you walk down that road you don't want to actually offend anyone who may actually in essence, have a similar tic. Eventually we had sort of a mini arbitration at the end of each take asking ourselves whether we should get less or more."

The film was released in the USA on 12 September 2003 and Europe a week later. Reviews were mixed: Roger Ebert in the *Chicago Sun-Times* thought that the Griffins' screenplay was an "an achievement of Oscar caliber—so absorbing that when it cuts away from 'the plot,' there is another, better plot to cut to . . . [the film] looks with dispassionate honesty at what, after all, people must believe who do this sort of thing for a living." Peter Travers in *Rolling Stone* asked why Scott, "who usually works in the epic mode" would be prompted to direct an intimate character piece: "Credible? Not really. But Cage and Rockwell play off each other with devilish finesse . . . [and] Scott . . . knows how to build suspense you can also take to heart." Neil Norman in the

Evening Standard thought that this was "a minor work, [of Scott] a chamber piece for three actors . . . And the use of music is tantalisingly eccentric, ranging from Sinatra and Bobby Darin to, hilariously, [the British music-hall comic] George Formby. Only a very confident Brit could have got away with 'I'm Leaning on a Lamppost' in a Hollywood movie." However Nigel Andrews of the *Financial Times* thought that *Matchstick Men* represented a serious waste of the Scott's talent: "The new movie is a common comedy thriller straight off the assembly line . . . no one is who they seem in these movies. No one at all: except possibly a gifted British director whose best movie invited comparisons with Orson Welles and who has now, in dismaying career replication, descended to his own version of F for Fake."

Audiences thought otherwise: by December 2003 *Matchstick Men* had taken $36 million in the United States alone and $65 million worldwide.

Matchstick Men focuses on two issues characteristic of Scott's oeuvre: MASCULINITY and male bonding. At the beginning of the film, Roy shows an almost unnatural obsession with cleanliness as he washes the sink, wipes down the kitchen counter, and lets the faucet run. The curtains are drawn, JOHN MATHIESON's photography underlining the fact that very little natural daylight enters Roy's apartment. He lives like a recluse, almost as if he is frightened of life. While talking to Dr. Klein (BRUCE ALTMAN) he explains why; his last relationship with a woman took place more than five years previously, with his ex-wife Heather, and since then he has consciously shied away from meeting new people. Roy understands his shortcomings: when Klein tells him that his long-lost child—who might be a boy—is "fourteen [and] ready to be a man," Roy winces, breathes hard and responds, "If he's a he. If he is at all." If the father is not a man himself, how can he be expected to cope with an offspring who is about to enter adulthood? The only way he can engage with life is with the help of pills—even if he has no idea what they are. Roy only assumes a confident manner while impersonating someone else—as for example, when he speaks to the housewife on the telephone as "John Goodhew, regional vice-president at Allied Affiliates." The film emphasizes this chameleon-like aspect of Roy's character in a short sequence where he rummages through his professional costume closet, containing "several suits, high- to low-end, plus a gallery of pristine shoes, [and] a number of pairs of eyeglasses."

However, the film shows him gradually assuming an identity of his own as he learns to care for Angela. At one point he describes her as "a beautiful, bright, innocent girl, and I'm not gonna screw that up like everything else." The observation might be clichéd, but the sentiment certainly isn't; Angela replies "you think that . . . I'm beautiful?" as if she has never heard that kind of thing before. Roy retreats

into his emotional shell ("No"), but the seeds of change have already been sown. By the end of the film, he has not only visited a lawyer to enquire about joint custody of Angela but has resolved to change his career for good, in the belief that it might prove detrimental to his daughter's future. Although he later discovers that he has been the victim of an elaborate con designed to deprive him of his money, which involved Angela pretending to be his daughter, Roy has acquired sufficient emotional strength to strike out on his own. He takes a job in a carpet store; and, although he still appears as unremarkable as ever in his nondescript short-sleeve shirt and dark gray trousers, "his bearing has changed; he is a man at ease." Angela unexpectedly enters the store with her boyfriend in search of a cheap carpet, and apologizes for having stolen the money. The "new-at-ease" Roy replies, "You didn't take it. I gave it to you." *Matchstick Men* ends with a scene showing the newly remarried Roy returning home to his pregnant wife Kathy (Sheila Kelley); the house is now "open and unencumbered by shades" as he walks into the kitchen, exchanges kisses, and lays his palm gently on her belly. Peter Bradshaw of *The Guardian* described this moment as "yuckily sentimental . . . a reassuring little sugary moment to take away the [film's] cynical taste." On the contrary, this ending suggests that, once Roy learns to trust those around him, he has no further need to indulge in role-play. He acquires a renewed strength of character, which can help him develop a new understanding of masculinity.

Matchstick Men begins by emphasizing the strength of Frank's attachment to Roy—so much so that Frank becomes jealous when Angela invades his partner's life: "This is no good for you, Roy. Or us." When the two finally break up, however, Frank admits that he enjoyed the experience of working together. Having fleeced Roy of all his savings, he tells Roy, "If it's any consolation, you're the best I ever saw. I'd never find a better partner. Now I won't have to." But what kind of an existence has Frank got to look forward to? Although rich, he no longer has anyone to share his life with, either professionally or personally. *Matchstick Men* represents a departure from other Scott films, which emphasize the strength of male bonding as a way of protecting oneself from harm. In this film, Roy and Frank's friendship is dependent solely on financial concerns; one partner can easily exploit the other.

Yet this is perhaps typical of Scott's jaundiced view of AMERICANISM in this film, which so enraged Stephen Himes of *Flak Magazine* that he accused the director of being "an imperialist thug whose contempt for America is barely held in check." While the comment is somewhat intemperate—especially about someone who has spent most of his directorial career in Hollywood—*Matchstick Men* does suggest that Americans prefer to make money as quickly as possible without having to work to fulfill their ambitions.

This renders them ripe for exploitation. Mr. Schaffer (Steve Eastin) berates his wife for being "too trusting. You gotta be more careful of people," without realizing that he himself has been fooled into disclosing both the name of his bank and his account number. Similarly, the housewife in the laundromat (Beth Grant) notices the lottery ticket Angela has dropped on the floor. Angela remarks that it's "probably a loser"; the housewife nods, but then turns, adding, "We should at least see if it hit." From then on she is easy prey for the con, as she hands over three hundred dollars to Angela as her supposed share of the winning ticket. Although Roy makes Angela hand the money back, the housewife remains "utterly befuddled" as she realizes how easily she has been fooled. Scott's view of America is aptly summed up in a short sequence taking place at Los Angeles airport, when Roy and Frechette (BRUCE McGILL) exchange suitcases filled with cash. Frechette riffles through Roy's suitcase to check whether the cash is genuine; Roy follows suit by exploring Frechette's gym bag, which is loaded with hundred dollar bills. He looks up with a smile and says, "It looks like we have a trade." Frank replies, "God bless America"; and the three of them toast their deal with club soda and Scotch whisky.

However, *Matchstick Men* ends optimistically; it depicts the conmen as victims of their own cons who, despite their abilities to deprive victims of money, can never find emotional security for themselves. The script bristles with references to families and children, imagined or otherwise: in the role of "John Goodhew" Roy tells the housewife that he "has a six- and two-year-old at home," who in his opinion are "our most precious resource." At the end of the scene where Roy first meets Angela, we hear Frank in voice-over proclaiming "What's more important than family?" Frechette tells Roy that he has two children, "fifteen and twelve," to which Roy replies "I have a fourteen-year-old." The housewife in the laundromat tells Angela that she has three boys: "Simon's about your age, but you'd never guess; he's so hyper. You know, girls really do mature much faster than boys." Angela responds, "That's what I keep telling my brothers." Roy muses in voiceover that "it's strange. Two weeks ago this was ancient history. Now suddenly I have a daughter"; later, however, he admits to Angela, "She [her mom] left me because of you. So you wouldn't grow up with me as your dad." Angela runs out on him; and he is left moaning to Dr. Klein, "I lost my little girl! I lost my little girl!" The ideas raised here are similar to those in other Scott-produced comedies such as *MONKEY TROUBLE*. Frechette and the housewife in the laundromat are represented as bad parents who put self-interest before their children's welfare. On the other hand, Roy yearns for the stability of family life, which might offer him the chance to care for others. He eventually finds it through his MARRIAGE to Kathy, the supermarket checkout girl bearing a strong visual resemblance to his ex-wife. Like *THE GATHERING STORM*, the film's final message suggests that marriage and the nuclear family are the keys to success, especially personal success.

To date there have been no critical essays published on *Matchstick Men*, except for a reprinted interview with Scott included in *Ridley Scott Interviews*.

References

Nigel Andrews, "Matchstick Men," *Financial Times*, 18 September 2003, 19; Peter Bradshaw, "The Art of the Con," *Guardian Section 2*, 19 September 2003, 18–19; Roger Ebert, "Matchstick Men," *Chicago Sun-Times*, 12 September 2003, http://rogerebert.suntimes.com/apps/pbcs.dll/article?AID=/20030912/REVIEWS/309120303/1023 (accessed 7 January 2009); Nick and Ted Griffin, "*Matchstick Men*: Shooting Draft" (14 October 2002), www.imsdb.com/scripts/Matchstick-Men.html (accessed 4 January 2009); Stephen Himes, "Matchstick Men," *Flak Magazine*, 19 September 2003, www.flak-mag.com/film/matchstick.html (accessed 12 August 2008); Tim Lammers, "*The Movies* Interviews: Ridley Scott, Alison Lohman: Director, Actress Enlightened by '*Matchstick Men*,'" KSBW.com posted 11 September 2003, www.ksbw.com/entertainment/2475348/detail.html (accessed 7 August 2008); Rebecca Murray, "*Matchstick Men*'s Impressive Young Talent, Alison Lohman," About.com (January 2003), http//movies.about.com/cs/matchstickmen/a/matchlohman.htm (accessed 7 January 2009); Neil Norman, "A Pro with the Cons," *Evening Standard*, 18 September 2003, 48; Production Information: *Matchstick Men* (Los Angeles: Warner Bros. Pictures, 2003), 5, 7; Ridley Scott, "Director's Commentary" to the 2004 DVD release of *Matchstick Men* (London: Warner Home Video UK, 2004); Peter Travers, "Matchstick Men," *Rolling Stone*, 8 September 2003, www.rollingstone.com/reviews/movie/5947865/review/5947866/matchstick_men (accessed 7 January 2009).

Bibliography

Daniel Robert Epstein, "Matchstick Men," in *Ridley Scott Interviews*, ed. Laurence F. Knapp and Andrea F. Kulas (Jackson: University Press of Mississippi, 2005), 223–28; Christian Jauberty, "Pour L'Humour du Risque," *Premiere* (French ed. no. 319) (September 2003): 98; Tim Swanson, "In the Works: Matchstick Men." *Premiere* Vol. 16, no.5 (January 2003): 36; "Tricks of the Trade: Making *Matchstick Men*," Documentary accompanying the 2004 DVD release of the film (London: Warner Home Video UK, 2004).

MATHIESON, JOHN (1958–)

John Mathieson came up through the traditional camera ranks and worked as an assistant to Gabriel Beristáin for several years. Mathieson was first recognized for his work on the music video "Peek-A-Boo" by Siouxsie and the Banshees. He also worked on "Marriage à Trois," the second episode in the first series of *THE HUNGER* (1997). Mathieson's camerawork foregrounds the bright colors of an old, disabled woman's (Karen Black's) bedroom—the bright red curtains concealing the windows, the shiny brown linoleum on the floor. She spends her life on morphine, which encourages her to dream almost incessantly of sex.

Engaged as director of photography for *GLADIATOR*, Mathieson and Scott were inspired by nineteenth-century painters such as Sir Lawrence Alma-Tadema, who painted Greek and Roman environments with great historical accuracy. They sought to invest the film with an epic quality—something that could be achieved by wide-angle lenses and battle scenes shot with handheld cameras.

Mathieson worked again with Scott on *HANNIBAL*. At the outset he and Scott decided that the film's look should be very different from that of the earlier *THE SILENCE OF THE LAMBS* (1991): "The film [*Hannibal*] has a lot of dull locations, such as little rooms with people tapping away on computers or on telephones. It's a little more fidgety, and let's face it that kind of thing can be quite boring to shoot." The film was shot entirely on location in Florence and Virginia; its intense psychological mood is created through lighting, in effects which Mathieson compared to the paintings of WILLIAM BLAKE, "which reveal the form of objects but not the detail." Mathieson found difficulty shooting in Florence, which has "narrow buildings with old, faded but glorious interiors, where the sunlight hardly penetrates . . . It would be nice to see everything in those wonderful palaces, but you don't really want to . . . You have to work at keeping the drama and a sense of distance in small rooms because they feel small; you have to keep the light controlled, or else it will bounce everywhere." The American sequences were colder, grayer; so Mathieson worked "to create a dirtier, more miserable look."

Mathieson's major contribution to *MATCHSTICK MEN* lay in his skillful use of light and shadow to emphasize the dark interior of Roy Waller's (NICOLAS CAGE's) house. As with the buildings in *Hannibal*, the sunlight hardly penetrates into his living room, save for the odd shafts of light at the side of the blinds. This is exactly how Roy wants it; he shuts himself away from everyone and resents the presence of intruders—even the sunlight. NICK AND TED GRIFFIN's script emphasizes this in a stage direction: "He raises the blinds, wincing at the flood of sunlight. He checks the window's lock, relocks it for good measure, then closes the shade again."

Mathieson collaborated for a fourth time with Scott on *KINGDOM OF HEAVEN*. They were inspired by J. M. W. Turner's landscapes, as well as lesser-known scenes by David Roberts. His biggest challenge was to photograph the siege sequences: "The people inside the wall are trying to keep the other people out, so it's not that interesting photographically. It's not sweeping vistas with cavalries charging . . . It's people getting anxious and harrowed by a bombardment of big rocks and running out of food and water." Unlike *GLADIATOR*, the battle-sequences in *Kingdom of Heaven* were not so personalized—consequently more wide-angle shots were employed.

References

Douglas Bankston, "A Pound of Flesh," *American Cinematographer* 82, no.2 (February 2001): 37–39; Nick and Ted Griffin, "*Matchstick Men*: Shooting Draft" (14 October 2002), http://www.imsdb.com/scripts/Matchstick-Men.html (accessed 4 January 2009); Patricia Thomson, "Holy War," *American Cinematographer* 86, no.6 (June 2005): 72.

Bibliography

Douglas Bankston, "Death or Glory," *American Cinematographer* 81, no.5 (May 2000): 34–45; Bankston, "Veni, Vidi, Vici," *American Cinematographer* 81, no.5 (May 2000): 46–53; "Glory, Glory in the Colosseum," in *Camera*, July 2000, 1–3; Charles Hewitt, "A Slave to His Craft." *Eyepiece* 22, no.4 (August 2001): 12–15; "John Mathieson, BSC," *British Cinematographer* 14 (April 2005): 21–23; Andy Stout, "Grading the Crusades," *British Cinematographer* 15 (August 2005): 15, 17.

MATSUDA, YUSAKU (1950–1989)

Born in Yamaguchi, Japan. In 1966 he lived for one year in the United States; back in Japan he started acting in a theatrical company, making his film debut in 1973. Thereafter he appeared in various television series and films until his death from bladder cancer at the young age of thirty-nine.

Cast as the yakuza leader Sato in *BLACK RAIN*, Matsuda relishes the opportunity given by Scott to portray an out-and-out villain, having spent much of his previous career in comedy. One of his most telling moments comes at the end of a sequence where he is removed from the plane taking him to Japan from America by some of his associates masquerading as police officers. He turns towards Nick Conklin (MICHAEL DOUGLAS) and silently points his fingers at him, as if he were firing a pistol. From then on we know that he will seek revenge for the humiliation of being in Nick's custody. Sato's ruthlessness is evident not only in his decapitation of a rival yakuza leader in a New York bar but also in the calm manner in which he slices off Charlie Vincent's (ANDY GARCIA's) head with a samurai sword. The extent of his domination over the city of Osaka is cleverly suggested by a reverse shot showing him looking out of an apartment window at the teeming streets below.

Scott told PAUL M. SAMMON that, despite Sato's outrageous villainy in the film, Matsuda was essentially a comedian: "A bit of an icon with the female population . . . What was he personally like? A sweetheart. Really a very nice guy." Already dying of cancer when he filmed *Black Rain*, Matsuda passed away on 6 November 1989, slightly less than two months after the film's American release.

Reference

Ridley Scott, quoted in Paul M. Sammon, *Ridley Scott Close-Up: The Making of his Movies* (New York: Thunder's Mouth Press, 1999), 95.

MAX, ARTHUR (1946–)

Born Arthur Max Shafransky in New York City and trained in the theater and on music videos before making his debut as art director on *Insignificance* (1985) and *Se7en* (1995). He also worked as a stage lighting designer for Pink Floyd when they performed live during the 1970s.

Production designer on *G.I. JANE, GLADIATOR, BLACK HAWK DOWN, KINGDOM OF HEAVEN, AMERI-CAN GANGSTER*, and *BODY OF LIES*. In *G.I. Jane* Max and Scott resolved to use as many authentic locations as possible but found that they were too dull; in an interview with PAUL M. SAMMON Scott recalled, "we were constantly trying to make the locations and the few sets we built visually interesting, while not making them seem excessively unrealistic." Filming mostly took place in Washington and Florida, as well as at the State Capitol Building in Richmond, Virginia. The war games were shot in Beaufort, South Carolina, and Lone Pine, California (where George Stevens shot *Gunga Din* [1939]). In the Sammon interview, Scott told how Max built the Naval Intelligence Center in Florida, where O'Neil (DEMI MOORE) works—"as a sort of take-off on the Pentagon . . . our biggest set . . . [with] about two hundred monitors and projection screens in there . . . [and] a slightly fantastic, almost Bondian edge."

In *Gladiator*, Max and Scott recalled in an interview with *American Cinematographer*, they tried to create an ambience inspired by the nineteenth-century painters Jean-Leon Gérome and Sir Lawrence Alma-Tadema, known as the "Master of Marble," believing that the story "has a lot of sinister intrigue and mental manipulation, with people living in fear of the emperor." Scott was also inspired by the futuristic set designs of Fritz Lang's *METROPOLIS*, as well as other ANCIENT EPICS such as *Ben Hur* (1959) and *THE FALL OF THE ROMAN EMPIRE* (1964), and Nazi propaganda films such as *TRIUMPH OF THE WILL*.

In *Black Hawk Down* Max worked mostly on location in Morocco, creating an entire neighborhood for Somalia. The film's production notes explain how he took advantage of "a rich array of walled cities from Crusader times, old medinas, half-completed new towns, coastal roads, cemeteries, areas of abandonment, and some very fine architecture." Facades of residential buildings were convincingly recreated as downtown Mogadishu, and pockmarked with bullet holes. Street after street of dilapidated buildings were strewn with rubbish, burnt-out vehicles and other detritus of war. To serve as the US MILITARY base in Mogadishu, Max, Scott, and producer JERRY BRUCKHEIMER took over a working Royal Moroccan Air Force field some twenty miles north of the capital city Rabat. The only set that was not built on location was the Joint Operations Center, the headquarters from which Garrison (SAM SHEPARD) conducts the mission. This was constructed in the Moroccan city of Sale, inside an abandoned warehouse.

For *Kingdom of Heaven* Max returned once again to Morocco. In a preproduction interview, he claimed that "the basic model for architecture was a layering of styles from these European painters [Belly, Fromentin, and Loffler] that would give a romantic imagined Jerusalem . . . We don't try to duplicate the historical places with total fidelity, though where possible the general layout and many details are based on research . . . Exercising our passion for historical accuracy is a game that we all like to play . . . and combining research with imagination to create these deeply textured worlds. The actors get a better feel for the period if they can meander through an environment where life is taking place on lots of different levels. The set should be a living place."

In *American Gangster* Max worked hard to recreate the ambience of early 1970s NEW YORK; filming was mostly completed twenty blocks north of Frank Lucas's infamous 116th Street, focusing in particular on 136th Street and switching those street signs to complete the look. Vietnam was recreated in Thailand, where Max built a traditional village and rice barn in the middle of a peanut field to represent the opium-processing center where Lucas seals his first deals with military drug suppliers (likely members of Chiang Kai-Shek's former Kuomintang army). He also recreated the market, even though matters were not helped by the fact that the Thai government had recently been disbanded in a *coup d'état*, and production had to rely on local workers and a changing political structure to create a city with never-ending nightlife that served as a docking station for service members. The film's production information drew a comparison between this set and that used in *BLADE RUNNER*.

For *Body of Lies* Max was faced with the task of recreating Jordan in the filming location of Morocco. Max recalled in the film's production notes that "We didn't construct gigantic sets as we would do on most epic films, but the scale of the street scenes we did was epic . . . At every location, we tried to complete a 360-degree set so that the actors had an environment in which they could immerse themselves." Max's team dressed the sets to the widest perimeters so they would appear realistic in these highly detailed aerial shots. They also needed to neutralize much of Morocco's vibrant, colorful landscape with more muted tones. Some of the transformations in Morocco included redressing the Olympic Stadium into the beautifully manicured exterior of the U.S. Embassy in Jordan. With no fencing to protect the shrubbery the landscaper planted, locals allowed their sheep and goats to graze freely at the site after hours. For a pivotal confrontation between Ferris (LEONARDO DICAPRIO) and Hani (MARK STRONG) that takes place in a massive landfill, Max's team dressed the steep, formerly spotless hillside with tons of artificial rubbish. Mark Strong was quoted as saying that "It looked so authentic, I had no idea that it had been created for the film."

References

American Gangster: Production Information (Los Angeles: Universal Pictures, 2007), 18; Diana Landau, ed., *Kingdom of Heaven: The Ridley Scott Film and the History behind the Story* (London: Simon and Schuster Ltd., 2005), 124; Ron Magid, "Rebuilding Ancient Rome," *American Cinematographer* 81, no.5 (May 2000): 47–60; "Production Notes: *Black Hawk Down*," in Ken Nolan, *Black Hawk Down: The Shooting Script* (New York: Newmarket Press, 2002), 167; "*Production Notes: Body of Lies*" (Los Angeles: Warner Bros. Entertainment, 2008), http://mix96tulsa.com/movies/notes/body-of-lies/note/4 (accessed 16 January 2009); Paul M. Sammon, "Joining the Club: Ridley Scott on *G.I. Jane*," in *Ridley Scott Interviews*, ed. Laurence F. Knapp and Andrea F. Kulas (Jackson: University Press of Mississippi, 2005), 140, 143.

Bibliography

"Production Design Primer: Arthur Max," Documentary included in *Gladiator: 3-disc Extended Special Edition* (Los Angeles: Universal Studios, 2005); "Production Design Primer"; "Production: Spain: Creative Accuracy"; "Production: Morocco: Unholy War"; "Production: Morocco: Mounting the Siege," Documentaries included in *Kingdom of Heaven: 4-Disc Director's Cut* (Beverly Hills: Twentieth Century-Fox Home Entertainment LLC, 2006).

MAY, JACK (1922–1997)

Gravelly-voiced British supporting actor, for many years the voice of Nelson Gabriel in the BBC radio soap opera *The Archers* (1951–1997).

He made his name playing William P. Simms, the long-suffering butler in *ADAM ADAMANT LIVES!* May was not the original choice for the role, but took over when the original actor John Dawson had to pull out due to a back injury. Clearly modeled on Alfred the butler (Alan Napier) in the ABC television series *Batman* (1966–1968), May's Simms exhibited a paternal concern for his employer's welfare, even though Adam Adamant (GERALD HARPER) took little notice of him. In "THE LEAGUE OF UNCHARITABLE LADIES," directed by Ridley Scott, the two of them indulge in lighthearted banter: while Georgina tells of her experiences at the ladies' club, Simms recalls the fact that he once had an uncle in the Antediluvian Order of Buffalo, and ascribes Georgina's condition to the effects of drink. Adam

smiles, but silences him with the observation—"Not in this one" [i.e. the ladies' club].

MAYLE, PETER (1939–)

Prolific novelist and writer who gave up a successful career in advertising and reinvented himself as the author of *A Year in Provence; French Lessons; Provence A–Z; Adventures with Knife, Fork and Corkscrew*, and eight other books set in PROVENCE. It was over a bottle of wine that Mayle and Scott cooked up the idea for the 2004 novel *A GOOD YEAR*. According to the pressbook Scott saw an article in the London *Times* about a Briton who was making money selling wine and suggested that Mayle write a book about it.

Mayle's text shows how much Max enjoys the Provençal atmosphere: "Bursts of laughter came rolling across the square, as did fragments of speeches, complete with interruptions and applause, and a quavering rendition of 'La Vie en Rose.' This started as a solo by an elderly man, standing with one hand on the shoulder of the bride and the other conducting the other guests, as they joined in, with a glass of champagne . . . He tilted his face up to the sun, closed his eye against the glare, and gave in to the impulse to doze."

Mayle collaborated with MARC KLEIN on the screenplay for the film. Interviewed in the pressbook Mayle claimed that the "characters are often reflections of what you yourself feel, and Max is representative of a very strong feeling that I had when I was his age, which is I wanted to basically get out of London and try something else. Of course, Max does it in a rather more dramatic fashion than I did. You live with these characters by yourself all the time in your own head."

References

Peter Mayle, *A Good Year* (London: Time Warner Books, 2005), 80; *Pressbook: A Good Year* (Los Angeles: Twentieth Century-Fox Film Corporation, 2006), 2, 4.

Bibliography

Kim Willsher, "A Good Year? It's No Vintage Scott, say French Critics," *The Guardian*, 4 January 2007, 17; *Peter Mayle Biography*. www.petermayle.com/bio.php (accessed 30 January 2009).

MCBURNEY, SIMON (1957–)

Actor and theater director whose credits include *Tom & Viv* (1994), *Bright Young Things* (2003), and *The Manchurian Candidate* (2004). He also wrote and directed the comedy hit *Mr. Bean's Holiday* (2007).

Cast as the computer geek Garland in *BODY OF LIES*, McBurney has a small role as someone so obsessed with his job that little else matters to him. He offers Roger Ferris (LEONARDO DICAPRIO) some fresh strawberries, but it is clear that he has no particular interest in them. Rather, he sits hunched over his desk stacked with laptops, offering everything potential spies could wish for in their endeavors. Scott adds a whimsical visual touch to the *mise-en-scène* by having a parrot sitting on his perch right by the desks repeating phrases mechanically, rather like Long John Silver's bird in R. L. Stevenson's *Treasure Island*.

Bibliography

John O'Mahony, "Anarchy in the UK," *The Guardian*, 1 January 2005, www.guardian.co.uk/stage/2005/jan/01/theatre2 (accessed February 20, 2009).

MCCARTHY, CORMAC (1933–)

Born Charles McCarthy in Providence, Rhode Island, McCarthy has written ten novels, as well as plays and screenplays. *Blood Meridian* (1985) was among *Time* magazine's poll of one hundred best English-language books published between 1925 and 2005. Scott announced in June 2008 that he wanted to film the novel; but recently the initiative for filming has passed on to Todd Field.

MCCORMACK, ERIC (1963–)

Born in Ontario, Canada, McCormack made his name in the television sitcom *Will & Grace* (1998–2006).

Cast as the investigative journalist Nash, a newly created character in MIKAEL SALOMON's remake of *THE ANDROMEDA STRAIN*, McCormack plays a recovering coke addict who will stop at nothing to uncover the truth about the US MILITARY's campaign to cover up the truth about regarding the source of the Andromeda Strain. If the scientists make their discovering through painstaking research and lengthy speeches, Nash is the all-action hero, traveling all over the state of Utah both in search of the story and to escape the army, which is looking to exterminate him. McCormack himself emphasized the relevance of his role in a media-dominated world in a preproduction interview: "We have a trillion media people who would kill for the scoop . . . it's almost impossible for the government to hide everything because you guys are going to find out about it. Well, not you. *People* magazine's probably not going to break the story but *Time* might. Or actually, this guy [Nash] isn't a magazine, he's *CNN*. It's that constant twenty-four hour news thing that doesn't allow anybody to get away with anything." Nash provides some of the few moments of comic relief as he forms a chalk-and-cheese partnership with a lonely drifter Suzie Travis (Magda Apanowicz), as the two of them travel across the Utah desert in a truck.

Reference

Fred Topel, "Eric McCormack Talks about *Andromeda Strain*," *About.com: Hollywood Movies*, http://movies.about.com/od/interviews withactors/a/andromeda51208_4.htm (accessed 15 February 2009).

MCDONALD, AUDRA (1970–)

Born in Berlin, Germany, McDonald has won four Tony awards in eleven years for her stage performances in *Carousel* (1994), *Ragtime* (1998), *Master Class* (1996), and *A Raisin in the Sun* (2004).

Cast as the liberal campaigning journalist Barbara Manning in *THE LAST DEBATE*, McDonald offers a penetrating study of how money can persuade individuals to forget their integrity and perpetuate the illusion that television news is nothing more than extended soap opera. Although politically opposed to conservative radio journalist Henry Ramirez (MARCO SANCHEZ) she agrees to appear in a regular Sunday morning program with him entitled *Hank and Barb*. Although ostensibly about politics, this show actually focuses on the hosts themselves and their carefully stage-managed struggles to command the camera's attention. Nothing they say is of any great interest; what matters more is whether their onscreen love affair can attract high ratings.

MCDONALD, CHRISTOPHER (1955–)

Born in New York, Christopher McDonald studied at the Royal Academy of Dramatic Art in London, and the Stella Adler Acting Conservatory in New York.

Cast as Darryl in *THELMA & LOUISE*, McDonald offers a buffoonish caricature of the smothering husband to Thelma (GEENA DAVIS). His only saving grace is that he is completely unaware of his own foolishness. Scott recalled that perhaps he might have gone a little too far "with the burlesque side of Darryl . . . But as things progressed . . . I thought . . . if nothing else, *Thelma and Louise* will be comic . . . And don't forget—Chris was playing the archetypal jerk husband. Any laughs he got helped humanize him."

McDonald also had a supporting role in the Ridley Scott-produced comedy *MONKEY TROUBLE*. As Tom, the stepfather of the central character Eva (THORA BIRCH), McDonald has a comparatively insignificant role. His one major quirk is that he has an allergy to animals, which reduces him to a sneezing wreck when the monkey Dodger is in the house. Unlike other police officers, his principal concern is for his stepdaughter's welfare—something that contrasts with similar characters in other Scott films, notably *SOMEONE TO WATCH OVER ME* and *BLACK RAIN*. According to the pressbook, McDonald enjoyed the experience of *Monkey Trouble*: "Working with kids and animals is great because they're spontaneous . . . and Thora [Birch] has the spontaneity of a normal little girl but it's blended with a knowledge that goes well beyond her years."

References

Ridley Scott, quoted in Paul M. Sammon, *Ridley Scott Close-Up: The Making of His Movies* (New York: Thunder's Mouth Press, 1999), 103–4; Pressbook, *Monkey Trouble* (London: Entertainment Film Distibutors, 1994), 14.

MCDOUGALL'S PASTRY MIX

GB 1972 Commercial r/t 28 sec col. *Production Company*: RSA Films for J. Walter Thompson. *Director*: Ridley Scott.

A commercial produced by Hovis McDougall, most notable for the fact that it shows the evolution of Ridley Scott's cinematic style. Its narrative is straightforward: a mother and daughter are shown shopping in a small village buying fresh fruit and vegetables. The action cuts to an interior shot of the kitchen, where the mother is shown making pastries, pies, and cakes with the pastry mix, with the daughter helping her. The son is shown looking at the feast on offer from outside the kitchen window. When the mother has finished, she puts the pastry mix back on the shelf. The entire sequence is accompanied by a lyric (sung to the tune of the popular English song "Floral Dance"): "Roll the pastry nice and thin,/ Line the dish and put them in,/ Steak and kidney, eggs and ham/ Cherries and berries and damson jam,/ Golden-brown they're sure to be/ Some for dinner and some for tea,/ Look at your pieces for the family,/ On a beautiful baking day."

This commercial associates baking with family values—the daughter is shown helping her mother, while the advertisement ends with a shot of a wedding ring on the mother's left hand as she places the pastry mix back on the shelf. More importantly, it shows how Scott transforms the advertisement into a mini-narrative, proving the truth of his assertion (expressed in a 1984 interview) that he has "always looked at each commercial as a film." In its twenty-eight-second running time, there are a total of thirty-two shots.

The commercial demonstrates a meticulous concern for visual detail within the *mise-en-scène* (or "layering' as Scott put it later on in *BLADE RUNNER*)—as shown, for example, in the open shot of a village green, where a cyclist is shown crossing the frame. In the background we see a baker's shop with the name "Hovis" outside. The camera zooms in to focus on the mother and the daughter, both of whom are shown waving goodbye to someone outside the frame. In this short one-second sequence, Scott not only alerts the viewer to the product being sold, but suggests an atmosphere of happy domesticity on a glorious summer's day.

Reference

Ridley Scott, interviewed in "The Making of the Apple Commercial, 1984," www.youtube.com/watch?v=AD2Xs0Spj_8 (accessed 4 February 2008).

MCGILL, BRUCE (1950–)

Born in San Antonio, Texas, McGill began his acting career on the stage. He enjoyed an early success as Daniel Simpson "D-Day" Day in *National Lampoon's Animal House* (1978). Thereafter he pursued a career as a character actor on films and television, playing Day once again in thirteen episodes of *Delta House* (1979).

Cast as Frechette in *MATCHSTICK MEN*, McGill comes across as outwardly affable, yet with a hint of menace lurking underneath. This surfaces late on in the film when he confronts Roy (NICOLAS CAGE) and Angela (ALISON LOHMAN) in Roy's house. He sits in the armchair, languidly smoking a cigarette, and murmurs: "In my business you need a few friends on the force. Your little girl's in their books. And your ex-wife doesn't know well enough not to give out your home address. Well, once I found you, sniffing out your buddy Frank wasn't such a big deal." He gesticulates towards the corner of the room, where Frank (SAM ROCKWELL) crouches, "eyes bloodied, nose blackened, the crap knocked out of him." Although we later discover that this is all part of Frank's con, designed to deprive Roy of his savings, the fact remains that Frechette is a thoroughly nasty piece of work—someone more than willing to resort to violence if his demands are not satisfied.

Reference

Nick and Ted Griffin, "*Matchstick Men*: Shooting Draft" (14 October 2002), http://www.imsdb.com/scripts/Matchstick-Men.html (accessed 4 January 2009).

MCGREGOR, EWAN (1971–)

Scottish leading actor who made his name in the British films *Shallow Grave* (1995) and *Trainspotting* (1999).

Cast as Grimes in *BLACK HAWK DOWN*, McGregor's role was based on the real exploits of John Stebbins, who had been awarded a Silver Star for bravery at Mogadishu. Unfortunately, in 2000 Stebbins had been court-martialed for abusing a child under the age of twelve, and sentenced for thirty years at Leavenworth military prison in Kansas. To avoid embarrassment and controversy, officials at the Pentagon asked that his name be changed for the film. In preparation for the role McGregor (along with the other actors) trained for a week at Fort Benning, Georgia.

Initially Grimes seems a typical bureaucrat—someone given an office job because he knows how to type. His other major ability consists of making coffee for the troops: "I made coffee through Desert Storm. I made coffee through Panama, while everyone else got to fight, got to be a Ranger." However, this campaign proves different, and Grimes at last gets the chance to serve. In one of the film's few moments of semi-comic relief, Grimes takes the advantage of a lull in the action to prepare coffee. Sanderson (WILLIAM FICHTNER) asks him "What the hell are you doing?" to which Grimes replies in a matter-of-fact tone, "It's all in the grind, Sarge. Can't be too fine, can't be too coarse. Grimesy, you are squared away." He understands the importance of thinking of something else just for a few moments so that he can prepare for the next phase of the battle. Like most of his colleagues, Grimes never knows when he is beaten—despite a horrific foot injury he resolves to carry on. Even in the football stadium he refuses any help to walk. Sanderson looks at him admiringly as Grimes runs into the medical tent "under his own power." McGregor described his character thus in an interview: "I quite liked his [Grimes's] arc . . . somebody [who was] terrified and descending into absolute chaos, and then somehow, through this desire to survive, he turned out to be a good soldier—he didn't relent and didn't lose his head in there."

References

Ken Nolan, *Black Hawk Down: The Shooting Script* (New York: Newmarket Press, 2002), 25, 105, 118; Fred Schruers, "The Way We War," *Premiere* 15, no.6 (February 2002): 84.

Bibliography

"Boys' Own Story," *Times Magazine*, 12 January 2002, 16, 19–20.

MEAD, SYD (1933–)

A former designer for the Ford Motor Company, US Steel, and Philips Electronics, Syd Mead established himself as a "futurist" consultant working for companies such as Sony and Chrysler and on films like *BLADE RUNNER*.

Originally Ridley Scott engaged Mead to design the futuristic CARS, having read *Sentinel*, Mead's book of illustrations. But once Scott failed to secure the services of the designer Jean Giraud (aka Moebius), he asked Mead to design the entire city look. IVOR POWELL, the film's associate producer, recalled in "The *Blade Runner* Chronicles," "we were influenced by the work of an sf illustrator called John Harris, who has done some very nice stuff on cities of the future. It's really only an extension of what America is today . . . we were doing traffic jams in the air, incredible stuff really, things that had never been attempted before."

Mead, in the same article, said, "We arrived at a kind of a sociological idea which was that the city had risen up from one, two, three story structures in the older sections . . . That's how we arrived at the sloped pyramidal look—essentially like the foothills of a mountain range." Twenty-five years later Mead suggested in an interview with Ian Nathan that the designs were conceived as "retro-deco" in line with Scott's intention to make a "noir-style film" in which the city of LOS ANGELES was transformed into "a sodden and shadowy noir hellhole . . . a perpetual night of the damned, illuminated by the soulless beams of advertising hoardings."

The FILM NOIR context is very strong in *Blade Runner*. Mead's designs create a dark city of mean streets, moral ambiguities, and an air of uncertainty—something that penetrates the characters' consciousness. Witness Deckard's (HARRISON FORD's) struggle to retain or regain his humanity.

The designs are distinguished by what Scott Bukatman calls "retrofitting," in which "a noir narrative is retrofitted onto science fictional speculations about human definition and development . . . Retrofitting could even be a metaphor for science fiction in general, since familiar characters and narratives ground its extrapolations." *Blade Runner* offers an urban experience of a world of surfaces, in which everything shines bright but proves ultimately meaningless. The film begins with a long shot of Los Angeles, combining its industrial overgrown with a panoramic view. The next shot shows a huge puff of smoke punctuating the hellish space, which is then reflected in a disembodied eye. The camera moves forward to identify the headquarters of the Tyrell Corporation. After an interlude involving Leon (BRION JAMES) the camera shows Deckard walking along the streets where there are advertising hoardings, neon signs, "traffications," futuristic costumes, and umbrella handles. A street vendor uses an electronic microscope. Technology reigns supreme; humanity does not matter.

Some reviewers admired Mead's designs: John Pym of the *Financial Times* described them as "perpetually rain-swept . . . the Information Age is declining (public TV stations have graffiti on their screens) and the Devil himself lives atop a futurist pyramid." On the other hand, David Robinson made the now-familiar complaint that Scott seemed "much less concerned with the story than with visual effects." *Blade Runner* was released at a time when science fiction—particularly CYBERPUNK—sought to construct a new position from which humans could interface with the global, yet hidden, realm of data circulation; a new identity to occupy the emergent electronic sphere. The film's heavy metal vision strongly influenced this movement: William Gibson, the author of *Necromancer* (1984), has made no secret of *Blade Runner*'s impact on his work. This perhaps helps to explain why Mead's designs have been so influential. Scott himself was inspired by them for his 1984 commercial for APPLE COMPUTERS.

References

Scott Bukatman, *Blade Runner*, BFI Modern Classics (London: British Film Institute, 1997), 52; Phil Edwards and Alan McKenzie, "The Blade Runner Chronicles," *Starburst* 50 (October 1982): 22, 30; Ian Nathan, "Retro-Deco, Trash-Chic," *Empire*, August 2007, 120–21; John Pym, "Blade Runner," *Financial Times*, 10 September 1982, 17; David Robinson, "Blade Runner," *The Times*, 10 September 1982, 7.

Bibliography

Blade Runner: Collector's Edition (Los Angeles: Warner Bros. Entertainment, Inc., and the Blade Runner Partnership, 2007), disc 2; Dietrich Neumann, *Film Architecture: Set Designs from Metropolis to Blade Runner* (Munich: Prestel Verlag, 1999), 148–60; Paul M. Sammon, *Future Noir: The Making of Blade Runner*, 2nd ed. (London: Gollancz, 2007), 71–82.

MESSIDOR

France/Switzerland 1979 r/t 123 min col. *Production Companies*: Action, Citel Films, Societé des Établissements L.Gaumont, and Télévision Suisse-Romande. *Producers*: Yves Gasser and Yves Peyrot. *Writer/ Director*: Alain Tanner. *Directors of Photography*: Renato Berta, Hugues Ryffel, and Carlo Varini. *Music*: Arié Dzierlatka. *Cast*: Clémentine Amoroux (*Jeanne Saleve*), Catherine Rétoré (*Marie Correncon*), Franziskus Abgottspon, Gerald Battiaz, Hanjorg Bedschard, René Besson.

The original inspiration for *THELMA & LOUISE*, concerning two young women who kill a rapist, steal an army officer's gun, rob some stores, and finally commit murder. The film has been described thus by Howard Schumann: "*Messidor* is a haunting personal film that authentically captures a mood of ennui. What was their life really about? . . . What led these two intelligent young women to undertake a self-destructive odyssey? Since they hardly talk about their lives, their thoughts or their feelings, we'll never know. That's what is so maddening. We'll never know." Yet perhaps Tanner is suggesting that it is not necessary for people to *know* or *understand* their motives. Knowledge is power, and this is usually assigned to men. By refusing to give the audience that knowledge, Tanner assigns power to the women.

Reference

Howard Schumann, "*Messidor*: Directed by Alain Tanner," www.talkingpix.co.uk/ReviewsMessidor.html (accessed 7 July 2008).

"METROPOLIS"

Projected title for a sequel to *BLADE RUNNER*, which was mooted (given consideration) but fell through due to rights issues. The idea is still on the table: according to an article by John Howell published in January 2009, Travis Wright (one of the writers of the thriller EagleEye) has been working on a script: "Whether anyone ever reads it or cares about it remains to be seen."

References

John Howell, "Blade Runner Sequel" (28 January 2009), http://sff-media.com/films/science-fiction-films/285-blade-runner-sequel.html (accessed February 28, 2009).

Bibliography

Corey Mandell, "Metropolis" (unpub. script, no date). www.angelfire.com/movies/ridleyscott/script/Metropolis.txt (accessed 28 February 2009).

METROPOLIS (1927)

Germany 1927 r/t 153 min (original release) b/w, silent. *Production Company*: UFA. *Producer*: Erich Pommer. *Director*: Fritz Lang. *Writers*: Fritz Lang and Theo von Harbou. *Director of Photography*: Karl Freund. *Production Designers*: Otto Hunte, Erich Kettelhut, and Karl Vollbrecht. *Cast*: Brigitte Helm (*Maria/Robot Maria*), Alfred Abel (*Jon Fredersen*), Gustav Frohlich (*Freder Fredersen*), Rudolf Klein-Rogge (*Rotwang*), Fritz Rasp (*the slim one*).

A futuristic story of a city whose workers are doomed to spend all of their lives underground while the privileged classes enjoy the fresh air above ground. The son of one of the elite families ventures below and discovers the world there; he also encounters a beautiful girl who ministers to the workers. Worried about her influence on him and the workers, his father encourages an inventor to create a robot that looks like her. Scott acknowledged that he was inspired by this film (as well as the Nazi propaganda film *TRIUMPH OF THE WILL*) in his designs for *GLADIATOR*.

MIDLAND BANK

GB c.1985 Commercial r/t 32 sec col. *Production Company*: RSA for Collett Dickenson Pearce. *Director*: Ridley Scott.

This commercial begins with a zoom in to a primitive man sitting in the desert, making music with a hollow tube. The action subsequently moves forward in time to show a group of aborigines playing their didgeridoos to the sound of a drumbeat. Scott cuts to the following shots in succession; three Arabs beating drums, followed by a close-up of a westerner in Arabic robes providing a vocal accompaniment to the music; a long line of men in capes walking away from the camera with crosses on their back—again suggesting that we are moving forward in time from the Crusades to the Reformation; the Tudor period, signaled by musicians playing flute, sackbut, and drum, one dressed to look like Queen Elizabeth I. Finally, we move forward in time to the present, with a shot of a full orchestra playing in the desert, the wind blowing around them as they play a symphonic work. The camera pans the orchestra and the choir in the background. The commercial ends with the camera tracking backwards to show a panoramic view of the desert with an aborigine on the left of the frame looking at the orchestra playing music. A voice-over informs us that "we only learn by listening," while their slogan, "Midland: the Listening Bank," appears on the screen.

The Midland Bank, founded in 1836, was one of the big four banks in Great Britain whose catch phrase, "The Listening

Bank," was popular throughout the 1970s and 1980s. It was acquired by HSBC in 1992. This commercial is notable for its desert sequences, filmed in bright sunlight with minute attention paid to the composition of each shot. In many ways the visual style, with its emphasis on human beings set against a vast landscape that appears to extend as far as the eye can see, anticipates that used in *THELMA & LOUISE*, *THE HIRE*, and *GLADIATOR*.

MILCHAN, ARNON (1944–)
Born in Palestine, Milchan began his career as producer with *The King of Comedy* (1982) and Sergio Leone's *Once Upon a Time in America* (1984).

Milchan enjoyed a reasonable working relationship with Scott on *LEGEND*, but was powerless to prevent the film being heavily cut before its American release. Scott recalled in an article by Sean Murphy as a result he "got totally paranoid. I started to hack away at the movie . . . I figured that maybe we'd been too adventurous with our expectations of a full blown fairy story, and therefore, maybe the combination of the [JERRY GOLDSMITH] score and the visual was actually too sweet."

Milchan was not involved in the creation of *LEGEND*: THE DIRECTOR'S CUT (2002). However, he recalled in the Murphy article that if he had known as much about the film business in 1984 as he did eighteen years later, he "would probably have convinced Ridley to fight for his original cut, which I felt was more true to his vision." Whether he would have actually honored his promise is a matter for conjecture.

Reference
Sean Murphy, "History of the *Legend* DVD," *Legend*: Frequently Asked Questions, www.figmentfly.com/legend/different4k.html (accessed 25 April 2008).

THE MILL (aka MILL FILM)
Special effects company based in London founded by Scott. The company provides the visual effects for *GLADIATOR* and *BLACK HAWK DOWN*.

MILLER, CHRISTA (1964–)
Born in New York City, Christa Miller has been associated with several television series, notably *The Drew Carey Show* (1995–2002), *Clone High* (2002–2003), and *Scrubs* (2001–2009).

Cast as Dr. Angela Noyce in *THE ANDROMEDA STRAIN*, Miller plays the ex-lover of Dr. Jeremy Stone (BENJAMIN BRATT), who has sacrificed her feelings in pursuit of her work. Her role is a comparatively minor one: the *Cinefantastique* reviewer saw it as "thinly defined," and overwhelmed by "the morass of confusing subplots" and paling into insignificance beside some of the more startling

moments, including "the sight of a character deliberately impaling himself with a chainsaw."

Reference
Peter McGarvey, "*The Andromeda Strain*" (2008), *Cinefantastique Online* May 5, 2008, http://cinefantastiqueonline.com/2008/05/05/tv-revew-the-andromeda-strain-2008/ (accessed 13 February 2009).

MILTON, JOHN (1608–1674)
BLADE RUNNER makes frequent allusions to Milton's *Paradise Lost* (1667). Milton's portrayal of hell as "A Dungeon horrible, on all sides round,/ As one great Furnace flam'd," resembles Scott's LOS ANGELES; the only difference being that "hope never comes" to Milton's protagonists. Milton's Satan vows to bring down God, and when he finds that impossible, turns to man instead. In *Blade Runner*, the satanic character is embodied in Batty (RUTGER HAUER), who seeks vengeance against Tyrell (JOE TURKEL) "in dubious Battel on the Plains of Heaven." Batty turns his attention to man—personified by Deckard—while confronting his creator. If Batty is Satan, then Deckard is Adam, seeking to come to terms with his existence. At one point in *Paradise Lost* Adam explains his emptiness ("In solitude/ What happiness, who can enjoy alone,/ Or all enjoying, what contentment find?"). Similarly, Deckard feels discontented with the world around him. In both texts God (or Tyrell) creates an Eve-like figure: one might argue that Rachael (SEAN YOUNG) was specifically created for Deckard, who rejects the life in "paradise" (i.e., as a retired adventurer) before he met her. Rachael, like Eve for Adam, provides "meet help." Milton attempts to redress the prevailing notion that Eve is an evil temptress; likewise, Scott shows Rachael and Deckard redeemed and redeeming each other. At the end of both poem and film, the Adam-and-Eve figures depart together. Milton shows the two of them expelled from Paradise after the Fall, to prepare the way for Christ's entrance. In the film there is neither Fall nor redemption; redemption comes to Deckard and Rachael through the power of love.

By recalling Milton's poem, Scott not only invests *Blade Runner* with an epic quality but invites viewers to rethink mythic motifs of good, evil, redemption, and transcendence. Other Miltonic echoes are also evident in Scott's later work such as *LEGEND*, with the appearance of Darkness (TIM CURRY) who seeks to take revenge on all humankind by depriving the world of light, while Jack (TOM CRUISE) is the adventurer-figure coming to terms with his existence as he endeavors to rescue Lily (MIA SARA) from Darkness's clutches. In *WHITE SQUALL* the *Paradise Lost* theme recurs in the notion of loss of innocence, notably when Frank Beaumont (JEREMY SISTO) shoots a dolphin, apparently without any motive for doing so.

THE COMPANY has Leo Kritzky (ALESSANDRO NIVOLA) quoting the line "They also serve who only stand and wait," from Milton's Sonnet XIX "When I consider how my Light is Spent." The original line suggests that , if people seek political stability, standing still and waiting for an order is just as important as obeying it. In the context of the film, however, the allusion is profoundly ironic, as Kritzky is actually a spy, who serves not his employers (the CIA) but his paymasters in the Soviet Union—the KGB.

Bibliography

David Desser, "The New Eve: The Influence of *Paradise Lost* and *Frankenstein* on *Blade Runner*," in *Retrofitting Blade Runner: Issues in Ridley Scott's Blade Runner and Philip K. Dick's Do Androids Dream of Electric Sheep?* ed. Judith B. Kerman (Bowling Green: Bowling Green State University Popular Press, 1997), 53–66; Mary S. Weinkauf, "Edenic Motifs in Utopian Fiction," *Extrapolation* 11, no.1 (December 1969): 15–23.

MOBY DICK

GB/ US, 1956 r/t 118 min col. *Production Company*: Moulin Productions, Inc. *Producer/Director*: John Huston. *Writers*: John Huston and Ray Bradbury, from the book by Herman Melville. *Director of Photography*: Oswald Morris. *Production Designers*: Geoffrey and Stephen Drake. *Music*: Louis Levy. *Cast*: Gregory Peck (*Ahab*), Richard Basehart (*Ishmael*), Leo Genn (*Starbuck*), James Robertson Justice (*Capt. Boomer*), Harry Andrews (*Stubb*), Bernard Miles (*Manxman*), Orson Welles (*Father Mapple*).

Charles Hamblett's *The Crazy Kill*, a fictionalized account of the making of this film, gives a good account of the eccentric monomaniac film director determined to make the adaptation his way; the stars, technicians and stunt people trying to carry out his wishes, and the Canary Islanders, who pursued their own agenda.

Ridley Scott viewed the film, together with *MUTINY ON THE BOUNTY*, as part of his research for *WHITE SQUALL*. Although the subject matter is very different, Peck's portrayal of Ahab provided him with the inspiration for the character of Sheldon (JEFF BRIDGES). TODD ROBINSON's script makes this clear in an allusion (eventually deleted from the final film version): "He [Sheldon] was everything I expected, part Ahab part Queeg and even Bligh. He spoke in whispers and answered all queries with efficiency and directness. He had gone to sea for the first time at fifteen . . . And as he looked upon us that first day it must have been as though he were staring into a mirror."

References

Charles Hamblett, *The Crazy Kill—A Fantasy* (London: Sidgwick and Jackson, 1956); Todd Robinson, *White Squall: Revised First Draft*, Unpub. script, dated 31 October 1994, http://sfy.ru/sfy.html ?script=white_squall (accessed 8 September 2008).

MODINE, MATTHEW (1959–)

Matthew Modine made his name in films such as *Full Metal Jacket* (1986), *Orphans* (1987)—in which he co-starred with ALBERT FINNEY—and *Memphis Belle* (1990).

Cast as the devil-may-care Frank Hunter in the Ridley Scott-produced film *THE BROWNING VERSION*, Modine portrays him as a fundamentally weak man who gives in to his passions rather than suppressing them (and thereby creating the image of an ideal schoolteacher in the boys' private school). Modine admitted that it was Frank's "personal weakness that makes him become susceptible to her [Laura Crocker-Harris's] wanton charms." Although popular with the boys on account of his scientific experiments which inevitably culminate with an explosion, he cannot cope with complex relationships. As an American on an exchange visit to a British school, he has in a sense become more British than the British; not only aping their rituals—for example, offering Laura (GRETA SCACCHI) a cup of tea—but proving equally reticent when it comes to expressing his emotions. Laura's description of him is brutally accurate: he has been imprisoned by male guilt, Puritanism, and her husband's ideals of teaching. She can even anticipate his excuses for not pursuing their relationship further: he is "not ready to settle down." The sequence ends with a shot showing Frank looking out of the barred window at the village street below; like Crocker-Harris (ALBERT FINNEY), he is literally and symbolically imprisoned by his emotional shortcomings.

Modine recalls other heroes of Scott films, such as Mike Keegan (TOM BERENGER) in *SOMEONE TO WATCH OVER ME*, who experiences similar feelings of guilt when falling for Claire Gregory (MIMI ROGERS), even while being married to his wife Ellie (LORRAINE BRACCO).

Reference

Production Information: The Browning Version (Los Angeles: Paramount Pictures, 1994), 3–4.

MOLINA, ALFRED (1953–)

Early British television and cinema successes include *Letter to Brezhnev* (1985) and *Prick Up Your Ears* (1987). More recently Molina has starred in Hollywood films such as *Spiderman 2* (2004) and *The Da Vinci Code* (2006).

Cast as the hard-drinking agent Harvey Torriti (aka "The Sorcerer") in *THE COMPANY*, Molina plays an agent of the old school who teaches Jack McCauliffe (CHRIS O'DONNELL) that the first rule of spying is to bend the rules. Molina himself described the character thus in the production notes: "My character represents the earlier generation of spies—former military men who relied on improvisation in the field and were willing to do business with dirty characters." In another interview Molina explained that "Harvey was essentially just a really brilliant spy and just understood the game . . . And he refers to the craft of espionage constantly, and when he's exercising his skill, as it were; it was always very, very clear in the script." Despite Harvey's skill as a spy, however, we wonder whether he has any sense of morality at all. At the end of the first episode, Jack returns to base in West Berlin and asks Harvey directly whether he was involved in sacrificing Lilli (Alexandra Maria Lara), one of the CIA's operatives based in the eastern sector of the city. Harvey denies any knowledge, but his hasty change of subject ("onwards and upwards") suggests that he might be lying.

At the end of the film Harvey confidently proclaims that all his efforts on behalf of the CIA helped America win the Cold War against the Soviets: "The Soviet Union wasn't a country, it was a metaphor for an idea that looked good on the drawing-board but in practice it was flawed . . . and we clobbered them in the end . . . It was always black-and-white, kid. Right versus wrong. There were good guys and there were bad guys." However, Jack's rejoinder ("Which side were we on, Harvey?" suggests that neither of them understand exactly who the bad guys and the good guys are. This is one of the disadvantages of spying: operatives are so preoccupied with illusions that they no longer have any understanding of right and wrong.

Reference

Production Notes: The Company, www.tnt.tv/series/thecompany/bts/ (accessed 12 August 2008); "The Company of Wolves," *TV Zone* 219 (September 2007): 58.

MOLINA, ANGELA (1955–)

The daughter of Spanish actor and singer Antonio Molina and sister of actor Miguel Molina; she made her film debut in 1974 in the Spanish film *No Mataras* (1974).

Cast as Beatrix, Columbus's partner in *1492: CONQUEST OF PARADISE*, Molina has a minor role. At one level she acts the part of the dutiful wife who (like Ellie Keegan in *SOMEONE TO WATCH OVER ME*) is given the responsibility of looking after the children while her husband devotes himself to his work. Even that responsibility is taken away from her, as Columbus arranges for the children to be taken into Queen Isabel's (SIGOURNEY WEAVER's) care. Her emotions at this point are well summarized in Robert Thurston's novelization of the screenplay: "Beatriz [*sic*] felt as if a sword had been suddenly thrust though her stomach. Everything has been so fine, so happy, for the last three months . . . Now, in this fine manor house, with a life she had always dreamed of, Columbus was telling her he was taking her son away." Although she remains outwardly passive, Scott's film suggests that she acquires an inner strength through solitude. In one sequence towards the end of the film, however, the camera tracks her walking alone through the cavernous exteriors of Columbus's (GÉRARD DEPARDIEU's) house, clearly suggesting that she has learned to fend for herself during his absence. Clearly things will never be the same as before: Columbus will have to learn to adapt himself to a different domestic situation. Whether he will do so or not is left deliberately unexplained.

Reference

Robert Thurston, *1492: Conquest of Paradise Based on a Screenplay by Roselyne Bosch* (London: Penguin Books, 1992), 138.

Bibliography

"Angela Molina," *Cineinforme* 506–507 (March 1987): lxiv–lxv.

MONAHAN, WILLIAM (1960–)

Monahan began his career as a journalist and editor for the now-defunct *Spy*, which developed a cult following during the 1980s. He also published *Light House: A Trifle* (1998), which was critically praised and bought by Warner Bros., for possible filming.

In 2001 Twentieth Century-Fox bought Monahan's screenplay "TRIPOLI," the true story of the nineteenth-century American army officer William Eaton who attempted to restore the rightful heir to the throne of Tripoli from his usurper brother. This script appealed to Ridley Scott on account of its subject matter—that of a hero trying to live by a moral code but being opposed by a structure of evil or misfortune. Monahan claimed that he was inspired by *THE DUELLISTS* to write the script.

Scott and Monahan met and gradually came up with the idea of writing a screenplay about knights, a project Scott had wanted to do ever since his early film career. Monahan recalled that he "thought immediately of the Latin Kingdom of Jerusalem, and the leper king Baldwin IV." A year later Monahan delivered the Crusades script (later renamed *KINGDOM OF HEAVEN*) to Scott: "Tripoli" had been pulled from production, and Scott instead agreed to go ahead with the Crusades film, with the backing of Twentieth Century-Fox. Monahan recalled that "from that moment on he [Scott] became a force of nature, prepared to demolish anything in his path to get the movie made. He willed *Kingdom of Heaven* into existence." Monahan soon realized that the material would assume a different meaning in the post-9/11 world: "The two civilizations [Christianity and Islam], arguably, being again at war, I was interested in examining a time when there was a period of . . . if not peace, then accommodation—when the Muslim world and 'Christendom' were at an equal strength." In researching the history of the period, he used primary sources—for example, the accounts of William of Tyre (c.1130–1185), regarded as one of the greatest chroniclers of any age: "I also used the Lyon Eracles (an anonymous French chronicler), and a lot of Muslim writers such as Imad ad-Din and Usama Ibin Munquidh, for incident, color and perspective."

The script altered many historical details. Balian (ORLANDO BLOOM) was an established lord, not a French artisan (as in the script). Monahan invented other characters such as Godfrey of Ibelin (LIAM NEESON) and the Hospitaler (DAVID THEWLIS). Other characters were deliberately altered for story purposes while remaining true to historical fact. The princess Sibylla, according to most chroniclers, was actually devoted to Guy de Lusignan, choosing him over increasingly worthy suitors put forth by the king after her first husband died. Monaghan transformed her into a stronger, wiser woman, who was not sure whether she loved Guy or not.

The script went through major changes once filming began. One of these was to recreate the opening, with Balian arriving at the Kingdom of Jerusalem after a long journey from France. However, the overall structure remained much the same as Monahan had originally created it—something that the screenwriter himself really appreciated: "I attacked ambitiously and wrote about themes highly personal to me … The film proposes that it is better to live together than to be at war. That reason is better than fanaticism. That kindness is better than hate. That it's better to discard the world—money, position, power, whatever your times are telling you to do—than to endanger your integrity. If that gets across, then I did my job."

After production on *Kingdom of Heaven* completed, Monahan was hired to collaborate once again with director Ridley Scott on an adaptation of CORMAC MCCARTHY's ultra-violent Western novel *BLOOD MERIDIAN* for producer Scott Rudin. To date, the film has not yet gone into production. Meanwhile, the release of *Kingdom of Heaven* was plagued by controversy: author James Reston Jr. claimed that much of the plot had been stolen from his novel *Warriors of God: Richard the Lionheart and Saladin in the Third Crusade* (2001). Monahan denied all claims, and Reston did not pursue the matter any further.

Kingdom of Heaven was released theatrically in May 2005 to mixed reviews; it was only when *KINGDOM OF HEAVEN: THE DIRECTOR'S CUT* was released a year later that Monahan's achievement as a screenwriter received due recognition. Monahan went on to write *The Departed* (2006) for Martin Scorsese, for which he won the Oscar for Best Adapted Screenplay.

Monahan's second screenplay for Scott began as a commission to adapt DAVID IGNATIUS's novel *Penetration*. The script was retitled *BODY OF LIES* in April 2007. In a preproduction interview Scott said he was drawn to the book because "there were so many interesting dimensions to the story, the way the plot develops and the characters have to adjust and change." Monahan's script was much appreciated

by star LEONARDO DICAPRIO: "He's [Monahan is] great with information and disinformation, and cat-and-mouse dilemmas between characters." Monahan himself liked the book because "the story showed the intelligence world more or less as it is, with, if anything, more pragmatism and less political coloring than you find in the actual CIA. The frailties of Ed Hoffman [RUSSELL CROWE] appealed to me … we all know a Hoffman. Ferris's story was appealing to me in that it is all about individual conscience." Monahan's original script was significantly revised prior to production by STEVEN ZAILLIAN. Whole sections were rewritten, and the tone softened to remove overtly racist references to Baghdad as "the asshole of Arabia," or describing Iraqis as badasses or cockroaches, referring to the stench of jihadis, or describing the Jordanian Secret Service chief Hani's (MARK STRONG's) men as goons. However, Monahan retained screen credit as the script's sole author.

References

Diana Landau, ed., *Kingdom of Heaven: The Ridley Scott Film and the History behind the Story* (London: Simon and Schuster Ltd., 2005), 24, 25, 47, 48, 59; *Production Notes: Body of Lies* (Los Angeles: Warner Bros. Entertainment, 2008), http://mix96tulsa.com/movies/notes/body-of-lies/note/4 (accessed 16 January 2009).

MONKEY TROUBLE

US/ Japan 1994 r/t 96 min col. *Production Companies*: Effe Productions, New Line Cinema, Percy Main, Ridley Scott Productions, and the Victor Company of Japan (JVC). *Executive Producer*: Ridley Scott. *Producers*: Mimi Polk Gitlin and Heide Rufus Isaacs. *Director*: Franco Amurri. *Writers*: Franco Amurri and Stu Krieger. *Production Designer*: Leslie Dilley. *Director of Photography*: Luciano Tovoli. *Music*: Mark Mancina and Hans Zimmer. *Cast*: Thora Birch (*Eva*), Finster (*Dodger*), Harvey Keitel (*Azro*), Mimi Rogers (*Amy*), Christopher McDonald (*Tom*), Adrian & Julian Johnston (*Jack*), Kevin Scannell (*Peter*), Adam LaVorgna (*Mark*).

Originally titled "Pet," this project started at Warner Bros., where executives toyed with the script for more than a year before passing on it. Ridley Scott stepped in as executive producer through his company PERCY MAIN, bringing along production designer LESLIE DILLEY.

In the film's pressbook, Amurri was quoted as saying that his daughter was the inspiration behind *Monkey Trouble* (as the film was now known): "I wanted to tell a story based on my own experiences and observations of my daughter's world," he said. "If I was going to dedicate two or three years to a project, I wanted to make a film my daughter wouldn't have to wait ten years to see. In the end, I wanted to make a film that families can enjoy together." Producer MIMI POLK added: "*Monkey Trouble* is about a little girl's adventures when a monkey comes into her life. On a deeper level, it's about the healing that takes place in this family when a young girl takes responsibility for something outside herself."

Amurri suggested in an interview that to work on an independent film like *Monkey Trouble* was "more exciting," particularly as he managed to secure a top-notch cast including HARVEY KEITEL, MIMI ROGERS, and CHRISTOPHER McDONALD at very low cost: "The film touches something in all of us, especially those of us who are parents. Harvey Keitel, for example, had lots of other projects coming along. But his daughter kept asking, 'Are you going to do that monkey movie?' Here he is making the monkey movie."

In the pressbook Scott claimed he liked the story because "it took a very funny look at sibling rivalry, and had some very serious things to say on the subject at the same time. But Franco's passion for the project was one of the main reasons I got involved with *Monkey Trouble*." The film cost $16 million to make, and had a limited release both in the United States and Europe. Reviews (when they appeared) were generally enthusiastic: the *Variety* critic remarked that while the film "makes good use of Venice and other colorful LA locations," it was still rather predictable: "[A]udiences are always ahead of the tarn, and whatever bits of narrative are used to cement the girl and her pet's escapades, the film becomes a bit stale and uninvolving—but not for long." The *Daily Telegraph* described the film as slight, but "[nonetheless] scripted with an ingenious wit, shot and edited with plenty of pace—[it] swings along very nicely." Other reviewers praised the hard-working cast: The *Evening Standard* congratulated Thora Birch on steering clear of the sentimentality normally associated with animal-child films, while *The Independent* found Keitel's presence in the film "mind-boggling . . . I especially liked his no-nonsense answerphone message (to be delivered in a threatening growl): "It's a machine. You know what to do!" The longest review for the film appeared in *Sight and Sound*, which felt that it "leaves little breathing space to dwell on character and performance . . . Attempts to match up the two, such as Eva's attempt to toilet-train [the monkey] Dodger, are perfunctory at best, and the rather cruel way that Azro's [Harvey Keitel's] embittered son (the monkey's "true" parent) loses his pet to her at the end sours whatever good humour the film has gathered."

Monkey Trouble returns to themes familiar in Scott's early work: home, family, and CHILDHOOD. Like *SOMEONE TO WATCH OVER ME*, Eva's stepfather Tom (Christopher McDonald) is a police officer, one who might be more dedicated to his family than Mike Keegan (TOM BERENGER), but still neglects his parental duties—just like his wife Amy who, while concerned with keeping a clean house, is far more interested in her little son Jack (Adrian/Julian Johnson) rather than Eva. Eva herself is left to her own devices. Ellen Leroe's novelization of the screenplay makes this point clear:

"Even though the door was closed, she [Eva] could hear her mom and Tom singing that spider song to Jack. If she heard that dumb song one more time, she'd scream. She clapped her hands over her ears, she hummed loudly, but still she could hear them."

Similarly, the gypsy Azro proves himself a poor parent, who has not only driven away his wife and son Mark (Adam LaVorgna), but proves himself incapable of looking after the monkey Dodger. He treats the animal like an unpaid slave, training him to steal gold and jewels from unsuspecting customers and beating him when he fails to come up with the goods. Azro is the perfect example of a hypocrite who, while professing love for his children (whether human beings or animals), just exploits them. This theme is one that recurs in Scott's work, notably in *BLADE RUNNER*, where the scientist Tyrell (JOE TURKEL) treats the REPLICANTS in similar fashion, prompting Batty (RUTGER HAUER) to rebel.

The ideal parent in *Monkey Trouble* turns out to be Eva herself, who looks after Dodger the monkey by giving him food, training him to use the potty, and eventually weaning him away from stealing jewelry and other valuables. The novelization makes this clear: "Now you know how responsible I can be—I took care of him [the monkey] so good, you [Amy] didn't even know I had him!" Amurri draws a deliberate visual parallel between Eva's half-brother Jack and Dodger the monkey by dressing them both in colored diapers. Both of them need to be looked after all the time, and in this film it is the little girl Eva who proves more adept at it than her mother. In the film's final sequence, Amurri has Dodger choosing between his adoptive parent Eva and his "real" parent Mark (who has looked after Dodger for Azro in the past). Initially the monkey runs towards Mark as if he were a long-lost parent—thereby suggesting that Eva's love and care has counted for nothing—but eventually comes running back to Eva. The novelization describes this moment thus: "He landed on her neck and hugged her tight. Screaming for joy, Eva hugged him back even harder. Dodger had chosen her, and they'd never be parted again." Meanwhile Tom and Amy have at last relented and allowed Eva to keep a pet for herself, in the belief that she has now learned responsibility.

Whether the parents have learned anything from the experience is debatable. Even at the end they seem more concerned with the return of the jewelry stolen by Dodger than with their daughter's welfare; they do not notice that she is in danger of being abducted by Azro (who needs her to tell him how to find the money). Even though everything turns out happily, Amurri reminds us of the fact that children often prove wiser than their supposed peers.

Visually speaking, Dodger the monkey bears a strong resemblance to the alien in *ALIEN*, with its row of front teeth and its high-pitched chattering noises. This is no coincidence; in the earlier film Scott characterized MOTHER-HOOD as something dangerous: the alien reproduces by implanting its young in human beings. The birth of the new alien is equally horrific in the famous "chestbusting" scene involving Kane (JOHN HURT). In *Monkey Trouble* Amurri is less apprehensive of the idea of motherhood, but suggests that the monkey needs a good mother (just like Eva does) in order to grow and develop. Otherwise it might become like the alien—a menace to the existing social order.

Perhaps uniquely for a film involving Scott, the location is one of perpetual sunshine in Venice and other areas of LOS ANGELES. This is a world whose inhabitants spend a lot of time on the beach, or walking beside the beach, watching the various sideshows on offer. The film shows several images of happy couples walking together; of families enjoying the sunshine; of young people swimming and flying kites. Leroe's novelization describes the scene thus: "There was a party going on, and it was all happening at Venice . . . On this sunny afternoon, the smell of cotton candy, grilling hot dogs, and suntan lotion filled the air. So did music." The streets are as crowded as those in *Blade Runner* and *BLACK RAIN*; the only difference being that the Los Angeles of *Monkey Trouble* does not seem a threatening place. Yet the word "seems" here is significant; even by the seaside there remains the perpetual threat of crime, with Dodger stealing purses and jewelry on command.

The same sense underlines a comic chase sequence in which Eva and Dodger are pursued by Azro. Dodger escapes from the back of Eva's bicycle, and leads the gypsy on a wild goose chase—flying kites, crawling under cars, concealing himself beneath a cardboard box, and upsetting a sunbather's umbrella. The gypsy runs after the monkey, steals a skateboard and a bicycle, and grabs the ropes controlling the kite; but still he cannot catch him. Eventually the monkey jumps back into the back of Eva's bicycle and the two of them escape. The sequence is very funny, handled at a brisk pace by Amurri; but throughout these remains the uneasy feeling that, were Azro to catch them, then the girl and the monkey would be in great danger. Utopias can very easily be transformed into DYSTOPIAS. Leroe's prose captures this sense well by means of repetition and alliteration: "Dodger was desperate. Shorty [Azro] was coming closer. Any minute Shorty would turn and see him . . . There was only one thing to do. Dodger jumped off the bike and scampered over to a pile of cardboard boxes and trash cans . . . Using the box for cover, Dodger stumbled across the boardwalk. He blindly bumped into hairy knees, skateboards, and baby strollers. He was going to get away, until a barking dog tipped the box over."

There have been no critical essays published on the film; but it has been referenced in *Kicking and Screaming* (1995) and *Pirates of the Caribbean: The Curse of the Black Pearl* (2003).

References

Hugo Davenport, "Monkey Trouble," *Daily Telegraph*, 14 October 1994, 24; Nick James, "Monkey Trouble," *Sight and Sound*, November 1994, 50; Sheila Johnston, "Monkey Trouble," *Independent*, 13 October 1994, 44; Ellen Leroe, *Monkey Trouble: A Novel Based on the Screenplay by Franco Amurri and Stu Krieger* (New York: Minstrel Books, 1994), 1, 20, 83, 144, 149; "Monkey Trouble," *Variety*, 21–27 March 1994, 57–58; Neil Norman, "Monkey Trouble," *Evening Standard*, 13 October 1994, 45; *Pressbook, Money Trouble* (London, Entertainment Film Distributors Ltd., 1994), 11, 13; Holly Willis, "Monkey Business," *Hollywood Reporter*, 1 August 1993, 39.

MOORE, DEMI (1962–)

Born Demetria Gene Guynes in New Mexico. Left school at sixteen to try to become an actor. Her breakout film was *St. Elmo's Fire* (1985); two years later she met Bruce Willis, whom she married. Her biggest hit, *Ghost,* was in 1990, and her subsequent films included *A Few Good Men* (1992) and *The Scarlet Letter* (1996).

Evidently it was Moore who initiated the project to film *G.I. JANE* and engaged Scott to direct. Scott felt "it would be a good film for Demi. I'd also wanted to work with her—I think she's one of the best actors we've got." The film's publicity made much of the arduousness of Moore's role, the fact that she not only trained hard, but did all her own stunts. Interviewed for a 1990 biography, she claimed that "it would be death to just sit where I might be safe. Either I'm a fool or have some sense of risk-taking or courage. There are too many things in life that I want to know and to taste and, as an actor, I get that kind of opportunity. If I can walk away from this film knowing just a little bit more . . . of what might be, it's mine and it has changed me for the rest of my life." The *Sunday Times* reported that the experience of filming proved tough for her: "Her set dispatches include tales of chronic sunburn, one-arm push-ups and 'surf torture,' a process that involved floating motionless in near-freezing sea water for hours at a time." However, she particularly enjoyed being part of an almost entirely male set: "I had a feeling from them of support and respect that was so fantastic and not even remotely about gender."

As with her other roles, Moore's performance in the film is competent, but we get the feeling that we are being manipulated throughout: any obstacle in her path will be overcome so that she can achieve her goal. Alexander Walker observed in the *Evening Standard* that "it [her performance] is the ultimate proof of what the movie-makers have manoeuvred us into accepting—namely, that women who want to claim the same rights as men must possess the same attributes as men." Critics generally disliked her interpretation of the role; and she was nominated for the 1997 award for Worst Actress of the Year, despite her efforts to publicize the film by doing one-armed push-ups on talk shows. However, perhaps they were being unfair: in a thoughtful piece published in *Sight and Sound*, Linda Williams suggested that the film was not just about Jordan O'Neil, but an attempt by Moore to manipulate her star image: "What we see isn't just Lieutenant Jordan O'Neil taking control of her career by taking control of her body . . . but Demi Moore giving herself a Number One. The 'mondo' pleasure of the scene lies in this—the collision of star and role, with what the scene says about the star as important as how the character develops in the film . . . [it] is in the end *not* primarily a film about a solitary woman trying to forge a path for other women to follow in a sexist institution. It is about Jordan's (mythically American) war with her personal weakness . . . That she [Moore] does so little to disguise her thirst for control makes her . . . a hard but compelling female icon."

References

Nigel Goodall, *Demi Moore: The Biography* (Edinburgh and London: Mainstream Publishing, 2000), 168; "The Prisoner of Gender," *Sunday Times Magazine*, 12 October 1997, 42; Ridley Scott, quoted in Paul M. Sammon, "Joining the Club: Ridley Scott on *G.I. Jane*," in *Ridley Scott Interviews*, ed. Laurence F. Knapp and Andrea F. Kulas (Jackson: University Press of Mississippi, 2005), 135; Alexander Walker, "The War on Womanhood," *Evening Standard*, 30 June 1997, 9; Linda Williams, "Body Talk," *Sight and Sound* 7, no.11 (November 1997): 20–21.

Bibliography

Julia Holt, *Demi Moore* (London: Hodder and Stoughton Educational), 1999.

MOORE, JULIANNE (1960–)

Born Julie Anne Smith in Fayetteville, North Carolina. Moore first came to prominence in *The Hand That Rocks the Cradle* (1992). Later successes included *Boogie Nights* (1997) and *The End of the Affair* (1999).

Moore was cast as Clarice Starling in *HANNIBAL* when JODIE FOSTER decided not to play the role again. There was considerable speculation in the press that Moore was just a stop-gap, but producer DINO DE LAURENTIIS claimed in an interview that "Jodie Foster is wrong for Starling here. She is a more mature woman. It's ten years later, so she is supposed to be nearly forty. She has a different job. She is full of sex appeal." Moore herself described the experience of the film in a publicity interview as "exciting . . . like doing several different kinds of movies at once. The FBI scenes were heavy-duty, dialogue-driven stuff. The fish market was completely action-oriented. The climax of the movie was dark, almost like a gothic thriller."

Moore's Clarice is dedicated to her work—so much so that she prefers to hide herself away in the FBI's Lecterium rather than enjoying the daylight. However, she is not prepared to put up with any nonsense from anyone—particularly her immediate superior Krendler (RAY LIOTTA). In the film's script by STEPHEN ZAILLIAN, when Krendler indecently suggests that he would not mind "having a go" with her, Clarice replies acidly "In the gym, anytime. No peds." At the same time, we are left unsure as to whether she is in love with Hannibal or not. In one shot a tear rolls down her cheek; the director could not decide whether it was an expression of anguish, loneliness, or disgust. In the documentary "The Making of *Hannibal*" included in the film's DVD release Scott claims that the affair between the two of them was "metaphorical"; while costar ANTHONY HOPKINS has been quoted in the *Wikipedia* entry on the film as saying that "it's not exactly a romance." Whatever the status of their relationship, it is clear that Clarice is profoundly affected by Hannibal's presence. At the end of the film he kisses her hard on the mouth, saying as he does so, in Zaillian's script, that "whenever you see the scar—the quality of the stitching—you'll remember this moment." This is certainly the case: Clarice snaps a pair of handcuffs on her own and Hannibal's wrists, and refuses to give him the key. The only way for Hannibal to escape is to cut his own hand off with a meat-cleaver. The fact that he is prepared to go to such extremes emphasizes the depth of affection between the two of them.

References

"*Hannibal*," http://en.wikipedia.org/wiki/Hannibal_(film) (accessed 22 December 2008); "The Making of *Hannibal*," Documentary included in the 2005 DVD release of the film (Los Angeles: Universal Pictures, 2005); Joe Mauceri, "Dino de Laurentis: King of Producers," *Shivers* 88 (April 2001): 32; Julianne Moore, "My Dinner with Hannibal," *Premiere* 14, no.6 (February 2001): 106; Steven Zaillian, "*Hannibal*: Screenplay Based on the Novel by Thomas Harris," Revision (9 February 2000), http://sfy.ru/sfy.html?script =hannibal2001 (accessed 15 December 2008).

Bibliography

Alison Boshoff, "Hannibal Lecter? He Wouldn't Eat a Girl Like Me," *Daily Mail* (London), 6 February 2001, 7; Douglas Eby, "Hannibal," *Cinefantastique* 32, no.6 (February 2001): 8–9, 13; Daniel Fireman, "Killer Instinct," *Entertainment Weekly* 531 (17 March 2000): 24–29; "The Right Woman for Lecter 2," *Evening Standard*, 6 February 2001, 9; Damon Wise, "Is That You, Clarice?" *Observer Screen*, 19 March 2000, 8–9.

MORE FACES OF JIM

GB 1963 TV Series 6 × 30 min episodes b/w. *Production Company*: British Broadcasting Corporation. *Producer/ Director*: Douglas Moodie. *Writers*: Frank Muir and Denis Norden. *Director of Photography*: Tony Leggo. *Production Designers*: Malcolm Goulding and Ridley Scott. *Music*: Bill McGuffie. *Cast*: Jimmy Edwards (*Mr. Padgett / Patient /*

Hadrian Maximum), Ronnie Barker *(The Psychiatrist / Las-civius)*, June Whitfield *(Mrs. Craybrooke / Mrs. Padgett / Rowena)*, Derek Nimmo *(Mr. Smeed)*.

A six-part comedy series designed to showcase the talents of British television and radio comedian Jimmy Edwards. Ridley Scott designed Episode 1 ("A Matter of Amnesia," broadcast 28 June 1963), Episode 2 ("A Matter of Growing Up," broadcast 5 July 1963), and Episode 3 ("A Matter of Spreadeagling," broadcast 19 July 1963).

MORROW, ROB (1962–)

Born in New Rochelle, New York, Morrow's television appearances include *Northern Exposure* (1993–1996), *The Thin Blue Lie* (2000) and *Street Time* (2002–2003). Film appearances include *Quiz Show* (1994).

Cast as the FBI agent Don Eppes in *NUMB3RS*, Morrow portrays a character so dedicated to his job that he simply does not have a personal life. Even though he has plenty of female friends, he cannot sustain a relationship for any length of time. The only true friends he possesses are his brother Charlie (DAVID KRUMHOLTZ) and his father Alan (JUDD HIRSCH). Don Eppes experiences the classic conflict of LOVE VS. DUTY, and finds that his duty to his work supersedes almost everything else. Nonetheless he works hard to sustain his "family" at work, by leading the FBI team as best he can. Don's finest hour comes in episodes such as "Rampage" (Series 2, Episode 21), where he has to cope with an intruder into his office who kills one of his agents. Charlie cannot stomach the experience; he goes home to Alan and admits that he does not have "enough heart to take what life is gonna throw at you." By contrast, Don not only delegates tasks to his subordinates, but ensures that the culprit is successfully apprehended.

Morrow has described his character in an interview with *Emmy* magazine as one "who's sacrificing himself for the greater good . . . He's totally committed to the job, he doesn't have much of a life outside the job and he ends up seeing a lot of things that he has difficulty talking about later. I admire people like that because their lives are tough . . . Family is an equation that makes sense to him. And that—not math—is the heart of the show."

Reference

Kathleen O'Steen, "Math Blaster," *Emmy* 27, no.3 (May 2005): 184.

Bibliography

Mark Nollinger, "Strength in Numbers," *TV Guide*, 17 April 2005, 42–3; *Official Web site of Rob Morrow*, www.robmorrow.net (accessed 22 February 2009).

MORTENSEN, VIGGO (1958–)

Mortensen came to prominence in films such as *The Portrait of a Lady* (1996) as Caspar Goodwood, and *Daylight* (also 1996).

Cast as Master Chief John Urgayle in *G.I. JANE*, Mortensen went to the Naval Base in Coronado, California where he watched the actual training and talked to as many active and retired SEALs as he could. His performance in the film has been well summarized by Richard A. Schwartz: "Urgayle firmly believes that women endanger their male comrades because the men will instinctively feel compelled to protect them. This instinct, Urgayle maintains, will cause men to recklessly expose themselves to danger or, when captured, to reveal secret information in order to prevent their female comrades from being tortured or actually molested. This is in fact Urgayle's greatest fear about himself, and it motivates much of his behavior towards Jordan [DEMI MOORE]."

The film's most dramatic moment also stems from Urgayle's fear of his own instinct to protect women. He brutally tortures her on the grounds that he does not want her to continue; if she does, he will be faced with responsibility of protecting her in battle. DAVID TWOHY's script sums up his view of the camp and its inhabitants: "This is my [male] island. My world. And here I can get away with shit that would get me arrested anywhere else in the world. Take another scan of my little joy-boy outside. If I can do that to a Navy SEAL, what's gonna happen to you [Jordan]?" But O'Neil subverts his intention by refusing to succumb to his brutality, and the scene closes with Urgayle acknowledging to his underlings that the women are not the problem: "We are."

In an interview with PAUL M. SAMMON, Scott praised Mortensen's performance, which "exhibited a certain strength which was offbeat, and because it was offbeat, it was quite threatening." Occasionally he quotes poems by D. H. Lawrence and Pablo Neruda, suggesting "other dimensions in the man. Urgayle's definitely a special kind of individual." Mortensen himself recalled in 1999 that playing Urgayle was "a little embarrassing but once I got into it, it was all right. . . The other day I came across a *Mad* magazine. For the first time I felt I had arrived when in it I saw a *G.I. Jane* parody of me called GI Shame. My favorite part was the idea that the candidates were dropping out of the SEALs not from the physical abuse but from my awful poetry readings."

References

"*G.I. Jane*: Production Notes," (Los Angeles: First Independent Distributors, 1997); Dennis Hensley, "The Hot New 39-Year-Old" (interview with Viggo Mortensen), *Movieline* 9, no.11 (August 1999): 73; Paul M. Sammon, "Joining the Club: Ridley Scott on *G.I. Jane*," in *Ridley Scott Interviews*, ed. Laurence F. Knapp and Andrea F. Kulas (Jackson: University Press of Mississippi, 2005), 147–48; Richard A. Schwartz, *The Films of Ridley Scott* (Westport, CT and London: Praeger Publishers, 2001), 133; David Twohy, "*G.I. Jane*: First Draft" (6 August 1995), Unpub Screenplay, http://sfy.ru/sfy.html?script=gi_jane (accessed 21 October 2008).

MOTHERHOOD

The theme of motherhood and its relationship to FEMI-NISM has been explored in *ALIEN*, where it is clear that motherhood is going to be an important issue from the outset. The logo used in promoting the film was cracked. The film opens with a "birth" scene in which the crew members of *NOSTROMO* are seen wearing diapers and sleeping in cradles. RON COBB's design for the spacecraft is peculiarly "maternal" in appearance with its plethora of tube-like corridors with smooth, curved walls.

The film views the entire concept of mothering and motherhood with great suspicion. For example, the computer that maintains the ship is called Mother; but there is nothing maternal about her. She is remote and detached from the crew and ultimately destroys the ship housing her "children." Ripley's (SIGOURNEY WEAVER's) relationship to Mother is based on hostility. She calls the computer "a bitch" as she realizes that Mother will destroy the ship, despite the fact that Ripley has keyed in the codes to prevent it. Mother follows her own rules; for her, the crew is expendable. In *THE COMPANY* James Angleton (MICHAEL KEATON) is known as "Mother"; as someone responsible for directing the work of CIA operatives both at home and abroad, he exerts tremendous influence. However, sometimes his behavior seems particularly erratic; like the computer in *Alien* he operates according to his own rules. Once again it seems that the idea of motherhood is something unpredictable and not to be trusted—especially for the "sons" working within the CIA.

In *Alien* the fear of motherhood is also expressed through its horrific birth imagery. The alien reproduces by implanting its young in human beings. The birth is equally horrific in the chest-busting scene. What differentiates women from men—the capacity for childbearing—is characterized as something alien, inhuman. Pregnancy is not part of the *Nostromo*'s natural order. Dennis Patrick Slattery relates this theme to the myth of Demeter and Persephone. Scott expresses an opposite view in *MONKEY TROUBLE*, showing the central character, Eva (THORA BIRCH), learning to become a good mother by looking after the monkey Dodger. She sets such a good example that her real-life mother Amy (MIMI ROGERS) has to follow suit.

Cara J. MariAnna identifies the theme of motherhood in *THELMA & LOUISE*, particularly in the landscape imagery, which for her represents Mother Earth, a "center of power . . . a center of dreaming and weaving and creating . . . a center of the spiral." This represents the obverse of the imagery employed in *Alien*; Mother Earth here inspires the eponymous central characters in their search for independence and alternative ways of living. For someone like Orson Welles (LIEV SCHREIBER) in *RKO 281*, the mother figure provides an important influence in his life. In a deleted scene

from JOHN LOGAN's script, his mother tells him, "[you] must have a dream. A great dream worthy of you." The same also applies to *WHERE THE MONEY IS*, where Carol MacKay (LINDA FIORENTINO) acts as a surrogate mother figure for Henry Manning (PAUL NEWMAN) when he enters the care home apparently suffering from a stroke. Carol's patience is rewarded when she transforms herself from a mother figure into Manning's partner in crime—a symbolic "reward" for her devotion.

HANNIBAL offers two constructions of motherhood—the first involves the drug dealer Evelda Drumgo (Hazelle Goodman), who carries her baby in a harness in front of her during a botched FBI attempt to capture her. Although the baby survives in the end, Evelda dies; and Clarice Starling (JULIANNE MOORE) is censured by her employers for putting the baby's life in danger, even though she had wanted the entire operation canceled before it had even begun. Evelda knows this, which is why she carries the baby in front of her in the first place. She has no concern for her child, who is just a pawn in the mother's struggle to survive. Clarice herself has a difficult relationship with her mother—as Hannibal Lecter (ANTHONY HOPKINS) observes. By devoting herself to her career, Clarice hoped to improve herself socially, to avoid having to follow in her mother's footsteps as "a chambermaid in a hotel on Route 66." Sadly, the daughter's efforts prove futile; even having dedicated herself to her career instead of motherhood and children, she is eventually suspended from the FBI. Hannibal's query as to what she will do now is a pertinent one: "I want to know what it is you think you will do, now that all you cared about in the world is gone."

This theme is extended in the Scott-produced film *IN HER SHOES*, where the two sisters Maggie and Rose Feller (CAMERON DIAZ, TONI COLLETTE) have been so traumatized by their mother's death when they were children that they have spent their lives trying to forget it. It is only when they seek the truth by meeting up with their grandmother Ella (SHIRLEY MACLAINE) and confronting their father Michael (Ken Howard) that they understand how much their mother Caroline had cared for them in spite of her mental illness. In a film peopled with inadequate parents—including Ella, Michael, and his second wife Sydelle—Caroline was the only one who really loved her offspring. No one can bring her back, of course; but at least the sisters have the chance to rebuild their family life once Michael and Ella have resolved their differences. *In Her Shoes* takes this discourse further by suggesting that perhaps the idea of the nuclear family with two parents should be superseded by a community based on mutual love and understanding. In *A GOOD YEAR*, both Max Skinner (RUSSELL CROWE) and Christie Roberts (ABBIE CORNISH) grew up in dysfunctional families: Max's parents died when he was young, while Christie never knew her father: Max's Uncle Henry (ALBERT FINNEY). Both come to understand the significance of companionship at the end of the film as they set up a new life in Henry's château with Duflot (DIDIER BOURDON), his wife Ludivine (Isabelle Candelier), and Fanny (MARION COTILLARD). No one knows how long it will last, so they opt for *carpe diem*.

Louise J. Kaplan takes a cynical view of motherhood in Scott's films, citing the mother-child relationship in *Thelma & Louise* as "another way of disavowing female sexuality and the sexual difference. The body of the hysterical woman is one conventional disguise for the potentially traumatic sensitivities of the female. Another disguise . . . is the fantasy of a reunion with mother nature." However this is certainly not characteristic of *In Her Shoes*, or in the reality series *AMERICAN FIGHTER PILOT*, where motherhood is viewed as something positive—especially by the male recruits who congratulate their spouses on their self-sacrificing devotion to the responsibility of sustaining a family.

References

Louise J. Kaplan, "Fits and Misfits: The Body of a Woman," *American Imago* 50, no.4 (Winter 1993): 456; John Logan, "Draft Script for *RKO 281*" (dated 1 May 1997), http://sfy.ru/sfy.html?script =rko218 (accessed 16 November 2008); Cara J. MariAnna, "The Seven Mythic Cycles of *Thelma and Louise*," *Trivia* 21 (1993): 84; Dennis Patrick Slattery, "Demeter-Persephone and the *Alien*(s) Cultural Body," *New Orleans Review* 19, no.1 (Spring 1992): 30–35; Steven Zaillian, "*Hannibal*: Screenplay Based on the Novel by Thomas Harris" Revision (9 February 2000), http://sfy.ru/sfy.html ?script=hannibal2001(accessed 15 December 2008).

Bibliography

Valerie Gray Hardcastle, "Changing Perspectives of Motherhood: Images from the Aliens Trilogy," *Film and Philosophy* 3 (1996): 167–75; Chad Hermann, "Some Horrible Dream About (S)mothering: Sexuality, Gender and Family in the *Alien* Trilogy," *Post Script* 16, no.3 (Summer 1997): 36–50; Krin Gabbard, "*Aliens* and the New Family Romance," *Post Script* 8, no.1 (October 1988): 30–42; John L. Cobbs, "Alien as an Abortion Parable," *Literature/Film Quarterly* 18, no.3 (1990): 198–201; Stephen A. Scobie, "What's the Story, Mother? The Mourning of the Alien," *Science Fiction Studies* 20, no.1 (March 1993): 80–94; Thomas Vaughn, "Voices of Sexual Distortion: Rape, Birth and Self-Annihilation Metaphors in the *Alien* Trilogy," *Quarterly Journal of Speech* 81, no.4 (November 1995): 423–35.

MOTHER'S PRIDE BREAD

GB 1971 Commercial 28 sec b/w. *Production Company*: RSA Films. *Producer*: Ridley Scott.

A commercial produced by the same company who would subsequently use Scott for McDOUGALL'S PASTRY MIX and HOVIS BREAD. The story begins with a harassed supermarket manager, desperately trying to organize his staff for the visit of "Mother," who has come to inspect the quality of his Mother's Pride Bread to ensure that it is "as fresh when it reaches you [i.e., the viewer] as it is when it leaves her." "Mother" arrives in a Rolls-Royce (license-plate number MP1) flanked by two bodyguards. She enters the store, feels the bread for freshness, and then gives the manager an approving glance. As she leaves the store and drives away, the manager mops his brow and takes his glasses off. The voice-over drives home the point: "Mother knows best."

Like the 1972 commercial for McDOUGALL'S PASTRY MIX, this commercial emphasizes the importance of family values. "Mother" has to decide what is best for people to eat. The idea of "Mother" as the head of a large company resurfaces in *ALIEN*, when the name is given to the computer which dictates what the crew on the spaceship *NOSTROMO* should and should not do. This commercial was voiced by JOHN HURT, who went on to play Kane in *Alien*.

MOYA, BERCELIO (?–)

Played the Indian boy in *The Mission* (1986) and took on a similar role in *1492: CONQUEST OF PARADISE*. As Utapan in the later film, Moya's role is largely symbolic—as a member of the NATIVE PEOPLES plucked from his homeland to be "civilized" in Spain, he is the classic example of the colonized person, who puts his native culture at risk by allowing himself to become an object of derision in Spain. Robert Thurston's novelization of the screenplay makes this clear: "Utapan laid the way for the Tainos, his face painted black and red, a squawking parrot on his shoulder . . . While Fernando saw that their [the Indians'] painted faces and nearly naked bodies made them seem primitive, he was disturbed by the way the [Spanish] people mocked their visitors from the Indies." However, Utapan understands the folly of his actions; in a significant cluster of sequences, he is shown shaving his head, removing his fine clothes and donning his native garb. As the great city is destroyed in a storm, he runs off into the forest, pausing only to accuse Columbus (GÉRARD DEPARDIEU) of being colonialist in assumption, of never having bothered to learn the native Indian language.

Reference

Robert Thurston, *1492: Conquest of Paradise Based on a Screenplay by Roselyne Bosch* (London: Penguin Books, 1992), 120.

MULCAHY, RUSSELL (1953–)

Australian-born director of action thrillers such as *Highlander* (1986) and *Highlander II—The Quickening* (1991).

Mulcahy worked on several episodes of *THE HUNGER*—TELEVISION in both series, including "Necros" (Series 1, Episode 3), "The Secret Shih Tan" (Series 1, Episode 9), "I'm Dangerous Tonight" (Series 1, Episode 17), "Wrath of God" (Series 2, Episode 4), "Nunc Dimittis" (Series 2, Episode 5), and "The Sacred Fire" (Series 2, Episode 17). None of these episodes are especially distinguished: they are photographed in rock-video style with plenty of fast cuts, and include obligatory sex scenes (which was one of the series' main selling points on US cable television).

MULRONEY, DERMOT (1963–)

American character actor who made his name in *Young Guns* (1988) Starred as the groom and Julia Roberts's sought-after best friend in *My Best Friend's Wedding* (1997). Cast as the heavy Wayne MacKay in the Ridley Scott-produced *WHERE THE MONEY IS*, Mulroney liked the script: "I think it's rare to find a project that has just three characters and if you do they're usually sitting around a dining room in some family drama that's a little less fun than a caper."

Alexander Walker thought his performance adequate, even though "this hunky junior is no march for a seasoned oldster [like PAUL NEWMAN]. It is the kid who turns out to be lacking in valour, stamina, loyalty, competence and—who can doubt it with Newman around?—sex appeal." By contrast, Anthony Quinn felt sorry for the actor, whose presence for the reviewer "was an albatross around the film's neck, slowing it down just when it seems about to soar." Mulroney's role is a thankless one—that of playing second fiddle to Newman, as well as portraying a husband interested more in the ideal of domesticity than in his wife Carol (LINDA FIORENTINO). His shortcomings are well illustrated in a sequence in which he is shown diving into the lake for the benefit of the elderly care home residents. If he thought that they might admire his physique, he experiences a rude awakening; one of them berates him for not entering the water straight.

References

Dermot Mulroney, quoted in the pressbook for *Where the Money Is* (London: Intermedia 2000), 15, 20; Anthony Quinn, "The King of the Hustlers Pulls Off One More Sting," *The Independent*, 6 October 2000, 10; Alexander Walker, "A Con, a Pro and a Caper to Treasure," *Evening Standard*, 5 October 2000, 29.

MURPHY, DONNA (1959–)

Donna Murphy achieved fame for her stage work such as *Passion* (filmed in 1996) and *The King and I*. Her television appearances included *Murder One* (1995–1996), and *Law and Order* (1993–2000).

Cast as the anchor Joan Naylor in *THE LAST DEBATE*, Murphy offers a portrait of a family woman dedicated to her job, who achieves celebrity as one of the four panelists who expose Republican presidential candidate Richard Meredith's (Stephen Young's) shady past on a live television debate.

As a result she is offered the role of anchor on one of the major networks, replacing long-established incumbent Don Beard (JOHN BADHAM). Although Naylor continues to carry out her job in a professional manner, it is clear that she has worked hard on her image—improving her wardrobe and deepening her voice so that it seems more authoritative on television. Like everyone else in the media, she realizes that surface impressions count for much more than journalistic integrity.

MUTINY ON THE BOUNTY

US 1935 r/t 133 min b/w. *Production Company*: Metro Goldwyn-Mayer. *Producers*: Frank Lloyd and Irving Thalberg. *Director*: Frank Lloyd. *Writers*: Talbot Jennings, Jules Furthman, and Carey Wilson, from the book by Charles Nordhoff and James Norman Hall. *Director of Photography*: Arthur Edeson. *Production Designer*: Cedric Gibbons. *Music*: Herbert Stothart. *Cast*: Clark Gable (*Fletcher Christian*), Charles Laughton (*William Bligh*), Franchot Tone (*Roger Byam*), Henry Stephenson (*Sir Joseph Banks*), Dudley Digges (*Bacchus*), Spring Byington (*Mrs. Byam*).

Producer Irving Thalberg made a film celebrating the British Navy, a weapon of freedom in a threatening world. What did it matter if the whole fleet mutinied just ten years after the *Bounty* and thirty-six men were hanged? What did it matter if flogging went on in the navy for forty years after the mutiny? Thalberg's message was that the act of mutiny, wrong in itself, had good effects. The reason was that institutions of power ultimately respond to people with good intentions.

Ridley Scott acknowledged that he looked at the film as an inspiration for *WHITE SQUALL*. Although the subject matter is very different, *Mutiny on the Bounty* does portray a good study in obsession, chiefly due to the performance of Laughton, which dominates the film. This might have provided the inspiration for Sheldon (JEFF BRIDGES)—even though he lacks Bligh's malignancy.

MYLES, SOPHIA (1980–)

When Sophia Myles was sixteen, she was spotted by Oscar-winning screenwriter Julian Fellowes in a school production of *Teachers* by John Godber which led to her being cast in the BBC film *The Prince & The Pauper* (1996). Since then, Sophia Myles has appeared in such film and TV projects as *From Hell* (2001), *Thunderbirds* (2004), and most recently *Moonlight* (2007–2008).

Cast as Isolde in *TRISTAN + ISOLDE*, Myles identified a similarity between herself and the character: "[W]e are both very, kind of headstrong young women. I mean, I've always done what I wanted to do and have never allowed anyone to dictate how I should live my life or what I should be doing with my time and so in that sense we are similar." She insisted on a no-nudity clause in the contract because she felt that it was not necessary in this kind of film, "and my body is a very, kind of precious thing to me. So when I was first sent the script and I opened it and flicked through it, and it says she enters and she disrobes I thought no way and threw it across the other side of the room."

Initially it seems as if Isolde is an independent young woman, who resists her father Donnchadh's (DAVID PATRICK O'HARA's) will. She also has a considerable amount of self-possession; when she discovers Tristan (JAMES FRANCO) washed up on a beach, almost dead of exposure, she drags him back to a hut on the seafront and checks his condition. When it seems as if he is about to die, she immediately strips off her clothes and hugs him in the belief that body heat is the best way to aid his recovery. At this point she seems to be in control of the situation: "You've been sleeping a long time. You're in Ireland. Did you know that? Shh … It's all right. You're safe here. No one knows. Don't be scared. Just sleep … sleep." As the film unfolds, however, Isolde becomes less and less responsible for her own fate, as she is forced into an unwanted MARRIAGE to King Marke (RUFUS SEWELL) and thereby denied the opportunity to pursue her love for Tristan. She can only achieve her wish at the moment of Tristan's death as he lies by the riverside and she murmurs: "Know that I love you, Tristan. And wherever you go, whatever you see, I will always be with you."

References

Paul Fischer "Sophia Myles for Tristan and Isolde" (13 January 2006), www.darkhorizons.com/news06/tristan2.php (accessed 8 August 2008); "Tristan + Isolde, Written by Dean Georgaris, Transcript by Chani at tristanandisolde.net," www.imsdb.com/Movie %20Scripts/Tristan%20and%20Isolde%20Script.html (accessed 23 January 2009).

MYTHS

GB 2009 TV series 6 × 5 min episodes col. *Production Companies*: BBC Switch and RSA Films. *Executive Producers*: Ridley Scott, Geoff Goodwin, and Caspar Delaney. *Producer*: Rhun Francis. *Director*: Henry Mason. *Writers*: Vikki Lewis and Grant Black. *Director of Photography*: Ed Rutherford. *Art Director*: Sarah Jenneson.

Series 1

"Paris and the Goddesses" (broadcast 10 January 2009). *Cast:* Tommy Knight, Joshua Bowman, Scarlett Sabet.
"The Syrens Call" (broadcast 17 January 2009). *Cast:* Jamie Doyle, Una Healy, Mollie King.
"The Fall of Icarus" (broadcast 24 January 2009). *Cast:* Jamie Blackley, Michael McKell, Georgina Leonidas.
"The Eye of the Cyclops" (broadcast 31 January 2009). *Cast:* Jamie Doyle, Mark Noble, Jamie Di Spirito.
"The Love of Narcissus" (broadcast 7 February 2009). *Cast:* Lewis Bradley, Jessica Bell.
"Escape from the Underworld" (broadcast 14 February 2009). *Cast:* Charles Mnene, Rebekah Brookes-Murrell.

A series of programs, designed for teenage audiences, in which Greek myths have been modernized. The show was originally commissioned to run online, but was broadcast as part of BBC Switch's new multimedia programming. The stories revolve around the lives of teenagers living in the fictional village of Delphi. The programs can be accessed online only in the United Kingdom, at www.bbc.co.uk/switch/myths/launch.shtml.

NADAL, LYMARI (1978–)

Born in Puerto Rico, Nadal earned her master's degree in chemistry before turning to acting. As Ana, a former beauty queen and wife of Frank Lucas (DENZEL WASHINGTON) in *AMERICAN GANGSTER*, Nadal exudes what Scott described in the production information as "pleasant innocence," having contracted a potentially idyllic MARRIAGE to a rich and prosperous man. Eventually the dream turns sour: Ana survives a shooting and then tries to make a quick getaway. STEVEN ZAILLIAN's script describes how she "pulls a drawer open. Takes out their passports [and] begins packing." Despite Frank's best attempts to calm her, she will not be pacified; she returns to Puerto Rico, leaving Frank a lonely and isolated man when he is finally released from prison. Only Richie, his former rival, is there to meet him: "Frank steps out into sunlight, free but owning nothing but the cardboard box in his arms. [He] looks out across the parking lot to see if anyone has come to pick him up. [He] sees Richie by his car, hand raised above his head like a flag."

References

American Gangster: Production Information (Los Angeles: Universal Pictures, 2007); Steven Zaillian, "*American Gangster*: Final Shooting Script" (27 July 2006), www.roteirodecinema.com.br/scripts/files/american_gangster.htm (accessed 8 February 2009).

NATIVE PEOPLES

In *1492: CONQUEST OF PARADISE* Scott portrays Native Americans as fundamentally self-sufficient, not in need of colonization from Columbus's (GÉRARD DEPARDIEU's) invading forces. Robert Thurston's novelization makes it clear that the Indians are in many ways superior to the Spaniards; and well aware of the colonists' real motives: "Columbus said to Utapan; 'Tell him we admire his people.' Utapan translated, listened to [Chief] Guacanagari's words, then said: 'Chief says he knows you like his . . . 'Utapan searched for he wanted, '. . . His women.'" At the same time the film objectifies Native Americans—particularly the women—by its focus on their nakedness, especially during one sequence in which an Indian servant brings food to Moxica (MICHAEL WIN-

COTT) and Guevara (Arnold Vosloo), and the two Spaniards (as well as the director) focus lovingly on her breasts.

In *WHITE SQUALL* the youthful crew disguise themselves as natives, carrying spears and wearing only shorts. They roam about the Galapagos Islands, claiming the almost deserted territory as their own. Although not actually intending to settle there, they consider themselves sufficiently mature and self-reliant to live like the natives. Chuck Gieg (SCOTT WOLF) emphasizes the point in a voiceover: "We wanted to stake a claim [to the land] as our own." In TODD ROBINSON's original script, the boys perform primitive rituals reminiscent of William Golding's *Lord of the Flies*: "Neptune's an Indian brave, whooping and hollering as he does a rain dance . . . Frenetic chaos . . . Neptune and his court lead a procession around the perimeter of the deck." They subsequently go to the islands, where "like Darwin before us, we would witness the bliss of nature in the absence of man" and subsequently engage in native pastimes, such as hunting goats: "Pounding through the waterline like the wild horses of Sable, the hunters charge after the hunted, closing. The goat's eyes are full of a terror it has never known." Although the intention is to try to distinguish the boys from colonists, it is clear that they are simply mimicking native rituals; after a brief respite, they will return to (white) civilization.

References

Todd Robinson, *White Squall: Revised First Draft*, unpub. script, dated 31 October 1994, http://sfy.ru/sfy.html?script=white_squall (accessed 8 September 2008); Robert Thurston, *1492: Conquest of Paradise Based on a Screenplay by Roselyne Bosch* (London: Penguin Books, 1992), 117.

NEESON, LIAM (1952–)

Liam Neeson made his major film debut in *EXCALIBUR* (1981) and *Krull* (1983). The chance to work with Ridley Scott on a film story of depth and substance gave him incentive enough to work on *KINGDOM OF HEAVEN*. In the book on the making of the film, Neeson described his character Godfrey as one who "earned his living from fighting and all that encompasses, and yet [had] a sensitivity to the idea that Christian and Muslim have to live together. Godfrey has come to this realizing only after many years of senseless killing. And then he must somehow get through to Balian, whom he's just met—convince him to come out to Jerusalem, and that there is a way forward for all of us . . . We're still feeling the effects of the Crusades to this day, with great mutual mistrust and confusion and ignorance between Muslim and Christian. I think this film goes some way towards explaining that confusion and showing where these wars came from."

Neeson's role is very similar to that of RICHARD HARRIS's Marcus Aurelius in *GLADIATOR*. Although not on screen for very long, he sets an example to Balian (ORLANDO BLOOM) of someone willing to repent for his past sins—ignoring Balian as his bastard child—and favoring right action instead. He hopes to go to Jerusalem to establish "a kingdom of conscience" in which Christians and Muslims can live in peaceful coexistence. When fate dictates otherwise (Godfrey is mortally wounded in the forest) Godfrey confers a knighthood on Balian and instructs him to protect the people of Jerusalem; as he does so, he strikes Balian across the face in the hope that the younger man will remember his words. In *KINGDOM OF HEAVEN*: THE DIRECTOR'S CUT Godfrey's role is expanded slightly, Scott showing how he was driven to the Holy Land to ensure the firstborn son's right to exclusive inheritance.

Reference

Diana Landau, ed., *Kingdom of Heaven: The Ridley Scott Film and the History behind the Story* (London: Simon and Schuster Ltd., 2005), 71.

NEGRON, JESSE (?–)

Jesse Negron earned his Masters in Film Production from UCLA in 1993. He worked as a sales specialist in film and video for manufacturers Alesis and Fairlight. In 1996, he founded RocketWerks in his Santa Clarita home with Garrard Whatley and Jeff Laity. After a few years of full-time editing and mixing independent films, he decided to follow his interests in film production. A series of film editing positions culminated in *Pop and Me*, a documentary which won Best Picture in the 1999 LA Independent Film Festival. He then moved to Florida to begin production on a documentary on fighter pilot training. This project went on to become *AMERICAN FIGHTER PILOT*, which aired on CBS in March 2002. His co-executive producers on the project were Ridley and TONY SCOTT.

NERI, FRANCESCA (1964–)

Italian actress who worked for Pedro Almodóvar on *Live Flesh* (1997) and Carlos Saura on *Dispara!* (1993).

As Allegra Pazzi, wife of the police inspector in *HANNIBAL*, Neri plays a social climber whose desire to procure the best opera tickets "no matter what the cost" drives her husband (GIANCARLO GIANNINI) into corruption. He informs the FBI as to Hannibal's whereabouts in the hope of obtaining the $3 million reward, even though that means destroying his reputation as an honest cop. Pazzi's efforts to please his wife prove fruitless, as Allegra ends up by falling in love with *Hannibal*. STEVEN ZAILLIAN's script has the inspector looking helpless "*as he watches Fell [Hannibal] rape his wife with a kiss of her hand. His [Hannibal's] head stays there longer than it should as he savors the aroma emanating from her wrist. Finally the head rises up and Pazzi all but shoves Allegra into the cab.*" Neri explained in an interview with *Cinefantastique* that at this moment "there's a feeling of sadness between the two of us [Allegra and Hannibal] because we know a passage by heart. So we play with a double entendre of the text and there's a little game going on there."

References

Roberto D'Onofrio, "Francesca Neri: The Cannibal's Ill-Fated Opera Flirt," *Cinefantastique* 32, no.6 (February 2001): 12; Steven Zaillian, "*Hannibal*: Screenplay Based on the Novel by Thomas Harris," Revision (9 February 2000), http://sfy.ru/sfy.html?script=hannibal2001 (accessed 15 December 2008).

NETWORK

US 1976 r/t 121 min col. *Production Companies*: Metro Goldwyn-Mayer and United Artists. *Producer*: Howard Gottfried. *Director*: Sidney Lumet. *Writer*: Paddy Chayefsky. *Director of Photography*: Owen Roizman. *Production Designer*: Philip Rosenberg. *Music*: Eliot Lawrence. *Cast*: Faye Dunaway (*Diana Christensen*), William Holden (*Max Schumacher*), Peter Finch (*Howard Beale*), Robert Duvall (*Frank Hackett*), Wesley Addy (*Nelson Chaney*), Ned Beatty (*Arthur Jensen*), Arthur Berghardt (*Great Ahmed Khan*).

In 1975 terrorist violence is the stuff of network nightly news programming and the corporate structure of the UBS television network is changing. Meanwhile, Howard Beale (Peter Finch), the aging UBS news anchor, has lost his once strong ratings share and so the network fires him. He goes on the air by insisting that people go to the windows and yell, "I'm mad as hell, and I'm not going to take it [media trivialities] anymore." His ravings make him an icon and help to improve the network's ratings. The subject matter is very similar to that of *THE LAST DEBATE*, and might have proved an inspiration for the later film.

NEWMAN, PAUL (1925–2008)

American leading actor, best known for films such as *The Hustler* (1961), *Cool Hand Luke* (1967), *Butch Cassidy and the Sundance Kid* (1969), and *The Sting* (1973).

Newman played a starring role in the Ridley Scott-produced film *WHERE THE MONEY IS*. He got on well with his leading lady LINDA FIORENTINO, despite her reputation for being difficult. Transcending the script, Newman is a charismatic presence as veteran crook Harry Manning, projecting a tough authority. On the dance floor, Manning demonstrates natural rhythm. His involuntary "business" relationship with Carol MacKay (Fiorentino) gradually turns into something deeper. The plot builds to an armored car heist, with predictable twists and turns. It comes as no surprise when Carol chooses Manning over her weak, treacherous husband Wayne (DERMOT MULRONEY), and the upbeat, crime-does-pay ending is cheerfully amoral.

Newman chose to do the film because he "hadn't done a caper in a long while . . . There's an element of Butch Cassidy in Henry." Apparently, Newman enjoyed the experience of filming a role that recalled this famous role. He told his biographer Daniel O'Brien that "larceny is always a very attractive and wonderful thing to play . . . I like the fact that the actors had to carry the film and not the special-effects guys . . . No one got shot. No one got stabbed. There isn't any profanity in the film and it still, I think, is funny and suspenseful." Kim Newman in *Sight and Sound* described Newman's performance thus: "[it] affords a fine late opportunity . . . to exert blue-eyed charisma and gravelly charm as the spry senior citizen . . . who would rather talk his way out of a situation . . . than use more brutal methods."

References

Kim Newman, "Where the Money Is," *Sight and Sound*, November 2000, 66; Paul Newman, quoted in *Daniel O'Brien, Paul Newman* (London: Faber and Faber Ltd., 2004), 296; Paul Newman, quoted in the pressbook for *Where the Money Is* (London: Intermedia 2000), 15, 17; Paul Newman, quoted in *Daniel O'Brien, Paul Newman* (London: Faber and Faber Ltd., 2004), 296.

NEW YORK

Some of Scott's films make use of specific locations to reinforce their thematic points. In *SOMEONE TO WATCH OVER ME* the script uses an opening description of the Manhattan skyline to represent the city as the ultimate source of man's desire and fulfillment. The film subsequently contrasts two neighborhoods to emphasize the CLASS DIFFERENCES between the two main characters, Mike Keegan (TOM BERENGER) and Claire Gregory (MIMI ROGERS). Claire lives on affluent Fifth Avenue opposite Central Park where people stroll happily, apparently without a care in the world. Compare this landscape with downtown Queens where Mike lives—a world of tightly packed houses comprising a front room, dining room and kitchen, with a small fenced backyard. Fifth Avenue foregrounds style and gracious living; Queens intimacy and friendliness. Despite the

differences between the two areas, Queens does possess certain virtues such a security and warmth denied to people like Claire. It is chiefly for this reason that she agrees to address the students at Milton Gregory high school (founded by her father) in an attempt to experience the thrill of animated chatter. The fact that no one talks to her only emphasizes the social gulf separating her from the other people in the school.

The city of New York assumes a living presence in *BLACK RAIN*. The film's opening shots depict the skyline at sunset with a song "I'll Be Holding On" (written by HANS ZIMMER) played over the soundtrack. Scott's camera focuses on a group of leather-clad bikers, including police officer Nick Conklin (MICHAEL DOUGLAS), racing along the banks of the Hudson River, the Brooklyn Bridge in the background and the Manhattan skyscrapers in the distance. The action cuts to a more mundane sequence in the suburbs: Nick briefly encounters his children outside their mother's house and promises to see them again soon, then drives off in pouring rain. Scott cuts to an aerial shot of the Manhattan skyline and then dollies downwards to focus on Nick traveling to work on his bike. Such sequences represent New York as a quasi-dream world—the summit of Nick's ambitions as he speeds along the river. At the same time the city is the principal source of his frustration as he cannot enjoy even five minutes alone with his children. As in *Someone to Watch Over Me*, Scott contrasts Manhattan with the suburbs; but in *Black Rain* this is used to emphasize the contradictory aspects within Nick's existence.

American Gangster is set in the Harlem of the early 1970s; a teeming, run-down area full of drug dealers, where shootings are commonplace and the police officers turn a blind eye to almost every crime. As described in an article published in *The Reeler* (2007), Harlem at that time was just "a big party every day, and you did whatever you had to do to be relevant. It was like being bigger than a movie star." The film brings this out with the portrayal of Nicky Barnes (CUBA GOODING JR.), who spends much of his time either stoned or playing around with naked women. DENZEL WASHINGTON was quoted in the same Reeler article as saying that the film was "a Harlem story . . . about a guy who's a kingpin . . . a guy from uptown."

Reference

S. T. VanAirsdale, "When Kingpins Collide: Searching for 'The Real Harlem' in *American Gangster* and *Mr. Untouchable*," *The Reeler*, 1 November 2007, www.thereeler.com/features/when_kingpins _collide.php (accessed 12 February 2009).

NICHOLSON, WILLIAM (1948–)

Nominated for an Academy Award for his screenplay of *Shadowlands* (1983). Other writing credits include *Nell* (with

JODIE FOSTER), *First Knight* (with Sean Connery), and *Sarafina!* with Whoopi Goldberg.

Nicholson was brought in as a third writer on *GLADIATOR* to make day-to-day revisions. He was quoted as saying that when he came on board for the production, "Maximus (RUSSELL CROWE) was just a killing machine. I changed the story so that he was acting out of love, not hate." He worked his friendship with Juba (DJIMON HOUNSOU) and developed the afterlife thread in the film, saying he "did not want to see a film about a man who wanted to kill somebody." The original screenwriter DAVID FRANZONI was later brought back to revise the rewrites of Nicholson and co-writer JOHN LOGAN, and in the process gained a producer's credit. When Nicholson was brought in, he started going back to Franzoni's original scripts and putting certain scenes back in. Franzoni helped creatively manage the rewrites and in the role of producer he defended his original script, and nagged to stay true to the original vision. The screenplay bore the brunt of many rewrites and revisions due to Russell Crowe's script suggestions. Crowe questioned every aspect of the evolving script and strode off the set when he did not get answers. Nicholson claimed that Crowe told him, "Your lines are garbage but I'm the greatest actor in the world, and I can make even garbage sound good." Nicholson goes on to say that "probably my lines were garbage, so he was just talking straight."

References

William Nicholson, quoted in James Russell, *The Historical Epic and Contemporary Hollywood: From* Dances with Wolves *to* Gladiator (New York and London: The Continuum International Publishing Group Inc., 2007), 167; William Nicholson, speech at the launching of the International Screenwriters Festival (January 2006), www.screenwritersfestival.com/news.php?id=3 (accessed 6 December 2008).

NIELSEN, CONNIE (1965–)

Born Connie Inge-Lise Nielsen in Elling, Frederikshavn, Denmark. She made her debut in American films in *Devil's Advocate* (1997) and *Soldier* (1998), before being unexpectedly cast as Lucilla in *GLADIATOR*.

Nielsen described herself in the book of the film as someone "caught between the ambitions of her brother and the will of Maximus, with whom she has a past . . . She lives in a time when women did not have a voice, at least officially . . . But she is her father's daughter and has been raised in the center of much political intrigue, so she is definitely capable of using whatever is at her disposal to survive." Her performance encapsulates the difficulties of being a woman in an aggressively masculine world, subject to the whims of her father and her brother Commodus. Early on in the film she is seen kissing Marcus's (RICHARD HARRIS's) cheek. But this is not a sign of filial affection; rather, it is something she has become accustomed to as one of the emperor's subjects. Her real relationship to her father is summed up in a terse exchange: Marcus asks of her, "pretend that you [Lucilla] are a loving daughter and I a good father." Lucilla replies with heavy irony: "This is a pleasant fiction, isn't it?" The same applies to her relationship with Commodus (JOAQUIN PHOENIX), where she has to play the dutiful sister to a man with incestuous designs on her, while continually looking out for her son Lucius's (Spencer Treat Clark's) welfare. Eventually the task proves too great for her; Commodus discovers her part in the plot to unseat him from the Emperor's throne and declares that she will love him as he loved her: "You will provide me with an heir of pure blood so that Commodus and his progeny will rule for a thousand years. Am I not merciful?" The script continues: "[*He gets close to her face and tries to kiss her but Lucilla turns away. Commodus grabs her by the jaw and turns her face towards him, screaming* 'AM I NOT MERCIFUL?!' *Tears slowly come down Lucilla's face*]." The strain of living in a male-dominated world has become too much for her. When Commodus is killed by Maximus (RUSSELL CROWE), it is not surprising that she should come down into the arena, look at Maximus adoringly, and exclaim "Go to them!" (his wife and son). Maximus can now die himself, having fulfilled the responsibility of freeing Rome—and Lucilla in particular—from tyranny.

Nielsen's character is something of a victim in a world which, as Jennifer Barker remarks, is dominated by "a deceptively 'new' masculinity that is tragically resistant to a dialogics of self, or of democracy, deliberation, reflection and meaning, and instead [people] assert, much like the fascist doctrine they so often mirror, that the male mind must remain locked in the fortress of pure unquestionable certainty."

References

Jennifer Barker, "The Myth of the Fascist Man in *Fight Club* and *Gladiator*," *Literature/Film Quarterly* 36, no.3 (2008): 184; "*Gladiator* by David Franzoni, revised by John Logan," transcribed from the film, http://sfy.ru/sfy/html?script=gladiator_ts (accessed 29 November 2008); Connie Nielsen, quoted in Diana Landau, ed., *Gladiator: The Making of the Ridley Scott Epic* (Basingstoke and London: Boxtree, 2000), 54.

Bibliography

Lesley O'Toole, "On a Mission," *Evening Standard Hot Tickets*, 13 April 2000, 3–4.

NIKE—MAX MAKES TRAX

GB 2008 Commercial 35 sec col. *Production Company*: RSA Films. *Director*: Ridley Scott.

A commercial produced by RSA Asia that shows a runner going through various locations—a cityscape, a lonely mountainous location (recalling *THELMA & LOUISE*), an urban jungle, past skyscrapers, and past a fat slovenly man in a café watching the world go by. As he runs, the voiceover intones the following rhyme: "Look, it's Mark, he likes to run, out in the sun/ He runs past cows, and fields, and trees,/ Runs past fat guys with TVs/ Rains can rain, dogs can bite,/ Stop he won't, he'll run all night,/ So he wants shoes, cushy and light,/ Then he'll feel the runner's joy,/ You can't find in a lazy boy,/ 'I like to run,' he says with a smile,/ I'll think I'll go another mile." The music sounds vaguely comic; but the slogan certainly is not: "Just Do It."

The commercial shows Scott's feeling for landscape; the bare landscape in the middle of a blazing hot day; the yellows and oranges of sunset, the blues and grays of nighttime. It suggests that if anyone buys Nikes, they can run all the time.

NINETEEN EIGHTY-FOUR

George Orwell's landmark DYSTOPIAN novel about life in a dictatorship as lived by Winston Smith, an intellectual worker at the Ministry of Truth, and his degradation when he runs afoul of the totalitarian government of Oceania, the state in which he lives in the year 1984. *Nineteen Eighty-Four* was published in 1949 and has been translated to sixty-two languages. The novel's title, its terms and its language (Newspeak), and its author's surname are bywords for personal privacy lost to national state security. The adjective "Orwellian" denotes totalitarian action and organization; the phrase "Big Brother is watching you" connotes pervasive, invasive surveillance.

Orwell's novel exerted a significant influence over Ridley Scott's early work. In a 1984 interview he suggested that in a film like *ALIEN*, "the value of humans could be diminished. I'm now thinking on the level of the Big Brother idea of a lifeless megastructure and its attitude toward human employees, who are considered expendable. In this instance, the machinery, information data, and cargo are of more importance to corporations than the individuals on their ships."

Scott was to explore the 1984 theme more directly in a famous commercial advertising the APPLE COMPUTERS, broadcast on American television in January 1984.

Reference

"Directing *Alien* and *Blade Runner*: An Interview with Ridley Scott by Danny Peary," in *Omni's Screen Flights: Screen Fantasies: The Future According to Science Fiction Cinema*, ed. Danny Peary (New York: Doubleday Dolphin, 1984), 295.

NISSAN 300ZX TWIN TURBO

US 1990 Commercial r/t 1.5 min. *Production Company*: RSA. *Director*: Ridley Scott.

This commercial has an off-screen narrator admitting that he is "having this dream" of being pursued by enemies in a jet aircraft and a motorcycle, "but they can't catch me." The car is seen driving fast along a racetrack, and is intercut with rapid shots of the pursuers. Just when they are about to catch the car, the driver switches into turbo mode; the car rises off the ground and launches into space (rather like the final scene of *THELMA & LOUISE*). The Nissan logo appears onscreen with the slogan "Built for the Human Race."

This commercial was only aired once during Super Bowl 1990. Evidently Nissan withdrew it on the grounds that it might encourage street racing.

NIVOLA, ALESSANDRO (1972–)

Born in Boston, Massachusetts, Nivola attended Yale University. His screen roles include *Face/Off* (1997), *Mansfield Park* (1999), and *Goal!* (2005). Cast as Leo Kritzky in the television miniseries *THE COMPANY* (2007), Nivola seems an ideal CIA operative—educated, well-groomed, and able to offer sound advice on ways of dealing with the Soviets. He contracts an apparently perfect MARRIAGE to Adelle, the daughter of a high-ranking government official (Kristin Booth) and lives in a nice place in the suburbs of Washington, DC. It is only at the end that we discover that this is all a façade: Kritzky leads a double life as Sasha, and is responsible for passing all the CIA's secrets on to the KGB. In a climactic sequence in part three, Kritzky explains why he pursued this particular course: "I did it because I believed in serving a country whose system of government offered the best hope for the future. That system was socialism . . . I was assigned to her [Adella] to get secrets out of her father." However, the job of being a double agent was not always an easy one: "Do you think this is what I had in mind when I joined [the CIA]? Do you think this is what I signed up for? . . . I want to protect my children. That's why I stayed, to protect my kids."

However, Kritzky's political commitment eventually proves futile, as he is forced to spend the remainder of his life in a Soviet Union undergoing rapid democratization during the Gorbachev era. It comes as no surprise to find Kritzky observing to Yevgeny Tsipin (RORY COCHRANE) that this kind of government was "not the ideal [he] fought for all these years."

NO COUNTRY FOR OLD MEN

US 2007 r/t 122 min col. *Production Companies*: Paramount Vintage, Miramax Films, Scott Rudin Productions, and Mike Zoss Productions. *Producers*: Scott Rudin, Ethan and Joel Coen. *Directors*: Ethan and Joel Coen. *Writers*: Ethan and Joel Coen, based on the book by Cormac McCarthy. *Director of Photography*: Roger Deakins. *Production Designer*: Jess Gonchor. *Music*: Carter Burwell. *Cast*: Tommy Lee Jones

(*Sheriff Ed Tom Bell*), Javier Bardem (*Anton Chigurh*), Josh Brolin (*Llewelyn Moss*), Woody Harrelson (*Carson Wells*), Kelly Macdonald (*Carla Jean Moss*).

Oscar-winning adaptation released in America at the same time as *THE ASSASSINATION OF JESSE JAMES BY THE COWARD ROBERT FORD*. The Western theme might be the same; but this film veers towards comedy in its depiction of a man who finds and takes the money from a drug deal gone wrong, and finds himself pursued by a psychopath who also wants the money. Director of photography ROGER DEAKINS also worked on *The Assassination*.

NOLAN, KEN (1967–)

Screenwriter, educated at the University of Oregon, who was brought in by producer JERRY BRUCKHEIMER to work on the script of *BLACK HAWK DOWN*—his first produced screenplay. He wrote several drafts before Scott was confirmed as director; even when filming took place, he was still writing and rewriting the script. Nolan recalled that his primary aim was to move the story along at a breakneck pace: "We knew that this was an important story. None of us wanted to disrespect the memories of the brave soldiers who fought and died on the streets of Mogadishu. None of us wanted to make a mediocre film that would somehow trivialize what the soldiers did. But . . . some things simply had to be changed or they wouldn't make sense to the viewer . . . I wanted to make the story as realistic as possible, but also deliver a piece of entertainment that would grip readers by the throat for two and a half hours and not let them go . . . I wanted every draft of the script to read the way Mark's book did for me the first time I read *Black Hawk Down*—an incredibly visceral story that kept me turning the pages and wondering what would happen next . . . My job was to thrust the reader onto the streets of Mogadishu, and keep him or her there. My job was to make the reader care about the characters, and to keep turning the pages."

Some of the soldiers involved in the original raid had their names changed: Grimes (EWAN McGREGOR) was based on John Stebbins, who had been awarded a Silver Star for bravery during the conflict, but had subsequently been convicted of molesting his daughter (hence the name-change). Eversmann (JOSH HARTNETT) was a composite character based on more than one real person; so was Sanderson (WILLIAM FICHTNER). Nolan also changed certain characters' roles from the book: when Steele (JASON ISAACS) tours the Olympic Stadium, he speaks to Ruiz (Enrique Murciano) who cries "Don't go back there [into battle] without me. I can still do my job." In MARK BOWDEN's original book, Steele speaks to someone else.

Nolan introduced new scenes that did not exist in the original book—for example, the conversational exchange between Eversmann and Hoot as they discuss the morality of the forthcoming conflict: "You don't think we should be here"/ "*Hoot*: Know what I think? Don't really matter what I think. Once that first bullet goes past your head—politics, and all that shit—just goes right out of the window." Ruiz's (Enrique Murciano's) part was expanded; he now had a soliloquy delivered in voice-over at the end of the film where he talks to his family: "Keep smiling and never give up, even when things get you down. So in closing my love, tonight, tuck my children in bed warmly. Tell them I love them." Even though he has perished in battle, he dies thinking of his family first. Other scenes were inserted so as to increase the film's action—for example, Durant (Ron Eldard) being attacked by the Somali mob.

In an interview with Alan Waldman, Nolan admitted that the experience of working on the film taught him gave him a renewed understanding of his generation. Whereas many cynics believed that young men of the late 1990s were part of Generation X, which did not really believe in anything, Nolan emphasized how *Black Hawk Down* showed that people did believe in traditional values such as patriotism, family, and doing one's duty: "I realized it was important for the audience to care for the characters, lest it [the film] became a cold, distant movie that lacks gut punch."

Nolan's subsequent work includes writing the teleplay for the miniseries *THE COMPANY*, produced by Scott. He recalled in the production notes that he "was approached by JOHN CALLEY about doing an adaptation of Robert Littell's novel, so I read the book and was totally hooked after the first sixty pages. I did a draft in about six months, but it was still too long—there was so much story to tell. So I trimmed about 150 pages and got it to the point where I could then work with David W. Zucker (co-executive producer) to format it for television." The experience of writing the film proved problematic: "I wasn't sure which characters were real and which were fictitious, so I visited Robert at his home in France. We talked a bit about the project, but it only seemed to add to the mystery. Who was really who? Did he ever work for the CIA? Was he a spy? I still don't know." Among the changes Nolan introduced to the script was to make the central character Jack McCauliffe (CHRIS O'DONNELL) a single man who never managed to find a suitable partner throughout his long career in the CIA (in Littell's book he was a married man). This alteration emphasized the loneliness of the spy's existence; he could never trust anyone sufficiently to settle down.

References

Ken Nolan, *Black Hawk Down: The Shooting Script* (New York: Newmarket Press, 2002), xx, 31, 125, 128; Production Notes: The Company, www.tnt.tv/series/thecompany/bts/ (accessed 12 August 2008); Alan Waldman, interview with Ken Nolan (January 2002), www.gather.com/viewArticle.jsp?articleId=281474976744830 (accessed 2 January 2009)

Bibliography

Mark Bowden and Ken Nolan, Commentary to the 2-disc DVD release of *Black Hawk Down* (Los Angeles: Revolution Studios Distribution Company LLG & Jerry Bruckheimer, Inc.), 2004.

NORTON, EDWARD (1969–)

Born Edward Harrison Norton in Boston, Massachusetts. Made his debut in the courtroom thriller *Primal Fear* (1996), for which he received an Oscar nomination. In *KINGDOM OF HEAVEN* Norton has a small (uncredited) role as King Baldwin IV of Jerusalem, a role he apparently played "for kicks," using his best "James Mason voice." A victim of leprosy, he appears in an iron mask covering up his ravaged face. Baldwin remains a figure of decency throughout the film; while concerned for his people's welfare, he nonetheless makes sterling efforts to forge a peaceful solution to the ongoing conflict with Saladin (GHASSAN MASSOUD). Despite his illness, he insists on leading his troops into battle and, once a truce has been forged, promises to deal with those who have acted disloyally—for example, Reynald de Chatillon (BRENDAN GLEESON), who has massacred innocent Muslims in cold blood. Baldwin is acutely conscious of his role as a figurehead: "I am Jerusalem and you, Reynald, will give me the kiss of peace!"

In *KINGDOM OF HEAVEN*: THE DIRECTOR'S CUT Baldwin's role is expanded slightly; he is shown refusing the Last Sacrament from the Patriarch (Jon Finch), in the belief that he has failed his people. On his death, the Director's Cut shows Baldwin IV being succeeded by Baldwin V, son of Sibylla (EVA GREEN) and her first husband William of Montferrat. The boy is discovered to have leprosy, so the queen kills him as an act of mercy by dropping poison in his ear. Only then does she marry Guy de Lusignan (MARTON CSOKAS). Norton's performance was described by Jack Moore of *Movie Insider* as "phenomenal, so far removed from anything that he has ever done that we see the true complexities of his talent."

References

Jack Moore, "Movie Reviews: *Kingdom of Heaven* (2005)," *The Movie Insider*, www.themovieinsider.com/reviews/rid/615/Kingdom_of_Heaven (accessed 15 January 2009); Edward Norton, quoted on his website, www.edward-norton.org/kingdomofheaven.html (accessed 15 January 2009).

NOSTROMO

First appeared in book form in 1904. In *ALIEN* Ridley Scott acknowledges Conrad's influence by naming the spaceship *Nostromo* (it was once called the *Snark*), and the module (that blasts off from the spaceship at the end of the film) *Narcissus* (after the novel *The Nigger of the Narcissus*). Reviewers felt that the Conradian echoes were largely insignificant: Derek Elley in *Films and Filming* observed that they were "left dangling for what it is worth." Perhaps Scott has a motive for including such allusions: Robert Hampson writes that *Nostromo*'s general historical context was the emergence of the United States as an imperial power. Costaguana was conceived as a South American state in general, where the practice of COLONIALISM was rife. *Alien* likewise explores the concept of imperialism through the Company, which sends the *Nostromo* into space and asks the crew to bring back the alien for the purposes of experimentation. No one—especially the crew—should think for themselves; to ensure this, Ash (IAN HOLM) is placed among them.

Hampson also suggests that *Nostromo* is about the destructive effects of capitalism, how colonizers destroy the lives of the indigenous people in Costaguana and subsequently exploit them. This is precisely what happens to the crew in *Alien*: as Ash observes, they are expendable in the Company's scheme of things, so long as the alien is safely returned to earth.

Conrad's novel explores the concept of "layering"; the creation of a city which, although ruled by a colonial power, nonetheless allows for the creation of a composite space, a milieu that is heterogeneous and multiple in its effect. The city Sulaco is an unstable space in which readers can never confidently orientate themselves. *Alien* uses a similar effect of layering by means of sound, music, and vision within a single shot, to establish a similarly unstable space. This is especially evident when Ripley (SIGOURNEY WEAVER) escapes in the *Narcissus*, and strips down to T-shirt and panties, in the mistaken belief that she is now safe. There is no such thing as certainty for her; she can never be free of the alien's influence. More significantly, Ripley's presence in this scene is ambiguous: is she actually in control of the situation, a dominant woman reasserting control, or an object of desire for alien and (male) spectator alike? Scott refuses to provide answers, his photography, romantic music and characterization encouraging multiple responses.

References

Derek Elley, "Alien," *Films and Filming*, October 1979, 32; Robert Hampson, "Conrad's Heterotopic Fiction: Composite Maps, Superimposed Sites, and Impossible Spaces," in *Conrad in the Twenty-First Century*, ed. Carola M. Kaplan, Peter Lancelot-Mallios, and Andrea White (London and New York: Routledge, 2005), 132–33.

NUMB3RS

US 2005 TV series 79 × 42 min episodes (to 16 May 2008). *Production Companies*: Paramount Network Television, Scott Free and the Barry Schindel Company. *Executive Producers*: Nicolas Falacci, Cheryl Heuton, Ridley Scott, Tony Scott, and

David W. Zucker. *Producers*: Christine Larson, Michael Attanasio, Bobby Roth, Timothy Silver. *Directors*: John Behring (eleven episodes 2005–2008), J. Miller Tobin (eleven episodes 2005–2007), Alex Zakrzewski (nine episodes 2005–2008), Dennis Smith (eight episodes 2005–2008). *Writers*: Nicolas Falacci, Cheryl Heuton (all episodes). *Directors of Photography*: Ronald Victor Garcia (forty-three episodes 2005–), Bing Sokolsky (thirty-three episodes 2006–). *Production Designer*: Bill Eigenbrodt (seventy-four episodes 2005–). *Music*: Charles Clouser (seventy-two episodes 2005–). *Cast*: David Krumholtz (*Charlie Eppes*), Rob Morrow (*Don Eppes*), Judd Hirsch (*Alan Eppes*), Alimi Ballard (*David Sinclair*), Peter MacNicol (*Dr. Larry Fleinhardt*), Navi Rawat (*Amita Ramanujan*), Dylan Bruno (*Colby Granger*), Diane Farr (*Megan Reeves*) (from Series 2 onwards), Aya Sumika (*Liz Warner*) (from Series 2 onwards), Sabrina Lloyd (*Terry Lake*) (Series 1 only).

Episodes List (to the end of Series 4 [May 2008])

Series 1

1. "Pilot" (broadcast 23 January 2005). *Directors*: Davis Guggenheim and Mick Jackson. To help capture a serial rapist-turned-killer, Don Eppes (ROB MORROW) recruits his academic brother Charlie (DAVID KRUMHOLTZ), who uses math to identify the killer's point of origin.
2. "Uncertainty Principle" (broadcast 28 January 2005). *Director*: David von Ancken. Charlie accurately predicts where a band of bank robbers will strike next, but is shocked and withdraws from the case when Don and his team become involved in a deadly gun battle.
3. "Vector" (broadcast 4 February 2005). *Director*: David von Ancken. Don and Charlie fight a race against time when a deadly virus hits LOS ANGELES.
4. "Structural Corruption" (broadcast 11 February 2005). *Director*: Tim Matheson. Charlie does not believe the death of an engineering student was a suicide and asks Don to investigate. The trail leads to a high-rise building full of structural faults.
5. "Prime Suspect" (broadcast 18 February 2005). *Director*: Lesli Linka Glatter. The five-year-old daughter of a mathematician is kidnapped, and Don and Terry must rely on Charlie's help when it becomes apparent that the crime revolves the Riemann Hypothesis.
6. "Sabotage" (broadcast 25 February 2005). *Director*: Lou Antonio. A series of train wrecks yields only one clue—a cryptic note left at each site.
7. "Counterfeit Reality" (broadcast 11 March 2005). *Director*: Alex Zakrzewski. A counterfeiting case involving small amounts of dollars is complicated by the kidnapping of a talented artist.

8. "Identity Crisis" (broadcast 1 April 2005). *Director*: Martha Mitchell. The murder of a stock-fraud suspect has Don questioning a previous arrest.
9. "Sniper Zero" (broadcast 15 April 2005). *Director*: J. Miller Tobin. Los Angeles is under siege as a sniper goes on a shooting spree. With Lou Diamond Phillips.
10. "Dirty Bomb" (broadcast 22 April 2005). *Director*: Paris Barclay. Thieves hijack a truck carrying radioactive material and demand a ransom of $20 million or they will detonate a bomb somewhere in Los Angeles.
11. "Sacrifice" (broadcast 29 April 2005). *Director*: Paul Holahan. A computer researcher is murdered in his home in the Hollywood hills; missing from his computer are files containing data on a secret government project.
12. "Noisy Edge" (broadcast 6 May 2005). *Director*: J. Miller Tobin. Fears of a terrorist attack are raised when eyewitnesses report a mysterious unidentified craft flying dangerously close to downtown Los Angeles.
13. "Man Hunt" (broadcast 13 May 2005). *Director:* Martha Mitchell. Don teams up with a former partner after a prison bus allows a violent felon to escape. With Lou Diamond Phillips.

Series 2

1. "Judgment Call" (broadcast 23 September 2005). *Director*: Alex Zakrzewski. Don helps to capture the killer of a federal judge's wife, with the help of newly recruited FBI academy graduate Megan Reeves (DIANE FARR).
2. "Better or Worse" (broadcast 30 September 2005). *Director*: J. Miller Tobin. An upscale jewelry store owner's family is kidnapped and held for ransom.
3. "Obsession" (broadcast 7 October 2005). *Director*: John Behring. A popular singer is receiving death threats from an obsessed stalker—or stalkers.
4. "Calculated Risk" (broadcast 14 October 2005). *Director*: Bill Eagles. A female CEO of a powerful energy company is murdered and her son is the sole witness.
5. "Assassin" (broadcast 21 October 2005). *Director*: Bobby Roth. Don uncovers a code that triggers a hunt for an assassin pursuing a Colombian exile in Los Angeles.
6. "Soft Target" (broadcast 4 November 2005). *Director*: Andy Wolk. Thousands of commuters are put at risk by a lethal chemical carried by mysterious people on the city's subway system.
7. "Convergence" (broadcast 11 November 2005). *Director*: Dennis Smith. Don investigates a connection between a series of robberies and the murder of a rich person.
8. "In Plain Sight" (broadcast 18 November 2005). *Director*: John Behring. An explosion at a methamphetamine laboratory leaves Megan feeling responsible for an agent's death.

9. "Toxin" (broadcast 25 November 2005). *Director:* Jefery Levy. Don and his team investigate mysterious poisonings linked to a manifesto published in a local paper.

10. "Bones of Contention" (broadcast 9 December 2005). *Director:* Jeannot Szwarc. The murder of a researcher at a Native American museum brings the FBI in to investigate.

11. "Scorched" (broadcast 16 December 2005). *Director:* Norberto Barba. Charlie investigates a series of arson attacks that have plagued the city.

12. "The O.G." (broadcast 6 January 2006). *Director:* Rod Holcomb. The murder of a Los Angeles gang member brings Don and his team in to investigate the death of a fellow agent.

13. "Double Down" (broadcast 13 January 2006). *Director:* Alex Zakrzewski. A Russian blackjack player ends up dead at a Los Angeles card club after a winning streak.

14. "Harvest" (broadcast 27 January 2006). *Director:* John Behring. The discovery of a girl tortured in a downtown hotel leads to a black market organ-harvesting scheme.

15. "The Running Man" (broadcast 3 February 2006). *Director:* Terrence O'Hara. The college campus where Charlie works is hit with the theft of a DNA synthesizer.

16. "Protest" (broadcast March 3, 2006). *Director:* Dennis Smith. An antiwar protest from the 1970s resurfaces at the time of the Iraq war.

17. "Mind Games" (broadcast 10 March 2006). *Director:* Peter Markle. A psychic offers to help Don solve the murders of three women killed under bizarre circumstances.

18. "All's Fair" (broadcast 31 March 2006). *Director:* Rob Morrow. Don investigates the murder of an Iraqi woman and discovers a connection to Saddam Hussein.

19. "Dark Matter" (broadcast 7 April 2006). *Director:* Peter Ellis. Charlie traces two culprits responsible for a shooting at a school, and finds a third person may be involved.

20. "Guns and Roses" (broadcast 21 April 2006). *Director:* Stephen Gyllenhaal. Don discovers that a murder victim was one of his old girlfriends.

21. "Rampage" (broadcast 28 April 2006). *Director:* J. Miller Tobin. A shooter terrorizes the FBI's office.

22. "Backscatter" (broadcast 5 May 2006). *Director:* Bill Eagles. The FBI investigates the disappearance of two bank employees and a case of bank fraud.

23. "Undercurrents" (broadcast 12 May 2006). *Director:* J. Miller Tobin. The sea yields the bodies of several young Asian girls linked to a sex-slave ring operating in the USA.

24. "Hot Shot" (broadcast 19 May 2006). *Director:* John Behring. A killer drugs women, murders them, and then carefully dresses them before placing them in their cars in their own driveways.

Series 3

1. "Spree" (broadcast 22 September 2006). *Director:* John Behring. Don tries to catch a young couple whose seven-state robbery spree has turned to murder.

2. "Two Daughters" (broadcast 29 September 2006). *Director:* Alex Zakrzewski. Megan is kidnapped by a pair of killers.

3. "Provenance" (broadcast 6 October 2006). *Director:* David von Ancken. A valuable painting belonging to the Nazis is stolen and its theft leads to murder.

4. "The Mole" (broadcast 13 October 2006). *Director:* Stephen Gyllenhaal. The team is drawn into a fascinating case when a Chinese interpreter is found dead.

5. "Traffic" (broadcast 20 October 2006). *Director:* J. Miller Tobin. The FBI team discovers links between a series of apparently random attacks on Los Angeles highways.

6. "Longshot" (broadcast 27 October 2006). *Director:* John Behring. Don and his team investigate a mysterious death at a racetrack.

7. "Blackout" (broadcast 3 November 2006). *Director:* Scott Lautanen. Los Angeles is plagued by a series of power failures; are they the result of an accident or something more sinister?

8. "Hardball" (broadcast 10 November 2006). *Director:* Fred Keller. A minor league baseball player winds up dead, and the investigation leads to a major doping ring involving the entire team.

9. "Waste Not" (broadcast 17 November 2006). *Director:* J. Miller Tobin. The investigation of a sinkhole in a schoolyard leads to a toxic case involving illegal waste disposal.

10. "Brutus" (broadcast 24 November 2006). *Director:* Oz Scott. Don uncovers a connection between two murder victims—a California state senator and a psychiatrist.

11. "Killer Chat" (broadcast 15 December 2006). *Director:* Chris Hartwill. Larry Fleinhardt (PETER MACNICOL) prepares for a mission with NASA while Don and Charlie track a killer who has murdered several sex predators.

12. "Nine Wives" (broadcast 5 January 2007). *Director:* Julie Hébert. A polygamist lands on the FBI's wanted list.

13. "Finders Keepers" (broadcast 12 January 2007). *Director:* Colin Bucksey. An expensive yacht sinks off the California coast and becomes an attractive prospect for thrill-seekers.

14. "Take Out" (broadcast 2 February 2007). *Director:* Leslie Libman. A series of robberies at upscale Los Angeles restaurants bring the FBI team in when one of them turns to murder.

15. "End of Watch" (broadcast 9 February 2007). *Director:* Michael Watkins. A police badge found at a construction site leads to the investigation of an unsolved murder committed seventeen years before.

16. "Contenders" (broadcast 16 February 2007). *Director:* Alex Zakrzewski. David Sinclair (ALIMI BALLARD) is stunned to discover that one of his childhood friends is accused of murder.

17. "One Hour "(broadcast 23 February 2007). *Director:* J. Miller Tobin. In Don's absence Granger (DYLAN BRUNO) leads the team in a hunt for a kidnapper demanding a $3 million ransom.

18. "Democracy" (broadcast 9 March 2007). *Director:* Steve Boyum. Several local deaths are tied to a voter fraud; the case becomes personal when Don's old colleague becomes one of the victims.

19. "Pandora's Box" (broadcast 30 March 2007). *Director:* Dennis Smith. Charlie investigates the crash of a corporate jet while trying to deal with a burglary at home.

20. "Burn Rate" (broadcast 6 April 2007). *Director:* Frederick J. Keller. A series of explosions are similar to the work of a long-imprisoned bomber. Is he at it again, or is there a copycat?

21. "The Art of Reckoning" (broadcast 27 April 2007). *Director:* John Behring. Don becomes suspicious when a hit man wants to confess to his crimes and help the FBI solve his wrongdoings.

22. "Under Pressure" (broadcast 4 May 2007). *Director:* J. Miller Tobin. The threat of a terrorist attack on Los Angeles involving the city's water supply puts everyone on edge.

23. "Money for Nothing" (broadcast 11 May 2007). *Director:* Stephen Gyllenhaal. Medical supplies earmarked for Africa are stolen.

24. "The Janus List" (broadcast 18 May 2007). *Director:* John Behring. A barricaded bomber reveals information that has a profound effect on the FBI team.

Series 4

1. "Trust Metric" (broadcast 28 September 2007). *Director:* Tony Scott. Was Granger really a double agent working for the Chinese? He escapes from prison and the FBI team attempt to track him down. With Val Kilmer.

2. "Hollywood Homicide" (broadcast 5 October 2007). *Director:* Alex Zakrzewski. Granger is back on the job but only temporarily until he is reassigned. The team investigates a murder among the Hollywood jet-set.

3. "Velocity" (broadcast 12 October 2007). *Director:* Fred Keller. The team investigates an out-of-control car driven by a teenager which smashes into a coffee shop, killing one person.

4. "Thirteen" (broadcast 19 October 2007). *Director:* Ralph Hemecker. A serial killer is obsessed with replicating the deaths of Jesus Christ's apostles, and leaves biblical verses at the site of each murder.

5. "Robin Hood" (broadcast 26 October 2007). *Director:* J. Miller Tobin. Larry contemplates the prospect of leaving his monastery; while a bank vault is raided by apparent "do-gooder."

6. "In Security" (broadcast 2 November 2007). *Director:* Stephen Gyllenhaal. One of Don's ex-lovers is murdered and he fears that he might have led the killer right to her.

7. "Primacy" (broadcast 9 November 2007). *Director:* Chris Hartwill. Amita Ramanujan (NAVI RAWAT) is forced to introduce the team to the obsessive world of video games after a man plunges to his death while participating in one such game.

8. "Tabu" (broadcast 16 November 2007). *Director:* Alex Zakrzewski. An extremist group targets an heiress to punish her rich father, but he refuses to negotiate. With William Atherton.

9. "Graphic" (broadcast 23 November 2007). *Director:* John Behring. David takes an interest in a theft of an extremely rare comic. With Christopher Lloyd and Will Wheaton.

10. "Chinese Box" (broadcast 14 December 2007). *Director:* Dennis Smith. Sinclair is trapped in an elevator with a gun-toting paranoid.

11. "Breaking Point" (broadcast 11 January 2008). *Director:* Craig Ross Jr. Charlie becomes the subject of a thuggish intimidation which inhibits his ability to carry out his job.

12. "Power" (broadcast 18 January 2008). *Director:* Julie Hébert. A serial rapist uses his position as a police officer to ensnare and assault his victims.

13. "Black Swan" (broadcast 4 April 2008). *Director:* John Behring. The team suspects they have stumbled upon a member of a terrorist cell planning an attack on Los Angeles.

14. "Checkmate" (broadcast 11 April 2008). *Director:* Stephen Gyllenhaal. Don's ex-girlfriend Robin Brooks tries to prosecute a criminal leader but finds herself on the leader's hit list. The FBI team tries to protect her.

15. "End Game" (broadcast 25 April 2008). *Director:* Dennis Smith. A man's father and sister are kidnapped by a gang of military thieves because they believe he knows the location of stolen money in Iraq.

16. "Atomic No. 33" (broadcast 2 May 2008). *Director:* Leslie Libman. A mass poisoning at a cult compound leads Don and his team into a complex murder plot.

17. "Pay to Play" (broadcast 9 May 2008). *Director:* Alex Zakrzewski. The murder of a rap star leads to the discovery of a conspiracy of embezzlement and bribery.

18. "When Worlds Collide" (broadcast 16 May 2008). *Director:* John Behring. Don and Charlie find themselves in conflict over differing beliefs as they investigate a case involving national security.

Until the husband-and-wife team Cheryl Heuton and Nicolas Falacci managed to sign a deal with SCOTT FREE and CBS Television, they had not had a single script accepted during their fifteen-year writing career. The inspiration for *Numb3rs* came from Falacci, who had been reading math books for at least a decade. In an interview published on the MIT website, Heuton admitted that she had experienced a lot of problems with the subject at school: "I won't say I disliked it, but I had a lot of trouble understanding it, and I remember . . . I would end up in these really advanced math courses, not by my choice—my counselors always thought I should be in them." In other interviews the creators insisted that they wanted to "set a different tone for this show. In the real world, cops often have that sardonic attitude towards work. Here we have this cast of gifted comic actors who are really dealing with an offbeat premise. It helps make the math—and the crime—not too dour."

Numb3rs gave both writers the chance to popularize math; after consultations with leading scholars and reading up on the subject, they pitched the idea to David L. Zucker of Scott Free. Scott admitted in another interview with *Broadcasting & Cable*, "Within a page of *Numb3rs*, I'm fully in, holding my breath and hoping to God they [the writers] don't drop the ball. I'm intrigued." The creators told *Emmy* magazine that their most difficult task was to find interesting metaphors, as a way of "translating [mathematical] things into simple terms . . . But it's the most fun, too." *Numb3rs* could also appeal to viewers who were not so keen on math on account of its basic theme: "It's all about family . . . about two brothers who look at the world very differently but who have come together to do very important work."

CBS commissioned a half-season of thirteen episodes beginning in early 2005. Originally the series was to have been situated at the Massachusetts Institute of Technology (MIT). When Gary Lorden, the chairman of the math department at Caltech agreed to consult on the series, however, the creators shifted the location there, using Los Angeles landscapes as a backdrop to the series. The pilot was first shown at Caltech and it received a standing ovation from the audience. Viewers were equally enthusiastic: *TV Guide* reported in May 2005 that *Numb3rs* had "has held steady in its regular Friday-night time slot, averaging 11.7 million viewers. That kind of reception has [David] Krumholtz feeling pretty good about the odds of CBS renewing the show." The main reason for the show's success was that it not only made math seem attractive but focused on "the complicated relationship between Charlie [DAVID KRUMHOLTZ] and Don [ROB MORROW]—under the watchful eye of their widowed father [JUDD HIRSCH]." The *Starburst* reviewer went further: And, get this—it [the series] works wonderfully. *Numb3rs* is quite reminiscent of *The X-Files* in its early seasons, suggesting much and explaining only in part the paranormal elements that both shine a light and cast darkness over the situation."

The mathematics used on the show is real—approved by a team of scholars working as consultants on the program. Heuton stressed in the MIT interview that "The math is all . . . applications. We have often applied them in ways that haven't been applied in real life. On the show they tend to be more efficacious and more quick than they would be in real life. All of it is fairly plausible, some of it is exactly. It's funny; some of the things that have been most questioned by mathematicians is stuff that has actually been done and is completely plausible. And sometimes when it's really been out there, no one has said anything."

Since 2005 the series has gone from strength to strength, regularly topping the ratings in its regular Friday night slot. By November of that year the stars were regularly appearing at regional conferences promoting the "We All Use Math Everyday" education program. This unique outreach initiative, promoted in conjunction with the National Council for Teachers of Mathematics (NCTM), used the math featured in the television series to engage and interest more students in the subject and help them see how it affects their world. Krumholtz was reported as saying that "it's really an honor to be part of such an innovative and successful program while at the same time, part of a terrific show . . . One of my favorite things about being an actor is finding ways to use my job to help others . . . It has been both a fun and rewarding learning experience for me as well." This initiative has led to the publication of numerous textbooks using the series as a basis for teaching math, notably *Igniting Creativity in Gifted Learners, K–6: Strategies for Every Teacher* (2008).

TONY SCOTT directed the first episode of series 4 ("Trust Metric"), which re-energized the series for the stars. Morrow likened him in an interview with *The Ledger* to "a conductor, a ramped-up conductor or a circus ringleader in the middle of everything, controlling everything, whipping everything up into a frenzy, every department." Krumholtz hoped that "maybe Tony's episode will be so good that Ridley will get jealous. That brotherly competition will come in. I wouldn't be surprised if one day Ridley Scott directed." To date Scott has not directed any episodes.

Numb3rs follows THE COMPANY and THE ANDROMEDA STRAIN in recognizing the abilities of the expert. While pursuing his own research, Charlie methodically collects data and applies different mathematical theories to it to help solve various crimes for the FBI. Early episodes of *Numb3rs* characterize him as a pedagogue, outlining his ideas in front of the FBI agents with the help of slides, blackboards or other visual aids. From the second series onwards, Charlie collaborates with his colleague (and lover) Amita Ramanujan (NAVI RAWAT) and his former teacher Larry Fleinhardt (PETER MACNICOL). Rather than talking directly to the agents, he explains his ideas in voice-over while the directors of each episode interrupt the narrative with fantasy sequences designed to render his ideas more comprehensible. In other episodes Amita and Larry assume the responsibility of explaining their findings to the viewers and the FBI. Such alterations help to humanize Charlie—he no longer appears like an academic marooned in an ivory tower. In "Man Hunt" (Series 1, Episode 13) he is shown conducting a class, "Math for Non-Mathematicians," for the general public; one of the attendees is his father Alan (Judd Hirsch). By the third series he discovers that there are other things to life besides scientific research; in "Waste Not" (Series 3, Episode 9) his department chair Mildred Finch (Kathy Najimy) encourages him to take more interest in university affairs. He also pursues a long-term relationship with Amita. Moreover, in certain episodes he discovers that mathematics is not the be-all and end-all of existence; sometimes the human element can confound even the most watertight of theories. In "Structural Corruption" (Series 1, Episode 4) he discovers how a student's obsession with work led to the breakup of his family and may have prompted him to commit suicide. In "When Worlds Collide" (Series 4, Episode 18), Charlie defends the reputation of a colleague Phil Sanjrani (Ravi Kapoor), a Pakistani national arrested by the FBI for suspected terrorist activities. This combination of humanity and mathematical acumen has proved particularly attractive to viewers. One fan site outlines his philosophy of life thus: "We all use math everyday to predict weather, to tell time, to handle money. Math is more than formulas and equations, it's logic, it's rationality, it's using your mind to solve the biggest mysteries we know."

Numb3rs emphasizes the importance of the family structure both at home and at work. While Charlie and his brother Don (Rob Morrow) inhabit two different worlds, they are nonetheless very alike in terms of character: "one part exuberance, two parts obsession," as someone puts it in "Counterfeit Reality" (Series 1, Episode 7). We learn a lot about their past lives: Charlie was a mathematical prodigy who went to Princeton when he was thirteen years old, which left Don (who is five years older) feeling jealous of his brother's academic success. Nonetheless, it is clear that they always look out for one another, despite the occasional dispute: Don cannot help but worry about Charlie's safety when Charlie decides to take lessons in shooting and unarmed combat from the FBI ("Checkmate"—Season 4, Episode 14). Their father Alan provides a source of stability for two workaholic sons, offering advice where necessary and providing a shoulder to cry on whenever they run into trouble. In "Two Daughters" (Series 3, Episode 2), Don acts unprofessionally upon learning that Megan Reeves (DIANE FARR) has been kidnapped; Alan takes him aside and reminds him that caring too much for people often leads

them to act unreasonably. To be a good "father"—both at home and at work—a man should learn to detach himself and reflect on the most suitable course of action.

The family structure is equally important in the workplace: Granger (DYLAN BRUNO) at one point remarks that FBI agents can only function effectively when they are part of a team. When he is arrested on suspicion of spying for the Chinese (Season 3, Episode 24), the news proves particularly shocking for his colleagues. Eventually the accusations prove unfounded, and Granger is admitted back into the fold; but the experience demonstrates how everyone in the workplace "family" needs to be vigilant in order to maintain its stability. Otherwise the FBI could resemble some of the dysfunctional "families" (e.g., the gangs) that pose a perpetual threat to the city's social stability. The point is well illustrated in "Spree" (Season 3, Episode 1), where the FBI pursue a Bonnie and Clyde-like couple Crystal Hoyle (Kim Dickens) and Buck Winters (David Gallagher) who commit a series of murders all around the state of California. We learn that Crystal's actions are promoted by revenge, as well as the desire to find her illegitimate daughter who had been placed with foster parents at birth. Family responsibilities mean nothing to her—all she cares about is personal satisfaction, even if it means sacrificing her teenage lover Buck in the process. By contrast, every agent within the FBI fulfills their expected role in helping to apprehend her.

Numb3rs recalls *BLADE RUNNER* in its critique of capitalism—particularly the kind of capitalism that sacrifices individuals in the pursuit of money. In "Toxin" (Season 2, Episode 9) the head of a chemical company tries to discourage the FBI from investigating an outbreak of viral disease, in the belief that it could affect its public image. In "Waste Not" (Series 3, Episode 9) the FBI discover that a large construction firm has been burying toxic waste underneath a school while bribing the principal (Erica Gimpel) to keep quiet about it. When she tries to blow the whistle on them after the playground caves in, leaving some of her students badly injured, the company poisons her. "Democracy" (Series 3, Episode 18) shows how J. Everett Tuttle (William Sadler) deliberately manipulates a local election, while arranging for some of his former employees to be killed off, in case they should make their knowledge public. Putting someone like him behind bars is not only important for the FBI, it will also determine "the fate of democracy" in America (as Don observes).

Like many FILMS AFTER 9/11, *Numb3rs* is not afraid to deal with the threat posed by potential terrorists. "Protest" (Series 2, Episode 16) evokes the spirit of the anti-Vietnam protests of the late 1960s to show how much the world has changed; now innocent people are being blown up for no apparent reason. "All's Fair" (Season 2, Episode 18) describes the world of the early 2000s as "crazy times," as an Iraqi woman visiting America to film an interview on atrocities on women back home is murdered. The action eventually culminates in a shoot-out at a Los Angeles mosque, where the culprit turns out to be an Iraqi national taking revenge on the woman for being "a disgrace to [her] family." Apart from the orientalist slant of the material (Islam is automatically equated with terrorism and violence), the episode suggests that no one is safe anymore. "Blackout" (Season 3, Episode 7) shows the entire city of Los Angeles under threat from potential terrorists who cut the electrical supply to various suburbs. Although the suspect turns out to be a US national, the implication remains that many citizens will exploit the current political situation to cause mayhem. "When Worlds Collide" (Season 4, Episode 18) shows a counter-terrorism expert (Zeljko Ivanek) suspecting a charitable organization, the Pakistan International Fund, of links to Al-Qaeda. Not unreasonably, one employee of that company accuses the FBI of suspecting all Muslims on account of their skin color or religion. Eventually the criminal turns out to be Shane O'Hanahan (Shawn Doyle) a former Irish Republican Army (IRA) member, who has deliberately disguised himself as a Pakistani in order to escape suspicion. We are left to reflect on the fact that the standoff between Christians and Muslims, explored both in *KINGDOM OF HEAVEN* and *BODY OF LIES*, remains unresolved—especially when white law-enforcement officers make erroneous assumptions about innocent Asian people, and Irish terrorists exploit such prejudices to pursue their own activities.

All episodes of *Numb3rs* are set in and around LOS ANGELES, which is depicted as a city of almost perpetual sunshine and imposing skyscrapers. Caltech is a typical campus university with its redbrick buildings, roomy classrooms and offices, and grassy walkways—the ideal milieu for Charlie and his colleagues to work. Such appearances prove deceptive; every street in the city, whether downtown or in the suburbs, can witness the most appalling crimes. Even the SMALL TOWNS outside the city are vulnerable: the action of "Toxin" (Series 2, Episode 9) takes place in Sibley, California, where the deserted streets are very reminiscent of Piedmont, Utah, in *TheAndromeda Strain*.

Numb3rs has spawned several tie-in books such as *The Numbers behind Numb3rs: Solving Crime with Mathematics* by Keith Devlin and Gary Lorden (a consultant to the series), which explains real-life mathematical techniques used by the FBI and other law-enforcement organizations to catch criminals. Julian Havil's *Impossible? Surprising Solutions to Counterintuitive Conundrums* suggests that the series provides a good way of learning how to solve mathematical problems.

Karen Heyman's "Talk Nerdy to Me" explains how the series celebrates the nerd as personified by Charlie Eppes. An article published in the *Journal of Blacks in Higher Education* (2005) shows how life follows art, as the Harvard mathematician (and consultant to *Numb3rs*) Jonathan Farley proposed to use lattice theory to fight the war on terrorism. *Numb3rs*— and Ridley Scott's involvement in it—is also mentioned in Paul Michael Atallah's article "A Usable History for the Study of Television" (2007), while Sasha Torres looks at the series in relation to the criminal mind in America since 9/11.

References

Paul Michael Atallah, "A Usable History for the Study of Television," *Canadian Journal of American Studies* 37, no.3 (2007): 325–49; Jillian Berry, "Creator Examines the Success of the Show and Bemoans Loss of MIT Setting," http://tech.mit.edu/V126/N40/40Numbers.html (accessed 20 February 2009); Keith Devlin and Gary Lorden, *The Numbers behind Numb3rs: Solving Crime with Mathematics* (New York: Plume, 2007); Jim Finkle, "Follow the Numb3rs," *Broadcasting & Cable*, 23 January 2005, www.broadcastingcable.com/article/101609-Follow_the_Numb3rs_.php (accessed 20 February 2009); "Harvard's Summa cum Laude Mathematician Proposes to Use Lattice Theory to Help Win the War on Terrorism," *Journal of Blacks in Higher Education* 48 (Summer 2005): 43; Julian Havil, *Impossible? Surprising Solutions to Counterintuitive Conundrums* (Princeton: Princeton University Press, 2008); Karen Heyman, "Talk Nerdy to Me," *Science* 320, no.5877 (May 9, 2008): 740–41; Mark Nollinger, "Strength in Numbers," *TV Guide*, April 17, 2005, 42–43; "*Numb3rs* Star David Krumholtz to Appear at NCTM Western Regional Conference and Exposition in Denver" (9 November 2005), http://education.ti.com/education-portal/sites/US/nonProductSingle/about_press_release_news74.html (accessed 20 February 2009); Kate O'Hare, "*Numb3rs* Counts on Tony Scott for Action," *The Ledger*, September 28, 2007, D2; Kathleen O'Steen, "Math Blaster," *Emmy* 27, no.3 (May 2005): 180, 185; Joan F. Smutny and Sarah E. von Fremd, *Igniting Creativity in Gifted Learners, K–6: Strategies for Every Teacher* (New York: Corwin Press, 2008); Sasha Torres, "Criminal Minds: Thinking and National Culture Since 9/11," *Review of Education, Pedagogy and Cultural Studies* 30, nos. 3–4 (July 2008): 275–95; Stuart Weightman, "Numbers," *Starburst* 323 (May 2005), 92; "Welcome to Charlie Eppes' World," www.charlieeppes.com/home.htm (accessed February 22, 2009).

Bibliography

Numbers.org Forums. www.fanrush.com/forums/forumdisplay.php?f=15, accessed 20 February 2009); *TV Com: Numb3rs News*. www.tv.com/numb3rs/show/25043/news.html?sort=sls (accessed 20 February 2009).

O'BANNON, DAN (1946–)

Dan O'Bannon first burst on to the fantasy cinema scene with *Dark Star* (1974), which he co-wrote with director John Carpenter. O'Bannon also took a leading role in the film. The next two years proved lean ones—one project, "They Bite" (featuring bizarre carnivorous organisms attracting their prey by camouflaging themselves as everyday objects), came to nothing. O'Bannon was subsequently hired on a project to direct Frank Herbert's *DUNE* for the screen. Again, the idea foundered; but it nonetheless brought together some of the world's finest fantasy artists, including Jean ("Moebius") Giraud, Chris Foss, and H. R. GIGER. Giger would later play a prominent role in designing *ALIEN*.

By early 1975 O'Bannon had teamed up with fellow writer RON SHUSETT to produce a new story based on an uncompleted screenplay "Memory" and another scenario entitled "Gremlins." After further work, the composite structure was transformed into something called "Star Beast." This was the basic story for *Alien*. "Star Beast" begins with the military craft *Snark* encountering a distress call in outer space. Tracing its origins to a desolate planet, the crew investigates and discovers the burnt-out wreckage of another spaceship. The pilot was a being from another world, but is now nothing more than a fossilized shell; the crew takes it back to the *Snark* as a keepsake. However, a small creature has concealed itself within the skull—once in the ship, this creature grows and grows and becomes even more ravenous. One by one the crew members are devoured by the creature, until at the end it is expelled from the *Snark* through an airlock.

O'Bannon worked this story into a screenplay, making minor changes, including the idea of an alien spreading itself over one of the crew members' face and implanting itself within that person (which is what happens to Kane in the finished film).

At this stage the film was planned as a low-budget homage to 1950s sci-fi films such as *THE THING FROM ANOTHER WORLD* and *INVASION OF THE BODY SNATCHERS*. O'Bannon wanted to direct it himself. Eventually the script found its way to the offices of Brandywine Productions, jointly run by WALTER HILL, DAVID GILER,

and GORDON CARROLL. They were attracted to it because of its shocking central "chestbuster" scene (incorporated in O'Bannon's screenplay) in which the alien emerges from the crew member's stomach.

Eventually O'Bannon's script was reworked by Hill and Giler, with O'Bannon relegated to the position of Visual Design Consultant. O'Bannon soon voiced his displeasure at the way in which the script had been altered: a nasty period of arbitration followed, with Giler and Hill on one side and O'Bannon on the other. Eventually it was decided to give O'Bannon sole screenplay credit.

O'Bannon's subsequent career included the screenplay for *The Return of the Living Dead* (1985) and two Canadian films: *Screamers* (1995) and *Bleeders* (1997). More recently, he received a screen story credit for *ALIEN VS. PREDATOR* (2004), on the basis that the filmmakers used material from the first *Alien* screenplay that never actually made it into the film.

Bibliography

David Konow, "*Alien*: 25 Years Later Dan O'Bannon Looks Back on His Scariest Creation," *Creative Screenwriting* 11, no.5 (2004): 70–73; Mark Kermode, "What a Carve Up!" *Sight and Sound*, December 2004, 12–15; Paul Scanlon and Michael Gross, *The Book of Alien* (London: Star Books, 1979); Paul M. Sammon, ed. and intro., *Alien: The Complete Illustrated Screenplay* (London: Orion Books Ltd., 2000); Adam Smith, "Taming the Beast: The Making of the Alien Saga," *Empire*, November 2002, 164–69; "The Starburst Vaults," *Starburst* 349 (1 May 2007): 68–71.

O'DONNELL, CHRIS (1970–)

Early successes included D'Artagnan in the remake of *The Three Musketeers* (1993), Ernest Hemingway in *In Love and War* (1996), and Wardell Pomeroy in *Kinsey* (2004).

Cast as Jack McCauliffe in *THE COMPANY*, O'Donnell plays an Ivy League graduate freshly recruited for service in the CIA. He begins the story as an idealist—he believes that he is genuinely helping to win the Cold War; his view of life is very different from that of old-style operatives such as Harvey Torriti (ALFRED MOLINA), whose "penchant for creativity and a bottle of whiskey a day [is] somewhat removed from what he [Jack] was taught back in Washington." As the story unfolds, however, Jack begins to realize that there is no such thing as right and wrong: operatives have to try and act as best they can, according to the demands of the situation.

By comparison with other members of the cast (notably Molina), O'Donnell gives rather a statuesque performance. But perhaps this is deliberate on director MIKAEL SALOMON's part, to show how well Jack has absorbed Torriti's advice to proceed "onwards and upwards"—in other words, forget what has happened in the past and look to the future. This is the only way to preserve oneself in the spying game.

Reference

Production Notes: The Company, www.tnt.tv/series/thecompany/bts/ (accessed 12 August 2008).

O'HARA, DAVID PATRICK (1965–)

Also known as David O'Hara, his early films include *Braveheart* (1995) and *The Slab Boys* (1997), followed in the next decade by *Hotel Rwanda* (2004).

Cast as the Irish King Donnchadh in *TRISTAN + ISOLDE*, O'Hara plays someone who according to producer Jim Lemley was simultaneously "malevolent and powerful . . . [who] has a hair trigger temper, but is also powerful and stoic." His best moments come early on in the film when he emphasizes the importance of duty to his daughter Isolde (SOPHIA MYLES). It is evident he has no real feeling for her; she is just a pawn in his struggle to assume absolute power over the English. He utters his lines with malevolent relish, taking care to emphasize the consonants in every word: "You have a duty to your King . . . Then obey me, daughter"; "You'll find no refuge in a new religion. Your place is here, with Morholt." Although his assault on King Marke's (RUFUS SEWELL) castle is repelled, we do not know what happens to Donnchadh at the end of the film. Initially we learn that the English have driven the Irish back, but that they are still in an offensive position; but then a title card informs us that Marke eventually defeated the Irish, rebuilt his castle and lived in peace until his death. It would have been helpful to learn the Irish king's fate—particularly as he seems to have such an overwhelming physical presence.

References

Jim Lemley, quoted in *Production Notes: Tristan + Isolde* (Los Angeles: Twentieth Century-Fox, 2005), viii; "*Tristan + Isolde*, Written by Dean Georgaris, Transcript by Chani at tristanandisolde.net," www.imsdb.com/Movie%20Scripts/Tristan%20and%20Isolde%20Script.html (accessed 23 January 2009).

OLDMAN, GARY (1958–)

British actor and director, the star of successful films such as *Prick Up Your Ears* (1987), *JFK* (1991), and *Bram Stoker's Dracula* (1992).

Cast as Mason Verger in HANNIBAL, Oldman described the character to Helen Keier as "the villain, I'd say. It's [the film is] melodrama, you know, and it's very humorous, like black humor, dark humor. I find the film very funny." He takes a positive pleasure in playing the educated villain who cannot be brought to trial because of his wealth. By contrast, someone like Clarice Starling (JULIANNE MOORE) will always suffer from "the stigma of [her] recent dishonor"—in other words, the botched drug-raid where she was responsible for the death of five people. STEVEN ZAILLIAN's script stresses that, as a result of Hannibal's violence in *THE SILENCE OF THE LAMBS*, Verger "has no face to speak of . . . He looks like some kind of creature that resides in the lowest depths of the sea." However the notion of "facelessness" sums up Verger's character—unlike either Hannibal or Clarice, he has no particular aim in life except revenge. He meets a grisly fate at the end of the film, eaten up by the hungry boars that he hoped would devour Hannibal.

Oldman had his name removed from the film's final credits. While he claimed to Keier that it was done as a joke ("The man with no face and no name, and sort of do it anonymously. It's no secret that I'm in the film. We just had fun with it, really"), some critics have suggested that the decision sprang from an argument over star billing.

Oldman has a cameo role in *THE HIRE*: "BEAT THE DEVIL," where he hams it up outrageously as the Devil, getting the chance to peel eggs (in a shot recalling Robert De Niro in *Angel* (1987).

References

Helen Keier, "Interview with Gary Oldman" (26 February 2001), http://uk.movies.ign.com/articles/035/035937p1.html (accessed 5 August 2008); Steven Zaillian, "*Hannibal*: Screenplay Based on the Novel by Thomas Harris," Revision (9 February 2000), http://sfy.ru/sfy.html?script=hannibal2001 (accessed 15 December 2008).

OLMOS, EDWARD JAMES (1947–)

Edward James Olmos's first big break was in Luis Valdez's play *Zoot Suit* (1978) which earned him a Tony nomination. The production was filmed three years later.

As Gaff in *BLADE RUNNER*, Olmos is one of the most memorable characters; a multilingual company man with a penchant for model-making. In one scene the camera cuts from Deckard's (HARRISON FORD's) hands doing police work to Gaff's hands creating a matchstick figure with an erection. This moment calls Deckard's status into question—is he human or a REPLICANT? In the DIRECTOR'S CUT of the film (1992), this question is apparently answered as Gaff's aluminum foil model of a unicorn (briefly glimpsed towards the end) reminds us of Deckard's dream of a unicorn, and thereby suggests that the thought has been artificially implanted in Deckard's mind.

At the beginning of *Blade Runner* Gaff seems dedicated to his work and nothing else. By the end he has changed; having watched Deckard from the sidelines, Gaff comes to understand a little more about the significance of life and death. This explains why he compliments Deckard on having completed "a man's job" (in PAUL M. SAMMON's phrase) and subsequently lets Rachael (SEAN YOUNG) live.

Perhaps best known for his work as Lieutenant Castillo in *Miami Vice* (1984–1989), Olmos received an Oscar nomination for his role in *Stand and Deliver* (1988). He made his directing debut with *American Me* (1992). He was once married to LORRAINE BRACCO, who played Ellie Keegan in *SOMEONE TO WATCH OVER ME*.

Reference

Paul M. Sammon, *Future Noir: The Making of Blade Runner*, 2nd ed. (London: Gollancz, 2007), 198–99.

ORANGE: FUTURE THOUGHTS

GB 1998 Commercial r/t 45 sec col. *Production Company:* RSA Films for WCRS. *Writers:* Leon Jaume and Larry Barker. *Director:* Ridley Scott.

A commercial produced to advertise the company as a cutting-edge technology company. Filmed in other-worldly colors, Scott's ad takes a tongue-in-cheek look at a future where technology has become oppressive. Its subject matter recalls his science-fiction movies such as *ALIEN* and *BLADE RUNNER*. It opens with a postman delivering letters to some delighted children as the voiceover declares, "E-mail will make the written word a thing of the past." With similar irony, the narrator declares that, in the future, people will no longer need to travel because video conferencing will make it redundant; children won't need to play football because of video games, and no one will go to the movies since films will be available at home through cable and satellite television. Finally, the commercial dares to suggest there will be no place for different sexes in this technologically advanced future. At this stage, however, we realize this bleak vision is not from our world at all, as the camera pulls back to reveal the earth hanging in the night sky where the moon would normally be. It is all happening on another planet. "Orange don't think technology should change the world—just make it a better place," the voiceover concludes.

This commercial was first broadcast in Great Britain after the main news bulletin *News at Ten* on Independent Television on 28 April 1998. It was Scott's first for eight years, and returns to the futuristic subjects covered in Scott's APPLE COMPUTER commercial as well as in his science fiction movies. The boy-on-a-bicycle shot during the early part of the commercial deliberately recalls Scott's earliest work, *BOY ON BICYCLE*.

Bibliography

Karen Yates, "Ridley Scott Returns to Ads with Orange Work," *Campaign*, 24 April 1998, 6.

ORBACH, JERRY (1935–2004)

Jerry was born in the Bronx. He slowly pushed to get acting roles in television and movies, but was frequently overlooked because of his musical roots.

As Lieutenant Garber in *SOMEONE TO WATCH OVER ME*, Orbach had a cameo role as the representative of established police values: to be committed to one's job, to maintain a good family life; and to keep work and personal lives separate. Garber is never going to understand Mike Keegan's (TOM BERENGER's) predicament, as Mike falls in love with rich socialite Claire (MIMI ROGERS) and thereby endangers his family life. Rather, the lieutenant upbraids Mike for his apparent negligence of duty: "I heard a lot . . . Anything you want to deny, Mike? . . . I gotta protect the Precinct, too. You're on suspension, pending disciplinary hearings. Don't hold your breath." Garber is sorry to make this decision, but feels that he is duty bound to do it ("Heavy with sadness, Garber turns and heads toward the women [Ellie and Helen]"). This focus on duty at the expense of love or friendship is something Mike cannot accept.

ORPHEUS

US 2006 TVM r/t 60 min col. *Production Companies:* Paramount Network Television Productions and Scott Free. *Executive Producers:* John McNamara, Nicholas Meyer, Ridley Scott, Tony Scott, and David W. Zucker. *Director:* Bruce Beresford. *Writer:* Nicholas Meyer. *Production Designer:* Michael S. Bolton. *Cast:* Patrick J. Adams (*Barry*), Fairuza Balk (*Karen*), Nicholas D'Agosto (*Guy*), Mena Suvari (*Sue Ellen*), Eion Bailey (*Brother*).

Planned as a follow-up to the highly successful series *NUMB3RS*, this pilot, written by Nicholas Meyer (*The Human Stain*), involved a young man whose girlfriend is involved in a sophisticated, modern-day cult and draws him to it, has been given the green light to produce a pilot.

The script caused controversy—according to the *Los Angeles Times* in March 2006: According to a copy of the script, *Orpheus* concerns Guy (Nicholas D'Agosto), a young would-be lawyer whose whirlwind romance with small-town siren Sue Ellen (Mena Suvari) sidetracks him into a shadowy, menacing group called "Grand Design," or GD. GD attracts new believers with a bestselling quasi-philosophical book akin to Hubbard's "Dianetics" and which, like Scientology, uses a complicated ranking system for followers. GD-ers even boast of their exploits on behalf of victims of Hurricane Katrina, recalling similar missions publicized by Scientologists. Asked about the similarities with Scientology, Lauri Metrose, a spokesperson for CBS Paramount Network Television, replied in an e-mail, "You are reading an early draft and there have been (as with any pilot) many changes big and small. The cult is an amalgamation of all cults throughout history." The draft that Channel Island obtained is dated 20 January 2006. A spokesman for the Church of Scientology did not return a phone call seeking comment.

The pilot has not yet led to any series being commissioned.

Reference

Scott Collins, "Nicholas Meyer's CBS Pilot Suggests Scientology-like Design," *Los Angeles Times*, 28 May 2006, http://articles.latimes.com/2006/mar/28/entertainment/et-channel28 (accessed 12 August 2008).

ORTIZ, JOHN (1968–)

Born in Brooklyn, Ortiz made his film debut in *Carlito's Way* (1993). More recently he has been in *Take the Lead* (2006) and the film version of *Miami Vice* (also 2006).

Cast as Richie Roberts's (RUSSELL CROWE's) sidekick Javier Rivera in *AMERICAN GANGSTER*, Ortiz offers a study of an officer whose heroin habit has blinded him to the distinctions between right and wrong. He cannot understand why Richie should censure him for killing and robbing a drug dealer—especially when Richie persuaded him to turn in a million dollars, much against his better judgment. STEVEN ZAILLIAN's script has Rivera criticizing Richie for "making that kind of accusation against your own kind . . . I listened to you and turned in a million fucking dollars. You'll know who'll work with me after that? Same as you. *No one*." Eventually Rivera dies of an overdose; and Richie looks sorrowfully at the sight of his former sidekick's corpse in a cadaver drawer, his miserable personal effects resting on his chest: "[A] few bucks, the Corvette key, a half-empty packet of heroin in blue cellophane."

Reference

Steven Zaillian, "*American Gangster*: Final Shooting Script" (27 July 2006), www.roteirodecinema.com.br/scripts/files/american_gangster.htm (accessed 8 February 2009).

OUT OF THE UNKNOWN: "SOME LAPSE OF TIME"

GB 1965 TVM r/t 50 min b/w. *Production Company*: British Broadcasting Corporation. *Producer*: Irene Shubik. *Director*: Ray Jenkins. *Writer*: Leon Griffiths from a story by John Brunner. *Production Designer*: Ridley Scott. *Cast*: Ronald Lewis (*Max Harrow*), Jane Downs (*Diana Harrow*), Peter Bowles (*Policeman*), Blake Butler (*Anderson*)

A fifty-minute adaptation of a story by John Brunner, broadcast on 6 December 1965 (Season 1, Episode 10) in a highly successful BBC science fiction anthology series that ran for a total of thirty-six episodes (1965–1971).

OUTLAWS

The outlaw is a central figure in American mythology, which embraces not only the idea of the rugged individual but the notion of the landscape as a realm where the "real" men are those who follow a different law from that practiced by the majority of the people. Roy Batty in *BLADE RUNNER* and Sato in *BLACK RAIN* are two examples of the outlaw figure that recurs in Scott's films. The same also applies to Henry Manning (PAUL NEWMAN) and Carol McKay (LINDA FIORENTINO) in *WHERE THE MONEY IS*, who form a spring-and-autumn partnership reminiscent of Bonnie and Clyde. *THELMA & LOUISE* is also an outlaw film with origins in films such as *Bonnie and Clyde* (1967) or *Butch Cassidy and the Sundance Kid* (1969). However, it puts a novel twist on the theme: the difference, of course, being that the two central characters are women. Scott makes much of the process of transformation: Thelma (GEENA DAVIS) acquires a personality of her own, eventually reminding Louise (SUSAN SARANDON) of why they went on the run in the first place. Louise herself overcomes the disappointments she experienced in her past life to become someone able to control her own destiny, as she rejects Jimmy (MICHAEL MADSEN) and steps out on her own. Marita Sturken observes that both characters are transformed as they take as their own several signifiers of MASCULINITY and the road—the cowboy hat, jeans and T-shirt, and baseball cap.

In placing two women as outlaws, the film recasts the genre. They are accidental outlaws who happen into crime and then spend the rest of the film trying to escape the law. As they do so, however, they discover that the law (as understood by mainstream society) is not that important. Elizabeth V. Spelman and Martha Minow suggest that "had Thelma and Louise turned themselves over to the law—whether to the sheriff or to an attorney—they would have become subject to constraints much like those from which they found themselves fleeing, constraints that among other things make their versions of themselves and of the world irrelevant. Screenwriter Calli[e] Khouri thus might be said to have this to say to observers of law: We have as much to learn about the law from those who find themselves (in both senses of that phrase) outside it as those who enforce it, wield it, or study it."

References

Elizabeth V. Spelman and Martha Minow, "Outlaw Women: Thelma and Louise," in *Legal Realism: Movies as Legal Texts*, ed. John Denvir (Urbana and Chicago: University of Illinois Press, 1996), 275–76; Marita Sturken, *Thelma & Louise*, BFI Modern Classics (London: BFI Publishing, 2000), 29–30.

Bibliography

Peter N. Chumo II, "At the Generic Crossroads with *Thelma and Louise,*" *Postscript* 13, no.2 (Winter/Spring 1994): 3–14.

OWEN, CLIVE (1964–)

British leading actor who made his name in television series such as *Chancer* and plays such as *Close My Eyes* (1990). Owen's early films included *Bent* (1996) and *Gosford Park* (2001).

Cast as The Driver in *THE HIRE*, a series of commercials for BMW, Owen was suddenly brought to the attention of Hollywood producers. The more action-packed installments of these glossy short films saw him tracking down drowning hostage victims under the direction of JOHN WOO, or protecting DON CHEADLE from helicopter-borne militia intent on destabilizing the state. His role was that of the super-cool yet caustic agent under fire. Woo likened him to James Bond with a smile.

Sometimes he could play light comedy too; Guy Ritchie cast his wife Madonna in need of a driving lesson, while in "BEAT THE DEVIL: he permits himself a mischievous smile as he endures the experience of driving JAMES BROWN around in a wild competition with The Devil (GARY OLDMAN).

OWEN, MEG WYNN (1939–)

Meg Wynn Owen shot to fame in the 1970s as Hazel Bellamy in the television series *Upstairs Downstairs* (1973–1974).

In *THE DUELLISTS*, she plays Armand's (KEITH CARRADINE's) sister Leonie, who comments on the advantages of a good MARRIAGE. She believes that it will help Armand settle down. Armand does not like the idea—chiefly because, as an honorable man, he believes that it will destroy his fiancée Adele's (CRISTINA RAINES's) life. The irony here is that Armand's life will be destroyed if he does *not* settle down: marriage may be the only thing that would help him forget the duel that hitherto has blighted his existence. His sister understands this; and brings the discussion to an abrupt close by telling him to go and play billiards.

When Meg Wynn Owen made *The Duellists*, she was still a big star. Scott himself recalled how privileged he felt when she accepted the part of Leonie. Since then she has appeared mostly in supporting roles in films such as *Gosford Park* (2001), *Love Actually* (2003), and *Vanity Fair* (2004).

Reference

Ridley Scott, "Director's Commentary," to the 2000 release of *The Duellists* by Paramount DVD in the "Special Collector's Edition" (London: Paramount Home Entertainment, 2000).

PANJABI, ARCHIE (1972–)

Previous films include *Yasmin* (2004) and *The Constant Gardener* (2005). Cast as Max Skinner's (RUSSELL CROWE's) long-suffering personal assistant Gemma, Panjabi acts as part-time secretary, confidante, and nursemaid to a man who has little idea of how to cope with anything except making more and more money. In most of her sequences she is shown talking on her cell phone; the living embodiment of a world where person-to-person contact is no longer valued. The ethics of this world are summed up by Max's line "Oh, please—come to papa," as he tries to reach up from the bottom of the swimming pool to answer his cell phone, which lies on the edge. Spouses and children are no longer important; all an individual needs is something to do business with. Gemma fades out of the film as Max gradually leaves the London world behind and opts for a new life as a château-owner in PROVENCE. But perhaps this is appropriate in a film that depicts the central character's gradual discovery of self-awareness.

Reference

Marc Klein, "*A Good Year:* Screenplay" (Draft dated 5 September 2005), www.dailyscript.com/scripts/A-GOOD-YEAR-2.pdf (accessed 26 January 2009).

PAPER MOON

US 1973 r/t 102 min b/w. *Production Companies:* The Directors Company, Paramount Pictures, and Saticoy Productions. *Producer/Director:* Peter Bogdanovich. *Writer:* Alvin Sargent, from the novel *Addie Pray* by Joe David Brown. *Production Designer:* Polly Platt. *Director of Photography:* László Kovács. *Music:* Jack Hylton, Dick Powell, Nat Gonella (among others). *Cast:* Ryan O'Neal (*Moses Pray*), Tatum O'Neal (*Addie Loggins*), Madeline Kahn (*Trixie Delight*), John Hillerman (*Deputy Hardin*), P. J. Johnson (*Imogene*), Jessie Lee Fulton (*Miss Ollie*), Jim Harrell (*The Minister*).

Classic caper film for which Tatum O'Neal the Oscar for Best Actress in a Supporting Role. Addie teams up with small-time conman Moses in Depression-era America, and the two of them travel across the country, making money in every dishonest way imaginable, looking for the ultimate con. In the production notes MATCHSTICK MEN, the screenwriters NICK AND TED GRIFFIN acknowledged the fact that they had been inspired by Bogdanovich's film.

Reference

Production Information: *Matchstick Men* (Los Angeles: Warner Bros. Pictures, 2003), 3–4.

PARKER, MARY-LOUISE (1964–)

Dubbed by some critics as "the long-suffering girl next door," Parker's films include *Grand Canyon* (1991), *Naked in New York* (1993), and *Boys on the Side* (1995). She plays another long-suffering role as Jesse James's (BRAD PITT's) wife Zee in *THE ASSASSINATION OF JESSE JAMES BY THE COWARD ROBERT FORD*, who becomes accustomed to a nomadic existence as her husband travels from place to place to avoid the clutches of the law. In a preproduction interview, Parker claimed that Zee was not entirely subservient: "Considering how she helped him [James] regain his strength after the war, she must have had some power in the relationship. Plus, she was entrusted with keeping his secrets." Zee obviously has great love for her husband, despite his dubious past; in director ANDREW DOMINIK's screenplay she rushes over and cradles James's head in her arms as he dies, murmuring "a syllable like 'God'" as he does so.

References

"About the Production," http://party931.com/common/movies/notes/54706-1-full.html (accessed 12 August 2008); Andrew Dominik, "The Assassination of Jesse James by the Coward Robert Ford," Final White Draft Screenplay dated 17 August 2005, www.simplyscripts.com/oscar80.html (accessed 5 February 2009).

PAT GARRETT AND BILLY THE KID

US 1973 r/t 121 min col. *Production Company:* Metro Goldwyn-Mayer Inc. *Producer:* Gordon Carroll. *Director:* Sam Peckinpah. *Writer:* Rudolph Wurlitzer. *Director of Photography:* John Coquillon. *Art Decorator:* Ted Haworth.

Music: Bob Dylan. *Cast*: James Coburn (*Pat Garrett*), Kris Kristofferson (*William "Billy the Kid" Bonney*), Richard Jaeckel (*Sheriff Kip McKinney*), Chill Wills (*Lemuel*), Barry Sullivan (*Chisum*).

Classic American BUDDY MOVIE that inspired ANDREW DOMINIK's film *THE ASSASSINATION OF JESSE JAMES BY THE COWARD ROBERT FORD*, produced by Scott. Whereas Peckinpah's film looks affectionately back at the West, Dominik adopts a more hardheaded approach, suggesting that the two central characters are in a sense victims of their own celebrity. The director of photography on *The Assassination*, ROGER DEAKINS, admitted that *Pat Garrett* influenced him while working on the latter film.

Reference

Stephen Pizzello and Jean Oppenheimer, "Western Destinies," *American Cinematographer* Vol. 88, no.10 (October 2007): 31–35.

PEOPLES, DAVID (1940–)

David Peoples's first work as a screenwriter was on *The Day After Trinity* (1981), having previously worked as a director on *How We Stopped the War* (1969) and an editor on *Doctor Dracula/Svengali* (1978) and *Steel Arena* (1973).

The story of how Peoples came to be involved in *BLADE RUNNER* as a scriptwriter has been exhaustively told by PAUL M. SAMMON in his book *Future Noir*, and in the documentary "Dangerous Days: Making *Blade Runner*" included as part of the five-disc *Blade Runner*: Collector's Edition (2007).

Although brought in to work on HAMPTON FANCHER's original script, Peoples felt that his writing style was sufficiently similar so as not to cause too many production difficulties. He told James van Hise, "It was like somebody'd opened my brain up or something and I look around and she was reading from an old draft that Hampton had written. In other words, I was writing exactly the same dialogue that Hampton had written months before because I'd just been presented with the same situation. So I felt that I had picked up and gotten right in tune with what he was doing."

Peoples recalled in a 2007 interview that he was brought in to work on *Blade Runner* after many drafts of the screenplay had already been written by Hampton Fancher. According to Ian Nathan, Scott invited Peoples to work on the script because the director "was perturbed that the characters 'never went outside the door' in his ongoing draft."

Nathan also quotes Peoples's statement that his major contribution to the script was that he came up with the pivotal term REPLICANTS: "I just felt that 'androids' was an overused word and kind of comic-booky in the negative sense." The idea of replication focused viewer attention on "What exactly makes us human beings or not human beings? . . . Are we people because we have memories? That

is the underlying question of the film. And it's not answered and not answerable."

Peoples told Nathan that the film itself had (and still has) a resonance with viewers: "Is he [Deckard] human? Isn't he human? What is human? It's in a large degree down to Hampton and Ridley both; their brilliance is to put something there without giving it talky explanations. You can't escape it, but you don't talk about it."

References

Ian Nathan, "Empathy Test: Screenwriter David Peoples on the Meaning of *Blade Runner*," *Empire*, August 2007, 110–11; Paul M. Sammon, *Future Noir: The Making of Blade Runner*," 2nd ed. (London: Gollancz, 2007), 57–63; "Incept Date—1980: Screenwriting and Dealmaking," Disc 2 of *Blade Runner: Collector's Edition* (Los Angeles: Warner Bros. Entertainment and the Blade Runner Partnership, 2007); James Van Hise, "The *Blade Runner* Screenwriters: Hampton Fancher and David Peoples," *Starlog* 55 (May 1982): 23.

PEPSI COLA MIAMI VICE

US 1985 Commercial r/t 40 sec col. *Production Company*: RSA. *Director*: Ridley Scott. *Cast*: Don Johnson, Philip Michael Thomas.

At the time of its first broadcast the two stars of this commercial were playing Crockett and Tubbs in the hit television series *Miami Vice* (1984–1990). In an obvious bid to attract younger consumers, Scott associates the act of drinking Pepsi-Cola with the characters' "cool" lifestyles. The action begins a shot of Miami at night and cuts to a shot of a dancer gyrating in a night club window. The two men speak ("Do you see that?"/ "What"/ "That?") and as they do so we see the image of Pepsi Cola reflected in their car windscreen. Scott cuts to close-ups of the actors asking "So where we going, anyway?" and then refreshing themselves with a can of Pepsi. The advertisement finishes with the two of them in their squad car traveling the Miami streets with a voice-over ("Hey, I'm everywhere, pal") followed by a close-up of the Pepsi can. The slogan, "Pepsi: The Choice of a New Generation," appears on screen.

PERCY MAIN

Ridley Scott's production company, responsible for *THELMA & LOUISE*, *1492: CONQUEST OF PARADISE*, *THE BROWNING VERSION*, and *MONKEY TROUBLE*. Percy Main changed its name to SCOTT FREE in the mid-1990s.

PERFORMANCE

GB 1970 r/t 105 min col. *Production Company*: Goodtimes Enterprises. *Producer*: Sanford Lieberson. *Writer/Director*: Donald Cammell. *Production Designer*: John Clark. *Director of Photography*: Nicolas Roeg. *Music*: Jack Nitzsche. *Cast*:

James Fox (*Chas*), Mick Jagger (*Turner*), Anita Pallenberg (*Pherber*), Michèle Breton (*Lucy*), Ann Sidney (*Dana*), John Bindon (*Moody*), Stanley Meadows (*Rosenbloom*).

Chas, a violent and psychotic East London gangster, needs a place to lie low after a hit that should never have been carried out. He finds the perfect cover in the form of a guesthouse run by the mysterious Mr. Turner, a one-time rock superstar, who is looking for the right spark to rekindle his faded talent.

Cult gangland thriller set in London in the late 1960s and early 1970s. The film's success derives mostly from its two central performances: Jagger makes a creditable stab at the role of Turner. His performance provided the inspiration for GARY OLDMAN's portrayal of The Devil in *THE HIRE*: "BEAT THE DEVIL."

PHILLIPPE, RYAN (1976–)

Began his career in the soap opera *One Life to Live*, the first-ever gay character on American television. Described himself in one interview as a member of the new Hollywood generation: "hardworking, ambitious, grounded. Uninterested in drugs. Or sleeping around. Or trashing hotel rooms. Or the fast, fierce burn-out."

As Gil Martin in *WHITE SQUALL*, Phillippe undergoes a considerable process of growth, both emotional and physical. Initially he seems completely unsuited to life on board ship, as he is paralyzed by fears, including fear of heights. In a brutally sadistic act, Captain Sheldon (JEFF BRIDGES) forces the young man to confront his fears by climbing the rigging, despite the young man being petrified of doing so. However, Sheldon's shock treatment has a positive effect: as Frank Beaumont (JEREMY SISTO) leaves the *Albatross* for the last time, Martin climbs to the top of the crow's nest, holding the ship's bell triumphantly over his head and waving to Frank. This gesture not only emphasizes the crew's unity of purpose, but shows how Martin has grown up. It is not surprising, therefore, that the rest of the crew begins to cheer.

Reference

Sheila Johnston, "The Life of Ryan," *Evening Standard Hot Tickets*, 29 July 1999, 2.

PHOENIX, JOAQUIN (1974–)

Real name Joaquin Rafael Bottom, born in Puerto Rico to Children of God missionaries John Bottom Amram and Arlyn Dunetz Jochebed. As a youngster he took his cue from older siblings River Phoenix and Rain Phoenix and changed his name to Leaf to match their names.

Cast as the eponymous Clay in the Ridley Scott-produced film *CLAY PIGEONS*, Phoenix admitted in an interview, "The toughest part about the role was that there's so much happening to this character, that I never got to catch my breath. During most of Clay's dialogue scenes, he's covering up for something that's just happened, or is about to get hit with something new. He tried to do the logical thing, but events keep conspiring against him." Phoenix gives a convincing characterization of a basically well-meaning young man perpetually subject to the vagaries of fate. In spite of his best intentions, he keeps being in the wrong place at the wrong time, and is thereby accused of murders he did not commit. Compared to his costar VINCE VAUGHN, who gives a much showier performance in the role of Lester Long, Phoenix is quite restrained; but director DAVID DOBKIN has obviously encouraged this kind of approach, to show how Clay maintains his integrity even when the fates seem to be against him (as signaled, for instance, in the repeated use of shots of the sky juxtaposed with close-ups of Clay, suggesting his insignificance in the overall scheme of things.)

Cast as Commodus in *GLADIATOR*, Phoenix had doubts about his capacity to play the part using an English accent. In an interview with *Film Review* he recalled that as he attended the first rehearsal "dressed in my jeans, I was thinking, 'What the hell am I doing?' Then I put on the layers of armour and I felt different. Costume and make-up really do make a big difference, especially because I'm obsessed with the physicality of a character." In another interview with *Time Out* Phoenix asserted that "[t]he great thing about Ridley . . . is that, yes, this [*Gladiator*] is a huge film, a big spectacle, but within all of that there are strong characterisations. Ridley didn't want any black-and-white, heroes-and-villains stuff, and I think audiences are much more fucking advanced than that. If you are going to feed them *Die Hard* where you have the hero and the bad guy with the dodgy English accent and that's what you want, then fine. But this has much more . . . there is so much going on, there is this whole arc. He [Commodus] can go from, like, screaming lunatic to spoilt kid. And that's basically what he is—a kid who never got any love from his dad."

With his cleft palate and perpetual sneer on his face, Phoenix makes a convincing bad guy. The contrast between his diminutive stature and the sheer scale of his ambitions is palpable, most notably in his exchanges with Lucilla (CONNIE NIELSEN). As he talks about his dreams of providing the Roman people with "a vision" that will help them "forget the tedious sermonizing of a few dry old men [the Senate]," he has to look up to his sister, as if seeking approval from her for his ideas. At the same time he possesses a great sense of theater. His return to Rome is celebrated by means of a vast pageant: an honor guard, cheering crowds, and a welcoming party of senators waiting for him on the steps of the Senate. The sheer scale of the scene recalls the fascist parades of Hitler or Mussolini, the only difference being that Commodus has not done anything to deserve it. Gracchus

(DEREK JACOBI) observes somewhat sardonically that "He [Commodus] enters Rome like a conquering hero. But what has he conquered?" The answer is obvious—the Praetorian guard. Until the film's final moments, when Quintus (Tomas Arana) tells them to defy orders and "sheath their swords," Commodus's position is secure. Once he loses the guard's support, however, he is no match for Maximus (RUSSELL CROWE) in the final duel.

Even though Commodus conceives of himself as a villain, perhaps he is rather to be pitied than despised. Phoenix himself observed in the book of the film that "he has all the emotions that go with being that age without having had the guidance he needed to handle that power. He's vulnerable and sad one minute and throwing a tantrum the next. He desperately wants the love of the people, but the irony of the story is that the gladiatorial games he decrees to get the masses to love him are ultimately what bring his nemesis [Maximus] to Rome." Perhaps the problem can be attributed to his father Marcus (RICHARD HARRIS), whose obsession with military glory rendered him totally oblivious to his son. Commodus at one point cries: "Father, I would have butchered the whole world if you would only have loved me!!" On this view, perhaps his despotic rule of Rome represents an attempt both to assert his authority and erase his father's memory.

References

"*Gladiator* by David Franzoni, revised by John Logan," Transcribed from the film, http://sfy.ru/sfy/html?script=gladiator_ts (accessed 29 November 2008); Martyn Palmer, "Royal Flush," *Time Out*, 10–17 May 2000, 24; Joaquin Phoenix, interviewed in "Production Notes: *Clay Pigeons*," included on the European DVD release of the film (Frankfurt: BY Internationale Medien und Film, 1998); Joaquin Phoenix, quoted in Diana Landau, ed., *Gladiator: The Making of the Ridley Scott Epic* (Basingstoke and London: Boxtree, 2000), 55; "Phoenix Rising," *Film Review Special* #51 (2004): 65.

Bibliography

Anne Hanley, "Even an Emperor Likes a Good Day," *Evening Standard* (London), 19 May 2000, 36.

PICARDO, ROBERT (1953–)

Robert Picardo began his screen career in series such as *Kojak* and minor roles in films such as *Oh, God! You Devil* (1984).

Cast as Meg Mucklebones in *LEGEND*, Picardo's cameo role offers him the chance to savor his lines in an evil, threatening tone as s/he contemplates the prospect of eating Jack (TOM CRUISE) for dinner. Actually, Scott's decision to cast a tall male in a female role reaffirms his belief in the tradition of the monstrous-feminine; no woman can actually convey the monster's sheer awfulness. This provides further

evidence of how skeptically the director approaches the question of FEMINISM.

PILEGGI, NICHOLAS (1933–)

Writer of hit GANGSTER FILMS such as *GoodFellas* (1990), *Casino* (1995), and *City Hall* (1996). Pileggi introduced author MARK JACOBSON to Frank Lucas, which inspired the story that was eventually turned into the film *AMERICAN GANGSTER*. Pileggi also appeared in the television profile of Lucas, broadcast in October 2006 as part of the *American Gangster* series.

PIRATES OF SILICON VALLEY

US 1999 TVM r/t 95 min col. *Production Companies*: Haft Entertainment, St. Nick Productions, and Turner Network Television. *Producer*: Leanne Moore. *Director*: Martyn Burke. *Writer*: Martyn Burke, from the book *Fire in the Valley* by Paul Freiberger and Michael Swaine. *Director of Photography*: Ousama Rawi. *Production Designer*: Jeff Ginn. *Music*: Frank Fitzpatrick. *Cast*: Noah Wyle (*Steve Jobs*), Joey Slotnick (*Steve Wozniak*), Anthony Michael Hall (*Bill Gates*).

The men behind Apple and Microsoft—Steve Jobs (Noah Wyle) and Bill Gates (Anthony Michael Hall)—are profiled in this made-for-TV movie, focusing in particular on their early years and how they created their respective companies. Ridley Scott appears as a character in the film, portrayed by J. G. Hertzler; in the opening sequence he is shown directing the famous commercial for APPLE COMPUTERS. The role is a small one; what comes across in the film is that Scott is a dedicated filmmaker, perfectly at home in the world of the studio and perfectly able to deal with large crowds and elaborate settings. He has a brief exchange with Jobs, but seems more concerned with the set-up, making sure that the actors know their moves. The commercial itself was supposed to represent the apotheosis of Jobs's achievement; the film suggests that it was the beginning of the end. Whereas Jobs believed that his main enemy was IBM computers (the "Big Brother") of the commercial, in truth it was Microsoft, then a fledgling organization run by Gates, which was about to take over as the major player in the global PC market. It was Jobs's tragedy that he failed to take note of this.

PITT, BRAD (1963–)

Born in Oklahoma and raised in Springfield, Missouri, Pitt never formally trained in acting. He began his screen career in TV sitcoms (*Growing Pains* in 1985, *Head of the Class* in 1986).

THELMA & LOUISE represented his big break in films. Cast as the young drifter JD, he is portrayed as beautiful object and roguish subject, the means to Thelma's independence, even if he does abuse and abandon her like every other man in her life. Pitt embodies such "equality" of female desire, subjectivity, and self-identification, as well as a moral instruction that women cannot act on their own desires without repercussion. Screenwriter CALLIE KHOURI welcomed his presence in the film in an interview with Bernie Cook: "Brad had a tremendous impact on the film because he's just so damn beautiful. And it really did kind of take it into the realm of fantasy . . . again, if you flipped it and had two guys and they picked up a woman, if would have to have been the female equivalent of Brad Pitt. It would have been extremely appealing to men. I think women looked at Brad in that same context, a sexual fantasy figure. He served several purposes. Good for the plot, easy on the eyes."

JD was an important figure in Thelma's process of development. Khouri told David Konow that "[The fact] that Thelma would get to have one insanely fulfilling sexual experience [with JD] before the end was really important to me . . . She was in an awful marriage with a guy who didn't care about her much, I never imagined the sex with them was that great, and he [JD] was probably her first one. There was a whole world goin' on out there that she didn't know anything about." Even though JD eventually makes off with the women's money, he unwittingly provides the catalyst for Thelma's change of character, as she transforms herself from a naïve innocent into someone responsible for her own destiny. The sex scene involving JD and Thelma (described by Pitt himself as "the six-thousand-dollar orgasm") was apparently very difficult to shoot, with Pitt being concerned about what his mother would think.

Pitt's role in *Thelma & Louise* has been identified as representative of "a particular shift in thinking about masculinity," as well as changing conceptions of sexualization and objectification, female agency, and volition. While he was initially presented as the ideal sexual object—youthful, attractive, self-conscious, and eager to please—Pitt's JD signifies a more complicated masculine celebrity, perpetually youthful (and therefore somewhat unformed), elusive, and feminized.

In the Ridley Scott-produced film *THE ASSASSINATION OF JESSE JAMES BY THE COWARD ROBERT FORD* (2007), Pitt plays the eponymous central character in a performance that according to director ANDREW DOMINIK "captures all the nuances and brings such authority to the part that you understand why people claimed Jesse James's mere presence could fill a room with warmth or tension." Scott himself applauded Pitt's performance as "a true character study that, on the surface, carries none of the usual trappings of a leading man 'hero.' It really demonstrates Brad's maturity and depth as an actor." In another interview with the British film magazine *Empire* Pitt described James's life as very contemporary in the sense that he had to contend with being a celebrity: "I was surprised to see how much of a quotient of tabloid media was alive and well at

that time. They were operating with sensationalism, and not much has changed."

While James appears a devoted family man, frequently seen playing with his two children, Pitt suggests that an undercurrent of violence lurks beneath the apparently mundane exterior. This is especially evident when he believes that he has been betrayed by members of his gang—first Ed Miller (Garret Dillahunt) and later Dick Liddil (Paul Schneider). He takes each of them out riding on a horse: although James does not say much, his silence speaks volumes. Miller rides on ahead of James in terror at what will happen next; but James soon puts him out of his misery by shooting him. Although Dick's life is spared, he is made well aware of the potential risks of deceiving James.

As the film unfolds, James experiences rapid changes of mood. Although a considerable celebrity, he is also a very lonely man who mistrusts everyone around him, something that eventually affects his state of mind. As he sits by the fire with Bob Ford (CASEY AFFLECK) and Charley (SAM ROCKWELL), he tells the two men what he will do in the next bank-robbery. Suddenly he grabs Charley by the neck and holds him at knifepoint; and then bursts out laughing. For once the narrator's (HUGH ROSS's) description in the screenplay is unfailingly accurate: "Jesse was increasingly cavalier, merry, moody, fey, unpredictable. He camouflaged his depressions with masquerades of extreme cordiality, courtesy and goodwill towards others." In many ways, he welcomes death as a merciful release from torment.

Pitt's performance won him the Best Actor Award at the Venice Film Festival. Kenneth Turan in the *Los Angeles Times* believed that "the casually charismatic aspect of Jesse James (described by novelist Hansen as someone who 'ate all the air in your lungs and the thoughts right out of your mind') is second nature to Pitt, but there is also an air of unsettling mystery around James and, as the film progresses, expressions of darker things as well."

References

"About the Production" [*The Assassination of Jesse James*], http://party931.com/common/movies/notes/54706-1-full.html (accessed 12 August 2008); Amy Dempsey, *The Unofficial Brad Pitt* (Bristol UK: Parragon Book Service, 1996); Andrew Dominik, "The Assassination of Jesse James by the Coward Robert Ford," Final White Draft Screenplay dated 17 August 2005, www.simplyscripts.com/oscar80.html (accessed 5 February 2009); David Konow, "Sisters Are Doin' It for Themselves" (Interview with Callie Khouri), *Creative Screenwriting* 8, no.5 (September 2001); Callie Khouri, interviewed by Bernie Cook in *Thelma & Louise Live!: The Cultural Afterlife of an American Film* (Austin: University of Texas Press, 2007), 187; Brad Pitt, "Just Like Jesse James," *Empire* 222 (December 2007): 28; Kenneth Turan, "The Assassination of Jesse James by the Coward Robert Ford," *Los Angeles Times*, 21 September 2007, www.calendarlive.com/tv/radio/cl-et-jesse21sep21,0,5224342.story (accessed 8 February 2009).

Bibliography
Brian J. Robb, *Brad Pitt: The Rise to Stardom* (London: Plexus Publishing Ltd., 2002), 47–61; Cynthia Fuchs, "What All the Fuss Is About: Making Brad Pitt in *Thelma & Louise*," in *Thelma & Louise Live!: The Cultural Afterlife of an American Film*, ed. Bernie Cook (Austin: University of Texas Press, 2007), 146–67; John Hiscock, "Brad Pitt: What I Share with Jesse James," *Daily Telegraph*, 14 December 2007, www.telegraph.co.uk/culture/film/starsandstories/3668742/Brad-Pitt-What-I-share-with-Jesse-James.html (accessed 8 Febuary 2009); Susan Knobloch, "Interplaying Identities: Acting and the Building Blocks of Character in *Thelma & Louise*," in *Thelma & Louise Live!: The Cultural Afterlife of an American Film*, 91–122.

PLAYTEN, ALICE (1947–)

Born Alice Plotkin in New York City, Playten's screen credits include *The Pirates of Penzance* (1983).

Cast as Blix in *LEGEND*, Playten wore a mask which Scott described as being modeled on Keith Richards of The Rolling Stones. She occupies a central role in the early part of the film, but fades away as the action centers more on Darkness's (TIM CURRY's) conflict with Lily (MIA SARA). The most interesting aspect is her relationship with Darkness; while being wholly based on fear, it leaves plenty of room for trickery. The first time we see the two of them is inside the Great Tree, where a nervous Blix is beckoned closer by his master. One of the long, curved nails of Darkness's hand comes rather too close to Blix's nose and, as Blix's nose is similar in shape to the nail, the effect (according to Matthew Aitken) resembles a perverted version of Michelangelo's "Creation of Adam." However the only "creation" that binds the two together is that of fear, which is created whenever Darkness comes on the scene. His evil, oppressive nature is emphasized later on when Blix dares to usurp his authority (having vanquished one unicorn and put the other to flight). Darkness not only cuffs Blix around the head, but reduces him to a quivering heap of jelly as he reasserts his rule.

References
Matthew Aitken, "LEGEND: Ridley Scott (the Remnants of a Masterpiece)," *Legend: Frequently Asked Questions*, www.figmentfly.com/legend/different4i.html (accessed 25 April 2008); Ridley Scott, interviewed in "The Making of *Legend*" (2002 documentary directed by J. M. Kenny), included on *Legend: The Ultimate DVD* (Los Angeles: Universal Studios, 2002).

POLK, MIMI (–)

Also known as Mimi Polk Gitlin, she started working with Ridley Scott on *LEGEND*, where she ran a small development company. She was associate producer on *SOMEONE TO WATCH OVER ME*, production associate on *BLACK RAIN*, and full producer on *THELMA & LOUISE, 1492: CONQUEST OF PARADISE* (where she is listed as Mimi Polk Sotela), *WHITE SQUALL* (where she is listed as Mimi Polk Gitlin), *MONKEY TROUBLE*, and *THE BROWNING VERSION*.

For *1492: Conquest of Paradise* Polk found the original treatment by ROSELYNE BOSCH "very interesting . . . she had clearly done her research and her approach was to tell the truth about Columbus—his obsessions, what he did in order to try and fulfill his dreams: both the positive and the negative results for the pursuit of this quest."

Having worked for PERCY MAIN (the feature film development company Scott established in 1980), which later morphed into SCOTT FREE, she left the company in 1996 and became an independent producer.

Reference
Pressbook, 1492: Conquest of Paradise (Los Angeles: Paramount Pictures, 1992), 3.

POSTER, STEVEN (1944–)

Steven Poster was born and raised in Chicago, and was first interested in still photography. He first filmed commercials and documentaries, and then worked in a second unit photographer on *BLADE RUNNER*.

Poster's experiences with Scott were almost uniformly favorable. He recalled in an interview that he did additional photography on *Blade Runner*. Then Scott hired him to shoot several commercials and tests for *LEGEND* before being hired as director of photography on *SOMEONE TO WATCH OVER ME*. In an interview with *American Cinematographer* published soon after the film's release, Poster emphasized the fact that the production used familiar NEW YORK locations so as to underline the conflict going on within Mike Keegan (TOM BERENGER's) mind. Poster later recalled in a conversation with Bob Fisher that "it [filming in New York] was a wonderful, intensely creative experience. He [Scott] was very supportive and amazingly collaborative." He admired Scott's "intensity and his ability to see what he wanted in a frame at any given moment. Ridley has an ability to change everything in every shot and make it flow and have continuity. It drives script supervisors crazy, but it works. He has that kind of an eye and that kind of a mind that allows him to create and build every shot separately." In a third interview with Ron Magid, Poster recalled that unlike Scott's earlier films, *Someone* was "not a very large budget film . . . I think he wanted to make a much simpler movie." The key to working with Scott, Poster believed, "was the ability to give him just about any look he wanted as soon as possible . . . I find it a very exciting process of discovery with Ridley, a very creative process where we're sharing ideas back and forth."

Poster's work is most evident in the series of memorable images that pervade the film—from the shot at Win Hockings's (Mark Moses's) chic club, where the celebrities enter in blinding white light, with the silhouettes of the photographers at the back of the frame, to the shot of Mike in medium close-up in the subway, with the lights of the train flashing on his face, to the gilded interior of Claire Gregory's (MIMI ROGERS's) apartment with its beautiful drapes and ornate furniture, and (most memorably) the shot of the Manhattan skyline at the beginning of the film, described thus in the script: "the ultimate object of man's desire and fulfillment, Oz, the city unfolding itself before and beneath us, till *dazzling shafts of light* sizzling up—*kleig lights*—stab our eyes and bring us down into their *blinding brightness*." Poster received an ASC (American Society of Cinematographers) nomination for Best Cinematography for this film.

References

Bob Fisher, "A Conversation with Steven Poster, ASC," *International Cinematographers' Guild*, www.cameraguild.com/interviews/chat _poster/poster_interview.htm (accessed 7 June 2008); Howard Franklin, Danilo Bach, and David Seltzer, "Someone to Watch Over Me" (revised 4 December 1986), www.imsdb.com/scripts/Someone-To-Watch-Over-Me.html (accessed 9 June 2008); Ron Magid, "*Someone to Watch Over Me*: A Story of Love and Terror," *American Cinematographer* 68, no.10 (October 1988): 57–58; Steven Poster, "Something To Watch . . . Is Something to See," *American Cinematographer* 69, no.4 (April 1988): 58–59.

POSTMODERNISM

BLADE RUNNER's status as postmodern text has been debated by several critics including Giuliana Bruno and Varun Begley.

Bruno argues that the film "posits questions of identity, identification and history." In a postmodern age, memories are contained in photographs which, as the film argued, might be real or constructed for ideological purposes. Consequently, viewers "like the REPLICANTS, are put in the position of reclaiming a history by means of its reproduction." As a result, "a simulacrum of history is established." This might be true on one level; but the film refuses to judge as to whether "history" (as depicted, for instance in Deckard's past life) is actually "real" or a "simulacrum." Viewers are left to make up their own minds.

Begley believes that Bruno's reading contains "a strangely traditional hermeneutic practice"; although it concentrates on the supposed "death of the author" associated with postmodernism, it nonetheless suggests that Scott might be "the author of postmodernity." Begley contends that the film actually combines postmodern and modern elements—the modernist elements include "the juxtaposition of the old and the new, the DYSTOPIAN vision of the

urbanized future, the persistent doubling of copy and original epitomized in the two heroes and their two distinct narratives, and the anguished redemption of the human through heroic suffering, sacrifice and disalienation."

References

Varun Begley, "*Blade Runner* and the Postmodern: A Reconsideration," *Literature/Film Quarterly* 32, no.3 (October 2004): 187, 191; Giuliana Bruno, "Ramble City: Postmodernism and *Blade Runner*," in *Alien Zone: Cultural Theory and Contemporary Science Fiction Cinema*, ed. Annette Kuhn (London: Verso, 1990), 193.

Bibliography

Michael Boughn, "Representations of Postmodern Spaces in *Black Hawk Down*," *West Coast Line* 39, no.1 (2005): 5–16; Nick Lacey, "Postmodern Romance: The Impossibility of (De)Centering the Self," in *The Blade Runner Experience: The Legacy of a Science Fiction Classic*, ed. Will Brooker (London and New York: Wallflower Press, 2005), 190–203; Kevin McNamara, "Los Angeles 2019: Two Tales of a City," in *Productive Postmodernism: Consuming Histories and Cultural Studies*, ed. John N. Duvall and Linda Hutcheon (Albany: State University of New York Press, 2002), 123–36; Gloria Pastorino, "The Death of the Author and the Power of Addiction in *Naked Lunch* and *Blade Runner*," in *Science Fiction, Critical Frontiers*, ed. Karen Sayer and John Moore (Basingstoke and New York: Macmillan Press Ltd., 2000), 100–15; Rolanda Romero, "The Postmodern Hybrid: Do Aliens Dream of Alien Sheep?" in *The Effects of the Nation: Mexican Art in an Age of Globalization*, ed. Carl Good and John V. Waldron (Philadelphia: Temple University Press, 2001), 196–213; Vivian Sobchack, "Postfuturism," in *Liquid Metal: The Science Fiction Film Reader*, ed. Sean Redmond (London and New York: Wallflower Press, 2004), 220–27.

POWELL, IVOR (–)

Powell began his career as a publicist and second assistant director working on films such as *2001: A Space Odyssey* (1968) and *Carry on Doctor* (1969).

He worked as Scott's associate producer on *THE DUELLISTS, ALIEN*, and *BLADE RUNNER*. He persuaded Scott to direct *Alien*: many of its design ideas were based on storyboards Scott had created for *TRISTAN AND ISEULT*, a follow-up to *The Duellists* that eventually came to nothing. He told Mike Childs and Alan Jones that "the space suits, for example, were based on Samurai armor, including colored pieces.

Powell also claimed responsibility for the film's ending, by suggesting that the alien should be front-lit so that the audience could see yet not see it. This greatly increased the film's shock effect. Following the success of *Alien*, Powell told Childs and Jones that he was enthusiastic about the possibilities of filming *Tristan and Iseult* in the belief that it contained "fantasy elements placing it in a category near *Alien*."

Once again the project failed to materialize; and Scott went on to direct *Blade Runner.*

Powell was heavily involved in the financing and the script-writing of the film. According to Phil Edwards and Alan McKenzie he worked hard to secure the services of SYD MEAD and DOUGLAS TRUMBULL, as well as collaborating with Scott on making most of the important script decisions. It was Powell's idea that Scott should borrow footage from Stanley Kubrick's *The Shining* (1980) for Blade Runner: PAUL M. SAMMON suggests that Kubrick obliged by giving Scott free access to *The Shining*'s wilderness shots (which had been filmed from a helicopter).

Powell recalled that the experience of working on *Blade Runner* was an ambivalent one. He felt "disappointed with the disjointed narrative, mainly caused by us not being able to shoot all of the sequences that we wanted to." On the other hand he admitted to Sammon that it had a significant impact on audiences: "[I]t feels like *BR* implicitly warns us that the twenty-first [century] will probably be the most dangerous century that mankind has ever faced . . . it does seem that the tail of the electric sheep is now wagging the dog."

References

Mike Childs and Alan Jones, "Ivor Powell: Associate Producer," in Mark Patrick Carducci and Glenn Lovell, "Making *Alien*: Behind the Scenes," *Cinefantastique* 9, no.1 (October 1979): 32; Phil Edwards and Alan McKenzie, "The *Blade Runner* Chronicles: Ivor Powell," *Starburst* 50 (October 1982): 26–30; Paul M. Sammon, *Future Noir: The Making of Blade Runner*, 2nd ed. (London: Gollancz, 2007), 303, 473–74.

PROVENCE

Scott had previously filmed in FRANCE when he made *THE DUELLISTS.* For *A GOOD YEAR* he returned there—specifically to the Provence region. Provence itself dates back to 600 BC, when Phocaean Greeks settled in Massalia, now modern-day Marseilles on the Mediterranean coast, and the region's most populous city. Scott has owned a house there for many years; in 2005–2006 he chose to film *A Good Year* there. Scott used quaint villages and other locations scattered throughout the hills and valleys of the Luberon valley. Those included Gordes (four days at Cafe Renaissance, dubbed Fanny's Café in the film), Cucuron, Lacoste, Avignon, and Menerbes (where author PETER MAYLE used to reside, and whose former house is still a popular stop on guided tours that frequent the village). The company also spent three days at another local vineyard, Chateau Les Eydins, which doubled for the home of the story's gruff vigneron, Duflot (DIDIER BOURDON).

Scott said, in an interview with Emanuel Levy, "London's a great place to live, [but] Provence is [also] a fantas-tic place to live. Is it better? No, it's different. For me, I live in Provence . . . because I live in London. So, I need one to have the other."

Reference

Emanuel Levy, "*Good Year*: Interview with Ridley Scott," www .emanuellevy.com/article.php?articleID=3485 (accessed 12 August 2008).

PSYCHO

US 1960 r/t 109 min b/w. *Production Company*: Shamley Productions. *Producer/Director*: Alfred Hitchcock. *Writer*: Joseph Stefano, from the novel by Robert Bloch. *Production Designers*: Robert Clatworthy, Joseph Hurley, and George Milo. *Director of Photography*: John L. Russell. *Music*: Bernard Herrmann. *Cast*: Anthony Perkins (*Norman Bates*), Janet Leigh (*Marion Crane*), Vera Miles (*Lila Crane*), John Gavin (*Sam Loomis*), Martin Balsam (*Milton Arbogast*), John McIntire (*Sheriff Al Chambers*).

Although Scott does not attribute any direct influence, Harvey R. Greenberg argues that there are specific parallels to be drawn between Hitchcock's classic shocker and *ALIEN.* Most viewers rushed to see *Psycho* on a dare in the belief that they would experience a new dimension in terror; the same thing happened when *Alien* premiered in 1979 (with the famous tagline "In space, no one can hear you scream"). *Psycho* is affected by "the taint of cannibalism": Norman Bates (Anthony Perkins) and his mother feast upon each other's egos. Mrs. Bates's withered frame provides evidence of the result; the ghastly image of her skull, her lips pulled back into a sepulchral grin, evoke an all-consuming orality. Such cannibalism finds its way into *Alien* in the famous chestbusting sequence involving Kane (JOHN HURT).

Other parallels are evident in the moment where Brett (HARRY DEAN STANTON) looks for Jones the cat in the *NOSTROMO*'s store-room. Through subjective camera-work, the gates seem to advance towards him, suffused with menace—just as the doors of the Bates house seem to move towards Lila Crane (Vera Miles) as she investigates the mystery lurking behind them. The adult alien is photographed so obliquely in the original 1979 release of *Alien* that its shape can only be guessed at. When it descends upon Brett it resembles a huge tube; during Lambert's (VERONICA CARTWRIGHT'S) death we only see its tail crawling round her legs. Most of the close-ups concentrate on the alien's head and jaws, designed by H. R. GIGER—its skull, cruel lips, and teeth dripping saliva. This bears a strong visual resemblance to Norman Bates's skull in *Psycho.*

Like *Psycho*, *Alien* is a prime example of what Greenberg called "cruel cinema," that offers a pessimistic view of "sacrosanct American values . . . notably of family life, and . . . the social contract under capitalism."

Reference

Harvey R. Greenberg, "Reimagining the Gargoyle: Psychoanalytic Notes on *Alien*," *Camera Obscura* 15 (October 1986): 90, 92, 105.

PUTTNAM, DAVID (1941–)

Producer and studio executive who was created a life peer in 1997.

David Puttnam began his career as a photographer's agent, which led him into producing low-budget British films such as *That'll Be The Day* (1973), *Stardust* (1974), and *Bugsy Malone* (1976), for which he also wrote the music.

THE DUELLISTS was the first production for Puttnam's own company Enigma Productions, which later produced Oscar-winning hits such as *Chariots of Fire* (1981). By employing Ridley Scott—who hitherto had only worked on commercials and in television—Puttnam was taking something of a gamble. However, Puttnam himself had worked in advertising, so he was well aware of Scott's capabilities (as well as those of others with an advertising background such as Alan Parker and Hugh Hudson).

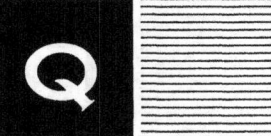

Q

QUICK, DIANA (1946–)

A former president of the Oxford Union at Oxford University, Diana Quick first came to the notice of the filmgoing public in *Nicholas and Alexandra* (1971).

In *THE DUELLISTS*, Quick plays the cameo role of Laura, D'Hubert's (KEITH CARRADINE's) girlfriend, who encounters him after one of his battle campaigns and wonders where he has been. Despite his experiences in battle, D'Hubert is still keen to continue his feud with Feraud (HARVEY KEI-TEL), prompting Laura to state rather bitterly that "nothing cures a duellist." Laura herself has fallen on hard times: her husband—a soldier—has died of typhus; and now all she can do for money is to beg and "strike up friendships." She asks whether she can return to Feraud; Feraud does not reply, and Laura finishes the sequence by running away, exclaiming that this time D'Hubert will kill him. Once again we are made aware of how Feraud's and D'Hubert's preoccupation with the duel renders them impervious to human suffering.

RADIANT WASHING POWDER

GB 1970 Commercial r/t 30 sec b/w. *Production Company*: RSA Films for J. Walter Thompson. *Director*: Ridley Scott.

A little boy homes come with his hands dirty, his handkerchief bloodied, and his face filthy. His mother makes him take off his shirt, and puts it in to soak and wash in Radiant washing powder. Next day the son, wearing the clean shirt, stands opposite his father; just for a joke, the father tells the little boy to hit him softly on the cheek. The little boy does not listen to him, however: when the father's back is turned the son hits him hard on the nose, making it bleed profusely. The mother sighs, and then smiles, as she realizes that this occasion provides her with another chance to use Radiant—"for the whiter white."

A serio-comic story designed to show how "Radiant's action is thoroughly biological. In the soak, in the wash, cleaning, brightening, bringing out the total brilliance of the whiter white." The advertisement provides a good example of Scott's use of natural light to create a mood; at one point the father and son are shown standing next to a pair of spotless net curtains while the morning sun streams in to illuminate their newly cleaned shirts. This technique has been frequently used in Scott's films, notably in the third duel sequence taking place in the stables in *THE DUELLISTS*. The commercial is voiced by IAN HOLM, later to appear as Ash in *ALIEN*.

RAINES, CRISTINA (1952–)

Cristina Raines (birth name Tina Herazo) was born in Manila, the Philippines. Her early films included *Sunshine* (1973) and *Nashville* (1975).

She was cast as Adele, D'Hubert's wife in *THE DUELLISTS* because of being KEITH CARRADINE's current girlfriend. Scott recalled in the "Director's Commentary" to the film's DVD release that he asked Carradine whether she wanted to play the role; the actor replied that, as she was going to accompany him on set anyway, she would be more than willing to accept.

Adele has a minor role within the film as the loving wife; the source of security in D'Hubert's life who persuades

him that the duel itself is ultimately futile. However, D'Hubert fights the duel (even though it seems ludicrous to do so), as Feraud casts aspersions on his HONOR.

Reference

Ridley Scott, "Director's Commentary" to the 2000 release of *The Duellists* by Paramount DVD in the "Special Collector's Edition" (London: Paramount Home Entertainment, 2000).

RAPE/REVENGE FILMS

Often identified by critics as challenging phallocentricism. Examples from the last three decades might include *Bloodsucking Freaks* (1976), *Carrie* (1976), *Fatal Attraction* (1987), and *Heathers* (1989).

Joy McEntee identifies *THELMA & LOUISE* as a good example of the genre; for her the film "illustrates why rape-revenge abstains from tackling the 'law' proper in the modern political context: the institutions which house systemic corruption—the judicial bureaucracy and the police army—are just now too big." Hence the two women have to enact their own form of justice by taking revenge on those men who seek to abuse them.

Reference

Joy McEntee, "Ladies, Bring a Poisoned Plate: Cinematic Representations of the Vengeful Woman," *Media Information Australia* 72 (May 1994): 41.

Bibliography

Jacinda Read, "Popular Film/ Popular Feminism: The Critical Reception of the Rape-Revenge Film," *Scope* 11 (June 2008): www.scope.nottingham.ac.uk/reader/chapter.php?id=3 (accessed 3 August 2008).

RATTIGAN, TERENCE (1911–1977)

British dramatist who dominated the West End of London in the late 1940s and early 1950s. He went out of fashion with the coming of the so-called "Angry Young Men" in the theater in the mid-1950s but has retained his popularity to this day, not least as a writer of dramas of narrowly reclaimed opportunity.

The Browning Version was first performed in 1948 as part of a double bill (*Playbill*) with *Harlequinade*. This has now become one of the most popular one-act plays in the repertoire on both sides of the Atlantic, and deservedly so. It has the characteristic Rattigan theme of the power of the weak over the strong, the power of the good-natured schoolboy Taplow over the dry, unpopular disciplinarian Crocker-Harris, once a brilliant Greek scholar, now merely the teacher of classics to the Lower Fifth at a minor private school. The play has a wonderful double climax as Taplow gives the teacher a copy of Robert Browning's version of the Agamemnon as a leaving present; Crocker-Harris finds this so affecting that he breaks down in front of the boy. That is the first climax; the second occurs right at the end, when Crocker-Harris insists on making his farewell speech in front of the entire school (although he has previously ceded this right to Frank Hunter, a more popular teacher). Despite a lifetime of failure, Crocker-Harris has at last summoned up the courage to admit his failings in public. The play was adapted as *THE BROWNING VERSION* (1951) with Michael Redgrave in the title role and Jean Kent as his wife and remade by Scott in 1994, with MIKE FIGGIS as director.

It is not surprising that Scott found this play suitable for filming, as it focuses once again on familiar preoccupations in his work such as the relationship between LOVE VS. DUTY. Crocker-Harris is trapped by his desire to be accepted by the school, by the boys and by his society, and needs to rediscover his sense of dignity.

Bibliography

Sean O'Connor, *Straight Acting: Popular Gay Drama from Wilde to Rattigan* (London and Herndon, VA: Cassell, 1998), 188–201.

RAWAT, NAVI (1977–)

Born in Malibu, California, Rawat starred in six episodes of *24* and thirteen of *The O.C.* before becoming a regular member of the cast of *NUMB3RS*.

As the mathematical genius Amita Ramanujan, Rawat offers a perfect foil to Charlie Eppes (DAVID KRUMHOLTZ) as someone who can match his academic ability, yet continually looks for him to show his affection. As the series develops, so Charlie's attitude towards her changes, so much so that the two contemplate moving in to the Eppes family house, with Alan Eppes (JUDD HIRSCH) finding a place of his own. Nothing comes of the idea, however. In Series 3 and 4, Amita has a larger role within the action, as the creators Cheryl Heuton and Nicholas Falacci decided to give more screen-time to the female characters.

Bibliography

Deepa Kamath, "The Many Faces of Navi Rawat," *Nirali Magazine* 4 April 2005, http://niralimagazine.com/2005/04/the-many-faces-of-navi-rawat/ (accessed 22 February 2009).

RAWLINGS, TERRY (1933–)

Born in London, Rawlings began his career as a sound editor, working with directors such as Ken Russell, Karel Reisz, and Jack Clayton.

Rawlings's last sound editing assignment was *THE DUELLISTS*. His contribution can be seen in the way he uses different sounds for the duels. The first of these has the two sounds clanging together in a series of dull thuds, drawing attention to how heavy the weapons actually are. As the duel becomes more intense, so the thuds increase, leading into a snatch of violin music, making us aware of the potential danger facing both D'Hubert and Feraud. This is not just a fight, but a fight to the death.

By contrast, the dawn duel scene takes place with rapiers—thin swords that sound just like whips when wielded by the two men. All we can hear on the soundtrack are a series of bell-like rings as the two swords clash; nothing much seems to happen until D'Hubert turns away clutching his chest and collapsing to the ground. Again, the sounds make us aware of how lethal each duel actually is; they might be fought with different weapons, but either participant is likely to die.

Rawlings next worked with Scott as a picture editor on *ALIEN*. He exerted a significant influence over the film's choice of music, especially in the final scene, as he put together a "temp track" to give Scott a better sense of how the ending would play to an audience. Rawlings inserted a movement from Howard Hanson's Symphony No. 2 ("Romantic") over the film's end credits: Scott liked it so much that he cut out the original score that JERRY GOLDSMITH had created for the end.

Rawlings worked again with Scott on *BLADE RUNNER*, where he was heavily involved in the editing of the final print for the 1982 release. According to William M. Kolb, Scott and Rawlings disapproved of Deckard's (HARRISON FORD's) voice-overs, on the grounds that they held up the narrative and prevented viewers from making their own decisions about the characters and their motives. Rawlings was also in favor of including Deckard's unicorn dream, a sequence that was eventually incorporated in the 1992 DIRECTOR'S CUT. The sequence originally began as a series of intercuts, designed to show Deckard going through photographs and turning over the memories stimulated by those photos in his mind. Rawlings told PAUL M. SAMMON that: "He [Deckard] mulled these images over and then shook the memories out of his head."

Rawlings was also heavily involved in creating the various versions of *LEGEND* for European and American audiences, once it was decided by the distributors (Universal/MCA) that the original version had to be cut to render it more attractive to audiences.

References
William M. Kolb, "Script to Screen: Blade Runner in Perspective," in *Retrofitting Blade Runner*, ed. Judith M. Kerman, 2nd ed. (Bowling Green: Bowling State University Popular Press, 1997), 143; Terry Rawlings, interviewed in Paul M. Sammon, *Future Noir: The Making of Blade Runner*, 2nd ed. (London: Gollancz, 2007), 358.

THE REAL WHITE SQUALL

Ridley Scott based his film of the same name on the autobiographical account of the incident *The Last Voyage of the Albatross* by CHUCK GIEG. However, the account of Gieg and screenwriter TODD ROBINSON was criticized by an anonymous writer who posted his version online in 2007. He claimed that "The only truth in the film is that the *Albatross* did sink in a white squall at 3.5 N. 85 W. The problem with the film is that Gieg's book was written by a ghost writer and the rights were bought by Hollywood . . . The Cuban gunboat incident never happened; the spearing of the dolphin never happened; *Albatross* was actually boarded by a group of Mexican marines at Progresso . . . Sheldon never forced anyone to do anything they were afraid to do . . . There was no court of inquiry . . . as was the agoraphobic Gill Martin. . . . Scott, [ROCKY] LANG, and Robinson foisted a fraud on the critics and audiences."

Reference
"The Real White Squall," www.mrcranky.com/movies/whitesquall/137.html (accessed 14 September 2008).

REDGRAVE, VANESSA (1937–)

Early film appearances include *A Man for All Seasons* (1966), *Camelot* (1968), *Isadora* (1968), and *Oh What a Lovely War!* (1968). Gained a reputation as much for her political activities as for her acting, which often put her into conflict with her employers.

As Clemmie Churchill in the Ridley Scott-produced film *THE GATHERING STORM*, Redgrave provides a source of moral, physical, and emotional support for her husband Winston (ALBERT FINNEY). Tall and angular, with faintly graying hair, Redgrave comes across as the dominant force in the MARRIAGE, even though she refuses to become involved in her husband's political activities. This appears to contradict what she said in a preproduction interview: "She [Clemmie] threw herself into politics with him [Churchill] and, although they later had children, she went through the vicissitudes of changing parties and his losing all position of any power whatsoever. It cost him a lot. Clementine was an extremely political woman." After many discussions with Mary Soames, Churchill's only surviving daughter, Redgrave "felt an enormous connection with this lady [Clementine] who I never knew or never even saw. Through the warmth in Mary's voice and eyes and what she told me about her mother, I came to feel an affinity with Clemmie."

It is interesting that Redgrave should have accepted the role; in her 1991 autobiography she recalls that as a child she was very much influenced by her nanny "and her worship of Churchill." However, her views about Churchill were to change, once she learned in later life that her father, the actor Sir Michael Redgrave, had espoused the socialist cause: "His political experiences . . . were of central importance in shaping his life, and mine . . . his political horizons were dominated by the menace of Fascism, the horrors of Nazi Germany, and the defeat of the Spanish revolution . . . he was certainly a socialist." The BBC eventually banned him from speaking on the radio on account of his political views; but the protest (from listeners and filmmakers alike) was so vehement that Churchill was forced to intervene and persuade the BBC to change its mind, even though his political views were very different from Redgrave's.

References
The Gathering Storm: Information Pack issued 17 June 2002 (London: BBC, 2002), www.bbc.co.uk/pressoffice/pressreleases/stories/2002/06_june/17/gathering_storm_pack.pdf (accessed 24 December 2008); Vanessa Redgrave, *An Autobiography* (London: Faber and Faber, 1991), 22.

REED, OLIVER (1938–1999)

Born in London, the son of Peter Reed, a sports journalist. His uncle was Sir Carol Reed, the film director of classics such as *Odd Man Out* (1946) and *THE THIRD MAN*. Reed made his debut in British B-pictures such as *Beat Girl* (1959) and comedies such as *The Rebel* (1960).

As much noted for his off-screen antics as for his film performances, Reed's finest films include the title role in *Hannibal Brooks* (1968) and Ken Russell's *Women in Love* (1969). He described himself in a 1974 biography by Susan D'Arcy as someone possessing "animal magnetism . . . I have no worries about the parts I play. Today I can play fathers and uncles and airline pilots. And that is why I can play fathers and uncles and airline pilots. And that is why I am confident about life." By the late 1990s, however, the leading roles had dried up: Reed was now perceived as being unemployable, on account of his excessive drinking and rowdy behavior. Ridley Scott needed a lot of persuasion before he agreed to employ Reed in *GLADIATOR*, so long as the actor promised to stay out of trouble. Reed was offered the part of Proximo, an aging former gladiator, and a $1 million fee. Reed observed in the book of the film that he was playing "a gladiator trainer who in the past was a gladiator himself, and who won his freedom . . . I'm responsible for finding out if Maximus [RUSSELL CROWE] can fight, taking him to Rome, and putting him into the big game. Proximo's a wonderful character—but then, if you're involved in something this big, you have to believe that your character can compete with everything else that's going on. His performance is encouragingly low-key; a world-weary cynic who was once a gladiator himself, and as a result is well aware of what will happen to those who live life to the limits. The actor and the character are as one: Proximo's colorful life parallels that of Reed's.

Oliver Reed died of heart failure some three weeks before filming on *Gladiator* had been completed. He once described himself to the journalist Cliff Goodwin as "only an actor—not a priest beyond reproach. I am not a villain. I have never hurt anyone. I am just a tawdry character who explodes now and again." This perhaps stands as a fitting epitaph for his life.

References

Susan D'Arcy, *The Films of Oliver Reed* (London: Barnden Castell Williams Ltd., 1974), 9, 11; Cliff Goodwin, *Evil Spirits: The Life of Oliver Reed* (London: Virgin Publishing Ltd., 2001), 3; Oliver Reed, quoted in Diana Landau, ed., *Gladiator: The Making of the Ridley Scott Epic* (Basingstoke and London: Boxtree, 2000), 56.

Bibliography

Garth Pearce, "A Barbaric World . . ." *Total Film* 41 (June 2000): 46–55.

THE RELUCTANT BANDIT

GB 1965 TV Series 5 × 25 min episodes b/w. *Production Company*: British Broadcasting Corporation. *Producer/ Director*: Paddy Russell. *Writer*: Colin Morris. *Production Designer*: Ridley Scott. *Cast*: William Mervyn (*Carson*), Michael Balfour (*Luigi*), Maggie Fitzgibbon (*Lili*), William Dexter (*Robert*).

A thriller first broadcast from 15 February–15 March 1965 about a British officer who serves in Sicily during World War II, who returns there to find himself involved in Mafia activity. Unfortunately the tapes of the production no longer exist.

RENNER, JEREMY (1971–)

Born in Modesto, California, Renner made his name in *S.W.A.T.* (2003) and *28 Weeks Later* (2007). Cast as Wood Hite in *THE ASSASSINATION OF JESSE JAMES BY THE COWARD ROBERT FORD*, Renner welcomed the role: although too old for the part he believed that "the character Wood Hite is more of a screen presence and how he affects other characters. The character's main purpose for the story is to instill paranoia in Jesse James. Just like every other character, he serves a specific purpose. As events unfold, Jesse James's paranoia causes him to only trust his blood. Since there is a reward for Jesse and his brother Frank, Jesse knows that Wood Hite, his cousin, will not turn on him."

Reference

Ryan Parsons, "Exclusive: Jeremy Renner Talks Assassination of Jesse James," *CanMag* 3 May 2006, www.canmag.com/news/4/3/3755 (accessed 7 February 2009).

REPLICANTS

The term used to describe those human beings manufactured by the Tyrell Corporation in *BLADE RUNNER*. Originally titled "androids" in the original novel by PHILIP K. DICK, they were renamed in line with screenwriter DAVID PEOPLES's wishes. He felt the term "android" was too reminiscent of a comic book.

Peoples told Ian Nathan that the term originated from a conversation with his eldest daughter, who was at UCLA at the time of the film's making, studying chemistry and biology. She said that the creatures of the film had been "replicated." Either Peoples or his daughter said "replicant," and the idea stuck.

The film defines replicants thus: "a being virtually identical to a human . . . they were superior in strength and ability, and at least equal in intelligence, to the genetic engineers who created them. Replicants were used offworld as slave labor in the hazardous explanation and colonization of other planets. After a bloody mutiny . . . Replicants were declared illegal on earth under penalty of death." Blade Runners like Deckard (HARRISON FORD) are ordered to exterminate them—or "retire" them, as the film puts it.

Reference

Ian Nathan, "Empathy Test: Screenwriter David Peoples on the Meaning of *Blade Runner*," *Empire*, August 2007, 110.

Bibliography

Ian Barns, "The Human Genome Project and the Self," *Soundings* 77, nos. 1–2 (Spring/Summer 1994): 99–128; Nick Land, "Machinic Desire," *Textual Practice* 7, no.3 (Winter 1993): 471–82; Michael J. Shapiro, "'Manning the Frontiers: The Politics of (Human) Nature in *Blade Runner*," in *In the Nature of Things: Language, Politics and the Environment*, ed. Jane Bennett and William Chaloupka (Minneapolis and London: University of Minnesota Press, 1993), 65–84; Jason P. Vest, "Double Jeopardy: The Sexual Dynamics of *Blade Runner*," in *The Image of the Twentieth Century: Proceedings, 2000 Conference, Society for the Interdisciplinary Study of Social Imagery*, ed. Will Wright and Steven Kaplan (Pueblo, CO: University of Southern Colorado, 2001), 349–58.

REY, FERNANDO (1917–1994)

Born Fernando Casado Arambillet in Spain, and made his debut in the 1939 Spanish film *Los Cuatros Robinsons*. Rey worked with Luis Buñuel on *The Discreet Charm of the Bourgeoisie* (1972), which earned him an award from the Cannes

Film Festival. He also received considerable plaudits for his role in the two *FRENCH CONNECTION* films (1971, 1975).

Cast in the cameo role of Antonio de Marchena, Columbus's associate in *1492: CONQUEST OF PARADISE*, Rey has little to do other than to assume a steadying role in the adventurer's life, advising him to remain true to his beliefs in the face of adversity. He assumes a dark, shadowy role; his face is seldom shown in light, suggesting that he will always act as the voice of conscience in Columbus's mind, even when he (the father) is not physically present. It is only at the end that he comes into his own, telling Columbus that he was proud of him: "You were like a willful child. You wouldn't accept what others told you. You had to find things out for yourself, and others, in the process."

Reference

Robert Thurston, *1492: Conquest of Paradise Based on a Screenplay by Roselyne Bosch* (London: Penguin Books, 1992), 201.

REYNOLDS, KEVIN (1952–)

Reynolds qualified as a lawyer before entering film school, where he was later recognized for a student film, which later became *Fandango* (1985). Reynolds's most well known films include *Robin Hood: Prince of Thieves* (1991) and *WATERWORLD* (1995). Reynolds was engaged by Scott to direct *TRISTAN + ISOLDE* on the basis of their friendship and his track record as director of the previous two films. In the production notes to the film Reynolds claimed that he was attracted to the story on account of it being "intensely romantic and sad, a beautiful tragedy that's Romeo and Juliet-esque in the way it unfolds."

Reynolds approaches the film as a love story which nonetheless emphasizes the importance of duty. Together with designer MARK GERAGHTY, he creates a world of the Dark Ages—all blacks, grays, and drab colors—which can only be enlightened by the two main characters' love affair. His achievement was recognized by one online reviewer who congratulated him on creating a prehistoric world "that may not have ever really existed, but it is one that certainly everyone wishes they could live in."

References

Keith Breese, "*Tristan + Isolde*," *FilmCritic.com*, www.filmcritic.com/misc/emporium.nsf/reviews/Tristan-and-Isolde (accessed 26 January 2009); Kevin Reynolds, quoted in *Production Notes: Tristan + Isolde* (Los Angeles: Twentieth Century-Fox, 2005), vii.

RKO 281

US/GB 1999 TVM r/t 90 min col. *Production Companies*: HBO Pictures, British Broadcasting Corporation, Labrador Films, Scott Free, and WGBH. *Executive Producers*: Ridley and Tony Scott. *Producer*: Su Armstrong. *Director*: Benjamin Ross.

Writer: John Logan, from the documentary *The Battle over Citizen Kane* written by Richard Ben Cramer and Thomas Lennon. *Production Designer*: Maria Djurkovic. *Director of Photography*: Mike Southon. *Music*: John Altman. *Cast*: Liev Schreiber (*Orson Welles*), James Cromwell (*William Randolph Hearst*), Melanie Griffith (*Marion Davies*), John Malkovich (*Herman Mankiewicz*), Liam Cunningham (*Gregg Toland*), David Suchet (*Louis B. Mayer*), Roy Scheider (*George Schaefer*), Brenda Blethyn (*Louella Parsons*).

RKO 281 was first proposed as a feature film in 1996, with Scott directing a cast that included Edward Furlong as Welles, Marlon Brando as William Randolph Hearst, and Madonna as Marion Davies, and a supporting cast including George C. Scott, Bette Midler, and Dustin Hoffman. The projected budget was over $40 million, with a script written by JOHN LOGAN, who had previously collaborated with Scott on the abortive project to film *I AM LEGEND*. However, the project could not find a home at any of the studios, particularly when it was rumored in newspapers such as *South Coast Today* that David Fincher was developing a rival project, tentatively called "Mank," based on the career of Herman Mankiewicz (which likewise came to nothing). Another report published in *Screen International* claimed that, as Scott's film was based on a PBS television documentary (*THE BATTLE OVER CITIZEN KANE*), which many viewers might not have seen, the studios felt that it would be difficult to recoup their investment.

Eventually the project was picked up by HBO with the participation of the BBC, and given a $10 million budget. Scott took on the role of producer, while handing over the directorial reins to BENJAMIN ROSS, a young British director whose previous films included *The Young Poisoner's Handbook* (1995). While including such well-known performers such as JOHN MALKOVICH and MELANIE GRIFFITH, the leading actor LIEV SCHREIBER had hitherto only taken supporting roles in films such as *Ransom* (1996) and *Scream* a year later. The cast also included such well-known television actors as BRENDA BLETHYN and DAVID SUCHET (as Louis B. Mayer), to attract British viewers.

For reasons of expense, *RKO 281* was filmed at Bray Studios in Great Britain, with locations in and around the area. According to an article published in Creation magazine, a large banqueting sequence, ostensibly taking place at William Randolph Hearst's mansion, was actually filmed at the Guildhall in central London. Two *Citizen Kane* sets were recreated in the studio.

The film received its first airing in the USA and Great Britain at Christmas 1999. In *Film Comment* J. Hoberman observed that Welles's *Citizen Kane* "dramatized the technique of filmmaking and manufactured celebrity, signaling the end of a classic, invisible cinema even as it prophesied the role of movies in a larger media system. *Kane*'s essential subject is the fake newsreel to which the drama provides a grandiose, authentic fictional footnote. *RKO 281* footnotes that footnote—demonstrating *Kane*'s thesis that what passes for history is a narrative hastily contrived to meet the needs of the present." He found Schreiber's Welles, and JAMES CROMWELL's Hearst repellent and manipulative, "as willful as . . . [they are] charmless." *Sight and Sound* suggested that Ross's Hearst and Welles "were two of a kind and that it's possible to cast Welles as a bully and Hearts as the tragic frustrated great man as the reverse. *RKO 281* may not transcend its Saturday night television gloss status, but thematically at least it's a brave try."

From the outset we are made aware that *RKO 281* will follow other Scott films—as director or producer—in dealing with an obsessive male central character. Like Columbus (GERARD DÉPARDIEU) in *1492: THE CONQUEST OF PARADISE*, Orson Welles in Logan's script is described as "unstoppable and resolute . . . Orson's a real barreler." Welles himself is well aware of his traits—in a line deleted from the finished film he calls himself the "Boy Wonder . . . a genius since the moment [he] was born." However, he is so wrapped up in himself that he remains totally indifferent to others; he deletes Herman Mankiewicz's (John Malkovich's) name from the script and justifies his action thus: "I own your [Mankiewicz's] script and I can do anything I goddamn want!" John Houseman's (Simeon Andrews's) observation is pertinent here: "Welcome to the world of Orson Welles," in which everything revolves around Welles himself. When he wants Mankiewicz to return to his side, Welles put on an act worthy of any barnstorming nineteenth century actor in an attempt to appeal to the older man's sympathies. It works like a charm: Welles "quickly bites off the end of his cigar—his expression is one of 'Gotcha!'—even as his cheeks are still wet with tears." Even when his employer George Schaefer (ROY SCHEIDER) offers some home truths about Welles's manipulative nature, Welles remains impervious, "lost in the dream factory" of his own self-image.

Scriptwriter Logan repeatedly draws parallels between Welles and William Randolph Hearst. Welles describes the media baron as "a titanic figure of limitless influence . . . living in a palace, a glorious palace on a hill, and controlling the permutations of everyone beneath him," who "loves in his own way. On his conditions. Because those are the only conditions he has ever known." Like Joe Tyrell in *BLADE RUNNER*, Hearst identifies himself as a godlike figure wielding "power like you couldn't begin to imagine"—as shown, for instance, in his reaction to the proposed release of *Citizen Kane*, when he calls all the Hollywood studio chiefs to a meeting and threatens to expose them, unless they conspire to destroy all the film's prints. Such behavior is also typical of Welles, who controls every aspect of the filmmaking process—acting, music, cinematography—even though he

has experienced professionals to assist him. Logan explicitly links the two of them in a stage direction, as they unexpectedly meet in an elevator: "Both men of mad grandeur and malevolent passion and stunning inspiration—both men of incalculable achievement and measureless poignancy."

One outcome of a world ruled by such megalomaniacs is that relationships become corrupted, both in the public and private spheres. Welles's father was an alcoholic; Hearst treats his lover Marion Davies (whom she calls "Pops") as a convenience; Schaefer likewise regards Welles as a petulant child who has to say thank you to his employer for suggesting the title *Citizen Kane*. Hearst treats his employees in a similarly offhand manner; he threatens Louella Parsons (Brenda Blethyn) with dismissal unless she tells him all the gossip relating to Hollywood that she can unearth.

A similar logic determines the film's representation of MASCULINITY. At first Welles and Mankiewicz are inseparable as they construct the script by bouncing ideas off one another. However, Welles soon reveals that friendship is expendable; once the script has been completed, he has no further use for the older man. Although the two are reunited later on, we understand that Welles embraces and dispenses with people at will; like a vampire he sucks the blood out of them and leaves them for dead. This metaphor runs throughout Logan's script: Louella demands Welles's blood in retribution for his having lied to her.

The film also suggests that in the dog-eat-dog world of early 1940s Hollywood women have to be as ruthless as men in order to survive. Louella and her fellow gossip columnist Hedda Hopper (Fiona Shaw) use their position to manipulate others. In a scene deleted from the finished film, Logan describes the two of them thus: "They occasionally glance back and forth at each other like ravenous hyenas eyeing the last bit of carrion." By contrast Marion's childlike devotion to Hearst appears as something unusual, almost foolhardy, as she sacrifices her star status and faces the prospect of living in penury after Hearst's downfall.

Hearst's description of the world he and Welles create is telling: "men will do anything to sell their newspapers and their movies . . . where no price is too high for fame and power? Where we will all scratch each other to pieces just to be heard? Can we truly envision such . . . horror?" This is a world where AMERICANISM is identified with "good red-white-and-blue [white] Americans, and the way they [the media] see it you can't be a good American and a Jew." The studio bosses—all of whom are Jewish—try to deny their ethnic backgrounds, passing off themselves instead as "real Americans," rather than "bedraggled foreigners and swarthy refugees." This recalls a theme explored in *BLACK RAIN* about what constitutes a "true" American, and whether American identity as represented on the screen can allow for plural interpretations. *RKO 281* suggests that this is unrealistic in a context where everyone dedicates themselves to self-interest.

At one point Welles describes Xanadu in *Citizen Kane* as nothing except "a matte painting and a camera trick." However, this film-world is so overpowering that it takes over people's lives. Welles, Mankiewicz, and cinematographer Gregg Toland (Liam Cunningham) emerge from the studio into the RKO backlot after an all-night filming session. There they see actors in costume bustling about on their way to work. The studio dedicates itself to illusions, which might be financially profitable but which have the capacity to destroy individual lives. This is precisely what happens to Welles—despite the fact that he makes *Citizen Kane* and achieves celebrity status, he is left isolated and uncertain in his private life. Mankiewicz observes somewhat trenchantly that Welles has made his masterpiece at twenty-six: "It's a bitch. I mean, where do you go from here?" Given the struggles Welles faced in the next half-century, as his career foundered amidst a welter of half-fulfilled projects and unrealized ideas, the answer is clearly downwards. Like Hearst he was "a man who could have been great, but was not."

To date there has been no critical comment on *RKO 281*. The making of *Citizen Kane* however, has been discussed in detail, most notably by Robert L. Carringer in *The Making of Citizen Kane* (rev. ed. 1996).

References

Connie Benesch, "Welles Finally Becomes Hollywood Hot Property," *South Coast Today*, 7 September 1997, http://archive.south-coasttoday.com/daily/09-97/09-07-97/e08ae191.htm (accessed 18 November 2008); Robert L. Carringer, *The Making of Citizen Kane*, rev. ed. (Berkeley and London: University of California Press, 1996); Charles Hewitt, "Timelords," *Creation* (December 1999), 13–14, 16; J. Hoberman, "RKO 281," *Film Comment* 36, no.1 (Jan/Feb 2000): 75–6; John Logan, "Draft Script for *RKO 281*" (dated 1 May 1997), http://sfy.ru/sfy.html?script=rko218 (accessed 16 November 2008; *Screen International*, 3 July 1998, 6; *Sight and Sound* 10, no.1 (January 2000): 8–9.

Bibliography

"The Big O," *Vanity Fair*, November 1999, 42–51.

ROACHE, LINUS (1964–)

British character actor who made his debut in the soap opera *Coronation Street* playing Peter Barlow, son of Ken Barlow (played by Roache's real-life father William Roache).

Roache made his name in low-budget British films such as *Priest* (1994) before being cast as Merton Densher in Iain Softley's *Wings of the Dove* (1997). Cast as Wigram in the Ridley Scott-produced *THE GATHERING STORM*, Roache gives a performance combining a degree of steeliness with a genuine concern for the future of his family, as he willfully breaks the law by passing on confidential documents to Churchill (ALBERT FINNEY), in the belief that appeasing Hitler must be prevented at once. Eventually the struggle to reconcile personal and governmental loyalties proves too much for him, and he apparently kills himself. In a preproduction interview Roache described the character as complex: "I went through two different opinions on that [his suicide]; I was convinced he did and then, as I started playing it, I thought well, maybe he just had a complete nervous breakdown and a heart attack . . . He's a man of conscience . . . He wants something to be done about it, but he doesn't really want to do it himself." Sometimes Ralph's nerve fails—on one occasion he tells Churchill that "Perhaps the Prime Minister's right. Perhaps we should try to find a compromise with Herr Hitler." However, Ralph is talked out of his doubts by Churchill, who remains convinced that it is truly his destiny to save England and the Empire. Ralph comments admiringly: "You're an extraordinary man, Winston." Sadly Ralph is not an extraordinary man; torn between love for his family and duty towards his country, he eventually commits suicide.

References

The Gathering Storm: Information Pack issued 17 June 2002 (London: BBC, 2002), www.bbc.co.uk/pressoffice/pressreleases/stories/2002/06_june/17/gathering_storm_pack.pdf (accessed 24 December 2008), 14; "*The Gathering Storm*: Transcript of the Screenplay by Hugh Whitemore," www.script-o-rama.com/novie_scripts/g/gatheringstorm-script-transcript.html (accessed 23 December 2008)

ROAD MOVIES

Classic road films—*Easy Rider* (1969), *Badlands* (1973)—are normally about male privilege, the right to hit the road without worrying about work, children, or family. Women are not normally the protagonists; they are often what the men seek to run away from. Timothy Corrigan defines the classic road movie according to four specific characteristics: (a) a breakdown of the family unit; (b) a context where obstacles are consistently presented for the male characters to overcome; (c) a protagonist readily identified with a certain means of transportation (e.g., a motorcycle); and (d) a focus on men alone.

BLACK RAIN begins by alluding to the road film, with the shot of Nick Conklin (MICHAEL DOUGLAS) driving along the Hudson River on his motorcycle. A divorced man committed to his work, his main leisure-time activity consists of proving his manhood by racing (and ultimately emerging victorious) over his (male) fellow-bikers. The same situation is repeated in *THE HIRE*: "HOSTAGE," as The Driver (CLIVE OWEN) races along the streets of San Francisco in a desperate search for a kidnapped woman Linda (Kathryn Morris), whose car has been driven into the Pacific Ocean.

In *THELMA & LOUISE* the protagonists follow the tradition of the road movie in the fact that they are most happy when they are moving. They encounter numerous obstacles. However, Scott reverses the tradition of the genre by showing the two women as active while their male counterparts are the ones left behind. Thelma's husband Darryl (CHRISTOPHER McDONALD) remains virtually housebound, while Louise's boyfriend Jimmy (MICHAEL MADSEN) is seldom photographed in exterior shots, despite making the effort to find Louise.

Tom Conley sees this reversal as a means for the two women to forge new lives, unfettered by patriarchal power: "The heroines never accede to an interstate highway where they would not be lost, nor do they take advantage of 'welcome centers' at rest stops that would afford them free maps of the states (Texas excepted) in which they drive. The fact that they don't know where they are going affords us, in turn, thanks to the story of their demise; to act out fantasies of getting lost in a world where cinema figures in a growing network of roads that foster illusions of boundlessness." By contrast the British critic Leslie Dick believes that "Puritanism is built in" to the women's dreams: "Whenever Thelma has fun with men, something terrible happens . . . The very end, when the grrrls drive their car over the cliff, is one of those times you feel, 'Shit, these women have to die because they are about to turn to each other and say, 'I love you.'" While it is certainly true that "something terrible [always] happens" to the two women, this is a characteristic of the road film genre. And perhaps the final moment where they turn to one another should be viewed in a positive light as an acknowledgement that they have at last escaped from the patriarchy. The same scene is repeated once again in *WHERE THE MONEY IS*; but this time the two protagonists are an older man (PAUL NEWMAN) and a much younger woman (LINDA FIORENTINO). They drive over a pier into a lake; but emerge later on to resume their lives as a spring-and-autumn Bonnie and Clyde, free from the constraints of their world.

The road movie conventions are inverted in *CLAY PIGEONS*, as Clay (JOAQUIN PHOENIX) is shown returning in his truck from the wilds of the Montana desert back to Mercer, the small town where he has spent most of his life. In this case the road symbolizes imprisonment. It is only at the of the film, when Clay has been cleared of any potential crimes and escaped the cloying friendship of the serial killer Lester Long (VINCE VAUGHN), that he can hit the road once again and seek permanent freedom from his past life.

References

Tom Conley, *Cartographic Cinema* (Minneapolis: University of Minnesota Press, 2007), 172; Timothy Corrigan, *A Cinema without Walls: Films and Culture after Vietnam* (New Brunswick NJ: Rutgers University Press, 1991), 143–45; Leslie Dick, "R:Road," *Sight and Sound* 7, no.11 (November 1997): 22.

Bibliography

Jack Boozer, "Seduction and Betrayal in the Heartland: *Thelma & Louise*," *Literature/Film Quarterly* 23, no.3 (1995): 188–96; Manohla Dargis, "*Thelma & Louise* and the Tradition of the Male Road Movie," in *Women and Film: A Sight and Sound Reader*, ed. Pam Cook and Philip Dodd (London: Scarlet Press, 1993), 86–93; Jessica Enevold, "The Daughters of *Thelma and Louise*: New? Aesthetics of the Road," in *Gender, Genre and Identity in Women's Travel Writing*, ed. Kristi Siegel (New York: Peter Lang Publishing, Inc., 2004), 73–97; Carmen Indurain Eroso, "*Thelma & Louise*: Easy Riders in a Male Genre," *Atlantis: Revista de la Associacion Espanola de Estudios Anglo-Norteamericanos* 23, no.1 (June 2001): 63–73.

ROBINSON, TODD (1969–)

Film writer and director whose credits include the screenplay for *WHITE SQUALL*, plus *Lonely Hearts* (2006) as director.

Bibliography

"Lonely Hearts' Todd Robinson," www.comingsoon.net/news/movienews.php?id=19734 (accessed 1 March 2009)

ROCKWELL, SAM (1968–)

American character actor who made his film debut in *Clownhouse* (1989). His subsequent films include *The Green Mile* (1999), *Charlie's Angels* (2000), and *Confessions of a Dangerous Mind* (2002).

Cast as Frank, Roy Waller's (NICOLAS CAGE's) sidekick in *MATCHSTICK MEN*, Rockwell forms part of a double-act, in which both of them can play any roles they desire. Scott suggested in a pre-production interview that Frank could be "anything from earnest to outrageous, quiet, loud, indignant—you name it." For most of the film he acts as subordinate—until the final con, when Frank admits in the script that "he [Roy] taught me most of what I know, so I suppose I owe you better than this . . . But you always said if I got a shot at a big score, I should take it . . . I'd never find a better partner. Now I won't have to." The pupil has now become the master conman. On the other hand the film suggests that Frank's triumph is a hollow one, as Roy discovers far more important things about life—for example the importance of MARRIAGE and family.

As Charley Ford in *THE ASSASSINATION OF JESSE JAMES BY THE COWARD ROBERT FORD*, Rockwell begins the film as a traditional older brother, by turns teasing and protecting, but, as Ford grows closer to Jesse and more confident in his own abilities, their roles begin to reverse. Before long, it's Bob who calls the shots and an increasingly passive and conflicted Charley struggling to keep up. Meanwhile Charley experiences a conflict of loyalty between his brother and his friend Jesse; but remains unable to do much about it on account of his disability. Rockwell suggested in a pre-production interview that "There's the alpha male and the beta, and Charley will always be the beta. He had a clubfoot, a disability that he always took great care to camouflage, and he was always a little hungry and vulnerable and just grateful, really, to be in the gang." While Charley eventually connives in James's murder, he is overcome by guilt. In ANDREW DOMINIK's screenplay the narrator describes his state of mind: "He began to look at his younger brother with spite, as if he suspected that in some future performance [of James's killing] he might present himself to a live cartridge in Robert Ford's gun." His death by suicide is shot in extended close-up as he shoots himself through the heart.

References
"About the Production [*Assassination of Jesse James*]," http://party931.com/common/movies/notes/54706-1-full.html (accessed 12 August 2008); Andrew Dominik, "The Assassination of Jesse James by the Coward Robert Ford," Final White Draft Screenplay dated 17 August 2005, www.simplyscripts.com/oscar80.html (accessed 5 February 2009); Nick and Ted Griffin, "*Matchstick Men*: Shooting Draft" (14 October 2002), www.imsdb.com/scripts/Matchstick-Men.html (accessed 4 January 2009); *Production Information: Matchstick Men* (Los Angeles: Warner Bros. Pictures, 2003), 8–9.

ROGERS, MIMI (1956–)
Born Miriam Sprickler in Coral Gables, Florida. In the early 1980s she began to carve a career out for herself in Hollywood, appearing in television and films. Her major break came in *SOMEONE TO WATCH OVER ME*, where she played Claire Gregory. Scott recalled in an interview with Brian Case that her part "would've been a lot easier to cast twenty years ago. It could've been Deborah Kerr, Grace Kelly, but actresses don't look like that anymore. They have a different kind of persona now . . . I went through a very lengthy casting process because I wanted a woman who could project some sort of class." Rogers herself recalled to Jann Wenner that "the screen test [for *Someone*] went very well. Tom Berenger and I hit it off immediately. Tom [Cruise] and I were leaving for New York the next day, and I figured I probably wouldn't hear anything till the end of the week. But we heard on the plane."

Like TOM BERENGER's Mike Keegan, Rogers's Claire is distinguished by a singular lack of emotion; her background and EDUCATION as an upper-class NEW YORKER has taught her to suppress her emotions in order to sustain a veneer of social respectability. The only time she deems it appropriate to smile is when in the company of her social equals—for example, at the Guggenheim reception when she allows Antonia, an elegant older woman (Meg Mundy), to fall into her arms: "Antonia, almost emotionally overcome that Claire has managed it [to come to the party." To fall in love with Mike represents a significant step for her; it is the first time she has acknowledged her emotions, even if it means putting her social position at risk. In the end the relationship is doomed to fail. Claire has to say goodbye to Mike while vainly endeavoring to sustain a civilized veneer: "(*[B]arely able to speak*) I'll miss you, Mike . . . (*half-laugh, half cry*) You have a weakness for Lady Cops."

Rogers was later cast as Amy in the Ridley Scott-produced comedy *MONKEY TROUBLE*. In a largely secondary role, she is shown initially as a poor parent, whose obsessive love for her stepson Jack (Adrian/Julian Johnson) means that she ignores her daughter Eva (THORA BIRCH). Eva herself learns to become a "good" parent by looking after the monkey Dodger. However, all turns out well at the end of the film: Amy appears to learn to care for both her children, while at the same time realizing that she must allow Eva some freedom to act on her own. According to the pressbook Rogers enjoyed the experience of the film: "[I]t challenged everyone to be better. Everyone working on this film had to be even more focused than usual because of the large number of difficult things the monkey had to do. When the monkey got it perfect, no one else could afford to screw it up."

References
Brian Case, "Great Scott," *Time Out* (London), 2–9 March 1988, 15; Howard Franklin, Danilo Bach, and David Seltzer, "Someone to Watch Over Me" (revised 4 December 1986), www.imsdb.com/scripts/Someone-To-Watch-Over-Me.html (accessed 9 June 2008); *Pressbook, Monkey Trouble* (London: Entertainment Film Distributors ltd., 1994), 14; Jann Wenner, "The Seduction of Mimi: Mimi Rogers," *Interview*, December 1987, 103.

RONA, JEFF (1957–)
Born in Los Angeles and worked mostly in television before making his film debut in *WHITE SQUALL*.

This is the Scott film with the most source music, in this case early 1960s rock and roll. Like the film, the music is something of a gem, combining a poetic and ambient sensibility with inventive use of percussive instruments. HANS ZIMMER produced the soundtrack album.

Bibliography
"Now Showing," *Music from the Movies* 28 (August 2000): 9–10.

"RONNIE AND LEO"
An unfilmed black comedy with a heist theme, slated to star Michael York and Ernest Borgnine, which was slated to be Scott's first feature film, but never made it to the screen.

ROSS, BENJAMIN (1964–)

Born in London, Ross's debut film was *My Little Eye* (1992). He worked on the successful low-budget black comedy *The Young Poisoner's Handbook* (1994), and wrote the screenplay for *Simon Magus* (1999).

Engaged by Scott to work on the television film RKO 281, Ross created what he described in *American Cinematographer* as a factionalized version of history: "I've tried to give dramatic weight—and equal claim—to both [Herman] Mankiewicz and [Orson] Welles, even though we present a very fudged version of what happened . . . The trick was to give the movie the potential for visual sophistication without forcing it upon the audience, because a lot of people who watch it may not have seen *Kane* . . . ." The film was shot in London rather than America (as a co-production between HBO and the BBC, as well as for economy's sake). Ross believed that the film did not lose its dramatic effect because "London is fantastically rich. You can shoot practically anything in London. It's a great joy to find 1940s California on your doorstep."

Reviewers liked Ross's efforts. One online correspondent commended him for creating "an absorbing . . . docudrama . . . [that] imparts some marvelously juicy insider lore, such as the real meaning behind the famous dying despatch in the history of movies: 'Rosebud' [a pet name given by Hearst for Marion Davies's vagina]."

References

Laura Mirsky, "RKO 281," www.amazon.com/RKO-281-Battle-Over-Citizen/dp/0783116764 (accessed 23 November 2008); Mark Salisbury, "Raising Kane," *American Cinematographer* 80, no.10 (October 1999): 83.

ROSS, HUGH (?–)

Attended St. Andrew's University in Scotland for two years, but dropped out and became a teacher. Ross subsequently studied at the Royal Academy of Dramatic Arts, London. His films and television series include *Charlotte Gray* (2001), *Taggart* (2002–2003), and *Hannibal Rising* (2007).

Cast as the (unseen) narrator in *THE ASSASSINATION OF JESSE JAMES BY THE COWARD ROBERT FORD*, Ross's sonorous tones encourage us to believe that he is somehow reliable: "The month of October came, and Jesse began seeing Pinkerton operatives in every floor walker, street sweeper, and common man poking about in a store." However, as the film unfolds, we gradually understand that the narrator is simply a journalist who (like everyone else in a celebrity-obsessed culture) is searching for a good story which might only have a passing relationship to historical truth. Some of his conclusions are unutterably banal ("Men who choose to be outlaws cannot afford to be in one place for very long"; on other occasions, he allows his penchant

for elaborate language to run away with him: "Jesse was sick with wounds and aches, and lung congestions. Insomnia stained his eye sockets like soot. He read augeries [*sic*] in the snarled intestines of chickens, or the blow of cat hair released to the wind."

Reference

Andrew Dominik, "The Assassination of Jesse James by the Coward Robert Ford." Final White Draft Screenplay dated 17 August 2005, www.simplyscripts.com/oscar80.html (accessed 5 February 2009).

RSA (RIDLEY SCOTT ASSOCIATES)

Formed in 1967 by Ridley and Tony Scott, it now has offices in London, New York, Los Angeles, and Hong Kong. The company has provided a training-ground for directors and other creative personnel to produce groundbreaking commercials. Among its current staff listed on the website (www.rsafilms.com) are Ridley Scott, TONY SCOTT, JORDAN SCOTT, JAKE and LUKE SCOTT, ANDREW DOMINIK, JOE CARNAHAN, and HUGH JOHNSON. The site also contains examples of some of Ridley Scott's best commercials—ORANGE: FUTURE THOUGHTS, MIDLAND BANK, EDEN ROC CHANEL NO.5.

Bibliography

"Hot Shots," *Creation*, March 1999, 14; Richard Natale, "Commercial Break" (1999), in *Ridley Scott Interviews*, ed. Laurence F. Knapp and Andrea F. Kulas, 172–79; Brendan Tapley, "Bond of Brothers" (2002), in *Ridley Scott Interviews*, ed. Laurence F. Knapp and Andrea F. Kulas (Jackson: University Press of Mississippi, 2005), 218–23.

R3

GB 1964–5 TV Series 26 × 50 min episodes b/w. *Production Company*: British Broadcasting Corporation. *Producers*: Andrew Osborn, John Robins (thirteen episodes each). *Directors*: Bill Hays (six episodes), Paul Bernard (four episodes), Moira Armstrong (three episodes), Terence Williams (three episodes), Douglas Hurn (three episodes), Peter Dews, Michael Leeson-Smith (six episodes each). *Writers*: N. J. Crisp (six episodes), Bill McIlwraith (four episodes), Donald Bull (three episodes), William Emms (two episodes). *Production Designers*: Tim Gleeson, Ridley Scott (one episode each). *Music*: Ken Thorne. *Cast*: Patricia Healey (*Jill Travers*), Betty Cooper (*Nora Gerrard*), Alex Scott (*Dr. Max Rankel*).

The adventures of staff at Research Center Number Three who deal with all manner of scientific ideas and issues, including drugs, technology, space flight, and underwater exploration. Scott designed the episode "And No Birds Sing" (Series 2, Episode 8), written by Bill Hays and directed by Douglas Young.

RUBINSTEIN, JOHN (1946-)

The multi-faceted actor/singer/composer/director John Rubinstein was born in Los Angeles in 1946. His biggest claim to fame would occur on Broadway in the late 1970s when he starred in *Children of a Lesser God*, which won him the Tony, Drama Desk, and L.A. Drama Critics Circle awards. However, he lost out in the film version to William Hurt.

Rubinstein has a thankless role in *SOMEONE TO WATCH OVER ME* as Neil Steinhart, the rich boyfriend of Claire Gregory (MIMI ROGERS). His main function is to provide a contrast to Mike Keegan (TOM BERENGER). Whereas the police officer is portrayed as fundamentally decent, torn between the responsibilities of family life and his desire for Claire, Neil is someone who will neither show his emotions nor make the effort to relate to people from different social classes. The script suggests that Neil treats Mike like a servant rather than a police officer: "When you're through with it [the book], put it back, please, exactly where you found it, and don't use the library again. I have to leave town for a few days. Let's do everything we can to make this [ordeal for Claire] less of a trial for her, shall we?" Mike's reaction is predictable: "when NEIL leaves, he makes a mock 'military salute,' a click of the heels." Nonetheless the script makes clear that Neil loves Claire as much as Mike: "NEIL takes her in his arms, holding her tightly, affectionately, protectively . . . [and] KISSES CLAIRE gently on her neck."

Reference

Howard Franklin, Danilo Bach, and David Seltzer, "Someone to Watch Over Me" (revised 4 December 1986), www.imsdb.com/scripts/Someone-To-Watch-Over-Me.html (accessed 9 June 2008).

SALOMON, MIKAEL (1945–)

Born in Denmark and worked there until 1988 as a cinematographer when he made his debut in Great Britain with *Stealing Heaven*. His first film as director was A *Far Off Place* (1993). Salomon moved to America in the late 1990s, where he worked mostly in television on films such as Stephen King's *Salem's Lot* (2004) and *The Grid* (also 2004).

Engaged by Scott as director on THE COMPANY (after Scott abandoned plans to appoint different directors—including himself—for each of the three episodes), Salomon answered the charge that he was romanticizing the Cold War period in his story of the CIA in an interview with *TV Zone*: "I don't think it ever is a comfortable time to be a spy, and I think we're showing that because O'Donnell's [CHRIS O'DONNELL's] character, who is a very idealistic character, and I think in the end the question remains, what really happened? Was it worth it? Did we make all those sacrifices, and what for? . . . we took a lot of inspiration from the old spy thrillers, from FILM NOIR, definitely from *THE THIRD MAN* . . . it became more of a brain thriller than an action thriller . . . you follow the characters and really feel for them, and you understand what's going on. This cat-and-mouse game that goes on, to me, set the mood."

As a former cinematographer Salomon was also concerned about the look of the films. He told *American Cinematographer* that he had been inspired by the chiaroscuro techniques of artists such as Rembrandt, Caravaggio, and van Honthorst: "Rather than use backlight, I crosslit the actors with a fairly dynamic contrast range and then silhouetted the dark side against a lit area on the background. This gave the images a sense of depth and cohesive style."

Salomon's second film as director with Scott as producer was the 2008 television miniseries THE ANDROMEDA STRAIN. In an interview with *If Magazine*, he and screenwriter Robert Schenkkan wanted to update Michael Crichton's novel for "a sophisticated and demanding viewing audience." While the novel was "the original Techno-thriller," "audiences are now quite familiar with this genre and its various tropes and you have to work a bit harder to stay ahead of them today. And the world has changed so much. It feels more complicated, faster-paced and, frankly, more dangerous on a number of levels. We are so much more aware now of how interconnected everything is and how fragile life itself is. It would have been a disservice to our viewing audience not to give that reality expression."

References

Peter Brown and A. C. Ferrante, "Robert Schenkkan Gets Infected for the Andromeda Strain Mini-Series," *If Magazine*, 24 June 2008, www.ifmagazine.com/feature.asp?article=2819 (accessed 15 February 2009); Simon Gray, "Covert Ops," *American Cinematographer* 88, no.8 (August 2007): 28; "The Company of Wolves," *TV Zone* 219 (September 2007): 60.

SAMMON, PAUL M. (1949–)

Indefatigable chronicler of Ridley Scott's films, especially *ALIEN* and *BLADE RUNNER*. He has also interviewed Scott for *G.I. JANE*. His books include *Splatterpunks: Extreme Horror* (1991), *Tales of Elvis Post-Mortem* (1994), *The Making of Starship Troopers* (1998), and *Conan the Phenomenon* (2007). A witness to the making of *Blade Runner*, Sammon's book *Future Noir* (2nd ed. 2007) chronicles the film's origins and subsequent fortunes over the past twenty-five years in exhaustive detail. Sometimes the sheer amount of factual information tends to overwhelm the reader; but the book is nonetheless a valuable record of how the film was made, as well as providing a unique insight into Scott's working practices. Sammon has also published a study of Ridley Scott's entire oeuvre (*Ridley Scott Close Up: The Making of his Movies* [1999]) and written the introduction to *Alien: The Complete Illustrated Screenplay* (2001). Most recently Sammon has appeared in many of the featurettes and documentaries included in the five-disc *Blade Runner: Collector's Edition* (2007).

Bibliography

"Bibliography of Paul M. Sammon's Books," *Fantastic Fiction*, www.fantasticfiction.co.uk/s/paul-m-sammon/ (accessed 12 February 2009).

SANCHEZ, MARCO (1970–)

Television actor who made his name with the series *SeaQuest DSV* (1993–1995).

Cast as the conservative journalist Henry Ramirez in *THE LAST DEBATE*, Sanchez offers a penetrating study of an apparently committed conservative journalist, full of self-righteous belief in the Republican presidential candidate Richard Meredith (Stephen Young), who eventually succumbs to the lure of money. He not only agrees to sacrifice his principles, but agrees to a name-change as he becomes half of a new double-act in *Hank and Barb*, a network show presented with his fellow panelist Barbara Manning (AUDRA McDONALD). Whereas earlier in the film we see him as a fanatic committed to purity of body and soul (he regularly visits the gym as well as refusing to be compromised on any of his principles), he is now seen eating buttered toast and bantering with his fellow presenter in the hope that this will sustain the show's high ratings.

SANDERSON, WILLIAM (1944–)

William Sanderson began his career in the theater and graduated to small roles in television (*Starsky and Hutch*) and on screen (*Coal Miner's Daughter* [1980]).

Cast as Sebastian, Tyrell's engineer in *BLADE RUNNER*, Sanderson based his interpretation on Einstein's image of the little man, suffering from Methuselah's syndrome, "the boy who looked middle-aged," in Howard Maxford's phrase. Clearly more at home with machines rather than human beings, Sebastian nonetheless seems strangely unfamiliar with REPLICANTS—especially Batty (RUTGER HAUER), who uses the chess game between Sebastian and Tyrell (JOE TURKEL) to arrange a confrontation with his maker. Sebastian quite literally makes friends to pass the time; when faced with women, even replicant women like Pris (DARYL HANNAH), he remains painfully shy. This underlines the extent to which technology has undermined the capacity of human beings to think and feel in the LOS ANGELES of 2019.

Reference

Howard Maxford, "Early Aging," *Starburst* 271 (March 2001): 66.

SANDS, JULIAN (1958–)

Made his name during the 1980s with films such as *The Killing Fields* (1986), *A Room with a View* (1987), and *The Turn of the Screw* (1992).

Cast as Tom Gilbert, the new member of staff in *THE BROWNING VERSION*, Sands has a largely minor role. His function is largely symbolic—as a tall, fair-haired man with an enthusiasm for his new post as Head of Modern Languages (replacing the aging classics teacher Crocker-Harris [ALBERT FINNEY]) he is a representative of the new order that is gradually superseding the old. Although sympathetic to Crocker-Harris's plight, it is clear that Tom is more concerned with trying to establish his reputation amongst the boys. As the film unfolds, however, we discover that Gilbert is also a classical scholar, who can readily translate the inscription written by Taplow (BEN SILVERSTONE) inside the *Browning Version* (the version of the Agamemnon translated by Robert Browning). The camera focuses on his face as he looks up, visibly moved at the boy's description of Crocker-Harris as "a gentle master." At this point he realizes that teaching is only partially concerned with subject delivery; it requires a great deal of humanity as well. Even Crocker-Harris, cruelly described by the boys as "the Hitler of the Lower Fifth," possesses that quality.

SARA, MIA (1967–)

Born Mia Sarapocciello in Brooklyn Heights, New York, on 19 June 1967. At sixteen, Mia won her first feature starring role, debuting as Princess Lily in Ridley Scott's fairy tale adventure, *LEGEND*. According to Mia's own account given to Daniel O'Neill: "I saw Ridley, read about half a scene, and he said, 'Stop. Don't read anymore.' I did a videotape here [in Los Angeles], and then I was flown to London." The experience of the film proved interesting for her as she tried to portray a princess as someone possessing "innocence with an edge. She's passionate and manipulative but very lovely . . . She's much like Scarlett O'Hara . . . She starts off innocent and becomes a great deal more sophisticated." This was evident, for example, in the discovery of her willfulness; her insatiable desire to touch the unicorns plunges the forest into a new Ice Age, despite the fact that Jack (TOM CRUISE) had expressly forbidden her to do so. Scott begged to differ from Sara's interpretation of the character, as he suggested in an interview quoted by PAUL M. SAMMON that "[b]asically, she was a brat . . . it was Lily's manipulative streak that let her be seduced to the side of evil."

However, much of this aspect of her character was cut out of the film's original version. Lily has a largely passive role; her major scene is the mock dance of death with Darkness (TIM CURRY) where she is put under a spell and transformed into a devil-like figure, complete with a long gown and black lipstick. Although Scott makes it clear that she has been bewitched, there remains the distinct suggestion that she has the capacity for evil within herself; she is not quite the purer-than-purer heroine that Jack imagines her to be.

In *LEGEND*: THE DIRECTOR'S CUT Lily appeared more like the person Scott had originally envisaged. A self-interested person, she was not especially concerned about Jack's feelings; she kisses him once, and Jack is afraid to respond for fear that Lily might break his heart. In this new version, even Jack realizes that Lily is not quite what she seems. This foreshadows the revised ending when Jack promises to be there for her always. The two of them run away in a long shot, followed by a close-up where Lily holds a flower and kisses Jack on the cheek. However, the film ends with a shot of Jack running away without Lily towards the sun, followed by another shot of Jack waving to the fairies. This suggests that the two of them have separated: Lily has gone her own way, and we doubt whether she has reformed. Perhaps the spell cast upon her has had a greater effect than anyone anticipated.

References

Patrick Daniel O'Neill, "Mira Sara: Innocence with an Edge," *Starlog* 105 (April 1986): 16; Ridley Scott, quoted in Paul M. Sammon, *Ridley Scott Close-Up: The Making of His Movies* (New York: Thunder's Mouth Press, 1999), 78.

SARANDON, SUSAN (1946–)

Born Susan Abigail Tomalin in New York. Sarandon made her name as Janet in the cult film *The Rocky Horror Picture Show* (1975). She took a major role in *THE HUNGER*, directed by TONY SCOTT.

Cast as Louise in *THELMA & LOUISE*, Sarandon recalled in an essay by Karen Hollinger that she and Scott "fought about things. We changed scenes." Sarandon claims she only took the part because Scott met her demand that the ending not be changed: "The first thing I demanded from the director was that I die in the last scene. I didn't want the movie to end with me in Club Med. Once he assured me I was definitely on the death list, I accepted the part." She also demanded other changes: that in packing for the trip, Louise should show her meticulousness by packing her belongings in ziplock bags; that the women had to get progressively more dirty as they continued their journey; that Louise would at some point exchange her jewelry for the old man's dirty hat; and that she should have a pensive moment of reflection in the middle of the Grand Canyon landscape. Sarandon also considered it inappropriate to have a love scene with Jimmy (MICHAEL MADSEN): "Not only would the film lose some of its tension, but also a woman who's just killed somebody because she's remembering having been raped—it's pretty hard to have sex under the circumstances and have it be great. Somehow that would cost us a lot of credibility." Sarandon also claims she persuaded Scott not to have GEENA DAVIS do a topless shot in the film. Davis claimed in an interview that Sarandon said "'Oh, for heaven's sake, Ridley. Geena is not going to take her shirt off in this scene.' He said, 'Okay, okay.'" Finally, Sarandon introduced the kiss at the end of the film: "They [the producers] weren't sure about me kissing Geena at the end, because of the gay thing, but the sun was setting, we had to finish it in two takes, so I knew they'd have to go with it."

According to an interview with the actress given on National Public Radio, Louise is clearly someone who, although outwardly strong, is nonetheless keen to erase her past—especially the experience of being raped in Texas. However, as the action progresses she understands that she is engaged in "some kind of search for an understanding of this moment"—in other words, to make sense of her present experiences and use them as part of a process of self-development. This process is not an easy one—especially after the two women have been robbed by JD (BRAD PITT), Louise succumbs to a fit of despair. Once she is out on the road again, however, she recovers herself. In an interview with *Premiere* magazine, Sarandon describes it: "In the movie, I get out of the car, kind of look around, and see that old guy sitting there alone. I take off my watch and my rings and trade them for his hat. Louise is really seeing things differently, and I think condensing things into a short period of time—staying up for four days straight—helps you lose perspective. I was trying to figure out a way you'd get to a point where you really would drive off a cliff."

Like her costar Geena Davis, Sarandon was unaware of just how much impact the film had on audiences at the time of its premiere. In the *Premiere* interview she recalled, "I don't think we understood what a challenge that was to the way things are. It's a primal threat—a woman with a gun. She's pissed off and she can give back what she got. It's something women aren't supposed to do."

Sarandon's role in the film has contributed greatly to the development of her public persona, most aptly summarized by Susan Knobloch as "a full-grown, desirable woman, who believes in sexual freedom when it comes both to herself (at any age, the idea of any kind of sensuality from celibacy to promiscuity is hers to choose) and to her partners (younger men, an older woman, or no one at all). She is also her own woman in the corridors of public power, and she relates to other women without undue jealousy and without always putting men first. If this persona is not clearly enough influenced by the feminism of the American 1960s through the 1980s, the public image of 'Susan Sarandon, celebrity' is one of a far left activist, a well- and outspoken critic of immigration policy."

References

Juliann Garey and Bronwen Hruska, "Road Worriers," *Premiere* 14 no.10 (June 2001): 84, 105; Karen Hollinger, *The Actress: Hollywood Acting and the Female Star* (New York and Abingdon, UK: Routledge, 2006), 131–32; Susan Knobloch, "Interplaying Identities: Acting and the Building Blocks of Character in *Thelma and Louise*," in *Thelma & Louise Live!: The Cultural Afterlife of an American Film*, ed. Bernie Cook (Austin: University of Texas Press, 2007), 97; Susan Sarandon, interviewed by Terry Gross on "Fresh Air," National Public Radio, 16 December 1999.

Bibliography

Graham Fuller, "Susan Sarandon: It's Your Duty as an American to Question Your Government," *Interview* 21, no.6 (June 1991): 104–7, 112; Marc Shapiro, *Susan Sarandon: Actress-Activist* (Amherst, NY: Prometheus Books, 2001).

SAVAGE, JOHN (1950–)

Dependable Hollywood character actor. Early films include *Steelyard Blues* (1972) with Jane Fonda, followed by a guest role in the TV series *Cade's County*. Described himself once as an actor who was "always a victim because I love it. In my own life, I can feel myself victimised but at the same time I recognise the egocentric state of mind that allows me to feel that way." He enjoyed working with Ridley Scott on *WHITE SQUALL*, as it fulfilled his desire (expressed in a 1981 interview) to work with the best directors. As the Shakespeare-quoting McCrea, Savage portrays an old sea-dog—initially perceived by the young crew members as an eccentric, but whose fondness for literary allusions eventually assumes importance for them as well. This is especially evident when the boys visit the Galapagos Islands, and Gieg (SCOTT WOLF) observes in a voiceover that he at last understood Homer's dictum about the importance of the journey.

Reference

Minty Clinch, "The Winning Victim," *Ms. London*, 23 March 1981, 17.

SAVIDES, HARRIS (1957–)

The native New Yorker had long been one of the most respected cinematographers in the fields of commercials and music videos before making the move to feature television and, in 1996, to feature films, starting with Phil Joanou's *Heaven's Prisoners* (1996) and David Fincher's *The Game* (1997).

As director of photography on *AMERICAN GANG-STER*, Savides made liberal use of a handheld camera, creating what Scott described in the production notes as a "guerilla filmmaking" style, appropriate to the film's status as a drama-documentary. In an interview with *American Cinematographer*, Savides explained why he chose to use a palette of faded colors for the film: he hoped not only to recreate the authentic style of the early 1970s (appropriate to the film's historical context), but wanted his photography to "feel like part of the story, rather than be something that draws attention to itself . . . We didn't want to ape those films [of the early 1970s] but I think their color palette is what evokes that period in people's minds—or helps to sell it . . . If this movie had the color and resolution of modern films, it wouldn't play as well."

References

American Gangster: Production Information (Los Angeles: Universal Pictures, 2007), 14; Jay Holben, "Blood on the Streets," *American Cinematographer* 88, no.12 (December 2007): 49.

SCACCHI, GRETA (1960–)

Born in Milan, Greta Scacchi made her name in costume dramas such as *Heat and Dust* (1982) and *White Mischief* (1987).

Cast against type as Laura Crocker-Harris in the Ridley Scott-produced film *THE BROWNING VERSION*, Scacchi described her role thus to the *Sunday Times Magazine*: "I think my character has got this passion burning over . . . you can look at it metaphorically as the environment of the school being very much a man's world, and we live in a man's world. There's so little sympathy for the woman, she's judged more harshly, she's expected to be a martyr, to love unconditionally and that's her duty . . . She frets slightly that people will see this character as another super-bitch—the script pivots on an instant of her throwaway cruelty: But she's not a bitch. She just didn't want to keep up the façade. Where's her voice and expression? Nobody's recognizing her at all." Her performance is engagingly low-key, distinguished more by what she does not say than by what she says. In one sequence, taking place at the Crocker-Harris's breakfast table, she sits down at the table opposite her husband (ALBERT FINNEY) and reads a letter from Frank (MATTHEW MODINE). Her head inclines slightly, and she gets up again, pausing only to look at Crocker-Harris before leaving the room. She is expected to fulfill the role of dutiful wife and it is clear that she cannot tolerate this anymore. The next sequence shows her riding her bicycle through the lush green landscape, as she steals a few hours away from the stifling environment of the school.

However, perhaps we should not always sympathize with her: in one scene of indescribable verbal cruelty, she deliberately destroys her husband's illusions. Having received the gift of the eponymous *Browning Version* (the Agamemnon translated by Robert Browning) from Taplow (BEN SILVERSTONE), Crocker-Harris enters the tea-tent and tells all of his colleagues about his good fortune. Laura's face remains expressionless once again, until she can stand it no longer; calling Taplow a "cunning little brat," she alleges that the boy deliberately bought the book as a bribe so as to expedite his transfer from the classics to the science section. Utterly deflated, Crocker-Harris gets up from the table and leaves the tent without a word. Laura has obviously had enough: it is time for plain speaking. What is sad about the whole scene is that Crocker-Harris lacks the strength to cope with such cruelty; life in the school has transformed him into an emotional cripple. Mick Brown observed in the *Daily Telegraph* that Scacchi's performance "confirms that . . . [she] is a much better actress than she has ever been given credit for. She gives a bravura performance as the teacher's wife, capturing perfectly the tension of a middle-aged woman trapped in a marriage where feeling has long been sublimated into icy politeness. It is a very different, and very welcome, role for her."

Scacchi's characterization of the suffering wife, trying to point out the realities of existence to her husband recalls other performances in Scott films, such as Ellie Keegan (LORRAINE BRACCO) in *SOMEONE TO WATCH OVER ME*, having to put up with her husband living in the man's world of the NEW YORK Police Department.

References

Mick Brown, "You Mean She Can Act Too?" *Daily Telegraph*, 18 October 1994, 21; Greta Scaachi, interviewed in *The Sunday Times Magazine*, 16 October 1994, 34.

Bibliography

Philip Thomas, "You Know Me . . ." *Empire*, July 1995: 86–87 (on Scaachi's star image).

SCALIA, PIETRO (1960–)

Italian-American film editor whose work includes *Wall Street* (1987), *Talk Radio* (1988), *JFK* (1991)—for which he won an Oscar for Film Editing—*Good Will Hunting* (1997), and *Hannibal Rising* (2006). His work for Scott includes *GLADIATOR, HANNIBAL, BLACK HAWK DOWN* (for which he won his second Oscar), *AMERICAN GANGSTER*, and *BODY OF LIES*.

Interviewed about his work on *Body of Lies*, Scalia claimed that Scott encourages input on major narrative and expressive strategy. "It is only directors who are insecure who don't want to hear suggestions . . . ." In the same interview he recalled his favorite shot in *Gladiator*—that of a hand moving through a field of wheat: "This was a shot intended for another sequence that Scalia relocated on his own initiative. The juxtaposition of that image with the close-up of RUSSELL CROWE's Maximus on the eve of battle implies, Scalia says, that the image is an internal one, a memory or a dream. It's a way of "beginning the story inside the character and then moving outward. You position the entire story as a human drama rather than an action movie."

Bibliography

"Pietro Scalia '82, MFA '85: *Body of Lies* Oscar-winning Editor," www.tft.ucla.edu/profiles/industry/pietro-scalia/ (accessed 20 February 2009).

SCHEIDER, ROY (1932–2008)

Roy Scheider studied drama at Rutgers before making his debut with the New York Shakespeare festival. His film career really took off following his performance alongside fiery Gene Hackman in the crime drama *THE FRENCH CONNECTION*. Four years later he played perhaps his most well-known role—police chief Brody in *Jaws* (1975) and subsequently *Jaws 2* (1978). By the late 1990s, Scheider's career had dipped somewhat; but in *RKO 271* he gave a convincing portrayal of George Schaefer, the harassed boss of RKO Pic-

tures, who not only offered Orson Welles (LIEV SCHREIBER) a contract to make whatever pictures he wished, but tried to support him throughout the long, torturous process of bringing *Citizen Kane* to the screen. Schaefer's relationship with Welles is certainly stormy; but Schaefer claims he would repeat the experience again, given the chance ("You know something, Orson, you haven't done anything but lie to me from the moment we met. But, ya know, I'd do it again in a second"). Sadly, Schaefer will never have that chance—at least with RKO, as the studio dispenses with his services.

Reference

John Logan, "Draft Script for *RKO 281*" (dated 1 May 1997), http://sfy.ru/sfy.html?script=rko218 (accessed 16 November 2008).

SCHINDEL, BARRY (1958–)

Television executive and writer who began his career as a lawyer. Schindel was widely credited with transforming *NUMB3RS* from a mundane police series into a major ratings triumph from the sixth episode onwards by improving "the clarity and power of the storytelling," according to the series' co-creator Cheryl Heuton. He was executive producer of the series from 2005 to 07, being responsible for fifty-three episodes. He also wrote the pilot program *LAW DOGS*, produced in association with SCOTT FREE.

Reference

Jim Benson, "*Numb3rs*' Schindel Inspired by Past Job," *Broadcasting & Cable*, 9 July 2006, www.broadcastingcable.com/article/105710-Numb3rs_Schindel_Inspired_By_Past_Job.php (accessed 1 March 2009).

SCHREIBER, LIEV (1967–)

Born Isaac Liev Schreiber, the son of actor Todd Schreiber. Early films include *Scream* (1996), *Ransom* (1996), and *Scream 2* (1997).

Cast as Orson Welles in *RKO 281*, Schreiber lacks on stature but nonetheless makes a great effort to replicate the gestures and mannerisms of the tortured genius. This Welles is like a chameleon, able to charm and/or persuade people through a series of convincing performances. However, as the film unfolds, we have the distinct impression that Welles is a man totally obsessed with himself, to the exclusion of everyone else. At one point JOHN LOGAN's script describes him thus: "We see Welles strutting, raging, boasting, dancing. And again towering." George Schaefer (ROY SCHEIDER) sums up Welles's character thus: "Did you ever think about that old man [Hearst] and Marion having to watch as you tore them apart? . . . Do you ever think for one second that you might have some responsibility for what you're doing? For cutting and slashing everything in your way so you can have your goddam movie?"

Schreiber's performance was described thus by director BENJAMIN ROSS in an interview with *TV Guide*: "Welles operated on a speed that is 150 times faster than the average person . . . He had a deep-seated insecurity that manifested itself as tremendous productivity." JAMES CROMWELL, playing Hearst, insisted in the same interview that Schreiber "shows the more vulnerable side. Liev stressed his humanity." However, this does not emerge in the finished film.

References
John Logan, "Draft Script for *RKO 281*" (dated 1 May 1997), http://sfy.ru/sfy.html?script=rko218 (accessed 16 November 2008); "RKO 281," *TV Guide*, 20 November 1999, 27–28.

SCHRODER, RICKY (1970–)
Famously made his debut in films in 1979 in the remake of *The Champ* opposite Jon Voight. More recently he has appeared in twelve episodes of *24*.

Cast as Major Bill Keane in *THE ANDROMEDA STRAIN*, Schroder initially comes across as a self-willed xenophobe, unwilling (or perhaps unable) to contemplate points of view other than his own. He is particularly antipathetic towards the Chinese dissident Dr. Tsi Chou (DANIEL DAE KIM). As the action unfolds, however, we discover that this aggression is nothing more than a front to cover his homosexuality. The assignment in the Wildfire laboratory represents an attempt to prove to that, despite his sexuality, he can perform his job in a manner beyond reproach. This might seem somewhat archaic; but director MIKAEL SALOMON implies that the US MILITARY is still very skeptical about the capabilities of someone who has openly "outed." Keane perishes in the attempt to close down the laboratory's computer system but his legacy lives on, as Dr. Jeremy Stone (BENJAMIN BRATT) has to cut off his thumb to secure access to the system.

SCOTT FREE
The company owned by Ridley and Tony Scott that superseded PERCY MAIN. Responsible for numerous film and television productions, including *CLAY PIGEONS, WHERE THE MONEY IS, RKO 281, HANNIBAL, BLACK HAWK DOWN, THE GATHERING STORM, MATCHSTICK MEN, KINGDOM OF HEAVEN, IN HER SHOES, TRISTAN + ISOLDE, A GOOD YEAR, THE ASSASSINATION OF JESSE JAMES BY THE COWARD ROBERT FORD, AMERICAN GANGSTER, THE COMPANY, THE ANDROMEDA STRAIN,* and *BODY OF LIES.*

Bibliography
Peter Keighron, "Looking for Big-Name Brits," *Broadcast* 3 August 2007, 23.

SCOTT, JAKE (1965–)
Film director, son of Ridley, who has worked mostly in music videos and in commercials for RSA. His feature films include

Plunkett and Macleane (1999) and *Welcome to the Rileys* (2009). Also directed "Marriage à Trois" (Series 1, Episode 2) in the *THE HUNGER* (TELEVISION) series. Jake Scott has also been responsible for the output of BLACK DOG.

Bibliography
Richard Natale, "Commercial Break" (1999), in *Ridley Scott Interviews*, ed. Laurence F. Knapp and Andrea F. Kulas (Jackson: University Press of Mississippi, 2005), 172–79.

SCOTT, JORDAN (1977–)
Daughter of Ridley Scott who played a Dutch schoolgirl in *WHITE SQUALL*. Scott co-directed *ALL THE INVISIBLE CHILDREN*: "JONATHAN" with her father, as well as a multi-million dollar series of commercials for RSA, launching Miuccia Prada's first designer fragrance (2005). The first of these, THUNDER PERFECT MIND, premiered in December of that year. Interviewed in *The Independent* at the time of the commercial's British release, Scott admitted that working with her father proved daunting: "I was like, 'How are we not going to kill each other?' At the end of the day, who would turn down an opportunity to work with someone as amazing as him? I know what he does and we've had a million conversations about it, but I realised that I'd never gotten to see what he does, one on one, every day."

Reference
Alice Jones, "It's the Family Business," *The Independent*, 16 December 2005, 10.

SCOTT, LUKE (1968–)
Son of Ridley Scott who has directed commercials for RSA, as well as "Skin Deep" (Series 2, Episode 2) in *THE HUNGER*: TELEVISION series.

SCOTT, TONY (1944–)
Sometimes characterized by reviewers as Ridley's more commercial little brother, Tony Scott has been one of mainstream Hollywood's more reliable and stylish action filmmakers since the mid-1980s.

After nearly a decade of art school and an abortive career as a painter, Scott entered filmmaking through the world of advertising. He has been a director and partner in his brother's commercial production company RSA. In 1981, Scott made a striking feature directorial debut with *THE HUNGER*, starring DAVID BOWIE and Catherine Deneuve, which was later turned into a television series. Five years later JERRY BRUCKHEIMER asked him to direct *TOP GUN*, an entertaining love story punctuated by high-flying effects, which established TOM CRUISE as the industry's most bankable movie star. After directing Eddie Murphy in the blockbuster follow-up *Beverly Hills Cop II* (1987), Scott's subsequent films included *Crimson Tide* (1995), a submarine-set thriller of nuclear brinkmanship that pitted DENZEL WASHINGTON against Gene Hackman.

Scott partnered with his brother in the production company SCOTT FREE, together purchasing London's SHEPPERTON STUDIOS in 1995. Two years later, Scott Free produced the Showtime series *THE HUNGER*, inspired by Scott's film of the same name, for which he and his nephew JAKE SCOTT each directed an episode. The following year, the Scott brothers co-produced the underrated *CLAY PIGEONS*, followed by the 1999 Emmy-nominated HBO drama *RKO 281*, *WHERE THE MONEY IS* (2000), and *THE GATHERING STORM* (2002). They produced the second series of *THE HIRE*, with Tony Scott contributing one episode as director—*THE HIRE: "BEAT THE DEVIL."* Like the episode "Sanctuary" in *The Hunger*, this film was about excess—this time the excess of the singer JAMES BROWN, who sought to renew his pact with The Devil (GARY OLDMAN) to prolong his eternal youth. Meanwhile The Driver (CLIVE OWEN) was faced with the task of chauffeuring Brown: a task Scott likened in the "Director's Commentary" to that insane upriver journey by Martin Sheen in *Apocalypse Now* (1979).

The 2002 reality television series *AMERICAN FIGHTER PILOT*, following the exploits of three pilots as they experienced a 112-day training course at the Tyndall Air Force Base in Florida, was also produced by the Scott brothers, with Tony Scott serving as advisor (using his experience gained on *Top Gun*).

Scott then segued to directing BRAD PITT and Robert Redford in the lackluster thriller *The Spy Game* (2001). His latest projects as producer and director include *NUMB3RS*, *THE ANDROMEDA STRAIN*, and *THE ASSASSINATION OF JESSE JAMES BY THE COWARD ROBERT FORD*.

Reference

Tony Scott, "Director's Commentary" to the DVD release of *The Hire: "Beat the Devil"* (Los Angeles: BMW North America, 2003).

Bibliography

Robert Arnett, "*True Romance*: Quentin Tarantino as Screenwriting Auteur," *Creative Screenwriting* 5, no.1 (1998): 50–55, 62; Thomas C. Carlson, "The Comeback Corpse in Hollywood: Mystery Train, *True Romance*, and the Politics of Elvis in the 90s," *Popular Music and Society* 22, no.2 (1998): 1–10; Mike D'Angelo, "Ridley v. Tony," *Esquire* 146, no.5 (2006): 58–60; Joan Gordon and Veronica Hollinger, eds., *Blood Read: The Vampire as Metaphor in Contemporary Culture* (Philadelphia: University of Pennsylvania Press, 1997); Ellis Hanson, "Lesbians Who Bite," in *Out Takes: Essays on Queer Theory and Film*, ed. Hanson (Durham and London: Duke University Press, 1999), 183–222; Robin Latimer, "Gridding the Vampire Filmography: Tony Scott's *The Hunger* (1983), Jonathan Demme's *The Silence of the Lambs* (1991) and Francis Ford Coppola's Bram Stoker's *Dracula* (1993)," *Niekas* 45 (July 1998): 44–8; Maria Pramaggiore, "Straddling the Screen: Bisexual Spectatorship and Contemporary Horror Film," in *RePresenting Bisexualities: Subjects and Cultures of Fluid Desire*, ed. Donald E. Hall and Maria Pramaggiore (New York: New York University Press, 1996), 272–97.

SELBY, DAVID (1941–)

Best known for his work as a villain in long-running soap operas. Following many years on the stage, Selby attracted infamous attention when he signed on as Quentin Collins, a werewolf, on the gothic daytime drama *Dark Shadows* (1968). After the series' demise, he made his movie debut with *Night of Dark Shadows* (1971), the second film based on the cult series. Cast as Francis Beaumont in *WHITE SQUALL*, Selby plays another bad guy as a father with little concern for anyone except himself. He treats Captain Sheldon (JEFF BRIDGES) as a social inferior, and shows little regard for proprieties on board, stubbing out a cigarette on the newly cleaned deck. Francis's treatment of his son is equally ruthless; when Frank insults him in a restaurant and storms out, Francis chases after him and they brawl in the street. In the film's final sequences, Francis gets his comeuppance as his son ignores him altogether and joins his fellow crew members in a celebration of unity and support for the captain. They offer role models far superior to "fathers" like Francis.

SERPICO

Italy/ US 1973 r/t 130 min col. *Production Companies*: Produzioni De Laurentiis International Manufacturing Company and Artists Entertainment Complex. *Producer*: Martin Bregman. *Director*: Sidney Lumet. *Writers*: Norman Wexler and Waldo Salt, based on the book by Peter Maas. *Director of Photography*: Arthur J. Ornitz. *Production Designer*: Charles Bailey. *Music*: Mikis Theodorakis. *Cast*: Al Pacino (*Frank Serpico*), John Randolph (*Sidney Green*), Jack Kehoe (*Tom Keough*), Biff McGuire (*Captain McClain*).

Archetypal early 1970s crime classic based on the experiences of an honest NEW YORK police officer who helped to expose corruption within the police. This film was acknowledged as one of the inspirations for *AMERICAN GANGSTER*. Nick James observes that this was part of a movement in contemporary Hollywood to replicate the standards of early 1970s American cinema: "there's a consistency of troubled undertones, or unease about manhood as well as nationhood."

Reference

Nick James, "Dealing Dope and Death," *Sight and Sound* 17 no.12 (December 2007): 40.

THE SEVENTH SEAL (DET SJUNDE INSEGLET)

Sweden 1957 r/t 96 min b/w. *Production Company*: Svensk Filmindustri. *Producer*: Allan Ekelund. *Writer/Director*: Ingmar Bergman. *Director of Photography*: Gunnar Fischer. *Production Designer*: P-A. Lundgren. *Music*: Erik Nordgren. *Cast*: Max Von Sydow (*The Knight*), Gunnar Bjornstrand (*The Squire*), Bengt Ekerot (*Death*), Nils Poppe (*Jof*), Bibi Andersson (*Mia*), Ake Fridell (*Plog, the Smith*), Inga Gill (*Lisa, Plog's Wife*).

Legendary film set in fourteenth-century Sweden that begins and ends with a powerful sense of omen and wonder. Bergman himself stressed that the film was designed to serve "the glory of God . . . The ability to create was a gift. In such a world flourished invulnerable assurance and natural humility." Scott acknowledged the film's inspiration in his treatment of *KINGDOM OF HEAVEN*: "I think the knight has always been in my sights since I was brought up on a diet of Ingmar Bergman." However, Bergman's existential questions of life, death and destiny have been superseded by individual choice; it is up to the knights (Balian and Godfrey) to choose whether they wish to pursue a religious life. As Balian (ORLANDO BLOOM) observes in *KINGDOM OF HEAVEN: THE DIRECTOR'S CUT*, he makes time to pray in the belief that it is his responsibility to do so.

References

Ingmar Bergman, "Introduction," *The Seventh Seal*, trans. Lars Malmstrom and David Kushner (London: Lorrimer Publishing, 1968), 8; Ridley Scott, quoted in Diana Landau, ed., *Kingdom of Heaven: The Ridley Scott Film and the History Behind the Story* (London: Simon and Schuster Ltd., 2005), 22.

Bibliography

Birgitta Steene, ed., *Focus on "The Seventh Seal"* (Englewood Cliffs, NJ: Prentice-Hall Inc., 1972).

SEWELL, RUFUS (1967–)

Films include *A Knight's Tale* (2001), *Helen of Troy* (TVM, 2003), and *The Legend of Zorro* (2005).

Cast as King Marke in *TRISTAN + ISOLDE*, Sewell observed in the production notes that he liked the part because he was not only playing a king but also "a great leader—but for the fact that, because he'd lost his right hand, he literally can't defend . . . He is no longer the best warrior amongst them because that was the greatest qualification." Director KEVIN REYNOLDS observed in the production notes that Sewell embodied "not only [the] strength, nobility and paternal qualities of Marke, but also . . . reveal[s] a vulnerability without being weak. Although he is known more for his darker roles, Rufus is actually quite charming with a very sharp wit. We hope to show another side to his work that people have not seen of him yet."

Sewell's Marke is fundamentally a decent man, concerned to rule his kingdom effectively yet heavily dependent on Tristan's (JAMES FRANCO's) skill in battle. Marke tries his best to make sure that Isolde (SOPHIA MYLES) enjoys her life as his queen—which makes the scene where he discovers her affair with Tristan all the more painful. Marke's climactic speech is delivered in a quiet, almost businesslike tone, as the king tries his best to conceal his resentment: "I've been selfish, arrogantly thinking that perhaps I'd given enough. At least enough to merit if not your [Tristan's] love, then at least your respect. You have a home. A kingdom. Why was it not enough? Tell me! You do not know what you have done." He then goes to Isolde's room, asks "How long?" and then leaves in silence, unable (or unwilling) to say any more. Although he releases both Tristan and Isolde at the end (he needs Tristan to help him repel the invading Irish forces), it is clear that Marke's personal life has been ruined. He might be a great king, but has fundamentally failed as a husband.

References

Kevin Reynolds, Rufus Sewell, quoted in *Production Notes: Tristan + Isolde* (Los Angeles: Twentieth Century-Fox, 2005), vii–viii; "*Tristan + Isolde*. Written by Dean Georgaris. Transcript by Chani at tristanandisolde.net," www.imsdb.com/Movie%20Scripts/Tristan %20and%20Isolde%20Script.html (accessed 23 January 2009).

SEYMOUR, MICHAEL (?–)

Michael Seymour began his career as production designer on films such as *Entertaining Mr. Sloane* (1970) and *Gumshoe* (1971).

On Ridley Scott's *ALIEN*, Seymour created a spaceship that in his opinion (as expressed to *American Cinematographer*) resembled "a sort of intergalactic supertanker aboard which people lived and worked . . . collecting ore and oil and minerals, potentially for huge profits. But basically they lived on this craft and maintained it . . . Their clothes were sort of casual and they were all a tiny bit greasy and they had relaxed relationships with one another."

This design gives the impression of normal life (and thereby renders the horrific tale more believable), but it brings home the fact that the crew are nothing more than employees carrying out the Company's instructions. They are "possessed" by others, just like the alien possesses Kane (JOHN HURT). According to Alan Jones, Seymour's designs also suggest claustrophobia: "[T]he interiors were all completely self-contained and enclosed, the rooms were four-sided and had ceilings."

References

Alan Jones, "Michael Seymour: Production Design," *Cinefantastique* 9, no.1 (October 1979): 30–31; Michael Seymour, "Out-of-

This-World Production Design," *American Cinematographer* 60, no.8 (August 1979): 776–77, 804.

SHEPARD, SAM (1943–)

Born Sam Shepard Rogers in Fort Sheridan, Illinois. Well-known as a playwright, his major successes include *The Tooth of Crime* (1972), *Angel City* (1976), *True West* (1980), and *Fool for Love* (1983). As an actor, his credits include *The Right Stuff* (1983), *Crimes of the Heart* (1986), *The Pelican Brief* (1993), and *The Good Old Boys* (1995).

Cast as Major-General William F. Garrison in *BLACK HAWK DOWN*, Shepard wrote most of his own dialogue. Described in KEN NOLAN's script as "laconic [and] steady," Garrison tries his best to do his job, even though the odds are stacked against him. He understands that working in Somalia is "a lot more complicated than Iraq" (this was before the American invasion in 2003). However, even Garrison is shocked by the level of casualties as a result of the botched campaign. In a significant moment towards the end of the film, he walks through the chaos in the medical tent as if in a trance, trying to make sense of what has happened. One wounded soldier bleeds profusely, with the doctors literally slipping in his blood on the floor. Galvanized into action, Garrison seizes a mop and "doing his duty, mops the bloody floor." In this kind of situation rank counts for nothing; everyone has to work as part of a team to create the best medical conditions possible.

Shepard has sometimes scoffed at his own movie career, crediting his success in this area more to his cheekbones than to his acting abilities, and more about financing than about art. In *THE ASSASSINATION OF JESSE JAMES BY THE COWARD ROBERT FORD* (2007) he takes on the powerful but understated role of Jesse's (BRAD PITT's) elder brother, Frank James, who gives up the OUTLAW life for a respectable and safer existence as a landowner and advises Jesse to do the same.

In a preproduction interview CASEY AFFLECK, playing Robert Ford, paid tribute to Shepard's performance, particularly at the point where "Robert approaches Frank first and tries to charm him, tries to pass himself off as someone . . . worthy of riding with the James Gang, and Frank just dismisses him . . . That look Sam gives me, as Frank, that mixture of boredom and contempt and just plain weariness, would be enough to discourage anyone—but not Ford." Eventually Frank exchanges the life of an outlaw for respectability as he departs Kansas for a new life in Baltimore—much to his brother's disgust. ANDREW DOMINIK's script describes his transformation thus: "*Frank James* and family are assembled in traveling clothes around a *Phaeton Carriage* . . . [He] receives her [Zee James's] kiss like medicine, and then turns to the backyard to see his younger brother angrily looking away."

References

Casey Affleck, interviewed in "About the Production" [*The Assassination of Robert Ford*], http://party931.com/common/movies/notes/54706-1-full.html (accessed 12 August 2008); Andrew Dominik, "The Assassination of Jesse James by the Coward Robert Ford," Final White Draft Screenplay dated 17 August 2005, www.simplyscripts.com/oscar80.html (accessed 5 February 2009); Ken Nolan, *Black Hawk Down: The Shooting Script* (New York: Newmarket Press, 2002), 6–7, 124.

SHEPPERTON STUDIOS

Formerly known as Sound City, this complex outside London opened in 1931. Since then the studios have had a checkered career, with periods of prosperity followed by lean times. Ridley Scott filmed *ALIEN* there in 1979. The Scott brothers acquired Shepperton Studios in 1995; but six years later the studios were bought by the larger Pinewood Studios, to enable the joint company to attract big-budget filmmakers. The company now characterizes itself on its website as "a home away from home for many filmmakers such as Ridley Scott and Paul Greengrass."

Reference

"Pinewood and Shepperton Studios Win BAFTA" (5 February 2009), www.pinewoodgroup.com/gen/z_sys_storyNews.aspx?intNewsId =181 (accessed 1 March 2009).

Bibliography

Shepperton Studios: A Visual Celebration. London: Southbank Publishing, 2000.

SHUSETT, RON (?–)

Born in Pittsburgh, Ron Shusett moved to Los Angeles when he was three and grew up there. He attended UCLA for two years, and in 1967 began producing stage plays including *The Impossible Years* and *Barefoot in the Park*. Over the next few years he wrote several stories and screenplays.

Shusett met DAN O'BANNON in 1974 to discuss story concepts each had been toying with. Shusett offered his idea for *Total Recall* and O'Bannon his concept for *ALIEN*. While O'Bannon liked Shusett's idea, the latter did not think much of *Alien*: "I thought it was just a good B-Movie," said Shusett in a 1991 interview with Bill Florence, "which showed a lack of vision on my part."

The two of them later collaborated on the final script of "Star Beast" (the prototype of *Alien*), after O'Bannon's abortive involvement in a project to film Frank Herbert's *DUNE*, directed by Alejandro Jadorowsky. O'Bannon wrote the scenario while Shusett contributed ideas and made connections where appropriate. Shusett told Florence that he had the idea that the monster should grow and emerge from a human body—a hybrid monster: "It's in there, and we don't know until it comes out and escapes in the ship, and all during the movie, it's chasing him and changing into different forms." Shusett subsequently took the script to a Samuel Goldwyn executive named Mark Haggard, who passed it on to Brandywine Productions, run by WALTER HILL, DAVID GILER, and GORDON CARROLL. Thereafter Shusett only had limited involvement in the production, even though he received a credit as executive producer and co-story creator.

Reference

Bill Florence, "Alien's Stepchild: the 15-Year Saga," *Cinefantastique*, April 1991, 35.

SIDDIG, ALEXANDER (1965–)

Born Siddig El Tahir El Fadil El Siddig Abderhman Mohammed Ahmed Abdel Karim El Mahdi in the Sudan, raised and educated in London, Siddig made his film debut in *A Dangerous Man: Lawrence After Arabia* (1990) a made-for-television sequel to David Lean's *LAWRENCE OF ARABIA*. During that time he changed his stage name from Siddig El Fadil to Alexander Siddig. He then embarked on a seven-year run in *Star Trek: Deep Space Nine* (1993–2000). Cast as Imad in *KINGDOM OF HEAVEN*, Siddig plays a soldier preoccupied with the idea of honor. When vanquished in combat, he expects Balian (ORLANDO BLOOM) to kill him; Balian shows his compassion and spares him. Later on in the film the tables are turned: Imad gets the better of Balian but, returning the favor, spares the Christian's life. At one point in the film Saladin (GHASSAN MASSOUD) tells Imad that perhaps he should have killed Balian when he had the chance. Imad responds, "Perhaps I should have had a different teacher." Once again the Muslims are portrayed as fair-minded, in stark contrast to the bloodthirsty Christians.

Siddig was reportedly dissatisfied with the film's original release and campaigned hard for Scott to produce *KINGDOM OF HEAVEN: THE DIRECTOR'S CUT* on the grounds that the longer version gave much more opportunity for character development.

THE SILENCE OF THE LAMBS

US 1991 r/t 118 min col. *Production Companies*: Orion Pictures Corporation and Strong Heart/ Demme Productions. *Producers*: Edward Saxon, Kenneth Utt, and Ron Bozman. *Director*: Jonathan Demme. *Writer*: Ted Tally, from the novel by Thomas Harris. *Director of Photography*: Tak Fujimoto. *Production Designer*: Tim Galvin. *Music*: Howard Shore. *Cast*: Anthony Hopkins (*Dr. Hannibal Lecter*), Jodie Foster (*Clarice Starling*), Scott Glenn (*Jack Crawford*), Ron Vawter (*Paul Krendler*), Anthony Heald (*Dr. Frederick Chilton*), Roger Corman (*FBI Director Hayden Burke*).

Multiple Oscar-winning adaptation of THOMAS HARRIS's novel. Following the film's runaway success, a sequel was planned; but did not emerge until 1999. Originally JONATHAN DEMME was slated to direct, with the two principals repeating their roles; but neither Demme nor JODIE FOSTER liked Harris's novel. They were eventually replaced by Scott and JULIANNE MOORE. The release of *HANNIBAL* provoked a significant reassessment of the earlier film: Andrew Schopp argues that *Hannibal* "replaces the gaze with the voice [and] . . . thereby impeding the possibility for the kind of visual exchange that signified so much in *Silence*. At the same time, Scott's film provides excessively lush visuals, a feast for the audience's eyes . . . coupled with excessively graphic representations of Hannibal's monstrous acts." By doing so it "turns cannibalism into a spectacle while at the same time removing the act's symbolic meaning" which was so evident in *Silence*.

Reference

Andrew Schopp, "The Practice and Politics of 'Freeing the Look': Jonathan Demme's *The Silence of the Lambs*," *Camera Obscura* 18, no.3 (September 2003): 7–8.

SILVERSTONE, BEN (1979–)

Ben Silverstone was born in Primrose Hill, an affluent area of north London. His parents were Anthony and Beverly Silverstone, who sent him to the exclusive private St Paul's School in Barnes, London. Ben's breakthrough was via a family friend, MIKE FIGGIS, who gave him a major role in *THE BROWNING VERSION* (1994) as Taplow. He is shown to be from a divorced family: Crocker-Harris (ALBERT FINNEY) and his wife Laura (GRETA SCACCHI) become his surrogate parents as they give him encouragement, whether in the form of extra tuition or glasses of lemonade. Taplow's development is evident throughout the film as he progresses from a shy, mouse-like character into someone eventually taking revenge on the school bully by putting locusts in his bed. The camera focuses on Taplow's joy after this, as he exclaims "Yes!!!" before going to sleep.

SISTO, JEREMY (1975–)

Sisto began his career in films such as *The Shaggy Dog* (1994) and *Moonlight and Valentino* (1995). As Frank Beaumont in *WHITE SQUALL*, Sisto undergoes a rite of passage from young boy into man. He begins the film as a sullen, silent personality, dominated by his father (DAVID SELBY). As time progresses, however, he gradually develops; but his progress is hindered by the unexpected reappearance of his father, who takes him off the ship and forces him to dine out. Frank's resentment at his father reaches boiling point and he storms out of the restaurant. The two of them brawl in the street; Frank responds to his treatment by getting drunk and smashing some streetlights. It is only due to the care and support of his fellow crew members that he manages to return safely to the *Albatross*.

From then on, however, Frank remains a disturbed personality. He kills a dolphin with a harpoon, and reacts to it "as if waking from a dream." Although expelled from the boat for this act of wanton destruction, he shakes Captain Sheldon's (JEFF BRIDGES's) hand, as if grateful for the experience of working on the boat. It is this which eventually prompts him, in the final sequence, to join the remaining crew members in a show of unity, ringing the ship's bell (salvaged from the wreck) in a symbolic gesture to show that the fundamental spirit of the *Albatross* will never die. His father might look on disapprovingly, but there is nothing he can do to intervene. TODD ROBINSON's script describes the scene thus: "[Frank] slowly rises. Tears streaming down his face. Tightly in his hands he grips the ship's bell. Ding ding. Ding ding. Ding ding. It is the ringing of the truth. The tolling of their unity."

Reference

Todd Robinson, *White Squall: Revised First Draft* (unpub. script, dated 31 October 1994), http://sfy.ru/sfy.html?script=white_squall (accessed 8 September 2008).

SIZEMORE, TOM (1961–)

Sizemore's first break came when Oliver Stone cast him in a bit part in *Born on the Fourth of July* (1989). In 1994 he played Bat Masterson in Kevin Costner's star-studded biopic *Wyatt Earp,* as well as in Oliver Stone's *Natural Born Killers.* Cast as McKnight in *BLACK HAWK DOWN,* Sizemore told Fred Schruers that he tried to portray the character as someone trying to "keep his cool . . . A lot of these kids are eighteen, and when they start getting hit, they need to look to someone who's not panicking. This character never flinches." Even in the midst of adversity, he tries to rally his troops: "We're gonna be home in a second, we're gonna be home in a second. Hang on! God dammit, you guys hang on!" However, he is enough of a pragmatist to realize when it is necessary to retreat: "With the amount of wounded we have, we'd do more harm than good. We need to come back to base, rearm and regroup and then we can go back out." Like most of his fellow soldiers, he places duty above personal safety; in the Olympic Stadium he urges the medic to hurry up and treat his wounds, even though one of them "missed [his] jugular by about three millimeters."

References

Ken Nolan, *Black Hawk Down: The Shooting Script* (New York: Newmarket Press, 2002), 86–87, 124; Fred Schruers, "The Way We War," *Premiere* 15, no.6 (February 2002): 84.

SKERRITT, TOM (1933–)

Lean, ruggedly handsome leading man and supporting actor whose looks have improved with age, Tom Skerritt attended Wayne State University and UCLA, and was first noticed in a UCLA production of *The Rainmaker* before making his movie debut in *War Hunt* (1962). However, he spent most of the next decade in television, regularly appearing in *The Virginian, Gunsmoke* and *12 O'Clock High.* Skerritt's next big break was appearing in *MASH* (1970).

Cast as Dallas in *ALIEN,* Skerritt reinforces his (patriarchal) authority, overruling Ripley's (SIGOURNEY WEAVER's) decision not to let Kane back into the *NOSTROMO,* once Kane has been infected by the alien. However, Dallas proves as incapable of dealing with the alien as any other member of the ill-fated crew. In a scene cut from the 1979 release but restored in *ALIEN—THE DIRECTOR'S CUT,* Skerritt is shown undergoing a gradual process of decomposition. No longer a symbol of MASCULINITY, he is being reduced into matter. This emphasizes the extent to which Scott's film deconstructs established concepts of gender.

SMALL TOWNS

Small towns are inevitably associated with stereotypical characteristics such as friendliness, honesty, and old-fashioned politeness. Such mythologies form the basis for the Ridley Scott-produced film *CLAY PIGEONS.* Set in the fictional small town of Mercer, Montana, it depicts the population as insular, fixed in their ideas, and ripe for exploitation by the serial killer Lester Long (VINCE VAUGHN). However, the small-town values emerge triumphant in the end, as Sheriff Mooney (SCOTT WILSON) successfully concocts a scheme to entrap Lester. Posing as a farmer with a pick-up truck, he offers Lester a lift out of Mercer and the two of them drive off—closely followed by a police car. One expects an arrest to be made soon. Even though Mooney has had to contend with an apparently efficient FBI Agent Shelby (JANEANE GAROFALO) whose metropolitan ideas are very different from his own, director DAVID DOBKIN suggests that small-town values are valuable. In a world populated by serial killers, it is good that everyone in Mercer knows everyone else.

In *THE ANDROMEDA STRAIN,* the small-town values of Piedmont, Utah, are completely destroyed by the onset of the deadly virus. Before it strikes, the townsfolk are shown happily playing cards; afterwards almost everyone is dead except for one alcoholic, Kyle Tobler (Tom McBeath), and a newborn baby with colic. The implication is clear—even the most apparently stable societies are vulnerable to attack from unseen forces. The only way of resisting them is for everyone to pull together and work for the common cause—the scientists, the US MILITARY, the government and civilians alike.

SOMEONE TO WATCH OVER ME

US 1987 r/t 105 min col. *Production Company*: Columbia Pictures Corporation. *Executive Producer*: Ridley Scott. *Producers*: Thierry de Ganay and Harold Schneider. *Director*: Ridley Scott. *Writers*: Howard Franklin, Danilo Bach, and David Seltzer. *Director of Photography*: Steven Poster. *Production Designer*: Jim Bissell. *Music*: Michael Kamen. *Cast*: Tom Berenger (*Mike Keegan*), Jerry Orbach (*Lt. Garber*), Lorraine Bracco (*Ellie Keegan*), Mimi Rogers (*Claire Gregory*), John Rubinstein (*Neil Steinhart*), Andreas Katsulas (*Joey Venza*).

Someone to Watch Over Me is perhaps one of Scott's most audience-friendly films, the product of a period in the director's career when he was somewhat wary of creating radical, experimental work following the commercial failure of *BLADE RUNNER* and *LEGEND*. The film's basic storyline was pitched to him by screenwriter HOWARD FRANKLIN. At the time Scott has been trying to develop a project tentatively called "Johnny Utah" (eventually renamed *Point Blank* and directed by Kathryn Bigelow in 1991). However the idea foundered and Scott told PAUL M. SAMMON that he took on *Someone* instead in the belief that the film's basic story of two people "thrown together into a high-pressure situation" sounded attractive. Scott appreciated "the contrast and coming together of the two main characters' different social classes."

Filming took place over eleven weeks in Manhattan, Queens, and Los Angeles, where different areas stood in for New York locations. One scene was filmed in Los Angeles' Mayan Theater, while the initial murder scene was shot inside a swimming-pool in the old *Queen Mary*, the luxury liner now permanently in dry-dock in Long Beach, California. Scott told Sammon that the experience of the film as "an absolute walk in the park, because the scale of my three previous movies had been so huge. This was a more intimate drama . . . I also felt comfortable filming in New York."

Reviews were modest to say the least: *Variety* believed that the central love story posed "a hurdle for the audience to believe," while the "highly contrived climax" was "incredible and unconvincing." Vincent Canby of the *New York Times* criticized Scott for his "dependence on a few, comparatively easy-to-achieve effects that pass for style . . . all supplemented by a music track that contrasts cocktail-piano pop and high-toned classical tidbits." Pauline Kael summed up her experience of the film thus: she wondered why "such morbid finicky care" had been lavished over "this silly little story," as the director had done nothing more than "worried the fun out of it." By contrast Richard Corliss of *Time* appreciated Scott's glamorous realization of "Manhattan in the '40s, with its twin thrills of grandeur and menace. The sidewalks gleam like a Bakelite floor. A hired gun jogs into a Fifth Avenue foyer." British reviewers enjoyed the film: Iain Johnstone of the *Sunday Times* recognized Scott's ability "to

make his characters not just figures in, but tangible constituents of their own landscape"; Simon Cunliffe of the *New Statesman* saw the film as a criticism of yuppie culture; while Scarth Flett of the *Sunday Express* (with a concern for sibilants) called it "a stark, stylish thriller."

Someone was released in September 1987 with virtually no publicity (the victim of an administrative regime at Columbia Pictures which failed to support the film). The film disappeared rapidly from the few theaters in which it had been booked, grossing only $10 million from its American release. Scott himself enjoyed the experience of the film, but its box-office failure made him philosophical. He recalled to Sammon: "I thought, 'There goes another one. I did it right, but it didn't really go. Oh, well, time to move on to the next one.'"

Nonetheless the film contains distinct echoes of Scott's earlier work, not least in its representation of NEW YORK as a living presence. The opening sequence begins with a spectacular aerial shot of the dusky Manhattan skyline (recalling the city in *Blade Runner*), focusing on the Chrysler Building before sweeping across the Hudson River and coming to rest on the more mundane apartment block where Mike (TOM BERENGER) and Ellie Keegan (LORRAINE BRACCO) reside. Scott told Sammon that the Chrysler Building was "real fantasy architecture, and one of the most beautiful buildings of its era . . . A spectacular achievement." However, this romanticized view is abruptly superseded by images of the city as a threatening presence: the pavements thronged with pedestrians staring into the distance; the interior of Win Hockings's (Mark Moses's) ultra-chic nightspot, where individual faces can only be briefly glimpsed in the flashing strobe lights; and the ever-present smoke emanating from the sewers, forming a background to most exterior sequences. Franklin's script describes New York City as "the ultimate object of man's [*sic*] desire and fulfillment."

However this proves nothing but an illusion; like the futuristic city in *Blade Runner*, New York is a DYSTOPIA where no one looks after each other, where people are endlessly on the move with no specific objective in mind. The smoke not only reminds us how polluted the city is, but assumes a symbolic function, a reminder of how seldom the characters express their feelings for one another. They would rather put a smokescreen in front of themselves. The script makes this clear in some of the exchanges between Claire Gregory (MIMI ROGERS) and Mike. When Mike tells her that Ellie knows about their love affair, Claire absorbs it the information without making any emotional response. She decides that the most suitable course of action would be to leave town; however, her body language demonstrate a reluctance to express herself honestly.

At the end of the film Mike and Ellie are reunited after a shoot-out in which Venza (ANDREAS KATSULAS) dies and Claire is driven off by the police. The camera focuses briefly on the smiling face of Mike's son Tommy (Harley Cross) as he watches his parents embracing from another police car. Yet this apparently happy denouement is undercut by the ever-present smoke, which not only occupies the rear of the frame but occasionally interposes between the characters and the lens of cinematographer STEVEN POSTER's camera. Although Mike and Ellie seek to "find some place to start over," they are still reluctant to talk to one another openly. If this is the case, then the future of their MARRIAGE might still be in doubt.

Someone makes ingenious use of city locations to emphasize the CLASS DIFFERENCES between the two main characters. Claire's world of privilege is dominated by exotic locations discreetly lit for maximum dramatic effect—a society reception at the Guggenheim Museum, a Fifth Avenue shop where no one actually pays for their purchases but puts them on their accounts. By contrast, Mike's more mundane existence in Queens is suggested by shots of grimy buildings, modest gardens, and dirty sedans. When Mike and Ellie go out for a celebratory meal, they book a table "that looks out on the East River. It's an OK restaurant, not the poshest in the world" whose customers (if they are old enough) "qualify for the Senior Citizens' Early-Bird Special."

Even though Claire inhabits a world of plenty, she can never enjoy it. Throughout the film Scott emphasizes the artificiality of her world; no one voices a sincere opinion for fear of being found out. At the Guggenheim Museum Mike encounters a pretty young woman (Susi Gilder) who asks him whether shooting anyone gives him an erection. Not surprisingly, Mike's eyes register utter astonishment at the suggestion. Claire yearns for the simplicity of Mike's existence with a spouse and a child; she describes it as "nice" but the expression on her fact suggests that "her envy is plain." By contrast her existence seems fractured and sterile; Scott emphasizes this by focusing on parts of her BODY—her legs or her upper torso—rather than photographing her in close-up. In one sequence Claire and Mike are shown kissing tenderly; in the rear of the frame we see the shadow of the window-blinds projected on to the wall, creating a prison image that aptly sums up her existence. Like Rachael in *Blade Runner*, Claire is like a REPLICANT, doomed to living a pseudo-existence in a gilded cage. The soundtrack—which includes popular operatic arias, Al Bowlly's romantic ballad "What More Can I Ask?" as well as the Gershwin song that provides the film's title—becomes an expression of her repressed yearning for a more fulfilling existence.

Mike experiences similar feelings, especially when it comes to following his instincts. This is brought out in a touching sequence late in the film when he returns to Claire's apartment, despite being expressly forbidden to do so. He pauses outside her lounge, his eyes filled with long-ing. Scott cuts to a shot of Claire staring out of the window, then returns to Mike entering the room. The two of them stand wordlessly opposite one another; neither wants to move or speak for fear of destroying the moment. Eventually Mike sighs and starts the conversation, realizing that such experiences cannot last. Life must go on, in spite of everything.

Mike's experiences invoke a theme common to several of Scott's films: the notion of LOVE VS. DUTY—both to work and family. Even though Mike believes that his interest in Claire is purely professional, his motives are willfully misunderstood by his colleagues. When he arrives at the Guggenheim reception, a cop opens the door of Claire's limousine and is "stunned to see MIKE step out, in suit and new tie—looking like he belongs there." Despite Mike's insistence that he is on duty, the cop asks him whether he has become a gigolo. The same also applies to his family life; while protesting his innocence, Ellie understands that Mike has actually fallen in love and tells him to "get off this case and come home!" Scott shows the potential consequences facing Mike if he neglects his MARRIAGE and his job in a sequence where Mike moves in with his colleague Scotty (Daniel Hugh Kelly). The camera focuses on the empty bedroom decorated with a boy's paraphernalia—posters, skateboards—and cuts back to Scotty's melancholy face as he informs Mike how his son stays there "on Wednesdays, and every other weekend." Scotty might protest that "our relationship has never been better"; the *mise-en-scene* suggests the reverse, as Scotty is doomed to live in perpetual isolation. The same fate is shared by other police officers, notably in *BLACK RAIN* and *AMERICAN GANGSTER*.

Someone illustrates another theme characteristic of Scott's work—that of gender roles. Mike's community of police officers value MASCULINITY; they communicate far more easily with one another than with women. Mike sees himself as a strong person who should protect his family, as well as Claire, from harm. He considers himself the decision-maker; when Ellie tells him that she has already taken steps to remove him from the evening shift at Claire's apartment, Mike is outraged: "My wife talks to his [Garber's] wife about what shift I'm gonna take!" His sense of masculinity is under threat.

Little critical material exists on the film, save for short essays in most of the Ridley Scott reference books. Sammon's *Ridley Scott Close-Up* gives an account of the making of the film; Knapp and Kulas's *Ridley Scott: Interviews* devotes one page to the film, while Richard Alan Schwartz's *Films of Ridley Scott* likens it to *THELMA & LOUISE* in its plot; that is, driven by "understandable violations of responsible behavior that result from extraordinary emotional circumstances, and both suggest that we must pay the consequences of our lapses, even when circumstances create almost irresistible emotional pressures that confuse our internal compasses." Steven Prince's *New Pot of Gold: Hollywood under the Electronic Rainbow* (2002) calls it "formulaic." James Clarke calls it "a triumph of characterisation and mood over the familiar mechanics of an urban thriller."

References

Vincent Canby, "Film: *Someone to Watch Over Me*," *New York Times*, 8 October 1987, B36; James Clarke, *Ridley Scott* (London: Virgin Books Ltd., 2002), 107; Richard Corliss, "High-Risk Love in an Alien World," *Time*, 12 October 1987, 27; Simon Cunliffe, "A Real Man," *New Statesman*, 11 March 1988, 38; Scarth Flett, "Watching-Brief Encounter," *Sunday Express*, 13 March 1988, 16; Howard Franklin, Danilo Bach, and David Seltzer, "*Someone to Watch Over Me*" (revised 4 December 1986), www.imsdb.com/scripts/Someone-To-Watch-Over-Me.html (accessed 9 June 2008); Iain Johnstone, "Glittering Vision of Less Than Fatal Attraction," *Sunday Times*, 13 March 1988, C9; Pauline Kael, "Someone to Watch Over Me," *New Yorker*, 2 November 1987, 140; François Guérif and Alan Garel, "Ridley Scott," in *Ridley Scott Interviews*, ed. Laurence F. Knapp and Andrea F. Kulas (Mississippi: University Press of Mississippi, 2005), 57–61; Lor, "Someone to Watch Over Me," *Variety*, 30 September 1987, 36; Stephen Prince, *A New Pot of Gold: Hollywood under the Electronic Rainbow* (Berkeley and London: University of California Press, 2001), 190; Richard Alan Schwartz, *The Films of Ridley Scott* (New York: Praeger Publications, 2001), 68; Ridley Scott, quoted in Paul M. Sammon, *Ridley Scott Close-Up: The Making of His Movies* (New York: Thunder's Mouth Press, 1999), 88, 90–91.

Bibliography

Brian J. Robb, *Ridley Scott* (Harpenden: Pocket Essentials, 2002), 49–51.

SOUTHON, MIKE (?-)

Joined the BBC television film unit as a trainee and became a regular camera operator on arts programs for the corporation. Then he turned freelance, making commercials for RSA, as well as music videos. His film credits include *Gothic* (1986), *A Kiss Before Dying* (1991), *Little Man Tate* (1991), and *Air Bud* (1997).

Southon served as director of photography on *RKO 281*. Although set in Hollywood, the production was actually filmed in London and at Bray Studios (where many classic Hammer horror productions originated). Southon recalled that the opulent atmosphere of many of the scenes—particularly in Xanadu, William Randolph Hearst's legendary mansion—were photographed in "warm, light colours on the ceiling to reflect uplighting back down into the rooms, bathing them in soft warm light. This wash was then accented with globes and the whole effect, when it hit long flowing gowns especially, was to create a lustrous, cin-

ematic glow on anyone in the room. Most of the scenes were night interiors and even the day interiors tended to be deep inside buildings and lit with artificial light."

Reference

"Practically Kane," *Eyepiece* 21, no.2 (April/May 2000): 41.

SPAIN

In *1492: CONQUEST OF PARADISE* Scott portrays fifteenth-century Spain as a place of inherent corruption, torn apart with political strife and social conflict. Queen Isabel's (SIGOURNEY WEAVER's) court is a place of opulence, full of ornate gardens and caged animals. This is contrasted with the anarchy outside—the mob of penitents crawling on bended knees or flagellating themselves, and the crowd behaving like animals while witnessing the public ceremony where the heretics are burned. The country is dominated by the Inquisition, which reinforces its authority through tyrannical means. Robert Thurston's novelization of the screenplay makes this clear through graphic description: "To the left and right, corpses slumped from center posts, but in the middle a still-living man struggled against the ropes that bound him to the thick wooden stake. The fire at his feet had evidently just been ignited. Hooded men with torches, the executioners, backed away from the flames . . . Fernando's last sight of the half-charred corpse was watching its neck snap like burning wood from the weight of the head. The head began to fall, its skin continuing to dissolve into pieces that looked almost like flakes, black flakes. Then the whole body seemed to collapse into the fire." Columbus (GÉRARD DEPARDIEU), as a foreigner, tries to create a world that dispenses with such violent punishments; but even he at the end is reduced to hanging his crew members who dared to mutiny. The effect of such moments uncomfortably recalls similar events in American history—notably the work of the Ku Klux Klan.

Reference

Robert Thurston, *1492: Conquest of Paradise Based on a Screenplay by Roselyne Bosch* (London: Penguin Books, 1992), 25–26.

SPENCER, JOHN (1946–2005)

Born John Speshock in New York. In 1963 he landed a recurring role in *The Patty Duke Show*, and returned to acting following his education at Farleigh Dickenson and New York Universities. His credits as a supporting actor included *War Games* (1983), *Miami Vice* (1986), and *Far From Home* (1989).

As Superintendent Oliver in *BLACK RAIN*, Spencer plays the kind of aggressive bureaucrat who seems to recur in Scott's work—witness EDWARD JAMES OLMOS's Gaff in *BLADE RUNNER*. A stickler for propriety, he resents Nick

Conklin's (MICHAEL DOUGLAS's) presence in the police force; a maverick with a shady past represents a potential threat to the existing order. Oliver is one of the "suits" as Nick puts it, whose obsession with process actually impedes a police officer's work. His view of life parallels that of the Japanese superintendent Ohashi (SHIGERU KOYAMA). Despite the obvious cultural differences, the American and Japanese police forces both seek to stifle individual initiative. While Oliver's role is a small one, it is nonetheless important as a way of showing how the odds are stacked against Nick's approach to policing. The fact that Nick overcomes them is proof of his determination.

SPENCER, NORRIS (1943–2006)

Started his career working for RSA on some of Ridley Scott's commercials. Spencer made his film debut with Lindsay Anderson's *Britannia Hospital* (1982) and subsequently worked as Scott's production designer on *BLACK RAIN, THELMA & LOUISE, 1492: CONQUEST OF PARADISE,* and *HANNIBAL*.

Interviewed prior to the opening of *Hannibal*, Spencer remarked that the film's look "comes from whatever is in the script, and primarily from speaking with Ridley Scott. I liked *Silence of the Lambs*, a lot, personally, but I have to say that Ridley's interpretation of *Hannibal*, then reading the book, with its intensity, was far more riveting to me than *Silence*. I didn't really look at it again, until two or three weeks into principal photography, because I didn't want it to influence me . . . Shooting in the Palazzo Vecchio [in Florence] was mind-boggling, and of course, shooting in Florence, with all that art stuff, and that history. It was really wonderful . . . always with Ridley's blessing, of course."

Reference
Douglas Eby, "Hannibal," *Cinefantastique* 32, no.6 (February 2001): 9.

STAMP, TERENCE (1939–)

Born in London, Terence Stamp became a star in the mid-1960s with films such as *Billy Budd* (1962) and *Far From the Madding Crowd* (1967). In latter years he has become a character actor of note on both sides of the Atlantic.

Cast as the host of the first series of *THE HUNGER:* TELEVISION, Stamp introduces each episode in measured, calm tones, as if lulling viewers into believing that the action to follow will not seem horrific at all. He appears in a variety of situations and disguises—shooting an ox-heart with a bow and arrow and driving a model train-set being only two. His introduction to each episode is something between a lecture and a sermon. For "Marriage à Trois" he asks the viewer: "How well do you know yourself? Inside—the body—the cerebellum?" for "The Secret Shih Tan" he tells us

that we must "eat what we must" and kill "for what he or she desires"; and before "I'm Dangerous Tonight" he asks whether clothes are a way of understanding the person wearing them or whether they are simply "a matter of happenstance." Sometimes he seems to be enjoying a huge joke at the viewers' expense, rather like Alfred Hitchcock in the classic *Alfred Hitchcock Presents*. In a preproduction interview, he described his character in tongue-in-cheek fashion as someone who has "lived for many lifetimes," and now resides in a mausoleum with many strange things around him. Terence Stamp was replaced for the second series by DAVID BOWIE.

Reference
Frank Barron, "*The Hunger:* Showtime's Adult Horror," *Cinefantastique* 28, no.12 (June 1997): 7.

STANTON, HARRY DEAN (1926–)

Born in West Irvine, Kentucky, Stanton served in World War II and then returned to the University of Kentucky to appear in a production of *Pygmalion*, before heading out to California and honing his craft at the prestigious Pasadena Playhouse. His film career took off with supporting roles in *Cool Hand Luke* (1967), *Kelly's Heroes* (1970), *Dillinger* (1973), and *The Godfather: Part II* (1974).

Cast as the laid-back crew member Brett in *ALIEN*, Stanton starts off the film as the classic rebel—someone who will not do anything unless he receives a suitable remuneration. He meets a sticky end during the film, being attacked by the alien and ultimately being transformed into spores (in a sequence deleted from the original 1979 release). Stanton is a favorite of Roger Ebert, who has said that "no movie featuring either Harry Dean Stanton . . . in a supporting role can be altogether bad."

Reference
Roger Ebert, "Dream a Little Dream," *Chicago Sun-Times*, 3 March 1989, 17.

STEPHENS, ROBERT (1931–1995)

Robert Stephens made his name during the 1960s as a leading member of the National Theatre of Great Britain under Sir Laurence Olivier. He was widely regarded as Olivier's heir; but following his departure from the company in 1970, his career slumped. His most celebrated film role was that of Sherlock Holmes in Billy Wilder's *The Private Life of Sherlock Holmes* (1970).

In *THE DUELLISTS* Stephens plays General Treillard who, like many of the supporting characters in the film, cannot understand why D'Hubert (HARVEY KEITEL) and Feraud (KEITH CARRADINE) persist in their duel, even though they have no idea why it started in the first place. In one sequence Treillard summons Feraud to his office and forbids the soldier from fighting any more duels while serving under his command. Scott's camera photographs Treillard from below, he looks down at the audience, rather like a teacher reprimanding a student. This is Feraud's strongest warning yet; the fact he chooses to ignore it by continuing to fight D'Hubert shows the extent to which the code of HONOR has corrupted his notions of right behavior.

STING (1951–)

Born Gordon Matthew Sumner in Wallsend, Northumberland, United Kingdom. His mother was Audrey, and his father was Ernest. He received his name Sting from his striped sweater, in which Gordon Solomon said that he looked like a bee. Primarily a musician, he worked in the band The Police until 1984, when he went solo. Before his music career he was a ditch digger, a schoolteacher who taught English, and a soccer coach.

Ridley Scott has twice used songs by Sting during credits for his films—singing George Gershwin's "Someone to Watch Over Me" for the film of the same name, and "Valparaiso" for WHITE SQUALL. On both occasions Scott makes use of Sting's voice to emphasize the emotion lurking behind each film; loneliness in SOMEONE TO WATCH OVER ME and the casting off of one's youth and passage into manhood in White Squall.

ST. JOHN, MARCO (1939–)

Graduated in 1960 from Fordham University. Played minor roles in film and television in Remington Steele (1984), Friday the 13th Part V: A New Beginning (1985), and This Gun for Hire (TV remake, 1991).

Cast as the pig-headed trucker in THELMA & LOUISE, St. John portrays him as a crude man whose estimation of women is so low that he expects them to have sex with him willingly. He receives his just deserts, however, as the two women riddle the man's vehicle with bullets.

STREITENFELD, MARC (?–)

Born in Germany, Streitenfeld served as music consultant on KINGDOM OF HEAVEN and music supervisor on TRISTAN + ISOLDE. Numerous composers were attached to A GOOD YEAR during preproduction (including HANS ZIMMER), but eventually Streitenfeld was given screen credit. His work here is a fairly pleasant surprise, a blend of Nino Rota and Ennio Morricone at their most pleasant and playful. Despite a couple of blah techno cues towards the beginning, most of the score is breezy romantic material with a French twist, sometimes with a bit of a pop feel. It's fun and pleasant, if not quite passionate; but then neither is the movie. There's a fairly memorable main theme crops up quite a few times.

Streitenfeld was also responsible for the musical score in AMERICAN GANGSTER, where he tried to create a score appropriate to the film's dark mood. It received a nomination for a British Academy (BAFTA) Award for Best Score. He also composed the score for BODY OF LIES, which was described by Jonathan Broxton on the MoviesMusicUK website as "fairly unremarkable . . . It relies heavily on little more than shifting orchestral textures and percussive rhythms to drive along the action, and is given a sense of geographic specificity through the regular inclusion of various ethnic percussion instruments and a number of Middle Eastern timbres, notably a trio of lute-like plucked instruments—a saz, a tanbur and an oud—and an Iranian santur hammered dulcimer . . . Part of the problem is that it lacks any kind of individual identity; there's nothing to make it stand out from the crowd. Dozens and dozens of political thrillers have received scores like this since Spy Game in 2001, and they're now beginning to all sound the same."

Reference

Jonathan Broxton, "Body of Lies: Marc Streitenfeld," www.moviemusicuk.us/bodyliescd.htm (accessed 20 February 2009).

Bibliography

Clark Douglas, "A Good Year: Marc Streitenfeld," www.moviemusicuk.us/agoodyear.htm (accessed 30 January 2009); Scott Gwin, "Interview—Marc Streitenfeld," www.cinemablend.com/soundtracks/INTERVIEW-Marc-Streitenfeld-7411.html (accessed 20 February 2009).

STRONG, MARK (1963–)

Born Marco Giuseppe Salussolia in London to an Italian father and an Austrian mother. His films and television work includes Anna Karenina (2000), Oliver Twist (2005) directed by Roman Polanski, and Syriana (also 2005).

Cast as Wicktred (originally named Geraldo) in TRISTAN + ISOLDE, Strong plays a treacherous power-seeker who will try and outwit anyone—whether through force or through scheming—to achieve his ends. His bête noire is Tristan (JAMES FRANCO), whom he unsuccessfully challenges to a fight at a tournament in Ireland. He lures Melot (Henry Cavill) into his schemes through flattery, telling him that "too long the ablest among us has been denied his rightful place. I pledge you [Melot] my allegiance and offer him my services as my second." Eventually this turns out to be nothing but a ruse, as Wicktred persuades Melot to show him the secret passage, so that Wicktred can invade King Marke's (RUFUS SEWELL's) castle. However, when they are in the passage, Wicktred stabs Melot to death. Wicktred's treachery leads him nowhere in the end, as Tristan cuts his head off in the climactic conflict.

Strong gives a scene-stealing performance as Hani, the head of the Jordanian Secret Service, in BODY OF LIES. He received considerable praise in the production notes for his role: LEONARDO DICAPRIO described how his father "talks about how cool Hani is, and how he wants to dress like him because he's such a badass." Strong himself described the character as someone able "to achieve things in a much more delicate, less obvious way than [Ed] Hoffman [RUSSELL CROWE]. His methods consist very much of not rattling the cage, but gently reeling in the fish." Nonetheless, Hani is capable of violence if necessary; on one occasion he takes the agent Roger Ferris (DiCaprio) to a prison cell and forces him to watch a criminal being ritualistically given several lashes.

If we discount the fact that Strong engages in a colonialist act of mimicry (like Alec Guinness in *LAWRENCE OF ARABIA* he is a European essaying the role of an Arab), he gives a convincing characterization of someone who trusts Ferris, so long as Ferris observes the principle of never lying to him. As he tells the CIA agent, this represents an important aspect of a culture "where friendship matters. It can save your life." Dressed in immaculately tailored in suits from London's Savile Row, Hani understands the importance of appearance; hence his willingness to entertain Ferris and Hoffman (Crowe) in the opulent surroundings of his office, complete with antique furniture and rich ornaments. His catchphrase is "my dear" (recalling Fagin in Carol Reed's *Oliver!* [1968]) denoting his willingness to collaborate with the Americans, so long as they observe the principle of reciprocity. In the production notes Scott claims that Ferris is duty-bound to double-cross Hani, "by virtue of his job." The film appears to contradict this by suggesting that Ferris ignores the notion of collaboration in his attempts to capture the extremist leader Al-Saleem (ALON ABOUTBUL). By doing so he betrays Hani's notions of goodwill and trust and thereby endangers any future diplomatic cooperation.

Critics admired Strong's performance: the *San Francisco Chronicle* felt that he lifted up the film "just by walking onto the screen . . . Strong dominates the handful of scenes he's in. He's a character of conscience and refinement, set up in contrast to his slovenly American counterpart (Crowe)." Scott Foundas in the *Village Voice* went further: "But as good as DiCaprio is, *Body of Lies* is stolen early and often right out from under him by a British actor named Mark Strong . . . Tailored to the nines in Savile Row couture, calling everyone 'my dear' in his mellifluous, dulcet tones, Strong's Hani Pasha supplies information . . . all without unsettling a hair on his elegantly coiffed head. 'Never lie to me,' he advises Ferris upon their first meeting, though it's quite clear that Hani doesn't risk trusting anyone. Which, in the world of *Body of Lies*, is the only sure way of keeping your head above water."

References

Scott Foundas, "Ridley Scott's *Body of Lies* is the Post 9/11, Tech-Savvy Terror Thriller We Deserve," *Village Voice*, 7 October 2008, www.villagevoice.com/2008-10-08/film/ridley-scott-s-body-of-lies-is-the-post-9-11-tech-savvy-terror-thriller-we-deserve/ (accessed 17 February 2009); Mick LaSalle, "Muddled *Body of Lies*," *San Francisco Chronicle*, 10 October 2008, E1; *Production Notes: Body of Lies* (Los Angeles: Warner Brothers Entertainment, 2008), http://mix96tulsa.com/movies/notes/body-of-lies/note/4 (accessed 16 January 2009); "*Tristan + Isolde*. Written by Dean Georgaris. Transcript by Chani at tristanandisolde.net," www.imsdb.com/Movie%20Scripts/Tristan%20and%20Isolde%20Script.html (accessed 23 January 2009).

Bibliography

Todd Gilchrist, "Best Supporting Actor: Mark Strong" (October 9, 2008), http://movies.ign.com/articles/918/918433p1.html (accessed 20 February 2009).

SUCHET, DAVID (1946–)

Best known in Great Britain and America for his performance as Agatha Christie's Poirot, which he has played off and on since the late 1980s. His film roles include Sigmund Freud in the miniseries *Freud* (1984), Aaron in *Moses* (1995).

Cast as Louis B. Mayer in *RKO 281*, Suchet portrays the mogul as someone who, like many of his contemporaries, has no time for things such as loyalty and devotion. JOHN LOGAN's script describes him thus: "A short, crafty, bespectacled man in his 50s. His cloying, avuncular exterior only fleetingly disguises the film titan's outrageous barbarism." Like William Randolph Hearst (JAMES CROMWELL), he is primarily interested in himself. However, Mayer is also shown to possess an Achilles heel: when faced with the threat of exposure as a Jew by Louella Parsons (BRENDA BLETHYN), he immediately agrees to have all prints of Orson Welles's (LIEV SCHREIBER's) film *Citizen Kane* either destroyed or removed from RKO's possession, even if it costs over $800,000 to do so.

Reference

John Logan, "Draft Script for *RKO 281*" (dated 1 May 1997), http://sfy.ru/sfy.html?script=rko218 (accessed 16 November 2008).

SULIMAN, ALI (1977–)

Born in Nazareth, Ali Suliman made his name in films such as *Paradise Now* (2005) and *The Kingdom* (2007).

Cast as Omar Sadiki in *BODY OF LIES*, Suliman plays the part of the fall guy caught up in a world of intrigue. Although an honest businessperson, he is ruthlessly exploited by Roger Ferris (LEONARDO DICAPRIO), and eventually meets a sticky end at the hands of extremist leader Al-Saleem (ALON ABOUTBUL). Sadiki is simply a victim of the "war on terror," whom no one really cares about.

TAKAKURA, KEN (1931–)

Born Oda Toshimasa in Kita-Kyushu City, Japan. Known as the Clint Eastwood of JAPANESE cinema, Takakura acquired his tough-guy persona watching yakuza battles in post-1945 Fukuoka. He gained international recognition after co-starring with Robert Mitchum in Sydney Pollack's *The Yakuza* (1974).

Cast as Inspector Masahiro in *BLACK RAIN*, Takakura offers a fascinating contrast in acting style to the film's two stars, MICHAEL DOUGLAS and ANDY GARCIA. Whereas the two Hollywood actors tend to act direct to camera, Takakura is much quieter, low-key, delivering his lines in a semi-whisper. Douglas called him "the silent warrior." Although berated by the American police officers for his lack of adventure, conformity, and obsession with protocol, Takakura's Masahiro understands the importance of loyalty. It is this quality that encourages him to ignore Superintendent Ohashi's orders and join Nick in his pursuit of Sato (YUSAKU MATSUDA).

Takakura has something of a thankless task in the film—to portray a detective without conforming to accepted Hollywood stereotypes of the Japanese (as represented for example, in Peter Lorre's characterization of Mr. Moto in a cycle of B-pictures for Twentieth Century-Fox in the late 1930s). It is a credit to Takakura's skills as an actor that he delivers the kind of self-effacing performance that makes us understand how hard a detective's life can be in 1980s Osaka, where a combination of repressive authority and lack of opportunities for self-expression (symbolized by Masahiro's tiny apartment) reduce him to an automaton.

Reference

Michael Douglas, interviewed in "*Black Rain*: The Script, The Cast," Special Feature included in the *Special Collector's Edition* DVD release of *Black Rain* (d. Laurent Bouzereau) (Los Angeles: Paramount Pictures, 2006).

Bibliography

Mark Schilling, *The Encyclopedia of Japanese Pop Culture* (Trumble, CT: Weatherhill Publishers, 1997).

THE TALISMAN

Sir Walter Scott's famous tale of the Crusades, first published in 1825, was based on the events of the Third Crusade (1188–1192), in which the chief Christian leaders were Richard I of England (Richard the Lionheart) and Philip II of France. The incidents of the story, however, were mainly Walter Scott's invention.

At the time of the novel's first publication, it was welcomed as a balanced account of the Crusades, focusing on the warriors' heroic qualities—Christian and Muslim alike. *The Talisman* gives a vivid picture not only of the bitter dissensions, but also of the heroism, the chivalry, and the fervor of the Crusades. While an exciting romance, it is also a novel that tries to reinterpret the events in the light of early nineteenth-century thought.

Ridley Scott's *KINGDOM OF HEAVEN* was accused by some critics of expressing a view of the Crusades similar to that found in Scott's novel, which seemed inappropriate to the spirit of the new millennium. Jonathan Riley-Smith, a professor of Ecclesiastical History at Cambridge University, was most vociferous in his criticism: "It sounds absolute balls. It's rubbish. It's not historically accurate at all. They [the characters in the film] refer to *The Talisman*, which depicts the Muslims as sophisticated and civilised, and the Crusaders are all brutes and barbarians. It has nothing to do with reality." Note, however, that Riley-Smith had not actually seen the film when he made this comment ("It *sounds* absolute balls").

Reference

Jonathan Riley-Smith, quoted in Charlotte Edwardes, "Ridley Scott's New Film 'Panders to Osama Bin Laden,'" *Daily Telegraph*, 17 January 2004, www.telegraph.co.uk/news/worldnews/northamerica/usa/1452000/Ridley-Scotts-new-Crusades-film-panders-to-Osama-bin-Laden.html (accessed 13 January 2009).

Bibliography

E. Gilliat, *Scott's The Talisman* (London: Percival & Co., 1892); *The Knight of the Leopard: A Tale of the Wars of the Cross Adapted from Sir Walter Scott's Novel The Talisman* (Edinburgh: Oliver and Boyd, 1904).

TALLY, TED (1952–)

A writer and playwright who made his name adapting *THE SILENCE OF THE LAMBS* for the screen (1991). Tally was originally slated to write *HANNIBAL*, but passed on the project. Tally claimed in an interview with *Shivers* magazine that both he and original director JONATHAN DEMME felt unable to work on the film: "We didn't want to end up in sequel hell as we thought that someone else should take a fresh approach to it [the novel]." Perhaps their decision was occasioned as much by dislike of writer THOMAS HARRIS's book as a reluctance to work on a sequel. Eventually DAVID MAMET produced a script that was later refined by STEVEN ZAILLIAN. Tally returned to write *Red Dragon* (2002), with ANTHONY HOPKINS once again repeating his role as Hannibal Lecter.

Reference

David Grove, "He's Back," *Shivers* 99 (October 2002): 8.

TANGERINE DREAM

Tangerine Dream was hired by Scott to complete the score of *LEGEND*, after the director (in collaboration with Sidney Sheinberg, president of MCA, Universal's parent company) decided to replace JERRY GOLDSMITH's original score with new, contemporary score that would render it appealing to young audiences. They completed the job in three weeks. Until 2002 (when *LEGEND*: THE DIRECTOR'S CUT was released), only European audiences could see the film with the Goldsmith score.

The Tangerine Dream score includes "Loved by the Sun," a vocal version of the "Unicorn Theme," with vocals written and sung by Jon Anderson of Yes. The vocals were added after Tangerine Dream had composed the instrumental music. It was originally recorded with vocals by Susanne Pawlitzki based on WILLIAM BLAKE's poem, "The Angel," but was rejected in favor of the Jon Anderson version. "Unicorn Theme" has been played live by the band at several concerts. "Is Your Love Strong Enough?" played over the end credits, has vocals written and sung by BRYAN FERRY with guitar by David Gilmour and bass by Guy Pratt; it was an outtake of the recording sessions for *AVALON*, the eighth and last Roxy Music album. All of the other tracks are Tangerine Dream instrumentals. "Is Your Love Strong Enough?" was also released as a twelve-inch single and included an extended version of the same song and an instrumental.

The soundtrack LP was released in 1986, but fans had to wait nearly ten years before the Tangerine Dream soundtrack was finally available on CD, because copyright problems had made a rerelease of the original LP impossible. The album was finally released in 1995.

THELMA & LOUISE

US 1991 r/t 129 min col. *Production Companies*: Metro Goldwyn-Mayer, Pathé Entertainment and Percy Main. *Producers*: Mimi Polk, Callie Khouri, Dean O'Brien, and Ridley Scott. *Director*: Ridley Scott. *Writer*: Callie Khouri. *Production Designer*: Norris Spencer. *Director of Photography*: Adrian Biddle. *Music*: Hans Zimmer. *Cast*: Susan Sarandon (*Louise*), Geena Davis (*Thelma*), Harvey Keitel (*Hal Slocombe*), Michael Madsen (*Jimmy*), Christopher McDonald (*Darryl*), Stephen Tobolowsky (*Max*), Brad Pitt (*JD*).

Scott discovered *Thelma & Louise* in mid-1990, almost a year after the release of *BLACK RAIN*. This was a period when he had turned to producing commercials once again, as well as expanding the activities of RSA (Ridley Scott Associates), which by 1990 was operating a Los Angeles as well as a London office. The origins of the film came about when screenwriter CALLIE KHOURI took her script to MIMI POLK, who had worked with Scott since *LEGEND*. Polk passed the script on to Scott, who liked it for several reasons, which he explained in the pressbook: "[t]he main reason I chose to do this film . . . was that I've never done anything like it before. This is a film where the emphasis—the driving force, if you will—is almost totally on character, rather than where a spaceship comes from . . . One highlight of the material is the way it puts the male/female relationship into perspective. Hopefully, after seeing the film, both male and female audience members will recognize something about themselves. If they like what they see, they'll keep it. If not, maybe they'll change it."

Eventually Scott secured funding from MGM, Pathé Entertainment and United International Pictures, once he had agreed to produce and direct the film. The total budget was only $16 million, comparatively small by the standards of his previous work. Casting was completed in several stages. SUSAN SARANDON was cast first, followed by GEENA DAVIS. Khouri's screenplay went through several changes before it was considered suitable for production. Among the deleted scenes were one in which Slocombe's wife was asked by her husband if she could shoot another person and one showing police procedures as they deal with information. The original screenplay has two interviews with Jimmy, which cut down to one in the film. Other deleted scenes showed the phones in Thelma's and Louise's houses being tapped. Several of the road scenes have been cut or edited. Linda J. Cowgill discusses how the finished film introduces new scenes: Louise trading her ring to Major, the old man (Ken Swofford); Louise stopping her car and surveying the beauty of the landscape (demonstrating her symbolic union with it).

Principal photography for *Thelma & Louise* began on 11 June 1990 and wrapped on 31 August of the same year.

The production was filmed entirely on location in fifty-four locations in and around Los Angeles, and in Utah's Arches National Park and Canyonlands National Park (also in Utah) which stood in for Arizona and New Mexico. Filming also took place in Bakersfield, California. Scott's work in the desert landscapes recalls the commercial for MIDLAND BANK; in an interview with PAUL M. SAMMON he recalled that this was the first time he had completed an entire feature with two cameras running simultaneously throughout, a technique which allowed him to "get multiple angles of the same shot" as well as keeping the actors' performances "loose and spontaneous." He subsequently employed the same technique in all of his films.

Immediately before the film's theatrical release, Scott altered the ending. In his interview with Sammon, he discussed how the film originally included footage of the Thunderbird car dropping down into the Grand Canyon and reaction shots from Slocombe as well as a shot of him walking back towards the hordes of police officers, followed by a reprise of the same wide shot that opens *Thelma & Louise* of an empty road leading to a distant mountain. On the soundtrack, B.B. King sang "Better Not Look Down." However Scott replaced this with a freeze-frame shot of the characters' car taking off from Grand Canyon into space.

Thelma & Louise generated an extraordinary range of critical opinion on its American premiere in June 1991. Male critics in general loathed the film for its apparent glorification of female violence, while female critics defended the film, rationalizing its violence as a legitimate response to patriarchal domination and sexual assault. Susan Sarandon's and Geena Davis's photographs appeared on the covers of *Time* and *Newsweek*. Bumper stickers and buttons began to appear: "*Thelma & Louise* Finishing School." To "Thelma-and-Louise" someone became a verb. Sharon Willis commented in 1993: "Like *Fatal Attraction*, *Thelma & Louise* plugged into ambient anxieties about sexual difference, and men's and women's places as organized by the 'battle of the sexes.'" Gina Fournier assembles some interesting extracts from contemporary reviews, ranging from the *US News and World Report* ("[The film] is just one of the current bumper crop of women-kills-man movies, but it is clearly the most upsetting"), to *Newsweek* ("[The central characters] are triumphant in an end-of-the-road finale that may shock feminists (and others) but it is true to the mythic nature of a big-hearted movie"), *The Houston Chronicle* ("Its execution is lovely and you'll make a tight emotional connection with the story and the characters") and the *Christian Science Monitor* ("[the film] proves that Hollywood still has a long way to go before its feminist credentials can be called respectable"). Fournier subsequently focuses in great depth on the main issues raised by the film in the media, including the portrayal of the male characters, the question of

whether one should sympathize with or reject the central characters' motives and whether the film's subject matter was feminist or antifeminist. More importantly, she argues that *Thelma & Louise* had a profound effect on American culture in the sense that "it revitalized attention toward important social, cultural and political issues [of gender]." A distraught reader complained to the *Village Voice*'s mock advice columnist Problem Lady: "You know you cannot go to dinner, or to a party, or even to the corner to buy carrot juice without hordes of people running up to you and saying, 'So, *Thelma & Louise*, what about that ending, huh? Was it a feminist movie or what the hell was it? Was the violence okay or is it bad for women? What about role models?'" The *Washington Post Magazine* concluded in 1993 that "More people had more gut-level discussions about the anger between men and women after seeing *Thelma & Louise* than after reading any gray Op-Ed piece in any paper or watching any balanced report on *Nightline*."

British critics were perhaps less divided in their opinions, despite an article appearing in the film magazine *Empire*, which predicted that the film might become "one of the most talked-about movies in recent times." The *Independent* called the film "Ridley Scott's warmest and loosest film to date . . . His un-American eye finds a number of new angles on Americana, though it is also in its way a limitation." The *Sunday Telegraph* enthused: "The whole film is an exhilarating celebration of popular culture's ability to turn stories of ordinary people into myths with a social resonance." Alexander Walker of the *Evening Standard* liked the acting, but thought that the director was too concerned to make "politically correct points."

Audiences responded to the film in different ways. Brenda Cooper's research into male and female reactions among university students in an American western rural town showed that "most women applauded the film for its empowering representation of women 'who dare to feel anger against male violence and domination,' while the majority of men denounced it as 'degrading to men, with pathetic stereotypes of testosterone-crazed behavior.'" For most of the women she interviewed, "*Thelma & Louise* clearly represents more than shoot-outs and car chases—its relevancy emerges from the film's empowerment of women in their struggle to transcend sexism and their subsequent marginalized status." The film earned over three times its cost in the United States alone, grossing $46 million. The European and Asian box-office proved equally strong, with $4 million each earned in Great Britain and France during the film's first six weeks of release. It subsequently won an Academy Award for Callie Khouri for Best Screenplay Written Directly for the Screen. The film certainly had a profound effect on North American culture. According to *The Independent*, two young women were arrested in Canada in

1995 and charged with a string of crimes against men seeking sexual favors. They were immediately dubbed "Thelma and Louise" by the local press.

Thelma & Louise follows the example of *ALIEN* in focusing on the construction of gender. As in the earlier film, the main characters are women; they drive not only the Thunderbird but also the film's plot, and thereby challenge the traditional cinematic association of activity with MASCULINITY. They refuse to be defined entirely by their relationships with men; instead, they form at the film's conclusion a symbolic MARRIAGE of sisterhood that transcends personal attachment. Theirs is a union of two abused women who revolt against a society that has not adequately protected them from crimes of male violence.

The film shows the protagonists constructing their own versions of "femaleness"—Thelma (Geena Davis) transforms herself from an innocent into someone responsible for her own destiny, while Louise (Susan Sarandon) learns to make sense of her previous experiences—including the rape in Texas—and embraces the freedom associated with the landscape. Both of them understand that patriarchy's rules are not only intolerable but also outrageous, laughable. The film's ending, showing the Thunderbird suspended in mid-air, summarizes their state of mind: they decide to continue their lives on their own, while defiantly rejecting the (male) police officers' order to "freeze," to become inert and inactive.

By contrast, Scott portrays the majority of the male characters as either childish or untrustworthy. Thelma's husband Darryl (CHRISTOPHER McDONALD) is petulant and self-important, while Louise's boyfriend Jimmy (MICHAEL MADSEN), though appearing to sympathize with her point of view, actually turns out to be tough and violent. Both men are forced to undertake tasks commonly performed by women—cleaning tables, eating out of boredom, or waiting for their partners to call on the phone. JD (BRAD PITT) appears initially as an attractive young man, but eventually steals Thelma and Louise's money. Other characters include a rigidly authoritarian state trooper (JASON BEGHE) and the potential rapist Harlan (TIMOTHY CARHART), who is outwardly attractive and charming but turns violent when Thelma refuses a sexual encounter with him. The foul-mouthed trucker (MARCO ST. JOHN) embraces much the same views, seeing women purely as sex objects to be picked up and dispensed with at will.

The one sympathetic male character in the film is Slocombe (HARVEY KEITEL), who tries his best to understand the two women. He transgresses the space of gender relations by being too sympathetic to the women and hence loses the confidence of his fellow police officers. He runs towards the women at the end because he knows that the troopers will not shoot him in the back, believing that he can still save them. However, Hal is wrong: once Thelma and Louise decide to drive off the cliff, they are no longer subjects within the law of the patriarchal culture and they do not want to be saved by this well-intentioned man. While the film might be seen to advance the cause of FEMINISM, according to Bernie Cook it also promotes "new ways of seeing, not in the ways it confirms old, established polarities and boundaries."

Scott underlines the importance of discovering "new ways of seeing" as he shows how the male and female characters are perpetually unable to communicate with one another. In Marita Sturken's view they do not have the same understanding of words or ways of expressing themselves. Thelma thinks it odd that Darryl should have to work on a Friday evening selling carpets, a clear hint that she knows that he is doing something else. Darryl dismisses this, though, as naiveté ("Well then, it's a good thing you're not regional manager and I am"). Later on Slocombe asks Darryl whether he is close to Thelma, and he replies "I love Thelma," and then pauses: "Yeah, I guess, I mean, I'm about as close as I can be to a nutcase like that." Clearly he has no conception of what motivates his wife's behavior. The most crude example of this misunderstanding occurs when the trucker makes lewd gestures at Thelma and Louise while driving by, gestures they ask him about later on ("What's that supposed to mean, exactly?"). Such questions, of course, make no sense to him; here are two women driving a car on the open road, and it is "evident" to him that they should be available. When he stops the truck, he takes off his wedding ring and grabs a couple of condoms, asking them as he does so whether they are "ready to get serious." The humor of this exchange lies in his and their different interpretations of what it means to "get serious"—as shown later on, when the two women set his truck on fire. Such scenes underline the importance of establishing new ways of understanding the world, where men and women might understand one another better.

Thelma & Louise also subverts traditional forms of the gaze, where women are constructed as passive objects for male spectators. It is JD, rather than the female characters, who becomes objectified by the gaze upon him, and he uses that sexuality to get what he wants—power and money. Thelma and Louise reject the unwanted gazes of strange men upon them, yet take pleasure in other looks (from one another). They deprive men of the power of gazing upon them, either by staring back or pointing with a gun. They are subject to the gazes of the (patriarchal) law—the surveillance camera, the gaze from the approaching helicopter in the final scene—which they evade by driving out of sight. The film begins with the two women photographing themselves; they are objectified, but simultaneously control the camera as well, while being framed within the camera operated by the male director. Such images in Sturken's view reveal "the complexity of the power relations of looking."

Much critical energy has been spent on deconstructing these power relations. Taking as her starting-point the idea that the film was helmed by a male director, Suzanna Danuta Walters concludes that "[the] focus on the relationship between two women is made narratively possible by male sexuality." Likewise, the conservative critic Margaret R. Miles judges the film a failure on account of its reliance on Hollywood conventions that represent "theft, alcohol, and casual, unsafe sex as exhilarating, fun and the best revenge on a sexist society." Yvonne Tasker refers to the fact that, like *ALIEN*, *Thelma & Louise* might be considered little more than "a masculine revenge fantasy," whose effect is, perversely, to reinforce the message that women cannot win. However, she also argues that the film's representation of the male and female BODY allows for the redefinition of gender roles. This issue has also been taken up by Elizabeth Jones, who uses Heidegger and Derrida to show how "the formation of our concepts of the self and of humanity . . . . depend upon the recognition of the Other . . . The ideal excludes the Other. The pursuit of the ideal in cinema today and specifically in *Thelma & Louise* precipitates the crisis of identity which we witness all around us."

Feminists such as Jane Arthurs take a similarly cautious line: "*Thelma & Louise* does not offer a radical alternative to patriarchal cinema but rather moves inside it to disrupt the codes of gender in Hollywood film." Patricia Mellencamp adopts a more enthusiastic view of the film, especially at the end where the protagonists are shown "defy[ing] gravity, gaining mastery of themselves, becoming triumphant in death. The [film's] ending is courageous, profound, sublime." Lynda Hart's psychoanalytic reading of the film concludes that while "there is no place for them [the women] to go except the place designated for them in the masculine symbolic [the director's camera, for example]," the disappearance of the photograph of them at the end of the film, as they plunge to their deaths, "allows us to imagine an elsewhere that resists representation." Cara J. MariAnna relates the film's content to ancient mythic tales of origin and power, justice and freedom, neglect and abuse, retribution, transformation and rebirth.

Other critics treat the film as a pessimistic interpretation of femininity. Susan Morrison situates it in the women's film genre, showing how it differs from classical Hollywood films such as *Duel in the Sun* (1946) in the way "it [*Thelma & Louise*] consciously insists on the audience's response to its unhappy ending in the form of reflection on the nature of its cause . . . The tragedy of the film is that Thelma should have been perfectly free to enjoy herself in that bar . . . It was the society in which we live that permitted Harlan to feel that he could so anything he wanted to and get away with it."

Writing in 1996, the British critic Magdalen Carol called the film "rather tame," as it offered a perspective on "ism"

oppression" which was "very much of its time," despite the fact that it was "complex, multi-layered and deeply personal." Whether the "personal" view refers to the director, the screenplay or the characters themselves remains unclear. *Film Quarterly* published a symposium on the film, containing contributions from eight critics under the title "The Many Faces of *Thelma & Louise*." The American magazine *Cineaste* did the same thing, with contributions on "The Impotence of Women," "Feminism Gets the Hollywood Treatment," "The Bimbo and the Mystery Woman," "The Movie Management of Rape," and "Hollywood Sets the Terms of the Debate." A good summary of critical opinion on the film (from 1991 to 1997) in books, journals, and newspaper articles is provided by Tess Forbes and Andrew Ormsby's *Thelma & Louise and The Piano: Information Source Pack*.

More recent critics such as Karen Hollinger and Alistair Daniel have focused on the film's conscious reshaping of cinematic genres, while Martha McCaughey, Neal King, and Hilary Neroni discuss its portrayal of violent women as figures in the landscape of contemporary Hollywood cinema. A 2007 anthology *Thelma & Louise Live!* examines the initial reception and ongoing impact of the film both in academic and popular cultural circles. Cindy L. Griffin offers certain suggestions as to how the film can be taught in the classroom.

References

Jane Arthurs, "Thelma & Louise: On the Road to Feminism?" in *Feminist Subjects, Multi-Media: Cultural Methodologies*, ed. Penny Florence and Dee Reynolds (Manchester and New York: Manchester University Press, 1995), 104; Russell Blinch, "'Thelma and Louise' Fugitives Arrested," *The Independent*, 6 October 1995, 17; Magdalen Carol, "A Room of Our Own," *Black Film Bulletin* 4, no.4 (Winter 1996): 26; Bernie Cook, "Something's Crossed Over in Me: New Ways of Seeing *Thelma & Louise*," in Cook, ed., *Thelma & Louise Live! The Cultural Afterlife of an American Film* (Austin: University of Texas Press, 2007), 39; Brenda Cooper, "The Relevancy and Gender Identity in Spectators' Interpretations of *Thelma & Louise*," *Critical Studies in Mass Communication* 16, no.1 (March 1999):34, 36; Linda J. Cowgill, *Secrets of Screenplay Structure: How to Recognize and Emulate the Structure of Great Films* (Los Angeles: Lone Eagle Publishing Company Llc., 1999), 296–300; Alistair Daniel, "Our Idea of Fun: *Thelma & Louise* on Trial," in *Lost Highways: An Illustrated History of Road Movies*, ed. Jack Sergeant and Stephanie Watson (London: Creation Books, 1999), 169–81; Tess Forbes and Andrew Ormsby, *Thelma & Louise and The Piano: Information Source Pack* (London: British Film Institute Library, 1997), 7–18; Gina Fournier, *Thelma & Louise and Women in Hollywood* (Jefferson, NC and London: McFarland & Company Inc., 2007), 31; Cindy L. Griffin, "Teaching Rhetorical Criticism with *Thelma & Louise*," *Communication Education* 44 (April 1995): 165–76; Lynda Hart, *Fatal Women: Lesbian Sexuality and the Mark* of Aggression (Princeton: Princeton University Press, 1994), 80; Cynthia Heimel, "Tongue in Chic," Village Voice, 9 July 1991, 37; Karen Hollinger, In the Company of Women: Contemporary Female Friendship Films (Minneapolis and London: University of Minnesota Press, 1998); Elizabeth Jones, "The Failure of Imagination in Thelma and Louise," Film and Philosophy 3 (1996): 159; "The Many Faces of Thelma & Louise," Film Quarterly 45, no.2 (Winter 1991–92): 20–32; Cara J. MariAnna, "The Seven Mythic Cycles of Thelma and Louise," Trivia 21 (1993): 82–99; Adam Mars-Jones, "Getting Away From It All," The Independent, 12 July 1991, 18; Martha McCaughey and Neal King, eds., Reel Knockouts: Violent Women in the Movies (Austin: University of Texas Press, 2001); Patricia Mellencamp, A Fine Romance: Five Ages of Film Feminism (Philadelphia: Temple University Press, 1995), 150; Margaret R. Miles, Seeing and Believing: Religion and Values in the Movies (Boston: Beacon Press, 1995), 147; Susan Morrison, "Pearl, Hilda, Thelma & Louise: The 'Woman's Film' Revisited," CineAction 30 (1992): 49; Hilary Neroni, The Violent Woman: Femininity, Narrative and Violence in Contemporary American Cinema (Albany: State University of New York Press, 2005); Ridley Scott, quoted in the pressbook for Thelma & Louise (London: UA Entertainment Co., 1991), 2–3; Ridley Scott, quoted in Paul M. Sammon, Ridley Scott Close-Up: The Making of his Movies (New York: Thunder's Mouth Press, 1999), 102; "Should We Go Along for the Ride? A Critical Symposium on Thelma & Louise," Cineaste 18, no.4 (1991); Marita Sturken, Thelma and Louise (London: BFI Publishing, 2000), 44; Yvonne Tasker, Spectacular Bodies: Gender, Genre and the Action Cinema (London and New York: Routledge, 1993), 139; Philip Thomas, "Girls Just Wanna Have Fun . . ." Empire 26 (August 1991): 50; Christopher Tookey, "Wild Women, and They Don't React," Sunday Telegraph, 14 July 1991, xiv; Alexander Walker, "A Letter from Thelma's Hide-Out," Evening Standard, 11 July 1991, 35; Suzanna Danuta Walters, Material Girls: Making Sense of Feminist Cultural Theory (Berkeley and Los Angeles: University of California Press, 1995), 9–10; Sharon Willis, "Hardware and Hardbodies: What Do Women Really Want? A Reading of Thelma & Louise," in Film Theory Goes to the Movies, ed. Jim Collins, Hilary Radner, and Ava Preacher Collins (London and New York: Routledge, 1993), 120.

Bibliography

Brenda Cooper, "Chick Flicks as Feminist Texts: The Appropriation of the Male Gaze in Thelma & Louise," Women's Studies in Communication 23, no.3 (Fall 2000): 277–306; Judy Elsey, "Edward Abbey, Thelma & Louise and Me: How Women Live in the West," Encyclia: Journal of the Utah Academy of Sciences, Arts and Letters 69 (1992): 53–63; Linda Frost, "The Decentered Subject of Feminism: Postfeminism and Thelma and Louise," in Rhetoric in an Antifoundational World: Language, Culture and Pedagogy, ed. Michael Bernard-Donals and Richard R. Glejzer (New Haven and London: Yale University Press, 1998), 147–69; Peter Hoyng, "Schiller goes to the Movies: Locating the Sublime in Thelma and Louise," Die Unter-richtspraxis/Teaching German 30, no.1 (Spring 1997): 40–49; Barbara Johnson, "Lesbian Spectacles: Reading Sula, Passing, Thelma & Louise, and The Accused," in Media Spectacles, ed. Marjorie Garber, Jann Matlock, and Rebecca L. Walkowitz (New York and London: Routledge, 1993), 160–66; Beth Kraig, "Are We There Yet, Driver? Searching for the Automotive Human," Midwest Quarterly 48, no.2 (Winter 2007): 297–313; Maitland McDonough, "Thelma & Louise Hit the Road for Ridley Scott," in Ridley Scott Interviews, ed. Laurence F. Knapp and Andrea F. Kulas (Jackson: University Press of Mississippi, 2005), 70–75; Kathi Maio, "Women Who Murder for the Man," Rural Politics 12 (1992): 5–8; Glenn Man, "Gender, Genre and Myth in Thelma and Louise," in Gender and Culture in Literature and Film East and West: Issues of Perception and Interpretation: Selected Conference Papers, ed. Nitaya Masavisut, George Simson, and Larry E. Smith (Honolulu: Colleges of Languages, Linguistics and Literature, University of Hawaii, 1994), 113–23; Ann Putnam, "The Bearer of the Gaze in Ridley Scott's Thelma and Louise," Western American Literature 27, no.4 (Winter 1995): 291–302; David Russell, "I'm Not Gonna Hurt You: Legal Penetrations in Thelma and Louise," Americana: The Journal of American Popular Culture 1900 to Present (Spring 2002) www.americanpopularculture.com/journal/articles/spring_2002/russell.htm (accessed 3 August 2008); Amy Taubin, "Ridley Scott's Road Work," Sight and Sound, July 1991, 18–19; Kerstin Westerlund-Shands, "Female Fatality in the Movies," Moderna Sprak: Publication of the Modern Language Association of Sweden 87, no.2 (1993): 113–20.

THEWLIS, DAVID (1963–)

Born David Wheeler in Blackpool, England, Thewlis made his name in Mike Leigh's film Naked (1993). He has a small role as the Hospitaler in KINGDOM OF HEAVEN—someone well aware of the mayhem the Christians have caused in their defense of the Holy Land: "By the word religion, I've seen the lunacy of fanatics of every determination be called 'the will of God.' Holiness is in right action, and courage on behalf of those who cannot defend themselves. And goodness—what God deserves—is here and here [he points to his heart and his head.] And what you decide to do every day, you'll be a good man or not." Balian (ORLANDO BLOOM) never forgets this message, as he makes similar gestures while talking to Sibylla (EVA GREEN) immediately after forging a peace deal with Saladin (GHASSAN MASSOUD).

For all his common sense, the Hospitaler will never countermand his commanding officer's orders, even when he knows that they are wrong. Thus the Hospitaler leaves the city of Jerusalem to fight a fruitless battle against Saladin in the desert, though well aware that the Christians, unable to adapt to alien conditions (especially a shortage of water), will be massacred.

Thewlis's subsequent films include ALL THE INVISIBLE CHILDREN: "JONATHAN" where he plays a photojournalist traumatized by the experience of working in war zones.

However, he comes to learn the value of his work—especially as a way of recording how resilient children are at bonding together and surviving amidst scenes of devastation.

THE THING FROM ANOTHER WORLD

US 1951 r/t 87 min (81 min on reissue) b/w. *Producers*: Howard Hawks and Edward Lasker. *Director*: Christian Nyby. *Writers*: Charles Lederer, Howard Hawks, and Ben Hecht, from the story by John W. Campbell Jr. *Director of Photography*: Russell Harlan. *Production Designers*: Albert S. D'Agostino and John J. Hughes. *Music*: Dmitri Tiomkin. *Cast*: Margaret Sheridan (*Nikki*), Kenneth Tobey (*Captain Patrick Hendry*), Robert Cornthwaite (*Dr. Carrington*), Douglas Spencer (*Scotty*), James Young (*Lt. Eddie Dykes*), Dewey Martin (*Crew Chief*).

Christian Nyby's direction sustains a mood of tingling expectancy as a small group of US airmen and scientists stationed near the North Pole learn that a new, mysterious element is playing tricks with their compass-readings. Tension develops effectively as the expedition takes off to reckon with the unearthly intruder. The film was clearly intended as a response to current political events—particularly in its final suggestion that one's homeland should be protected against possible invaders, or those who try to upset the balance of the world with too much scientific research.

Although Scott has not acknowledged any direct influence, *ALIEN* clearly resembles this film, both in its social criticism and its portrayal of the sheer power of the beast. Certain scenes have distinct parallels: for example, the "chestbuster" scene from *Alien* and the geiger-counter scene from *The Thing*. Producer Howard Hawks's biographer Todd McCarthy observes that "*The Thing* was one of Hawks's most influential creations, still cited as a key film in the lives of such prominent directors as Ridley Scott . . . [it] received the sort of serious attention from the press that was customarily denied to examples of culturally despised genres. Most critics found it scary, entertaining, not unintelligent, and well made, almost as if Hawks had directed it himself."

Reference

Todd McCarthy, *Howard Hawks* (New York: Grove Press, 1997), 483.

THE THIRD MAN

GB 1949 r/t 104 min b/w. *Production Companies*: London Film Productions and British Lion Film Corporation. *Producers*: David O. Selznick, Carol Reed, and Alexander Korda. *Director*: Carol Reed. *Writer*: Graham Greene. *Director of Photography*: Robert Krasker. *Music*: Anton Kara. *Cast*: Orson Welles (*Harry Lime*), Joseph Cotten (*Holly Martins*), Alida Valli (*Anna Schmidt*), Trevor Howard (*Major Calloway*).

Classic FILM NOIR of the late 1940s, whose visual style (the use of dark passages and gloomy war-torn locations) inspired many films and miniseries, including *THE COMPANY* (2007); the story of the CIA from the mid-1950s through the Cold War period.

THIRTY-MINUTE THEATRE: "THE HARD WORD"

GB 1966 r/t TVM 30 min b/w. *Production Company*: British Broadcasting Corporation. *Producer*: Harry Moore. *Director*: Ridley Scott. *Writer*: Jim Allen. *Production Designer*: Raymond Cusick. *Cast*: Jack Woolgar (*Martin*), Tony Selby (*Danny*), Iain Anders (*Kelly*), Jeremy Young (*Boss*).

A contribution to the BBC's long running series (1965–1974), broadcast live on 16 May 1966 (Series 1, Episode 32). The setting is a lingering and harsh northern winter. Reluctantly taking the only jobs available, three men find themselves on a small building site.

THOMSON, ALEX (1929–2007)

After a career as a camera operator on films such as *A Funny Thing Happened on the Way to the Forum* (1966) and *Far From the Madding Crowd* (1967), Thomson made his debut as director of photography with *Here We Go Round the Mulberry Bush* (1967).

Thomson described his involvement in *LEGEND* thus, in an interview with Ron Magid published at the time of the film's American release: "We used shafts of light that I sometimes had moving . . . it followed through from the thing he [Scott] did in [*BLADE RUNNER*] with searchlights that moved about for no reason at all except that they looked quite good."

Thomson's work on *LEGEND* is most spectacularly evident in the management of lighting effects. The opening sequence announces the theme in spectacular fashion: shafts of blue moonlight shine through the branches of a shadowy forest, foreshadowing the battle between good and evil that is about to take place. To reemphasize the point, Thomson cuts away from Darkness's (TIM CURRY's) lair to a shot of a bright summer's day as Lily (MIA SARA) skips down the path of the enchanted forest. Another lighting effect in Darkness's first scene shows him lamenting his lack of power while bathed with a majestic purple light, his eyes and fingernails glowing green in the semi-gloom.

In another sequence Thomson underlines the hypnotic aspects of Lily's seduction by Darkness. As the masked dancer walks around the terrified princess, the action cuts to a close-up of the dancer's fingers clawing across her face. This is followed by an out-of-focus shot of the dancer moving rhythmically across the frame, at first obscuring and then revealing Lily's face, which gradually alters from fear to rapture. She is now Darkness's slave.

Thomson found Scott's attention to detail awe-inspiring, especially on a production the size and complexity of *Legend*. He observed to Magid that "a lot of the film's atmosphere comes directly from Ridley, because he dresses the sets impeccably and he creates a lot of that mood himself, just through his compositions and because he props the whole thing."

Reference

Ron Magid, "*Labyrinth* and *Legend*, Big Screen Fairy Tales," *American Cinematographer* 67, no.8 (August 1986): 67.

THUNDER PERFECT MIND

GB 2005 Commercial r/t 30 sec. *Production Company*: RSA Films. *Directors*: Ridley Scott and Jordan Scott.

A 2005 film by JORDAN SCOTT and Ridley Scott, that depicts Canadian supermodel Daria Werbowy moving through various urban scenes (such as a nightclub, the back of a taxi, and around Potsdamer Platz in Berlin), while a recitation from the fourteenth-century poem (entitled "The Thunder, Perfect Mind") is read in as a form of narrative commentary. A shortened version of the film was used in a Prada advertisement to promote the launch of the fashion house's first perfume. The advertisement can be viewed online at http://www.rsafilms.com/d/rsa/companies/rsa-uk/87.

Bibliography

Rae Ann Fera, "Thunder Perfect Prada," *Boards Magazine*, 1 May 2005, www.boardsmag.com/articles/magazine/20050501/prada .html (accessed 21 January 2009).

TIDY, FRANK (?–)

THE DUELLISTS was his first feature film. Pauline Kael, in her *New Yorker* review, praised Tidy for his "Géricault-like compositions" and lighting that would earn the approval of Vermeer himself. Gavin Millar in *The Listener* observed that the photography gave "a violently sensuous impression of a threatening physical world . . . the shrill grinding of a sword-edge upon a wheel, the panicky flutter of a trapped sparrow." The film also has a mastery of minute detail: D'Hubert's (KEITH CARRADINE's) slight dandyism is hinted at by the way in which the light catches his braided golden pigtails and the echoing pattern of his helmet strap.

Tidy's photography can be observed to best effect in some of the duel sequences. In the second of these, taking place in a late autumn morning, the camera focuses on a rural French landscape, the branches of the trees set starkly against a blue-gray sky, the sun peeping from behind the hills to the left of the frame. The camera tracks to the right, where we witness D'Hubert practicing his moves with an (unnamed) second. A farmhouse becomes visible on the right of the frame, the sun catching its honey-stone walls. In the background, a row of tall pine trees are visible, also illu-minated by the morning sun. On the soundtrack, the neighing of horses can be heard, as Feraud and his seconds emerge from the rear of the frame in preparation for the forthcoming conflict. Feraud rides to the front of the frame, draws his sword, and dismounts, while his seconds wish good morning to D'Hubert's seconds. Feraud subsequently walks away from the camera towards the farmhouse; all we can hear in the background is bird-song, the faint clip-clop of the horses' hooves and the baa-ing of unseen sheep. Scott holds the shot for nearly fifteen seconds, during which time we see the two duelists preparing for their conflict in the middle distance. By this means Scott and Tidy emphasize the sheer pointlessness of the conflict. It doesn't matter who wins: life in rural FRANCE will continue in the same way it always has done.

In his excellent "Director's Commentary" on the DVD version of the film, Scott states that he operated the camera himself, but maintains that Tidy's contributions were equally important. Indeed, he and Tidy had previously worked together on scores of commercials, so the cameraman was well acquainted with Scott's cinematic preferences. "I had no concerns about how much [of the imagery] was in the shadows," Scott notes. "Frank knew that this was what I liked . . . I don't mind if windows blow out . . . [and] I don't mind sometimes if [the frame] goes totally dark. Frank just really knew how far to go."

At another juncture, Scott huffs that some critics found the film "too beautiful" and "too gauzed," even though no gauze or diffusion was used during the shoot. In fact, the filmmakers achieved the striking look by staging scenes in authentic locations in France which they strategically enhanced with filters and liberal doses of smoke. Scott also feels that the production benefited from "overcast but beautiful weather," noting that mist, precipitation, and indirect sunlight enabled his team to create dramatic but naturalistic moods. He concedes that working in variable conditions occasionally affected shot-to-shot continuity, but is quick to add that neither he nor Tidy worried about this much. "By the time it's been cut together, most of the time you don't even notice." Tidy was nominated for a British Film Academy (BAFTA) award for his work on *The Duellists*.

References

Pauline Kael, "The Current Cinema," *New Yorker*, 23 January 1978, 80; Gavin Millar, "Monstrous Absurdity," *The Listener*, 8 February 1978, 184–85; Ridley Scott, "Director's Commentary," to the 2003 release of *The Duellists* by Paramount DVD in the "Special Collector's Edition" (London: Paramount Home Entertainment, 2003).

TINKER TAILOR SOLDIER SPY

GB 1979 TV series 7 × 50 min episodes col. *Production Companies*: BBC and Paramount Pictures. *Producer*: Jonathan

Powell. *Director*: John Irvin. *Writer*: Arthur Hopcraft, from the novels of John le Carré. *Director of Photography*: Tony Pierce-Roberts. *Production Designer*: Austen Spriggs. *Music*: Geoffrey Burgon. *Cast*: Alec Guinness (*George Smiley*), Michael Jayston (*Peter Guillam*), Ian Richardson (*Bill Haydon*), Terence Rigby (*Roy Bland*), Bernard Hepton (*Toby Esterhase*), Ian Bannen (*Jim Prideaux*).

Classic BBC drama of the Cold War, focusing on a spy coming out of retirement to cope with a serious problem at the "circus" involving MI5 and the CIA. This drama provided the inspiration—especially in visual terms, with all the darkened interiors—for Scott's 2007 miniseries *THE COMPANY*.

TOP GUN

US 1986 r/t 110 min col. *Production Company*: Paramount Pictures. *Producers*: Jerry Bruckheimer and Don Simpson. *Director*: Tony Scott. *Writers*: Jim Cash and Jack Epps Jr., from a story by Ehud Yonay. *Production Designer*: John F. DeCuir Jr. *Director of Photography*: Jeffrey Kimball. *Music*: Harold Faltermeyer. *Cast*: Tom Cruise (*Lt. Pete "Maverick" Mitchell*), Kelly McGillis (*Charlotte "Charlie" Blackwood*), Val Kilmer (*Lt. Tom "Iceman" Kazansky*), Anthony Edwards (*Lt. J. G. Nick "Goose" Bradshaw*), Tom Skerritt (*Cmdr. Mike "Viper" Metcalf*), Michael Ironside (*Lt. Cmdr. Rick "Jester" Heatherly*).

Maverick is a hot pilot. When he encounters a pair of MIGs over the Persian Gulf, his colleague is clearly scared. On almost no fuel, Maverick is able to talk him back down to the aircraft carrier. As a reward, Maverick is sent to the Top Gun Naval Flying School. There he fights the attitudes of the other pilots and struggles to be the best pilot, stepping on the toes of his other students and becoming attracted to Charlie, a civilian instructor. *Top Gun* provided the inspiration for the reality series *AMERICAN FIGHTER PILOT*, produced by TONY SCOTT (who had directed Top Gun). At least two of the three pilots featured in this series had seen the film.

TOVOLI, LUCIANO (1936–)

Born in Massa Marittima, Italy, Tovoli began his career in Italian films, making his Hollywood debut as director of photography with *Reversal of Fortune* (1990) and *Single White Female* (1992).

The Ridley Scott-produced comedy *MONKEY TROUBLE* was his third American film. The action is set entirely in LOS ANGELES, around Venice and other suburban locations. Tovoli pictures the city as a place of eternal sunshine, full of people walking by the sea, cycling, skateboarding, or engaging in street theater. Director FRANCO AMURRI seems to suggest that everything should be perfect in this kind of ambience; but this is certainly not the case, with the perpetual threat of crime: theft, and maybe worse—particularly if Azro (HARVEY KEITEL) catches Eva (THORA BIRCH) and Dodger the monkey. However, everything ends happily; family stability is restored; and Eva is allowed to keep Dodger (despite the fact that her stepfather Tom [Kevin Scannell] once had an allergy to animals).

Bibliography

"Luciano Tovoli Reminisces," *In Camera*, October 2002, 16–17.

"TRIPOLI"

A script written by WILLIAM MONAHAN, which was due to go into production in 2002 with Scott as director. However, filming was delayed due to the 9/11 attacks and the star RUSSELL CROWE's decision to take a break from acting.

The story was conceived as a historical epic set against the backdrop of the Barbary Wars of 1805. It focuses on the military and diplomatic campaign of US naval agent to the Barbary States William Eaton (Crowe) to restore to power Hamet Karamanli, the rightful but exiled Bashaw of Tripoli, in order to curb the piracy by Barbary corsairs against American merchant and military vessels. In other words, Eaton is a hawk who schemes to oust the brutal Yusuf Bashaw from power and install a ruler who will be friendly towards the fledgling United States and their commercial and military interests abroad. Eaton led his motley crew of US Marines, Berbers and assorted mercenaries hundreds of miles across the desert to battle Yusuf Bashaw's superior forces. According to a script review issued in 2003, Monahan's work was "a highly fictionalized work based on a historical event. It is not a biopic of either Eaton or Hamet; it focuses only on their campaign against Yusuf Bashaw. Monahan's script condenses events that transpired over the course of months and sometimes years, a creative license that is more than understandable."

Interviewed four years later, Monahan said he still owned the rights to the script and he hoped that it would get made when the time was right.

References

Interview with William Monahan, www.collider.com/entertainment/interviews/article.asp?aid=3700&tcid=1 (accessed 16 January 2009); "Stax," "The Stax Report: Script Review of *Tripoli*" (7 August 2003), http://movies.ign.com/articles/432/432011p1.html (accessed 16 January 2009).

"TRISTAN AND ISEULT"

After *THE DUELLISTS*, Scott planned to make a version of the TRISTAN AND ISOLDE myth with a script by GERALD VAUGHAN-HUGHES, but failed to find any funds. Eventually he abandoned the project and worked on *ALIEN* instead. The film was eventually made in 2005 as *TRISTAN*

+ *ISOLDE* with KEVIN REYNOLDS as director and Scott as producer.

TRISTAN + ISOLDE

Germany/Czech Republic/GB/US 2005 r/t 120 min col. *Production Companies*: Apollo Pro Media, Scott Free, and Twentieth Century-Fox. *Executive Producers*: Ridley Scott, Tony Scott, Frank Hubner, and John Hardy. *Producers*: Moshe Diamant, Elie Samaha, and Lisa Ellzey. *Director*: Kevin Reynolds. *Writer*: Dean Georgaris. *Director of Photography*: Arthur Reinhart. *Production Designer*: Mark Geraghty. *Music*: Anne Dudley. *Cast*: James Franco (*Tristan*), Sophia Myles (*Isolde*), Rufus Sewell (*Lord Marke*), David Patrick O'Hara (*King Donnchadh*), Mark Strong (*Lord Wicktred*), Henry Cavill (*Melot*).

Scott had been considering an adaptation of the TRISTAN AND ISOLDE myth as long ago as the early 1980s, after he had finished *THE DUELLISTS*, under the title "TRISTAN AND ISEULT." He explained why in an interview with Reg Seaton: "I was down in Dordogne, that part of France, which seems to be very applicable to that kind of romanticism . . . Basically, because of the legend, the love story always works. I think Shakespeare tried it closely in *Romeo and Juliet*. I mean, the love that shouldn't happen. I think Lancelot and Guinevere; those are all very similar exchanges of that human passion." Evidently he had planned to make a science fiction version of the tale, but opted for *BLADE RUNNER* instead. DEAN GEORGARIS's screenplay was sent to Scott on spec in the mid-1990s. In an article published in *Creative Screenwriting*, Georgaris suggested that he had created his own version of the story; having read the opera libretto of *TRISTAN AND ISOLDE* (WAGNER), the poem by A. E. HOUSMAN, and watched other TRISTAN AND ISOLDE FILMS, he decided "with a fist full of blasphemy" to create a version focusing on a young man "being forced to make a choice and to believe that he can turn his back on love." Scott himself preferred this version—although Wagner's retelling appealed to him, he felt that the basic storyline involving a cup of potion (which makes Tristan fall in love with Isolde) might not prove believable to his potential audience. There was also the problem of length; to retell the Wagner version might result in a three-hour film. Scott told Seaton that he worked on the Georgaris version by "tightening up the story, and improving the dialogue." In this version Tristan and Isolde are not brought together as a result of a political marriage; rather, Tristan is actually put on a boat and cast out to sea in the belief that he is actually dead. His boat washes up on the Irish coast, and there he meets Isolde; and the two of them fall in love on the spot. This transformed the story into a *Romeo and Juliet*-type tale, which Scott believed would be more accessible to audiences. He also altered Georgaris's script by rendering the protago-

nists much younger and having them make love for the first time on the Irish coast, very soon after they had met. He also omitted a scene at the beginning where Isolde (as an old woman) retells the story in flashback.

Twentieth Century-Fox agreed to finance the production so long as it contained a bankable star—consequently JAMES FRANCO was cast as Tristan in the belief that he would prove a box-office draw on the strength of his performances in the two *Spiderman* films (2002, 2004). SOPHIA MYLES played Isolde, having played Lady Penelope in the remake of *Thunderbirds* (2004); RUFUS SEWELL (Marke) had played in numerous costume dramas on film and television, notably *A Knight's Tale* (2001) and *Helen of Troy* (2003); while DAVID PATRICK O'HARA (Donnchadh) had a major role in the television series *The District* (2001). In the Seaton interview Scott recalled that he was unavailable to direct (as he was heavily involved in *KINGDOM OF HEAVEN*), so he passed the reins on to KEVIN REYNOLDS, who had apparently been offered *THELMA & LOUISE*: "He's [Reynolds] a great filmmaker, and I just thought he does well with period stuff. You know, not just a romp like *Robin Hood* [1991], which was a pretty big one, a pretty successful romp, but I also liked his version of *The Count of Monte Cristo* [2002]. In fact, seeing that again, I then realized that he'd done it, and that kind of started to resurrect the discussions [about directing Tristan] again."

Financing was provided by Twentieth Century-Fox and three European partners, while filming took place in the Republic of Ireland and the Czech Republic. Scott was quoted in the production notes as saying, "It's a story with epic scope, rooted in common human behavior that is timeless . . . I continue to be drawn by the tragic nature of the love story . . . It's so powerful dramatically that it transcends any setting or time."

Sadly the reviewers did not share his enthusiasm once the film opened in January 2006 (in the USA) and three months later in Great Britain. The *Sight and Sound* reviewer felt that "the film cannot survive Dean Georgaris's remarkably terrible screenplay, some of which sounds like an unhappy opera translation . . . Quite bizarrely, Isolde seems to have accessed literature from the distant future, murmuring lines from John Donne's 'The Good Morrow' (c. 1600)." Derek Malcolm in the *Evening Standard* felt that the casting was weak: "it would have taken two brilliant performers to make Dean Georgaris's screenplay zing into our hearts. And there's far too much rum-tum fake history and sword-flailing on the way." In particular, James Franco received much criticism for his "pouty woodenness that blighted his performance in the *Spiderman* movies" and his "glum, one-dimensional presence." *The Times* reviewer summed up the views of many fellow-critics: "A tale that inspired great opera has turned into something as murky as a long-running soap." Although the film was made for a comparatively low budget, it hardly set the box office on fire; by March 2006 it had grossed only $14.7 million at the US box office.

What is perhaps most interesting about *Tristan + Isolde* is the extent to which the screenplay appears to have been inspired by earlier Scott films. Like Maximus in *GLADIATOR* (RUSSELL CROWE) and Balian in *Kingdom of Heaven* (ORLANDO BLOOM), Tristan and King Marke suffer family tragedies, their immediate siblings killed by the marauding Irish. This traumatic experience prompts the desire to seek revenge by whatever possible means and thereby restore stability to the English kingdom. Georgaris's script makes this clear: "They [the Irish] are one day from their boats on the old Roman road. Now who will ride out with Tristan to fight them?" The Irish are portrayed as barbaric, with their King Donnchadh displaying a bloodthirsty relish for killing as many English as possible, rather like the warrior Reynald de Chatillon in *Kingdom of Heaven* (BRENDAN GLEESON): "If there are any more attacks we shall put out guests to death and raze this entire land." Both films end with sieges, in which one group (the Christians in *Kingdom of Heaven*, the English in *Tristan + Isolde*) struggle to protect their property against the invaders (Saladin and the Irish). *Tristan + Isolde* incorporates a tournament sequence reminiscent of *Gladiator*, with a Herald (Gordon Truefit) announcing the contests in a circular arena thronged with spectators, and Tristan—the central character—emerging the winner after several contests. In a later sequence King Marke appoints Tristan as his second, much to Melot's (Henry Cavill's) disappointment. This encourages him to plot against Marke by forming an alliance with Wicktred (MARK STRONG). Melot's reactions parallel those of Commodus (JOAQUIN PHOENIX) in *Gladiator*, who objects to his father Marcus Aurelius's naming of Maximus as heir to the throne of Rome. In the commentary to the film's DVD release, Georgaris recalls that some scenes reminiscent of *Gladiator* were removed from the *Tristan + Isolde* screenplay—for example, a sequence showing the young Tristan walking through a field of barley.

Tristan + Isolde suggests that male bonding is not only an important aspect of growing up; it is essential to the survival of the state. In one sequence Tristan, Melot, and Simon (Leo Gregory) discover the secret passage leading into Marke's castle; they think it might be "a burial crypt or something," but decide not to tell anyone in case it might put the king's authority at risk. The three friends are shown fighting for their lives against the marauding Irish. Both Simon and Tristan are stabbed; Simon dies, while Tristan appears to die (but actually remains alive). Devastated by the loss, Melot assumes (quite wrongly) that every man should look after themselves. This is what lies behind his decision to join Wicktred in the plot to overthrow King Marke. Melot only understands the error of his ways at the point of death

when he asks Tristan to "swear . . . that you are true." Tristan responds, "As we are brothers."

Tristan enjoys an equally close relationship with Marke; once the king loses his right hand in battle, Tristan quite literally assumes its function. The Biblical echo is quite deliberate: "Then the King will say to those on his right, 'Come, you are blessed by my Father; take your inheritance, the kingdom prepared for you since the creation of the World.'" Tristan becomes Marke's vice-regent on the battlefield—without him the kingdom cannot survive. Marke reminds him of his responsibilities while appointing him his second "Ever since you were a boy you sacrificed everything for me. All for one dream. Now that you reached that dream, it is natural that you would feel some loss. It doesn't matter if you want to be second. You are. I will only be king if you are my second. I'd put it more gently if I could." By conducting an illicit affair behind Marke's back, Tristan puts the future of his country at risk—as Tristan himself remarks: "For all time, they will say it was our love that brought down a kingdom" Tristan has no choice; he has to give up Isolde and reassume his position at Marke's side, as the two of them launch a counterattack against Wicktred and the marauding Irish forces.

Perhaps more so than any other film since *BLACK RAIN*, *Tristan + Isolde* focuses specifically on LOVE VS. DUTY. Director Reynolds suggests that both protagonists have to be aware of their responsibilities, even if they are in love with one another. Isolde has to comply with her father's wishes and marry Morholt (Graham Mullins); later, Tristan tells her that her MARRIAGE to Marke "will end a hundred years of bloodshed" between England and Ireland. Whether she likes it or not does not matter; she has to "live with this. We must." Isolde asks: "If things were different. If we lived in a place without duty . . . would you be with me?" Tristan responds pragmatically: "That place does not exist." Isolde herself soon understands that the stability of her husband's kingdom is more important that her own personal well-being. She cannot acknowledge her love for Tristan in public, however much pain that may cause her: "Yesterday at the market I saw a couple holding hands, and I realized we would never do that. Never anything like it. No picnics or unguarded smiles. No rings. Just stolen moments that leave too quickly."

Yet such denial is particularly important in a context where everyone has to participate to ensure the common good. Tristan understands this as he sends Isolde back to Ireland in a boat and leads the English in their defense of Marke's castle. He ends up by cutting off Wicktred's head and stepping out on to the drawbridge, proclaiming "Behold! The head of a traitor!" Marke sets aside the personal humiliation of learning about Tristan and Isolde's affair and releases Tristan from prison so that he can lead the army into battle. The king understands the importance of social responsibility as he urges his fellow barons to join the fight to expel the Irish from his homeland: "Will you always be little men, who cannot see what was and could be again? There is no middle ground! So slay us or slay him [Donnchadh]!"

At the same time, *Tristan + Isolde* suggests that "love conquers everything"—even if this particular theme undercuts the film's socio-political message. Isolde proclaims that personal qualities such as duty and HONOR are "the shells of life. And empty ones and in the end all they hold is days and days without love. Love is made by God. Ignore it and you can suffer as you cannot imagine." This speech prepares the ground for the final scene when Tristan declares that he does not know whether "life is greater than death, but love was more than either." Reynolds cuts away from his death scene to a shot of the two of them lying together, while Isolde's voice is heard reciting the concluding stanza of John Donne's lyric "The Good Morrow":

> My face in thine eye, thine in mine appears,
> And true plain hearts do in the faces rest;
> Where can we find two better hemispheres
> Without sharp north, without declining west?
> Whatever dies, was not mix'd equally;
> If our two loves be one, or thou and I
> Love so alike than none can slacken, none can die.

Her sentiments might be heartfelt, but the sequence seems rather incongruous in a film emphasizing the importance of responsibility, especially for men. Or perhaps we should approach the film not as a social commentary but rather as "a legend or fable, and therefore you can take all kinds of liberties [with the plot]."

To date there has been no published critical work on the film (even though there are plenty of online reviews). There are numerous books focusing on the Tristan and Isolde myth, notably Dorothy Roberts's *The Enchanted Cup* and Rosalind Miles's trilogy *Isolde, Queen of the Western Isle*, *The Maid of the White Hands*, and *The Lady of the Sea*. Denis de Rougemont's *Love in the Western World* explores the psychology of love from Tristan and Isolde to Hollywood, while Geoffrey Ashe looks at the myth in its historical context. Most recently Jeff Limke has retold the story in graphic novel format with illustrations by Ron Randall.

References

Geoffrey Ashe, *The Landscape of King Arthur* (London: Webb and Bower, 1987); *The Bible: Authorized Version*: Matthew 25:41; James Cameron-Wilson, "*Tristan + Isolde*: Celtic Myth Given Hollywood Treatment," *Film Review* 669 (May 2006): 107; Denis de Rougemont, *Love in the Western World* (Princeton: Princeton University Press, 1974); John Donne, "The Good Morrow," www.luminarium.org/sevenlit/donne/goodmorrow.htm (accessed 25 January 2009); Dean Georgaris, "Commentary" to the 2006 DVD release of *Tristan + Isolde* (Los Angeles: Twentieth Century-Fox Home Entertainment, 2006); David Jays, "*Tristan + Isolde*," *Sight and Sound* 16, no.4 (April 2006): 80; Ian Johns, "*Tristan + Isolde*," *Times 2*, 20 April 2006, 17; Will Lawrence, "*Tristan + Isolde*," *Empire* May 2006, 54; Jeff Limke and Ron Randall, *Tristan and Isolde: The Warrior and the Princess: A British Legend* (London: Graphic Universe, 2007); Derek Malcolm, "History Re-told to the Tune of Rum-Tum," *Evening Standard*, 26 April 2006, 35; Rosalind Miles, *Isolde, Queen of the Western Isle*; *The Maid of the White Hands*; *The Lady of the Sea* (Los Angeles, CA: Three Rivers Press, 2003, 2005); Dorothy Roberts, *The Enchanted Cup* (New York: Appleton-Century-Crofts, 1953); Ridley Scott interviewed by Reg Seeton, www.ugo.com/channels/dvd/features/tristanandisolde/interview2.asp (accessed 8 August 2008); Ridley Scott, quoted in *Production Notes: Tristan + Isolde* (Los Angeles: Twentieth Century-Fox, 2005), vi–vii; "*Tristan + Isolde*: Screenplay by Dean Georgaris," *Creative Screenwriting* 13, no.1 (2006): 32; "*Tristan + Isolde*. Written by Dean Georgaris. Transcript by Chani at tristanandisolde.net," www.imsdb.com/Movie%20Scripts/Tristan%20and%20Isolde%20Script.html (accessed 23 January 2009).

Bibliography

Jeremy May, "The Dark Ages in Britain—Via Prague," *Screen International* 1424 (10–16 October 2003): 13.

TRISTAN AND ISOLDE

A legend dating back to the twelfth century, of which there have been many different versions in different cultures. Claude D'Esplas reconstructs the legend thus: The giant Morhot comes to Cornwall to collect the tribute of young people which the country owes to Ireland. Tristan challenges Morhot and kills him in single combat; a chip of the edge of the sword remains, however, embedded in the giant's skull. Tristan himself receives a wound that becomes dangerously infected. No one can help him. In accordance with the Celtic funeral rites he is put into a boat without sails and left to the currents.

The boat drifts to the shores of Ireland. Tristan calls himself a minstrel and hides his identity under a disguised name; the magic drinks of Queen Isolt, sister of Morhot, who is assisted by her daughter, Isolt the Fair, cure him. Tristan leaves his benefactresses without having revealed his identity nor spoken of Morhot and returns to Cornwall. The story negotiates various twists and turns until the final scene when Tristan, away in Brittany, marries another Isolt—Isolt of the White Hands. While coming to the rescue of her brother Katherdin, Tristan receives a mortal wound which can only be healed by Isolt the Fair as she has done before. However Isolt of the White Hands grows jealous, and tells

Tristan that Isolt the Fair will not come; all Tristan can do is die. Isolt the Fair arrives, and falls lifeless on Tristan's body. King Marc buries them together.

Bibliography
Claude D'Esplas, *Tristan & Isolt: From Bayreuth to Monsegur* (Moscow, IMA Press, 1994).

TRISTAN AND ISOLDE FILMS
The *Internet Movie Database* lists fourteen films in addition to *TRISTAN + ISOLDE* that have been made using the same story. Of these, the most noteworthy are *L'Eternel Retour* (1943) directed by Jean Delannoy, *Tristan et Yseult* (1972) directed by Yvan Lagrange, *Lovespell* (1979) directed by Tom Donovan, and *Fire and Sword* (1981) directed by Veith von Furstenberg.

The attraction for most of these films has been the original myth's themes of consuming love and transfiguring death. The challenge of interpreting the myth cinematically has proved formidable, and those directors who have currently attempted it (including KEVIN REYNOLDS in *Tristan + Isolde*) have failed to satisfy most critics. Nevertheless, cinema has been the major medium for the exploration of these themes in the twentieth and twenty-first centuries.

Bibliography
Kevin J. Harty, "A Bibliography on Arthurian Film," in *Cinema Arthuriana: Essays on Arthurian Film*, ed. Harty (New York and London: Garland Publishing, 1981), 204–43 (includes references to reviews of all the Tristan films mentioned above); Meradith T. McMunn, "Filming the Tristan Myth: From Text to Icon," in *Cinema Arthuriana: Essays on Arthurian Film*, ed. Harty, 169–81.

TRISTAN AND ISOLDE (WAGNER)
Epic musical dramatic poem by Richard Wagner completed in 1865. Wagner reduces the TRISTAN AND ISOLDE myth to its simplest details. His main focus is on the longing for Death associated with love. This idea, commonly attributed to Schopenhauer, appears in Wagner's works long before he had heard of Schopenhauer. In a letter to Liszt (written in 1854), Wagner wrote: "His chief idea, the final negation of the desire of life, is terribly serious, but it shows the only salvation possible. To me of course that thought was not new, and, indeed it can be conceived by no one for whom it did not preexist; but this philosopher was the first to place it clearly before me." He elaborates the point in a letter written in January 1859, when he was scoring the second act of *Tristan*: "This Idea will then play an important part in the form of this experience; the purer and more elevated this Idea has been, so much the more unworldly and incomparable that experience will be. It will purify his will, his aesthetic interest will become a moral one, and the

highest moral consciousness will be added to the highest poetical Idea."

Screenwriter DEAN GEORGARIS listened to Wagner's version of the myth before composing his own version of *TRISTAN + ISOLDE*, which was eventually directed by KEVIN REYNOLDS and produced by Scott.

Reference
Richard Wagner, quoted in Alice Leighton Cleather and Basil Crump, *Tristan and Isolde: An Intepretation* (London: Methuen & Co., 1905), 8–9.

Bibliography
C. A. Barry, *A Preface to Richard Wagner's Music-Drama Tristan und Isolde* (London: A. S. Mallett, 1901); Eric Chafe, *The Tragic and the Ecstatic: The Musical Revolution of Wagner's Tristan and Isolde* (Oxford: Oxford University Press, 2005); Hans von Wolzogen, *Guide to the Legend, Poem and Music of Richard Wagner's Tristan and Isolde*, trans. B. L. Mosely (Leipzig: Breitkopf & Hartel, 1884).

TRIUMPH OF THE WILL (TRIUMPH DES WILLENS)
Germany 1935 r/t 110 min b/w. *Production Company*: Nationalsozialistische Deutsche Arbeiterpartei. *Producer/ Director*: Leni Riefenstahl. *Director of Photography*: Sepp Allgeier. *Production Designer*: Albert Speer. *Music*: Herbert Windt and Richard Wagner.

A visual record of the Nazi party's 1934 Nuremberg rally including speeches by Hitler, Hess, Goebbels, Sepp Dietrich, Hans Frank, Alfred Rosenberg, Baldur von Schirach, Julius Streicher. Ridley Scott acknowledged this film as an inspiration for *GLADIATOR*, not least in terms of the futuristic Nazi architecture, whose oblique lines provided designer ARTHUR MAX with an alternative concept to that expressed in other ANCIENT EPICS such as *Ben Hur* (1959). This is especially evident in the scene where Commodus (JOAQUIN PHOENIX) returns to Rome, to be greeted by a guard of honor, cheering crowds, and the senators waiting on the steps of the Senate to greet him. At this point he resembles Hitler enjoying similar acclaim in Riefenstahl's film.

TRUMBULL, DOUGLAS (1942–)
Visual effects pioneer Douglas Trumbull was one of the Special Photographic Effects Supervisors for Stanley Kubrick's *2001: A Space Odyssey* (1968). He also worked on *Close Encounters of the Third Kind* (1977) and *Star Trek: The Motion Picture* (1979) before coming to *BLADE RUNNER*.

Trumbull believed that the work done on Scott's film pushed the art form "to its ultimate leading edge . . . To really be able to create illusions that are significantly advanced from anything anybody's ever done is something I find very exciting." By 1983 Trumbull had quit the motion picture business and concentrated instead on supplying theme parks and hotels with special visual presentations—for example the "Back to the Future' ride at Universal Studios.

References

Paul M. Sammon, *Future Noir: The Making of Blade Runner*, 2nd ed. (London: Gollancz, 2007), 265.

TURKEL, JOE (1927–)

Joe Turkel's career began in television with roles in *The Untouchables* and *Bonanza*. His film credits included *The Hindenburg* (1975) and the supernatural bartender in Stanley Kubrick's *The Shining* (1980). It was this last film that persuaded Scott to cast him as Tyrell in *BLADE RUNNER*.

With his huge glasses and detached, aloof manner, Tyrell one who values control over anyone else. During Deckard's (HARRISON FORD's) meeting, Tyrell manipulates the sun light with the push of a button; it rises convincingly in the sky, making the view early in the morning towards the east. In Ancient Egypt the sun god Ra was considered the creator of all things, "the god of the whole world." Likewise according to William M. Kolb Tyrell is the creator—both father and mother of all the REPLICANTS.

The relationship between Tyrell and the replicants is understood by all the ecclesiastical trappings that surround Tyrell in a later sequence: the papal gown he wears, the bed, the ring on the little finger of his right hand and the devotional candles illuminating his rooms. However he makes one fatal mistake with Batty (RUTGER HAUER) by treating him as a comrade. Batty responds by kissing Tyrell and thrusting his hands into his creator's eyes. The eye imagery is important here, for it is only by doing this that Batty can make Tyrell see (in other words, understand) that replicants should be given a life of their own and not simply exist to serve their "parents.' Scott revealed in an interview with Harlan Kennedy that Batty was supposed to deliver the line "I want more life, fucker," at this point; but this was softened into "I want more life, father." This "funnily enough, works better."

Joe Turkel's subsequent career has been punctuated with occasional television roles in *Tales from the Dark Side* (1985) and *Miami Vice* (1988). For the most part he has kept a low profile, save for an appearance at a *BLADE RUNNER*—FINAL CUT panel in July 2007, where PAUL M. SAMMON witnessed him recalling how the kissing scene was the first time he had ever "kissed a man with passion."

References

Harlan Kennedy, "21st Century Nervous Breakdown," *Film Comment* 18, no.4 (July 1982): 64–68; William M. Kolb, "*Blade Runner* Film Notes," in *Retrofitting Blade Runner*, ed. Judith M. Kerman, 2nd ed. (Bowling Green: Bowling Green State University Popular Press, 1997), 158; Paul M. Sammon, *Future Noir: The Making of Blade Runner*, 2nd ed. (London: Gollancz, 2007), 472.

TWOHY, DAVID (1955–)

Early successes as a screenwriter included *The Fugitive* (1993), plus the screenplay for the Kevin Costner film *WATERWORLD* (1995).

Twohy was brought in to improve the script of *G.I. JANE* after it had been initially written by Danielle Alexandra. Scott told PAUL M. SAMMON that Twohy "came up with the action, as well as integrating my concerns into the script. He did a great job of grafting all that onto a good story with humorous and intelligent dialogue." Twohy's first draft for the film can be accessed online at http://sfy.ru/sfy.html?script=gi_jane.

References

Ridley Scott, quoted in Paul M. Sammon, "Joining the Club: Ridley Scott on *G.I. Jane*," in *Ridley Scott Interviews*, ed. Laurence F. Knapp and Andrea F. Kulas (Jackson, University Press of Mississippi, 2005), 137.

US MILITARY

Several of Scott's films contain a military theme, notably *THE DUELLISTS*. *G.I. JANE* is the first dealing directly with the US military. Scott admitted in an interview that he was fascinated with the SEALs on account of their status as "state-of-the-art spearheads in terms of avoiding warfare. These groups can infiltrate enemy territory months before a confrontation . . . In that sense, the SEALs actually save lives. Ultimately, I think that is what the concept of the military is all about. *Saving* lives."

When asked what he had achieved through the film, Scott responded. "We got a fairly good sense of really being inside the military and of how hidden agendas motivate politics." The film caused a stir on its first release, not least because it addressed an event very much on the political agenda at that time: the role of women in the armed forces. *Mad* magazine even published a parody of the film (*GI Shame*) in its issue of 1 January 1998.

In *AMERICAN FIGHTER PILOT* the life of the US military at the Tyndall Air Base in Florida is explored in a seven-part reality series. In general the tone is reverent, allowing both instructors and recruits to create an image of military life as firm but fair, training pilots to be harsh and ruthless yet concerned with maintaining group identity. This is particularly important in the post-9/11 era, when they are faced with the possibility of being killed in action as they seek to preserve the American ideals of freedom and democracy.

Simon Dalby has recently noted that *GLADIATOR*, *BLACK HAWK DOWN*, and *KINGDOM OF HEAVEN* all explore the morality and identity of the American soldier. They are set in exotic landscapes and settings that emphasize the confrontation with danger as external and frequently unknowable; political violence is presented as something that has both simple and very complicated geographies. The public discussion of the necessity for warfare and "intervention" in Western states is enmeshed in discourses of moralities, rights, and "just war." The professional fighter, whether in the guise of a Special Forces operative, gladiator, or garrison soldier in peacekeeping mode, is a key figure of the post-9/11 era, physically preserving the safety of the American nation, and simultaneously reinforcing its identity as the repository of virtue against barbaric threats to civilization. These themes are central to Ridley Scott's work. Analyzing them in terms of the soldier's life adds a specifically military dimension to the critical geopolitical literature on war and representation.

Despite the fact that the CIA makes use of sophisticated military hardware—Black Hawk helicopters, plus the latest surveillance equipment—they are ultimately outwitted by their enemies in *BODY OF LIES*. In the tight, closely-knit streets of Amman, or in the wastes of the desert, their equipment offers them little assistance in catching Al-Saleem (ALON ABOUTBUL). This is a new kind of warfare—one relying much more on stealth and cooperation than technology. In this changed world, the US military has yet to find an effective role.

References

Paul M. Sammon, "Joining the Club: Ridley Scott on *G.I. Jane*," in *Ridley Scott Interviews*, ed. Laurence F. Knapp and Andrea F. Kulas (Jackson: University Press of Mississippi, 2005), 166–67; Simon Dalby, "Warrior Geopolitics: *Gladiator, Black Hawk Down* and [The] *Kingdom of Heaven*," *Political Geography* 27, no.4 (May 2008): 439–55.

LES VACANCES DE M. HULOT
(MONSIEUR HULOT'S HOLIDAY)

France 1953 r/t 90 min b/w. *Production Companies*: Cady Films and Discina. *Producer*: F. Orain. *Director*: Jacques Tati. *Writers*: Pierre Aubert and Jacques Lagrange. *Directors of Photography*: Jacques Mercanton and Jean Mousselle. *Music*: Alain Romans. *Cast*: Jacques Tati (*M. Hulot*), Nathalie Pascaud (*Martine*), Michele Rolla (*The Aunt*), Raymond Carl (*The Waiter*), Lucien Frégis (*The Hotel Proprietor*).

Tati's classic slapstick comedy of an innocent man encountering all kinds of mishaps while on holiday in coastal FRANCE. Ridley Scott acknowledged the influence of this film on the tennis sequence involving Max Skinner (RUSSELL CROWE) and Duflot (DIDIER BOURDON) in *A GOOD YEAR*: "I have a court in France, and it's still the best game for me . . . [In Hulot] there's always this gentleman playing tennis and Tati has everyone watch him play . . . I like the scene a lot." Scott includes a more direct tribute to Tati by naming Duflot's Yorkshire terrier after him.

Reference
Ridley Scott, "Ripe on the Vine," *Fade In* 9, no.3 (October 2006): 53.

VANGELIS (1943–)

Born Evangelos Odysseus Papathanassiou in Greece. Vangelis came to *BLADE RUNNER* via a number of connections—Ridley Scott used music from his China album for his EDEN ROC CHANEL NO. 5 (1989) commercial, while TERRY RAWLINGS had cut the Vangelis-scored *Chariots of Fire* (1981), which won an Oscar for music.

Vangelis recalled that what interested him most about the film was the atmosphere and the general feeling rather than the distinct themes. The score borrows from a dazzling variety of musical genres, from the haunting love theme played as Deckard (HARRISON FORD) and Rachael (SEAN YOUNG) kiss, to the arabesque-style music-influenced "Tales of the Future" sung by Demis Roussos; from the 1940s throwback "One More Kiss, Dear" played after Zhora's (JOANNA CASSIDY's) death to the end titles theme.

Vangelis's methods mirrored Scott's own technique of layering: the musician improvised the basic melody of each track, laid down the melody on tape, and then refined it by piling other sounds on top of it, working the whole structure into a unified whole. The official soundtrack to *Blade Runner* was not released until 1994, entitled Blade Runner: *Vangelis* featuring twelve tracks overlaid with extracts of dialogue from the film.

Vangelis returned to work with Scott on *1492: CONQUEST OF PARADISE*, when HANS ZIMMER was unavailable. Scott admitted in an interview published by Brian J. Robb that "the film could have a traditional score to suit its fifteenth-century project . . . [but] that's the last thing I wanted. I knew Vangelis could give me something which was both appropriate for the period and is also contemporary . . . I hate it when people say you shouldn't notice the score. The score, if it's doing its job, should lift and elevate the movie." In the film, Vangelis's music is not triumphal; rather it emphasizes mystery, unease, and solemnity.

Reference
Ridley Scott, quoted in Brian J. Robb, *Ridley Scott* (Harpenden: Pocket Essentials, 2002), 64.

Bibliography
Ian Freer, "Synth Job," *Empire*, August 2007, 112–13; Michael Hannan and Melissa Carey, "Ambient Soundscapes in *Blade Runner*," in *Off the Planet: Music, Sound and Science Fiction in Cinema*, ed. Philip Hayward (Eastleigh, UK: John Libbey Publishing, 2004), 149–65.

VAUGHAN-HUGHES, GERALD (?–)

Vaughan-Hughes cut his teeth in television, working on series such as *ITV Playhouse* and *Armchair Theatre*. Before working on *THE DUELLISTS*, Vaughan-Hughes had written a screenplay based on The Gunpowder Plot of 1605. Scott wanted to produce this picture, but could not find the funding to do so.

In a 1977 interview Vaughan-Hughes emphasized the fact that he wanted to establish D'Hubert as the hero of *The Duellists*; to show him as someone with a private life. Hence he created a new character, Laura (DIANA QUICK) whom D'Hubert eventually marries. However, D'Hubert's obsession with dueling eventually takes over his life to such an extent that he forgets about Laura.

Vaughan-Hughes's screenplay went through several drafts; an early version (now in the British Film Institute, London) had D'Hubert being accused of rape by a maid—something that prompts Feraud to continue the duel. To emphasize the importance of Feraud's private life, Vaughan-Hughes incorporated two long scenes involving the soldier and Laura. D'Hubert admits at one point that he is nothing more than a savage brute, needing a woman to tame him. However this does not seem very likely as D'Hubert believes that Feraud will win in the end. These two sequences were deleted from the final script.

Vaughan-Hughes's original draft ends with D'Hubert acquiring a new self-confidence; not only does he emerge victorious, but he has the opportunity to condemn Feraud as a Bonapartist—someone who should take the chance to leave France and live in exile for the rest of his life. This dialogue was likewise removed from the final script: Scott replaces it with an image of Feraud standing on a hill, silhouetted against the landscape. Like Napoleon, Feraud has paid the price for overreaching himself.

Despite the cuts, Scott praised Vaughan-Hughes's script for its emphasis on character development that seemed "minimalistic, specific [and] loaded with humor." Iain Johnstone reports that Vaughan-Hughes actually wrote a draft script for *TRISTAN AND ISEULT*, which apparently was going to be produced by Paramount Pictures and filmed in the Dordogne (like *The Duellists*). However, the project was abandoned when Scott saw *Star Wars*, as the director believed that George Lucas "had beaten him to it in character design."

References

Iain Johnstone, *Tom Cruise: All the World's a Stage* (London: Hodder and Stoughton, 2006), 99–100; Ridley Scott, quoted in *Duelling Directors: Ridley Scott and Kevin Reynolds*, Documentary on the making of *The Duellists* included in the 2003 DVD release of the film (Los Angeles: Paramount Pictures Corporation, 2002).

VAUGHN, VINCE (1970–)

Born 1970 in Illinois and made his name in the film *Swingers* (1996), which immediately paved the way for a leading role in *CLAY PIGEONS*.

Vaughn plays a serial killer with a passion for his work. In an interview he claimed that "It's rare to find a piece of material that is both very funny and very dark. That combination is what interested me. It keeps an audience wondering what is going to happen next . . . [Lester Long] is a man with no conscience. Nevertheless, Lester is a charmer—women love him, and men easily become his friends."

Vaughn gives a compelling performance as the serial killer, whose basically amiable nature conceals an obsessive personality. We are made aware of this by the way he keeps laughing nervously, as if unsure of what to make of the people he befriends. When they double-cross him, he reacts violently; the only way he can be pacified is if they vow to remain loyal to him. This is clear in a scene towards the end of the film, when Lester holds the girl Kimberly as a hostage, a knife to her throat, and exclaims to Clay (JOAQUIN PHOENIX): "I've taken a lot of chances for you. Hell, I'm taking a chance tonight, but that's okay, because we've got a special kind of friendship." When Clay resists, Lester threatens him nastily: "I go down, you go down with me."

References

Matt Healy, *In Too Deep* (Draft Script for *Clay Pigeons* dated 7 January 1997) (Beverly Hills, CA: Scott Free, 1997); Vince Vaughn, interviewed in "Production Notes: *Clay Pigeons*," included on the European DVD release of the film (Frankfurt: BY Internationale Medien und Film, 1998).

WAG THE DOG

US 1997 r/t 97 min col. *Production Companies*: Baltimore Pictures, New Line Cinema, Punch Productions, and Tribeca Productions. *Producers*: Michael de Luca, Robert De Niro, and Barry Levinson. *Director*: Barry Levinson. *Writers*: Hilary Henkin and David Mamet from the novel *American Hero* by Larry Beinhart. *Director of Photography*: Robert Richardson. *Production Designer*: Wynn Thomas. *Music*: Mark Knopfler. *Cast*: Robert de Niro (*Conrad Brean*), Dustin Hoffman (*Stanley Motss*), Anne Heche (*Winifred Ames*), Denis Leary (*Fad King*), Willie Nelson (*Johnny Dean*), Andrea Martin (*Liz Butsky*), Kirsten Dunst (*Tracy Lime*).

The action takes place just before a presidential election in which the current president seems to have little chance of being reelected. One of his advisers contacts a top Hollywood producer in order to manufacture a war in Albania that the president can heroically end, all through the mass media. The subject of how the mass media can influence American politics is a popular one—although not actively credited, it is likely that this film inspired *THE LAST DEBATE*.

WAKAYAMA, TOMISABURO (1929–1992)

Born in Tokyo, Japan, Tomisaburo Wakayama made his debut in films in 1956. He was best known in his own country for playing Ogami Itto, the scowling, seventeenth-century ronin in six *Kozure Ogami* (*Lone Wolf and Cub*) samurai feature films.

Cast as the Sugai, the elderly yakuza leader in *BLACK RAIN*, Wakayama's most noteworthy speech comes late in the film on why he hates America, both for detonating nuclear weapons on his homeland and dominating the post-1945 cultural landscape. It is the Americans who created the "black rain" of the film's title with its nuclear experiments. Sugai explains that he runs the counterfeiting racket—to flood the market with millions of fake dollars—as a way of paying the Americans back. Sugai also considers it his duty to fight Sato (YUSAKU MATSUDA) for supremacy; in his system of values the young pretender has no right to challenge the elder man's authority.

Wakayama was an expert with a sword, a living legend in Japanese films; persuading him to play Sugai was no easy task. Scott told PAUL M. SAMMON that he had a formal meeting with Wakayama, in which "someone was sitting on one side of Tommy [Wakayama] lighting a cigarette every ten minutes and setting it into his cigarette holder. So our talk was very impressive, actually . . . Finally, at the end, he muttered something to the translator in Japanese, which meant 'Yes, I'll do it.'"

Reference

Ridley Scott, quoted in Paul M. Sammon, *Ridley Scott Close-Up: The Making of His Movies* (New York: Thunder's Mouth Press, 1999), 95.

WALSH, M. EMMET (1935–)

M. Emmet Walsh has carved out a reputation for playing deadly crooks, zany comedic roles, and corrupt cops since the 1970s. Cast as Bryant, the police chief in *BLADE RUNNER*, Walsh based his interpretation on members of his family, many of whom were civil servants: "I had no trouble playing a bureaucrat. And Bryant liked his job. He lived in that office. That's why I played him so cheerfully." Scott told PAUL M. SAMMON that he saw the character as a heavy character whose "stomach was all shot to hell. That's why he offered Deckard [HARRISON FORD] two glasses of whiskey in his office. Bryant liked to see other people drink because he couldn't."

Bright is an inherent racist who identifies the REPLICANTS as "skin jobs" and enjoys the power he wields over Deckard as he offers him a choice between being a killer (cop) or a victim (little people). Although appearing only briefly on screen, Walsh's Bryant embodies the inherent corruption of *Blade Runner*, manipulating people for his own ends with scant concern for their feelings.

Reference

Paul M. Sammon, *Future Noir: The Making of Blade Runner*, 2nd ed. (London: Gollancz, 2007), 119.

WASHINGTON, DENZEL (1954–)

Born Denzel Hayes Washington Jr., in Mount Vernon, New York. He made his first screen appearance in *Carbon Copy* (1981), and won the Oscar for Best Supporting Actor eight years later for his role in *Glory*. Other major films include *The Pelican Brief* (1993), *Courage Under Fire* (1996), and *Remember the Titans* (2000). Washington made his debut as a director with *Antwone Fisher* (2002). Washington was cast as Frank Lucas in the original production of *AMERICAN GANGSTER*, but the film was never made. He was persuaded to return to the production once the project had been green-lighted by Universal Pictures with Scott as the director.

To prepare for the role, Washington acknowledged in the production information that he "got in a room with Frank, turned on the recorder and talked with him. I didn't try to imitate him, necessarily, but Frank's such a charmer; that's key to his character . . . What interested me in the story was not to glorify a drug dealer, and I told Frank that when I met him." Washington evidently wrote the biblical passage Isaiah 48:22 ("There is no peace, saith the Lord, unto the wicked") on his shooting script to remind him of Lucas's journey and quest for redemption.

Washington gives an understated performance in the film—the very epitome of social respectability, it would seem, as he leads a quiet, inconspicuous life eating alone in a midtown NEW YORK diner, going to work, "dropping in on one of the several office buildings he owns. Nights, he usually stays at home. When he does go out, it's to a club or diner—with his new wife—friends, celebrities, sports figures . . . Sundays he takes his mother to church. Then drives out to change the flowers on Bumpy's [Bumpy Johnson's] grave." However there is a strong undercurrent of violence beneath this urbane surface—for example, when Frank leaves his diner, walks up to the local hoodlum Tango (Idris Elba), and shoots him in the head in broad daylight. Everyone stops dead in their tracks and looks at him: according to STEVEN ZAILLIAN's script, this is "maybe that's what he wants." He calmly reaches into Tango's suit pocket, takes out a money clip thick with cash, and sets it right next to the body saying that it is "for the cops." Frank subsequently returns to the diner and continues his lecture on good business practice ("What matters in business is honesty, integrity, hard work, loyalty, and never forgetting where you came from . . . That's basically the whole picture right there.") We discover the reason for such violence at the end of the film, when Frank admits to Richie Roberts (RUSSELL CROWE) that he harbors a lifelong contempt for authority figures or anyone who orders him around.

Washington's performance drew mixed reactions from reviewers. Writing in *The Guardian*, David Thomson felt

that *American Gangster* rehearsed "the same old bogus runaround we were given in *Heat*, where two outrageously great and self-satisfied actors played the routine that said: well, really, aren't cops and hoodlums cut from the same cloth? No, they are not, and why do our movies keep trying to insist on the iniquity? So, hear this cry for Denzel that at his peak he has to play such garbage . . . I'll believe in progress the day Denzel Washington plays a black man who has a full-blooded physical affair with a white woman."

References

American Gangster: Production Information (Los Angeles: Universal Pictures, 2007); "David Thomson's Biographical Dictionary of Film #25," *Guardian Film and Music*, 9 November 2007, 20; Steven Zaillian, "*American Gangster*: Final Shooting Script" (27 July 2006), www.roteirodecinema.com.br/scripts/files/american_gangster.htm (accessed 8 February 2009).

Bibliography

Douglas Brode, *Denzel Washington: His Films and Career* (New York: Citadel Press, 1997); Martyn Palmer, "Original Gangsters," *Empire* 221 (November 2007): 114–24; James Robert Parish, *Denzel Washington: Actor* (New York: Facts on File, Inc., 2005); Denzel Washington and Daniel Paisner, *A Hand to Guide Me* (New York: Meredith Corporation, 2006).

WATERWORLD

US 1995 r/t 130 min col. *Production Company*: Universal Pictures. *Producers*: Kevin Costner, John Davis, and Charles and Lawrence Gordon. *Director*: Kevin Reynolds. *Writers*: Peter Rader and David Twohy. *Music*: James Newton Howard and Artie Kane. *Directors of Photography*: Scott Fuller and Dean Semler. *Production Designer*: Dennis Gassner. *Cast:* Kevin Costner (*Mariner*), Dennis Hopper (*Deacon*).

In a future where the polar ice caps have melted and the earth is covered by water, the people travel the seas in search of survival. The Mariner leaves his solitary existence to care for a woman and a young girl while being pursued by the evil forces of the Deacon.

Legendary action film that cost over $200 million, at a conservative estimate, and made only $88 million in domestic distribution but recouped a total of $167 million including overseas distribution. Universal eventually returned a profit on the film, even though in the public mind the film was an expensive flop.

Waterworld creates a DYSTOPIAN vision of the future, where people are left rootless and wandering in an inhospitable world. It is only because the Mariner discovers some human feelings within himself that he learns to care for the young woman. Director KEVIN REYNOLDS was to create a similar kind of dystopia in *TRISTAN + ISOLDE*; an ancient world where no one really cares for anyone else.

Bibliography

Janine Pourroy, "The Making of *Waterworld*" (New York: Boulevard Books, 1995); James Robert Parish, *Fiasco: A History of Hollywood's Iconic Flops* (Hoboken, NJ: John Wiley and Sons. Inc. 2006), 249–70.

THE WAY OF THE GLADIATOR

Written by Daniel P. Mannix and originally published as *Those About to Die* in 1958, and reissued in 2001 under the new title. One of the major sources for the screenplay for *GLADIATOR*, this book tells the story of the Roman Games and the gladiators who fought in the various spectacles put on for the Emperors. It focuses not only on the risks taken by the gladiators themselves, but on the wanton cruelty of many of the activities: of gladiators mangled beneath chariots, slaughtered by wild beasts and maltreated by prison guards. Mannix also focuses on the Roman people's thirst for blood sports: once they had a set of games that lasted 122 days, at the end of which eleven thousand people and ten thousand animals had perished.

WEAVER, SIGOURNEY (1949–)

Born Susan Alexandra Weaver. The stately, intense dramatic lead entered film as Ripley in *ALIEN*.

Ridley Scott filmed several tests of Weaver for the studio executives: in one she runs through rather nicely constructed corridors; in another she asks for sexual "relief" from the captain, removing her top in the process. In Ximeria Gallardo's and C. Jason Smith's *Alien Woman*—a study of Weaver in the role—DAVID GILER is quoted as saying that the selection process even included a female audience: "Alan Ladd [of Twentieth Century-Fox] watched the screen test and had all the secretaries in the building come down and watch it. And then everybody asked—and they got in a big argument—did she look more like Jane Fonda or Faye Dunaway." The secretaries liked her, and Weaver was in.

Ripley takes her responsibilities seriously; in an early scene, a landing party returns from their exploration of an alien planet with the news that Kane (JOHN HURT) has been infected with the alien. Ripley refuses to let the party on board the ship; the infection could potentially contaminate the entire crew. Dallas (TOM SKERRITT) countermands her order, however; and the end result is disastrous.

Most reviewers agreed that Ripley is tough and Weaver's performance is compelling. *Alien Woman* quotes from some of them: Ripley is either "sexy," "pleasant to look at," or "gutsy"; she is "controlled," "earnest," "intelligent," "impressive," "funny," and "efficient." *Newsweek*'s David Ansen's labeling of Ripley as a "tough talking astronette" reveals a certain fascination with this confident female, who is very different from the heroines of the 1950s monster films that inspired Scott's conception.

Ripley's critical reputation has varied greatly over the years. In the late 1980s critics viewed her as a feminist heroine—someone who eventually defeats the alien and emerges successful. She became one of the main elements of the film's FEMINISM. In an interview with *Starburst* published in 1987, Weaver described the character as someone whose mind "never stopped working" as she embarked upon "an epic journey through personal hardship, trauma and a fiendish nightmare." But at what price success? The making of *Alien* had been fun; but according to her biographer Robert Sellers, she did feel as if she had been thrown in at the deep end. She had advanced and grown as an actress in the theater by playing supporting character parts, a successful *modus operandi* that she hoped to repeat in films. This was not to be; from now on Weaver would be cast solely as a leading player, associated with a certain type of (aggressive, feminine) role.

Weaver reprised her role in the three other films that make up the ALIEN QUADRILOGY. Her next project with Ridley Scott was playing Queen Isabel in *1492: CONQUEST OF PARADISE*, a role originally slated for Anjelica Huston. Scott said in an interview with *Empire*, "Sigourney had always been in my mind to do this [role] . . . I walked straight slap-bang into her." Weaver herself described the queen in the pressbook as someone who "always relied on her intuition . . . When Columbus speaks about what he wants to do, she feels that he can really do it—she feels his passion is the same as hers. She thought that he was her kindred spirit, doing the impossible even more than she. That was the start of her great admiration for him."

Weaver gives an understated performance—although a reigning monarch of the throne, she appears rather a passive personality. However, we know that she is actually the force behind Columbus's schemes; in one sequence she is shown peeping through the keyhole in an adjoining room while the admiral tries to convince Luis de Santangel (FRANK LANGELLA) of the value of traveling to the New World. Clearly she treats it as a charade—an opportunity for her to discover whether Columbus possesses the courage of his convictions. She will permit him to go, whatever he says. Even when he has been discredited she still believes in him and his dreams. Weaver's performance was dismissed by Amanda Hopkinson in *Empire* magazine as spurious, "with peals of silly giggles and seductive interest to afford spurious erotic interest."

References

"Aliens: Sigourney Weaver Talks About her Role of Ripley," *Starburst* 102 (February 1987): 17–18; Ximeria Gallardo, C. Jason Smith, *Alien Woman: The Making of Lieut. Ellen Ripley* (New York: Continuum, 2004), 18, 20; Amanda Hopkinson, "Conquest of History?" *Empire*, November 1992, 90; *Pressbook, 1492: Conquest of Paradise* (Los

Angeles: Paramount Pictures, 1992), 4; Ridley Scott, quoted in Mark Salisbury, "In Nineteen Hundred and Ninety Two . . . ," *Empire*, November 1992, 86; Robert Sellers, *Sigourney Weaver* (London: Robert Hale, 1992), 76.

Bibliography

Ros Jennings, "Desire and Design—Ripley Undressed," in *Immortal, Invisible: Lesbians and the Moving Image*, ed. Tamsin Wilton (London and New York: Routledge, 1995), 193–206; T. D. Maguffee, *Sigourney Weaver* (New York: St. Martin's Press, 1989).

WEINER, JENNIFER (1970–)

Born in Louisiana, Jennifer Weiner's first novel, *Good in Bed*, appeared in 2001. *IN HER SHOES* appeared a year later; and was filmed by CURTIS HANSON with Scott producing, in 2005. It is a good example of CHICK LIT, focusing on the existences of two sisters who have nothing in common but a CHILDHOOD tragedy, shared DNA, and the same size feet, but they are about to find out that they are more alike than they ever would have believed. Weiner did not have anything to do with the script for the film, which was written by SUSANNAH GRANT.

Reference

Jennifer Weiner, *In Her Shoes* (London: Simon and Schuster, 2005); Jennifer Weiner, interviewed (2006), www.readinggroupguides .com/guides3/in_her_shoes2.asp#interview (accessed 8 August 2008).

WELLES, ORSON (1915–1987)

Legendary actor, writer, and filmmaker, the subject of *RKO 281*. Scott counts Welles among his great inspirations, though he admitted in an interview that he was glad he was not directing when *Citizen Kane* came out in 1941: "The film was so good that, if I'd been a filmmaker at the time, it would have crushed the hell out of me. It was like a quantum leap forward in both technique and storytelling."

Scott envisaged his version of the making of *Citizen Kane* (i.e., *RKO 281*) as a big-budget feature film, but the studios didn't share his enthusiasm for a period film about filmmaking. "It really came down to the budget . . . really they [HBO, the producers of the film] cut me to size."

In terms of character, Scott shares with Welles a belief in the power of ambition. Welles's biographer Barbara Leaming remarks that while Welles "provoked hostility when he [first] got to Hollywood," he also "inspired . . . subsequent generations of filmmakers . . . he is responsible for inspiring more people to be film directors than anyone else in the history of cinema." Likewise, Scott's ambition has driven him to make films which otherwise would not have been made (e.g., *BLADE RUNNER*), and he has also launched the careers of other directors, not only as a pro-

ducer of their films, but as a cofounder of his advertising agency RSA.

References

Barbara Leaming, *Orson Welles* (Harmondsworth: Penguin Books, 1989), 199–200; Ridley Scott, quoted in Barry Garron, "*Kane* Explained," *Emmy* 21, no.6 (December 1999): 8.

WESTERNS

The Western has recently been subject to radical revision from Hollywood filmmakers. The back-to-back release of *3:10 to Yuma (2007)*, *NO COUNTRY FOR OLD MEN*, and the Ridley Scott–produced *ASSASSINATION OF JESSE JAMES BY THE COWARD ROBERT FORD* reveal the protagonists' desire to be heard—something that resonates with audiences of today, when many in the US feel they live in dark times ruled over by small minds. The Western's myths and rituals have served America well in earlier epochs—and if filmmakers and audiences continue to be drawn to them, perhaps it's because the genre still has something to say about America's past that people need to hear.

Bibliography

Jim Kitses, "Twilight of the Idol," *Sight and Sound*, 17 no. 12 (December 2007): 16–20; James Naremore, "Films of the Year, 2007," *Film Quarterly* 61, no.4 (Summer 2008): 59–60.

WHERE THE MONEY IS

Germany/USA/GB 2000 r/t 88 min col. *Production Companies*: Gramercy Pictures, IMF Internationale Medien und Film GmbH & Co., InterMedia Films, Pacifica Film, Polygram Filmed Entertainment, and Scott Free. *Executive Producers*: Moritz Borman, Guy East, Tony Scott, Chris Sievernich, and Nigel Sinclair. *Producers*: Ridley Scott, Christopher Dorr, Charles Weinstock, and Chris Zarpas. *Director*: Marek Kanievska. *Writer*: E. Max Frye. *Director of Photography*: Thomas Burstyn. *Production Designer*: André Chamberland. *Music*: Mark Isham. *Cast*: Paul Newman (*Henry Manning*), Linda Fiorentino (*Carol*), Dermot Mulroney (*Wayne*), Susan Barnes (*Mrs. Foster*), Anne Pitoniak (*Mrs. Tetlow*), Bruce MacVittie (*Karl*), Irma St. Paul (*Mrs. Galer*).

Busy with other commitments, the Scotts hired fellow director Marek Kanievska, whose only feature film credit was the British-made *Another Country* (1987). They cast PAUL NEWMAN in the leading role as an aging crook; his leading lady was LINDA FIORENTINO, who made a lasting impression in *The Last Seduction* (1993).

Budgeted at $18 million, *Where the Money Is* began shooting in Quebec, Canada, on 7 January 1998. For Newman, the production offered a return trip to Montreal, where he had filmed *Quintet* for Robert Altman two decades earlier. The script called for several car chases, Newman remaining behind the wheel throughout the filming. As director Kanievska explained to Newman's biographer Daniel O'Brien: "Paul can drive better than most stunt drivers. It was just another day on the race track for him, but it proved to be a pretty harrowing experience for Linda Fiorentino, who was sitting next to him in those vehicles." According to the pressbook, the director liked the experience of the production, which he felt was "colorful, playful and eccentric . . . It features all my favorite colors . . . When you get people in a tense or suspenseful situation and you put them in a colorful context, it all takes on a different tone." Director of photography Tom Burstyn agreed in another interview for the pressbook: "We decided every room in the nursing home should be a wild color . . . Each room is decorated with curtains of a very strong color and this gave me the excuse to light the scenes in an extremely colorful way—in green, violet, turquoise."

Reviews were favorable and sometimes enthusiastic. *The Guardian* thought that "there's a classical simplicity about such a narrative . . . Kanievska generates a momentum that carries events on at a considerable clip . . . [he] serves his cast—and audience—entertainingly enough." *Empire* thought of it as "a pacy little adventure with some marvelous one-liners and smart twists . . . Newman [gives] . . . a masterclass in timing, sardonic delivery and weathered charm." *Film Review* described the film in one review as "a beguiling caper that Hollywood film-makers sadly don't make anymore . . . the cinematic equivalent of a light snack" and in another as "a likeable comedy, which would fill your Sunday afternoon nicely, but fails to cash in fully on Newman's obvious charm."

Where the Money Is went on limited release in the United States on 14 April 2000, over two years after it was shot. It took only $5.65 million at the North American box office, less than a third of its production cost.

The film deliberately exploits Newman's screen image of MASCULINITY, which has been mostly aptly summed up by Mark Harris: "Newman became a star at a moment when two opposing images . . . were dominating the screen: the rough, tough unforgiving force of actors like John Wayne . . . and the newer, more sensitive, almost wounded approach exemplified by Montgomery Clift. He [Newman] belonged to neither category; rather . . . he found a way to be both brutal and tender, callous at one moment and vulnerable the next." In *Where the Money Is* Newman shows his toughness as he deliberately feigns a stroke in order to secure temporary release from prison. Even though Carol MacKay (Fiorentino) and her husband Wayne (DERMOT MULRONEY) expose him as a fraud by throwing him out of his wheelchair into the lake, Newman's Henry Manning demonstrates his mental toughness by stubbing a lighted cigarette out on his hand. By concentrating solely on his heartbeat,

he can render himself impervious to any other stimuli, whether physical, mental or visual.

Manning's tender side is revealed soon afterwards when he asks Carol to dance with him. While the two of them keep their distance from one another (especially as Wayne is sitting close by), it is evident that Manning understands Carol's desire to escape from the daily routine of married life. The two of them become unlikely partners in crime by hatching an elaborate scheme to steal $2 million from a security firm. Although it eventually fails, both find the experience so rewarding that they resolve to work as a team, with Carol pretending to be Manning's granddaughter. The film ends with them involved in another heist, this time in a jeweler's shop: Carol persuades the assistant (Vlasta Vrana) to help her remove her wedding-ring in the stockroom, leaving the counter unattended; meanwhile Henry (who hitherto has remained immobile in a wheelchair) looks through the display cases and puts whatever he likes into a small black bag.

Where the Money Is allows Newman to play a role strongly reminiscent of Henry Gondorff in *THE STING*. Like Gondorff, Manning comes out of retirement to teach an aspiring hustler how to stage the Big Con. The only difference between the two is that his sidekick is now a woman instead of a man.

Linda Fiorentino's role as Carol contains distinct echoes of *THELMA & LOUISE*. Like the two protagonists in the earlier film, she leads a humdrum life in a nondescript Californian suburb, working as a nurse in a care home and married to a dominant husband who demands that she should pursue a "normal" life—in other words, fulfill a subordinate role as a homemaker. She derives no pleasure from her existence—at one point she complains to Henry, "Me and Wayne don't make sense any more. [Soon] I'm gonna wonder where my life went. I'm the one who's dead here. I gotta do something." This explains her willingness to break the shackles of convention and join Manning in a life of crime.

Carol's dreams eventually come true, as the two of them give the police the slip and hit the road in a Mustang—one of those iconic CARS (like the 1966 Thunderbird in *Thelma & Louise*) which achieved prominence in the famous nine-minute car chase through the streets of San Francisco in the film *Bullitt* (1968). One of the car's designers summed up the experience of driving a Mustang thus: "It's a car you can drive fast and probably not get caught all the time." It sums up the significance of freedom in *Where the Money Is*.

The parallels between *Where the Money Is* and *Thelma & Louise* are also apparent in their plots. The earlier film ends with the eponymous central characters driving off a precipice into the Grand Canyon, and thereby freeing themselves of patriarchal culture. *Where the Money Is* employs a similar shot on two occasions: the first occurs in a black-and-white sequence right at the beginning, where the youthful Carol and Wayne are shown kissing and cuddling in their car. A truck suddenly appears in front of them; Wayne swerves to avoid it and loses control of the steering wheel. The car veers off the road, plunges into the undergrowth, and crashes into a lake. However, both Wayne and Carol emerge unharmed, with faces flushed in sheer exhilaration.

In the second sequence at the end of the film, Manning drives the Mustang into the water, with Carol once again as the passenger, in an attempt to escape the police. At first we think both of them have perished; but they make a speedy recovery and continue their lives as an aging Bonnie and Clyde. As in *Thelma & Louise*, the entire sequence demonstrates how the central characters reject the world of convention and pursue their dreams instead.

By contrast, Wayne remains a prisoner of his upbringing. While agreeing in principle to assist Carol in the security van robbery, he only does so in the belief that she will "go back to normal" afterwards—in other words, accept the fact that the two of them are "a husband and wife amateur hour." When she refuses to comply with his wishes, he reports her felony to the police, justifying his decision by asking Carol: "What am I supposed to do? I did it for us." Wayne's trust in her proves misplaced, as Carol runs out on him. In the patriarchal universe, it is the male who is expected to be active while the female passively accepts his opinions. *Where the Money Is* reverses this distinction: whereas Carol actively pursues her dreams, Wayne experiences them vicariously by playing video games. His fundamentally blinkered outlook on life is summed up through frequent prison images—for example, being photographed in close-up looking out of a barred window in his house at the rolling landscape outside.

Kanievska enjoys making fun of existing stereotypes of MASCULINITY. The corrupt nurse Karl (Bruce MacVittie), who exploits the care home residents by stealing their valuables while they are asleep, also fancies himself as a biker. In a sequence(recalling MICHAEL DOUGLAS's race along the Hudson River in *BLACK RAIN*, Karl dons his helmet and leathers and zooms away from the home in a cloud of exhaust fumes. What he does not know, however, is that Manning has immobilized his bike by severing the fuel injection pipe (as a way of taking revenge for the nurse's petty crimes). As a result Karl ends up quite literally on his backside—much to the amusement of the residents—losing a tooth in the process.

What the film proposes is that everyone should set aside existing gender preconceptions and adopt more fluid identities instead. At various points in the action Manning plays a stroke victim, a genial convict, a tough guy, a religious zealot encouraging people to achieve "a state of grace," a daredevil driver, a perfect gentleman (described by one of his fellow-residents as someone of "good breeding"), and an aging grandfather sitting comatose in his wheelchair. Carol plays Manning's surrogate mother (while he passes the time in the care home) and subsequently assumes the part of his granddaughter when the two of them rob the jeweler's shop. Her other roles include that of a telephone operator making hoax calls to facilitate the security firm robbery. Kanievska's view recalls that put forward by Virginia Woolf in *Orlando* (1928), which proposes that all identities—whether masculine or feminine—should be fluid, evanescent and subject to change.

Critical comment on *Where the Money Is* has been scant, to say the least. The only essay of note referring to it is one written by David Patrick Stearns (2007), which cites Newman's role as Henry Manning as one where the actor "crafts the details of his character and delineates private and public behavior in ways that add great dimensions." Stearns quotes a line from the film ("However easy it is, we have a job to do. Do your homework") as evidence of Newman's meticulous preparation for any role, "when an actor's performances blend life experience and cultivated technique."

References

Peter Bradshaw, "That Old Grey Magic," *The Guardian*, 6 October 2000, 15; Tom Burstyn, quoted in the pressbook for *Where the Money Is* (London: Intermedia 2000), 22; James Cameron-Wilson, "Where the Money Is," *Film Review Special Issue* 34 (2001): 122; Mark Harris, "Paul Newman 1925–2008," *Entertainment Weekly*, September 2008, www.ew.com/ew/article/0,,20230909,00.html (accessed 27 November 2008); "Interview: The Team Behind the 2008 Mustang Bullitt" (16 November 2007), http://autoshows.ford.com/189/2007/11/16/interview-the-team-behind-the-2008-mustang-bullitt/ (accessed 27 November 2008); Marek Kanievska, quoted in Daniel O'Brien, *Paul Newman* (London: Faber and Faber Ltd., 2004), 295; Marek Kanievska, quoted in the pressbook for *Where the Money Is* (London: Intermedia 2000), 15, 21–22; David Patrick Stearns, "Paul Newman as King Lear," *Obit Magazine*, 2 June 2007, www.obit-mag.com/viewmedia.php/prmMID/68 (accessed 27 November 2008); "Where the Money Is," *Empire*, October 2000, 54; "Where the Money Is," *Film Review*, May 2001, 73.

WHITE SQUALL

US 1996 r/t 129 min col. *Production Companies*: Hollywood Pictures, Largo Entertainment and Scott Free. *Executive Producer*: Ridley Scott. *Producers*: Mimi Polk Gitlin and Rocky Lang. *Director*: Ridley Scott. *Writer*: Todd Robinson from the book *The Last Voyage of the Albatross* by Charles ("Chuck") Gieg Jr. and Felix Sutton. *Production Designers*: Peter J. Hampton and Leslie Tomkins. *Director of Photography*: Hugh Johnson. *Music*: Jeff Rona. *Cast*: Jeff Bridges (*Captain Christopher "Skipper" Sheldon*), Caroline Goodall (*Dr. Alice Sheldon*), John Savage (*McCrea*), Scott Wolf (*Chuck Gieg*), Jeremy Sisto (*Frank Beaumont*), Ryan Phillippe (*Gil Martin*), David Lascher (*Robert March*).

The origins of this film came about in the early 1990s when screenwriter TODD ROBINSON was introduced to CHUCK GIEG, who told him of the story of his time on *The Albatross* thirty years before. Gieg subsequently served as a consultant, using the telephone and email to communicate with Robinson. Robinson himself took the script to producer Rocky Lang, and the two of them tried to find a suitable director. They were resolute in their determination to maintain the integrity of their story; this precluded them accepting a number of lucrative offers because they would have been required to alter the script to conform to someone else's ideas. Eventually, their patience and vision prevailed: they showed the script to Ridley Scott.

At this time Scott was considering directing *Mulholland Falls* (eventually directed by Lee Tamahori in 1996). When the *White Squall* script was shown to him, he read the material and announced ninety minutes later that he would make the film. In a preproduction interview with Neil Norman published in 1995, he said the film had attracted him on account of its historical value: "It's about a generation that is gone and lost . . . And I don't think it's ever going to come back. In a way this film is really about the rite of passage from adolescence into manhood and I think the process has evaporated. The real values, family values, have collapsed . . . Children have lost respect for their elders . . . Now there is far too much toleration of bullshit . . . If that [the disaster] had happened today everyone would have been sued . . . the most they would have done then would have been to have a hearing. In simple terms the boys defended the honour of their Captain. Consequently he was let off the hook."

Scott used several seafaring films as guides, including Frank Lloyd's *MUTINY ON THE BOUNTY* (1935) and John Huston's *MOBY DICK* (1956), both of which featured maverick captains obsessed with achieving their goals.

The film had an expansive location shoot, taking in the Caribbean islands of Grenada, St. Lucia, and St. Vincent before moving inland to Georgia and South Carolina. In the publicity for the production, most of the creative personnel stressed the fact that filming itself was an adventure. Scott was quoted in the production information as saying that the cast "function[ed] like a crew and are the most professional group I've ever worked with" (though SCOTT WOLF admitted to feeling "extremely nervous when I met Chuck Gieg, since I was portraying him"). Producer MIMI POLK made the same point in the production information: "The young cast, as well as the real crew came from different backgrounds and experiences, and were challenged by being put in a confined and often isolated environment. Finding a common bond, they all became friends and learned to work together as a crew." Likewise, cinematographer HUGH JOHNSON emphasized the fact that the crew had to contend with the elements, which made them bond together:

"Shooting in the Caribbean is difficult . . . The problem is that the sun is high at nine-thirty in the morning, especially out on the boat. It's very difficult, because the light goes up so quickly and we're trying to create images of light, shade and contrast when the sun there."

Reviews on the film's opening in 1996 were lukewarm, to say the least. The *Village Voice* critic considered it "[a] disappointing adventure [that] plays more like '*Dead Poets Goes to Sea*.'" The London *Guardian* voiced similar opinions; while the film contained "one of the best sequences of a yacht slowly sinking in a storm that I have ever seen [it is] . . . chock full of the kind of clichés one might expect from a bad Disney feature of ten years ago." Nigel Andrews of the *Financial Times* voiced the kind of criticism that has dogged Scott since the start of his career as a film director: "[The film] is low art with a high-art sheen. It looks like every sea painting you ever wanted to steal off a gallery wall. The resulting brigantine riding the high-clawing, silvered waves, the Turnerish storms blending their gloomy, glowing half-colours; the hot-hued exoticism of lulls ashore." Likewise Mark Kermode in *Sight and Sound* described *White Squall* as "[a] sustained and exhausting torrent of energy which threatens to drown the viewer in experiential overload. As the *Albatross* keels and groans its way into the ocean, with the soundtrack shaking our ear-drums and intestines, Scott metaphorically manacles us to the doomed ship's deck, dragging us down into the whirlpool, making us gasp for air as the waters envelope the screen."

White Squall had a budget of around $38 million. When it was released, the film failed to make much of an impact with the moviegoing public, grossing only around $10 million in North America. Nonetheless, the film's impact on audiences encouraged RICHARD E. LANGFORD, the English teacher on the original voyage, to publish his own reminiscences, written in the mid-1960s but hitherto unpublished. They appeared in 2001 as *White Squall: The Last Voyage of Albatross*.

The film returns to themes explored in previous Scott films, notably *1492: THE CONQUEST OF PARADISE* and *THE BROWNING VERSION*. Captain Sheldon resembles Columbus (GÉRARD DEPARDIEU) in his determination to continue the voyage at all costs and educate his charges. Described in Todd Robinson's script as "part Ahab part Queeg and even Bligh," he observes at one point that working on board ship "builds character . . . the kind you only find on mountain-tops, deserts or battlefields or across oceans." His dedication to character building prompts him to commit sadistic acts—for example, forcing Gil Martin (RYAN PHILLIPPE) to climb the rigging, despite the boy's fear of heights. Later on he challenges Frank Beaumont (JEREMY SISTO) to a fight, a knee-jerk reaction to the boy's having mortally wounded a dolphin. Such acts prompt Gieg

(Scott Wolf) to reflect on whether Sheldon is any different "from our fathers back home." On the other hand, Sheldon remains unselfishly devoted to his charges' welfare. In one sequence Cuban officers try to take one of the boys as a prisoner for failing to produce his American passport. Sheldon stands in front of the boy and announces that "nobody on my ship is going anywhere." If they want to take someone as a prisoner, they will have to make do with Sheldon himself. The Cuban officer (James Medina) climbs down and leaves the ship, pausing only to smash its compass with the butt of his rifle. Not to be outdone, Sheldon responds in Spanish (hitherto he has spoken only in English): "*Las estrellas es lo unico, que un marinero verdarero sa mesesita para encontrarse* [real sailors only need the stars]."

Sheldon fears no one; and although brutal in his methods, he harbors a genuine concern for his crew. The boys understand this, which helps to explain why they all join him in the final climactic sequence in the courtroom, exclaiming "you go one, we go all." In this respect, Sheldon is more successful at his job than Columbus—even Frank Beaumont (whose testimony provided the basis for the case against the captain) understands how much he has learned from the experience of being on the *Albatross*, and rejoins the group of boys, ringing the ship's bell (salvaged from the wreck) as he does so.

Once the boys reach the deserted Galapagos Islands, they take possession of it in a sequence strongly reminiscent of Columbus's arrival in the New World. In a voiceover, Gieg informs us that they wanted to "stake a claim [on the islands] as our own" as they roam over the vast landscape dressed in shorts and carrying staffs. Todd Robinson's script emphasizes the primal nature of this scene: "Pounding through the waterline like the wild horses of fable, the hunters charge after the hunted [goat], closing . . . The wind carries the sounds of ceremony across the water. The flames from the beach reflect off the water turning the white hull of the ship a deep flickering orange." In a sense the boys have discovered a new world—emotional rather than physical—as they come to understand the importance of teamwork and concern for one another.

This particular theme recalls *The Browning Version*, even though in the earlier film the focus of attention centers on the teacher rather than the boys in his charge. In both films a series of pivotal sequences are used to signal the characters' development. At the beginning of *White Squall* Robert March (DAVID LASCHER) is depicted as a bully, unceremoniously ejecting one of his fellow crew members from a bunk, and later grabbing another one's private parts, snarling as he does so, "Don't ever call me stupid." However, we soon discover that this aggression is nothing more than a cover-up for March's academic shortcomings; he has to cheat in order to pass his exams. The rest of the crew members volunteer to help him, and as a result he passes his exams. Gieg says to March, "It feels different, doesn't it?" (to have achieved something by his own efforts, and thereby discovered an identity for himself).

Martin undergoes a similar process of development as he climbs up to the crow's nest and rings the ship's bell triumphantly while waving to the departing Frank Beaumont (who has just been expelled from the ship). Immediately the crew raises a cheer, prompting Sheldon to observe to Frank, "They never gave up on you, you know." The final courtroom scene is strongly reminiscent of *The Browning Version*, both visually and thematically; it takes place in a crowded hall, with parents and their offspring witnessing the proceedings. Tiring of the repeated questions calling his integrity into question, Sheldon gets up from his seat, taking responsibility for the entire disaster, and strides through the audience (just like Crocker-Harris in the earlier film). The boys likewise move towards the door as Gieg tells Sheldon that the entire voyage was "something we made together," and emphasizes this by encouraging everyone—the captain included—to put their arms around one another in a final show of unity. Like Crocker-Harris, Sheldon comes to understand how everyone should "share his burden, the burden of sea-captains, and fathers, the burden of men . . . You can't win in the end. You face the music, you trim your sails, and you keep going."

White Squall also returns to familiar Scott territory in its emphasis on MASCULINITY. The boys can only survive if they stay together and look out for one another. This is emphasized in another pivotal sequence that begins when Francis Beaumont (DAVID SELBY) and his wife Peggy (Jill Larson) fly in to Panama to take their son Frank out for a meal. Francis strides on board ship, proclaiming, "We've come to give our boy a little break from the monotony." Immediately Frank is "full of rage. This is an invasion of his privacy. Everyone feels it." Frank's rage boils over in a local restaurant; he accuses his father of embarrassing him and storms out—closely followed by his father. The two of them are shown fighting in the street, with Frank predictably coming off second best. Frank is only prevented from causing more harm to himself by his fellow crew members, who discover him blind drunk in the street, smashing streetlights. They drag him into the darkness and ensure that he goes to sleep. Scott suggests that Frank's parents have abnegated their responsibilities to their son; it is the boys who are now responsible for his welfare. James Clarke comments: "It [the film] makes a good companion piece to Peter Weir's 1989 *Dead Poets Society*—both of them are about imposing father figures who their 'sons' must break away from."

The only critical comment to have appeared on the film is contained in the surveys of Scott's oeuvre as a whole. James Clarke draws our attention to the fact that apart from the final song "Valparaiso" sung by *STING* at the end of the film, accompanied by images of the boys landing in the Galapagos Islands, Scott is very sparing with his score: "There is no music used on the squall sequence which enhances its believability. Scott lets the terror speak for itself." Clarke highlights the parallels between *White Squall* and JOSEPH CONRAD, in its emphasis on "The marine setting with young men and story of honour and loss of innocence . . . The boat . . . is like a microcosm of the world at large as well as being a place removed from everyday routine in which the boys' adventure unfolds before returning them to the everyday at the conclusion." He also detects "a very military strain to the 'philosophy' of the film" which finds later expression in *G.I. JANE, GLADIATOR,* and *BLACK HAWK DOWN*. In a relentless search for literary antecedents, Clarke also likens the story to JOHN MILTON's *Paradise Lost,* notably when Frank shoots a dolphin with a harpoon.

Richard A. Schwartz seems more preoccupied with the film's manipulation of history: "For although the *Albatross* is boarded on Fidel Castro's personal orders and is rescued by the American fleet, the rescuing fleet is not engaged in the naval quarantine that Kennedy imposed during the crisis. Instead, Chuck tells us they are en route to the Bay of Pigs. But the Bay of Pigs invasion occurred in April 1961 . . . Similarly, Scott overlaps the storm that sinks the Albatross with the launch of Alan Shepard in the *Mercury 1* spaceship. But that flight occurred on 1 May 1961, about three weeks after the Bay of Pigs invasion. Presumably, both the invasion and *Mercury 1* flight occurred while the real *Albatross* was at sea in 1961, and Scott was trying to do justice to the actual history by inserting them. Treated differently, the historical intrusions might have intensified the drama or created suggestive parallels between the voyage into outer space and the one at sea. But as presented, the anachronisms merely confuse viewers who lived during those times."

Scott's grasp of history might not be entirely accurate, but the historical references are significant. The Bay of Pigs reference is used to contrast the American and the Cuban world-views; whereas Sheldon and the boys try to work together for mutual benefit, the Cubans seem far more preoccupied with an ostentatious display of power. By implication, Scott suggests that their unnecessary bravado—in violation of accepted maritime laws—provoked the Cuban Missile Crisis. Similarly the radio broadcast of the *Mercury 1* spaceship is used as a counterpoint to the white squall disaster. Whereas the launching of the craft symbolized American progress in the space race against the Soviet Union, the sea disaster emphasizes just how powerless human beings can be while contending against the elements. They might try to conquer them—through space travel—but such a task proves ultimately futile. This once again emphasizes the importance of community: to survive in a hostile world, people must stick together.

References

Nigel Andrews, "Growing Up and Rites of Passage," *Financial Times*, 9 May 1996, 15; Georgia Brown, "White Squall," *Village Voice*, 6 February 1996, 48; James Clarke, *Ridley Scott* (London: Virgin Books Ltd., 2002), 152; Mark Kermode, "White Squall," *Sight and Sound*, May 1996, 64; Derek Malcolm, "Drowning by Numbers," *The Guardian*, 9 May 1996, 9; Neil Norman, "Scott of the Caribbean," *Evening Standard* 18 May 1995, 28; *Production Information, White Squall* (Los Angeles: Hollywood Pictures, 1996); Todd Robinson, *White Squall: Revised First Draft*, Unpub. script, dated 31 October 1994, http://sfy.ru/sfy.html?script=white_squall (accessed 8 September 2008); Richard A. Schwarz, *The Films of Ridley Scott* (Westport, CT: The Greenwood Press, 2001), 123–24.

Bibliography

Estelle Shay, "*White Squall:* Stormy Weather," *Cinefex* 66 (June 1996): 33–34, 126; Michael Wilmington, "*White Squall:* Director a Visionary without Visual Strategy," in *Ridley Scott Interviews*, ed. Laurence F. Knapp and Andrea F. Kulas (Jackson: University Press of Mississippi, 2005), 129–32; "Young Men and the Sea." *Premiere* 9, no.6 (February 1996): 66–71 (photographs from the shoot by Jeff Bridges).

WHITEMORE, HUGH (1936–)

Hugh Whitemore began his career in television, writing plays and adapting literary classics by Dickens, Brontë, and Somerset Maugham. His film screenplays include *84 Charing Cross Road* (1987) with ANTHONY HOPKINS and *Utz* (1992).

Whitemore wrote the screenplay for the Emmy award-winning *GATHERING STORM*, produced by Scott. The script caused considerable controversy by celebrating the achievements of Ralph Wigram (LINUS ROACHE), a civil servant and committed anti-appeaser who worked in the Foreign Office, and who passed on secret documents to Churchill, in full knowledge that he was breaking the law by doing so. Whitemore defended his decision by insisting that Wigram received due mention in *THE GATHERING STORM: MEMOIRS*, Churchill's own account of World War II.

WICK, DOUGLAS (1955–)

Wick is the son of Charles Wick (a producer and in business and politics). His early hits included *Working Girl* (1988), and *Stuart Little* (1999).

Wick is credited with taking the script to *GLADIATOR* and convincing Scott to direct it. Wick asserted in the book of the film, "No one had done this kind of spectacle in thirty years . . . It was an opportunity that hadn't been visited in a long time. We felt that audiences were getting tired of space movies, and that to revisit Rome was to take them to extraordinary spectacle, extraordinary action—but all grounded in a human reality. And with the new technology, you could give them a much more realistic version than ever before."

Reference

Douglas Wick, quoted in Diana Landau, ed., *Gladiator: The Making of the Ridley Scott Epic* (Basingstoke and London: Boxtree, 2000), 16.

Bibliography

"Strength and Honor: Creating the World of *Gladiator*" (Los Angeles: Universal Studios, 2005).

WILKINSON, TOM (1948–)

British character actor associated with a variety of roles, often unsavory characters in costume dramas. His main roles include Pecksniff in the BBC version of *Martin Chuzzlewit* (1994), Mr. Dashwood in *Sense and Sensibility* (1995), and the Marquess of Queensberry in *Wilde* (1997).

As Robert Vansittart in THE GATHERING STORM, Wilkinson is back on familiar ground as a civil servant determined to reveal the truth about Ralph Wigram (LINUS ROACHE) passing confidential documents on to Churchill (ALBERT FINNEY), even while realizing that doing so will destroy Wigram's family. Vansittart is a man for whom duty is everything; no allowances can be made for any departure from the rules, even if it is in the interests of the country. In a short sequence in the Crush Bar at the Royal Opera House, Covent Garden, London, he talks quietly to Wigram, asking where Churchill gets his information and warning Wigram politely that it would be "unfortunate if something were to go wrong." Wilkinson delivers the lines in a soft, confidential tone; but his penetrating glance leaves us in no doubt as to the seriousness of his words. He knows what Wigram is doing, but rather than making his knowledge public, he hopes the younger civil servant will see reason and discontinue his actions. Wigram, however, believes that he has a greater loyalty—to his country rather than the Civil Service.

Reference

"*The Gathering Storm*: Transcript of the Screenplay by Hugh Whitemore," www.script-o-rama.com/novie_scripts/g/gathering storm-script-transcript.html (accessed 23 December 2008).

WILSON, SCOTT (1942–)

Early films include *In Cold Blood* (1967), *The Right Stuff* (1983), and *The Grass Harp* (1995).

Cast as Commanding Officer Salem in *G.I. JANE*, Wilson comes across as someone irritated with the idea of having a woman undergo military training at his Florida base.

The script describes his first reaction to Jordan O'Neil (DEMI MOORE) thus: "[he] takes stock of the female in his doorway, sizing her up like a fighter across the ring." He begins by addressing her stiffly, almost formally: "If a classmate or superior acts in a harassing or otherwise unbecoming manner, please inform me immediately so I can deal with it." Jordan is surprised by this response: "If . . . [she] was expecting a fight, the bell never sounded." Salem only reveals his true feelings in a conversation with Senator DeHaven (ANNE BANCROFT): "[There is] nothing I can do about it [the publicity surrounding Jordan's presence] unless you're suggesting I infringe on their civil liberties—which I'd happily do if you'll just trim a little fat off the Constitution." He resents Jordan in his camp, if only for the fact that she forces him to rethink the way in which he runs it. Although he eventually accedes to her request to share the men's quarters and to be treated no differently from them by the officers, it is clear that he cannot tolerate her presence. He is the venerable patriarch of a male-dominated world, which cannot and will not accept any redefinition of gender roles.

In *CLAY PIGEONS* (1998), produced by Scott, Wilson plays Sheriff Mooney, a SMALL-TOWN officer with a beer belly whose naïve trust in Clay's (JOAQUIN PHOENIX's) innocence causes Agent Shelby (JANEANE GAROFALO) to snort in derision. Although claiming to know Clay all his life, he has clearly not taught the young man to observe the law. Mooney's views are vindicated at the end of the film, however, when he participates in a sting operation to catch the serial killer Lester Long (VINCE VAUGHN). Mooney acts the part of a farmer in a pick-up truck with a horse in the back. Intrigued by the idea of making a new friend, Long asks whether he can hitch a lift with Mooney. The two of them drive off into the sunset, closely followed by a police vehicle. The film suggests that the small-town residents' trust in one another can go a long way to sustaining law and order, making Mooney's job that much easier. Wilson enjoyed the film, particularly when he learned that director DAVID DOBKIN had cast him on the strength of his performance in *In Cold Blood*: "[I]t makes me feel good that a film that I'm in has stood the test of time, and that a young filmmaker would still appreciate the film."

References

David Twohy, "*G.I. Jane*: First Draft" (6 August 1995), Unpub. screenplay, http://sfy.ru/sfy.html?script=gi_jane (accessed 21 October 2008); Scott Wilson, interviewed in "Production Notes: *Clay Pigeons*," included on the European DVD release of the film (Frankfurt: BY Internationale Medien und Film, 1998).

Bibliography

"Industry Central Profiles: Scott Wilson," http://industrycentral .net/content/actors/s_wilson.html (accessed 25 October 2008).

WINCOTT, MICHAEL (1958–)

Most of his roles prior to *1492: CONQUEST OF PARADISE* were in television, including *Miami Vice* (1988), *The Equalizer* (1987–1989), and *The Tragedy of Flight 103: The Inside Story* (1990).

Cast as Moxica in Scott's film, Wincott plays the classic role of the bad guy; in Robert Thurston's words—the "young surly nobleman" with "flashes of madness" in his eyes. Wincott was quoted in the pressbook as saying that Moxica "is a creature of his lineage, a man of absolute and corrupt power . . . To him, Columbus is a peasant and a foreigner, and taking orders from someone so beneath his station is a total humiliation. It would have been impossible for them to get along." As with YUSAKU MATSUDA's Sato in *BLACK RAIN*, Wincott enjoys playing the villain, calling the Indians "monkeys" and refusing to admit their existence. As a Spanish noble, he considers himself too grand to lower himself down to their level. In sequences reminiscent of the earlier film, Wincott, in an act of naked brutality, cuts off the hand of an Indian whom he suspects of lying. Later on, just before his death, he faces Columbus (GÉRARD DEPARDIEU), points his finger at the governor, and mutters: "You are nothing. Your bastards will never inherit the titles. We are everything. We are immortal." He then jumps off a precipice to his death, secure in the knowledge that he has not been defeated by a foreigner.

References

Robert Thurston, *1492: Conquest of Paradise Based on a Screenplay by Roselyne Bosch* (London: Penguin Books, 1992), 125; Michael Wincott, quoted in *Pressbook, 1492: Conquest of Paradise* (Los Angeles: Paramount Pictures, 1992), 5.

WINSTON CHURCHILL—THE GATHERING STORM

US/GB 1961 TVM 30 min b/w. *Production Companies*: Screen Gems Television, Le Vien International and the British Broadcasting Corporation. *Executive Producer*: Jack Levin. *Producers*: Ben Feiner, Patrick Macnee, and Robert D. Graff. *Director*: Ben Feiner. *Writers*: Quentin Reynolds, William L. Shirer, Richard Tregaskis, and Victor Wolfson. *Music*: Richard Rodgers.

An earlier version of the material broadcast in Scott's 2002 series *THE GATHERING STORM*, broadcast in the first series of *The Valiant Years* (episode number not specified), using news film, photographs, and sound recordings. The series aired on BBC in Great Britain and ABC in the United States and won two primetime Emmys.

One reader on the *Internet Movie Database* comments on the series thus: "This *Valiant Years* production was second to none in its use of archival motion picture footage. It also went that extra step in obtaining the services of two top acting talents of the English-speaking world in American

Gary Merrill as the narrator and British (Welsh-born) Richard Burton . . . The beautiful, majestic theme music and the incidental music in the original score are most haunting and unforgettable. They were composed by the American Richard Rodgers . . . who was the man responsible for the immortal score for NBC's *Victory at Sea*."

Reference

John T. Ryan, "Carefully Researched Telling of the Great Statesman's Life Story, Going Back to Early Days for Background! Question: Hey BBC, So Where're the DVDs Already?" (11 December 2007), www.imdb.com/title/tt0053548/combined (accessed 27 December 2008).

WITT, ALEXANDER (1952–)

A Hollywood filmmaker who has worked mostly as a camera operator and second unit director. His feature directorial debut came in 2004 with *Resident Evil: Apocalypse*, based on the popular Capcom video game series. Witt also became the second unit director on the James Bond remake *Casino Royale* (2006).

As director of photography in *BODY OF LIES*, Witt's most notable moment (according to the production notes) came when he collaborated with Scott on staging a frantic chase through a teeming Jordanian marketplace, with camera angles depicting Roger Ferris (LEONARDO DICAPRIO) from above as he's being tracked by the Predator System: "'The Predator System is like a "big brother" character that's always there,' says Scott, who simulated this POV [point of view] using an HD camera mounted on a helicopter hovering at ten thousand feet above the action on the ground."

Reference

Production Notes: Body of Lies (Los Angeles: Warner Bros. Entertainment, 2008), http://mix96tulsa.com/movies/notes/body-of-lies/note/4 (accessed 16 January 2009).

Bibliography

Jeff Otto, "Interview: Alexander Witt" (23 August 2004), http://movies.ign.com/articles/539/539681p1.html (accessed 20 February 2009).

WOLF, SCOTT (1968–)

Made his name as one of the stars of the American television series *Party of Five* (1994).

Cast as Chuck Gieg in *WHITE SQUALL*, Wolf recalled the experience in the British magazine *Empire* as "a blast . . . as much of an adventure for us as it was for our characters . . . It was parallel to the real story. We were all plucked from our homes and put in this foreign environment together." However, there was a serious side to the film: "You read this story and it sounds like some *Saturday Night Live* sketch . . .

I read this in the script before I knew it was a true story and it was like, 'Then the boat sinks and *then* sharks? Come on, that's pushing it a bit.' It just goes to show that truth *is* stranger than fiction."

Wolf was quick to emphasize that "this [film] is [not about] a bunch of young men without shirts" but rather focused on "that simple idea—being able to count on friends and have them be able to count on you. To have an incident like this shape your foundation can be very difficult to recover from. The survivors [on the real *Albatross*] never got a chance to do that, unfortunately, it was looked upon as just an accident on a little old school ship and it was belittled, so hopefully this [film] can be some catharsis for them in a way, redeem some of what they lost."

In another interview with *The Guardian* Wolf admitted that "there was so much responsibility in the role, because the events for Chuck were so life-altering . . ." Director Scott seems to concur—at one point Chuck is described metaphorically as the glue that holds the teenage crew together. He provides the emotional center of the film; in the final scene it is Gieg who stands up and tells Sheldon (JEFF BRIDGES) that everyone participated together in the experience of being on board ship. Gieg also offers the moral in a voiceover: "You can't win in the end. You face the music, you trim your sails, and you keep going."

References

Jeff Dawson, "Profiles—Scott Wolf—Uncanny Resemblance," *Empire* 84 (June 1996): 55; Robert Yates, "It Was 35 Years Ago Today," *Guardian Section* 2, 2 May 1996, 10–11.

WOO, JOHN (1946–)

Celebrated director of action films such as *Broken Arrow* (1996), *Face/Off* (1997), and *Mission Impossible II* (2000).

Woo's characteristically fast-paced style is evident in THE HIRE: "HOSTAGE," a short film made for Ridley Scott's RSA for BMW, where nonstop action is combined with throbbing music. In the Director's Commentary to the DVD release of the film, Woo describes how he was a fan of both Ridley and Tony Scott and his delight at being offered the chance to direct. Although *Hostage* was only a short film, he felt he had the chance to be able to experiment with complicated action sequences.

John Woo's subsequent work includes short films for *ALL THE INVISIBLE CHILDREN* (2005)—the Italian produced compilation for which Scott contributed the film "Jonathan"—"Stranglehold" (2007), and "Chi Bi" (2008).

Reference

John Woo, Director's Commentary to the DVD release of *The Hire: Hostage* (Los Angeles: BMW of North America, 2003).

YATES, JANTY (1950–)

Longtime costume designer for many of Ridley Scott's films, including *GLADIATOR, HANNIBAL, KINGDOM OF HEAVEN, AMERICAN GANGSTER,* and *BODY OF LIES.* She received a Goya Award for Best Costume Design in Spain for her work in *Kingdom of Heaven.* Other work in films includes *Plunkett and Macleane* (1999) directed by JAKE SCOTT, *Charlotte Gray* (2001), and *Miami Vice* (2006).

YOUNG, SEAN (1959–)

Born Mary Sean Young. A trained dancer, Sean Young studied at the school of American Ballet in New York. She tested for the role of Marion Ravenwood in *Raiders of the Lost Ark* (1981).

She was one of several actors who tested for the role of Rachael in *BLADE RUNNER* (others included Barbara Hershey). Ridley Scott was interested in Young for several reasons: he felt the heroine had to be inexperienced so as to provide a suitable love interest for Deckard; and he wanted her to recall Rita Hayworth—the classic film noir heroine. Scott told PAUL M. SAMMON that he considered Young perfect for the role, "as if she had just stepped out of the REPLICANT vat. I couldn't get that from a thirty-five or forty-year-old actress, no matter how talented they were. It just wouldn't work."

Young characterizes Rachael as emotionless, almost glacial. On her first appearance in Tyrell's (JOE TURKEL's) office, she is silhouetted against the sun, wearing a small-waisted black dress. Her attitude towards Deckard (HARRISON FORD) is severe; when he mentions a full-page photo of a nude girl, she responds sarcastically and glares at Tyrell. While proving to Deckard that she is not a replicant, her gestures also indicate her desire to keep her emotions under control. When he tells her that her memories are counterfeit, purloined from Tyrell's sixteen-year-old niece, she lets her photo fall to the floor amid Deckard's trash and slips out in an attempt to avoid a scene. The same happens later on when Deckard tries to kiss her: Young herself recalled in an interview with *Prevue* magazine that Rachael "becomes frantic . . . because she doesn't know the meaning of love . . . she's a woman without experience being forcibly endowed with emotions."

While Young's interpretation might be coherent in terms of the plot (as a replicant, she has no experience of anything other than what people have told her), she still lacks passion—especially in the love scenes. Even at the end, when Deckard and Rachael leave his apartment, there appears to be little sense of warmth between them. She responds without emotion to his statement ("I love you"); in the DIRECTOR'S CUT the scene ends with a close-up of her expressionless face as elevator door closes, "leaving the nature of her and Deckard's plight unresolved," in Sammon's phrase from a 1982 article. Pauline Kael noted Rachael's lack of passion in her review: "[She] seems more of a zombie than anyone else in the movie . . . she's cold at first, but she spends most of her screen time looking mysteriously afflicted, wet-eyed with yearning, and she never gets to deliver a zinger."

Yet perhaps Young's reactions were real rather than simply part of her characterization; she recalled later in an interview with Sammon for the book *Future Noir* that her experiences of *Blade Runner* were pleasurable, "except [for] my leading man . . . suffice it to say I wouldn't call Harrison Ford generous." An anonymous member of the crew put it more bluntly: "Between them, something didn't work. Whenever Harrison would come onto the set he wouldn't speak to her. Totally ignored her."

References

Pauline Kael, "The Current Cinema: Baby, the Rain Must Fall," *New Yorker,* 12 July 1982, 83; Paul M. Sammon, "The Making of *Blade Runner*," *Cinefantastique* 12, nos. 5–6 (June–July 1982): 46, 214–15; Ridley Scott, quoted in Paul M. Sammon, *Future Noir: The Making of Blade Runner,* 2nd ed. (London: Gollancz, 2007), 92; Sean Young, quoted in James Steranko, "Blade Runner," *Prevue* 48 (June–July 1982): 26.

Z

ZAILLIAN, STEVEN (1953–)

Graduated from San Francisco State University in 1975 with a degree in cinema. His first big success was *Awakenings* (1990), followed by screenplays for *Schindler's List* (1993) and *Mission: Impossible* (1996). Also known as an effective rewriter of other work, Zaillian was brought in to work on DAVID MAMET's draft of *HANNIBAL*. Zaillian originally thought that the work on the film would be fairly quick; it ended up taking six months. He told the horror magazine *Fangoria* that he initially did not want to do it, as he could not see "how it [the film] could be done in a way that wasn't [gruesome] and still be true to the book." The adaptation made numerous changes to THOMAS HARRIS's book. Zaillian gave the character [Verger] a degree of mobility by placing him in a wheelchair. A number of key supporting characters were dropped, including several who had appeared in *THE SILENCE OF THE LAMBS* film. The police officer Jack Crawford, who initially featured in Mamet's script, was jettisoned, as were some of the animals—for example, a live electric eel in the novel that is stuffed head first into Verger's mouth. Zaillian explained: "That image was too much for me. I said 'I don't want to see it and I don't want to write it.' That was one of the things where people would say it was so firmly entrenched in the minds of people who had read the book. I felt it was unnecessary, and that was one of the [script debates] that I won."

In the film, *Hannibal* (ANTHONY HOPKINS) removes Krendler's (RAY LIOTTA's) skull cap and scoops out pieces of his brain for the sauce pan. Krendler gobbles down the tasty morsels in a serene stupor. Clarice (JULIANNE MOORE) tries to bash in Hannibal's brains with a candlestick holder, but he's too quick. The next time we see Hannibal he is on a plane, offering an adventurous little boy a bite from his specially prepared meal—including (we assume) another tasty morsel of brain. In Harris's book Clarice eats Krendler's brain and fully gives in to Hannibal's spell. In what amounts to a supreme farewell gesture, Starling says goodbye to her disappointing career by literally eating the brains of a man who kept her from fulfillment with the FBI and by doing so

opens her heart to the love and the high-society pleasures of the monster she covets. Zaillian changed the ending to have Clarice seduced by Hannibal, but not going off and living together—therefore allowing for the possibility of another sequel: *Red Dragon* (2002).

Since *Hannibal*, Zaillian has written or collaborated on the screenplays for *BLACK HAWK DOWN, AMERICAN GANGSTER*, and *BODY OF LIES*. For the second film, Zaillian wrote two separate scripts—one telling the story of Frank Lucas (DENZEL WASHINGTON) and the other about the cop Richie Roberts (RUSSELL CROWE), and later combined them. In an interview with *Creative Screenwriting* Zaillian recalled that he found Lucas "very friendly, very open . . . He's well-spoken. He tells a good story. He has a great memory. I know some stuff about him, but none of the details." Lucas was involved in police corruption; something that caused Zaillian to write a note to himself on an index card: "Frank could not have done what he did without . . . corruption." Zaillian was inspired by *SERPICO* (1973) and *THE FRENCH CONNECTION* (1974), both gritty police films: "Coincidentally, Ridley is a great fan of those [same] films. So he put his interpretation on it. But we both had them in mind." The script contained 350 short scenes; with emphasis placed on Lucas's family life "He [Scott] wanted to make sure we didn't succumb to the drug-trade romance. Frank had lots of money, and we see the excess, the parties, the penthouse. [Ridley] wanted to show the other side." The two main characters don't meet till the end of the film. Zaillian originally wrote a scene showing them meeting earlier on, but for budgetary reasons it was cut.

Steven Zaillian also revised WILLIAM MONAHAN's script for *BODY OF LIES*. An entire subplot involving Roger Ferris (LEONARDO DICAPRIO) and his wife Gretchen was removed; in its place Ferris referred in passing to the fact that he was about to get a divorce. Another subplot involving Ferris's relationship with Alice, a beautiful French émigré, was replaced by a new love affair between Ferris and Aisha (GOLSHIFTEH FARAHANI), an Iraqi nurse who tends him in a Jordanian hospital. The sex scenes were removed, as were the long scenes of exposition involving Ferris, Hoffman (Russell Crowe), and Hani, the head of the Jordanian Secret Service (MARK STRONG). Zaillian also rewrote an entire section of the film where Ferris and Hoffman create a fake terrorist network to try and catch Al-Saleem (ALON ABOUTBOUL). In Monahan's script much of this took place at an English country house, and involved Special Forces (for example, the SAS) and British Asians working at a specially created surveillance center. Zaillian transposed the surveillance center to a small isolated house near the CIA headquarters in Langley, Virginia, and created a new character, the computer geek Garland (SIMON McBURNEY), who carried out all of Ferris's instructions. Other incidents in Monahan's script—for example an explosion in Afghanistan designed to attract Al-Saleem's attention, and an internal investigation of Ferris's and Hoffman's conduct by the CIA—were also omitted.

References

Abbie Bernstein, "Writing & Biting," *Fangoria* 202 (May 2001): 53–6; Michael Ventre, "Now Playing: *American Gangster*," *Creative Screenwriting* 14, no.6 (November 2007): 24–25.

Bibliography

Lance Carmichael, "Advance Script Review: *Body of Lies*," *CinCity 2000* website, www.cincity2000.com/content/index.php?option =com_content&task=view&id=1059&Itemid=2 (accessed 16 February 2009); Douglas Eby, "Hannibal." *Cinefantastique* 32, no.6 (February 2001): 8–9; David Orr, "Script-review: *Hannibal*," *Creative Screenwriting* 8, no.2 (March/April 2001): 31–36.

Z CARS: "ERROR OF JUDGMENT"

GB 1965 TVM r/t 45 min b/w. *Production Company:* British Broadcasting Corporation. *Producer:* David E. Rose. *Director:* Ridley Scott. *Writer:* Alan Plater. *Cast:* Brian Blessed (*PC "Fancy" Smith*), Stratford Johns (*Det. Insp. Barlow*), Michael Goodliffe (*Chief Insp. Parker*), Colin Welland (*PC Graham*), Frank Windsor (*Det. Sgt. Watt*).

Groundbreaking BBC police drama—one of the first to show the seamy side of life in the force. Ridley Scott directed one episode (Season 4, Episode 40) broadcast live on 9 June 1965, written by Alan Plater.

ZEMECKIS, ROBERT (1951–)

Born in Chicago, Illinois, Zemeckis made his name as a writer with films such as *1941* (1979), and as a director with *Romancing the Stone*, the three episodes of *Back to the Future* (1985, 1989, 1990), and *Who Framed Roger Rabbit?* (1988). Recently he has branched out into new territory as a producer; he owns two companies—ImageMovers and Dark Castle Entertainment. Originally planned to direct *MATCH-*

STICK MEN, but passed on the project. Ridley Scott took over, but Zemeckis remained as executive producer.

Bibliography

Norman Kagan, *The Cinema of Robert Zemeckis* (Lanham, MD: Taylor Trade Publishing, 2003).

ZIMMER, HANS (1957–)

German-born composer Hans Zimmer is recognized as one of Hollywood's most innovative musical talents, having first enjoyed success in the world of pop music as a member of The Buggles. The group's single "Video Killed the Radio Star" became a worldwide hit and helped usher in a new era of global entertainment as the first music video to be aired on MTV. A turning point in Zimmer's career came in 1988 when he was asked to score *Rain Man* for director Barry Levinson. The film went on to win the Oscar for Best Picture of the Year and earned Zimmer his first Academy Award Nomination for Best Original Score. It was on the strength of this score that Scott and producer STANLEY R. JAFFE engaged him for *BLACK RAIN*.

Hans Zimmer's experiences on the film were not entirely satisfactory. He recalled in an interview with producer Stanley R. Jaffe "hated everything I was doing. And hated it so much that I actually got shouted at after a screening at Paramount, and I fainted. So by the time we got to the dub stage, I was just living in fear. We were battling the system. And it's very odd because Monday night after the Oscars, I went to a little private party. Michael Douglas was there, and he said, 'You really saved my ass in *Black Rain*.' And I thought, 'Wow, great. Thank you, Michael, you realized what I did.'" Interestingly, Jaffe himself recalled that he admired some of Zimmer's work on the film. Zimmer composed an entire suite for the film, but it was removed from the final cut on the grounds that Jaffe thought it was "the worst piece of music he's every heard." It was restored to the original soundtrack album, issued one month later in October 1989. Zimmer's main contribution to the film is the title song "I'll Be Holding On."

For *THELMA & LOUISE* Zimmer used a restrained palette of sounds, dominated by synthesizers and electronically processed instruments. The sounds included "lonesome" notes from a slide guitar and harmonica, blues riffs for a solo electric guitar, and banjo and guitar for dynamic or comic moments. Such sounds were deliberately intended to echo similar scores from earlier composers working on American westerns such as Ennio Morricone in *A Fistful of Dollars* (1964) or *Once Upon a Time in the West* (1968) and Ry Cooder in *Paris Texas* (1984). For Claudia Gorman, Zimmer's music becomes "the music of heroism, but, rather than heroism of action, it is a heroism of thought and being" in a film that seeks to "dismantle the structures of gender in the Western."

Zimmer was slated to do the score for *1492: CONQUEST OF PARADISE*, but had to pull out at the last moment due to work commitments. His role was taken over by VANGELIS. After producing the soundtrack album for *WHITE SQUALL*, his next work for Scott was on GLADIATOR, where he tried to write "battle music" inspired by William Walton's score for *Battle of Britain* (1969). Eventually he acknowledged in an interview with Rudy Koppl that Gustav Holst provided a major inspiration: "he is talking about the same gods we're talking about in our movie . . . the difference between Holst and what I was trying to do with 'The Gladiator Waltz' is syntax." In another interview with Ford A. Thaxton, Zimmer spoke of his decision to write all the action sequences as waltzes: "I was trying to find them the most pleasant, formal form of music and then make it savage, turning beauty on its head and perverting it. If you go to Rome and look at the architecture . . . and what the emperor has given us, you realize it's built on blood, guts, savagery and slaves." He also suggested that the film is "not a sissy movie . . . I took a deeply emotional approach while taking a deeply savage one as well. It goes from the horror of battle into completely different scenarios . . . This is an opera."

HANNIBAL, however, was notable for the fact that Zimmer included ANTHONY HOPKINS's voice on the soundtrack. Zimmer explained in the Thaxton interview that Hopkins "had become part of the journey. At one point, he was the pianist on the project, and then things happened and Glenn Gould had become the pianist! . . . I do feel his voice is like an instrument." Zimmer used a symphony orchestra for the opera sequence, but would mostly use what he described as a "very odd orchestra . . . only cellos and basses all playing at the extreme ends of their range." The character of Mason Verger (GARY OLDMAN) had his own theme, which become more perverted as the movie progressed.

For *BLACK HAWK DOWN* Zimmer told Mikael Carlson that he tried to create a score combining two cultures: "The culture of Northern East Africa and basically our Western culture . . . [the score is peppered] with ethnic colours. I needed to pick somebody who could give voice to the whole African continent in a way, and of course Baaba Maai—who is one of the great singers of Senegal—comes

from a family well of tradition . . . I wanted him to sing about the tragedy of Africa. And very often he sings about how beautiful the land was, how everything came from the land and what it has turned into . . . The second part was not to do a big orchestral score. If you think about the participants in the movie, it's really about a small group of elite soldiers— so I thought that I would surround myself with a very small group of elite musicians and we would all work in a very confined space, very fast and under great pressure."

Zimmer's score for *MATCHSTICK MEN* was, according to "MC" in *Music from the Movies*, very much influenced by Nino Rota: "the main theme includes a few bars from . . . La Dolce Vita!" It included solo sounds for the accordion, organ, 1950s electro-acoustic guitar, human whistle, and vibraphone, creating "a sense of light-heartedness and naivety. This is what the score focuses on: the light aspects of the film as opposed to the elements of criminal activities and suspense."

References

Mikael Carlsson, "Hans Zimmer: *Black Hawk Down*," *Music from the Movies* 33 (May 2002): 12; Claudia Gorman, "Hearing *Thelma & Louise*: Active Reading of the Hybrid Pop Score," in *Thelma & Louise Live!: The Cultural Afterlife of an American Film*, ed. Bernie Cook (Austin: University of Texas Press, 2007), 88; Stanley Jaffe, interviewed in "*Black Rain*: Post-Production," Special Feature included in the *Special Collector's Edition* DVD release of *Black Rain* (d. Laurent Bouzereau) (Los Angeles: Paramount Pictures, 2006); Rudy Koppl, "Hans Zimmer: A Genre Awakes—Scoring *Gladiator* with Lisa Gerrard," *Music from the Movies* 27 (June 2000): 6, 9; MC, "Hans Zimmer: *Matchstick Men*," *Music from the Movies* 40 (December 2003): 40; Ridley Scott, interviewed in "*Black Rain*: Post-Production," Special Feature included in the *Special Collector's Edition* DVD release of *Black Rain* (d. Laurent Bouzereau) (Los Angeles: Paramount Pictures, 2006); Ford A. Thaxton, "Hans Zimmer: Dining with Hannibal, Waltzing with Gladiator," *Soundtrack* 20, no.77 (Spring 2001): 5–7; Hans Zimmer, interviewed by Edwin Black, *Film Score Magazine* (1998), www.filmscoremonthly.com/features/zimmer.asp (accessed 18 June 2008).

Bibliography

Jeff Bond, "Downbeat: The Sword and Sandal Sound." *Film Score Monthly* 5, no.3 (March 2000): 17–18; Jim Healey, "All This for Us: The Songs in *Thelma and Louise*." *Journal of Popular Culture* 29, no.3 (Winter 1995): 103–19; Daniel Schweiger, "In the War Zone." *Film Score Monthly* 7, no.1 (January 2002): 32–33, 48.

INDEX

Encyclopedia entries are in bold, as well as the pages for them. This index includes every reference to every actor mentioned in the text, plus critics and reviewers whose works are quoted regularly and other directors and film workers who have influenced Scott's work. Nothing in the reference and bibliography sections at the end of entries is included.

LAURENCE RAW teaches at Baskent University, Ankara, Turkey. His previous books include *Adapting Henry James to the Screen* (2006) and *Adapting Nathaniel Hawthorne to the Screen* (2008). In 2009 he published an anthology of theater reviews, *Nights at the Turkish Theatre*, focusing on how western plays have been adapted to local theaters in Turkey. Forthcoming projects include two coedited collections: *Teaching Adaptation Studies* and *Adapting America/America Adapted*.

Lightning Source UK Ltd.
Milton Keynes UK
UKOW07n2114271017
311668UK00019B/418/P